CW01494759

CIMA

STUDY TEXT

STRATEGIC

PAPER P9

MANAGEMENT ACCOUNTING – FINANCIAL STRATEGY

In this edition we:

- **Discuss** the **best strategies** for studying for CIMA exams
- **Highlight** the **most important elements** in the syllabus and the **key skills** you will need
- **Signpost** how each chapter links to the syllabus and the learning outcomes
- **Provide** lots of **exam focus points** demonstrating what the examiner will want you to do
- **Emphasise key points** in regular **fast forward summaries**
- **Test your knowledge** of what you've studied in **quick quizzes**
- **Examine your understanding** in our **exam question bank**
- **Reference all the important topics** in our **full index**

BPP Learning Media's **i-Learn** and **i-Pass** products also support this paper.

FOR EXAMS IN NOVEMBER 2007 AND MAY 2008

BPP LEARNING MEDIA

First edition 2004
Fourth edition May 2007

ISBN 9780 7517 4219 0
(previous edition 07517 2645 1)

British Library Cataloguing-in-Publication Data
A catalogue record for this book
is available from the British Library

Published by

BPP Learning Media Ltd
BPP House, Aldine Place
London W12 8AA

www.bpp.com/learningmedia

Printed in Great Britain by
WM Print
45-47 Frederick Street
Walsall
West Midlands
WS2 9NE

Your learning materials, published by BPP Learning Media Ltd, are printed on paper sourced from sustainable, managed forests.

We are grateful to the Chartered Institute of Management Accountants for permission to reproduce past examination questions. The suggested solutions in the exam answer bank have been prepared by BPP Learning Media Ltd.

Contents

Page

BPP LEARNING MEDIA

The BPP Learning Media Effective Study Package

Distance Learning from BPP Professional Education

You can access our exam-focussed interactive e-learning materials over the **Internet**, via BPP Learn Online, hosted by BPP Professional Education.

BPP Learn Online offers **comprehensive tutor support**, **revision guidance** and **exam tips**.

Visit www.bpp.com/cima/learnonline for further details.

Learning to Learn Accountancy

BPP Learning Media's ground-breaking **Learning to Learn Accountancy** book is designed to be used both at the outset of your CIMA studies and throughout the process of learning accountancy. It challenges you to consider how you study and gives you helpful hints about how to approach the various types of paper which you will encounter. It can help you **focus your studies on the subject and exam**, enabling you to **acquire knowledge**, **practise and revise efficiently and effectively**.

How the BPP Learning Media Study Text can help you pass

How the BPP Learning Media Study Text can help you pass

Tackling studying

We know that studying for a number of exams can seem daunting, particularly when you have other commitments as well.

- We therefore provide guidance on **what you need to study efficiently and effectively** – to use the limited time you have in the best way possible
- We explain the **purposes** of the **different features** in the Study Text, demonstrating how they help you and improve your chances of passing

Developing exam awareness

We never forget that you're aiming to pass your exams, and our Texts are completely focused on helping you do this.

- In the section **Studying P9** we introduce the key themes of the syllabus, describe the skills you need and summarise how to succeed
- The **Introduction** to each chapter of this Study Text sets the chapter in the context of the syllabus and exam
- We provide specific tips, **Exam focus points**, on what you can expect in the exam and what to do (and not to do!) when answering questions

And our Study Text is **comprehensive**. It covers the syllabus content. No more, no less.

Using the Learning outcomes and Syllabus

We set out the Learning outcomes and Syllabus in full.

- Reading the **Learning outcomes** will show you what **capabilities** (skills) you'll have to demonstrate.
- The topics listed in the **Syllabus** are the **key topics** in this exam. By quickly looking through the Syllabus, you can see the breadth of the paper. Reading the Syllabus will also highlight topics to look out for when you're reading newspapers or *Financial Management* magazine.
- Don't worry if the Syllabus seems large when you look through it; the Study Text will **carefully guide you** through it all.
- Remember the Study Text shows, at the start of every chapter, which **Learning outcomes** and **Syllabus areas** are covered in the chapter.

Testing what you can do

Testing yourself helps you develop the skills you need to pass the exam and also confirms that you can recall what you have learnt.

- We include **Questions** within chapters, and the **Exam Question Bank** provides lots more practice.
- Our **Quick Quizzes** test whether you have enough knowledge of the contents of each chapter.

Example chapter

How the BPP Learning Media Study Text can help you pass

Introduction

The Introduction sets the chapter in the context of the whole syllabus.

Introduction

This sample chapter will help you tackle the Study Text when you start studying the syllabus content in detail.

The chapter introduction explains **why** the topics in each chapter need to be studied. It links in with the **overall themes** of the Syllabus and exam, and signposts how the chapter relates to previous and future chapters. It also **highlights the main points** you should be looking out for as you go through the chapter.

Topic list

The Topic list gives an overview of the chapter.

Topic list	Learning outcomes	Syllabus reference	Ability required
1 The topic list helps you navigate each chapter	The Learning outcomes indicate what you will be expected to do as a result of studying this section	The Syllabus references show you how each topic fits into the Syllabus	The ability required references show you the depth of understanding you are expected to have
2 Each numbered topic is a numbered section within each chapter			
3 The topic list therefore emphasises the most important topics within each chapter			

BPP LEARNING MEDIA 1

HOW THE BPP LEARNING MEDIA STUDY TEXT CAN HELP YOU PASS

Knowledge brought forward from earlier studies

Knowledge brought forward boxes summarise information and techniques that you are **assumed to know** from your earlier studies. As the exam may test your knowledge of these areas, you should **revise** your previous study material if you are unsure about them.

1 Key topic which has a section devoted to it

FAST FORWARD

Fast forwards give you a **summary** of the content of each of the main chapter sections. They are listed together in the roundup at the end of each chapter to allow you to review each chapter quickly.

1.1 Important topic within section

The headings within chapters give you a good idea of the **importance** of the topics covered. The larger the header, the more important the topic is. The headers will help you navigate through the chapter and locate the areas that have been highlighted as important in the front pages or in the chapter introduction.

2 BPP LEARNING MEDIA

Knowledge brought forward

Knowledge brought forward shows you what you need to remember from previous exams.

Fast forward

Fast forwards allow you to preview and review each section easily.

Example

Examples show you how theory is put into practice.

Key term

Key terms are the core vocabulary.

Exam focus point

Exam focus points provide specific links to the exam.

Formula to learn

You must remember these formulae in the exam.

Question

Questions provide vital practice of what you've learnt.

Case Study

Case Studies link what you've learnt with the business environment.

HOW THE BPP LEARNING MEDIA STUDY TEXT CAN HELP YOU PASS

Example: Why examples are important

We include examples to illustrate how you should **apply key knowledge and techniques**. You therefore need to work through all examples very carefully.

Key term

Key terms are definitions of important expressions or concepts that can often earn you easy marks in the exam.

Exam focus point

Exam focus points tell you how specific topics may be examined, or if there are any **common weaknesses** in answers in these areas.

Formula to learn

This is a formula which you won't be given in the exam so you have to **learn** it. The best ways of learning it are using it in practice or writing it out a number of times until you're sure of all the terms.

Question — **Practice makes perfect**

Why should you attempt each question and what should you do with your answer?

Answer

You should attempt questions because they illustrate how well you **understand** what you've just read. You should check our answers against yours, and make sure you understand why they may have differed.

Case Study

Case studies show you how the topics you've covered come alive in the real world. Try to add to them with examples of your own experiences.

BPP LEARNING MEDIA 3

HOW THE BPP LEARNING MEDIA STUDY TEXT CAN HELP YOU PASS

Chapter Roundup

- Fast forwards give you a **summary** of the content of each of the main chapter sections. They are listed together in the roundup at the end of each chapter to allow you to review each chapter quickly.

Quick Quiz

1 What are the main purposes of the Quick Quiz?

2 What should you do if you get Quick Quiz questions wrong?

A Nothing as you now know where you went wrong
B Note the correct answer and go on to the next chapter
C Practise full questions on this topic when you revise
D Go back and look through the topic again to ensure you know it

Answers to Quick Quiz

1 The main purposes of the Quick Quiz are to check how much you've remembered of the topics covered and to practise questions in a variety of formats.

2 D Go back and look through the topic again to ensure that you know it.

Now try the questions below from the Exam Question Bank

Number	Level	Marks	Time
Questions that give you practice of what you've learnt in each chapter	Examination	25	45 mins

4 BPP LEARNING MEDIA

Chapter Roundup

The Chapter Roundup lists all the Fast forwards.

Quick Quiz

The Quick Quiz speedily tests your knowledge.

Exam Question Bank

Each chapter cross-references to further question practice.

Learning styles

BPP Learning Media's guide to studying, *Learning to Learn Accountancy*, provides guidance on identifying how you learn and the variety of intelligences that you have. We shall summarise some of the material in *Learning to Learn Accountancy*, as it will help you understand how to you are likely to approach the Study Text:

If you like	Then you might focus on	How the Study Text helps you
Word games, crosswords, poetry	Going through the detail in the Text	Chapter introductions, Fast forwards and Key terms help you determine the detail that's most significant
Number puzzles, Sudoku, Cluedo	Understanding the Text as a logical sequence of knowledge and ideas	Chapter introductions and headers help you follow the flow of material
Drawing, cartoons, films	Seeing how the ways material is presented show what it means and how important it is	The different features and the emphasis given by headers and emboldening help you see quickly what you have to know
Attending concerts, playing a musical instrument, dancing	Identifying patterns in the Text	The sequence of features within each chapter helps you understand what material is really crucial
Sport, craftwork, hands on experience	Learning practical skills such as preparing a set of accounts	Examples and question practice help you develop the practical skills you need

If you want to learn more about developing some or all of your intelligences, *Learning to Learn Accountancy* shows you plenty of ways in which you can do so.

Studying efficiently and effectively

What you need to study efficiently and effectively

Positive attitude

Yes there is a lot to learn. But look at the most recent CIMA pass list. See how many people have passed. They've made it; you can too. Focus on all the **benefits** that passing the exam will bring you.

Exam focus

Keep the exam firmly in your sights throughout your studies.

- Remember there's lots of **helpful guidance** about P9 in this first part of the Study Text.
- Look out for the **exam references** in the Study Text, particularly the types of question you'll be asked.

Organisation

Before you start studying you must organise yourself properly.

- We show you how to **timetable** your study so that you can ensure you have enough time to cover all of the syllabus – and revise it.
- Think carefully about the way you take **notes**. You needn't copy out too much, but if you can summarise key areas, that shows you understand them.
- Choose the notes **format** that's most helpful to you; lists, diagrams, mindmaps.
- Consider the **order** in which you tackle each chapter. If you prefer to get to grips with a theory before seeing how it's applied, you should read the explanations first. If you prefer to see how things work in practice, read the examples and questions first.

Active brain

There are various ways in which you can keep your brain active when studying and hence improve your **understanding** and **recall** of material.

- Keep asking yourself how the topic you're studying fits into the **whole picture** of this exam. If you're not sure, look back at the chapter introductions and Study Text front pages.
- Go carefully through every **example** and try every **question** in the Study Text and in the Exam Question Bank. You will be thinking deeply about the syllabus and increasing your understanding.

Review, review, review

Regularly reviewing the topics you've studied will help fix them in your memory. Your BPP Learning Media Texts help you review in many ways.

- Important points are emphasised **in bold**.
- **Chapter Roundups** summarise the **Fast forward** key points in each chapter.
- **Quick Quizzes** test your grasp of the essentials.

BPP Learning Media Passcards present summaries of topics in different visual formats to enhance your chances of remembering them.

Timetabling your studies

As your time is limited, it's vital that you calculate how much time you can allocate to each chapter. Following the approach below will help you do this.

Step 1 Calculate how much time you have

Work out the time you have available per week, given the following.

- The standard you have set yourself
- The time you need to set aside for work on the Practice & Revision Kit, Passcards, i-Learn and i-Pass
- The other exam(s) you are sitting
- Practical matters such as work, travel, exercise, sleep and social life

		Hours
Note your time available in box A.	A	

Step 2 Allocate your time

• Take the time you have available per week for this Study Text shown in box A, multiply it by the number of weeks available and insert the result in box B.	B	
• Divide the figure in box B by the number of chapters in this Study Text and insert the result in box C.	C	

Remember that this is only a rough guide. Some of the chapters in this Study Text are longer and more complicated than others, and you will find some subjects easier to understand than others.

Step 3 Implement your plan

Set about studying each chapter in the time shown in box C. You'll find that once you've established a timetable, you're much more likely to study systematically.

Short of time: Skim study technique

You may find you simply do not have the time available to follow all the key study steps for each chapter, however you adapt them for your particular learning style. If this is the case, follow the **Skim study** technique below.

Read the **Topic list, Introduction** and **Knowledge brought forward boxes.**

↓

Skim through the **explanations**, focusing on the points highlighted as important in the **Fast forward boxes**.

↓

Read the **Key terms** and **Exam focus points** carefully.

↓

Go through the **Examples** and **Case Studies**.

↓

Prepare **Answers** to the **Questions**.

↓

Revisit the Fast forwards in the **Chapter Roundups**.

↓

Answer the **Quick Quiz** and look back at any areas where you got questions wrong.

↓

Do a plan for the **Question(s) in the Exam Question Bank** and review our answers carefully.

↓

Brief notes may help you skim study, although you may simply rely on the **Passcards** for notes you can use for revision.

Revision

When you are ready to start revising, you should still refer back to this Study Text.

- As a source of **reference** (you should find the index particularly helpful for this)
- As a way to **review** (the Fast forwards, Exam focus points, Chapter Roundups and Quick Quizzes help you here)

Remember to keep careful hold of this Study Text – you will find it invaluable in your work.

Learning to Learn Accountancy

BPP Learning Media's guide to studying for accountancy exams, **Learning to Learn Accountancy**, challenges you to think about how you can study effectively and gives you lots and lots of vital tips on studying, revising and taking the exams.

Approaching Strategic level exams

Approaching Strategic level exams

When students start studying Strategic level subjects they are often puzzled about how these exams differ from Managerial level papers. What are the implications of having an exam consisting of scenario questions worth 25 or 50 marks, with no short questions? This section explains the key features of Strategic level exams, how to approach scenario questions, the importance of knowledge brought forward, links between Strategic papers, and how you can improve your chances of passing the exams.

1 Strategic level fundamentals

1.1 Knowledge and application

Even at Managerial level, you'll remember that passing didn't only mean reproducing knowledge; you also had to **apply** what you knew. At Strategic level, the balance is tilted much more towards application. You will need a sound basis of technical knowledge; the exams will detect whether you have the necessary knowledge. However you won't pass if you just spend your time acquiring knowledge; developing application skills is vital.

1.2 Application skills

What application skills do you need? Most Strategic level questions will include detail in a scenario about a specific organisation. The following skills are particularly important when you're dealing with question scenarios.

- **Identifying the most important features** of the organisation and the organisation's environment; clues to these will be scattered throughout the scenario. The technical knowledge that you have should help you do this, but you will also need business awareness and imagination
- **Using analysis techniques** that will give you more insight into the data that you're given
- **Selecting real-life examples** that are relevant to the scenario
- **Making informed judgements** that follow from your analysis about what the organisation is doing and should be doing
- **Communicating clearly and concisely** your analysis and recommendations. Perhaps you will be reporting to a specific individual; if so you should take into account the needs of this individual

1.3 Answering selectively

Examiners at Strategic level expect you to consider carefully what is relevant and significant enough to include in your answers. There are various signs that students are not making the necessary judgements:

- **Stating theories and concepts** rather than applying them
- **Quoting chunks of detail** from the question that don't add any value
- **Forcing irrelevancies into answers**, for example irrelevant theories or examples that don't relate to the scenario
- **Giving long lists or writing down all that's known** about a broad subject area, and not caring whether it's relevant or not

- **Failing to question the assumptions** made in the scenario or in the methods used to analyse the scenario
- **Focusing too narrowly on one area** – for example in P3 *Risk and Control Strategy* only covering financial controls when non-financial controls are also important

One aim of Strategic level papers is to prepare you for TOPCIMA; a number of marks will be available in TOPCIMA for distinguishing the relevant from the irrelevant and identifying the most important issues.

2 Answering scenario questions

You therefore need to develop techniques for dealing systematically with scenario questions.

2.1 Reading the requirements

When you first see a scenario question, it can be useful to have an initial quick look through the scenario before looking at the question requirements, to gain an idea of what the main issues are likely to be. However you should read the question requirements before analysing the scenario in detail. You need to identify what the requirements tell you about:

- The **syllabus areas** to be addressed
- What information will be **most significant** in the scenario
- The **techniques** you will need to analyse the data
- **Possible links and overlaps** between different parts of the question
- What the question is asking you to **provide** (determined by the question verb), also whether the requirements specify the way you should **structure** your answer
- **How long** to spend on each part (determined by the mark allocation)

2.2 Question verbs

CIMA stresses the importance of understanding what the verbs in question requirements are asking you to do. At Strategic level, the top level verbs, **evaluate**, **advise** and **recommend** are the most important. All of these test your ability to make good use of your assessment of the organisation's situation and plans.

2.2.1 Evaluate

CIMA defines evaluation as **appraising or assessing the value of**. Numerical techniques are therefore an important part of the evaluation process, and answers that don't include any calculations will not score well. However **depth of discussion** is also important. Discussions will often consist of paragraphs containing 2-3 sentences. Each paragraph should:

- **Make a point**
- **Explain the point** (you must demonstrate **why** the point is important)
- **Illustrate the point** (with material or analysis from the scenario, perhaps an example from real-life)

Evaluation questions also test your ability to do the following;

Identify what's relevant to the organisation	Consider what the organisation's strategy is, and whether the organisation will be easily able to do what it wants to do.
Select appropriate methods of assessment	This means choosing appropriate numerical techniques or theoretical models – assume you won't be told what method or model to use
Interpret fairly the results of your analysis	What does the analysis suggest about what the organisation is doing and should do?
Discuss the limitations of what you have done	What are the shortcomings of the data and problems with the techniques you've used (these should be relevant to the scenario)? Will other techniques such as sensitivity analysis give you additional insights?
Discuss the problems with the results you have obtained	Do the strategic decisions suggested by the results appear sensible? If not what other key factors are influencing strategy? You also need to consider the links between the decisions and implementing the decisions. What will be the impact upon management accounting, information and control systems?

2.2.2 Advise and Recommend

Don't be afraid to give advice. Even if you analyse a situation well, you will fail to pick up marks if you're told to recommend but don't provide any recommendations. The examiner may also want you to make a number of recommendations, rather than focusing exclusively on a single suggestion.

Other important qualities your recommendations or advice should have are:

- They should be in terms that the recipient(s) will **understand**. They shouldn't be too technical
- It should be **clear** what the recipient **has to do**. For example it wouldn't be enough to say – 'Improve risk management procedures' as you haven't explained how to improve them. Instead you would say improve risk management procedures by opening a risk register, appointing a risk officer, insuring the most serious risks
- The recommendations must be **appropriate** for the organisation's circumstances. For example if the organisation is small, that limits the sources of funding it can use and means that certain controls, such as a large internal audit function, will not be suitable

2.3 Analysing the situation

Even when you're reading the scenario more carefully, don't get too stuck in the detail, but look for the **key issues and information** in each paragraph. The importance of different information will be determined by the question requirements, but the following information will normally be important if it's included in the scenario:

- Financial and non-financial objectives
- Business strategies
- Financial and non-financial resources available to the organisation
- Constraints on the organisation or its directors
- Key persons/stakeholders within the organisation
- The organisation's size, structure and culture
- Management accounting, information and control systems

- Products, markets and competition
- Recent financial trends
- Likely changes in the business environment
- Major risks
- Other problems and weaknesses

Reviewing the numbers will be an important part of your analysis. You need to consider:

- What the numbers tell you
- What the numbers don't tell you

Often the question requirements will require you to consider the implementation and consequences of **significant changes**. Anything that will give you insights into the effects of change (the opportunities that will be provided, the internal consequences and the potential risks) will be important. You'll need to consider how far to analyse the **consequences** of the change. The level of **uncertainty** involved may be very significant, affecting the reliability of the techniques you use and meaning that you have to make reasonable estimates of what will happen.

2.4 Planning your answer

As you are reading the scenario, you should be putting the key points under the headings related to the requirements (by marginal notes by the scenario, highlighting key information or jotting down issues separately). This should form the basis of your answer plan. Answer planning will:

- Help you **focus** on the key issues
- Help you ensure that you **don't miss anything out** that's important
- Help you **link** your analysis with the actions the organisation should take to deal with the opportunities or problems it faces
- Stop you **repeating** the same material in different parts of the answer

A headed answer plan, spread out over a whole page, also creates a good impression on the marker. Don't however worry about making the plan too neat; abbreviations/short-hand will be fine. Think carefully about how much time you'll spend on each question part and how much time to spend on calculations; you need to leave sufficient time to discuss the issues raised by the calculations.

2.5 Writing your answer

Having completed your plan, don't then forget about it, but use it as the basis for your answer. In addition, remember everything you've learnt about exam technique for Managerial level papers. The following aspects of exam technique are particularly relevant in Strategic level exams.

- **Subheadings and leaving spaces between paragraphs** help to demonstrate that your answer is clearly structured and emphasise the points you're making
- **Short paragraphs** (2-3 sentences) help you keep to the point; however avoid 2-3 word bullet points
- **Clear numerical workings** can gain you many marks even if you make a mistake in your calculations
- **Time management** is likely to be less of a problem if you do the longest question (Question 1) first
- Because you'll often have to give advice, your answer may have to be in the form of a **report**; using a proper report style should gain you easy marks

3 Knowledge brought forward

The Strategic level examiners regard everything you studied at Managerial and Certificate level as knowledge that could be tested at Strategic level. It doesn't matter that this knowledge is not mentioned specifically in Strategic level syllabuses or learning outcomes; if it's relevant to the paper it could be tested.

4 Interaction of Strategic syllabuses

4.1 The main links between syllabuses

CIMA expects you to make links between the various papers and not see the three subjects in isolation.

- **Business strategy decisions** will **impact** upon the financial objectives, sources of finance chosen, the investment decisions, the risks the organisation faces and the controls necessary to counter those risks
- **Financial and risk and control strategies** must therefore fulfil the same criteria as business strategy; for example they should be **acceptable, suitable and feasible**
- At the same time **business strategy** will be **constrained** by the finance available and the level of risks the organisation is prepared to bear
- **Financial strategy decisions** will **impact** upon the **risks** the organisation bears and perhaps impose limitations on the controls the organisation can implement. Financial strategy will also be determined by the **financial risks** (some sources of finance may be thought too risky, the benefits of investment decisions too uncertain, risk may impact upon investment appraisal calculations)
- Remember that all three papers are management accounting papers. **Performance measurement** techniques such as ratio analysis may be useful in any paper. The **effectiveness of management accounting systems**, particularly in terms of the information provided and how useful they are as control mechanisms, could impact upon any of the papers

4.2 Other overlaps between syllabuses

The following areas are obvious overlaps between syllabuses, although it isn't a complete list:

- **Shareholder value added, Economic value added, Market value added** are important performance measures in P6 *Business Strategy* and useful valuation techniques in P9 *Financial Strategy*
- **Discounted cash flow calculations**, also cost of capital calculations, are key techniques in P9 *Financial Strategy*, but you will also need these techniques in P6 *Business Strategy*
- Various international aspects are relevant across Strategic level. **Political and international risks** will impact significantly upon strategic decisions, above all the decision of whether to invest abroad
- Similarly **information technology** issues are relevant for all three papers. Information strategy, critical success factors and how information systems are used are important for P3 *Risk and Control Strategy* and P6 *Business Strategy,* whilst the costs and benefits of investing in information technology and systems are significant in P9 *Financial Strategy*

- **Outsourcing** is a topical issue affecting many organisations. The decision to outsource may be a consequence of business strategy decisions, but the risks of doing so need to be managed. From the financial strategy viewpoint whether to outsource the financial functions (financial control and treasury) is an important decision

5 Helping yourself

5.1 Reading

Any reading you can do to develop your understanding of how businesses make strategic decisions, obtain finance and deal with risks will help. The business pages of quality newspaper, the Financial Times and Economist can help give you the insights you need and maybe provide some practical examples that you can use.

5.2 Post-exam guidance

Although Study Texts and Practice and Revision Kits refer to examiner's guidance, you should read all the post-exam guidance on CIMA's website for all the papers to see what questions are aiming to test, what receives credit, and the common mistakes students make. Post-exam guidance is **essential** reading.

5.3 Practice

The more practice you have, the more opportunity you will have to develop your application skills. The Study Text gives you opportunities by questions within chapters and particularly questions in the Exam Question Bank.

You will also significantly improve your chances of passing by leaving yourself enough time before the exam to **attempt questions in full** from all areas of the syllabus. BPP Practice and Revision Kits provide the large selection of questions that you need. As well as attempting the questions and comparing the approach and content of your answers to ours, it's useful to have another person review your answers, not just to mark them, but also to assess the basics, whether your analysis is clear, whether you answer has only included relevant material.

Approaching P9

Studying P9

1 What P9 is about

1.1 Formulation of financial strategy

In Chapters 1 to 4, we are concerned with how **financial objectives** of different types of organisation are identified and attained. We look at the links between investment, financing and dividend decisions and the **constraints** on formulating financial strategy. In Chapter 3 we look at the techniques of **ratio analysis** and **forecasting**. The emphasis in this exam is always on **discussion** of techniques you employ and using your calculations to support your **analysis.**

Probably the most important learning outcome in this paper is that you should be able to **recommend alternative financial strategies** and Chapter 4 takes you through the key features of this process.

1.2 Financial management

In Part B of this book we consider various aspects of financial management, starting with a look at the determination of **long-term capital structure** in the form of debt finance, equity finance and leasing. We then look at how **securities markets** work and towards the end of this part of the book, the roles of the finance and treasury functions.

There are some essential techniques that you need to use such as calculating the **cost of capital** and using the **capital asset pricing model**.

1.3 Business valuations and acquisitions

Part C of this book is concerned with **methods of calculating the valuations** of organisations of different types. The most important use of these techniques is in a merger or acquisition situation and this area is frequently examined.

1.4 Investment decisions and project control

The final part of this book covers issues connected with **investment appraisal**. The basic techniques involved should be revision but we do then go on to introduce more complex calculations and techniques which need to be practised.

2 What's required

You need to show understanding and ability to use techniques, and set your answers in context, above all in linking investment, financing and dividend decisions. Key higher level skills being tested are analysis, evaluation and advice.

The examiners are looking for:

- Clear presentation and conclusions
- Understanding of the key issues and tools
- Ability to analyse data and information (going beyond a description of the issues)
- Answers focussed on the scenarios.

3 Passing P9

3.1 Study the whole syllabus

You need to be comfortable with **all areas of the syllabus** as questions, particularly compulsory Question 1, will often span a number of syllabus areas.

3.2 Lots of question practice

You can **develop application skills** by attempting questions in the Exam Question Bank and later on questions in the BPP Practice and Revision Kit.

3.3 Analysing questions

Have another look at the guidance on tackling question scenarios in the *Approaching Strategic level exams* section of this Text. For P9 it's particularly important to focus on **how long** to spend on each part of the question and avoid spending too much time doing the calculations at the expense of the written parts. Make sure you pick up **scenario details** eg size of company, listed or unlisted, attitude to risk, dividend policy.

3.4 Answering questions

You need to show understanding and ability to use relevant techniques, but most importantly make sure that you set your answers in context and don't make recommendations which are unsuitable for the organisation in question.

3.5 Exam technique

The following points of exam technique are particularly relevant to this paper.

- Analyse questions during the 20 minute reading time – for example by putting notes in the question margin
- Make sure workings are presented clearly
- If short on time on an investment appraisal, remember that you will score significantly more method marks for calculating all the flows for 2 years, rather than a couple of the flows for 10 years
- Remember that doing calculations is not enough – you have to be able to comment on them as well. The error that a lot of students make is to overemphasise the theories and numbers in this paper
- Leave time to check your answers at the end to identify and correct any silly mistakes

4 Brought forward knowledge

The examiner may test knowledge or techniques you've learnt at Certificate or Managerial level. As P9 is part of the Financial Management pillar, the content of papers P7 and P8 will be significant. However material from other Managerial level papers is relevant as well, particularly information systems from P4, and investment appraisal from P2.

Remember however that brought forward knowledge will only be useful if it is linked to the particular organisation in the question.

5 Links with other Strategic level papers

We've discussed many of these already in the Approaching Strategic level exams section. Remember in particular that the **financial strategies** chosen must fulfil the same criteria as business strategy; for example they should be acceptable, suitable and feasible and financial strategy will be determined by the **financial risks**.

Learning outcomes and Syllabus

Paper P9 Management Accounting Financial Strategy

The syllabus comprises:

Topic and Study Weighting

A	Formulation of Financial Strategy	20%
B	Financial Management	30%
C	Business Valuations and Acquisitions	25%
D	Investment Decisions and Project Control	25%

Learning aims

Students should be able to:

- Understand and apply contemporary thinking on strategic financial management
- Understand and utilise appropriate tools for strategic management
- Evaluate strategic financial management options in light of the needs of management and the policy of the enterprise
- Characterise and describe the enterprise's financial strategy and use that characterisation to develop optimal financial strategy for all stages of the lifecycle
- Assess and evaluate proposed strategies

Learning outcomes and Syllabus content

A – Formulation of Financial Strategy – 20%

Learning outcomes

On completion of their studies students should be able to:

(i) Identify an organisation's objectives in financial terms and evaluate their attainment

(ii) Discuss the interrelationships between decisions concerning investment, financing and dividends

(iii) Identify and analyse the impact of internal and external constrains on financial strategy (eg funding, regulatory bodies, investor relations, strategy, and economic factors)

(iv) Evaluate current performance, taking account of potential variations in economic and business factors

(v) Recommend alternative financial strategies for an organisation

Syllabus content

(1) The financial and non-financial objectives of different organisations (eg, value for money, maximising shareholder wealth, providing a surplus)

(2) The three key decisions of financial management (by which we mean investment, financing and dividend) and their links

(3) Benefits of matching characteristics of investment and financing eg in cross border investment

(4) Identifying the financial objectives of an organisation and the economic forces affecting its financial plans, eg interest, inflation and exchange rates

(5) Assessing attainment of financial objectives

(6) Developing financial strategy in the context of regulatory requirements (eg price and service controls exercised by industry regulators) and international operations

(7) Modelling and forecasting cash flows and financial statements based on expected values for economic variables (eg interest rates) and business variables (eg volume and margins) over a number of years

(8) Analysis of sensitivity to changes in expected values in the above models and forecasts

(9) Identifying financing requirements (both in respect of domestic and international operations) and the impacts of different types of finance on the above models and forecasts

(10) Assessing the implications for shareholder value of alternative financial strategies, including dividend policy. Note: Modigliani and Miller's theory of dividend irrelevancy will be tested in broad terms. The mathematical proof of the model will not be required, but some understanding of the graphical method is expected

(11) Current and emerging issues in financial reporting (eg proposals to amend or introduce new accounting standards) and in other forms of external reporting (eg environmental accounting)

B – Financial management – 30%

Learning outcomes

On completion of their studies students should be able to:

(i) Identify and evaluate optimal strategies for the management of working capital and satisfaction of longer term financing requirements

(ii) Identify and evaluate key success factors in the management of the finance function and its relationship with other parts of the organisation and, where necessary, with external parties

(iii) Discuss the role and management of the treasury function

Syllabus content

(1) Working capital management strategies. (Note: No detailed testing of cash and stock management models will be set since these are covered at the Managerial level.)

(2) Types and features of domestic and international long-term finance; share capital (ordinary and preference shares; warrants), long-term debt (bank borrowing and forms of securitised debt, eg convertibles) and finance leases, and methods of issuing securities

(3) The lender's assessment of creditworthiness

(4) The lease or buy decision (with both operating and finance leases)

(5) The operation of stock exchanges (eg how share prices are determined, what causes share prices to rise or fall, and the efficient market hypothesis). (Note: No detailed knowledge of any specific country's stock exchange will be tested.)

(6) The capital asset pricing model (CAPM): calculation of the cost of equity using the dividend growth model (knowledge of methods of calculating and estimating dividend growth will be expected), the ability to gear and ungear betas and comparison to the arbitrage pricing model

(7) The ideas of diversifiable risk (unsystematic risk) and systematic risk (Note. Use of the two-asset portfolio formula will not be tested.)

(8) The cost of redeemable and irredeemable debt, including the tax shield on debt (numerical questions on the cost of convertible debt will not be tested)

(9) The weighted average cost of capital (WACC); calculation, interpretation and uses

(10) Criteria for selecting sources of finance, including finance for international investments

(11) The effect of financing decisions on balance sheet structure and on ratios of interest to investors and other financiers (gearing, earnings per share, price-earnings ratio, dividend yield, dividend cover gearing, interest cover.)

(12) Management of the finance function and relationships with professional advisors (accounting tax and legal), auditors and financial stakeholders (investors and financiers)

(13) The role of the treasury function in terms of setting corporate objectives, liquidity management, funding management, currency management

(14) The advantages and disadvantages of establishing treasury departments as profit centres or cost centres, and their control

C – Business Valuations and Acquisitions – 25%

Learning outcomes

On completion of their studies students should be able to:

(i) Calculate values of organisations of different types, eg service, capital intensive

(ii) Identify and calculate the value of intangible assets (including intellectual property)

(iii) Identify and evaluate the financial and strategic implications of proposals for mergers, acquisitions, demergers and divestments

(iv) Compare and recommend alternative forms of consideration for, and terms of, acquisitions

(v) Calculate post-merger or post-acquisitions value enhancement strategies

(vii) Discuss and illustrate the impact of regulation on business combinations

(viii) Evaluate exit strategies

Syllabus content

(1) Valuation bases for assets (eg historic cost, replacement cost and realisable value), earnings (eg price earning multiples and earnings yield) and cash flows (eg discounted cash flow, dividend yield and the dividend growth model)

(2) The strengths and weaknesses of each valuation method and when each is most suitable

(3) Recognition of the interest of different stakeholder groups in mergers, acquisitions and company valuations

(4) Application of the efficient market hypothesis to business valuations

(5) Selection of an appropriate cost of capital for use in valuation

(6) The impact of changing capital structure on the market value of a company. (Note: An understanding of Modigliani and Miller's theory of gearing, with and without taxes, will be expected, but proof of their theory will not be examined.)

(7) Forms of intellectual property and methods of valuation

(8) The reasons for merger or acquisition (eg synergistic benefits)

(9) Forms of consideration and terms for acquisitions (eg cash, shares, convertibles and earn-out arrangements), and their financial effects

(10) The post-merger or post-acquisition integration process (eg management-transfer and merger of business)

(11) The implications of regulation for business combinations. (Note: Detailed knowledge of the City Code and EU competition rules will not be tested.)

(12) The function/role of management buy-outs, venture capitalists

(13) Types of exit strategy and their implications

D – Investment Decisions and Project Control – 25%

Learning outcomes

On completion of their studies students should be able to:

(i) Analyse relevant costs, benefits and risks of an investment project

(ii) Evaluate investment projects (domestic and international) taking account of potential variations in business and economic factors

(iii) Recommend methods of funding investments, taking account of basic tax considerations

(iv) Evaluate procedures for the implementation and control of investment projects

(v) Recommend investment decisions when capital is rationed

Syllabus content

(1) Identification of a project's relevant costs (eg infrastructure, marketing and human resource development needs), benefits (including incremental effects on other activities as well as direct cash flows) and risks (ie financial and non-financial)

(2) Linking investments with customer requirements and product/service design

(3) Linking investment in IS/IT with strategic, operational and control needs (particularly where risks and benefits are difficult to quantify)

(4) Calculation of a project's net present value and internal rate of return, including techniques for dealing with cash flows denominated in a foreign currency and use of the weighted average cost of capital.

(5) The modified internal rate of return based on a project's "terminal value" (reflecting an assumed reinvestment rate)

(6) The effects of taxation (including foreign direct and withholding taxes) and potential restrictions on remittances on these calculations

(7) Recognising risk using the certainty equivalent method (when given a risk free rate and certainty equivalent values)

(8) Adjusted present value. (Note: The two step method may be tested for debt introduced permanently and debt in place for the duration of the project.)

(9) Capital investment real options (ie to make follow-on investment, abandon or wait)

(10) Project implementation and control in the conceptual stage, the development stage, the construction stage and initial manufacturing/operating stage

(11) Post completion audit of investment projects

(12) Single period for capital rationing for divisible and non-divisible projects, (Note: Multi-period rationing will not be tested.)

The exam paper

Format of the paper

		Number of marks
Section A:	A compulsory scenario-based question with up to 4 parts	50
Section B:	2 out of 4 questions, 25 marks each	50
		100

Time allowed: 3 hours, with 20 minutes reading time before the exam begins.

The examiner has stated that in all questions marks will be available for structure and presentation, and marks will be allocated for correct structure and approach. The marking scheme will apply 0.5 to 3 marks per valid point.

The examiner has given the following further guidance:

- The numerical content of the paper may be up to 50%, and may require calculations that are not specified in questions.
- The paper will usually include one question that contains no specific requirements for calculations.
- No new topic will be included in a compulsory question until it has featured in an optional question.
- All topics will be covered over three diets.
- Question weightings will be within 10% of the stated weightings for each syllabus section in each exam.

November 2006

Section A

1 Investment appraisal; forecast balance sheets; investment evaluation; roles and responsibilities of treasury and finance departments

Section B

2 Business valuation with intellectual capital

3 Venture capital valuation and as a source of finance

4 Investment appraisal, NPV, IRR and MIRR

5 Objectives; dividend, investment and financing policies

May 2006

Section A

1 Post-merger values; attainment of objectives; post-merger value enhancing strategies

Section B

2 Working capital requirements; financing policies; advantages and disadvantages of aggressive policy; treasury department structure

3 Debt finance, calculations of conversion value and yield to maturity; creditworthiness of an investment

4 APV; functions of project committee

5 NPV and profitability index; capital rationing in publicly owned entities.

November 2005

Section A

1 Investment; risk issues; share prices; rights issues

Section B

2 Corporate objectives and financing

3 Cost of capital; bid price; consideration

4 Financial data calculations; sources of finance

5 Forecast statements; company objectives

May 2005

Section A

1 Acquisition consideration, financing acquisition; value-enhancing acquired company; post-completion audits.

Section B

2 Financing new subsidiary; forecast balance sheet; gearing

3 Forecast balance sheet and income statement; cash flow analysis; financial management decisions

4 Cost of debt; lease or buy decision

5 Net present value; project control, real options

Pilot paper

Section A

1 Net present value of acquisition; MIRR ; contribution of new investment to objectives; real options

Section B

2 Sources of finance for an investment; overseas finance

3 Stock market ratios; cost of equity; share price; offer price; offer consideration; business implications

4 Inter-relation of investment, financing and dividend policies; treasury and financial control departments

5 Company valuation; venture capital or stock market funding

What the examiner means

The table below has been prepared by CIMA to help you interpret exam questions.

Learning objective	Verbs used	Definition
1 Knowledge What you are expected to know	• List • State • Define	• Make a list of • Express, fully or clearly, the details of/facts of • Give the exact meaning of
2 Comprehension What you are expected to understand	• Describe • Distinguish • Explain • Identify • Illustrate	• Communicate the key features of • Highlight the differences between • Make clear or intelligible/state the meaning of • Recognise, establish or select after consideration • Use an example to describe or explain something
3 Application How you are expected to apply your knowledge	• Apply • Calculate/ compute • Demonstrate • Prepare • Reconcile • Solve • Tabulate	• Put to practical use • Ascertain or reckon mathematically • Prove with certainty or to exhibit by practical means • Make or get ready for use • Make or prove consistent/compatible • Find an answer to • Arrange in a table
4 Analysis How you are expected to analyse the detail of what you have learned	• Analyse • Categorise • Compare and contrast • Construct • Discuss • Interpret • Produce	• Examine in detail the structure of • Place into a defined class or division • Show the similarities and/or differences between • Build up or compile • Examine in detail by argument • Translate into intelligible or familiar terms • Create or bring into existence
5 Evaluation How you are expected to use your learning to evaluate, make decisions or recommendations	• Advise • Evaluate • Recommend	• Counsel, inform or notify • Appraise or assess the value of • Advise on a course of action

Pilot paper

Paper P9

Management Accounting – Financial Strategy

Pilot paper

Instructions to candidates:

You are allowed three hours to answer this question paper.
In the real exam, you are allowed 20 minutes reading time before the examination begins during which you should read the question paper, and if you wish, make annotations on the question paper. However, you will **not** be allowed, **under any circumstances**, to open the answer book and start writing or use your calculator during this reading time.
You are strongly advised to carefully read the question requirement before attempting the question concerned.
Answer the ONE compulsory question in Section A.
Answer TWO of the FOUR questions in Section B.

DO NOT OPEN THIS PAPER UNTIL YOU ARE READY TO START UNDER EXAMINATION CONDITIONS

SECTION A – 50 marks

Answer this question

Question 1

Background

The Hi-clean Group is a UK-based unlisted company that imports, assembles and distributes laundry and cleaning equipment for hotels and restaurants and for public sector departments, such as hospitals, prisons and the armed forces. The company was formed in 19X5 with £24 million start-up capital in ordinary shares of £1. No other capital has been raised since then, except from the venture capital company explained below.

The company has seen growth in turnover and post-tax profits of around 20% each year over the past three years in all sectors of its customer base, although sales to the public sector now account for a much higher proportion of the total than five years ago: 38% in 20X4 compared with 18% in 20X0.

Details on major shareholder

A venture capital company owns 20% of the company's shares, bought three years ago for £25 million. The venture capital company also provided a £25 million loan with equity warrants attached. The loan carries a variable rate of interest, LIBOR +3%, and is repayable in 20X6. The warrants allow for the venture capital company to buy 1 share at 400 pence for every £10 of debt at the time the loan is repaid. This shareholder is looking to exit from its investment in Hi-clean in two to three years' time. Unless Hi-clean has obtained a share listing by then, the venture capital company has indicated it is unlikely to exercise its warrants. The venture capital company's usually required return is an average of 50% per annum (dividends plus capital gain as percentage of initial investment) over a five-year investment period.

Although the venture capital company has a seat on the Hi-clean Group board, it has taken a very 'hands-off' approach and had little involvement in the company's direction or management.

Forecast results for the year to 31 December 20X4

The accounts department has produced the following full-year forecasts for 20X4.

Results by sector

	Public sector	*Hotels and restaurants*	*Total*
	£ million	£ million	£ million
Turnover	83.60	136.40	220.00
Direct costs	45.98	68.20	114.18
Gross profit margin	37.62	68.20	105.82
Fixed overheads*	26.53	43.29	69.82
Operating profit	11.09	24.91	36.00

* Fixed overheads are apportioned to operating sectors on the basis of turnover.

Summary group profit and loss account

	£ million
Operating profit	36.00
Interest payable	1.75
Profit before taxation	34.25
Taxation	6.17
Profit after tax	28.08
Ordinary dividends	8.43

Summary group balance sheet

	£ million
Non-current assets (net book value)	124.00
Net current assets	48.00
Loan capital	25.00
Assets less liabilities	147.00
Capital and reserves	
Called up share capital (Ordinary shares of £1)	30.00
(Authorised share capital £35 million)	
Share premium account	18.00
Profit and loss account	99.00
Shareholders' funds	147.00

Future funding and request for study

Hi-clean's directors have, for some time, been considering a public listing for the company's shares to raise new finance and provide an exit route for the venture capital company. Assume you are the Financial Manager with Hi-clean. The directors have asked you for a study that includes a forecast of the company's financial situation at 31 December 20X5. You have spent the last month obtaining the following information from a variety of sources.

Growth in turnover and profits

You expect growth to continue but not at the high levels seen over the past few years. A complication is that a general election will take place shortly and the outcome will have an effect on Hi-clean's business. If Party A wins, it has promised more money for some public sector departments, which may increase Hi-clean's sales to its public sector customers. However, this increased spending would be paid for by an increase in certain taxes that would adversely impact on some of Hi-clean's private customers. If Party B wins, spending on public services will also increase, but not necessarily in areas serviced by Hi-clean. Opinion polls suggest Party A has a 60% chance of winning and Party B 40%.

Based on your informed opinion about prospects for the economy and the industry, you forecast the following range of turnovers and probabilities for 20X5, by sector, depending on which party wins the election.

		Public sector		*Hotels and restaurants*
If Party A wins:	Turnover *£ million*	102.00	112.00	123.00
	Probabilities	0.55	0.45	1
If Party B wins:	Turnover *£ million*	95.00	110.00	143.00
	Probabilities	0.50	0.50	1

Other information/assumptions

- Corporate tax will be payable at the current percentage level of 18% owing to availability of capital allowances. No capital expenditure is planned for 20X5.
- Gross profit margin percentage by sector is expected to remain unchanged irrespective of the election outcome.
- Fixed costs are expected to rise to £71.8 million.
- LIBOR is currently 4%. It is expected to fall to 3% in 20X5.
- Average P/E ratio and cost of equity capital for listed companies in this industry are currently 11 and 9% respectively. It is difficult to forecast how P/E ratios will move over the next 12 months but market professionals are expecting an upturn in the market generally, so anything between 12 and 15 is not unreasonable.
- The dividend payout ratio has been constant at 30% since 20X1.

Required

(a) For 20X5, calculate forecast of the following:

(i) Turnover, gross margin and operating profits by customer sector
(ii) A profit and loss account and earnings per share for the Hi-clean Group

Assume a full-year effect for all the changes forecast for 20X5. Provide comments to accompany your forecasts that explain any significant changes between 20X4 and 20X5. **(10 marks)**

(b) As Financial Manager, write a report to the directors of Hi-clean Group. In your report you should:

(i) Calculate a range of potential values as at the end of 20X5 for the entire Group and for the venture capital company's shareholding. Base your calculations on the information you have available and assume the Group remains a private, unlisted company. Accompany your calculations with a brief discussion of each valuation method.

(ii) Comment on the reasons for potential differences between the value of the entire company and the value of the venture capital company's shares (that is, why the value of the venture capital company's shares might not be strictly proportionate). **(18 marks)**

(c) Based on your forecasts, estimate whether the venture capital company will achieve its target return on investment in Hi-clean and identify exit strategies that might be available to the investor in 20X6. Evaluate how the venture capital company's situation might affect Hi-clean's future financial strategy. **(10 marks)**

(d) Identify the main risks and opportunities facing the company and advise on methods of managing the risks.

(12 marks)

(Total = 50 marks)

SECTION B – 50 marks

Answer TWO questions ONLY

Question 2

VID Inc is a US-based company, which was established 15 years ago. It makes and distributes videos, both for the general market and to customer specifications. Its common stock (shares) have been listed on a US stock exchange for the past 8 years. However, there are relatively few stockholders and the stock is not traded in large volumes. The founders of the company no longer participate in its management but own around 10% of the stock in issue.

VID Inc borrowed US$ 65 million to purchase new premises three years ago, which have recently been valued at US$ 85 million. The company is now considering diversifying into mainstream film production, which will require raising US$ 50 million for additional fixed and working capital. This new business will involve joint ventures with UK partners and much of the filming will be done in the UK or Spain. The new investment is not expected to have a significant effect on profits for at least 18 months.

The three months being considered for raising capital are:

(i) New equity in the UK, subject to US stockholders' approval
(ii) Long-term fixed rate US$ debt
(iii) Floating rate sterling-denominated Eurobonds

Summary financial statistics for the last financial year for VID Inc are as below.

	US$ millions
Turnover	175.00
Operating profit	45.00
Post-tax profits	31.36
Non-current assets (book value)	95.00
Net current assets	58.00
Long-term loans: 8% redeemable 20Z0	65.00
Common stock (in units of US$ 1)	25.00
Retained earnings	63.00
Share price (US$):	
High for year	28.56
Low for year	18.50
As at today (25 May 20X4)	22.58

Current annual fixed interest rates for secured long term borrowing are as follows.

US$	6%	UK £	7%	European common currency area €	5%

Floating rate sterling Eurobond notes are available at the bank base rate +0.5%. Tax will continue to be payable at 20% per annum.

Required

Assume you are a financial advisor to VID Inc. Evaluate the three methods of finance being considered at the present time and advise the directors of VID Inc. Support your advice with any calculations you consider appropriate. Assume, for the purposes of this evaluation, that the P/E ratio of the company will rise to 20 if equity finance is used, or 19 if fixed or floating rate debt is issued. Make any other simplifying assumptions you think necessary and appropriate. **(Total = 25 marks)**

Notes. Up to 10 marks are available for calculations. A report structure is not required for this question.

Question 3

TDC is a transport and distribution company listed on the New York Stock Exchange. On 14 November 20X3, the directors made a bid for a competitor, UED, that is based in the UK and listed on the UK stock market.

UED's directors are considering the bid but have indicated the terms are inadequate and would have to be improved if they were to feel able to recommend it to their shareholders.

The merger would create the fourth largest company in the industry worldwide, but it would still be substantially smaller than the three largest companies. TDC has suffered from slow growth over the past few years and has long been rumoured by market professionals to be a likely target of a hostile bid from one of the three larger companies, or even a reverse takeover by a smaller company. The bid for UED is therefore being seen by the market as defensive.

	TDC	*UED*
Market data		
Common stock/share price as at today (18 November 20X3)	US$ 11.36	425 pence
Common stock/share price on 18 October 20X3	US$ 12.45	305 pence
Common stock/shares in issue	120 million	145 million
P/E ratio as at today	11	13.5
Accounting data	US$ millions	£ millions
Forecast profit after tax for the current financial year	98.5	45.5
Net asset values at last balance sheet date (30 June 20X3)	825.2	230.5
Including cash balances of	125.5	65.2
Debt outstanding (market value)	250	75
[Repayable	20X7	20X8]

Other information

- The average P/E ratio for the industry is currently estimated as 10 in the UK and 13 in the USA.
- The average debt ratio for the industry internationally (long-term debt as a proportion of total funding) is 15% based on market values.
- TDC's cost of equity is 12% net of tax.
- The US$/£ exchange rate today is 1.53.

Terms of the bid

TDC's directors have made an opening bid of 1 TDC common stock for 2 UED shares. No cash alternative has been offered so far.

Required

Assume that you are the financial Manager with TDC. Write an internal memorandum for the board that:

(a) Discusses how the recent price movements of the two companies' shares might impact on the bid negotiations. **(6 marks)**

(b) Recommends revised bid terms that might be acceptable to the directors and shareholders of UED and also to your own board. Your recommendation should be fully evaluated. **(12 marks)**

(c) Evaluate the strategic implications of making a hostile bid compared with an aggressive investment programme of organic growth. **(7 marks)**

(Total = 25 marks)

Question 4

TMc is a large cosmetic and toiletries retail organisations based in a country within the European common currency zone. Its current turnover is approximately €1.4 billion and it has an asset base of €750 million.

The company is evaluating opening up to 10 new retail outlets in a country in Asia, to be financed by its existing cash or other highly liquid assets. It proposes to operate these new retail outlets itself for the first two years of operation. After that time, and subject to satisfactory commercial and financial performance, each outlet will be offered as a franchise to either the outlet manager/employees or to a third party.

Forecast nominal cash flows for the first two years of operation for a single outlet are as follows.

	Year 0	*Year 1*	*Year 2*
	Asian $ million	Asian $ million	Asian $ million
Initial investment	(15)		
Pre-tax operating cash flows		4.5	5.5

Exchange rate information is as follows.

Spot rate as at today €/Asian $	0.65

Forecast inflation rates (% per annum).

European common currency area	1.50
Asian country	3.50

Estimated cash flows beyond year 2 depend on the type of operation. If the company continues to operate the outlet, it assumes zero growth per year on year 2's post-tax Euro operating cash flows until the end of year 10. Cash flows beyond year 10 are ignored. If the outlet is franchised, there will be a one-off taxable payment by the franchisee at the beginning of year 3 of Asian $500,000 plus an annual payment in perpetuity of Asian $3.2 million (both figures in today's money), commencing at the end of year 3.

Additional information

- Corporate taxes in the Asian country are 30% per annum, payable or refundable the year in which the liability to tax arises. In the European country, they are 35% payable or refundable the following year. Double taxation agreements are in force between the two countries. Both countries allow 100% writing-down allowance for investments of this type.
- TMc uses 9% as the discount rate in its investment appraisals.
- All operating cash flows may be assumed to occur at the end of each year. The initial capital investment will be made at the beginning of year 1 and written off over 5 years.
- TMc evaluates international investments by converting the foreign currency cash flows to €s and applying its domestic cost of capital.

Required

Evaluate the proposed investment and recommend whether it should proceed. You should include in your evaluation some discussion of the risks that might be associated with the two alternative methods of operation being considered after year 2 and advise on how these risks might be managed.

(Total = 25 marks)

Notes. Up to 10 marks are available for calculations. A report structure is not required for this question.

Question 5

A regional police force has the following corporate objectives:

- To reduce crime and disorder
- To promote community safety
- To contribute to delivering justice and maintaining public confidence in the law

The force aims to achieve these objectives by continuously improving its resources management to meet the needs of its stakeholders. It has no stated financial objective other than to stay within its funding limits.

The force is mainly public-funded but, like other regional forces, it has some commercial operations, for example policing football matches when the football clubs pay a fee to the police force for its officers working overtime. The police force uses this money to supplement the funding it receives from the government. The national government is proposing to privatise (that is, sell off) these commercial operations and has already been in preliminary discussions with an international security company. This company's stated financial objectives are:

- To increase earnings per share year on year by 5% per annum
- To achieve a 20% per annum return on capital employed

Arguments put forward by government in favour of privatisation focus on the conflict of objectives between mainstream operations and commercial activities, and savings to the taxpayer. However, the proposals have met with strong opposition from most of the force's stakeholders.

Required

(a) Discuss the reasons for the differences in the objectives of the two types of organisation given above. Use the scenario details given above to assist your answer wherever possible. **(12 marks)**

(b) Discuss the influence the commercial operations might currently have on the police force's ability to meet its stated objectives. Include in your discussion an evaluation the possible effects on mainstream services and the various stakeholder groups if the commercial operations were to be privatised. **(13 marks)**

(Total = 25 marks)

Part A
Formulation of financial strategy

1

Objectives of organisations

Introduction

In Part A of this Study Text, we are concerned with how **financial objectives** of different types of organisation are identified and attained; the links between the investment, financing and dividend decisions; the **constraints** on formulating financial strategy; **non-financial objectives** and non-financial information; the analysis of the **performance of organisations**. Try not to get bogged down with these chapters; remember the most important learning objective of this paper is that you should **recommend alternative financial strategies** for an organisation. What the first few chapters provide you with are factors you should consider and tools you can use when formulating your recommendations.

In this chapter we concentrate on **financial objectives**. You need to understand what the most important objectives are and how you recognise that they have been achieved. However don't assume that you will always be asked about the financial objectives of businesses. Questions may ask you to consider the objectives of non-commercial bodies or public sector bodies such as hospitals. In addition the financial objectives will need to be seen in the context of potentially significant non-financial objectives.

The last section of this chapter deals with the inter-relationships between the decisions concerning **investment, financing and dividends**. In your earlier studies you may have come across the concept that these decisions are linked. For this paper these links may be a central part of your answer as you consider how organisations finance their investments.

Topic list	Learning outcomes	Syllabus references	Ability required
1 Objectives of companies	A(i)	A(1)	Evaluation
2 Stakeholders and objectives	A(i)	A(1)	Evaluation
3 Objectives of publicly owned and non-commercial bodies	A(i)	A(1)	Evaluation
4 Financial management decisions	A(ii)	A(2), (3)	Analysis

1 Objectives of companies 11/05

FAST FORWARD

In financial management of businesses, the key objective is the **maximisation of shareholders' wealth**.

1.1 Strategic financial management

Key term

Strategic financial management is defined in the *CIMA Official Terminology 2005 edition* (*OT 2005*) as 'the identification of the possible strategies capable of maximising an organisation's net present value, the allocation of scarce capital resources among the competing opportunities and the implementation and monitoring of the chosen strategy so as to achieve stated objectives'.

Strategy depends on stated **objectives** or **targets**. Therefore, an obvious starting point is the identification and formulation of these objectives.

Key term

Strategy is a course of action, including the specification of resources required, to achieve a specific objective. *(OT 2005)*

Case Study

The following statements of objectives, both formally and informally presented, were taken from recent Annual Reports and Accounts.

Tate & Lyle ('a global leader in carbohydrate processing')

The board of Tate & Lyle is totally committed to a strategy that will achieve a substantial improvement in profitability and return on capital and therefore in shareholder value. To that end we will:

- continue to develop higher margin, higher value-added and higher growth carbohydrate-based products, building on the Group's technology strengths in our world-wide starch business
- ensure that all retained assets produce acceptable returns
- divest businesses which do not contribute to value creation, and/or are no longer core to the Group's strategy
- conclude as rapidly as practicable our review of the strategic alternatives available to us in our US sugar operations
- continue to improve efficiency and reduce costs through our business improvement projects which include employee development and training programmes.

Kingfisher ('one of Europe's leading retailers concentrating on markets serving the home and family')

Customers are our primary focus. We are determined to provide them with an unbeatable shopping experience built on great value, service and choice, whilst rapidly identifying and serving their ever-changing needs.

This goal is pursued through some of Europe's best known retail brands and increasingly through innovative e-commerce channels which harness our traditional retailing expertise.

By combining global scale and local marketing we aim to continue to grow our business, deliver superior returns to our shareholders and provide unique and satisfying opportunities for our people.

Hilton Group ('A global company operating in the hospitality and gaming markets with the leading brand names of Hilton and Ladbroke')

The group intends to enhance shareholder value by exploiting its prime position in these international markets, both of which are expected to experience significant long-term growth.

1.2 Financial objectives of a company 5/06

Exam focus point

Any discussion of objectives should be **specific** to the company or organisation described in the question. Make sure you conclude with **valid recommendations** if required by the question.

The theory of company finance is based on the assumption that the **objective of management is to maximise the market value of the enterprise**. Specifically, the main objective of a company should be to **maximise the wealth** of its **ordinary shareholders**.

A company is financed by ordinary shareholders, preferred shareholders, loan stock holders and other long-term and short-term payables. All surplus funds, however, belong to the legal owners of the company, its ordinary shareholders. Any retained profits are undistributed wealth of these equity shareholders.

1.3 Measuring wealth and value

If the financial objective of a company is to **maximise the value** of the company, and in particular the value of its ordinary shares, we need to be able to put values on a company and its shares. How do we do it?

Methods of company valuation	
Going concern basis	Based on the company's balance sheet. Rising retained profits are an indication of potential dividends
Break-up basis	Only of interest if company is threatened with insolvency, or if individual assets are being sold to raise cash
Market values	Trading prices of stocks and shares, most relevant to financial objectives. Shareholder's return on investment comes from dividends received and increases in market value of shares (determined by expectations of future dividends)

When shares are in a non-quoted company, it can be hard to measure their **value** as there is no market price available. However the priorities of non-quoted shareholders will be the same, and therefore a company should be looking to maximise their wealth.

1.4 Increasing value

If a company's shares are **traded on a stock market**, the wealth of shareholders is increased when the share price goes up. **The price of a company's shares should go up when the company is expected to make additional profits**, which it will pay out as dividends or re-invest in the business to achieve future profit growth and dividend growth. However, to increase the share price the company should achieve its profits without taking excessive **business risks** and **financial risks** that worry shareholders.

1.5 Primary financial targets

If there is an increase in earnings and dividends, management can hope for an increase in the share price too, so that shareholders benefit from both higher revenue (dividends) and also capital gains (higher share prices).

Management should set **primary financial targets** for factors which they can influence directly, such as cash flows, profits and dividend growth. A financial objective might be expressed as the aim of **increasing profits**, earnings per share and dividend per share by, say, 10% a year for each of the next five years.

The shorter term financial objectives of companies include targets for **profitability**. Although profits do matter, they are not necessarily the best measure of a company's achievements.

(a) Accounting profits are not the same as 'economic' profits. **Accounting profits can be manipulated** to some extent by choices of accounting policies.

Question

Manipulation of profits

Learning outcome: A(i)

Can you give three examples of how accounting profits might be manipulated?

Answer

Here are some examples you might have chosen.

(i) Provisions, such as provisions for depreciation or anticipated losses
(ii) The capitalisation of various expenses, such as development costs
(iii) Adding overhead costs to inventory valuations

(b) A company might make an accounting profit **without having used its resources in the most profitable way possible**. There is a difference between the accounting concept of 'historical cost' and the economic concept of 'opportunity cost', which is the value that could have been obtained by using resources in their most profitable alternative way.

(c) Profits on their own take no account of the **volume of investment that it has taken to earn the profit**. Profits must be related to the volume of investment to have any real meaning. Hence measures of financial achievement include:

- Accounting rate of return on investment, return on capital employed
- Earnings per share
- Yields on investment, for example dividend yield as a percentage of stock market value

(d) Profits are reported every year (with half-year interim results for quoted companies). They are measures of **short-term** performance, whereas a company's performance should ideally be judged over a longer term.

1.6 Other financial targets

In addition to targets for earnings, EPS, and dividend per share, a company might set **other financial targets**. These will often be measured over a year.

Examples of other financial targets	
Restriction on gearing	Ratio of debt: equity shouldn't exceed 1:1 or finance costs shouldn't be higher than 25% of profit from operations
Profit retentions	Dividend cover (Profit for the year:Dividends) should exceed 2.5
Profit from operations	Target profit from operations: revenue ratio or minimum return on capital employed
Cash generation	As well as generating profits, businesses need to generate enough cash to ensure they remain liquid
Value added	Creation of economic value for shareholders, to be discussed later in this text

Case Study

In their annual report, Tate & Lyle identified the '**signposts to shareholder value**' as being:

- *Focus* – we focus on adding value to carbohydrates within a group that has clear objectives
- *Efficiency* – we initiate programmes to maximise efficiency, reduce costs and enhance the value on investment
- *Markets* – our extensive market knowledge and geographic reach enable us to serve global customers and maintain our leading market positions
- *Growth* – new products, innovative manufacturing processes and our strong brand portfolio deliver growth by adding value to consumer products
- *Investment* – selective investment, combined with volume manufacturing skills, enable us to grow our business and become a low-cost processor

These financial targets are not primary targets, but they can act as **subsidiary targets** or constraints that should help a company to achieve its main financial objective without incurring excessive risks.

In some countries private sector companies that were formerly run by the government act within regulatory financial constraints imposed by 'consumer watchdog' bodies set up by government. For example, BT (British Telecom) is overseen by the telecommunications regulator (OFCOM), which restricts price rises to protect consumers.

1.7 Short-term and long-term targets

In the long-term companies should be looking to **maximise shareholder wealth**.

Short-term targets can encourage a company to pursue short-term objectives at the expense of long-term ones, for example by deferring new capital investments, or spending only small amounts on research and development and on training.

1.8 Multiple financial targets

A major problem with setting a number of different financial targets, either primary targets or supporting secondary targets, is that they might not all be consistent with each other, and so might not all be achievable at the same time. When this happens, some compromises will have to be accepted.

1.9 Example: evaluation of the attainment of financial objectives

Lion Grange Co has recently introduced a formal scheme of long range planning. At a meeting called to discuss the first draft plans, the following estimates emerged.

(a) Revenue in the current year reached £10,000,000, and forecasts for the next five years are £10,600,000, £11,400,000, £12,400,000, £13,600,000 and £15,000,000.

(b) The ratio of profit for the year to revenues is 10%, and this is expected to continue throughout the planning period.

(c) Total assets less current liabilities will remain at around 125% of sales.

It was also suggested that:

(d) If profits rise, dividends should rise by at least the same percentage.

(e) An earnings retention rate of 50% should be maintained.

(f) The ratio of long-term borrowing to long-term funds (debt plus equity) is limited (by the market) to 30%, which happens also to be the current gearing level of the company.

Prepare a financial analysis of the draft long range plan and suggested policies for dividends, retained earnings and gearing.

Solution

The draft financial plan, for profits, dividends, assets required and funding, can be drawn up in a table, as follows.

	Current year	*Year 1*	*Year 2*	*Year 3*	*Year 4*	*Year 5*
	£m	£m	£m	£m	£m	£m
Revenues	10.00	10.60	11.40	12.40	13.60	15.00
Profit for the year	1.00	1.06	1.14	1.24	1.36	1.50
Dividends (50% of profit after tax)	0.50	0.53	0.57	0.62	0.68	0.75
Total assets less current liabilities (125% of sales)	12.50	13.25	14.25	15.50	17.00	18.75
Equity (increased by retained earnings)	8.75	9.28	9.85	10.47	11.15	11.90
Maximum debt (30% of long term funds)	3.75	3.98	4.22	4.49	4.78	5.10
	12.50	13.26	14.07	14.96	15.93	17.00
Funds available/(Shortfall in funds)*	0.00	0.01	(0.18)	(0.54)	(1.07)	(1.75)

* Given maximum gearing of 30% and no new issue of shares
= funds available minus total assets less current liabilities.

These figures show that the financial objectives of the company are not compatible with each other, and adjustments will have to be made.

(a) Given the assumptions about sales, profits, dividends and assets required, there will be an increasing shortfall of funds from year 2 onwards, unless new shares are issued or the gearing level rises above 30%.

(b) In years 2 and 3, the shortfall can be eliminated by retaining a greater percentage of profits, but this may have a serious adverse effect on the share price. In year 4 and year 5, the shortfall in funds cannot be removed even if dividend payments are reduced to nothing.

(c) The net asset turnover appears to be low. The situation would be eased if investments were able to generate higher revenues, so that fewer non-current assets and less working capital would be required to support the projected level of revenues.

(d) If net asset turnover cannot be improved, it may be possible to increase the profit to revenues ratio by reducing costs or increasing selling prices.

(e) If a new issue of shares is proposed to make up the shortfall in funds, the amount of funds required must be considered very carefully. Total dividends would have to be increased in order to pay dividends on the new shares. The company seems unable to offer prospects of suitable dividend payments, and so raising new equity might be difficult.

(f) It is conceivable that extra funds could be raised by issuing new debt, so that the level of gearing would be over 30%. It is uncertain whether investors would be prepared to lend money so as to increase gearing. If more funds were borrowed, profits would fall so that the share price might also be reduced.

1.10 Non-financial objectives

FAST FORWARD

Non-financial objectives such as welfare, service provision and fulfilment of responsibilities are also important for businesses.

A company's non-financial objectives may include the following.

Non-financial objectives	
Welfare of employees	Competitive wages and salaries, comfortable and safe working conditions, good training and career development
Welfare of management	High salaries, company cars, perks
Welfare of society	Concern for environment
Provision of service to minimum standard	For example regulations affecting utility companies (water, electricity providers)
Responsibilities to customers	Providing quality products or services, fair dealing
Responsibilities to suppliers	Not exploiting power as buyer unscrupulously
Leadership in research and development	Failure to innovate may have adverse long-term financial consequences
Maintaining competitive position & market share	Preventing rivals from becoming too large and enjoying benefits of size such as economies of scale

1.11 Non-financial targets

A business may have a variety of non-financial targets that reflect its non-financial objectives.

Non-financial targets	
Market share	As above, limiting the threat of competition
Customer satisfaction	A key target, because of the adverse financial consequences if businesses switch suppliers
Risk exposure	Risk limitation will be covered briefly where relevant in this text and in greater detail in your text for *Management Accounting Risk and Control Strategy*
Environmental targets	Fulfilling targets such as reducing emissions or use of recyclable material. We shall consider environmental reporting in more detail in a later chapter.

2 Stakeholders and objectives 11/06

FAST FORWARD

One of the most important influences on strategy is the **goals of different interest groups**, or **stakeholder groups**.

- Internal – managers, employees
- Connected – shareholders, banks, customers, suppliers
- External – Government, pressure groups, local communities

2.1 Stakeholder groups

Key term

Stakeholders are those persons and organisations that have an interest in the strategy of an organisation. Stakeholders normally include shareholders, customers, staff and the local community. *(OT 2005)*

As you will have gathered from Section 1, many objectives and targets are set in terms of satisfying the requirements of interested parties or stakeholders. In this section we consider in more depth the importance of stakeholders and their role.

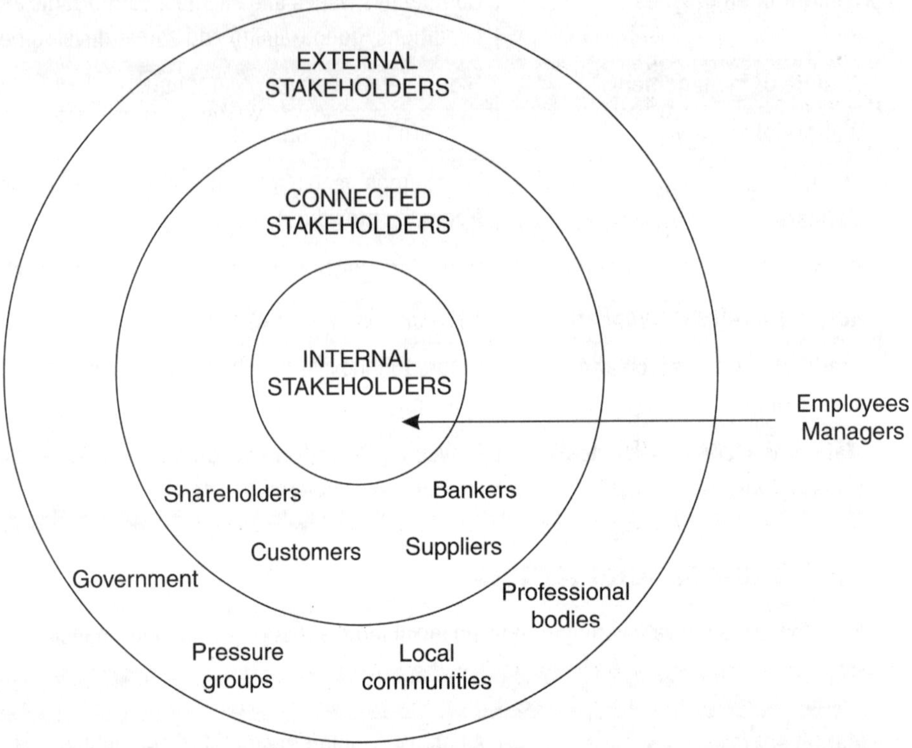

Exam focus point

You may be told in a question that a company aims to respect the interests of stakeholders, and determines its policies in the light of that aim. Even if you aren't, you will see at various times in this text circumstances when stakeholder interests become particularly important, for example in a merger and acquisition situation, or when a business is linking investments with customer desires.

2.2 Objectives of stakeholder groups

The various groups of stakeholders in a firm will have different goals which will depend in part on the situation of the organisation.

STAKEHOLDER GOALS	
Shareholders	Providers of risk capital, aim to maximise wealth
Suppliers	Often other businesses, aim to be paid full amount by date agreed, but want to continue long-term trading relationship, and so may accept later payment
Long-term lenders	Wish to receive payments of interest and capital on loan by due date for repayment
Employees	Maximise rewards paid to them in salaries and benefits, also prefer continuity in employment
Government	Political objectives such as sustained economic growth and high employment. We shall discuss in Chapter 2 how government policies affect organisations
Management	Maximising their own rewards

2.3 Stakeholder groups and strategy

The greater the power of stakeholders, the greater their influence will be. Each stakeholder group will have different expectations about what it wants, and the expectations of the various groups may conflict. Each group, however, will influence strategic decision-making.

Question

Learning outcome: A(i)

Describe and discuss the significance of the main stakeholders of a commercial bank.

Answer

(a) **Customers**

Customers are very significant to the bank because this group directly provides **income** for the business. Some customers, for example large corporate customers, are more significant than others.

(b) **Employees**

This group looks to the bank to be a **good employer**, offering fair and continuing employment. This group is very significant to the company, as banks are people-intensive businesses and good performance by employees can impact directly on customer satisfaction and hence company profitability.

(c) **Suppliers**

These may provide the company with **key technologies** that enable the bank to have a competitive advantage.

(d) **Government agencies**

There is a widespread feeling that banks abuse their position and exploit customers, for example through **cartel-type** agreements on cash machine charges. Government agencies may have powers to control activities of the bank. The competition authorities may recommend that a proposed takeover planned by the bank be blocked.

(e) **Intermediaries**

The bank sells some of its services (for example insurance policies) through intermediaries whose continued support is of significance.

2.4 Shareholders and management

Although ordinary shareholders (equity shareholders) are the owners of the company to whom the board of directors are accountable, the actual powers of shareholders tend to be restricted, except in companies where the shareholders are also the directors.

The day-to-day running of a company is the responsibility of the management, and although the company's results are submitted for shareholders' approval at the annual general meeting (AGM), there is often apathy and acquiescence in directors' recommendations. AGMs are often very poorly attended.

TOPCIMA link

> The views of investors may have a significant impact upon the strategies you discuss in the TOPCIMA exam; for example restive institutional investors being a major impetus behind change.

2.5 The agency problem

FAST FORWARD

The **agency problem** arises when agents (managers) do not act in the best interests of their principals (shareholders). The system of corporate governance – which is the directors' responsibility – should seek to ensure **goal congruence** between the objectives of the organisation and those of its teams or departments or individual team members.

Key term

Agency theory is the hypothesis that attempts to explain elements of organisational behaviour through an understanding of the relationships between **principals** (such as shareholders) and **agents** (such as **company managers and accountants**).

A **conflict** may exist between the actions undertaken by agents in furtherance of their own self-interest, and those required to promote the interests of the principals. *(OT 2005)*

The relationship between management and shareholders is sometimes referred to as an **agency relationship**, in which managers act as agents for the shareholders, using delegated powers to run the affairs of the company in the shareholders' best interests.

The agency relationship arising from the separation of ownership from management is sometimes characterised as the **agency problem**. For example, if managers hold none or very little of the equity shares of the company they work for, what is to stop them from:

- Working inefficiently?
- Not bothering to look for profitable new investment opportunities?
- Giving themselves high salaries and perks?

One power that shareholders possess is the **right to remove the directors from office**. But shareholders have to take the initiative to do this, and in many companies, the shareholders lack the energy and organisation to take such a step.

2.6 Goal congruence

Key term

In a control system, **goal congruence** is the state which leads individuals or groups to take actions which are in their self-interest and also in the best interest of the entity. *(OT 2005)*

Goal congruence may be better achieved, and the 'agency problem' better dealt with, by providing managers with incentives that are related to profits or share price, such as:

(a) Pay or bonuses related to the size of profits (**profit-related pay**).

(b) Rewarding managers with **shares**, eg when a private company is listed on a stock exchange and managers are invited to subscribe for shares in the company at an attractive offer price.

(c) Rewarding managers with **share options**. In a share option scheme, selected employees are given a number of share options, each of which gives the holder the right after a certain date to subscribe for shares in the company at a fixed price. The value of an option will increase if the company is successful and its share price goes up.

Such measures might encourage management to adopt '**creative accounting**' methods which will distort the reported performance of the company in the service of the managers' own ends.

An alternative approach is to attempt to monitor managers' behaviour, for example by establishing '**management audit**' procedures, to introduce additional reporting requirements, or to seek assurances from managers that shareholders' interests will be foremost in their priorities.

2.7 Shareholder value analysis

Shareholder value analysis (SVA) was developed during the 1980s from the work of Rappaport and focuses on value creation using the net present value (NPV) approach. Thus, SVA assumes that **the value of a business is the net present value of its future cash flows, discounted at the appropriate cost of capital**. Many leading companies (including, for example, Pepsi, Quaker and Disney) have used SVA as a way of linking management strategy and decisions to the creation of value for shareholders. We cover SVA in more detail in Chapter 15 of this text but a brief introduction now emphasises important considerations that are relevant through this text.

Key term

Shareholder value analysis is an approach to financial management which focuses on total return to shareholders in terms of both dividends and price growth, calculated as the present value of future free cash flows of the business discounted at the weighted average cost of capital of the business less the market value of its debt.

SVA takes the following approach.

(a) Key decisions with implications for cash flow and risk are specified. These may be **strategic, operational, related to investment** or **financial**.

(b) **Value drivers** are identified as the factors having the greatest impact on shareholder value, and management attention is focused on the decisions which influence the value drivers. Value drivers include:

- Sales growth and margin
- Working capital and fixed capital investment
- The cost of capital

SVA may help managers to concentrate on **activities which create value** rather than on short-term profitability. A problem with the approach is that of specifying a terminal value at the end of the planning horizon, which will extend for perhaps five or ten years.

2.8 Working with shareholders

A company's senior management should remain aware of who its major shareholders are, and it will often help to retain shareholders' support if the chairman or the managing director meets occasionally with the major shareholders, to exchange views.

(a) The company's management might learn about **shareholders' preferences** for either high dividends or high retained earnings for profit growth and capital gain.

(b) For public companies, changes in shareholdings might help to **explain recent share price movements**.

(c) The company's management should be able to learn about **shareholders' attitudes to both risk and gearing**.

(d) Management might need to know its shareholders in the event of an **unwelcome takeover bid** from another company, to identify key shareholders whose views on the takeover bid might be crucial to the final outcome.

Having a **wide range of shareholders** has advantages.

(a) Likelihood of **greater activity** in the market in the firm's shares, ie greater 'market liquidity'

(b) **Less likelihood** of one shareholder having a **controlling interest**

(c) Since shareholdings are smaller on average, **likelihood of less effect on the share price** if one shareholder sells his holding

(d) **Greater likelihood** of a **takeover bid** being **frustrated**

Having a large number of shareholders also has disadvantages.

(a) **High administrative costs** eg the costs of sending out copies of the annual report and accounts, counting proxy votes, registering new shareholders and paying dividends

(b) The **varying tax rates and objectives** of shareholder clientele groups, which make a dividend/retention policy more difficult for the management to decide upon

Exam focus point

The mix of shareholders may be important when a company considers how best to raise new finance.

2.9 Shareholders, managers and loan holders

The relationship between **loan holders** of a company, the **management** and the **shareholders** of a company encompasses the following factors.

(a) Management may decide to raise finance for a company by taking out long-term or medium term loans. They might well be taking **risky investment decisions** using outsiders' money to finance them.

(b) Investors who provide loan finance will rely on the company's management to generate enough net cash inflows to make **interest payments** on time, and eventually to **repay loans**.

However, long-term loan holders will often take **security** for their loan, perhaps in the form of a fixed charge over an asset (such as a mortgage on a building). Loan notes are also often subject to certain restrictive covenants, which restrict the company's rights to borrow more money until the loan notes have been repaid.

If a company is unable to pay what it owes its loan holders, the loan holders may decide:

- To exercise their security, or
- To apply for the company to be wound up

(c) The money that is provided by long-term loan holders will be **invested to earn profits**, and the profits (in excess of what is needed to pay interest on the borrowing) will provide extra dividends or retained profits for the shareholders of the company. In other words, shareholders will expect to increase their wealth using creditors' money.

3 Objectives of publicly owned and non-commercial bodies 11/06

FAST FORWARD

The prime objectives of publicly owned and non-commercial bodies will not be to make a profit. However they will have to **meet financial targets**. Some non-commercial bodies (eg charities) may be involved in profit-making activities to **raise funds** so that they can **fulfil their primary objectives**.

3.1 Not-for-profit organisations

Some organisations are set up with a prime objective which is not related to making profits. Charities and government organisations are examples. These organisations exist to pursue **non-financial aims**, such as providing a service to the community. However, there will be **financial constraints** which limit what any such organisation can do.

(a) A not-for-profit organisation needs finance to pay for its operations, and the major financial constraint is the **amount of funds that it can obtain** from its donors (its 'customers').

(b) Having obtained funds, a not-for-profit organisation will use the funds to help its 'clients', for example by alleviating suffering. It should seek to use the funds:

- **Economically**: not spending $2 when the same thing can be bought for $1
- **Efficiently**: getting the best use out of what money is spent on
- **Effectively**: spending funds so as to achieve the organisation's objectives

3.2 Government departments

Financial management in **government departments** is different from financial management in an industrial or commercial company for some fairly obvious reasons.

(a) Government departments **do not operate to make a profit**, and the objectives of a department or of a programme of spending cannot be expressed in terms of maximising the return on capital employed.

(b) Government services are provided **without the commercial pressure of competition**. There are no competitive reasons for controlling costs, being efficient or, when services are charged for (such as medical prescriptions), keeping prices down.

(c) Government departments have full-time professional civil servants as their **managers**, but decisions are also taken by **politicians**.

(d) The government gets its money for spending from **taxes, other sources of income and borrowing** (such as issuing gilts) and the nature of its fund-raising differs substantially from fund-raising by companies.

Since managing government is different from managing a company, a different framework is needed for planning and control. This is achieved by:

(a) **Setting objectives** for each department
(b) **Careful planning** of public expenditure proposals
(c) Emphasis on getting **value for money**

In the UK, **internal markets** have been created in the health sector whereby purchasers are separated from providers of health care and the providers of hospital and other healthcare facilities compete for purchasers' funds. The idea is that those providing the best value for money will gain an increasing share of funds available.

3.3 Objective setting

There are a number of issues to consider when objectives are set for not-for-profit organisations.

(a) **Who are the main stakeholders?**

There may be a complex mix of stakeholders, especially in the public sector. For example, a local government entity will be directed by a group of local politicians, controlled by the political party that won the last election. The local population will be the main stakeholders together with employees and central government.

(b) **Which are the most important objectives?**

Not-for-profit organisations tend to have **multiple objectives** so that even if they can all be clearly identified, it is impossible to say which is the overriding objective.

(c) **How will achievement of objectives be measured?**

Outputs can seldom be measured in a way that is generally agreed to be **meaningful.** (Are good exam results alone an adequate measure of the quality of teaching? How does one quantify the easing of pain following a successful operation?)

Bodies like local government, health services and so on can **compare** their performance **against each other** and against the historical results of their predecessors.

Question — Voluntary sector

Learning outcome: A(i)

Summarise the main strengths and weaknesses of a voluntary sector organisation.

Answer

Strengths

- There are **no shareholders** who would expect a short-term return on their investment.
- There is less chance of **conflict** between social goals and profit goals.
- Voluntary organisations may be **trusted** more by users than a comparable private sector organisation, for whom users may be suspicious of the company's profit motives.
- There may be greater **dedication** from staff who share the voluntary organisation's vision.
- 'Staff' may be prepared to give their services for **free**.

Weaknesses

- The **absence** of a **profit motive** may lead to **unfocused** management whose results are difficult to monitor.
- There may be a reluctance to act in a **business-like way**, thereby resulting in poor services to users.
- Users may **not** expect to **pay** for services provided, but overhead costs must still be covered.
- Voluntary workers may be **less committed** to their job as they will not lose pay for poor performance.

Exam focus point

You must always discuss the specific needs of the organisation in a scenario and make sure the issues you discuss are relevant.

4 Financial management decisions 5/05, 11/06

FAST FORWARD

In seeking to attain the financial objectives of the organisation or enterprise, a financial manager has to make the following decisions:

- Investment
- Financing
- Dividends

4.1 Investment, financing and dividend decisions

Maximising the wealth of shareholders generally implies maximising profits consistent with long-term stability. Often short-term gains must be sacrificed in the interests of the company's long-term prospects.

In the context of this overall objective of financial management, there are three main types of decisions facing financial managers: **investment** decisions, **financing** decisions and **dividend** decisions.

4.2 Investment decisions

The financial manager will need to **identify** investment opportunities, **evaluate** them and decide on the **optimum allocation of scarce funds** available between investments.

Investment decisions may be on the undertaking of new **projects** within the existing business, the **takeover** of, or the **merger** with, another company or the **selling off** of a part of the business. Managers have to take decisions in the light of strategic considerations such as whether the business wants to **expand internally** (through investment in existing operations) or **externally** (through expansion).

4.3 Interaction of investment with financing and dividend decisions

Managers will need to consider whether **extra finance** will be required, and if it will be, what will be the consequences of obtaining it. They will have to consider the demands of **providers of finance**, particularly of equity shareholders who require **dividends**. Will equity shareholders be content with projects that maximise their long-term returns, or will they require a minimum return or dividend each year?

4.4 Financing decisions

Financing decisions include those for both the long term (**capital structure**) and the short term (**working capital management**).

The financial manager will need to determine the **source, cost** and effect on **risk** of the possible sources of long-term finance. A balance between **profitability** and **liquidity** (ready availability of funds if required) must be taken into account when deciding on the optimal level of short-term finance.

4.5 Interaction of financing with investment and dividend decisions

When taking financial decisions, managers will have to fulfil the **requirements of the providers of finance**, otherwise finance may not be made available. This may be particularly difficult in the case of equity shareholders, since dividends are paid at the company's discretion; however if equity shareholders do not receive the dividends they want, they will look to sell their shares, the share price will fall and the company will have more difficulty raising funds from share issues in future.

Although there may be risks in obtaining extra finance, the long-term risks to the business of **failing to invest** may be even greater and managers will have to balance these up. Investment may have direct consequences for decisions involving the **management of finance**; extra working capital may be required if investments are made and sales expand as a consequence. Managers must be sensitive to this and ensure that a balance is maintained between receivables and inventory, and cash.

A further issue managers will need to consider is the **matching** of the **characteristics** of investment and finance. **Time** is a critical aspect; an investment which earns returns in the long-term should be matched with finance which requires repayment in the long-term.

Another aspect which we will consider in later chapters is the **financing of international investments**. A company which expects to receive a substantial amount of income in a foreign currency will be concerned that this currency may weaken. It can hedge against this possibility by borrowing in the foreign currency and using the foreign receipts to repay the loan. It may though be better to obtain finance on the international markets.

4.6 Dividend decisions

Dividend decisions may affect the view that shareholders have of the long-term prospects of the company, and thus the **market value of the shares**.

4.7 Interaction of dividend with investment and financing decisions

The amount of surplus cash paid out as **dividends** will have a direct impact on **finance** available for **investment**. Managers have a difficult decision here; how much do they pay out to shareholders each year to keep them happy, and what level of funds do they retain in the business to invest in projects that will yield long-term income. In addition funds available from retained profits may be needed if debt finance is likely to be unavailable, or if taking on more debt would expose the company to undesirable risks.

We shall consider dividend policies further in Chapter 4.

Exam focus point

> The examiner is particularly interested in the integration of the three decisions. Any exam answer must always focus on the specific entities involved rather than a regurgitation of text book knowledge.

Chapter roundup

- In financial management of businesses, the key objective is the **maximisation of shareholders' wealth**.
- **Non-financial objectives** such as welfare, service provision and fulfilment of responsibilities are also important for businesses.
- One of the most important influences on strategy is the **goals of different interest groups**, or **stakeholder groups**.
  - Internal – managers, employees
  - Connected – shareholders, banks, customers, suppliers
  - External – Government, pressure groups, local communities
- The **agency problem** arises when agents (managers) do not act in the best interests of their principals (shareholders). The system of corporate governance – which is the directors' responsibility – should seek to ensure **goal congruence** between the objectives of the organisation and those of its teams or departments or individual team members.
- The prime objectives of publicly owned and non-commercial bodies will not be to make a profit. However they will have to **meet financial targets**. Some non-commercial bodies (eg charities) may be involved in profit-making activities to **raise funds** so that they can **fulfil their primary objectives**.
- In seeking to attain the financial objectives of the organisation or enterprise, a financial manager has to make the following decisions:
  - Investment
  - Financing
  - Dividends

Quick quiz

1 On what management objective is the theory of company finance primarily based?

2 To which areas might non-financial objectives of a company relate?

3 List six types of stakeholder group.

4 **Fill in the blanks**

_________ theory sees employees as individuals, each with their own objectives, the relationship between managers and shareholders being an _________ relationship. If achieving individual and departmental objectives leads to achievement of the organisation's objectives, there is ___________________

5 Where external financing limits apply government-owned industries are not usually set financial targets.

True ☐

False ☐

6 To obtain value for money, a not-for-profit organisation should aim for the '**Three Es**', which are (**fill in the blanks**):

E _________

E _________

E _________

7 In the context of managing performance in 'not for profit' organisations, which of the following definitions is incorrect?

A Value for money means providing a service in a way which is economical, efficient and effective.

B Economy means doing things cheaply: not spending $2 when the same thing can be bought for $1.

C Efficiency means doing things quickly: minimising the amount of time that is spent on a given activity.

D Effectiveness means doing the right things: spending funds so as to achieve the organisation's objectives.

8 **Fill in the blanks**

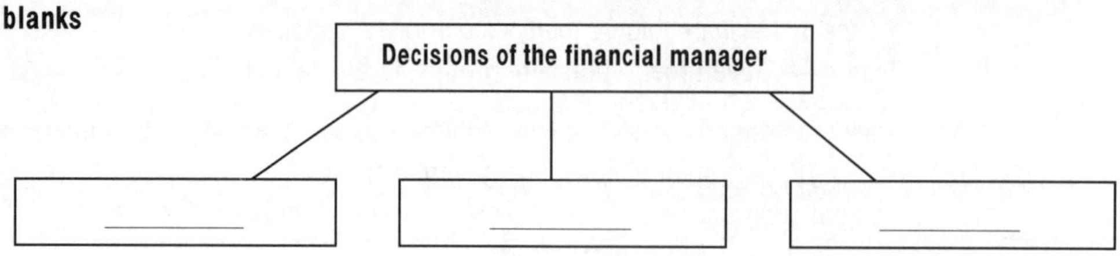

9 __________ is a course of action, including the specification of resources required, to achieve a specific objective.

Answers to quick quiz

1 The objective of management is to maximise the market value of the enterprise and the shareholders' wealth.

2 (1) Welfare of employees (2) Welfare of management
(3) Welfare of society (4) Quality of service provision
(5) Responsibilities to customers and suppliers (6) Leadership in research and development

3 Employees, managers, shareholders, bankers, customers, suppliers, government, local communities, pressure groups, professional bodies.

4 Agency; agency; goal congruence

5 False

6 Economy; efficiency; effectiveness

7 C Efficiency means doing things well: getting the best use out of what money is spent on

8 Investment; financing; dividend

9 Strategy

Now try the question below from the Exam Question Bank

Number	Level	Marks	Time
Q1	Examination	25	45 mins

2 Constraints on financial strategy

Introduction

We now examine the range of **factors** which may constrain financial strategy.

It is important to see how changes or differences in these factors may influence strategy. For example, a **change in government legislation** may limit (or maybe open up) opportunities. When seeking **investment opportunities in other countries**, the particular external factors which are important there will need to be considered.

Interest rates are a key influence on **investment** decisions, and you need to appreciate the main factors affecting interest rates, and why rates differ across the economy.

As well as influencing business decisions, many of the constraints will require direct action by businesses, possibly **costs of complying** with them, or (possibly costly) action to limit their effects.

Topic list	Learning outcomes	Syllabus references	Ability required
1 Internal constraints	A(iii)	A(4)	Analysis
2 The influence of governments	A(iii)	A(6)	Analysis
3 Legal and regulatory constraints	A(iii)	A(6)	Analysis
4 Economic constraints	A(iii)	A(4)	Analysis
5 International constraints	A(iii)	A(6)	Analysis

Exam focus point

Constraints on maximisation of shareholder wealth are likely to be the most significant constraints in the context of this paper.

1 Internal constraints 11/06

FAST FORWARD

Internal constraints on financial strategy include directors' views on financial structure, the need to **maintain good relations** with **investors**, and the **need for financial strategy to be compatible** with overall business strategy.

1.1 Limiting factors

You should be able to think of several examples of resource constraints that limit businesses' scope from your earlier studies.

Key term

A **limiting factor** or **key factor** is anything that limits the activity of an entity. *(OT 2005)*

Examples

- A shortage of production capacity
- A limited number of key personnel, such as salespeople with technical knowledge
- A restricted distribution network
- Too few managers with knowledge about finance, or overseas markets
- Inadequate research or design resources to develop new products or services
- A poor system of strategic intelligence
- Lack of money
- A lack of adequately trained staff

Once the limiting factor has been identified, the planners should do two things.

- In the short term, make best use of the resources available.
- Try to reduce the limitation in the long term.

1.2 Financial constraints

Businesses must consider financial constraints when formulating financial strategy. We shall discuss external financial constraints such as government policies or significant economic factors later in this chapter, and will consider sources of finance in depth in Part B of this text.

Businesses may be reluctant to **obtain extra funds themselves** for a variety of reasons. In smaller non-listed companies, equity funding from the small group of owners will be a significant source of finance. However owners may not have the **financial resources** to provide significant equity injections, and may also require the company to pay them a regular source of income. Larger companies listed on a stock exchange may be constrained when they are contemplating a share issue by fears that the issue will not be fully taken up or that they will have to issue shares at a low price in order to ensure full take-up.

Directors of companies of any size may be reluctant to obtain further debt finance because:

(a) They fear that the company may be unable to **service the debt**, to make the required capital and interest payments on time

(b) The tax position is such that they will be unable to use the **tax shield**, to obtain any tax benefit from interest payments

(c) The company lacks the **asset base** to be able to **generate additional cash** if needed or provide **sufficient security**

(d) The company wishes to **maintain access** to the capital markets on **good terms**, and hence needs a good credit rating

Smaller companies may be deterred from **obtaining debt finance** by lender requirements that the directors offer personal security.

1.3 Investor relations

Financial constraints are bound up with the need to keep investors happy. We have seen in Chapter 1 that investors need to be convinced that companies are investing in projects generating sufficient long-term returns, and that en route the company will also be able to generate enough dividends to satisfy investor requirements.

An important aspect of the corporate governance debate which we shall discuss later in this chapter is a company's relations with its investors, in particular the board's accountability to investors.

1.4 Strategy

Obviously a business's financial strategy is not independent of its overall business strategy. There may be occasions when an organisation departs from what appears to be the optimum financial strategy. It may for instance depart from its optimal capital structure to **raise funds** to seize a potentially **valuable investment opportunity**

2 The influence of governments

FAST FORWARD

Government involvement can **encourage business expansion** but also **restrict businesses** through regulations and tax. This reflects differing government aims, to encourage businesses and hence raise national prosperity, but also correct adverse consequences of markets.

2.1 Government interests

Governments do not have a direct interest in companies (except for those in which it actually holds shares). However, the government does often have a strong indirect interest in companies' affairs.

2.1.1 Taxation

The government raises taxes on sales and profits and on shareholders' dividends. It also expects companies to act as tax collectors for income tax and sales tax. The tax structure might influence investors' preferences for either dividends or capital growth.

2.1.2 Encouraging new investments

The government might provide funds towards the cost of some investment projects. It might also encourage private investment by offering tax incentives.

2.1.3 Encouraging a wider spread of share ownership

In the UK, the government has made some attempts to encourage more private individuals to become company shareholders, by means of attractive privatisation issues (such as in the electricity, gas and telecommunications industries) and tax incentives, such as ISAs (Individual Savings Accounts), to encourage individuals to invest in shares.

2.1.4 Legislation

The government also influences companies, and the relationships between companies, their directors, shareholders and other stakeholders. We shall consider the impact of legislation as it relates to corporate governance in Section 3.

2.1.5 Economic policy

A government's economic policy will affect business activity. For example, exchange rate policy will have implications for the revenues of exporting firms and for the purchase costs of importing firms. Policies on economic growth, inflation, employment, interest rates and so on are all relevant to business activities. We shall look further at government attempts to control key economic variables in Section 4 of this chapter.

2.2 Governments' attitude to businesses

Although governments have universal ambitions, this does not mean that they are immune to sectional interests. In the reasonably near past, it was relatively easy to identify the relationship between ruling political parties and interest groups. Socialist and labour parties represented the organised working class, and others represented business and capital.

The relationship between a government's philosophy and its attitudes to business is now no longer a simple one. In part, this is because a new consensus seems to have emerged on the value of market-based policies.

(a) **Work place regulation** (such as the Social Chapter of the Maastricht Treaty) is supported, in most of Europe, by parties of both left and right.

(b) Free trade promotes competition, but many pro-business governments do not wish to see **their** businesses affected. Some EU governments have, in the past, been hostile to Japanese investment in the UK. However, the single European market is designed to promote competition.

2.3 The encouragement of free market forces

Throughout the industrialised world, governments have tried to stimulate their economies by giving **encouragement to free market forces** through:

(a) **Greater liberalisation of markets**, by removing regulations and legislative restrictions on them (deregulation)

(b) A **reduction in the role of the government** in industry and commerce

(c) A **simplified tax system**, which encourages firms to take commercial decisions which are not influenced by tax advantages or disadvantages

(d) The **privatisation of state-owned assets** (such as British Gas, British Telecom and the electricity industry in the UK)

(e) **Opening up state-controlled activities** to competition from private firms

(f) **Encouraging competition**, by a judicious regulation of monopolies and mergers, and by giving encouragement to small firms

(g) The **removal or reduction of import restrictions**, to open up domestic markets to greater foreign competition

2.4 Dealing with market failure

By contrast, governments are also concerned with the **regulation of private markets** where these fail to bring about an efficient use of resources. As you should be aware from your earlier studies in economics, **market failure** is said to occur when the market mechanism fails to result in economic efficiency, and therefore the outcome is **sub-optimal**.

In response to the existence of market failure, and as an alternative to taxation and public provision of production, the state often resorts to regulating economic activity in a variety of ways. Of the various forms of market failure, the following are the cases where regulation of markets can often be the most appropriate policy response.

(a) **Imperfect competition**

Where monopoly power is leading to inefficiency, the state will intervene through controls on, say, **prices or profits** in order to try to reduce the effects of the monopoly.

(b) **Externalities**

A possible means of dealing with the problem of external costs and benefits is via some form of regulation. Regulations might include, **for example**, **controls on emissions of pollutants**, **restrictions on car use** in urban areas, **the banning of smoking in public buildings**, **compulsory car insurance** and **compulsory education**.

(c) **Imperfect information**

Regulation is often the best form of government action whenever informational inadequacies are undermining the efficient operation of private markets. This is particularly so when **consumer choice is being distorted. Examples** here would include **legally enforced product quality/safety standards**, **consumer protection legislation**, the **provision of job centres** and other means of improving information flows in the labour market and so on.

(d) **Equity**

The government may also resort to regulation to improve social justice. For example, legislation to prevent racial and/or sexual discrimination in the labour market; regulation to ensure equal access to goods such as health care, education and housing; minimum wage regulations and equal pay legislation.

Case Study

UK examples of government assistance include:

- The Loan Guarantee Scheme, assisting small businesses get loans from the bank that the bank would otherwise be unwilling to give because of the lack of security
- The Enterprise Initiative, including measures to help investors invest tax efficiently, regional selective grant assistance and local business advice centres
- Venture capital trusts, which are required to invest a large proportion of assets in unquoted companies. Investors gain 20% income tax relief on dividends, provided shares are held in the VCT for three years, and capital gains rollover relief if the gain is invested in a VCT.
- Regional aid, principally grants to businesses to set up in selected areas
- Measures to support innovation and technology including awards and training assistance.

2.5 Financial reporting and accounting

As you will be aware, limited companies and their directors are bound by the provisions of legislation and accounting standards. This legislation governs the preparation and publication of the annual financial statements of companies. We shall consider the particular impact of changes in accounting standards in Chapter 4 of this text.

2.6 Influencing government policy

As well as compliance, businesses also need to consider how they can actively influence policy. Influence may be by the industry or an individual business.

(a) **Initial influence**

Industry influence is perhaps most important during the **early stages** of legislation when legislation may be built upon good practice. Industry concerns may also be an important influence upon **fiscal policy.**

(b) **Comments**

Later in the legislative programme, when more specific proposals have been published businesses affected directly by the legislation may be given the chance to **comment** in detail.

(c) **Lobbying**

Whilst legislation is going through legislature, members may be **lobbied**, although lobbying of this sort has had much bad publicity in certain countries.

(d) **Enforcement**

When the legislation is in place, governments may require the help of businesses to **enforce** it. In any event governments regularly seek **feedback** on legislation through formal bodies such as Deregulation Taskforces or more informally.

Exam focus point

In the exam, you may wish to answer questions using your own country's legislation as an example. You will however need to understand how your own country's legislation deals with the issues that we have discussed.

3 Legal and regulatory constraints

FAST FORWARD

Companies must have procedures for **ensuring compliance** with **all relevant laws**. Costs of compliance may be significant.

3.1 Legal requirements

As you have seen in your earlier studies, businesses need to be aware of the whole range of legislation that affects their operations. This includes company, tax, health and safety and consumer legislation. These laws not only affect what companies do, but also the relationships between shareholders, creditors, management, employees and the general public. Relevant legislation will include **company legislation**, legislation on employment, health and safety regulations, legislation on consumer protection and consumer rights and environmental legislation.

3.1.1 Compliance with legislation

Organisations need to consider carefully the financial aspects of compliance with the law. Compliance with legislation may involve **extra costs**, including the extra procedures and investment necessary to conform to safety standards, staff training costs and legal costs. Higher costs of compliance, as well as costs of labour may mean that companies **relocate** to countries where costs and regulatory burdens are lower. However these costs may also act as a **significant barrier to entry**, benefiting companies that are already in the industry.

Businesses that fail to comply with the law run the risk of financial **penalties** and the financial consequences of accompanying **bad publicity**. Companies may also be forced into legal action to counter claims of allegedly bad practice that is not actually illegal; even a victory in such an action may not prevent much bad publicity.

Companies may therefore wish to take all possible steps to avoid the bad publicity resulting from a court action. This includes investing in systems that ensure that the company **keeps abreast** of **changes in the law**, and staff are kept fully informed. Internal procedures may be designed to minimise the risks from legal action. Ultimately businesses may prefer the costs of settling cases out of court, rather than the direct and indirect consequences of court action.

3.2 Corporate governance

FAST FORWARD

The **corporate governance debate** impacts upon the way companies make decisions, their financial organisation and their relations with investors and auditors.

Key term

Corporate governance is the system by which companies and other entities are directed and controlled. **Boards of directors** are responsible for the governance of their companies. The **shareholders'** role in governance is to appoint the directors and the **auditors** and to satisfy themselves that an appropriate governance structure is in place.

The responsibilities of the board include:

- setting the company's **strategic aims**
- providing the **leadership** to put them into effect
- supervising the **management** of the business
- **reporting** to shareholders on their stewardship

The board's actions are subject to laws, regulations and the shareholders in general meeting. *(OT 2005)*

Corporate governance has emerged as a major issue in the last ten to fifteen years in the light of several high profile collapses. Guidance has been given because of the lack of confidence perceived in financial reporting and in the ability of auditors to provide the assurances required by the users of financial accounts.

Exam focus point

Paper 3, Risk and Control Strategy covers this area and you can use **relevant** information from the other areas you have studied in the financial strategy exam.

3.2.1 UK guidance

A number of reports in the UK have addressed key corporate governance issues. A summary of their recommendations is given below. The UK Stock Exchange expects listed companies to follow a Combined Code that incorporates the recommendations of these reports.

SUMMARY OF UK CORPORATE GOVERNANCE REPORTS	
Board of directors	Board must **exercise effective control** by **meeting regularly** and **monitoring management**. No individual should exercise excessive power, and there should be a **balance** between executive and independent non-executive directors. Ideally the posts of Chairman and Chief Executive should be held by different people.
Directors' remuneration	Remuneration should be decided by a **remuneration committee**, staffed by independent non-executive directors. **Directors' service contracts** should **not last** for **excessive periods of time**, ideally the target should be one year or less. Remuneration must be clearly disclosed to shareholders.
Audit committees	Companies should establish an **audit committee**, which should ensure a **balance** between audit objectivity and value for money. The committee should also **review the provision of non-audit services**, and monitor and review internal audit and management systems.
Internal audit and control	Companies should consider **establishing an internal audit function**; auditors should report on internal controls.
Investor relations	Investors should receive **notice of meetings** in plenty of time. At general meetings, shareholders should be able to **vote separately** on each substantially separate issue. Shareholders should be able to **express their views** by voting on the annual report and accounts, as well as having the legal right to elect directors.

3.2.2 Other jurisdictions

In other jurisdictions the rules are much stricter. Most importantly **strengthened statutory rules** are being introduced in **America** as a result of the 2002 Sarbanes-Oxley Act, passed in the wake of corporate scandals, most notably Enron.

Under Sarbanes-Oxley companies will not be able to obtain a listing unless they have an **audit committee.** Auditors are prohibited from offering a variety of non-audit services to audit clients. Disclosure requirements are expanded. The Act also requires investigations to be undertaken in a number of areas including compulsory rotation of auditors and the areas of reporting that are most susceptible to fraud.

Exam focus point

How Sarbanes-Oxley will impact upon foreign companies trading in America is still under discussion, but bear its requirements in mind if you are considering companies with trading interests in America.

The changing corporate governance framework will particularly impact upon the finance function, something we shall consider further in Part B of this text.

3.2.3 Impact of corporate governance requirements on businesses

The consequences of **failure to obey corporate governance regulations** should be considered along with failure to obey any other sort of legislation. In regimes where corporate governance rules are **guidelines** rather than regulations, businesses will consider what the consequences might be of non-compliance, in particular the **impact** on **share prices**.

Obedience to requirements or guidelines can also have consequences for businesses. For example increased disclosure regulations have highlighted **director remuneration packages** that investors have thought to be excessively generous.

3.3 Regulatory bodies

FAST FORWARD

Depending on the sector in which they are involved, businesses may be subject to **industry regulators** or **self-regulation**.

Key term

Regulation can be defined as any form of state interference with the operation of the free market. This could involve regulating demand, supply, price, profit, quantity, quality, entry, exit, information, technology, or any other aspect of production and consumption in the market.

Where privatisation has perpetuated monopolies over natural resources, industry regulatory authorities have the role of ensuring that **consumers' interests** are not subordinated to those of other stakeholders, such as employees, shareholders and tax authorities. The regulator's role may be 'advisory' rather than statutory, and may extend only to a part of a company's business, necessitating a correct allocation of costs across different activities of the company.

3.3.1 Methods of regulation

The two main methods used to regulate monopoly industries are as follows.

(a) **Price control**

The regulator **agreeing the output prices** with the industry. Typically, the price is **progressively reduced** in **real terms** each year by setting price increases at a rate below that of inflation. This has been used with success by regulators in the UK but can be confrontational.

(b) **Profit control**

The regulator **agreeing the maximum profit** which the industry can make. A typical method is to fix maximum profit at x% of capital employed, but this does not provide any incentive to making more efficient use of assets: the higher the capital employed, the higher the profit.

In addition the regulator will be concerned with:

(a) Actively **promoting competition** by encouraging new firms in the industry and preventing unreasonable barriers to entry

(b) Addressing **quality** and **safety** issues and considering the **social implications** of service provision and pricing

3.4 Self-regulation

In many areas, the participants may decide to maintain a system of voluntary self-regulation, possibly in order to try to avert the imposition of government controls. Areas where self-regulation often exists are the professions and financial markets (the UK's Financial Services Authority).

3.5 Costs of regulation

The potential costs of regulation include the following.

3.5.1 Enforcement costs

Regulation can only be effective if it is properly monitored and enforced. **Direct costs** of enforcement include the setting up and running of the regulatory agencies – employing specialist staff, monitoring behaviour, prosecuting offenders (or otherwise ensuring actions are modified in line with regulations). **Indirect costs** are those incurred by the regulated (eg the firms in the industry) in conforming to the restrictions.

3.5.2 Regulatory capture

This refers to the process by which the regulator becomes **dominated and controlled by the regulated firms**, such that it acts increasingly in the latter's interests, rather than those of consumers. This is a phenomenon which has been observed in the USA (where economic regulation has always been more widespread).

3.5.3 Unintended consequences of regulation

An example is the so-called 'Aversch-Johnson effect'. This refers to the tendency of rate-of-return (profit) regulation to encourage firms to become **too capital-intensive** and hence minimise their return on capital. In other words, firms regulated in this way (which is a common method of economic regulation in the USA) have an incentive to choose a method of production which is not least-cost, because it involves too high a ratio of capital to labour.

TOPCIMA link

Problems with regulatory bodies may be a significant constraint on a strategy of expansion, which you have to discuss in a case study answer.

4 Economic constraints

FAST FORWARD

Economic constraints on strategy will be imposed by **inflation, interest rates** and **exchange rates**.

4.1 Inflation

The rate of **price inflation** in the economy is important because it affects:

- Costs of production and selling prices
- Interest rates
- Foreign exchange rates
- Demand in the economy (high rates of inflation limit real economic growth. However businesses' inability to meet demand might have caused high inflation levels in the first place).

4.1.1 The effects of inflation

Businesses faced with higher costs of production and higher interest rates may try to pass on their extra costs to customers by raising their selling prices (However if they wish to maintain demand levels, they may **cut** their prices, putting downward pressure on margins, costs and wages.) Some companies will be able to raise prices more easily than others, depending on the nature of demand in the industry's markets.

Inflation affects **asset values, costs and revenues** in the following ways.

(a) Since non-current assets and inventory will increase in money value, the **same quantities of assets** must be financed by **increasing amounts of capital**.

    (i) If the future rate of inflation can be predicted, management can work out how much extra finance the company will need, and take steps to obtain it (for example by **increasing retentions of earnings**, or **borrowing**).

    (ii) If the future rate of inflation cannot be predicted with accuracy, management should guess at what it will be and plan to obtain extra finance accordingly. However, plans should also be made to obtain '**contingency funds**' if the rate of inflation exceeds expectations.

(b) Inflation means higher costs and **higher selling prices**, creating a spiral of rising costs and prices and weakening demand from abroad for a country's products.

(c) Inflation results in a **redistribution** in **favour of borrowers** at the expense of lenders. The **real value of savings** is being **eroded**. Inflation also results in a redistribution of income away from people on fixed incomes and those lacking bargaining power.

4.1.2 Inflation and uncertainty

When managers evaluate a particular project, or when shareholders evaluate their investments, they can only guess at what the rate of inflation is going to be. Their expectations will probably be wrong, at least to some extent, because it is extremely difficult to forecast the rate of inflation accurately. This may adversely affect business confidence.

The effect of higher prices on demand is also not necessarily easy to predict. A company that raises its prices by 10% because the general rate of inflation is running at 10% might suffer a serious fall in demand.

The only way in which uncertainty about inflation can be allowed for in project evaluation is by **risk and uncertainty** analysis.

Question — Inflation

Learning outcome: A(iii)

Pellas is a small manufacturing company which specialises in the production of high quality electronic organisers, which are sold direct to the public by mail order. Summary figures from the Income Statements for the last three years are shown below.

Year	*20X5*	*20X6*	*20X7*
	£m	£m	£m
Sales	1.250	1.500	1.620
Cost of sales	0.650	0.830	0.967
Operating profit	0.600	0.670	0.653

Notes

(1) Unit selling price for the electronic organiser has been fixed by Pellas since the year 20W5. This is in response to low levels of demand in the UK consumer electronlcs market.

(2) 80% of the cost of sales in 20X5 is accounted for by electronic components purchased from a supplier who has increased prices by 10% in each of the last two years.

Government financial statistics for the same period reveal the following.

Retail price index		*Wholesale price index*	
December 20X5	150.7	December 20X5	132.4
December 20X6	154.4	December 20X6	134.8
December 20X7	159.5	December 20X7	137.5

Required

(a) Calculate and comment on the annual rate of inflation for 20X5/6 and 20X6/7, as measured by both the retail and wholesale price indices.

(b) In general terms describe how inflation affects companies.

(c) Write a report for the directors of Pellas, commenting on the way in which they have managed their sales and costs under inflationary conditions.

Answer

(a)

		Index at start of period	Index at end of period	Increase	Inflation %
RPI	20X5/X6	150.7	154.4	3.7	2.46
	20X6/X7	154.4	159.5	5.1	3.30
WPI	20X5/X6	132.4	134.8	2.4	1.81
	20X6/X7	134.8	137.5	2.7	2.00

The figures show that the rate of inflation in the RPI was higher than that in the WPI throughout the period in question, and that the gap between the two rates is increasing. To explain this difference it is helpful to understand exactly what is being measured by each index. The RPI measures the percentage changes month by month in the average level of prices of the commodities and services, including housing costs, purchased by the great majority of households. The WPI measures the rate of change in prices of goods leaving the factory gate. There are probably two main reasons for the disparity in the rates.

(i) During the period in question there were a number of rises in **interest rates**. Interest rate rises impact directly on the RPI through their effect on mortgage interest costs, while the effect will be felt more slowly on the WPI as suppliers have to renegotiate prices with their customers. The RPI will therefore respond more sharply to the increase in interest rates.

(ii) The WPI is related more directly to the manufacturing sector, while the RPI is linked to the prices of both goods and services.

(b) **Inflation** can affect all the financial areas of a business and impact upon its **profit performance** in a variety of ways.

(i) The rate of inflation will **affect the prices** that a business must pay for all the factors of production and the prices that it is able to charge to its customers. It will therefore affect the level of reported profits.

(ii) When inflation is high, **regular price reviews** will be necessary so as to ensure that there is no erosion of real returns. In times of low inflation it may be difficult to achieve any price increases due to a reduced level of inflationary expectations.

(iii) Where there is a high level of inflation, there is also a **high level of uncertainty** about the future. This tends to make businesses wary of committing themselves to new long-term investments.

(iv) Inflation places **pressure on cash flow**, particularly where the prices of raw materials are rising ahead of prices charged to customers. Even where sales prices do keep up, additional cash will still be required to cover the increased payments to suppliers that will have to be made in advance of monies being received in respect of credit sales.

(v) Companies may **increase their level of investment in inventory** as a hedge against anticipated price rises. This will also increase the amount of working capital required and restrict the funds available for new investment.

(vi) Different approaches may need to be taken to **financial reporting** and evaluation methods, such as current cost accounting techniques, which make it easier to understand the changing performance of a company over time.

(vii) The relationship between **inflation rates** and **interest rates** means that interest rates tend to rise during a period of inflation. This has implications both for the capital structure decisions and investment appraisal criteria used by companies.

(c) To: Board of Directors, Pellas
From: Accountant
Date: 12 June 20X8
Subject: Review of the management of sales and costs for the period 20X5 to 20X7

Introduction

The trading environment during the period in question has been difficult for Pellas. Due to price sensitivity, it has not been possible to increase prices to customers, even though the cost of key components has been rising at 10% per year, which is well above the rate of inflation. However, Pellas has been able to increase sales volumes during the period by 20% in the first year and 8% in the second, and to increase operating profits, despite the large increases in component costs.

Numerical analysis

It is helpful to analyse the figures to show the changes in the non-component costs, and the relationship of the different costs to sales.

	20X5		*20X6*		*20X7*	
	£'000	%	£'000	%	£'000	%
Sales	1,250		1,500		1,620	
Component costs	520	41.6	686	45.7	815	50.3
Non component costs	130	10.4	144	9.6	152	9.4
Operating profit	600	48.0	670	44.7	653	40.3

The figures show that although component costs have risen to over 50% of sales, the other operating costs have been tightly controlled and now represent 1% less of sales than they did in 20X5. Given that the growth in sales has come purely from volume increases and not from price, this is a very good achievement by the company. However, because the components make up such a large percentage of the total cost, it has not been possible to prevent a **fall in the rate of return on sales** during the period. Most worrying is the fact that in 20X6/X7 profits fell in absolute terms as well as percentage terms, despite the increase in sales, although they are still above the 20X5 level.

Conclusions

Pellas has done well to achieve sales growth in a market where demand is low. It has also managed to mitigate the effect of component price increases through the tight management of other costs. However, it now needs to consider in more detail the extent of **price sensitivity** in the market and the possibility of finding **alternative sources of components**, since a situation of declining profits is not sustainable in the long-term.

4.2 Interest rates

Interest rates are an important element in the economic environment, and are of particular relevance for financial managers.

(a) Interest rates **measure the cost of borrowing**. If a company wants to raise money, it must pay interest on its borrowing, and the rate of interest payable will be one which is 'current' at the time the borrowing takes place. When interest rates go up, companies will pay more interest on some of their borrowing (for example on bank overdrafts).

(b) Interest rates in a country **influence the foreign exchange value** of the country's currency.

(c) Interest rates act as a **guide to the sort of return** that a company's shareholders might want, and changes in market interest rates will affect share prices.

4.2.1 The general level of interest rates

Interest rates on any one type of financial asset will vary over time. In other words, the general level of interest rates might go up or down. The general level of interest rates is affected by several factors.

(a) **Need for a real return**

Investors normally want to **earn a 'real' rate of return** on their investment. The appropriate 'real' rate of return will depend on factors such as investment risk.

(b) **Inflation**

Nominal rates of interest should be sufficient to **cover expected rates of inflation** over the term of the investment and to provide a real return.

(c) **Uncertainty about future rates of inflation**

When investors are uncertain about inflation and therefore about what future nominal and real interest rates will be, they are likely to require **higher interest yields** to persuade them to take the risk of investing, especially in the longer term.

(d) **Liquidity preference of investors and the demand for borrowing**

Higher interest rates have to be offered to persuade savers to invest their surplus money. When the demand to borrow increases, interest rates will rise.

(e) **Balance of payments**

When a country has a continuing deficit on the current account of its balance of payments, and the authorities are unwilling to allow the exchange rate to depreciate by more than a certain amount, interest rates may have to be raised to **attract capital** into the country. The country can then finance the deficit by borrowing from abroad.

(f) **Monetary policy**

From mid-1997, decisions over UK interest rate policy have been made by the Monetary Policy Committee of the Bank of England. The Bank of England influences very short-term money market rates by means of **open market operations**. Usually longer term money market rates, and then banks' base rates, will respond to the authorities' wish for interest rate changes.

(g) **Interest rates abroad**

The rate of interest in one country will be influenced by **external factors**, such as interest rates in other countries and expectations about the exchange rate. When interest rates in overseas countries are high, interest rates on domestic currency investments must also be comparably high, to avoid capital transfers abroad and a fall in the exchange rate of the domestic currency.

4.2.2 Interest rates in different markets and market segments

(a) **Risk**

Higher risk borrowers must pay higher rates on their borrowing, to compensate lenders for the greater risk involved.

(b) **The need to make a profit on re-lending**

Financial intermediaries make their profits from re-lending at a higher rate of interest than the cost of their borrowing.

(c) **The duration of the lending**

Normally, long-term loans will earn a higher yield than short-term loans. You should be familiar with the reasons for this term structure of interest rates as illustrated by the **yield curve**, from your previous studies; the main points are summarised below.

(d) **The size of the loan**

Deposits above a certain amount with a bank or building society might attract higher rates of interest than smaller deposits.

(e) **International interest rates**

The level of interest rates varies from country to country. The reasons for these variations are:

(i) Differing rates of inflation from country to country
(ii) Government policies on interest rates and foreign currency exchange rates

(f) **Different types of financial asset**

Different types of financial asset attract different rates of interest. This reflects the competition for deposits between different types of financial institution.

4.2.3 The term structure of interest rates: the yield curve

Interest rates depend on the **term to maturity** of the asset. For example, government stock might be short-dated, medium-dated, or long-dated depending on when the stock is to be redeemed and the investor repaid.

The **term structure of interest rates** refers to the way in which the yield on a security varies according to the term of the borrowing, as shown by the **yield curve**.

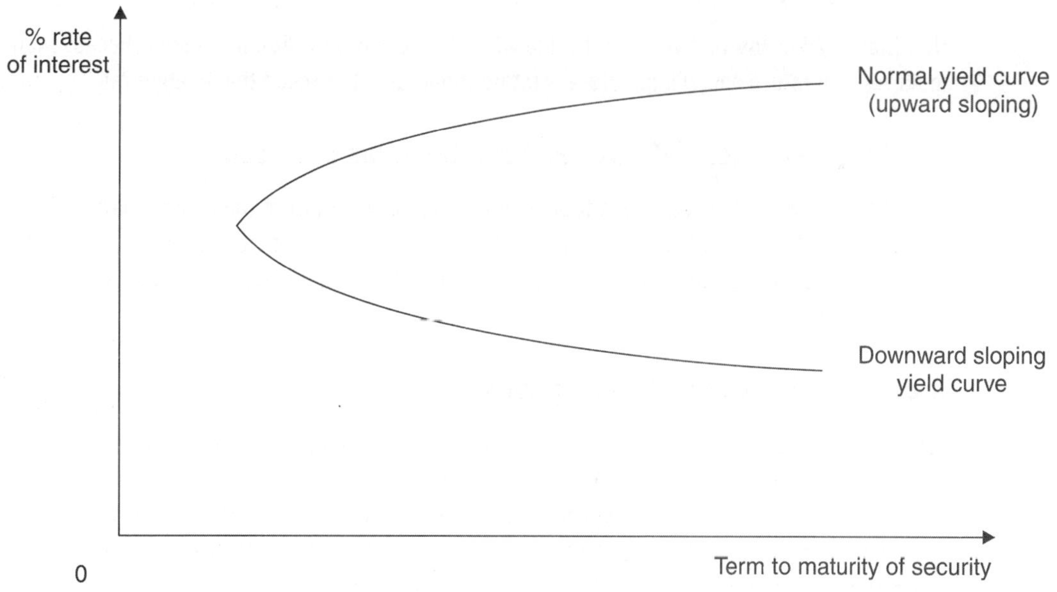

The reasons why, in theory, the yield curve will normally be upward sloping, so that long-term financial assets offer a higher yield than short-term assets, are as follows.

(a) **The investor must be compensated for tying up his money in the asset for a longer period of time**. The only way to overcome this **liquidity preference** of investors is to compensate them for the loss of liquidity; in other words, to offer a higher rate of interest on longer dated stock.

(b) **There is a greater risk in lending long-term than in lending short-term**. To compensate investors for this risk, they might require a higher yield on longer dated investments.

A yield curve might **slope downwards**, with short-term rates higher than longer term rates for the following reasons.

(a) **Expectations**. When interest rates are expected to fall, short-term rates might be higher than long-term rates, and the yield curve would be downward sloping.

(b) **Government policy**. A policy of keeping interest rates relatively high might have the effect of forcing short-term interest rates higher than long-term rates.

(c) The **market segmentation theory**. The slope of the yield curve will reflect conditions in different segments of the market. This theory holds that the major investors are confined to a particular segment of the market and will not switch segment even if the forecast of likely future interest rates changes.

4.2.4 Nominal rates and real rates of interest

Nominal rates of interest are the actual rates of interest paid. **Real rates of interest** are rates of interest adjusted for the rate of inflation. The real rate is therefore a measure of the increase in the real wealth, expressed in terms of **buying power**, of the investor or lender.

(a) The real rate of interest can be calculated as:

$$\text{Real rate of interest} = \frac{1+\text{nominal rate of interest}}{1+\text{rate of inflation}} - 1$$

If the nominal rate of interest is 12% and the rate of inflation is 8%, the real rate of interest would be 1.12/1.08 – 1 = 0.037 = 3.7%.

(b) The real rate of interest is sometimes estimated (for arithmetical simplicity) as the difference between the nominal rate of interest and the rate of inflation. In our example, this would be 12% – 8% = 4%.

Nominal rates of interest will tend to **rise** when the **rate of inflation increases,** because lenders will want to earn a real return and will therefore want nominal rates to exceed the inflation rate.

4.2.5 Interest rates, inflation and capital gains or losses

A positive real rate of interest adds to an investor's real wealth from the income he earns from his investments. However, when interest rates go up or down, perhaps due to a rise or fall in the rate of inflation, there will also be a potential capital loss or gain for the investor. In other words, the market value of interest-bearing securities will alter. **Market values will fall when interest rates go up and vice versa.**

4.2.6 Interest rates and share prices

When interest rates change, the return expected by investors from shares will also change. For example, if interest rates fell from 14% to 12% on government securities, and from 15% to 13% on company loan notes, the return expected from shares (dividends and capital growth) would also fall. This is because shares and debt are alternative ways of investing money. **If interest rates fall, shares become more attractive to buy**. As demand for shares increases, their prices rise too, and so the dividend return gained from them falls in percentage terms.

4.2.7 Changes in interest rates and financing decisions

Interest rates are important for financial decisions by companies.

(a) **When interest rates are low**, it might be financially prudent:

(i) To **borrow more**, preferably at a fixed rate of interest, and so increase the company's gearing

(ii) To **borrow for long periods** rather than for short periods

(iii) To **pay back loans which incur a high interest rate**, if it is within the company's power to do so, and take out new loans at a lower interest rate

(b) **When interest rates are higher:**

(i) A company might decide to **reduce the amount of its debt finance**, and to substitute equity finance, such as retained earnings

(ii) A company which has a large surplus of cash and liquid funds to invest might **switch some of its short-term investments out of equities and into interest-bearing securities**

(iii) A company might opt to raise new finance by **borrowing short-term funds and debt at a variable interest rate** (for example on overdraft) rather than long-term funds at fixed rates of interest, in the hope that interest rates will soon come down again

4.2.8 Interest rates and new capital investments

When interest rates go up, and so the cost of finance to a company goes up, **the minimum return that a company will require on its own new capital investments will go up too**. Some new capital projects might be in the pipeline, with purchase contracts already signed with suppliers, and so there will often be a time lag before higher interest rates result in fewer new investments.

A company's management should give close consideration, when interest rates are high, to keeping **investments in assets**, particularly unwanted or inefficient non-current assets, inventories and receivables, down **to a minimum**, in order to reduce the company's need to borrow. Management also need to bear in mind the deflationary effect of high interest rates in deterring spending by raising the cost of borrowing.

4.2.9 Other impacts of higher interest rates

Businesses are likely to face lower demand for the following reasons:

- Consumer spending falling because the higher interest rates **raise the cost of capital**
- The **value of investors' financial assets falling**, and their maintaining their total wealth by saving more and spending less
- The **exchange rates rising** as a result of an influx of foreign capital, attracted by higher interest rates. This rise will result in exports becoming more expensive

However the influx of foreign funds may also eventually mean that **more capital** is **available for British companies**.

4.3 Exchange rates 11/06

Key term

Exchange rate is the rate at which a national currency exchanges for other national currencies, being set by the interaction of demand and supply of the various currencies in the foreign exchange markets (**floating** exchange rate) or by government intervention in order to maintain a constant rate of exchange (**fixed** exchange rate). *(OT 2005)*

An **exchange rate** is the rate at which money in one currency can be exchanged for money in another currency. Exchange rates between different currencies on the world's foreign exchange markets are continually changing, and often by large amounts.

Foreign exchange rates are important for a business and its financial management because they affect:

- The cost of imports
- The value of exports
- The costs and benefits of international borrowing and lending

4.3.1 Impact of changes in exchange rates

Changes in the value of a currency will affect the cost of goods from abroad. For example, if a consignment of goods is shipped from the USA to Germany and the invoice price is US$420,000:

- If the euro-dollar exchange rate is €1 = $1.50, the cost of the imports would be €280,000
- If the euro fell in value to €1 = $1.25, the cost of the imports would be higher, at €336,000

Changes in the value of a currency affect buying costs, companies and households alike, because a large proportion of the raw materials, components and finished goods that we consume is imported.

Exchange rates affect **exporting companies**, for similar reasons, because changes in exchange rates affect the price of exported goods to foreign buyers.

(a) **When the local currency, say the yen, goes up in value**, goods sold abroad by a Japanese exporter, and invoiced in yen, will cost more to the foreign buyer (who must purchase yens with his own currency in order to pay).

(b) **When the yen falls in value,** goods sold abroad by a Japanese exporter and invoiced in yen will become cheaper to foreign buyers.

To the extent that demand is influenced by price, the demand for exports will therefore vary with changes in the exchange rate.

4.3.2 Exchange rate policies

Governments may choose to let currencies fluctuate completely freely (a 'free float'), or they can attempt to regulate the values of their national currencies. Under a system of **fixed or semi-fixed exchange rates**, a government acts to ensure that its currency keeps its value. This may be accomplished by market operations, or by legislation forbidding transactions at other than the official rate.

Under **managed floating**, a government will buy or sell its currency to prevent sharp fluctuations in its value, but will set no particular limits to the currency's value.

Businesses want both **certainty** and an exchange rate which will make them **competitive**. Fixed exchange rates offer the greatest certainty, followed by a managed float. However, rigidity of exchange rates can rapidly damage the competitiveness of exporting businesses in a country. While importers might benefit in the short term from fixed exchange rates if domestic inflation remained comparatively high, they could in the longer term find that foreign currency was simply not available.

4.3.3 Exchange rates and international capital investments

Exchange rates can affect **international capital investments** significantly. Suppose that an American company issues some shares. What is the likelihood that overseas investors will buy some of the shares? Obviously, prospects for capital growth and dividends will influence the investors' decision, but prospects of changes in the value of the dollar will be important too. A 20% increase in the market value of US company shares is worthless to a European investor if in the same period of time the value of the dollar falls by a corresponding amount against the euro, leaving no capital gain in euros.

Exam focus point

> If you are required to discuss external constraints on an entity, make sure you apply your knowledge to the specific scenario and do not simply regurgitate textbook information.

5 International constraints

FAST FORWARD

Companies that **trade internationally** must be aware of the risks of **interference** in their businesses, in particular blocking of remittance of earnings from abroad.

5.1 Trading abroad

Compared with companies that trade entirely within one country, companies that trade overseas will have to deal with a variety of international constraints. Multinationals are particularly vulnerable to these problems compared with businesses that export from their base in one country.

Key term

A **multinational company** or enterprise is one which owns or controls production facilities or subsidiaries or service facilities outside the country in which it is based. Thus, a company does not become 'multinational' simply by virtue of exporting or importing products: **ownership and control of facilities abroad** is involved.

5.1.1 Foreign exchange constraints

As we have already seen, any company that exports or imports faces the risk of **higher costs** or **lower revenues** because of adverse movements in foreign exchange rates. Multinationals that trade between one country and another therefore face this risk. A company that owns assets in different countries (subsidiaries abroad) faces the risk of accounting losses due to adverse movements in exchange rates causing a fall in the value of those assets, as expressed in domestic currency.

5.1.2 Political issues

A multinational can face risks of **economic or political measures** being taken by governments, affecting the operations of its subsidiaries abroad. An example was the import restrictions imposed by the USA on the British cashmere industry during 1999, in retaliation for EU restrictions on banana imports. Political risk is discussed further below.

5.1.3 Geographical separation

The **geographical separation** of the **parent company** from its subsidiaries adds to the problems of management control of the group of companies as a whole. Separation may enhance problems caused by **language** and **cultural differences**.

5.1.4 Litigation

The risk of litigation varies in different countries and to minimise this risk, attention should be paid to **legislation** and **regulations** covering the products sold in different countries. Care should be taken to comply with contract terms.

5.2 Political risks

Key term

Political risk is the risk that political action will affect the position and value of a company.

As stated above, when a multinational company invests in another country, by setting up a subsidiary, it may face a **political risk** of action by that country's government which restricts the multinational's freedom. The government of a country will almost certainly want to **encourage** the **development and growth of commerce** and industry, but it might also be suspicious of the motives of multinationals which set up subsidiaries in their country, perhaps fearing exploitation.

The government might offer **incentives** to encourage new investment from abroad, for example by offering cash grants towards the building of factories or the purchase of equipment.

On the other hand, the government might try to **prevent the exploitation of the country by multinationals**, and the various measures it might take include the following.

(a) **Import quotas** could be used to limit the quantities of goods that a subsidiary can buy from its parent company and import for resale in its domestic markets.

(b) **Import tariffs** could make imports (such as from parent companies) more expensive and domestically produced goods therefore more competitive.

(c) **Legal standards of safety or quality** could be imposed on imported goods to prevent multinationals from selling goods through their subsidiary which have been banned as dangerous in other countries.

(d) **Exchange control regulations** could be applied (see below).

(e) A government could **restrict the ability of foreign companies to buy domestic companies**, especially those that operate in politically sensitive industries such as defence contracting, communications, energy supply and so on.

(f) A government could **nationalise** foreign-owned companies and their assets (with or without compensation to the parent company).

(g) A government could insist on a **minimum shareholding in companies by residents**. This would force a multinational to offer some of the equity in a subsidiary to investors in the country where the subsidiary operates.

5.2.1 Dealing with political issues

(a) **Negotiations with host government**

The aim of these negotiations is generally to obtain a **concession agreement**. This would cover matters such as the transfer of capital, remittances and products, access to local finance, government intervention and taxation, and transfer pricing.

(b) **Insurance**

Government or private sector insurance companies may provide protection against various threats including nationalisation, currency conversion problems, war and revolution.

(c) **Production strategies**

It may be necessary to strike a balance between **contracting out to local sources** (thus losing control) and **producing directly** (which increases the investment and hence increases the potential loss.) Alternatively it may be better to locate key parts of the production process or the distribution channels abroad. Control of patents is another possibility, since these can be enforced internationally.

(d) **Contacts with markets**

Multinationals may have contacts with customers which interventionist governments cannot obtain.

(e) **Financial management**

If a multinational **obtains funds** in local investment markets, these may be on terms that are less favourable than in markets abroad, but would mean that local institutions suffered if the local government intervened. However governments often limit the ability of multinationals to obtain funds locally.

Alternatively guarantees can be obtained from the government for the investment that can be enforced by the multinational if the government takes action.

(f) **Management structure**

Possible methods include **joint ventures** or ceding control to local investors and obtaining profits by a management contract.

If governments do intervene, multinationals may have to make use of the advantages they hold or threaten withdrawal. The threat of expropriation may be reduced by negotiation or legal threats.

5.3 Exchange controls

Exchange controls restrict the flow of foreign exchange into and out of a country, usually to defend the local currency or to protect reserves of foreign currencies. Exchange controls are generally more restrictive in developing and less developed countries although some still exist in developed countries. Typically, a government might enforce regulations:

(a) **Rationing the supply of foreign exchange**. Anyone wishing to make payments abroad in a foreign currency will be restricted by the limited supply, which stops them from buying as much as they want from abroad.

(b) **Restricting the types of transaction** for which payments abroad are allowed, for example by suspending or banning the payment of dividends to foreign shareholders, such as parent companies in multinationals, who will then have the problem of **blocked funds**.

Ways of overcoming blocked funds include the following.

(a) The parent company could **sell goods or services** to the subsidiary and obtain payment. The amount of this payment will depend on the volume of sales and also on the transfer price for the sales.

(b) A parent company which grants a subsidiary the right to make goods protected by patents can charge a **royalty** on any goods that the subsidiary sells. The size of any royalty can be adjusted to suit the wishes of the parent company's management.

(c) If the parent company makes a **loan** to a subsidiary, it can set the interest rate high or low, thereby affecting the profits of both companies. A high rate of interest on a loan, for example, would improve the parent company's profits to the detriment of the subsidiary's profits.

(d) **Management charges** may be levied by the parent company for costs incurred in the management of international operations.

Chapter roundup

- Internal constraints on financial strategy include directors' views on financial structure, the need to **maintain good relations** with **investors**, and the **need for financial strategy to be compatible** with overall business strategy.
- Government involvement can **encourage business expansion** but also **restrict businesses** through regulations and tax. This reflects differing government aims, to encourage businesses and hence raise national prosperity, but also correct adverse consequences of markets.
- Companies must have procedures for **ensuring compliance** with **all relevant laws**. Costs of compliance may be significant.
- The **corporate governance debate** impacts upon the way companies make decisions, their financial organisation and their relations with investors and auditors.
- Depending on the sector in which they are involved, businesses may be subject to **industry regulators** or **self-regulation**.
- **Economic constraints** on strategy will be imposed by **inflation, interest rates** and **exchange rates**.
- Companies that **trade internationally** must be aware of the risks of **interference** in their businesses, in particular blocking of remittance of earnings from abroad.

Quick quiz

1 List two principal methods of regulating a monopoly industry.

2 Draw a 'normal' yield curve, labelling axes.

3 Fill in the following at (A), (B) and (C) in the equation below

- Nominal rate of interest
- Real rate of interest
- Rate of inflation

$$\frac{1+(A)}{1+(B)} - 1 = (C)$$

4 What effect does a high interest rate have on the exchange rate?

5 **Fill in the blank**

Corporate governance is ______________________________.

6 What is the best way to achieve a division of responsibilities at the head of a company?

7 Give four reasons for government intervention in markets.

8 Give three potential costs of regulation.

Answers to quick quiz

1 Price control; profit control.

2

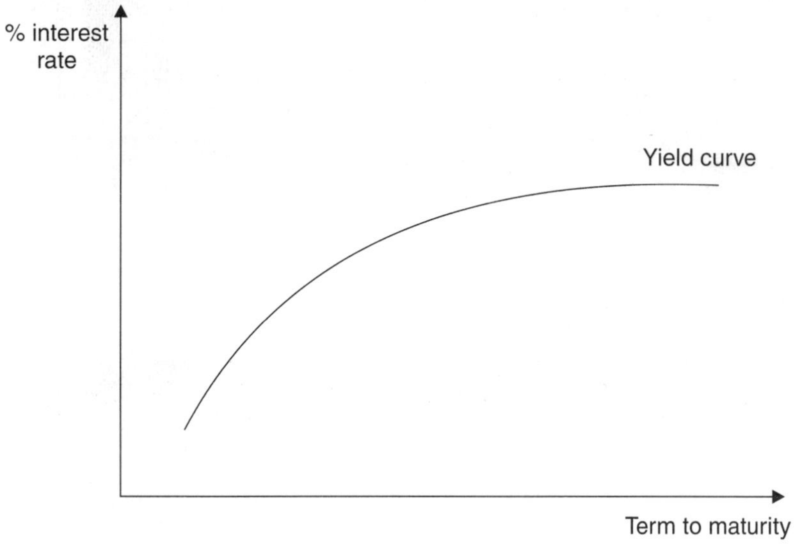

3 (A) Nominal rate of interest
(B) Rate of inflation
(C) Real rate of interest

4 It attracts foreign investment, thus increasing the demand for the currency. The exchange rate rises as a result.

5 The system by which companies are directed and controlled

6 Separation of the posts of Chairman and Chief Executive

7 (a) Imperfect competition
(b) Social costs/externalities
(c) Imperfect information
(d) Equity

8 (a) Enforcement costs
(b) Regulatory capture
(c) Unintended consequences

Now try the question below from the Exam Question Bank

Number	Level	Marks	Time
Q2	Introductory	N/a	30 mins

3

Performance analysis and forecasting financial statements

Introduction

We start this chapter by **revising ratio analysis** and other methods of **performance measurement**. You are unlikely to get a question that solely involves calculating and analysing ratios in this paper. You may be asked for example, to use ratio analysis to ascertain whether an organisation has met its objectives.

Ratio analysis will often highlight a problem with working capital so Section 2 looks at working capital management strategies.

Cash forecasting is vital to ensure that **sufficient funds** will be **available** when they are needed to sustain the activities of an enterprise, at an acceptable cost. Although you will have encountered forecasts before, again don't neglect this chapter as the examiners have highlighted this topic as important. You may well get a compulsory question on a cash forecast.

In Section 4 we look at how you should prepare forecast financial statements.

Section 5 deals with the links between the cash requirements forecast and decisions on funding.

Topic list	Learning outcomes	Syllabus references	Ability required
1 Performance analysis	A(iv)	A(5)	Evaluation
2 Working capital management strategies	B(i)	B(1)	Evaluation
3 Cash forecasts	A(iv)	A(7),(8)	Evaluation
4 Forecast financial statements: example	A(iv)	A(7),(8)	Evaluation
5 Sensitivity analysis and changes in variables	A(iv)	A(7),(8)	Evaluation
6 Financing requirements	A(iv)	A(7),(9)	Evaluation

1 Performance analysis

FAST FORWARD

Ratios provide a means of systematically analysing financial statements. They can be grouped under the headings **profitability**, **liquidity**, **gearing** and **shareholders' investment**. It is important to calculate **relevant ratios** and to take into account the **limitations of ratio analysis**.

1.1 Uses of ratio analysis

The key to obtaining meaningful information from ratio analysis is **comparison**: comparing ratios over time within the same business to establish whether the business is **improving** or **declining**, and comparing ratios between similar businesses to see whether the company you are analysing is better or worse than average within its own business sector.

A vital element in effective ratio analysis is understanding the needs of the person for whom the ratio analysis is being undertaken. **Investors** for example will be interested in the **risk and return** relating to their investment, so will be concerned with dividends, market prices, level of debt vs equity etc. **Suppliers** and **loan creditors** are interested in receiving the payments due to them, so will want to know how liquid the business is. **Managers** are interested in ratios that indicate how well the business is being run, and also how the business is doing in relation to its **competitors**.

Exam focus point

Try not to be too mechanical when working out ratios, and think constantly about what you are trying to achieve. You will only obtain credit in the exam for calculating ratios that are relevant and being able to explain the results.

1.2 Limitations of ratio analysis

Although ratio analysis can be a very useful technique, it is important to realise its limitations.

(a) **Availability of comparable information**

When making comparisons with other companies in the industry, industry averages may hide **wide variations** in figures. Figures for 'similar' companies may provide a better guide, but then there are problems identifying which companies are similar, and obtaining enough detailed information about them.

(b) **Use of historical/out-of-date information**

Comparisons with the previous history of a business may be of limited use, if the business has recently undergone, or is about to undergo, **substantial changes**. In addition, ratios based on published accounts suffer from the disadvantage that these accounts are filed some months after the end of the accounting period. Comparisons over time may also be distorted by **inflation**, leading to assets being stated at values that do not reflect replacement costs, and revenue increasing for reasons other than more sales being made.

(c) **Ratios are not definitive**

'Ideal levels' vary industry by industry, and even they are not definitive. Companies may be able to exist without any difficulty with ratios that are rather worse than the industry average.

(d) **Need for careful interpretation**

For example, if comparing two businesses' liquidity ratios, one business may have higher levels. This might appear to be 'good', but further investigation might reveal that the higher ratios are a result of higher inventory and receivable levels which are a result of poor working capital management by the business with the 'better' ratios.

(e) **Manipulation**

Any ratio including profit may be distorted by **choice of accounting policies**. For smaller companies, working capital ratios may be distorted depending on whether a big customer pays, or a large supplier is paid, before or after the year-end.

(f) **Ratios lack standard form**

For example, when calculating **gearing** some companies will include bank overdrafts, others exclude them.

(g) **Other information**

Ratio analysis on its own is not sufficient for interpreting company accounts, and there are other items of information that should be looked at. We shall consider this further below.

Exam focus point

> Bear these limitations in mind when calculating and interpreting ratios, as examiners' reports give many examples of misapplication of ratio analysis, and over-simplistic and misleading interpretations.

1.3 Categorisation of ratios

You may remember that ratios can be grouped into the following four categories:

- Profitability and return
- Debt and gearing
- Liquidity: control of cash and other working capital items
- Shareholders' investment ratios (or 'stock market ratios')

Within each heading we will identify a number of standard measures or ratios that are normally calculated and generally accepted as meaningful indicators.

The Du Pont system of ratio analysis involves constructing a pyramid of interrelated ratios like that below.

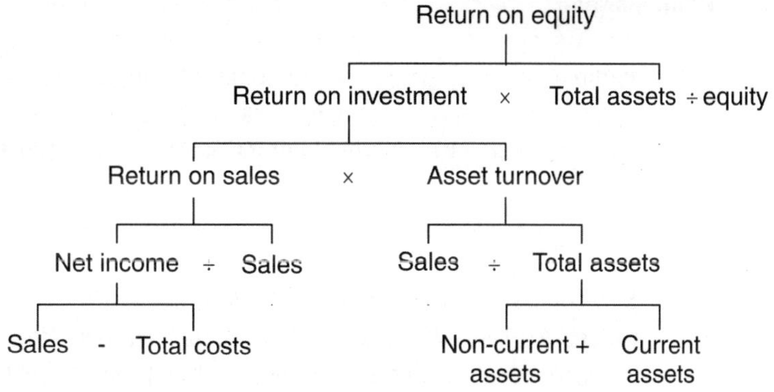

Such ratio pyramids help in providing for an **overall management plan** to achieve profitability, and allow the **interrelationships** between ratios to be **checked**.

1.4 Profitability and return

Knowledge brought forward from earlier studies

Return on capital employed

$$\text{ROCE} = \frac{\text{PBIT}}{\text{Capital employed}}\,\% = \frac{\text{Profit from operations}}{\text{Total assets less current liabilities}}\,\%$$

When **interpreting** ROCE look for the following.

- How risky is the business?
- How capital intensive is it?
- What ROCE do similar businesses have?
- How does it compare with current market borrowing rates, is it earning enough to be able to cover the costs of extra borrowing?

Problems: which items to consider to achieve comparability:

- Revaluation of assets
- Accounting policies, eg goodwill, research and development
- Whether bank overdraft is classified as a short/long-term liability

Return on equity

$$\text{ROE} = \frac{\text{Profit after tax and pref div}}{\text{Ordinary share capital + reserves}}\,\%$$

This gives a more **restricted view** of capital than ROCE, but the same principles apply.

ROCE = Profit margin × Asset turnover

Profit margin

$$\text{Profit margin} = \frac{\text{PBIT}}{\text{Sales}}\,\% \qquad \text{Gross profit margin} = \frac{\text{Gross profit}}{\text{Sales}}\,\%$$

It is useful to compare profit margin to gross profit % to investigate movements which do not match.

Gross profit margin

- Sales prices, sales volume and sales mix
- Purchase prices and related costs (discount, carriage etc)
- Production costs, both direct (materials, labour) and indirect (overheads both fixed and variable)
- Inventory levels and valuation, including errors, cut-off and costs of running out of goods

Net profit margin

- Sales expenses in relation to sales levels
- Administrative expenses, including salary levels
- Distribution expenses in relation to sales levels

Asset turnover

$$\text{Asset turnover} = \frac{\text{Sales}}{\text{Total assets less current liabilities}}$$

This measures the **efficiency** of the use of assets. Amend to just non-current assets for capital intensive businesses.

1.5 Debt and gearing

Knowledge brought forward from earlier studies

Debt ratio

$$\text{Debt ratio} = \frac{\text{Current and non-current liabilities}}{\text{Current and non-current assets}} \% \ (>50\%=\text{high})$$

Debt/equity

$$\text{Debt/equity ratio} = \frac{\text{Interest bearing net debts}}{\text{Shareholders' funds}} \% \ (> 100\% = \text{high})$$

Capital or Financial gearing (leverage) ratio

$$\text{Gearing} = \frac{\text{Prior charge capital}}{\text{Total capital}}$$

Operating gearing (leverage)

$$\text{Gearing} = \frac{\text{Contribution (sales minus variable cost of sales)}}{\text{PBIT}}$$

Demonstrates relationship between cost operating structure and profitability. Indication of business risks from rises or falls in volume.

Interest cover

$$\text{Interest cover} = \frac{\text{PBIT(incl int receivable)}}{\text{Interest payable}} \text{ or } \frac{\text{Profit from operations}}{\text{Finance costs}}$$

Is this a better way to measure gearing? Company must generate enough profit to cover interest. Certainly it's important to bankers and lenders.

Cash flow ratio

$$\text{Cash flow ratio} = \frac{\text{Net cash flow from operations}}{\text{Current and non-current liabilities}}$$

Indicator of whether company will be able to meet foreseeable debts and future commitments from cash generated by operations.

We shall consider gearing and investor ratios further in Chapter 10.

1.6 Liquidity

Knowledge brought forward from earlier studies

Current ratio

$$\text{Current ratio} = \frac{\text{Current assets}}{\text{Current liabilities}}$$

Assume assets realised at book level ∴ theoretical. 2:1 acceptable? 1.5:1? It depends on the industry. Remember that excessively large levels can indicate excessive receivables and inventories, and poor control of working capital.

Quick ratio

$$\text{Quick ratio (acid test)} = \frac{\text{Current assets - Inventory}}{\text{Current liabilities}}$$

Eliminates illiquid and subjectively valued inventory. Care is needed: it could be high if **overtrading** with receivables, but no cash. Is 1:1 OK? Many supermarkets operate on 0.3, as inventories of goods are very liquid and inventory turnover is very fast.

Receivable collection period

$$\text{Average collection period} = \frac{\text{Trade receivables}}{\text{Credit sales}} \times 365$$

Is it **consistent** with quick/current ratio? If not, investigate.

Inventory turnover

$$\text{Inventory turnover} = \frac{\text{Cost of sales}}{\text{Inventory}} \text{/Inventory days} = \frac{\text{Inventory}}{\text{Cost of sales}} \times 365$$

The quicker the turnover the better? But remember:

- Lead times
- Seasonal fluctuations in orders
- Alternative uses of warehouse space
- Bulk buying discounts
- Likelihood of inventory perishing or becoming obsolete

Payables payment period

$$\text{Payables payment period} = \frac{\text{Trade payables}}{\text{Purchases}} \times 365$$

Use **cost of sales** if purchases are not disclosed.

Cash cycle

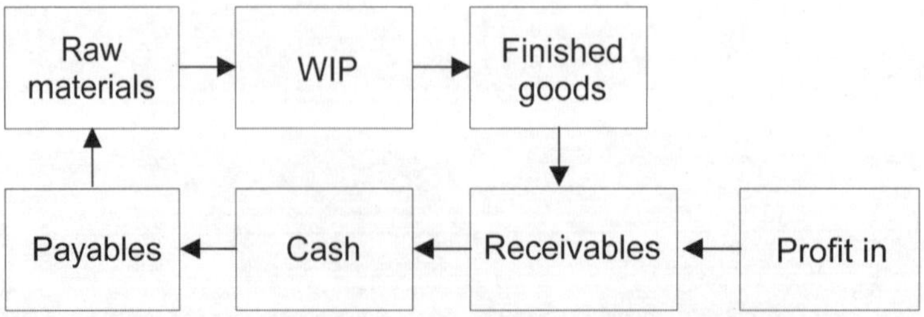

- Cash flow timing does not match sales/cost of sales timing as credit is taken
- Holding inventory delays the time between payments for goods and sales receipts

Reasons for changes in liquidity

- Credit control efficiency altered
- Altering payment period of suppliers as a source of funding
- Reducing inventory holdings to maintain liquidity

We shall look at the management of working capital in Section 2.

1.7 Shareholder investor ratios

Knowledge brought forward from earlier studies

Dividend yield

$$\text{Dividend yield} = \frac{\text{Dividend per share}}{\text{Market price per share}}\%$$

- **Low yield**: the company retains a large proportion of profits to reinvest
- **High yield**: this is a risky company or slow-growing

Dividend yield is generally less than interest yield. Shareholders will expect price rises, and wish for return (dividends + capital gains) to exceed return investors get from fixed interest securities.

Earnings per share (EPS)

$$\text{EPS} = \frac{\text{Profit after tax and preferred dividends}}{\text{Number of equity shares in issue}}$$

Investors look for growth; earnings levels need to be sustained to pay dividends and invest in the business. In order for comparisons over time to be valid, must be consistent basis of calculation. EPS can be manipulated.

Need to consider possibility of dilution through exercise of warrants or options, or conversion of loan notes

Dividend cover

$$\text{Dividend cover} = \frac{\text{EPS}}{\text{Div per share}}$$

$$\text{Or} \quad \frac{\text{Profit after tax and pref div}}{\text{Div on ordinary shares}}$$

This shows **how safe the dividend is**, or the extent of profit retention. Variations are due to maintaining dividend when profits are declining.

The converse of dividend cover is the dividend payout ratio.

$$\text{Dividend payout ratio} = \frac{\text{Dividend per share}}{\text{EPS}}$$

P/E ratio

$$\text{P/E ratio} = \frac{\text{Market price per share}}{\text{EPS}}$$

The **higher the better** here: it reflects the confidence of the market in high earnings growth and/or low risk. A rise in EPS will cause an increase in P/E ratio, but maybe not to same extent.

P/E ratio will be affected by interest rate changes; a rise in rates will mean a fall in the P/E ratio as shares become less attractive. P/E ratio also depends on market expectations and confidence.

Earnings yield

$$\text{Earnings yield} = \frac{\text{EPS}}{\text{Market price per share}}\ \%$$

This shows the dividend yield if there is no retention of profit. It allows you to compare companies with **different dividend policies**, showing growth rather than earnings.

Net assets per share

$$\text{Net assets per share} = \frac{\text{Net assets}}{\text{No of shares}}$$

This is a crude measure of value of a company, liable to distortion.

Other factors

Investors are also interested in current market price, past and future returns and security of investment.

We shall look at the major investor ratios again in Chapter 10.

Question — Ratios

Learning outcome: A(iv)

Calculate liquidity and working capital ratios from the accounts of a manufacturer of products for the construction industry, and comment on the ratios.

	20X8	*20X7*
	$m	$m
Revenue	2,065.0	1,788.7
Cost of sales	1,478.6	1,304.0
Gross profit	586.4	484.7
Current assets		
Inventory	119.0	109.0
Receivables (note 1)	400.9	347.4
Short-term investments	4.2	18.8
Cash at bank and in hand	48.2	48.0
	572.3	523.2
Creditors: amounts falling due within one year		
Loans and overdrafts	49.1	35.3
Taxes	62.0	46.7
Dividend	19.2	14.3
Payables (note 2)	370.7	324.0
	501.0	420.3
Net current assets	71.3	102.9

Notes

		20X8	*20X7*
		$m	$m
1	Trade receivables	329.8	285.4
2	Trade payables	236.2	210.8

Answer

	20X8	20X7
Current ratio	$\frac{572.3}{501.0} = 1.14$	$\frac{523.2}{420.3} = 1.24$
Quick ratio	$\frac{453.3}{501.0} = 0.90$	$\frac{414.2}{420.3} = 0.99$
Receivables collection period	$\frac{329.8}{2,065.0} \times 365 = 58$ days	$\frac{285.4}{1,788.7} \times 365 = 58$ days
Inventory turnover period	$\frac{119.0}{1,478.6} \times 365 = 29$ days	$\frac{109.0}{1,304.0} \times 365 = 31$ days
Payables payment period	$\frac{236.2}{1,478.6} \times 365 = 58$ days	$\frac{210.8}{1,304.0} \times 365 = 59$ days

As a manufacturing group serving the construction industry, the company would be expected to have a comparatively lengthy receivables collection period, because of the relatively poor cash flow in the construction industry. It is clear that the company compensates for this by ensuring that it does not pay for raw materials and other costs before they have sold their inventories of finished goods (hence the similarity of receivables' and payables' turnover periods).

The company's current ratio is a little lower than average but its quick ratio is better than average and very little less than the current ratio. This suggests that inventory levels are strictly controlled, which is reinforced by the low inventory turnover period. It would seem that working capital is tightly managed, to avoid the poor liquidity which could be caused by a high receivables' turnover period and comparatively high payables.

Payables payment period is ideally calculated by the formula:

$$\frac{\text{Average trade payables}}{\text{Purchases}} \times 365$$

However, it is rare to find purchases disclosed in published accounts and so cost of sales serves as an approximation. The payables turnover ratio often helps to assess a company's liquidity; an increase in payables' days is often a sign of lack of long-term finance or poor management of current assets, resulting in the use of extended credit from suppliers, increased bank overdraft and so on.

1.8 Other information

FAST FORWARD

As well as ratios, **other information** can be used to analyse a company's performance and identify possible problem areas. This will include information relating to **non-current assets** and **financial obligations**.

As well as ratios, other **financial** and **non-financial information** can give valuable indicators of a company's performance and position.

1.8.1 The revaluation of non-current assets

Non-current assets may be stated in the balance sheet at cost less accumulated depreciation. They may also be revalued from time to time to a current market value, which will lead to an increased depreciation charge.

1.8.2 Share capital and reserves

The **capital and reserves** section of a company's accounts contains information which appears to be mainly the concern of the various classes of shareholder. However, because the shareholders' interest in the business acts as a **buffer for the lenders** in the event of any financial problems, this section is also of some importance to lenders.

The nature of any increase in share capital and accumulated profits will be of interest including **share issues** and **substantial profit retentions**.

If a company has **issued shares in the form of a dividend**, are there obvious reasons why this should be so? For example, does the company need to retain capital within the business because of poor trading in the previous year, making the directors reluctant to pay out more cash dividend than necessary?

1.8.3 Loans and other liabilities

Two points of interest about loans and other liabilities are:

- Whether or not loans are **secured**
- The **redemption dates** of loans

For loans that are **secured**, the details of the security are usually included in the terms of a trust deed. Details of any **fixed or floating charges against assets** should be disclosed in a note to the accounts.

In analysing a set of accounts, particular attention should be paid to some significant features concerning **redemption**. These are:

(a) The **closeness of the redemption date**, which would indicate how much finance the company has to find in the immediate future to repay its loans. It is not unusual, however, to repay one loan by taking out another, and so a company does not necessarily have to find the money to repay a loan from its own resources.

(b) The **percentage interest rate** on the **loans being redeemed**, compared with the current market rate of interest. This would give some idea, if a company decides to replace loans by taking out new loans, of the likely increase (or reduction) in interest costs that it might face, and how easily it might accommodate any interest cost increase.

1.8.4 Earn-out arrangements

Key term

An **earn-out arrangement** is a procedure whereby owners/managers selling an entity receive a portion of their consideration linked to the financial performance of the business during a specified period after the sale. The arrangement gives a measure of security to the new owners, who pass some of the financial risk associated with the purchase of a new enterprise to the sellers. *(OT 2005)*

In the case of an earn-out arrangement, it is likely to be **very difficult to make reliable estimates** of the future amounts payable, where they will depend upon future profits of the acquired company, particularly if that company is in a transitional state. In these circumstances, at least those amounts that are reasonably expected to be payable would be recognised.

Thus any **minimum amount guaranteed** to be payable as part of deferred consideration must be initially provided. As information upon which any further obligations may be reasonably estimated becomes available (for example, short-term profit forecasts for the acquired company), **further provisions** must be made.

Clearly, when reviewing the financial statements of a company that includes such provisions, the **underlying uncertainty** surrounding the amount of the ultimate liability must be taken into account.

1.8.5 Contingencies

Contingencies are conditions which exist at the balance sheet date where the outcome will be confirmed only on the occurrence or non-occurrence of one or more uncertain future events.

Contingencies can result in contingent gains or contingent losses. The fact that the condition **exists at the balance sheet date** distinguishes a contingency from events occurring after the balance sheet date.

Some of the **typical types of contingencies** disclosed by companies are as follows.

- Guarantees given by the company
- Discounted bills of exchange
- Uncalled liabilities on shares or loan notes
- Lawsuits or claims pending
- Tax on profits where the basis on which the tax should be computed is unclear

Again, knowledge of such contingencies will enhance the quality of the information used in analysis.

1.8.6 Private finance initiative (PFI)

Under PFI contracts, the private sector provides a service to the public sector, eg the government, in return for a payment that covers both the use of any assets involved, and the cost of any ancillary services provided. Examples would include research and development, prison security, road maintenance and catering contracts.

In general, the private sector company has the responsibility for the upfront investment in the capital assets required, and then sells a service using those assets to the public sector. The three main types of PFI transaction are:

(a) **Services sold to the public sector** where the public sector pays only on delivery of specified services to specified quality standards

(b) **Financial free standing projects** where the private sector recovers its costs through direct charges on the private use of the asset (eg tolling) rather than from payments by the public sector

(c) **Joint ventures**, where the costs of the project are not met entirely through charges on the end users, but are subsidised from public funds

Thus under PFI contracts, private firms become long term providers of services rather than simply upfront asset builders, combining the responsibilities of designing, building, financing and operating assets in order to deliver the required services to the public sector.

Where a company enters into a PFI contract it will be generally taking on **long-term obligations**, with compensation payable if the company cancels the contact. There may also be the possibility of **penalties** if the service is not provided at the required level or quality. This will affect the analyst's view of the **risks and rewards** associated with the related assets.

1.8.7 Events after the balance sheet date

Key term

Events after the balance sheet date or **post balance sheet events** are favourable and unfavourable events that occur between the balance sheet date and the date the financial statements are authorised for issue. *(IAS 10)*

The following are examples of significant events occurring after the balance sheet date.

- Mergers and acquisitions
- The issue of new shares and loan notes
- The purchase and sales of major non-current assets and investments

- Losses of non-current assets or inventories as a result of a catastrophe such as fire or flood
- The opening of new trading activities
- The closure of a significant part of the trading activities
- A decline in the value of property and investments held as non-current assets
- Changes in exchange rates (if there are significant overseas interests)
- Government action, such as nationalisation
- Strikes and other labour disputes
- The augmentation of pension benefits to employees

Knowledge of such events allows the analyst to 'update' the latest published figures by taking account of their potential impact.

1.8.8 Segmental analysis

Segmental information can be useful in the following ways.

- Segmental information can **explain** factors which **contributed to company results.**
- Users can **compare the results** of **different products** from year to year.
- Users can **compare performance with companies within the same market**.
- Users can **assess the future risks and rewards** associated with the business.

Exam focus point

Make sure you look for and comment on relevant issues that are clear from the financial statements.

1.9 Corporate failure

FAST FORWARD

Business failure can be predicted by **Z-scores**, using a number of financial variables, or by models such as **Argenti's model**, which emphasises defects, mistakes and symptoms.

Liquidity ratios are a foundation for analysis of potential corporate failure. This is important to investors, as they wish to know whether **additional funds** could be lent to the company with **reasonable safety** and whether the company would **fail without additional funds**.

1.9.1 Z scores

E I Altman researched into the simultaneous analysis of several financial ratios as a combined **predictor of business failure**. The five indicators he identified were used to derive a **Z score**. Firms with a Z score above a certain level would be predicted to be financially sound, and firms with a Z score below a certain level would be categorised as probable failures.

Altman's Z score model (derived in 1968) emerged as:

$$Z = 1.2X_1 + 1.4X_2 + 3.3X_3 + 0.6X_4 + 1.0X_5$$

where X_1 = working capital/total assets
X_2 = retained earnings/total assets
X_3 = earnings before interest and tax/total assets
X_4 = market value of equity/book value of total debt (a form of gearing ratio)
X_5 = sales/total assets

Exam focus point

It is not necessary for you to memorise this formula.

In Altman's model, a Z score of 2.7 or more indicated non-failure, and a Z score of 1.8 or less indicated failure. Subsequent research based on the similar principle of identifying a Z score predictor of business failure has produced different prediction models, using a variety of financial ratios and different Z score values as predictors of failure.

1.9.2 Argenti's model

Other writers have put forward alternative models designed to predict whether a business will fail. From historical data on a wide range of actual cases, **Argenti** developed a model which is intended to predict the likelihood of company failure. The model is based on calculating scores for a company based on (a) defects of the company; (b) management mistakes and (c) the symptoms of failure. For each of the scores (a), (b) and (c) there is a 'danger mark'.

Among the most important factors in the model are:

(a) **Defects**

- Autocratic Chief Executive (Robert Maxwell is an example here)
- Passive board
- Lack of budgetary control

(b) **Mistakes**

- Over-trading (expanding faster than cash funding)
- Gearing – high bank overdrafts/loans
- Failure of large project jeopardises the company (eg Laker Airways)

(c) **Symptoms**

- Deteriorating ratios
- Creative accounting – signs of window-dressing
- Declining morale and declining quality

1.9.3 Weaknesses of corporate failure models

(a) In common with all correlation models, they **relate to the past**, without taking into account the current state of the macroeconomic environment (the level of inflation and interest rates, and so on).

(b) The models share the **limitations of the accounting model** (including the accounting concepts and conventions) on which they are based.

(c) The **publication** of accounting data by companies is subject to a **delay**. Failure might occur before the data becomes available.

(d) If the measures incorporated in the models become used as objectives, as some suggest, then the model is likely to become less useful as a predictive tool, as the measures will be subject to **manipulation**.

(e) The **definition** of **corporate failure** is not clear, given that various forms of rescue or restructuring are possible, short of liquidation, for a company which is in trouble.

Case Study

The **pressure to deliver earnings growth** may result in companies making poor decisions that eventually lead to their downfall. It is arguable that a deterioration a few years ago in the performance of Marks & Spencer was attributable to its policy of seeking short-term growth by cutting costs and failing to invest sufficiently in stores. Although this delivered growth in earnings for a while, the effects of this policy were eventually felt in a shrinking customer base and the consequences of a lack of investment in the underlying businesses.

1.9.4 Other indicators of financial difficulties

Ratio analysis of published accounts and **Z score analysis** are not the only ways of spotting that a company might be running into financial difficulties. There are other possible indicators too.

(a) **Other information in the published accounts**

- A worsening net liquid funds position, as shown by the cash flow statement
- Very large **potential or contingent liabilities**
- Important events after the balance sheet date

(b) **Information in the chairman's report**

- Difficulties that haven't been overcome
- Forthcoming problems

(c) **Information in the press**

(d) **Published information about environmental or external matters**

- **New legislation**
- **International events**
- **New and better products** being launched on to the market by a competitor
- A big **rise in interest rates**, which might affect a highly-geared company
- A big **change in foreign exchange rates**, which might affect an international trader

2 Working capital management strategies 5/06

FAST FORWARD

Working capital management involves achieving a balance between the requirement to minimise the risk of insolvency and the requirement to maximise profit.

2.1 Working capital management

Exam focus point

Questions on working capital management in this paper will focus more on the overall approach to management rather than the operational issues that are examined at lower levels. Working capital management is an important area in this paper.

The working capital that an organisation holds has to be financed, and investment in working capital can be a significant drain on the resources that a business has. In this section we consider strategies to manage working capital levels.

2.2 Working capital investment

Organisations have to decide what are the most important **risks** relating to working capital, and therefore whether to adopt a **conservative** or **aggressive** approach.

(a) A **conservative** working capital management policy aims to **reduce the risk of system breakdown** by holding high levels of working capital. Thus customers are allowed **generous payment terms** to stimulate demand, **finished goods inventories** are high to **ensure availability** for customers, and **raw materials and work in progress** are **high** to **minimise the risk** of running out of **inventory** and consequent downtime in the manufacturing process. **Suppliers** are **paid promptly** to ensure their goodwill, again to minimise the chance of stock-outs.

However, the cumulative effect on these policies can be that the firm carries a high burden of **unproductive assets**, resulting in a **financing cost** that can destroy profitability. A period of rapid expansion may also cause **severe cash flow problems** as working capital requirements outstrip available finance. Further problems may arise from inventory obsolescence and lack of flexibility to customer demands.

(b) An **aggressive** working capital investment policy aims to reduce this financing cost and increase profitability by **cutting inventories**, **speeding up collections from customers**, and **delaying payments to suppliers.**

The potential disadvantage of this policy is an increase in the chances of **system breakdown** through running out of inventory or **loss of goodwill** with customers and suppliers. However, modern manufacturing techniques encourage inventory and work in progress reductions through just–in–time policies, flexible production facilities and improved quality management. Improved customer satisfaction through quality and effective response to customer demand can also mean that credit periods are shortened.

2.3 Working capital financing

There are different ways in which the funding of the current and non-current assets of a business can be achieved by **employing long and short-term sources of funding**. The diagram below illustrates three alternative types of policy A, B and C. The dotted lines A, B and C are the cut-off levels between short-term and long-term financing for each of the policies A, B and C respectively: assets above the relevant dotted line are financed by short-term funding while assets below the dotted line are financed by long-term funding.

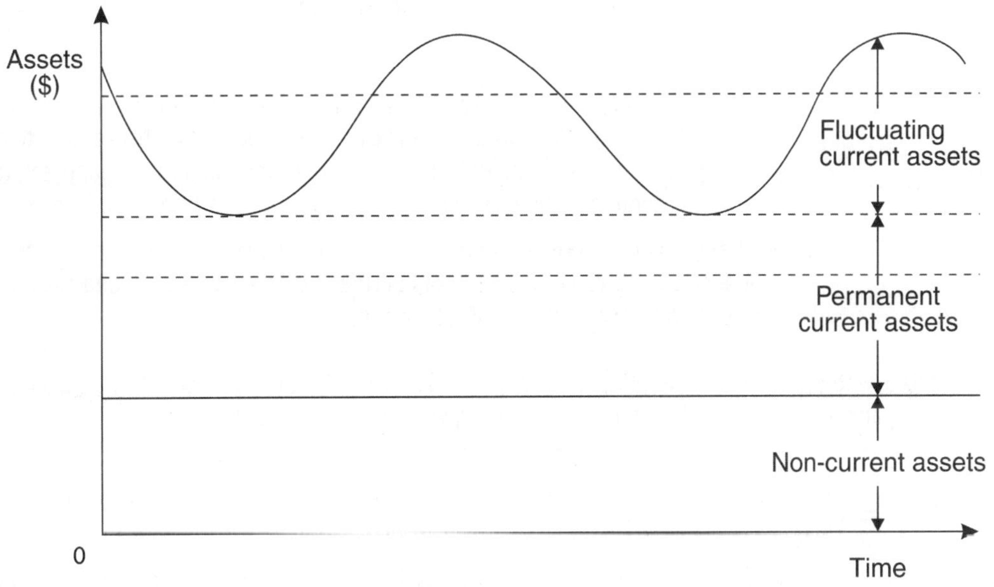

Fluctuating current assets together with permanent current assets (the core level of investment in inventory and receivables) form part of the working capital of the business, which may be financed by either long-term funding (including equity capital) or by current liabilities (short-term funding). This can be seen in terms of policies A, B and C. Once again a conservative or an aggressive approach can be followed.

(a) Policy A can be characterised as a **conservative approach** to financing working capital. All non-current assets and permanent current assets, as well as part of the fluctuating current assets, are financed by long-term funding. There is only a need to call upon short-term financing at times when fluctuations in current assets push total assets above the level of dotted line A. At times when fluctuating current assets are low and total assets fall below line A, there will be **surplus cash** which the company will be able to invest in marketable securities.

(b) Policy B is a more **aggressive approach** to financing working capital. Not only are fluctuating current assets all financed out of short-term sources, but so are some of the permanent current assets. This policy represents an **increased risk of liquidity and cash flow problems**, although potential returns will be increased if short-term financing can be obtained more cheaply than long-term finance. It enables **greater flexibility** in financing.

(c) A **balance** between risk and return might be best achieved by the **moderate approach** of policy C, a policy of maturity matching in which long-term funds finance permanent assets while short-term funds finance non-permanent assets.

Exam focus point

You may be required to draw a chart to show working capital financing as in May 2006.

2.4 Other factors

The trend of overall working capital management will be complicated by the following factors:

(a) **Industry norms**

These are of particular importance for the **management of receivables**. It will be difficult to offer a much shorter payment period than competitors.

(b) **Products**

The **production process**, and hence the amount of work in progress is obviously much greater for some products and in some industries.

(c) **Management issues**

How **working capital** is **managed** may have a significant impact upon the actual length of the working capital cycle whatever the overall strategy might be. Factors to consider include the degree of centralisation (which may allow a more aggressive approach to be adopted, depending though on how efficient the centralised departments actually are).

Differences in the **nature of assets** also need to be considered. Businesses adopting a more conservative strategy may well hold permanent safety inventory and cash balances, whereas there is no safety level of receivables balances.

TOPCIMA link

Working capital may be important in the TOPCIMA exam, for example the effect on working capital of expansion overseas, or methods of improving working capital management.

3 Cash forecasts 5/05

FAST FORWARD

Cash forecasting should ensure that sufficient funds will be available when needed, to sustain the activities of an enterprise at an acceptable cost.

3.1 Cash budgets

Key term

A **cash budget** (or **forecast**) is a detailed budget of estimated cash inflows and outflows incorporating both revenue and capital items. *(OT 2005)*

Cash forecasts (or budgets) provide an early warning of liquidity problems, by estimating:

- How much cash is required
- When it is required
- How long it is required for
- Whether it will be available from anticipated sources

A company must know **when** it might need to borrow and **for how long**, not just **what amount** of funding could be required.

Exam focus point

No detailed testing of cash management models will be set.

3.2 Cash forecasts based on the balance sheet

The balance sheet based forecast is produced for **management accounting purposes** and so not for external publication or statutory financial reporting. **It is not an estimate of cash inflows and outflows**. A number of sequential forecasts can be produced, for example, a forecast of the balance sheet at the end of each year for the next five years.

As an estimate of the company's balance sheet at a future date, a balance sheet based forecast is used to identify either the **cash surplus** or the **funding shortfall** in the company's balance sheet **at the forecast date**.

3.3 Estimating a future balance sheet 11/06

FAST FORWARD

Balance sheet based forecasts can be used to assess the scale of funding requirements or cash surpluses expected over time, and to act as a check on the realism of cash flow based forecasts.

A balance sheet estimate calls for some prediction of the amount/value of each item in the company's balance sheet, **excluding cash and short-term investments**, as these are what we are trying to predict. A forecast is prepared by taking each item in the balance sheet, and estimating what its value might be at the future date. The assumptions used are critical, and the following guidelines are suggested.

(a) **Intangible non-current assets and long term investments**

If there are any, they should be taken at their current value unless there is good reason for another treatment.

(b) **Property, plant and equipment**

Some estimate of **asset purchases** (and disposals) will be required. Revaluations can be ignored as they are not cash flows.

(c) **Current assets**

Balance sheet estimates of **inventory** and **receivables** are sometimes based on fairly simple assumptions, such as the following:

- **Same** as current amounts. This is unlikely if business has boomed.
- **Increase by a certain percentage**, to allow for growth in business volume. For example, the volume of receivables might be expected to increase by a similar amount.
- **Decrease by a certain percentage**, to allow for tighter management control over working capital.
- Assume to be a **certain percentage** of the company's estimated **annual sales revenue** for the year.
- The firm can assume that the **operating cycle** will more or less **remain the same**.

In other words, if a firm's customers take two months to pay, this relationship can be expected to continue. Therefore, if total annual sales are £12m and customers take two months to pay, receivables at the year end will be $^2/_{12} \times$ £12m = £2m.

If revenue increases to £18m, and the collection period stays at two months, receivables will amount to $^2/_{12} \times$ £18m = £3m. Similar relationships might be plotted for inventory and hence purchases and suppliers.

(d) **Current liabilities**

Some itemising of current liabilities will be necessary, because no single set of assumptions can accurately estimate them collectively.

(i) **Trade payables and accruals** can be estimated in a similar way to current assets, as indicated above.

(ii) Current liabilities include **bank loans** due for repayment within 12 months. These can be identified individually.

(iii) **Bank overdraft facilities**. Often there will be no overdraft in the forecast balance sheet. Any available overdraft facility can be considered when the company's overall cash needs are identified.

(iv) **Taxation**. Any corporation tax payable should be estimated from anticipated profits and based on an estimated percentage of those profits.

(v) **Dividends payable**. Any ordinary dividend payable should be estimated from anticipated profits, and any preference dividend payable can be predicted from the coupon rate of dividend for the company's preference shares.

(vi) **Other creditors** can be included if required and are of significant value.

(e) **Non-current creditors**

Non-current creditors are likely to consist of non-current loans, bond issues, debenture stock and any other non-current finance debt. Unless the company has already arranged further non-current borrowing, this item should include just existing long-term debts, minus debts that will be repaid before the balance sheet date (or debts transferred from long-term to short-term creditors).

(f) **Share capital and reserves**

With the exception of accumulated profits (retained earnings), the estimated balance sheet figures for share capital and other reserves should be the same as their current amount, unless it is expected or known that a new issue of shares will take place before the balance sheet date, in which case the total amount raised (net of issue expenses) should be added to the share capital/other reserves total.

(g) **Accumulated profits**

An estimate is required of the change in the company's **accumulated profits** in the period up to the balance sheet date. This reserve should be calculated as:

- The existing value of the retained earnings
- **Plus** further retained profits anticipated in the period to the balance sheet date (ie post tax profits minus estimated dividends)

3.4 Compiling a balance sheet

The various estimates should now be brought together into a balance sheet. The figures on each side of the balance sheet will not be equal, and there will be one of the following.

(a) A surplus of share capital and reserves over net assets (total assets minus total liabilities). If this occurs, the company will be forecasting a **cash surplus**.

(b) A surplus of net assets over share capital and reserves. If this occurs, the company will be forecasting a **funding deficit**.

Alpha has an existing balance sheet and an estimated balance sheet in one year's time before the necessary extra funding is taken into account, as follows.

	Existing		*Forecast after one year*	
	€'000	€'000	€'000	€'000
ASSETS				
Non-current assets		100		180
Current assets		90		100
Total assets		190		280
EQUITY AND LIABILITIES				
Share capital and reserves				
€1 ordinary shares	50		50	
Other reserves	20		20	
Accumulated profits	30		50	
		100		120
Non-current liabilities				
5% loan notes	20		20	
Deferred tax	10		10	
		30		30
Current liabilities		60		90
		190		240

The company is expecting to increase its total assets in the next year by €90,000 (€280,000 – €190,000) but expects accumulated profits for the year to be €20,000 (€50,000 – €30,000) and current liabilities to increase by €30,000. There is an excess of net assets over share capital and reserves amounting to €40,000 (€280,000 – €240,000), which is a **funding deficit**. The company must consider ways of obtaining extra cash (eg by borrowing) to cover the deficit. If it cannot, it will need to keep its assets below the forecast amount, or to have higher short-term payables.

A revised projected balance sheet can then be prepared by introducing these new sources of funds. This should be checked for realism (eg by **ratio analysis**) to ensure that the proportion of the balance sheet made up by non-current assets and working capital, etc is sensible.

Balance sheet-based forecasts have **two main uses:**

(a) As **longer-term (strategic) estimates**, to assess the scale of funding requirements or cash surpluses the company expects over time

(b) To act as a **check on the realism** of cash flow-based forecasts (The estimated balance sheet should be **roughly** consistent with the net cash change in the cash budget, after allowing for approximations in the balance sheet forecast assumptions.)

3.5 Deriving cash flow from income statement and balance sheet information

The previous paragraphs concentrated on preparing a forecast balance sheet, with estimated figures for receivables, payables and inventory. Cash requirements might therefore be presented as the 'balancing figure'. However, it is possible to derive a forecast figure for cash flows using both the **balance sheet** and **income statement**. The profit from operations is adjusted first of all for items not involving cash, such as depreciation. This is further adjusted for changes in the levels of working capital (eg receivables and payables) to arrive at operational cash flows.

This is examined in the example below. For the time being, assume that there is no depreciation. The task is to get from profit to operational cash flow, by taking into account movements in working capital.

	Profit	*Operational cash flow*
	£	£
Sales	200,000	200,000
Opening receivables (∴ received in year)		15,000
Closing receivables (outstanding at year end)		(24,000)
Cash in		191,000

	Profit	*Operational cash flow*
	£	£
Cost of sales	170,000	170,000
Closing inventory (purchased, but not used, in year)		21,000
Opening inventory (used, but not purchased, in year)		(12,000)
Purchases in year		179,000
Opening payables (∴ paid in year)		11,000
Closing payables (outstanding at year end)		(14,000)
Cash out		176,000
Profit/operational cash flow	30,000	15,000

This may be summarised as:

		£	£
Profit			30,000
(Increase)/Decrease in inventory	Opening	12,000	
	Closing	(21,000)	
			(9,000)
(Increase)/Decrease in receivables	Opening	15,000	
	Closing	(24,000)	
			(9,000)
Increase/(Decrease) in payables	Closing	14,000	
	Opening	(11,000)	
			3,000
Operational cash flow			15,000

In practice, of course, a business will make many other adjustments. The profit figure includes **items which do not involve the movement of cash,** such as the annual depreciation charge, which will have to be added back to arrive at a figure for cash.

Both 'receipts and payments' forecasts and forecasts based on financial statements could be used alongside each other. The cash management section and the financial controller's section should reconcile differences between forecasts on a continuing basis, so that the forecast can be made more accurate as time goes on.

3.6 Quality control of forecasts

When actual results differ from budget, it can be tempting to conclude that plans never work out in practice. However, as planning is a vital management activity, and if actual results differ from the plan, it is important to find out whether the **planning processes** can be improved.

Accuracy of cash flow forecasts can be enhanced by:

(a) **Reviewing actual cash flows** against the forecasts, learning from past mistakes, and

(b) **Preparing updated rolling forecasts** or revised forecasts, where useful, to replace earlier, less reliable forecasts

A constant monthly amount for receipts and payments will often indicate either sloppy cash forecasting practice, or a high degree of uncertainty in the forecast, since it is rare for a specific receivables and payables to remain unchanged except when there is a formal arrangement.

As a financial year progresses, the actual cash flows for the past months could show large variances from budget, but a rolling forecast indicates that the original budget for the end-of-year cash balance will still be achieved. This could occur if the rolling forecast has been prepared by adjusting the forecast for the unexpired months of the year, in order to keep the annual budget (on paper at least) for the end-of-year cash position. Where this occurs, suspicion must arise that the **rolling forecast has been prepared with little thought.**

Unchanged figures over a number of months of revised forecast submissions are also an indication of a weak forecasting system. It could be that business expectations have not changed; however there are few businesses that do not fluctuate with market conditions. A more likely explanation is that the rolling cash forecast has been prepared by copying the figures from the previous forecast or that a new revised forecast has not been prepared at all.

Exam focus point

Questions 2 and 3 in May 2005 required construction of a forecast balance sheet, and Question 3 required an income statement and cash flow analysis as well.
Question 5 in November 2005 required forecast income statements and cash flow forecasts.

4 Forecast financial statements: example 5/05, 11/05

FAST FORWARD

Forecast financial statements can be constructed for a period of several years, from first year data, given certain assumptions. You will not need to present cash flow statements in IAS 7 format.

4.1 Question requirements

In this paper, you could be presented with a requirement to construct forecast financial statements, which need not be presented in published accounts format, based upon first or base year data. Below, we work through such a question in detail.

4.2 Example: financial statement forecasting

You are a consultant working for a company called CC Drains, which started trading four years ago in 20X3 and which manufactures plastic rainwater drainage goods. You have the following information.

(a) Revenue and cost of sales are expected to increase by 10% in each of the financial years ending 31 December 20X7, 20X8 and 20X9. Operating expenses are expected to increase by 5% each year.

(b) The company expects to continue to be liable for tax at the marginal rate of 30%. You can assume that tax is paid or refunded 12 months after the year end.

(c) The ratios of **receivables to sales** and **trade payables to cost of sales** will remain the same for the next three years.

(d) Non-current assets comprise land and buildings, for which no depreciation is provided. Other assets used by the company, such as machinery and vehicles, are hired on operating leases.

(e) The company plans for dividends to grow at 25% in each of the financial years 20X7, 20X8 and 20X9.

(f) The company plans to purchase new machinery to the value of £500,000 during 20X7, to be depreciated straight line over ten years. The company charges a full year's depreciation in the first year of purchase of its assets. Tax allowable depreciation at 25% reducing balance is available on this expenditure.

(g) Inventory was purchased for £35,000 at the beginning of 20X7. The value of inventory after this purchase is expected to remain at £361,000 for the foreseeable future.

(h) No decision has been made on the type of finance to be used for the expansion programme. The company's directors believe that they can raise new medium-term secured loan notes if necessary.

(i) The average P/E ratio of listed companies in the same industry as CC Drains plc is 15.

The company's objectives include the following.

(a) To earn a pre-tax return on the closing book value of shareholders' funds of 35% pa
(b) To increase dividends per share by 25% per year
(c) To obtain a quotation on a recognised stock exchange within the next three years

A summary of the financial statements for the year to 31 December 20X6 is set out below.

CC DRAINS
SUMMARISED INCOME STATEMENT

FOR THE YEAR TO 31 DECEMBER 20X6	£'000
Revenue	1,560
Cost of sales	950
Gross profit	610
Operating expenses	325
Interest	30
Tax liability	77
Net profit	178
Dividends declared	68

SUMMARISED BALANCE SHEET AT 31 DECEMBER 20X6

	£'000
Non-current assets (net book value)	750
Current assets	
Inventories	326
Receivables	192
Cash and bank	50
Total assets	1,318

Financing	£'000
Ordinary share capital (ordinary shares of £1)	500
Retained profits to 31 December 20X5	128
Retentions for the year to 31 December 20X6	110
10% loan note redeemable 20Z0	300
	1,038
Current liabilities	
Trade payables	135
Other payables (including tax and dividends)	145
Total equity and liabilities	1,318

Required

Using the information given:

(a) Prepare forecast income statements for the years 20X7, 20X8 and 20X9, and calculate whether the company is likely to meet its stated financial objective (return on shareholders' funds) for these three years.

(b) Prepare cash flow forecasts for the years 20X7, 20X8 and 20X9, and estimate the amount of funds which will need to be raised by the company to finance its expansion.

Notes

(1) You should ignore interest or returns on surplus funds invested during the three-year period of review.

(2) You may ignore the timing of cash flows within each year and you should not discount the cash flows.

Solution

(a) CC DRAINS INCOME STATEMENTS

	Actual		*Forecast*	
	20X6	*20X7*	*20X8*	*20X9*
	£'000	£'000	£'000	£'000
Revenue (increase 10% pa)	1,560	1,716	1,888	2,076
Cost of sales (increase 10% pa)	(950)	(1,045)	(1,150)	(1,264)
Gross profit	610	671	738	812
Operating expenses (increase 5% pa)	(325)	(341)	(358)	(376)
Depreciation (10% pa × £500,000)		(50)	(50)	(50)
Profit from operations	285	280	330	386
Interest (assumed constant)	(30)	(30)	(30)	(30)
Profit before tax	255	250	300	356
Taxation (see working)	(77)	(53)	(77)	(101)
Net profit	178	197	223	255
Dividend (25% growth pa)	(68)	(85)	(106)	(133)
Retained profit	110	112	117	122
Reserves b/f	128	238	350	467
Reserves c/f	238	350	467	589

	Actual		*Forecast*	
	20X6	*20X7*	*20X8*	*20X9*
	£'000	£'000	£'000	£'000
Share capital	500	500	500	500
Year end reserves	238	350	467	589
Year end shareholders' funds	738	850	967	1,089
Pre-tax return on shareholders' funds	34.6%	29.4%	31.0%	32.7%

On the basis of these figures, the financial objective of a pre-tax return of 35% of year-end shareholders' funds is not achieved in any of the years.

Working: Tax payable

It is assumed that the company does not account for deferred taxation.

	Actual		*Forecast*	
	20X6	*20X7*	*20X8*	*20X9*
	£'000	£'000	£'000	£'000
Profit before tax	255	250	300	356
Add back depreciation		50	50	50
Less tax allowance (25% red./bal)		(125)	(94)	(70)
Taxable profit	255	175	256	336
Tax at 30%	77	53	77	101

Exam focus point

Make sure you can calculate the effect of tax-allowable depreciation (capital allowances) in the taxation figure.

(b) **Cash flow forecasts**

Exam focus point

There are many ways of computing the cash flow forecasts. However, some ways are quicker than others. Our answer shows one of the quickest methods first. Remember that you will need to complete calculations in the exam as quickly as possible.

The 20X6 balance sheet figure for 'other payables (including tax and dividends)' is simply the sum of tax and dividends in the income statement. It is assumed that this will continue to be the case in the following three years. The annual change in net current assets can be computed as follows.

Changes in net current assets	*Actual*		*Forecast*	
	20X6	*20X7*	*20X8*	*20X9*
	£'000	£'000	£'000	£'000
Inventories (scenario note (7))	326	361	361	361
Receivables (12.31% of sales) *	192	211	232	256
Trade payables (14.21% of cost of sales) *	(135)	(148)	(163)	(180)
Tax and dividends payable (sum of the figures)	(145)	(138)	(183)	(234)
Net current assets	238	286	247	203
Increase/(decrease) net current assets		48	(39)	(44)

* Alternatively receivables and payables can be computed as a 10% increase each year.

The cash flow forecasts can then be constructed.

Cash flow forecasts	*20X7*	*20X8*	*20X9*
	£'000	£'000	£'000
Retained profit for the year	112	117	122
Add back depreciation	50	50	50
(Investment in net current assets)/release of net current assets (see working)	(48)	39	44
Expenditure on non-current assets	(500)		
Surplus/(deficit) for the year	(386)	206	216
Cash/(deficit) b/f	50	(336)	(130)
Cash/(deficit) c/f	(336)	(130)	86

The company will need to find finance of £338,000 in 20X7 but this can be completely repaid in the following two years. However, interest costs have been ignored in this computation.

Exam focus point

Alternative presentations include:

- A detailed statement of cash receipts and payments, or
- A cash flow statement in IAS 7 format.

Answers by both of these methods are shown here, for comparison, but you should practise producing forecasts as quickly as possible.

Appendices

1 **Cash receipts and payments**

	20X7	*20X8*	*20X9*
Receipts	£'000	£'000	£'000
Cash from sales			
(revenue + opening receivables – closing receivables)	1,697	1,867	2,053
Payments			
For purchases (cost of sales + opening			
payables – closing payables)	1,032	1,135	1,248
Operating expenses	341	358	376
Additional inventory purchase	35		
Machinery	500		
Interest (current year)	30	30	30
Tax (previous year)	77	53	77
Dividends (previous year)	68	85	106
	2,083	1,661	1,837

	20X7	*20X8*	*20X9*
	£'000	£'000	£'000
Net cash flow	(386)	206	216
Cash/(deficit) b/f	50	(336)	(130)
Cash/(deficit) c/f	(336)	(130)	86

2 **IAS 7 format**

	20X7	*20X8*	*20X9*
	£'000	£'000	£'000
Net cash inflow from operations (see working)	290	373	429
Interest paid	(30)	(30)	(30)
Dividends paid	(68)	(85)	(106)
Tax paid	(77)	(53)	(77)
Net cash inflow	115	205	216
Investing activities:			
Non-current assets	(500)		
Net cash flow before financing	(385)	205	216

Working: net cash inflow from operations

	20X6	*20X7*	*20X8*	*20X9*
	£'000	£'000	£'000	£'000
Inventory	326	361	361	361
Receivables	192	211	232	256
Payables	(135)	(149)	(163)	(180)
	383	423	430	437
Incremental working capital		(40)	(7)	(7)
Gross profit before depreciation		671	738	812
Less: operating expenses		(341)	(358)	(376)
Net cash inflow from operations		290	373	429

Question

Definite variables

Learning outcome: A(iv)

Triassic produces smoke alarms for residential and office premises. The most recent balance sheet of the company is set out below.

Balance sheet as at 30 November 20X2

	£m	£m	£m
Non-current assets			
Freehold buildings at cost		24.4	
Less: accumulated depreciation		4.4	20.0
Plant and machinery at cost		37.9	
Less: accumulated depreciation		12.9	25.0
			45.0
Current assets			
Inventory	39.0		
Trade receivables	20.0		
Bank	8.3	67.3	
Less payables: amounts falling due within one year			
Trade payables	12.0		
Taxation	4.5		
Dividends	7.8	24.3	
			43.0
			88.0
Capital and reserves			
Ordinary £1 shares			20.0
Accumulated profits			68.0
			88.0

During the year to 30 November 20X2, the sales revenue for the business was £240m.

As a result of recent changes in government legislation, it has been predicted that the market for smoke alarms will increase significantly in the short-term. The directors of Triassic are planning to expand the business significantly during the forthcoming year in order to exploit these new market conditions. The following forecasts and assumptions for the forthcoming year have been prepared by the directors.

(i) Sales for the forthcoming year will be 25 per cent higher than the previous year. Sales are expected to be spread evenly over the year.

(ii) The gross profit margin will be 30 per cent of sales.

(iii) To prepare for the expansion in output, new machinery costing £57m will be purchased at the beginning of the year and a long-term loan will be taken out immediately to help finance this purchase. At the end of the year, the long-term debt to equity ratio is planned to be 1:3.

(iv) The average receivables collection period will be three times that of previous years and the average payment period for creditors will be one and a half months.

(v) The value of inventory at the end of the year will be £18m lower than at the beginning of the year.

(vi) Depreciation charges for freehold buildings and plant and machinery are calculated using the reducing balance method and will be 5 per cent and 20 per cent respectively. Other expenses for the period will be £54.6m. There will be no prepayments or accruals at the end of the year.

(vii) Dividends will be announced at the end of the year and the dividend payout ratio will be 50 per cent which is in line with previous years. The tax rate will be 30 per cent of net profits before taxation. The dividend and tax will be paid after the year end.

All workings should be in £millions and should be made to one decimal place. Workings must be clearly shown.

Required

(a) Prepare in as much detail as the information allows:

(i) A forecast income statement for the year ended 30 November 20X3, and
(ii) A forecast balance sheet as at 30 November 20X3.

(b) Comment briefly on the financial performance and position of the business using the financial statements prepared in (a) above.

Exam focus point

The discussion/explanation part of a forecasting question will be worth a significant proportion of the marks on offer, so make sure you practice answering these parts, in addition to the calculations.

Answer

(a) (i) There is no information about the cost of loan interest, and it is assumed that this cost is included within other expenses.

Triassic

Forecast income statement for the year to 30 November 20X3

	£m	£m
Revenue (£240m × 1.25)		300.0
Cost of sales (70%)		210.0
Gross profit (30%)		90.0
Expenses	54.6	
Depreciation of buildings (5% of £20m)	1.0	
Depreciation of plant and machinery (20% of £(25m + 57m))	16.4	
		72.0
Profit before taxation		18.0
Taxation (30%)		5.4
Profit after taxation		12.6
Dividend (50%)		6.3
Retained profit		6.3

(ii) *Triassic*

Forecast balance sheet as at 30 November 20X3

	£m	£m	£m
Non-current assets			
Freehold buildings at cost		24.4	
Less accumulated depreciation		5.4	
			19.0
Plant and machinery at cost		94.9	
Less accumulated depreciation (12.9 + 16.4)		29.3	
			65.6
			84.6
Current assets			
Inventory (39 – 18)		21.0	
Trade receivables (W1)		75.0	
		96.0	
Payables: amounts falling due within one year			
Bank overdraft (W4)	19.2		
Trade payables (W2)	24.0		
Taxation payable	5.4		
Dividend payable	6.3		
		54.9	
			41.1
			125.7
Payables: amounts falling due after more than one year			
Loan (W3)			31.4
			94.3
Share capital and reserves			
Ordinary shares of £1			20.0
Accumulated profits (68 + 6.3)			74.3
			94.3

Workings

(1) **Trade receivables**

Average debt collection period in year to 30.11.20X2 = (20/240) × 12 months = 1 month.

Average debt collection period in year to 30.11.20X3 = 3 times one month = 3 months.

Trade receivables as at 30 November 20X3 = (3/12) × £300 million = £75 million.

(2) **Trade payables**

Purchases in the year = closing inventory + cost of sales – opening inventory.

Purchases are therefore (given an £18m reduction in inventory levels)

21m + 210m – 39m = £192 million.

Trade payables at 30.11.20X3 = (1.5/12) × £192 million = £24 million.

(3) **Loan**

	£m
Share capital	20.0
Reserves as at 30 November 20X2	68.0
Accumulated profit, 20X3	6.3
Share capital and reserves at 30.11.20X3	94.3

	£m
Loan at 30.11.20X3 (one third of £94.3m)	31.4
Original loan	57.0
Loan repaid in the year	25.6

(4) **Cash**

> **Tutorial note**. The cash balance in the balance sheet can be calculated as the 'missing figure' to make the balance sheet net assets equal the share capital and reserves. A proof of the cash position, however, is shown here.

	£m	£m
Operating profit		18.0
Add back depreciation (1.0 + 16.4)		17.4
		35.4
Reduction in inventory	18.0	
Increase in receivables (75 – 20)	(55.0)	
Increase in trade payables (24 – 12)	12.0	
		(25.0)
Cash flow from operations		10.4
Tax paid		(4.5)
Dividends paid		(7.8)
Machinery purchase		(57.0)
Loan raised		57.0
Loan repaid		(25.6)
Cash flow in the year		(27.5)
Cash at start of year		8.3
Cash at end of year		(19.2)

(b) **The profit after tax next year** will be £12.6 million, giving a return on shareholder capital of (12.6/94.3) 13.4% and a profit margin on sales of (12.6/300) 4.2%. In the previous year, the profit after tax was £15.6 million (double the dividend), with a ROSC of (15.6/88) 17.7% and a profit/sales ratio of (15.6/240) 6.5%.

The forecast profit is therefore lower, with a lower ROSC and a lower profit/sales ratio, despite a 25% increase in sales.

Liquidity is also expected to deteriorate. The company is forecasting a bank overdraft of £19.2 million at the end of November 20X3, compared to a positive cash balance the previous year. The company will have to ensure that bank overdraft facilities are available if it goes ahead with its plan to increase sales.

The company will also have some long-term debt capital, having been ungeared in the year to 30 November 20X2.

On the basis of the forecasts, it is questionable whether there is any financial benefit to be obtained from expanding sales, and the company management should review its plans urgently, before implementing them.

5 Sensitivity analysis and changes in variables

FAST FORWARD

As part of a business's risk analysis, different forecasts should be prepared with **changing financial** or **business variables**. The links between these variables and the figures in the forecasts may not be straightforward.

5.1 Sensitivity analysis

In a well-designed forecast a great number of **'what-if'** questions can be asked and answered quickly by carrying out **sensitivity analysis** and changing the relevant data or variables. In a cash flow forecast model, managers may wish to know the cash flow impact if sales growth per month is nil, ½%, 1%, 1½%, 2½% or minus 1% and so on.

However businesses will also want to estimate the magnitude of changes in sales and ultimately profits if economic or business variables change. This will be more problematic.

5.2 Changes in economic variables

Businesses need to be aware of likely changes in inflation, interest rates and so on. Governments and central banks issue regular updates and forecasts, and the financial press is also helpful.

However businesses will also need to forecast:

- How the **predicted changes** will **affect demand**. The links may not be easy to forecast. Businesses should consider separately the effect of major increases on each type of product.
- How the **business** will **respond to changes in variables**. For example will the business automatically adjust prices upwards by the rate of inflation, or will it try to hold prices? What will its competitors do? If raw material prices increase, will the business try to change suppliers? What effect will this have on payment patterns?

5.3 Changes in business variables

Economic variables will clearly impact upon business variables such as **sales volumes** or **profit margins**. Businesses need to be aware of the other factors, such as changes in the competitive environment that could affect these variables and how this effect might work. The original forecast should itself have been based on **demand forecasts,** determined by market surveys and statistical models based on past changes in demand. However If factors such as taste change, businesses need to recognise this might not just require marginal changes in forecasts, but a re-visiting of the base data, since the changes will ultimately render the previous surveys or models redundant.

6 Financing requirements 5/05

FAST FORWARD

Cash deficits will be funded in different ways, depending on whether they are short or long-term. Businesses should have procedures for investing **surpluses** with appropriate levels of risk and return.

6.1 Deficiencies

Any forecast **deficiency** of cash will have to be funded.

(a) **Borrowing**. If borrowing arrangements are not already secured, a source of funds will have to be found. If a company cannot fund its cash deficits it could be wound up.

(b) The firm can make arrangements to **sell any short-term marketable financial investments** to raise cash.

(c) The firm can delay payments to suppliers, or pull in payments from customers. This is sometimes known as **leading and lagging**.

Because cash forecasts cannot be entirely accurate, companies should have **contingency funding**, available from a surplus cash balance and liquid investments, or from a bank facility. The approximate size of contingency margin will vary from company to company, according to the cyclical nature of the business and the approach of its cash planners.

Forecasting gives management time to arrange its funding. If planned in advance, instead of a panic measure to avert a cash crisis, a company can more easily choose when to borrow, and will probably obtain a lower interest rate.

6.2 Cash surpluses

Many cash-generative businesses are less reliant on high quality cash forecasts. If a **cash surplus** is forecast, having an idea of both its size and how long it will exist could help decide how best to invest it.

In some cases, the amount of **interest** earned from surplus cash could be significant for the company's earnings. The company might then need a forecast of its interest earnings in order to indicate its prospective **earnings per share** to stock market analysts and institutional investors.

Chapter roundup

- **Ratios** provide a means of systematically analysing financial statements. They can be grouped under the headings **profitability**, **liquidity**, **gearing** and **shareholders' investment**. It is important to calculate **relevant ratios** and to take into account the **limitations** of **ratio analysis.**
- As well as ratios, **other information** can be used to analyse a company's performance and identify possible problem areas. This will include information relating to **non-current assets** and **financial obligations**.
- Business failure can be predicted by **Z-scores**, using a number of financial variables, or by models such as **Argenti's model**, which emphasises defects, mistakes and symptoms.
- **Working capital management** involves achieving a balance between the requirement to minimise the risk of insolvency and the requirement to maximise profit.
- **Cash forecasting** should ensure that sufficient funds will be available when needed, to sustain the activities of an enterprise at an acceptable cost.
- **Balance sheet based forecasts** can be used to assess the scale of funding requirements or cash surpluses expected over time, and to act as a check on the realism of cash flow based forecasts.
- **Forecast financial statements** can be constructed for a period of several years, from first year data, given certain assumptions. You will not need to present cash flow statements in IAS 7 format.
- As part of a business' risk analysis, different forecasts should be prepared with **changing financial or business variables**. The links between these variables and the figures in the forecasts may not be straightforward.
- **Cash deficits** will be funded in different ways, depending on whether they are short or long-term. Businesses should have procedures for investing **surpluses** with appropriate levels of risk and return.

Quick quiz

1. What are the main limitations of ratio analysis?
2. Return on equity = ?
3. What is an earn-out arrangement?
4. Give three methods of funding a deficiency of cash.
5. What variables should typically be included in a cash budgeting model?
6. If a business is in financial difficulties, what type of assets should be sold off first?
7. What is the aim of a conservative working capital management policy?
8. From what sources might a business be able to obtain contingency funds?
9. What are permanent current assets?

Answers to quick quiz

1
- Lack of comparable industry information
- Historical information used for comparison may be out-of-date
- Ratio levels may not indicate situation fairly
- Ratios need careful interpretation
- Ratios can be manipulated
- Some ratios can be calculated in different ways
- Ratios shouldn't be used in isolation

2 Return on equity = $\frac{\text{Profit after tax and preferred dividend}}{\text{Ordinary share capital and reserves}} \times 100\%$

3 A procedure where owners/managers who are selling a business receive a portion of their consideration linked to the financial performance of the business during a specified period after the sale.

4 Borrowing; selling short-term financial investments; leading and lagging payables and receivables.

5
- Total sales
- Cash sales, perhaps as a percentage of total sales
- Credit sales, perhaps as a percentage of total sales
- Rate of growth in sales, or seasonal variations in sales
- Time taken by debtors to pay what they owe
- Purchases on credit
- Wages and salaries
- Other cash expenses
- Dividends
- Taxation payments
- Capital expenditure

6 Short-term marketable financial investments

7 To reduce the risk of system breakdown by holding high levels of working capital.

8
- Surplus cash balances
- Liquid investments
- Bank facility

9 The core level of investment in inventory and receivables. This is the minimum level of current assets that an entity needs to continue operation.

Now try the question below from the Exam Question Bank

Number	Level	Marks	Time
Q3	Introductory	n/a	35 mins
Q4	Examination	25	45 mins

Financial strategies

4

Introduction

Probably the most important learning outcome in this paper is that you should be able to '**recommend alternative financial strategies** for an organisation.' The syllabus requires you to assess the implications for shareholder value of alternative financial strategies. In the first section of this chapter, we draw together a number of the themes you have come across either earlier in this text, or in your previous studies, and demonstrate how they impact upon the development of financial strategies. We also will look at the key features of financial strategies.

As we've already seen, **dividend policy** is a key element in overall financial strategy, and in Section 2 we consider dividend policy in depth, in particular whether the amounts of profits that a company distributes has much or little impact on shareholders. Section 3 deals with **recent developments in financial reporting**. You won't be asked questions requiring a detailed knowledge of financial reporting standards; however you will be expected to know how recent changes and current issues might affect the financial strategies that organisations choose.

Topic list	Learning outcomes	Syllabus references	Ability required
1 Developing financial strategies	A(v)	A(10)	Evaluation
2 Dividends and retentions	A(ii), (v)	A(2), (10)	Evaluation
3 Issues in financial reporting	A(v)	A(11)	Evaluation

1 Developing financial strategies

Key term

A **strategy** is ' a course of action including the specification of resources required, to achieve a specific objective.' *(OT 2005)*

1.1 Choosing financial strategies

FAST FORWARD

The financial strategies that an organisation pursues should be developed taking into account all **relevant environmental factors**, the **views of stakeholders** and the **impact upon accounts** and **cash flows**.

The aim of this section is to provide a guide to financial strategies by highlighting the key considerations that will affect the choice of strategies and giving guidance on formulating strategies.

1.2 General considerations affecting strategies

We have covered many of these in the first few chapters of this book, but this section highlights the most significant factors.

- Investment, finance and dividends
- Profit effects
- Cash effects
- Shareholders
- Other stakeholders
- Economic and market considerations
- Restrictions
- Risks
- Time frame

1.2.1 Links between investment, finance and dividend

In other words:

- When formulating an **investment strategy**, always consider how the strategy will be financed and what the impact will be upon dividend payments
- When considering a **financing strategy**, consider whether its costs will mean reduced dividends, and how it will affect the resources the organisation can use for investment
- When considering a **dividend strategy**, remember that the organisation's investments have to generate the profits to pay dividends, and that high payout levels could mean less finance is available

1.2.2 Profits

The effect of **strategies chosen on profits** will obviously be a critical influence on how strategies are perceived, as a business's accounts present the public face of its financial strategies.

1.2.3 Cash

Though financial strategies should hopefully enhance long-term profitability, **cash flow considerations** will often be shorter-term but possibly rather more pressing. It's easy to just concentrate on operating and investing cash flows and ignore financing cash flows (interest and dividends). However a critical, and often finely balanced, question will be whether operating cash flows will be sufficient to pay the servicing costs of finance.

1.2.4 Shareholders

Enhancing shareholder value is of course a key objective, and although this is connected with dividend policy, you also need to assess the effect on **value of shares** (which we shall see later is not necessarily just a function of current and future dividends).

1.2.5 Other stakeholders

Many financial strategies will have major impacts upon stakeholders other than shareholders with whom the organisation wishes to maintain good relations. These include:

- **Managers and employees**, who will be affected by any fundamental decision about a business's direction such as a merger or acquisition
- **Other suppliers of finance**, who will be affected by decisions on capital structure
- The **government**, who might be concerned that major investment decisions have an adverse impact upon the outside environment (not just the natural environment but also the competitive environment)
- **Customers.** Clearly their goodwill needs to be retained. Businesses need to be sensitive not only to actions which directly affect customers (product pricing) but how other actions may impact (for example redundancies meaning that fewer staff are available to deal with customer demands)

1.2.6 Economic and market considerations

Business decisions are never taken in isolation in a perfect world. Therefore you have to evaluate the impact of factors such as **key economic indicators**. For this paper as well you need to consider the **international implications**, including exchange rates and conditions for investment abroad.

In addition the organisation's achievements may be assessed from distorted viewpoints, that place excessive emphasis upon certain factors and do not have all the necessary information. An assessment of **market efficiency** will thus often be helpful. Assessing market efficiency involves considering to what information the market is responding. We shall consider market efficiency further in Chapter 7.

1.2.7 Restrictions

Bear in mind that a business may not always be able to do what it wants. **Legal** restrictions may be a powerful restraining force, also restrictions imposed by **suppliers of finance** (restrictions imposed by loan arrangements or the need to maintain dividend levels to keep shareholders happy). Particularly for small companies, there may also be **restrictions** on the **funds available** to the business.

1.2.8 Risks

You will consider risks in detail in Paper P3 *Management Accounting – Risk and Control Strategy*, but you will often need to consider risk carefully in this paper. Remember also that it is not necessarily just financial risk you are considering. A good illustration of an area where other risks are important is investment in information technology, which we shall consider in Chapter 17 of this text.

You also need to have an awareness of **general risk issues** such as **limited data** and how the **changing environment** can be **measured**, also the impact of **uncertainty** (how difficult it is to measure the likelihood of outcomes). **Various measures** of risk may need to be considered (variation of possible outcomes, likelihood of an unsatisfactory outcome, worst possible outcome).

As well as the risks themselves, you also need to consider the organisation's (and its directors') **attitudes to risk.** It may be a good textbook answer to say that the business should obtain debt finance, but the current directors may be unwilling to put the business at risk by taking on extra debt.

1.2.9 Time scale

We've already mentioned timescale, but it's worth considering separately:

- Strategy is primarily concerned with long-term direction and businesses have to maximise shareholder value in the **long-term**. However you also should consider what objectives or conditions have to be fulfilled in the **short-term** (such as making enough money to carry on trading!)
- Decisions relating to a particular strategy are not always being made at a single time. In Chapter 19 we shall be looking at **real option theory**, which takes into account that businesses may choose one course, and then later on may decide on a different course of action depending on how the first course of action has gone.

1.3 Generating strategies

FAST FORWARD

The financial strategies chosen must be **clear**, **acceptable**, **feasible** and **suitable**.

The financial strategies you choose must be clear, which means that they need to specify certain things. From your studies of Paper 6 *Management Accounting – Business Strategy* you should also remember that strategies need to be:

- **Acceptable**, fulfilling stakeholder expectations
- **Feasible**, the organisation being able to carry it out
- **Suitable**, for enhancing the long-term prosperity of the organisation

1.3.1 Clarity

The considerations listed below will apply to strategies of **investment**. The focus of **financing strategies** will be on the provision of sufficient resources, although the resources required must also be spelt out for **investment strategies**.

(a) **Benefits**

The benefits to the **organisation** and **principal stakeholders** of strategies need to be spelt out, for example higher revenues or falling interest commitments meaning more funds being available for distribution to shareholders.

(b) **Direction**

The **activities** required to **implement the strategy** must be **directed** towards providing the benefits. Direction also means setting **financial targets**, enabling better control when the strategy is implemented.

(c) **Resource specification and management**

The **financial resources needed** to implement investment strategies should be specified in detail. Remember also the need to ensure **resources** are **managed carefully**. In your previous studies you should have encountered the concept of **over-trading**, where a business expands too quickly, failing to manage its working capital and cash flows properly.

(d) **Changes in the environment**

The strategy chosen should enable the business to cope with **environmental changes** and **complexity**. If environmental changes are likely to be a significant factor, it may be important to specify the responses that may be required, for example obtaining contingency funding.

(e) **Timescale**

The strategy chosen should be **relevant for the long-term**, that is going beyond short-term profit targets. What constitutes long-term will vary, but for an investing strategy it is likely to mean the **life-time of the investment**, for a financing strategy perhaps the **duration of long-term debt instruments**.

1.3.2 Acceptability

Stakeholder analysis is vital when assessing acceptability. Shareholders will obviously be concerned with how far the strategy chosen contributes to meeting the dominant objective of increasing shareholder wealth. Other suppliers of finance will be concerned with whether the organisation will be able to meet its commitments to them.

All stakeholders may be concerned with the potential **risks** of the strategies.

Financial acceptability will need to be **demonstrated,** by **investment appraisal** and by analysis of the effect on **profitability**, **liquidity** and **gearing** indicators. This may need to be supplemented by risk analysis.

Don't forget the other conditions (legal, loan covenant) etc imposed by other stakeholders. Acceptability may not just be a matter of fulfilling a set of rules, but also being a good citizen (acting sensitively towards the natural environment, paying suppliers on time).

1.3.3 Feasibility

As mentioned above, specification of **resources** required is a key aspect of clear exposition of strategy. These resources clearly have to be available in order for strategies to be **feasible.** Obviously for financial strategy decisions, financial resources will be critical, but businesses will also need to have access to **technology**, **materials** and **other natural resources**.

Businesses must also be able to **generate sufficient returns** in order to compensate resource providers for the resources consumed. They will need to be able to **supply sufficient goods and services** and be able to withstand competitor threats.

Again it will be important to demonstrate **financial feasibility** with supporting financial data. **Cash and funds flow forecasts** will be central to this.

Feasibility also relates to the **conditions** that will have to be fulfilled if a strategic decision is to be successful. If for example the success of an acquisition is dependent upon the key staff of the acquired company staying, how feasible is it that they will?

1.3.4 Suitability

Suitability relates to the **strategic logic** of decisions. Financial strategy should fit the situation of the business. The financial decisions taken should help businesses **generate and maintain competitive advantages**, **seize opportunities** and **exploit company strengths and distinctive competences**.

When considering the suitability of an option you are given in a question, you might also think about whether there are any **alternatives** not specified in the question that might be better. For example if a business is looking to acquire another, would it be better off trying to grow internally instead? It may be necessary to create a **framework** for ranking alternatives.

Exam focus point

> You cannot judge suitability by thinking wholly in numerical terms.

1.3.5 A trade-off?

If you are thinking that there may be problems with alternatives that are strategically **suitable** on the one hand, but which are perhaps not **acceptable** nor **feasible** on the other, you are probably right.

TOPCIMA link

> The TOPCIMA exam will often feature organisations which are facing imperative strategic decisions, but which currently lack the financial resources to implement those decisions.

One area of financial strategy where there may be significant problems is the business's optimal capital structure. We shall see in Chapter 10 that various strategic considerations may suggest a particular capital structure is suitable, but it may not be acceptable, and the finance not available.

Question

Financial strategy

Learning outcome: A(v)

As a general illustration of the principles we've just been discussing, consider the following outline scenario.

Getfitquick operates leisure clubs in a number of countries in Europe. The company is a major presence in the leisure club market, specialising in high care good facility operations. However this market is highly competitive and over the last few years a number of chains that have not been growing have been taken over. Getfitquick's performance over the last couple of years has been stagnant, with falling membership in existing clubs and newly-opened clubs taking time to become profitable.

The company is listed on a major European stock exchange, with a significant percentage of its shares being held both by its founders and by institutional investors. It also has significant loan finance, with loan creditors holding title deeds to some of the clubs, and in the past some of its loan commitments have had to be rescheduled.

Required

Getfitquick is considering whether to open a number of new clubs over the next few years. Draft notes suggesting how an expansion strategy would be judged against the criteria outlined above.

Answer

Factors to consider

(a) **Investment, finance and dividends**

A major investment is planned. There may be financing problems as equityholders may not subscribe if there is a prospect of low dividends.

(b) **Profit effects**

Growth in profit has to be sufficient to meet investor and market expectations. There may be problems initially with new clubs.

(c) **Cash effects**

There will be major expenditure on new clubs, paying finance providers, and possibly refurbishing old clubs. Again new clubs may not generate very much cash flow just after opening.

(d) **Shareholders**

There may be conflicts between initial investors who will accept a long-term return and want to retain active involvement in the business, and institutional shareholders with shorter-term interests who may be willing to accept a reasonably-priced takeover bid.

(e) **Other stakeholders**

Debtholders will be concerned whether investment will generate sufficient returns to guarantee sum lent and income. Managers will be worried about expansion/curtailment of their position. Employees will want to know how operational changes will affect their employment. Customers will be concerned with the fees charged and the services offered.

(f) **Economic and market factors**

The financial markets are not viewing the sector very positively. Investment in clubs that make initial losses may have an adverse effect on share price, if markets do not take potential long-term revenues into account.

(g) **Restrictions**

Takeover of another big sports chain may run into difficulties from competition authorities. Existing loan agreements may contain possible restrictions on taking on more debt or opening more clubs.

(h) **Risks**

Downturns in the economy may hit membership of sports clubs if it is perceived as a luxury item. The company may also be vulnerable to changes in property prices if it's investing in new sites, and changes in demand as leisure clubs become less popular. There may be some exposure to foreign exchange risks.

(i) **Time frame**

There's a potential conflict between the need for good short-term profits and cash flows, and longer-term returns.

Generating strategy

The strategy can be summed up as increasing profits and cash flows by opening of X new clubs over the next X years throughout Europe.

(a) **Benefits**

Benefits may accrue to shareholders in terms of dividend and market price appreciation.

(b) **Direction**

Monitoring of investments should be by financial performance indicators for new and existing clubs and overall targets for returns on capital employed.

(c) **Resources**

The company will need to specify sources of finance, amounts expected to be raised, commitments (return to suppliers and security). Also the directors should consider the generation of increased returns from existing operations by increasing membership charges and savings in operating costs.

(d) **Environment changes**

The scale of investment in new clubs should be reconsidered if property prices rise beyond a certain level, or if demand for existing clubs falls beyond a certain level.

(e) **Timescale**

Short-term investments may be limited by current funding problems. Finance may be available on better terms only when the existing network has generated higher returns.

Judging strategy

(a) **Suitability**

A strategy of expansion will maintain the position as a market leader, necessary in a highly competitive market. Merely maintaining current position without any investment may leave the company vulnerable to takeover. However there may be better ways of achieving its goals, taking over existing clubs or diversifying into other less costly areas.

(b) **Acceptability**

Will founder stakeholders maintain sufficient control, or will they prefer any combination of investment and financing to being taken over? Will institutional shareholders be satisfied with resultant dividend levels and movements in market prices? How will creditors view possible threats to their position? Will savings in operating costs adversely affect the service given to customers?

(c) **Feasibility**

Will required finance be available from all sources to support investments, or are the uncertainties or likely restrictions unacceptable? Will existing and new clubs generate enough cash flows to pay providers of finance and make their own contribution to future investment? Does the company have the management, personnel and systems needed to run a much-expanded network of clubs?

2 Dividends and retentions

FAST FORWARD

- **Retained earnings** are the most important single source of finance for companies, and financial managers should take account of the proportion of earnings that are retained as opposed to being paid as dividends.
- Companies generally **smooth out dividend payments** by adjusting only gradually to changes in earnings: large fluctuations might **undermine investors' confidence**.
- The dividends a company pays may be treated as a **signal** to investors. A company needs to take account of different clienteles of shareholders in deciding what dividends to pay.

Key term

A **dividend** is a distribution of profits to the holders of equity investments in proportion to their holdings of a particular class of capital. *(IAS 18)*

2.1 Dividend payments

Shareholders normally have the power to vote to **reduce** the size of the dividend at the AGM, but not the power to **increase** the dividend. The directors of the company are therefore in a strong position, with regard to shareholders, when it comes to determining dividend policy. For practical purposes, shareholders will usually be obliged to accept the dividend policy that has been decided on by the directors, or otherwise to sell their shares.

2.2 Factors influencing dividend policy

When deciding upon the dividends to pay out to shareholders, one of the main considerations of the directors will be the amount of earnings they wish to retain to meet **financing needs**.

Question

Retained earnings

Learning outcome: A(ii)

What are the major reasons for using the cash from retained earnings to finance new investments, rather than to pay higher dividends and then raise new equity funds for the new investments?

Answer

(a) The dividend policy of a company is in practice often determined by the directors. From their standpoint, funds from retained earnings are an attractive source of finance because **investment projects can be undertaken without involving either the shareholders or any outsiders.**

(b) The use of retained earnings as opposed to new shares or debentures **avoids issue costs.**

(c) The use of funds from retained earnings **avoids the possibility of a change in control** resulting from an issue of new shares.

As well as future financing requirements, the decision on how much of a company's profits should be retained, and how much paid out to shareholders, will be influenced by:

(a) The **need to remain profitable** (Dividends are paid out of profits, and an unprofitable company cannot for ever go on paying dividends out of retained profits made in the past.)

(b) The **law on distributable profits**

(c) Any **dividend restraints** that might be imposed by loan agreements

(d) The **effect of inflation**, and the need to retain some profit within the business just to maintain its operating capability unchanged

(e) The company's **gearing level** (If the company wants extra finance, the sources of funds used should strike a balance between equity and debt finance)

(f) The company's **liquidity position** (Dividends are a cash payment, and a company must have enough cash to pay the dividends it declares.)

(g) The need to **repay debt** in the near future.

(h) The ease with which the company could raise **extra finance** from sources other than retained earnings (Small companies which find it hard to raise finance might have to rely more heavily on retained earnings than large companies.)

(i) The **signalling effect** of dividends to shareholders and the financial markets in general – see below.

2.3 Dividends as a signal to investors

The ultimate objective in any financial management decisions is to **maximise shareholders' wealth**. This wealth is basically represented by the **current market value** of the company, which should largely be determined by the **cash flows arising from the investment decisions** taken by management.

Although the market would **like** to value shares on the basis of underlying cash flows on the company's projects, such information is **not readily available to investors**. But the directors do have this information. The dividend declared can be interpreted as a **signal** from directors to shareholders about the strength of underlying project cash flows.

Investors usually expect a **consistent dividend policy** from the company, with stable dividends each year or, even better, **steady dividend growth**. A large rise or fall in dividends in any year can have a marked effect on the company's share price. Stable dividends or steady dividend growth are usually needed for share price stability. A cut in dividends may be treated by investors as signalling that the future prospects of the company are weak. Thus, **the dividend which is paid acts**, possibly without justification, **as a signal of the future prospects of the company.**

The signalling effect of a company's dividend policy may also be used by management of a company which faces a possible **takeover**. The dividend level might be increased as a defence against the takeover: investors may take the increased dividend as a signal of improved future prospects, thus driving the share price higher and making the company more expensive for a potential bidder to take over.

Exam focus point

> You should show, whenever relevant in exam answers, that you appreciate the signalling effect of dividends. However, don't mention it if you're dealing with a private company as it won't be relevant.

2.3.1 Other signalling issues

Directors can signal to the market in other ways also: **the issue of debt**, which commits the company to paying interest, can be interpreted as a signal of strong project cash flows, as compared with the issue of equity. Such 'signals' are likely to be taken as more reliable than anything that the directors say, since they involve actual commitments or movements of cash.

2.4 Theories of dividend policy

2.4.1 Residual theory

A **'residual' theory** of **dividend policy** can be summarised as follows.

- If a company can identify projects with positive NPVs, it should invest in them.
- Only when these investment opportunities are exhausted should dividends be paid.

2.4.2 Traditional view

The **'traditional' view** of dividend policy, implicit in our earlier discussion, is to focus on the effects on share price. The price of a share depends upon the mix of dividends, given shareholders' required rate of return, and growth.

2.4.3 Irrelevancy theory

In contrast to the traditional view, **Modigliani and Miller** (MM) proposed that in a tax-free world, shareholders are indifferent between dividends and capital gains, and the value of a company is determined solely by the 'earning power' of its assets and investments.

MM argued that if a company with investment opportunities decides to pay a dividend, so that **retained earnings** are **insufficient** to finance all its investments, the shortfall in funds will be made up by **obtaining additional funds** from outside sources. As a result of obtaining outside finance instead of using retained earnings:

Loss of value in existing shares = Amount of dividend paid

In answer to criticisms that certain shareholders will show a preference either for high dividends or for capital gains, MM argued that if a company pursues a consistent dividend policy, 'each corporation would tend to attract to itself a clientele consisting of those preferring its particular payout ratio, but one clientele would be entirely as good as another in terms of the valuation it would imply for the firm'.

2.4.4 The case in favour of the relevance of dividend policy (and against MM's views)

There are strong arguments against MM's view that dividend policy is irrelevant as a means of affecting shareholder's wealth.

(a) **Differing rates** of **taxation** on **dividends** and **capital gains** can create a **preference** for a **high dividend** or one for **high earnings retention**.

(b) **Dividend retention** should be **preferred** by companies in a period of **capital rationing**.

(c) Due to imperfect markets and the possible difficulties of selling shares easily at a fair price, shareholders might need **high dividends** in order to have funds to **invest** in **opportunities** outside the company.

(d) **Markets** are **not perfect**. Because of **transaction costs** on the sale of shares, investors who want some cash from their investments will prefer to receive dividends rather than to sell some of their shares to get the cash they want.

(e) Information available to shareholders is imperfect, and they are not aware of the **future investment plans** and **expected profits** of their company. Even if management were to provide them with profit forecasts, these forecasts would not necessarily be accurate or believable.

(f) Perhaps the strongest argument against the MM view is that shareholders will tend to **prefer a current dividend** to future capital gains (or deferred dividends) because the future is more uncertain.

Exam focus point

Even if you accept that dividend policy may have some influence on share values, there may be other, more important, influences. Don't be tempted to regurgitate chunks of theory in the exam, you must focus on the entities involved.

Question

Dividend policy

Learning outcome: A(ii)

Ochre is a company that is still managed by the two individuals who set it up 12 years ago. In the current year the company was launched on the stock market. Previously, all of the shares had been owned by its two founders and certain employees. Now, 40% of the shares are in the hands of the investing public. The company's profit growth and dividend policy are set out below. Will a continuation of the same dividend policy as in the past be suitable now that the company is quoted on the stock market?

Year	*Profits*	*Dividend*	*Shares in issue*
	£'000	£'000	
4 years ago	176	88	800,000
3 years ago	200	104	800,000
2 years ago	240	120	1,000,000
1 year ago	290	150	1,000,000
Current year	444	222 (proposed)	1,500,000

Answer

Year	*Dividend per share pence*	*Dividend as %of profit*
4 years ago	11.0	50%
3 years ago	13.0	52%
2 years ago	12.0	50%
1 year ago	15.0	52%
Current year	14.8	50%

The company appears to have pursued a dividend policy of paying out half of after-tax profits in dividend. This policy is only suitable when a company achieves a stable EPS or steady EPS growth. Investors do not like a fall in dividend from one year to the next, and the fall in dividend per share in the current year is likely to be unpopular, and to result in a fall in the share price.

The company would probably serve its shareholders better by paying a dividend of at least 15p per share, possibly more, in the current year, even though the dividend as a percentage of profit would then be higher.

2.5 Scrip dividends

Key term

Scrip dividend is a dividend paid by the issue of additional company shares, rather than by cash. *(OT 2005)*

A scrip dividend effectively converts retained earnings into **issued share capital**. When the directors of a company would prefer to retain funds within the business but consider that they must pay at least a certain amount of dividend, they might offer equity shareholders the choice of a **cash dividend** or a **scrip dividend**. Each shareholder would decide separately which to take.

Recently **enhanced scrip dividends** have been offered by many companies. With enhanced scrip dividends, the value of the shares offered is much greater than the cash alternative, giving investors an incentive to choose the shares.

2.5.1 Advantages of scrip dividends

(a) They can **preserve** a company's **cash position** if a substantial number of shareholders take up the share option.

(b) Investors may be able to obtain **tax advantages** if dividends are in the form of shares.

(c) Investors looking to **expand their holding** can do so **without incurring** the **transaction costs** of buying more shares.

(d) A small scrip issue will **not dilute the share price significantly.** If however cash is not offered as an alternative, empirical evidence suggests that the share price will tend to fall.

(e) A share issue will **decrease** the company's **gearing**, and may therefore **enhance** its **borrowing capacity.**

2.6 Stock split

This possible advantage of a scrip issue is also the reason for a **stock split**. A stock split occurs where, for example, each ordinary share of £1 each is split into two shares of 50p each, thus creating cheaper shares with **greater marketability**. There is possibly an added psychological advantage, in that investors may expect a company which splits its shares in this way to be planning for substantial earnings growth and dividend growth in the future.

As a consequence, the market price of shares may benefit. For example, if one existing share of £1 has a market value of £6, and is then split into two shares of 50p each, the market value of the new shares might settle at, say, £3.10 instead of the expected £3, in anticipation of strong future growth in earnings and dividends.

The difference between a stock split and a scrip issue is that a scrip issue converts equity reserves into share capital, whereas a stock split leaves reserves unaffected. Both are popular with investors as they are seen as likely to lead to increased dividends. Scrip dividends can, however, lead to tax complications for individual investors.

2.7 Share repurchase

FAST FORWARD

Purchase by a company of its own shares can take place for various reasons and must be in accordance with any **requirements of legislation**.

In many countries companies have the right to **buy back shares from shareholders** who are willing to sell them, subject to certain conditions.

For a **smaller company** with few shareholders, the reason for buying back the company's own shares may be that there is no immediate willing purchaser at a time when a shareholder wishes to sell shares. For a public company, share repurchase could provide a way of withdrawing from the share market and 'going private'.

2.7.1 Benefits of a share repurchase scheme

(a) Finding a **use for surplus cash**, which may be a 'dead asset'.

(b) **Increase in earnings per share** through a reduction in the number of shares in issue. This should lead to a higher share price than would otherwise be the case, and the company should be able to increase dividend payments on the remaining shares in issue.

(c) **Increase in gearing**. Repurchase of a company's own shares allows debt to be substituted for equity, so raising gearing. This will be of interest to a company wanting to increase its gearing without increasing its total long-term funding.

(d) **Readjustment of the company's equity base** to more appropriate levels, for a company whose business is in decline.

(e) Possibly **preventing a takeover** or enabling a quoted company to withdraw from the stock market.

2.7.2 Drawbacks of a share repurchase scheme

(a) It can be **hard to arrive at a price** that will be fair both to the vendors and to any shareholders who are not selling shares to the company.

(b) A repurchase of shares could be seen as an **admission** that the company **cannot make better use of the funds** than the shareholders.

(c) Some shareholders may suffer from being **taxed on a capital gain** following the purchase of their shares rather than receiving dividend income.

Case Study

In July 2006 Microsoft announced the launch of a $20bn share buyback, despite seeing its profits fall over the past quarter. This was equivalent to 8% of its total stock, adding to the $30bn it had already bought in the past year.

Chief financial officer, Chris Liddell stated: 'With our share repurchase programs, we reaffirm our confidence and optimism in the long-term future of the company'.

3 Issues in financial reporting

FAST FORWARD

Companies must **carefully assess** the impact of **changes** in **accounting standards**. Changes may affect individual items (share-based payments) or the whole basis of accounts (value-based accounting), or may develop new types of accounting (environmental or human resource accounting).

3.1 Impact of financial reporting developments on the financial manager

The syllabus states that current and emerging issues in financial reporting and in other forms of external reporting are examinable in this paper. However as this is a financial management paper, the syllabus will not be testing the detail of the changes and developments in standards, but will take an overview, testing the impact of emerging issues on financial strategy decisions.

Question — Developments in financial reporting

Learning outcome: A(v)

What general impacts might developments in financial reporting have on financial strategy?

Answer

General impacts might include:

(a) **Relations with stakeholders**

Companies have to consider how changes in standards will affect the key indicators for various stakeholders. Changes that affect the **calculation of profit** will **influence shareholders** if profits become significantly more volatile as a result. Shareholders and lenders who are concerned with financial stability will be influenced by changes in the **treatment** and **classification of capital instruments**, for example changes that force companies to include previously off-balance sheet items or reclassify equity instruments as debt.

Other stakeholders may be affected by **new forms of accounting** or **increased disclosures**. Employees will be interested in developments in human resource accounting. Pressure groups and other interested stakeholders ('ethical investors') will be interested in how the organisation is reporting its impact upon the natural environment (considered further below)

(b) **Undertaking and form of transactions**

Changes in standards may also mean companies do **not undertake transactions** or stop doing what they previously have been doing. The introduction of more **volatility into accounts** may make certain transactions less attractive, for example granting of employee share options. Many companies in the United Kingdom have alleged that FRS 17, which introduced more onerous rules for accounting for pension liabilities, has forced them to close their final salary pension schemes and offer less generous arrangements instead. However other factors would have had a major influence on this decision as well.

Alterations to standards can also affect the **form transactions take**. There is evidence that some acquisitions in the United Kingdom have been structured in a certain way in order to be treated under the (more appealing) merger accounting rules than acquisition accounting rules. A proposed prohibition of the merger accounting treatment would remove the incentive to use unusual structuring arrangements.

(c) **Investments**

Having diverse requirements internationally arguably allows companies in some jurisdictions to shelter behind **doubtful arrangements**. Evidence from the USA suggests that having one set of strict standards forces companies to be more efficient and more competitive. It also lowers the risks of investment, reducing the cost of capital and hence making previously unattractive overseas investments feasible.

(d) **Costs of compliance**

In particular the costs of fundamental changes such as the introduction of international accounting standards may be significant. Not only will this impact upon companies' **financial accounting function**, but also may affect the **management accounting function's** work if compatibility between financial and management accounting is to be maintained.

3.2 Adoption of international accounting standards

In order to establish a single European market for financial services, the European Commission required all European Union (EU) companies with either debt or equity securities listed on a regulated market, to prepare their consolidated accounts in accordance with international accounting standards. The deadline for adoption of international standards by EU companies was **1 January 2005**, and this change is likely to put pressure on other jurisdictions to adopt international rules as well.

3.2.1 Advantages of international harmonisation

The advantages of harmonisation will be based on the benefits to users and preparers of accounts, as follows.

(a) **Investors**

Both individual and corporate investors would like to be able to compare the financial results of different companies **internationally** as well as nationally in making investment decisions. **Differences in accounting practice and reporting** can prove to be a barrier to such cross-border analysis. There is a growing amount of investment across borders and for example, it is not easy for an analyst familiar with UK accounting principles to analyse the financial statements of a Dutch or German company. Harmonisation would therefore be of benefit to such analysts.

(b) **Multinational companies**

Multinationals would benefit from harmonisation for many reasons including the following.

- **Better access** would be available to **foreign investor funds**.
- **Management control** would be improved, because harmonisation would aid internal communication of financial information.
- **Appraisal of foreign enterprises** for take-overs and mergers would be more straightforward.
- It would be easier to **comply** with the **reporting requirements** of overseas stock exchanges.
- **Consolidation of foreign subsidiaries** and associated companies would be easier.
- A **reduction in audit costs** might be achieved.
- **Transfer of accounting staff** across national borders would be **easier**.

(c) **Governments of developing countries**

Governments would **save time and money** if they could adopt international standards and, if these were used internally, governments of developing countries could attempt to **control the activities** of foreign multinational companies in their own country. These companies could not 'hide' behind foreign accounting practices that are difficult to understand.

(d) **Tax authorities**

It will be **easier to calculate the tax liability** of investors, including multinationals who receive income from overseas sources.

(e) **Regional economic groups**

Regional economic groups **promote trade** within a **specific geographical region**. This would be aided by common accounting practices within the region.

3.2.2 Barriers to harmonisation

However there are many barriers to international harmonisation: if there were not then greater progress would probably have been made by now. The main problems are as follows.

(a) **Different purposes of financial reporting**

In some countries the purpose of accounts is solely for **tax assessment**, while in others it is for investor decision-making.

(b) **Different legal systems**

These prevent the development of **certain accounting practices** and restrict the options available.

(c) **Different stakeholders**

Countries have different ideas about who the **relevant user groups** are and their respective importance. In the USA investor and creditor groups are given prominence, while in Europe employees enjoy a higher profile.

(d) **Needs of developing countries**

Developing countries are obviously behind in the standard setting process and they need to develop the **basic standards and principles** already in place in most developed countries.

(e) **Focus of standards**

IASs have been developed for the **consolidated accounts of listed companies**, and have not been designed for single entities or small and medium-sized companies.

(f) **Nationalism**

Nationalism is demonstrated in an unwillingness to accept another country's standards.

(g) **Cultural differences**

Cultural differences result in objectives for accounting systems differing from country to country.

(h) **Unique circumstances**

Some countries may be experiencing unusual circumstances which affect all aspects of everyday life and impinge on the ability of companies to produce proper reports, for example hyperinflation, civil war, currency restriction and so on.

(i) **The lack of strong accountancy bodies**

Many countries do not have strong independent accountancy or business bodies that would press for better standards and greater harmonisation.

3.3 Changes in the basis of accounting

Apart from overseeing the implementation of standards in EU countries, probably the most significant project that the International Accounting Standards Board is involved in is the development of fair value accounting. This will involve substantial changes to current standards, and mean that various concepts such as **historical costs** and **realisation** become **less significant**. It will also mean that the determination of taxable and distributable profits become purely legal, not financial reporting issues. A widening of the differences between financial reporting surpluses and taxable profits will complicate relations with the tax authorities.

This change will also mean a switch in emphasis to a **balance sheet model** where **assets and liabilities** are **measured at fair value**. Company performance will be reported in a **financial performance statement** that aggregates all income with all value changes, **realised and unrealised.**

The consequences of changing the way financial performance is measured will be fundamental. **Measures** such as earnings per share and profit from operations will become much **more volatile** and **less valuable**. There are likely to be **major impacts** on **performance incentives**; schemes that base rewards on performance figures that take into account estimated fair value changes will not be popular with investors.

3.4 IFRS 2 *Share based payments*

Transactions whereby entities purchase goods or services from other parties, such as suppliers and employees, by **issuing shares or share options** to those other parties are **increasingly common.** Share schemes are a common feature of director and executive remuneration and in some countries the authorities may offer tax incentives to encourage more companies to offer shares to employees. Companies whose shares or share options are regarded as a valuable 'currency' commonly use share-based payment to obtain employee and professional services.

The increasing use of share-based payments has raised questions about the accounting treatment of such transactions in company financial statements.

Share options are often granted to employees at an **exercise price** that is **equal to or higher than the market price** of the shares at the date the option is granted. Consequently the options have no intrinsic value and so **no transaction is recorded in the financial statements**.

This leads to an **anomaly:** if a company pays its employees in cash, an expense is recognised in the income statement, but if the payment is in share options, no expense is recognised.

3.4.1 Arguments against recognition of share-based payment in the financial statements

There are a number of arguments against recognition. The International Accounting Standards Board has considered and rejected the arguments below.

(a) **No cost therefore no charge**

There is no cost to the entity because the granting of shares or options does not require the entity to sacrifice cash or other assets. Therefore a charge should not be recognised.

This argument ignores the fact that a **transaction has occurred**. The employees have provided **valuable services in return for valuable shares or options**.

(b) **Earnings per share is hit twice**

The charge to the income statement for the employee services consumed reduces the entity's earnings, while at the same time there is an increase in the number of shares issued.

However, the dual impact on earnings per share simply **reflects the two economic events** that have occurred.

(i) The **entity has issued shares or options**, thus increasing the denominator of the earnings per share calculation.

(ii) It has also **consumed the resources** it received for those shares or options, thus reducing the numerator.

(c) **Adverse economic consequences**

Entities might be discouraged from **introducing or continuing employee share plans** if they were required to recognise them on the financial statements. However, if this happened, it might be because the requirement for entities to account properly for employee share plans reveals the economic consequences of such plans.

A situation where entities are able to obtain and consume resources by issuing valuable shares or options without having to account for such transactions could be perceived as a **distortion**.

3.4.2 Objective and scope

IFRS 2 requires an entity to **reflect the effects of share-based payment transactions** in its income statement and balance sheet.

IFRS 2 applies to all share-based payment transactions. There are three types.

(a) **Equity-settled share-based payment transactions**, in which the entity receives goods or services in exchange for equity instruments of the entity (including shares or share options)

(b) **Cash-settled share-based payment transactions**, in which the entity receives goods or services in exchange for amounts of cash that are based on the price (or value) of the entity's shares or other equity instruments of the entity

(c) Transactions in which the entity receives or acquires goods or services and either the entity or the supplier has a **choice** as to whether the entity settles the transaction in cash (or other assets) or by issuing equity instruments

3.4.3 Recognition: the basic principle

An entity should **recognise goods or services received or acquired in a share-based payment transaction when it obtains the goods or as the services are received.** Goods or services received or acquired in a share-based payment transaction **should be recognised as expenses unless they qualify for recognition as assets**. For example, services are normally recognised as expenses (because they are normally rendered immediately), while goods are recognised as assets.

If the goods or services were received or acquired in an **equity-settled** share-based payment transaction the entity should recognise **a corresponding increase in equity** (reserves).

If the goods or services were received or acquired in a **cash-settled** share-based payment transaction the entity should recognise a **liability.**

3.4.4 Equity-settled share-based payment transactions

The issue here is how to measure the 'cost' of the goods and services received and the equity instruments (eg, the share options) granted in return.

The general principle in IFRS 2 is that when an entity recognises the goods or services received and the corresponding increase in equity, it should measure these at the **fair value of the goods or services received**. Where the transaction is with **parties other than employees**, there is a rebuttable presumption that the fair value of the goods or services received can be estimated reliably.

If the fair value of the goods or services received cannot be measured reliably, the entity should measure their value by reference to the **fair value of the equity instruments granted.**

Where a transaction is measured by reference to the fair value of the equity instruments granted, fair value is based on **market prices** if available, taking into account the terms and conditions upon which those equity instruments were granted.

3.4.5 Cash-settled share-based payment transactions

Examples of this type of transaction include:

(a) **Share appreciation rights** granted to employees: the employees become entitled to a future cash payment (rather than an equity instrument), based on the increase in the entity's share price from a specified level over a specified period of time or

(b) An entity might grant to its employees a right to receive a future cash payment by granting to them a **right to shares that are redeemable**

The basic principle is that the entity measures the goods or services acquired and the liability incurred at the **fair value of the liability**.

The entity should **remeasure** the fair value of the liability **at each reporting date** until the liability is settled **and at the date of settlement**. Any **changes** in fair value are recognised in **profit or loss** for the period.

The entity should recognise the services received, and a liability to pay for those services, **as the employees render service.** For example, if share appreciation rights do not vest until the employees have completed a specified period of service, the entity should recognise the services received and the related liability, over that period.

3.4.6 Disclosures

IFRS 2 requires entities to disclose information that enables users of the financial statements to understand the **nature and extent** of share-based payment **arrangements that existed during the period**

(a) A **description** of each type of share-based payment arrangement that existed at any time during the period, including the general terms and conditions of each arrangement;

(b) The **number and weighted average exercise prices** of share options.

(c) For share options **exercised** during the period, the **weighted average share price** at the date of exercise

(d) For share options **outstanding** at the end of the period, the **range of exercise prices** and **weighted average remaining contractual life**

In addition, IFRS 2 requires disclosure of information that enables users of the financial statements to **understand how the fair value** of the goods or services received, or the fair value of the equity instruments granted, during the period **was determined**.

Entities should also disclose information that enables users of the financial statements to understand the effect of share-based payment transactions on the entity's **profit or loss for the period** and on its **financial position**.

3.5 Inclusion of published cash flow forecasts

Many believe that companies should publish cash flow forecasts. However, published cash flow forecasts have certain disadvantages.

(a) The **information** contained in them **may be manipulated** by unscrupulous managers wishing to show a favourable impression.

(b) They are **only as good as the assumptions on which they are based**. Clearly there is an element of subjectivity and uncertainty involved in preparing them. However, users of cash flow forecasts should be aware of their limitations.

(c) Cash flow forecasts are **very difficult to audit**, because they are **based on subjective prediction**. However, auditors can assess the accounting principles adopted and the consistency with which they are applied.

(d) It is possible that **competitors could make use of the information** disclosed in a cash flow forecast, although if they were compulsory for all companies no single company would benefit from this advantage.

(e) If **markets** are **fully efficient**, arguably the impact of publishing cash flow forecasts will be limited. However if markets are not efficient, an over-optimistic forecast may result in the **directors coming under fire** if the company does not achieve its targets; over-pessimistic estimates may however result in **immediate falls in the company's share price.**

3.6 Environmental accounting

In their capacity as information providers, accountants may be required to report on a firm's environmental impact and possible consequences. Most listed companies now produce environmental reports but disclosures are voluntary.

3.6.1 Environmental management accounting

Examples of environmental management accounting include the following.

(a) **Eco-balance**

The firm identifies the raw materials it uses and outputs such as waste, noise etc, which it gives a notional value. The firm can identify these outputs as a social 'cost'.

(b) **Cleaner technology**

This can be used in the manufacturing process to avoid waste. Simple waste-minimisation measures can increase profit on purely economic grounds.

(c) **Corporate liabilities**

Firms are being sued for environmental damage, and this might need to be recorded as a liability, with a suitable risk assessment. This might have to be factored into the project appraisal and risk.

(d) **Performance appraisal**

This can include reducing pollution.

(e) **Life cycle assessments**

The total environmental impact of a product is measured, from the resources it consumes, the energy it requires in use, and how it is disposed of, if not recycled. It may be that a product's poor ecological impact (and consequent liability or poor publicity) can be traced back to one component or material, which can be replaced.

(f) **Budgetary planning and control system**

These can be used to develop variances analysing environmental issues.

3.6.2 Environmental reporting

More companies are now producing an external report for external stakeholders, covering:

- What the **business does** and how it impacts on the environment
- **Environmental objectives** (eg use of 100% recyclable materials within x years)
- The **company's approach** to achieving and monitoring these objectives
- An **assessment of its success** towards achieving the objectives
- An **independent verification** of **claims made**

3.6.3 Widening the scope of environmental accounting

Companies are acknowledging the advantages of having an environmental policy, including **reduction/management of risk to the business, motivating staff** and corporate reputation enhanced by being a **good citizen**. Many believe that development of a policy will mean a **long term improvement in profitability**. According to Shell plc 'we believe long-term competitive success depends on being trusted to meet society's expectations.'

Pressure is increasing on companies to widen their scope of corporate public accountability. This pressure stems from **increasing expectations of stakeholders** and knowledge about the consequences of ignoring such pressures. There is an increasing expectation on companies to follow social policies of their business in addition to economic and environmental policies.

The United Nations has backed a Global Reporting Initiative (GRI). This Initiative sets out a framework for reporting, including a **statement of vision and strategy** from the CEO together with **performance indicators** divided into economic, environmental and social performance indicators against which performance can be **measured** and **independently verified**.

The development of measurement and independent verification techniques are important, as in the past companies' own valuation of their contribution to the environment has sometimes been accepted uncritically. Enron was awarded six environmental awards in 2000, voted the best company to work for three years in a row and boasted its achievements in a report on its economic, environmental and social performance.

3.7 Human resource accounting

In 2003 the UK government set up a *Taskforce on Human Capital Management Reporting* (Accounting for People). Its terms of reference were to 'consider best practice in human capital reporting, and the performance measures that are most valuable for stakeholders.' The Taskforce reported in late 2003 emphasising that **human resource activity** needs to be **measured**, otherwise it could **not** be **properly managed,** and investors interested in the long-term success of a company need good information on human capital resources.

A key recommendation was that organisations should communicate clearly how their **human resource policies link** with **business strategy and performance**. The taskforce also suggested that companies should report on:

- The **size** and **composition** of the **workforce**
- **Employee motivation** – data such as turnover and absentee rates and information for gathering employee's views
- **Staff training and development** – amount, cost and effectiveness

- **Remuneration and fair employment** – the approach to pay and incentives
- **Leadership and succession planning**

3.7.1 Advantages of human resource accounting

(a) Human resource accounting aims to analyse, measure and evaluate how people, policies and practices create value and thus **supports strategic decision-making**. Restructuring decisions for example will be aided by an understanding of the value staff add. In merger situations a large premium is often paid for staff expertise; human resource accounting helps ensure that this premium is calculated fairly, and by emphasising the value of human assets, should help ensure they are not dissipated after the merger.

(b) Human resource accounting can also be a sign of **strategic success**, for example the recruitment, retention and development of talented people where there is strong competition for them.

(c) It enables managers to demonstrate to external stakeholders, particularly shareholders, that the organisation is adopting **human resource procedures** that should result in **high performance**.

(d) **Development of best practice** may **encourage more companies to report**, since a number cite the absence of clear guidance and universal practice as a deterrent against reporting.

(e) It is a clear response to general pressures for **greater corporate openness**. Developments in reporting such as the Operating and Financial Review in the UK require businesses to comment on assets that may not be included in the balance sheet, such as human capital.

3.7.2 Problems with human resource accounting

(a) Human resource accounting may be an attempt to meet the **agendas of different stakeholders**, but the **benefits to shareholders** are **unclear**.

(b) The UK paper admits that all the approaches appear to suffer **from limitations** and that there is **no obvious best set of principles**.

(c) The **particular circumstances** of an **organisation** must be taken into account when reviewing its human resource procedures.

(d) If no general measures can be found, **measures** that only give **limited information** have to be used. However organisations may try to manage these at the expense of more important aspects of human resource development which cannot be measured.

(e) Organisations regard certain information as **commercially confidential** or sensitive.

(f) Evidence suggests that in certain regimes (South Africa for example) where legal requirements are onerous companies adopt a **mechanistic approach**. A more effective approach may be to encourage awards for good practice (Investors in people) and for governments themselves to set an example and require those with whom they contract to meet certain standards.

Chapter roundup

- The financial strategies that an organisation pursues should be developed taking into account all **relevant environmental factors**, the **views of stakeholders** and the **impact upon accounts** and **cash flows**.
- The financial strategies chosen must be **clear**, **acceptable**, **feasible** and **suitable**.
- **Retained earnings** are the most important single source of finance for companies, and financial managers should take account of the proportion of earnings that are retained as opposed to being paid as dividends.
- Companies generally **smooth out dividend payments** by adjusting only gradually to changes in earnings: large fluctuations might **undermine investors' confidence**.
- The dividends a company pays may be treated as a **signal** to investors. A company needs to take account of different clienteles of shareholders in deciding what dividends to pay.
- Purchase by a company of its own shares can take place for various reasons and must be in accordance with any **requirements of legislation**.
- Companies must **carefully assess** the impact of **changes** in **accounting standards**. Changes may affect individual items (share-based payments) or the whole basis of accounts (value-based accounting), or may develop new types of accounting (environmental or human resource accounting).

Quick quiz

1 Define what a strategy is.

2 Apart from clarity, what other qualities should strategies have?

3 **Fill in the blank**

Particular companies may attract particular types of shareholders. This is called the .... effect.

4 Give a definition of 'signalling' in the context of dividends policy.

5 **Fill in the blank**

A .... is a dividend payment which takes the form of new shares instead of cash.

6 Why might shareholders prefer a current dividend to a future capital gain?

7 Why would a company buy back shares from shareholders?

8 What are the main barriers to international harmonisation of accounting standards?

9 What disclosures might be included in an environmental accounting report?

Answers to quick quiz

1 A **strategy** is 'a course of action including the specification of resources required, to achieve a specific objective.'

2
- Acceptability
- Feasibility
- Suitability

3 Clientele

4 The use of dividend policy to indicate the future prospects of an enterprise

5 Scrip dividend

6 Tax advantages or because the future capital gain will be uncertain

7
- To find a use for surplus cash
- To increase EPS
- To increase gearing
- To readjust the equity base to more appropriate levels
- To prevent a takeover
- To withdraw from the stock market

8
- Different purposes of financial reporting
- Different legal systems
- Different stakeholders
- Needs of developing countries
- Focus of standards
- Nationalism
- Cultural differences
- Unique circumstances
- Lack of strong accountancy bodies

9
- How what the company does impacts upon the environment
- The environmental objectives
- The approach to monitoring and achieving those objectives
- Assessment of success in achieving its objectives
- Verification of claims made

Now try the question below from the Exam Question Bank

Number	Level	Marks	Time
Q5	Introductory	n/a	20 mins
Q6	Examination	20	36 mins

Part B
Financial management

5

Equity finance

Introduction

In Part B of this book we consider various aspects of financial management. In the first few chapters of this part, we shall look at how businesses determine their long-term capital structure, before moving on to examine the consequences of choosing a particular capital structure.

When sources of **long-term finance** are used, large sums are usually involved, and so the financial manager needs to consider all the options available with care, looking at the possible effects on the company in the long term.

In this chapter, we describe the different forms of **share capital**, and go on to consider other long-term sources of finance in Chapters 6 and 7. The learning outcomes require you to identify and evaluate optimal strategies for the satisfaction of long-term financing requirements. You should therefore concentrate on the **reasons** why different methods are used and their **advantages** and **disadvantages**. Don't get bogged down in the detail of each method.

1 Obtaining equity funds

FAST FORWARD

Companies seeking extra equity finance can obtain it by **retaining cash** in the business for investment or **issuing shares**.

1.1 Retained profits

For many businesses, the cash needed to finance investments will be available because the earnings the business has made have been retained within the business rather than paid out as dividends. We emphasised in Chapter 1 that this interaction of investment, financing and dividend policy is the most important issue facing many businesses.

Exam focus point

Strictly speaking it is the cash accumulated within the business that can be used as a source of finance and not the retained profits. This may seem a pedantic point, but it is one that examiners often pick up.

1.1.1 Advantages of using retentions

(a) Retentions are a **flexible source** of finance; companies are not tied to specific amounts or specific repayment patterns.

(b) Using retentions does **not involve** a **change in the pattern** of **shareholdings**.

1.1.2 Disadvantages of using retentions

(a) As mentioned above, shareholders may be **sensitive** to the **loss of dividends** that will result from retention for re-investment, rather than paying dividends.

(b) Not so much a disadvantage as a misconception, that retaining profits is a cost-free method of obtaining funds. There is an **opportunity cost** in that if dividends were paid, the cash received could be invested by shareholders to earn a return.

1.2 Ordinary (equity) shares

Key terms

Equity is share capital, retained earnings and other reserves of a single entity, plus minority interests in a group, representing the investment made in the entity by the owners.

Equity share capital is a company's issued share capital less capital which carries preferential rights. Equity share capital normally comprises ordinary shares.

Ordinary (equity) shares are those of the owners of a company.

Key term

Equity instrument is a contract that evidences a residual interest in the assets of the entity after deducting all of its liabilities. *(IAS 32)*

Equity instrument has a wider meaning than equity shares because it includes some non-equity shares, as well as warrants (see later in this chapter) and options to subscribe for or purchase equity shares in the issuing company.

The ordinary shares of UK companies have a nominal or 'face' value, typically £1 or 50p. Outside the UK it is not uncommon for a company's shares to have no nominal value.

The market value of a quoted company's shares bears **no relationship** to their **nominal value**, except that when ordinary shares are issued for cash, the issue price must be equal to or (more usually) *more than* the nominal value of the shares.

1.3 Reasons for share issues

A new issue of shares might be made in a variety of different circumstances.

(a) The company might want to **raise more cash**, for example for expansion of its operations.

(b) The company might want to issue new shares partly to raise cash but more importantly to obtain a **stock market listing**. When a UK company is floated, for example on the main stock market, it is a requirement of the Stock Exchange that at least a minimum proportion of its shares should be made available to the general investing public if the shares are not already widely held.

(c) The company might issue new shares to the shareholders of another company, in order to **take it over**.

1.4 Factors to consider when issuing shares

A lot of the factors involved are specific to the type of issue, as we shall see below.

However the following general factors apply to all types.

1.4.1 Costs

There will be administrative costs, but how great these are will vary enormously.

1.4.2 Income to investors

In Britain and other jurisdictions, companies are not obliged to pay dividends to shareholders in a particular year. However in the long-term shareholders will expect dividends and/or capital appreciation.

1.4.3 Tax

Unlike loan finance interest or charges, dividends paid are **not normally tax-deductible**.

1.4.4 Effect on control

Unless shares are issued to **existing shareholders** in proportion to their **current holdings**, the balance of voting power will change and there may ultimately be an impact on the **control** of the firm.

1.5 Timing of share issues

New equity issues in general will be more common when share prices are high than when share prices are low.

(a) When **share prices are high**, **investors' confidence** will probably be **high**, and investors will be more willing to put money into companies with the potential for growth.

(b) By issuing shares at a high price, a company will **reduce** the **number of shares** it must issue to raise the amount of capital it wants. This will reduce the dilution of earnings for existing shareholders.

(c) Following on from (b), the company's **total dividend commitment** on the new shares, to meet shareholders' expectations, will be **lower**.

(d) If **share prices are low**, business **confidence** is likely to be **low** too. Companies may not want to raise capital for new investments until expectations begin to improve.

2 Stock market listing

FAST FORWARD

A company can obtain a **stock market listing** for its shares through an offer for sale, a prospectus issue, a placing or an introduction.

2.1 Obtaining a listing

Directors must consider carefully the factors, positive and negative, involved in obtaining a listing.

2.2 Advantages of a listing

2.3 Disadvantages of a stock market listing

The owners of a company seeking a stock market listing must take the following disadvantages into account:

(a) There will be significantly greater **public regulation, accountability** and **scrutiny.** The legal requirements the company faces will be greater, and the company will also be subject to the rules of the stock exchange on which its shares are listed.

(b) A **wider circle of investors** with more exacting requirements will hold shares.

(c) There will be additional costs involved in making share issues, including **brokerage commissions** and **underwriting fees**.

2.4 Methods of obtaining a listing

An unquoted company can obtain a listing on the stock market by means of:

- Direct **offer by subscription** to the public
- **Offer for sale**
- **Placing**
- **Introduction**

Of these an offer for sale or a placing are the most common.

2.5 Direct offer by subscription to general public

Issues where the issuing firm sells shares directly to the general public tend to be quite rare on many stock exchanges, and the issues that are made tend to be quite large. These issues are sometimes known as **offers by prospectus**. This type of issue is very risky, because of the lack of guarantees that all shares will be taken up.

2.6 Offer for sale

Key term

> **Offer for sale** is an invitation to the public to apply for shares in a company based on information contained in a prospectus. *(OT 2005)*

An **offer for sale** is a means of selling the shares of a company to the public at large. When companies 'go public' for the first time, a **large** issue will probably take the form of an offer for sale. Subsequent issues are likely to be **placings** or **rights issues**, described later.

An offer for sale entails the **acquisition by an issuing house** of a large block of shares of a company, with a view to offering them for sale to the public.

An issuing house is usually a merchant bank (or sometimes a firm of stockbrokers). It may acquire the shares either as a direct allotment from the company or by purchase from existing members. In either case, the issuing house publishes an invitation to the public to apply for shares, either at a fixed price or on a tender basis.

The advantage of an offer for sale over a direct offer by the company to the public is that the issuing house **accepts responsibility** to the public, and gives to the issue the support of its own standing.

2.6.1 Offers for sale by tender

It is often very difficult to decide upon the price at which the shares should be offered to the general public. One way of trying to ensure that the issue price reflects the value of the shares as perceived by the market is to make an **offer for sale by tender.** A **minimum price** will be fixed and subscribers will be invited to tender for shares at prices equal to or above the minimum. The shares will be **allotted at the highest price** at which they will **all be taken up**. This is known as the **striking price**.

2.6.2 Example: offer for sale by tender

Byte Henderson is a new company that is making its first public issue of shares. It has decided to make the issue by means of an offer for sale by tender. The intention is to issue up to 4,000,000 shares (the full amount of authorised share capital) at a minimum price of 300 pence. The money raised, net of issue costs of £1,000,000, would be invested in projects which would earn benefits with a present value equal to 130% of the net amount invested.

The following tenders have been received. (Each applicant has made only one offer.)

Price tendered per share	*Number of shares applied for at this price*
£	
6.00	50,000
5.50	100,000
5.00	300,000
4.50	450,000
4.00	1,100,000
3.50	1,500,000
3.00	2,500,000

(a) How many shares would be issued, and how much in total would be raised, if Byte Henderson chooses:

(i) To maximise the total amount raised?

(ii) To issue exactly 4,000,000 shares?

(b) Harvey Goldfinger, a private investor, has applied for 12,000 shares at a price of £5.50 and has sent a cheque for £66,000 to the issuing house that is handling the issue. In both cases (a)(i) and (ii), how many shares would be issued to Mr Goldfinger, assuming that any partial acceptance of offers would mean allotting shares to each accepted applicant in proportion to the number of shares applied for? How much will Mr Goldfinger receive back out of the £66,000 he has paid?

(c) Estimate the likely market value of shares in the company after the issue, assuming that the market price fully reflects the investment information given above and that exactly 4,000,000 shares are issued.

Solution

(a) We begin by looking at the cumulative tenders.

Price	*Cumulative number of shares applied for*	*Amount raised if price is selected, before deducting issue costs*
£		£
6.00	50,000	300,000
5.50	150,000	825,000
5.00	450,000	2,250,000
4.50	900,000	4,050,000
4.00	2,000,000	8,000,000
3.50	3,500,000	12,250,000
3.00	6,000,000 (4,000,000 max)	12,000,000

(i) To maximise the total amount raised, the issue price should be £3.50. The total raised before deducting issue costs would be £12,250,000.

(ii) To issue exactly 4,000,000 shares, the issue price must be £3.00. The total raised would be £12,000,000, before deducting issue costs.

(b) (i) Harvey Goldfinger would be allotted 12,000 shares at £3.50 per share. He would receive a refund of 12,000 × £2 = £24,000 out of the £66,000 he has paid.

(ii) If 4,000,000 shares are issued, applicants would receive two thirds of the shares they tendered for. Harvey Goldfinger would be allotted 8,000 shares at £3 per share and would receive a refund of £42,000 out of the £66,000 he has paid.

(c) The net amount raised would be £12,000,000 minus issue costs of £1,000,000, £11,000,000.

The present value of the benefits from investment would be 130% of £11,000,000, £14,300,000. If the market price reflects this information, the price per share would rise to $\frac{£14{,}300{,}000}{4{,}000{,}000}$ = £3.575 per share.

2.7 A placing **5/05**

A **placing** is an arrangement whereby the shares are not all offered to the public, but instead, the sponsoring market maker arranges for most of the issue to be bought by a **small number of investors**, usually institutional investors such as pension funds and insurance companies.

2.7.1 The choice between an offer for sale and a placing

Is a company likely to prefer an offer for sale of its shares, or a placing?

(a) **Placings** are much **cheaper**. Approaching institutional investors privately is a much cheaper way of obtaining finance, and thus placings are often used for smaller issues.

(b) Placings are likely to be **quicker**.

(c) Placings are likely to involve **less disclosure** of **information.**

(d) However, most of the shares will be placed with a **relatively small number of (institutional) shareholders**, which means that most of the shares are **unlikely to be available for trading** after the flotation, and that **institutional shareholders** will have control of the **company**.

(e) When a company first comes to the market in the UK, the **maximum proportion of shares** that can be **placed** is **75%**, to ensure some shares are available to a wider public.

2.8 A Stock Exchange introduction

By this method of obtaining a quotation, no shares are made available to the market, neither existing nor newly created shares; nevertheless, the stock market grants a quotation. This will only happen where shares in a large company are already widely held, so that a market can be seen to exist. A company might want an **introduction** to obtain **greater marketability** for the shares, a known share valuation for inheritance tax purposes and easier access in the future to additional capital.

2.9 Underwriting

A company about to issue new securities in order to raise finance might decide to have the issue underwritten. **Underwriters** are financial institutions which agree (in exchange for a fixed fee, perhaps 2.25% of the finance to be raised) to buy at the issue price any securities which are **not subscribed** for by the investing public.

Underwriters **remove** the **risk** of a share issue's being under-subscribed, but at a cost to the company issuing the shares. It is not compulsory to have an issue underwritten. Ordinary offers for sale are most likely to be underwritten although rights issues may be as well.

Because of the costs of underwriting, there has been a trend in recent years for companies whose securities are marketable to adopt the practice known as the **'bought deal'**, whereby an investment bank buys the whole of a new issue at a small discount to the market.

2.10 Costs of share issues on stock market

Companies may incur the following costs when issuing shares.

- Underwriting costs
- Stock market listing fee (the initial charge) for the new securities
- Fees of the issuing house, solicitors, auditors and public relations consultant
- Charges for printing and distributing the prospectus
- Advertising in national newspapers

2.11 Pricing shares for a stock market launch

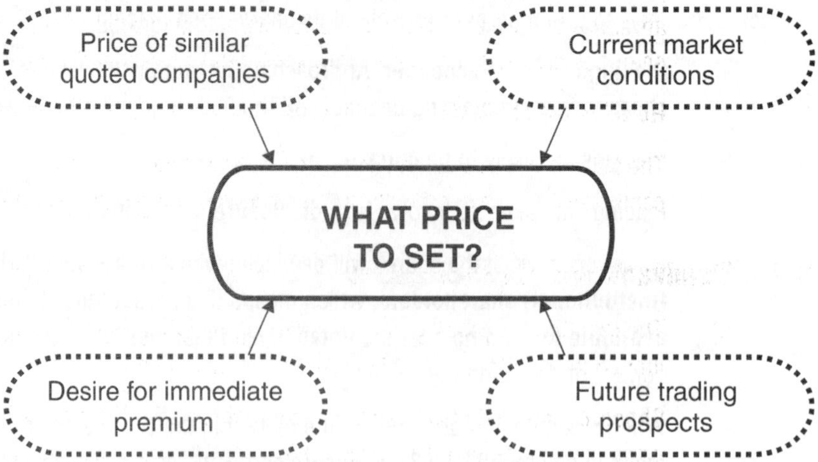

Companies will be keen to avoid **over-pricing an issue**, which could result in the **issue** being **under subscribed**, leaving underwriters with the unwelcome task of having to buy up the unsold shares. On the other hand, if the **issue price** is **too low** then the issue will be **oversubscribed** and the company would have been able to raise the required capital by issuing fewer shares.

The share price of an issue is usually advertised as being based on a certain P/E ratio, the ratio of the price to the company's most recent earnings per share figure in its audited accounts. The issuer's P/E ratio can then be compared by investors with the P/E ratios of similar quoted companies.

3 Rights issues 5/05

FAST FORWARD

A **rights issue** is an offer to existing shareholders for them to buy more shares, usually at lower than the current share price.

Key terms

A rights issue is the raising of new capital by giving existing shareholders the right to subscribe to new shares in proportion to their current holdings. These shares are usually issued at a discount to market price. A shareholder not wishing to take up a rights issue may sell the rights. *(OT 2005)*

A dilution is the reduction in the earnings and voting power per share caused by an increase or potential increase in the number of shares in issue. *(OT 2005)*

3.1 Pre-emption rights

Existing shareholders have **pre-emption rights** when new shares are issued. So that existing shareholders' rights are not diluted by the issue of new shares, legislation in many countries requires that before any equity shares are allotted for cash, they must first be offered to existing shareholders.

3.2 Advantages and disadvantages of rights issues

3.2.1 Advantages of rights issues

(a) Rights issues are **cheaper** than offers for sale to the general public. This is partly because no **prospectus** is generally required (provided that the issue is for less than 10% of the class of shares concerned), partly because the **administration** is **simpler** and partly because the cost of underwriting will be less.

(b) Rights issues are **more beneficial** to **existing shareholders** than issues to the general public. New shares are issued at a **discount** to the current market price, to make them attractive to investors. A rights issue secures the discount on the market price for existing shareholders, who may either keep the shares or sell them if they wish.

(c) **Relative voting rights** are **unaffected** if shareholders all take up their rights.

(d) The finance raised may be used to **reduce gearing** in book value terms by increasing share capital and/or to pay off long-term debt which will reduce gearing in market value terms.

3.2.2 Disadvantages of rights issues

(a) The **amount of finance** that can be **raised** by rights issues of unquoted companies is limited by the funds available to existing shareholders.

(b) **Choosing the best issue price** may **be problematic**. If the price is considered too high, the issue may not be fully subscribed; if too low, the company will not have raised all the funds it conceivably could have done.

(c) During the time between the **announcement of the rights issue** and the **date of subscription** the **market price of shares** may **fall**, and the issue price of rights will be above the market price, with the result that the rights issue will fail.

(d) Rights issues **can't be used** to **widen the base** of shareholders.

Exam focus point

Question 2 in May 2005 asked candidates to compare a rights issue and a placing.

3.3 Pricing a rights issue

A company making a rights issue must set a price which is low enough to **secure the acceptance** of shareholders, who are being asked to provide extra funds, but not so low that earnings per share are excessively diluted. Other possible problems include getting the issue **underwritten** and an excessive **fall** in the **share price.**

Exam focus point

Question 1 in November 2005 required candidates to calculate a rights price given a capital requirement in a foreign currency.

A question might ask for discussion on the effect of a rights issue, as well as calculations, eg of the effect on EPS.

3.4 Example: rights issue (1)

Seagull can achieve a profit after tax of 20% on the capital employed. At present its capital structure is as follows.

	£
200,000 ordinary shares of £1 each	200,000
Retained earnings	100,000
	300,000

The directors propose to raise an additional £126,000 from a rights issue. The current market price is £1.80.

Required

(a) Calculate the number of shares that must be issued if the rights price is: £1.60; £1.50; £1.40; £1.20.

(b) Calculate the dilution in earnings per share in each case.

Solution

The earnings at present are 20% of £300,000 = £60,000. This gives earnings per share of 30p. The earnings after the rights issue will be 20% of £426,000 = £85,200.

Rights price	*No of new shares (£126,000 ÷ rights price)*	*EPS (£85,200 ÷ total no of shares)*	*Dilution*
£		Pence	Pence
1.60	78,750	30.6	+ 0.6
1.50	84,000	30.0	–
1.40	90,000	29.4	– 0.6
1.20	105,000	27.9	– 2.1

Note that at a high rights price the earnings per share are increased, not diluted. The breakeven point (zero dilution) occurs when the rights price is equal to the capital employed per share: £300,000 ÷ 200,000 = £1.50.

3.5 The market price of shares after a rights issue: the theoretical ex-rights price

After the announcement of a rights issue, **share prices generally fall**. This temporary fall is due to **uncertainty in the market about** the consequences of the issue, with respect to future profits, earnings and dividends. After the issue has actually been made, the market price per share will normally fall, because there are more shares in issue and the new shares were issued at a discount price.

When a rights issue is announced, all existing shareholders have the **right to subscribe for new shares**, and so there are **rights attached to the existing shares**. The shares are therefore described as being traded as 'cum rights'. On the first day of dealings in the newly issued shares, the rights no longer exist and the old shares are now 'ex rights' (without rights attached).

In theory, the new market price will be the consequence of an adjustment to allow for the discount price of the new issue, and a theoretical ex rights price can be calculated (the shares are ex rights because the new shares have been issued and the rights no longer exist).

3.6 Example: rights issue (2)

Fundraiser has 1,000,000 ordinary shares of £1 in issue, which have a market price on 1 September of £2.10 per share. The company decides to make a rights issue, and offers its shareholders the right to subscribe for one new share at £1.50 each for every four shares already held. After the announcement of the issue, the share price fell to £1.95, but by the time just prior to the issue being made, it had recovered to £2 per share. This market value just before the issue is known as the cum rights price. What is the theoretical ex-rights price?

Solution

Value of the portfolio for a shareholder with 4 shares before the rights issue:

	£
4 shares @ £2.00	8.00
1 share @ £1.50	1.50
	9.50

so the value per share after the rights issue (or TERP) is 9.50/5 = £1.90.

Exam Formula

An alternative method would be to use formula given to you in the exam.

$$\text{Theoretical ex-rights price} = \frac{1}{N+1}((N \times \text{cum rights price}) + \text{issue price})$$

where N = number of shares required to buy one new share.

$$\text{Theoretical ex-rights price} = \frac{1}{4+1}((4 \times £2) + £1.50) = \frac{£9.50}{5} = £1.90$$

Exam focus point

Question 1 of November 2005 required the calculation of a TERP before and after adjusting for project cash flows.

3.7 Yield adjusted ex-rights price

We have assumed so far that the additional funds raised by the rights issue will generate the same rate of return as existing funds. If the new funds are likely to earn a different return from what is currently being earned, the yield-adjusted theoretical ex-rights price should be calculated. The yield-adjusted price demonstrates how the market will view the rights issue, and what will happen to the market value.

Formula to learn

Yield-adjusted theoretical ex-rights price =

$$\left[\frac{\text{Cum rights price} \times N}{(N+1)}\right] + \left[\frac{\text{Issue price}}{(N+1)} \times \frac{\text{Yield on new funds}}{\text{Yield on existing funds}}\right]$$

3.8 Example: rights issue (3)

Using the same data for Fundraiser as above, with the additional information that rate of return on new funds = 12%, and on existing funds = 8%, calculate the yield-adjusted theoretical ex-rights price.

Solution

$$\text{Yield-adjusted theoretical ex-rights price} = \left(\frac{2 \times 4}{5}\right) + \left[\frac{1.50}{5} \times \frac{0.12}{0.08}\right] = £2.05$$

3.9 The value of rights

Exam formula

$$\text{Value of a right} = \frac{\text{Rights on (cum rights) price} - \text{Issue price}}{N+1} = \frac{\text{Theoretical ex-rights price} - \text{Issue pice}}{N}$$

Using the above example:

$$\text{Value of a right} = \frac{2.00 - 1.50}{5}$$

$$= \frac{1.90 - 1.50}{4}$$

$$= 10p$$

This means that the value of a right attaching to each **existing** share is 10p. If a holder of four existing shares exercises his rights to buy one new share, and then sells it, his gain will be 1.90 – 1.50 = 40p, in other words (4 × 10p) or the difference between the theoretical ex-rights price and the rights issue price.

The value of rights is the **theoretical gain** a shareholder would make by exercising his rights.

Question — Effects of rights issue

Learning outcome: B(i)

Devonian has the following long-term capital structure as at 30 November 20X3.

	$m
Ordinary shares 25c fully paid	50.0
General reserve	22.5
Retained profit	25.5
	98.0

The company has no long-term loans.

In the year to 30 November 20X3, the profit from operations (net profit before interest and taxation) was $40m and it is expected that this will increase by 25 per cent during the forthcoming year. The company is listed on a major stock exchange and the current share price is $2.10.

The company wishes to raise $72m in order to re-equip one of its factories and is considering making a one-for-five rights issue at a discounted price of $1.80 per share. It is expected that the price earnings (P/E) ratio will remain the same for the forthcoming year.

Assume a tax rate of 30 per cent.

Required

(a) Assuming the rights issue of shares is made, calculate

(i) The theoretical ex-rights price of an ordinary share in Devonian, and
(ii) The value of the rights for each original ordinary share.

(b) Calculate the price of an ordinary share in Devonian in one year's time assuming a rights issue is made,

Answer

(a)

	$
Current market value of 5 existing shares (× $2.10)	10.50
Rights issue price of one new share	1.80
Theoretical value of 6 shares	12.30

(i) Theoretical ex-rights price = $12.30/6 shares = $2.05 per share.

(ii) The value of the rights for each new share is $2.05 – $1.80 = $0.25. The value of the rights for each existing share is therefore $0.25/5 shares = $0.05 per share.

(b) (i) *Rights issue*

Number of shares in issue ($50 million/$0.25 per share)	200 million
New shares in rights issue (1 for 5)	40 million
Total number of shares after the issue	240 million

Current earnings = $40 million less 30% tax = $28 million.
Current EPS = $28 million/200 million shares = $0.14
Current P/E ratio = 2.1/0.14 = 15 times.

	$m
Profit before taxation (+ 25%)	50
Taxation at 30%	(15)
Profit after tax (earnings)	35

Earnings per share = $35 million/240 million shares = $0.146
Assumed P/E ratio (no change) = 15
Assumed share price in one year's time: $0.146 × 15 = $2.19

3.10 The theoretical gain or loss to shareholders

Possible courses of action open to shareholders

(a) **'Take up' or 'exercise' the rights**

That is, to buy the new shares at the rights price. Shareholders who do this will maintain their percentage holdings in the company by subscribing for the new shares.

(b) **'Renounce' the rights and sell them on the market**

Shareholders who do this will have lower percentage holdings of the company's equity after the issue than before the issue, and the total value of their shares will be less (on the assumption that the actual market price after the issue is close to the theoretical ex rights price).

(c) **Renounce part of the rights and take up the remainder**

For example, a shareholder may sell enough of his rights to enable him to buy the remaining rights shares he is entitled to with the sale proceeds, and so keep the total market value of his shareholding in the company unchanged.

(d) **Do nothing**

Shareholders may be protected from the consequences of their inaction because rights not taken up are sold on a shareholder's behalf by the company. The Stock Exchange rules state that if new securities are not taken up, they should be sold by the company to new subscribers for the benefit of the shareholders who were entitled to the rights.

The decision by individual shareholders as to whether they take up the offer will therefore depend on:

(a) The **expected rate of return** on the investment (and the risk associated with it)
(b) The **return obtainable** from other investments (allowing for the associated risk)

Question — Rights issue

Learning outcome: B(i)

Gopher has issued 3,000,000 ordinary shares of £1 each, which are at present selling for £4 per share. The company plans to issue rights to purchase one new equity share at a price of £3.20 per share for every three shares held. A shareholder who owns 900 shares thinks that he will suffer a loss in his personal wealth because the new shares are being offered at a price lower than market value. On the assumption that the actual market value of shares will be equal to the theoretical ex rights price, what would be the effect on the shareholder's wealth if:

(a) He sells all the rights
(b) He exercises half of the rights and sells the other half
(c) He does nothing at all

Answer

Value of the portfolio for a shareholder with 3 shares before the rights issue

	£
3 shares @ £4.00	12.00
1 share @ £3.20	3.20
4	15.20

so the value per share after the rights issue (or TERP) is 15.20/4 = 3.80.

Alternative solution

The theoretical ex rights price = $\frac{1}{3+1}$ ((3 × £4) + £3.20)) = £3.80 per share

	£
Theoretical ex rights price	3.80
Price per new share	3.20
Value of rights per new share	0.60

The value of the rights attached to each existing share is $\frac{£0.60}{3}$ = £0.20.

We will assume that a shareholder is able to sell his rights for £0.20 per existing share held.

(a) If the shareholder **sells all his rights**:

	£
Sale value of rights (900 × £0.20)	180
Market value of his 900 shares, ex rights (× £3.80)	3,420
Total wealth	3,600
Total value of 900 shares cum rights (× £4)	£3,600

The shareholder would neither gain nor lose wealth. He would not be required to provide any additional funds to the company, but his shareholding as a proportion of the total equity of the company will be lower.

(b) If the shareholder **exercises half of the rights** (buys 450/3 = 150 shares at £3.20) and sells the other half:

	£
Sale value of rights (450 × £0.20)	90
Market value of his 1,050 shares, ex rights (× £3.80)	3,990
	4,080
Total value of 900 shares cum rights (× £4)	3,600
Additional investment (150 × £3.20)	480
	4,080

The shareholder would neither gain nor lose wealth, although he will have increased his investment in the company by £480.

(c) If the shareholder **does nothing**, but all other shareholders either exercise their rights or sell them, he would lose wealth as follows.

	£
Market value of 900 shares cum rights (× £4)	3,600
Market value of 900 shares ex rights (× £3.80)	3,420
Loss in wealth	180

It follows that the shareholder, to protect his existing investment, should either **exercise his rights** or **sell them** to another investor. If he does not exercise his rights, the new securities he was entitled to subscribe for might be sold for his benefit by the company, and this would protect him from losing wealth.

Exam focus point

Make sure you practise the calculations in this chapter so that you can do them competently and quickly if required.

3.11 Other types of share issue

You may see examples of other types of share issue in the financial press.

SHARE ISSUES	
Open offer	Offer of shares to existing shareholders, but unlike rights issue, not necessarily pro rata, and offer not made on renounceable documents
Vendor consideration	Issue of shares by acquiring company in a takeover, as payment to target company's shareholders for their shares
Employee share scheme	Share option schemes, giving employees rights to subscribe for new shares at later date at predetermined price. When the options are exercised, the option price ought to be below the issue price.

4 Scrip dividends, scrip issues and stock splits

FAST FORWARD

Scrip dividends, **scrip issues** and **stock splits** are not methods of raising new equity funds, but they *are* methods of altering the share capital structure of a company, or in the case of scrip dividends and scrip issues, increasing the issued share capital of the company.

4.1 Scrip dividends

We discussed scrip dividends, the dividends paid by the issue of additional company shares, in the last chapter.

4.2 Bonus issues

Key term

A **bonus/scrip/capitalisation issue** is the capitalisation of the reserves of an entity by the issue of additional shares to existing shareholders, in proportion to their holdings. Such shares are normally fully paid-up with no cash called for from the shareholders. *(OT 2005)*

For example, if a company with issued share capital of 100,000 ordinary shares of £1 each made a one for five scrip issue, 20,000 new shares would be issued to existing shareholders, one new share for every five old shares held. Issued share capital would be increased by £20,000, and reserves (probably share premium account, if there is one) reduced by this amount.

By creating more shares in this way, a scrip issue does not raise new funds, but does have the advantage of making shares **cheaper** and therefore (perhaps) **more easily marketable** on the Stock Exchange. For example, if a company's shares are priced at £6 on the Stock Exchange, and the company makes a one for two scrip issue, we should expect the share price after the issue to fall to £4 each. Shares at £4 each might be more easily marketable than shares at £6 each.

4.3 Stock splits

The advantage of a scrip issue mentioned above is also the reason for a **stock split** which we discussed in the last chapter.

5 Preference shares

FAST FORWARD

Preference or preferred shares carry priority over shareholders with regard to dividend payments. They do not carry voting rights. They may be attractive to corporate investors, as (unlike interest receipts) dividends received are generally not subject to tax. However, for the issuing company, dividend payments (unlike interest payments) are generally not tax-deductible.

Key terms

Preference shares are shares carrying a fixed rate of dividends, the holders of which, subject to the conditions of issue, have a prior claim to any company profits available for distribution. They are an example of prior charge capital.

Preferred shareholders may also have a prior claim to the repayment of capital in the event of winding up.

Prior charge capital is capital which has a right to the receipt of interest or of preferred dividends in precedence to any claim on distributable earnings on the part of the ordinary shareholders. On winding up, the claims of holders of prior charge capital also rank before those of ordinary shareholders.

Cumulative preference shares are preference shares where any arrears of dividend are carried forward. When eventually the company decides to pay a dividend, the cumulative preference shareholders are entitled to all their arrears before ordinary shareholders are paid a dividend.

Participating preference shares are shares that have an additional entitlement to dividend over and above their specified rate. Participating preferred shareholders are however entitled to participate along with ordinary shareholders in available profits, normally once the ordinary shareholders have themselves received a specified level of dividend.

5.1 Why issue preference shares?

From the company's point of view, preference shares have some positive features.

(a) Dividends do **not have** to be **paid** in a year in which **profits are poor**, while this is not the case with interest payments on long-term debt.

(b) Since they do not normally carry voting rights, preference shares **avoid diluting** the **control** of existing shareholders while an issue of equity shares would not.

(c) Unless they are redeemable, issuing preference shares will **lower** the company's **gearing**. Redeemable preference shares are normally treated as debt when gearing is calculated.

(d) The issue of preference shares does **not restrict** the company's **borrowing power**, at least in the sense that preference share capital is not secured against assets of the business.

(e) The non-payment of dividend does **not give** the preference shareholders the **right** to **appoint a receiver**, a right which is normally given to debenture holders.

However, **dividend payments on preference shares may not be tax deductible** in the way that interest payments on debt are. Furthermore, for preference shares to be attractive to investors, the level of payment needs to be **higher than** for **interest on debt** to compensate for the additional risks.

From the point of view of the investor, preference shares are less attractive than loan stock because:

(a) They **cannot be secured** on the company's assets.

(b) The **dividend yield** traditionally offered on preferred dividends has been much **too low** to provide an attractive investment compared with the interest yields on loan stock in view of the additional risk involved.

In recent years preferred shares have formed a very small proportion only of new capital issues.

6 Warrants

FAST FORWARD

Share **warrants** give their holder the right to apply for new shares at a specified exercise price in the future. They might be issued as an 'add-on' to a new issue of loan notes.

Key terms

A **warrant** is a financial instalment that gives the holder the right to purchase ordinary shares. *(IAS 33)*

The **exercise price** is the price at which an option to purchase or sell shares or other items (**call option** or **put option**) may be exercised. *(OT 2005)*

6.1 Purpose of warrants

A **warrant** is a right given by a company to an investor, **allowing him** to **subscribe** for new shares at a future date at a fixed, pre-determined price (the **exercise price**).

Warrants are usually issued as part of a package with unsecured loan notes: an investor who buys stock will also acquire a certain number of warrants. The purpose of warrants is to make the loan stock more attractive.

6.2 Sale of warrants

Once issued, warrants are detachable from the stock and can be sold and bought separately before or during the 'exercise period' (the period during which the right to use the warrants to subscribe for shares is allowed). The market value of warrants will depend on expectations of actual share prices in the future.

During the exercise period, the price of a warrant should not fall below the higher of:

- **Nil**
- The **'theoretical value'**, which equals:

(Current share price – Exercise price) × Number of shares obtainable from each warrant

If, for example, a warrant entitles the holder to purchase two ordinary shares at a price of £3 each, when the current market price of the shares is £3.40, the minimum market value ('theoretical value') of a warrant would be (£3.40 – £3) × 2 = 80p.

For a company with good growth prospects, the warrant will usually be quoted at a premium above the minimum prior to the exercise period. This premium is known as the **warrant conversion premium.** It is sometimes expressed as a percentage of the current share price.

6.3 Example: warrant conversion premium

An investor holds some warrants which can be used to subscribe for ordinary shares on a one for one basis at an exercise price of £2.50 during a specified future period. The current share price is £2.25 and the warrants are quoted at 50p. What is the warrant conversion premium?

Solution

The easiest way of finding the premium is to deduct the current share price from the cost of acquiring a share using the warrant, treating the warrant as if it were currently exercisable:

	£
Cost of warrant	0.50
Exercise price	2.50
	3.00
Current share price	2.25
Premium	0.75

In the short run the warrant price and share price normally move fairly closely in line with each other. In the longer term the price of the warrant and hence the premium will depend on:

- The length of time before the warrants may be exercised
- The current price of the shares compared with the exercise price
- The future prospects of the company

As the exercise period approaches, the premium will reduce. Towards the end of the exercise period the premium will disappear because, if there were a premium, it would be cheaper to buy the shares directly rather than via the warrant.

Let us now recalculate the premium, assuming a 50p rise in the share price and a 50p rise in the warrant price.

	£
Cost of warrant (50p + 50p)	1.00
Exercise price	2.50
	3.50
Current share price (£2.25 + 50p)	2.75
Premium	0.75

The premium has stayed the same.

Note also that the share price is now above the exercise price. The warrants now have an 'intrinsic' value of 25p (ie 275p – 250p).

6.4 Advantages of warrants for investors

You may be wondering why an investor would prefer to buy warrants at 50p when this means that it will cost him more to get the ordinary shares than if he bought them directly. The attractions of warrants to the investor are:

(a) **Low initial outlay**

He only has to spend 50p per share as opposed to £2.25. This means that he could buy $4^1/_2$ times as many warrants as shares or, alternatively, he could invest the remaining £1.75 in other, less risky investments.

(b) **Lower downside potential**

His maximum loss per share is 50p instead of £2.25. Of course the risk of the loss of 50p is much greater than the risk of losing £2.25. The share price of £2.25 is below the exercise price. If it remained at this level until the beginning of the exercise period, the warrants would become worthless as it would not be worthwhile exercising them.

(c) **High potential returns**

Warrants offer the investor the possibility of making a high profit as a percentage of initial cost. This is because the price of the warrants will tend to move more or less in line with the price of the shares. Thus, if the share price rises by 50p the increase in the value of the warrant will be similar. Using the previous prices, a 50p increase in share price is about 22% but a 50p increase in the warrant price is 100%. This illustrates the gearing effect of warrants.

(d) **Capital gains**

As warrants provide no interest at all, all profits are in the form of capital gains, which will be attractive to higher-rate taxpayers who have not used up their annual tax-free allowance.

6.5 Advantages of warrants

(a) Warrants themselves **do not involve** the **payment** of any **interest or dividends**. Furthermore, when they are initially attached to loan stock, the interest rate on the loan stock will be lower than for a comparable straight debt.

(b) Warrants make a loan stock issue more attractive and may make an issue of unsecured loan stock possible where adequate security is lacking. (**Loan stock**, as a form of debt finance, is covered in the next chapter.)

(c) Warrants provide a means of **generating additional equity** funds in the future without any immediate dilution in earnings per share. The cost will be the right that warrants holders to buy at the **possibly reduced exercise price**.

6.6 Disadvantages of warrants

The disadvantages of warrants are:

(a) When exercised, they will result in the **dilution** of **share capital.**

(b) Warrants may be exercised when a business **does not need additional capital**.

(c) The company has **less control** over the exercise of warrants than it does over the exercise of share capital.

7 Euro-issues 5/05

FAST FORWARD

Euro-issues are issues outside a company's own domestic stock market.

7.1 Euro-equity issues

A **euro-equity issue** may be defined as an **issue of equity** in a **market outside** the **company's own domestic market**.

(a) A company may find it appropriate to raise funds by **selling shares outside its domestic capital market** if this is too small for its needs.

(b) A company may wish to **attract shareholders** based in the markets in which it trades overseas. The **liquidity** of the company's shares and the international standing of the firm can be improved.

(c) The **wider spread of shareholdings** that might be achieved could act as a defence against **hostile takeovers**.

(d) An **issue overseas** may also be **convenient** if compliance with domestic capital market listing requirements is a complex or lengthy process.

(e) It may reduce the company's exposure to **foreign exchange** and **political risks**.

Conventional share issues have been made on the euro-equity markets, as for example when there were attempts to place large numbers of shares of US corporations and of Japanese companies in Europe. These attempts were largely unsuccessful: the absence of a sufficiently liquid after-market or secondary market in such shares is the main limitation on such euro-equity issues.

'Sweeteners' are often added to the shares issued on the market, to make the issue more attractive to investors. For example, a 'rolling put option' might be added to a convertible preference share, giving the purchaser the right to sell the convertible preference share back to the company at any time between, say, five and ten years after the issue.

Exam focus point

Many students forget that Euro finance means funds obtained outside a company's own domestic market in **any currency, not just in Euros**.

Chapter roundup

- Companies seeking extra equity finance can obtain it by **retaining cash** in the business for investment or **issuing shares**.
- A company can obtain a **stock market listing** for its shares through an offer for sale, a prospectus issue, a placing or an introduction.
- A **rights issue** is an offer to existing shareholders for them to buy more shares, usually at lower than the current share price.
- **Scrip dividends**, **scrip issues** and **stock splits** are not methods of raising new equity funds, but they are methods of altering the share capital of a company, or in the case of scrip dividends and scrip issues, increasing the issued share capital of a company.
- **Preference shares** carry priority over shareholders with regard to dividend payments. They do not carry voting rights. They may be attractive to corporate investors, as (unlike interest receipts) dividends received are generally not subject to tax. However, for the issuing company, dividend payments (unlike interest payments) are generally not tax-deductible.
- Share **warrants** give their holder the right to apply for new shares at a specified exercise price in the future. They might be issued as an 'add-on' to a new issue of loan notes.
- **Euro-issues** are issues outside a company's own domestic stock market.

Quick quiz

1 Which of the following sources of finance to companies is the most widely used in practice?

A Bank borrowings
B Rights issues
C New share issues
D Retained earnings

2 Identify four reasons why a company may seek a stock market listing.

3 A company's shares have a nominal value of £1 and a market value of £3. In a rights issue, one new share would be issued for every three shares at a price of £2.60. What is the theoretical ex-rights price?

4 A company offers to pay a dividend in the form of new shares which are worth more than the cash alternative which is also offered. What is this dividend in the form of shares called?

5 Match A/B to (i)/(ii), to express the difference between a stock split and a scrip issue.

A	A scrip issue	(i)	.... converts equity reserves into share capital
B	A stock split	(ii)	.... leaves reserves unaffected

6 Explain what a warrant is in not more than 30 words.

7 Which of the following is least likely to be a reason for seeking a stock market flotation?

A Improving the existing owners' control over the business
B Access to a wider pool of finance
C Enhancement of the company's image
D Transfer of capital to other uses

8 Which of the following is not true of a rights issue by a listed company?

A Rights issues do not require a prospectus
B The rights issues price can be at a discount to market price
C If shareholders do not take up the rights, the rights lapse
D Relative voting rights are unaffected if shareholders exercise their rights

9 Preference shares have become increasingly popular.

True ☐

False ☐

Answers to quick quiz

1 D Retained earnings

2 Four of the following five: access to a wider pool of finance; improved marketability of shares; transfer of capital to other uses (eg founder members liquidating holdings); enhancement of company image; making growth by acquisition possible

3 $((£3 \times 3) + £2.60) \div 4 = £2.90$

4 An enhanced scrip dividend

5 A(i); B(ii)

6 A right given by a company to an investor, allowing him to subscribe for new shares at a future date at a fixed, pre-determined price (the exercise price)

7 A Flotation is likely to involve a significant loss of control to a wider circle of investors.

8 C Shareholders have the option of renouncing the rights and selling them on the market.

9 False. Preference shares have formed a very small proportion of new capital issues in recent years.

Now try the questions below from the Exam Question Bank

Number	Level	Marks	Time
Q7	Introductory	n/a	35 mins
Q8	Examination	15	27 mins

6 Debt finance

Introduction

As well as being financed by its owners, the **shareholders**, a company is likely to be financed by lenders who provide it with **debt finance**. We look in this chapter at the most important forms of long-term debt finance. We finish off by examining the **practical factors** that determine whether lenders provide finance, how much they provide and on what terms. Remember that you may need to use the detail in this chapter to explain **why** organisations choose particular sources of finance.

Go slowly through the calculations, to confirm your understanding, as calculations remain an important element in this paper. The last two sections should be studied more carefully, as they cover the areas of international finance and assessment of creditworthiness that are both significant in this paper.

Topic list	Learning outcomes	Syllabus references	Ability required
1 Bank loans	B(i)	B(2)	Evaluation
2 Loan capital	B(i)	B(2)	Evaluation
3 Convertible securities	B(i)	B(2)	Evaluation
4 International debt finance	B(i)	B(2)	Evaluation
5 Lenders' assessment of creditworthiness	B(i)	B(3)	Evaluation

1 Bank loans

FAST FORWARD

Bank loans tend to be a **source** of **medium-term finance**, linked with the purchase of specific assets. Interest and repayments will be set in advance.

1.1 Loans and overdrafts

Banks often provide term loans as medium or long-term financing for customers. The customer borrows a fixed amount and pays it back with interest over a period or at the end of it. You hopefully will remember that this contrasts with an overdraft facility, when a customer, through its current account, can borrow money on a short-term basis up to a certain amount. Overdrafts are repayable on demand.

1.2 Loan or overdraft

A customer might ask the bank for an overdraft facility when the bank would wish to suggest a loan instead; alternatively, a customer might ask for a loan when an overdraft would be more appropriate.

(a) In most cases, when a customer wants finance to help with 'day to day' trading and cash flow needs, an **overdraft** would be the **appropriate method** of financing. The customer should not be short of cash all the time, and should expect to be in credit in some days, but in need of an overdraft on others.

(b) When a customer wants to borrow from a bank for only a **short period of time**, even for the purchase of a major asset such as an item of plant or machinery, an overdraft facility might be more suitable than a loan, because the customer will stop paying interest as soon as his account goes into credit.

(c) When a customer wants to borrow from a bank, but cannot see his way to repaying the bank except over the course of a few years, the **medium– or long-term nature** of the financing is best catered for by the provision of a loan rather than an overdraft facility.

1.2.1 Advantages of an overdraft over a loan

(a) The customer **only pays interest when he is overdrawn**.

(b) The bank has the flexibility to **review** the customer's overdraft facility periodically, and perhaps agree to additional facilities, or insist on a reduction in the facility.

(c) An overdraft can do the same job as a loan: a facility can simply be **renewed** every time it comes up **for review**.

(d) Being short-term debt, an overdraft will not **affect** the calculation of a company's **gearing**.

1.2.2 Advantages of a loan over overdraft

(a) Both the customer and the bank **know exactly** what the repayments of the loan will be and how much interest is payable, and when. This makes planning (budgeting) simpler.

(b) The customer does not have to worry about the bank deciding to reduce or **withdraw** an overdraft facility before he is in a position to repay what is owed. Overdrafts are normally **repayable on demand**. There is an element of 'security' or 'peace of mind' in being able to arrange a loan for an agreed term.

(c) Loans normally carry a **facility letter** setting out the precise terms of the agreement.

1.3 Bank loan or other loan capital

A choice businesses often have is whether to seek funding through a bank loan or through other types of loan capital.

1.3.1 Advantages of bank loan over other forms of loan capital

(a) **Flexibility**. It may be possible to alter the terms of the bank loan as the finance requirements of the company change.

(b) **Confidentiality**. Although the bank will require information, the customer will not have to fulfil the publicity requirements that an issue of loan stock on the financial markets would need.

(c) **Speed**. It will be rather quicker to arrange a bank loan than fulfilling all the requirements of a public issue.

(d) **Costs**. A bank loan will mean that the issue costs of loan stock are avoided.

1.3.2 Disadvantages of bank loan over other forms of loan capital

(a) **Restrictions**. Restrictions such as collateral and possible restrictive covenants are required, as opposed to none for certain types of loan capital.

(b) **Financial information**. Detailed financial information such as budgets and management accounts may have to be submitted periodically to the bank, whereas other lenders will not require information in this detail.

1.4 Time scale of loan

For purchases of a non-current asset the **term of the bank loan should not exceed** the **economic or useful life** of the asset purchased with the money from the loan. A business manager will often expect to use the revenues earned by the asset to repay the loan, and obviously, an asset can only do this as long as it is in operational use.

2 Loan capital

2.1 Loan notes

FAST FORWARD

The term **bonds** describes various forms of long-term debt a company may issue, such as loan notes, which may be **redeemable** or **irredeemable**. Bonds or loans come in various forms, including **floating rate loan notes, zero coupon bonds** and **convertible loan notes.**

Key term

Loan capital is debentures and other long-term loans to a business.

Loan capital has a **nominal value**, which is the debt owed by the company, and interest is paid at a stated **'coupon'** on this amount. For example, if a company issues 10% loan notes, the coupon will be 10% of the nominal value of the notes, so that £100 of notes will receive £10 interest each year. The rate quoted is the gross rate, before tax.

Unlike shares, debt is often issued **at par**, ie with £100 payable per £100 nominal value. Where the coupon rate is fixed at the time of issue, it will be set according to prevailing market conditions given the credit rating of the company issuing the debt. Subsequent changes in market (and company) conditions will cause the market value of the bond to fluctuate, although the coupon will stay at the fixed percentage of the nominal value.

2.2 Debentures

Key term

A **debenture** is a written acknowledgement of a debt by a company, usually given under its seal and normally containing provisions as to payment of interest and the terms of repayment of principal. A loan note may be secured on some or all of the assets of the company or its subsidiaries.

Debentures are defined as the written acknowledgement of a debt incurred by a company, normally containing provisions about the payment of interest and the eventual repayment of capital.

A **trust deed** would empower a trustee (such as an insurance company or a bank) to **intervene** on behalf of loan note holders if the conditions of borrowing under which the debentures were issued are not being fulfilled. This might involve:

(a) **Failure** to **pay interest** on the due dates

(b) An **attempt** by the company to **sell off important assets** contrary to the terms of the loan

(c) A company taking out **additional loans** and thereby exceeding previously agreed borrowing limits established either by its constitution or by the terms of the loan note trust deed (A trust deed might place restrictions on the company's ability to borrow more from elsewhere until the loan notes have been redeemed.)

2.3 Debentures with a floating rate of interest

These are loan notes for which the coupon rate of interest can be changed by the issuer, in accordance with changes in market rates of interest. They may be attractive to both lenders and borrowers when interest rates are volatile, and preferable to fixed interest loan notes.

For example, suppose that a company issues 6% fixed rate loan notes at par when the market rate of interest is 6%, and the debentures have a term to maturity of 20 years. If interest rates suddenly rise to 12%, the market value of the debentures would fall by half to £50 per cent (that is, per £100 nominal value). However, if the debentures had carried a floating rate of interest, the interest rate would have been raised to 12% and the debentures would have retained their market value at par (£100 per cent).

2.4 Deep discount bonds

Key term

Deep discount bond is a bond offered at a large discount on the face value of the debt so that a significant proportion of the return to the investor comes by way of a capital gain on redemption, rather than through interest payment. *(OT 2005)*

Deep discount bonds will be redeemable at par (or above par) when they eventually mature. For example a company might issue £1,000,000 of loan notes in 2002, at a price of £50 per £100, and redeemable at par in the year 2017. For a company with specific cash flow requirements, the **low servicing costs** during the currency of the bond may be an attraction, coupled with a high cost of redemption at maturity. The company can deduct notional interest each year in computing profits.

Investors might be attracted by the **large capital gain** offered by the bonds, which is the difference between the issue price and the redemption value. However, deep discount bonds will carry a much **lower rate of interest** than other types of loan notes. The only tax advantage is that the gain gets taxed (as **income**) in one lump on maturity or sale, not as amounts of interest each year.

2.5 Zero coupon bonds

Key term

> **Zero coupon bond** is a bond offering no interest payments, all investor return being gained through capital appreciation. *(OT 2005)*

Zero coupon bonds are bonds that are issued at a discount to their redemption value, but no interest is paid on them. The investor gains from the difference between the issue price and the redemption value, and there is an implied interest rate in the amount of discount at which the bonds are issued (or subsequently re-sold on the market).

(a) The advantage for borrowers is that zero coupon bonds can be used to **raise cash immediately**, and there is no cash repayment until redemption date. The cost of redemption is known at the time of issue, and so the borrower can plan to have funds available to redeem the bonds at maturity.

(b) The advantage for lenders is restricted, unless the rate of discount on the bonds **offers a high yield**. The only way of obtaining cash from the bonds before maturity is to sell them, and their market value will depend on the remaining term to maturity and current market interest rates.

The tax advantage of zero coupon bonds is the same as that for deep discount bonds.

2.6 Security 5/06

FAST FORWARD

> Charges (**fixed** or **floating**) may be given over debt.

Loan notes and debentures will often be secured. **Security** may take the form of either a **fixed charge** or a **floating charge.**

(a) **Fixed charge**

Security would be related to a **specific asset** or group of assets, typically land and buildings. The company would be unable to dispose of the asset without providing a substitute asset for security, or without the lender's consent.

(b) **Floating charge**

With a floating charge on **certain assets** of the company (for example inventory or receivables), the lender's security in the event of a default of payment is whatever assets of the appropriate class the company then owns (provided that another lender does not have a prior charge on the assets). The company would be able, however, to dispose of its assets as it chose until a default took place. In the event of default, the lender would probably appoint a receiver to run the company rather than lay claim to a particular asset.

Not all loan notes are secured. Investors are likely to expect a higher yield with **unsecured loan notes** to compensate them for the extra risk. The rate of interest on unsecured loan notes may be around 1% or more higher than for secured debt.

2.7 The redemption of loan notes

Loan notes are usually **redeemable**. They are issued for a term of ten years or more, and perhaps 25 to 30 years. At the end of this period, they will 'mature' and become redeemable (at par or possibly at a value above par).

Key term

> **Redemption** is repayment of the principal amount (for example a bond) at the date of maturity. *(OT 2005)*

Most redeemable notes have an earliest and a latest redemption date. For example, 12% Loan Notes 2007/09 are redeemable at any time between the earliest specified date (in 2007) and the latest date (in 2009). The issuing company can choose the date. The decision by a company when to redeem a debt will depend on **how much cash** is available to the company to repay the debt, and on the **nominal rate of interest** on the debt.

Some loan notes do not have a redemption date, and are **'irredeemable'** or **'undated'**. Undated loan notes might be redeemed by a company that wishes to pay off the debt, but there is no obligation on the company to do so.

Exam focus point

The examiner has stated that irredeemable preference shares should be treated as equity and redeemable preference shares as debt.

2.7.1 Valuation of redeemable loan notes

The normal principles apply so that the valuation depends upon future expected receipts.

Formula to learn

Value of debt = (Interest earnings × annuity factor) + (Redemption value × Discounted cash flow factor)

Similar principles apply to the valuation of convertible debt which we shall discuss later.

2.7.2 Yield to maturity **5/06**

The yield to maturity (or redemption) is the effective yield on a redeemable bond which allows for the time value of money and is effectively the **internal rate of return** of the cash flows.

For example, a five year unsecured bond with a coupon of 5% per annum, redeemable at par and issued at a 6% discount to par will have a yield to maturity of 6.47%. This is calculated by assuming a nominal value of $100 and calculating NPVs at 5% and 7% discount rates.

Year	*Cash flow*	*Discount factor*	*Present value*	*Discount factor*	*Present value*
	$m	5%	$m	7%	$m
0	(94)	1.000	(94.00)	1.000	(94.00)
1-5	5	4.329	21.64	4.100	20.50
5	100	0.784	78.40	0.713	71.30
		NPV	6.04	NPV	(2.20)

$$\text{Yield to maturity} = 5\% + \left(\frac{6.04}{(6.04+2.20)}\right) \times 2\% = 6.47\%$$

2.7.3 How will a company finance the redemption of long-term debt?

There is no guarantee that a company will be able to raise a new loan to pay off a maturing debt, and one item to look for in a company's balance sheet is the **redemption date** of **current loans**, to establish how much new finance is likely to be needed by the company, and when.

(a) If the redemption is to take place using **current funds** (assuming there are enough available), the business needs to consider the **alternative uses** to which these funds could be put.

(b) The company may decide to issue **new debt** to replace the old debt. The company will incur **issue costs** using new debt, and will also need to consider the **future pattern of interest rates**.

(c) Alternatively the company could use an issue of **equity** to provide the funds for redemption. **Issue costs** will again be a factor, and the directors will need to consider whether to issue shares to **new shareholders**, or use a **rights issue** to existing shareholders.

(d) If the redeemable debt has been **issued** on the stock market, it can be bought and hence redeemed by the company at any time. The directors will choose to redeem it if other possible sources of finance have a lower cost.

2.8 Companies that are unable to repay debt capital

A company might get into difficulties and be unable to pay its debts. The difficulty could be an inability to repay the debt capital when it is due for redemption or an inability, perhaps temporary, to pay interest on the debt, before the capital is due for redemption.

When this occurs, the debenture holders or loan note holders could exercise their right to appoint a **receiver** and to make use of whatever **security** they have.

2.9 Debt or equity? 11/05

A common theme in exam questions is whether a company should issue debt or equity. In this section we shall consider the most significant relative advantages and disadvantages of debt and equity finance. In Chapter 10 we shall look further at how a business decides between the two methods and determines its capital structure.

2.9.1 Advantages of debt

(a) Debt is a **cheaper form of finance** than shares because, unlike preferred shares, debt interest is tax-deductible in most tax regimes.

(b) Debt should be **more attractive** to investors because it will be **secured** against the assets of the company.

(c) **Debt holders** rank above **shareholders** in the event of a liquidation.

(d) **Issue costs** should be **lower** for debt than for shares.

(e) There is **no immediate change** in the existing structure of control, although this will change over time as conversion rights are exercised.

(f) There is **no immediate dilution** in earnings and dividends per share.

(g) Lenders do not participate in high profits compared with shares

2.9.2 Disadvantages of debt

(a) **Interest** has to be paid on debt no matter what the company's profits in a year are. In particular the company may find itself locked into long-term debt at unfavourable rates of interest. The company is not legally obliged to pay dividends.

(b) Money has to be made available for **redemption** or **repayment** of debt. However redemption will be cheaper in real terms during a time of inflation.

(c) Heavy borrowing **increases the financial risks** for ordinary shareholders. A company must be able to pay the interest charges and eventually repay the debt from its cash resources, and at the same time maintain a healthy balance sheet which does not deter would-be lenders. There might be insufficient security for a new loan.

(d) Shareholders may demand a **higher rate of return** because an increased interest burden increases the risks that dividends will not be paid.

(e) There might be restrictions on a company's power to borrow. The **company's constitution** may limit borrowing. These borrowing limits cannot be altered except with the approval of the shareholders at a general meeting of the company. **Trust deeds of existing loan notes** may **limit borrowing**. These limits can only be overcome by redeeming the loan notes.

3 Convertible securities

FAST FORWARD

Convertible securities give investors the opportunity to turn their stock into shares at a later date if they wish and, because of this, they usually carry a lower rate of interest than a similar non-convertible security. For the companies issuing them, convertibles may be viewed as a delayed form of equity which does not immediately affect EPS.

3.1 Convertible loan notes

FAST FORWARD

Convertible loan notes are a loan that gives the holder the right to convert to other securities, normally ordinary shares, at a pre-determined price/rate and time. *(OT 2000)*

Conversion terms often vary over time. For example, the conversion terms of convertible notes might be that on 1 April 20X0, £2 of notes can be converted into one ordinary share, whereas on 1 April 20X1, the conversion price will be £2.20 of notes for one ordinary share. Once converted, convertible securities cannot be converted back into the original fixed return security.

3.2 The conversion value and the conversion premium 5/06

The current market value of ordinary shares into which a unit of notes may be converted is known as the conversion value. The **conversion value** will be below the value of the notes at the date of issue, but will be expected to increase as the date for conversion approaches on the assumption that a company's shares ought to increase in market value over time.

Conversion premium = Issue value of notes – Conversion value of notes

Question — Convertible debt

Learning outcome: B (i)

The 10% convertible loan notes of Starchwhite are quoted at £142 per £100 nominal. The earliest date for conversion is in four years time, at the rate of 30 ordinary shares per £100 nominal. The share price is currently £4.15. Annual interest on the notes has just been paid.

Required

(a) What is the average annual growth rate in the share price that is required for the noteholders to achieve an overall rate of return of 12% a year compound over the next four years, including the proceeds of conversion?

(b) What is the implicit conversion premium on the notes?

Answer

(a)

Year	*Investment*	*Interest*	*Discount factor*	*Present value*
	£	£	12%	£
0	(142)		1.000	(142.00)
1		10	0.893	8.93
2		10	0.797	7.97
3		10	0.712	7.12
4		10	0.636	6.36
				(111.62)

The value of 30 shares on conversion at the end of year 4 must have a present value of at least £111.62, to provide investors with a 12% return.

The money value at the end of year 4 needs to be £111.62 ÷ 0.636 = £175.50.

The current market value of 30 shares is (× £4.15) £124.50.

The growth factor in the share price over four years needs to be:

$$\frac{175.50}{124.50} = 1.4096$$

If the annual rate of growth in the share price, expressed as a proportion, is g, then:

$$(1 + g)^4 = 1.4096$$
$$1 + g = 1.0896$$
$$g = 0.0896, \text{ say } 0.09$$

Conclusion. The rate of growth in the share price needs to be 9% a year (compound).

(b) The conversion premium can be expressed as an amount per share or as a percentage of the current conversion value.

(i) As an amount per share $\frac{£142 - £(30 \times 4.15)}{30} = £0.583$ per share

(ii) As a % of conversion value $\frac{£0.583}{£4.15} \times 100\% = 14\%$

3.3 The issue price and the market price of convertible loan notes

A company will aim to issue loan notes with the **greatest possible conversion premium** as this will mean that, for the amount of capital raised, it will, on conversion, have to issue the lowest number of new ordinary shares. The premium that will be accepted by potential investors will depend on the company's growth potential and so on prospects for a sizeable increase in the share price.

Convertible loan notes issued at par normally have a **lower coupon rate of interest** than straight debt. This lower yield is the price the investor has to pay for the conversion rights. It is, of course, also one of the reasons why the issue of convertibles is attractive to a company, particularly one with tight cash flows around the time of issue, but an easier situation when the notes are due to be converted.

When convertible loan notes are traded on a stock market, the ***minimum* market price** will be the price of straight debentures with the same coupon rate of interest. If the market value falls to this minimum, it follows that the market attaches no value to the conversion rights.

The actual market price of convertible notes will depend on

- The **price of straight debt**
- The **current conversion value**
- The **length of time** before conversion may take place
- The **market's expectation** as to future equity returns and the risk associated with these returns

Most companies issuing convertible notes expect them to be **converted**. They view the notes as delayed equity. They are often used either because the company's ordinary share price is considered to be particularly depressed at the time of issue or because the issue of equity shares would result in an immediate and significant drop in earnings per share. There is no certainty, however, that the security holders will exercise their option to convert; therefore the notes may run their full term and need to be redeemed.

3.4 Example: convertible debentures

CD has issued 50,000 units of convertible loan notes, each with a nominal value of £100 and a coupon rate of interest of 10% payable yearly. Each £100 of convertible loan notes may be converted into 40 ordinary shares of CD in three years time. Any notes not converted will be redeemed at £110 (that is, at £110 per £100 nominal value).

Estimate the likely current market price for £100 of the loan notes, if investors in the loan notes now require a pre-tax return of only 8%, and the expected value of CD ordinary shares on the conversion day is:

(a) £2.50 per share
(b) £3.00 per share

Solution

(a) Shares are valued at £2.50 each

If shares are only expected to be worth £2.50 each on conversion day, the value of 40 shares will be £100, and investors in the debt will presumably therefore redeem their debt at 110 instead of converting them into shares.

The market value of £100 of the convertible debt will be the discounted present value of the expected future income stream.

Year		*Cash flow*	*Discount factor*	*Present value*
		£	8%	£
1	Interest	10	0.926	9.26
2	Interest	10	0.857	8.57
3	Interest	10	0.794	7.94
3	Redemption value	110	0.794	87.34
				113.11

The estimated market value is £113.11 per £100 of debt.

(b) Shares are valued at £3 each

If shares are expected to be worth £3 each, the debt holders will convert their debt into shares (value per £100 of stock = 40 shares × £3 = £120) rather than redeem their debt at 110.

Year		*Cash flow/value*	*Discount factor*	*Present value*
		£	8%	£
1	Interest	10	0.926	9.26
2	Interest	10	0.857	8.57
3	Interest	10	0.794	7.94
3	Value of 40 shares	120	0.794	95.28
				121.05

The estimated market value is £121.05 per £100 of debt.

3.4.1 Advantages of convertibles

(a) Convertibles serve as a **sweetener** for debt by allowing the investor to participate in increases in price of share capital.

(b) The issuer can pay **lower interest** than on straight debt. This may be significant if funds are tight during the early years of issue of the stock.

(c) The **attractions of the conversion rights**, the possibility of a significant capital gain and the hedge against risk (the right to have the debt repaid if conversion is not worthwhile), should mean the lender is willing to accept fewer other conditions.

(d) Convertibles may provide a means of issuing equity ultimately at a **higher price** than **current** market price.

(e) There may be provisions in the issue terms allowing the issuer to **force conversion** if the market price of the stock is greater than the conversion price.

(f) If the company issued straight loan notes initially and then equity to redeem the loan notes, two lots of issue costs would be paid, whereas with convertible debt, issue costs would only be **paid once**.

(g) The **debt ratio** is **reduced** if conversion takes place.

3.4.2 Disadvantages of convertibles

(a) If the company had waited for funds, and the **market price increases significantly** above the conversion price, it would be better off issuing shares at a higher price, rather than having to issue shares at the lower conversion terms.

(b) The company has to **repay the debt** if the share price does not increase.

(c) Some borrowers may be reluctant to invest because of the **lower yield** on convertible shares compared with securities not having conversion rights.

(d) As compared with warrants, the exercise of convertibles does **not provide extra funds** to the firm, whereas the exercise of warrants does.

Exam focus point

Question 3 in May 2006 required a comparison of a convertible bond with an unsecured bond and an unsecured loan.

4 International debt finance 5/05

FAST FORWARD

Multinational companies will have access to international debt, such as **Eurobonds**.

4.1 International borrowing and equity markets

Borrowing markets are becoming increasingly internationalised, particularly for larger companies. Companies are able to borrow long-term funds on the eurocurrency (money) markets and on the markets for eurobonds. These markets are collectively called 'euromarkets'. Large companies can also borrow on the syndicated loan market where a syndicate of banks provides medium to long-term currency loans.

4.2 Eurocurrency markets

Key terms

Eurocurrency is currency which is held by individuals and institutions outside the country of issue of that currency.

Eurodollars are US dollars deposited with, or borrowed from, a bank outside the USA. *(OT 2005)*

A UK company might borrow money from a bank or from the investing public, in sterling. However it might also borrow in a foreign currency, especially if it trades abroad, or if it already has assets or liabilities abroad denominated in a foreign currency. When a company borrows in a foreign currency, the loan is known as a **eurocurrency loan**. (As with euro-equity, it is not only the euro that is involved, and so the 'euro-' prefix is a misnomer.) Banks involved in the euro currency market are **not subject to central bank reserve requirements** or regulations in respect of their involvement.

The eurocurrency markets involve the **depositing of funds** with a **bank outside the country** of the currency in which the funds are denominated and **re-lending these funds for a fairly short term**, typically three months, normally at a floating rate of interest. Eurocredits are medium to long-term international bank loans which may be arranged by individual banks or by **syndicates of banks**. Syndication of loans increases the amounts available to hundreds of millions, while reducing the exposure of individual banks.

4.3 Eurobonds

Key term

> A **eurobond** is a bond sold outside the jurisdiction of the country in whose currency the bond is denominated. *(OT 2005)*

In recent years, a strong market has built up which allows very large companies to borrow in this way, long-term or short-term. Again, the market is not subject to national regulations.

Eurobonds are **long-term loans raised by international companies** or other institutions and **sold to investors in several countries** at the same time. Such bonds can be sold by one holder to another. The term of a eurobond issue is typically 10 to 15 years. Although eurobond funds may be raised at **lower cost** than direct borrowing from banks, issue costs are generally higher than the costs of using the eurocurrency markets. Funds are also lent on fixed dates at set rates on the eurobond market, whereas the eurocurrency market is a more flexible and speedier place to raise money. Eurobonds may be the most suitable source of finance for a large organisation with an excellent credit rating, such as a large successful multinational company, which:

(a) **Requires a long-term loan to finance a big capital expansion programme** (with a loan for at least 5 years and up to 20 years)

(b) **Requires borrowing** which is **not subject** to the **national exchange controls** of any government

The interest rate on a bond issue may be fixed or variable and is paid **gross**. Many variable rate issues have a minimum rate which the bond holders are guaranteed, even if market rates fall even lower. Eurobonds are issued in **bearer** form and holders do not have to declare their identities.

Exam focus point

> Question 2(a) in May 2005 required comparison of Eurobank loans and Eurobonds.

4.4 Eurobond issues and foreign exchange risk

A borrower contemplating a eurobond issue must consider the **foreign exchange risk** of a long-term foreign currency loan. If the money is to be used to purchase assets which will earn revenue in a currency different to that of the bond issue, the borrower will run the risk of exchange losses if the currency of the loan strengthens against the currency of the revenues out of which the bond (and interest) must be repaid.

4.5 Eurocommercial paper

Key term

> **Commercial paper (CP)** is a short-term financial instrument:
>
> (a) Issued in the form of unsecured promissory notes with a fixed maturity of up to one year, typically between seven days and three months (A promissory note is a written promise to pay.)
>
> (b) Issued in bearer form
>
> (c) Issued on a discount basis (so the rate of interest on the CP is implicit in its sale value)

A large company can raise short-term finance by issuing commercial paper. The term **eurocommercial paper** refers to CP issued in any currency (often US dollars or euros)-

Commercial paper is an example of **securitisation** – the raising of loans in the form of debt securities. Banks raise finance for their customers by packaging and selling the customers' securities, such as commercial paper, rather than by lending them money.

4.5.1 Advantages of eurocommercial paper

(a) **Interest rates** are **determined** by **market conditions** but companies which issue commercial paper can hope to obtain slightly lower interest rates on their borrowing than if they borrowed direct from a bank.

(b) A company that issues CP **does not** have to be **formally 'rated'**. However, companies that are rated will be able to issue paper at better rates.

(c) If a company has surplus cash, it can **invest** it in **commercial paper** rather than in a bank deposit, and hope to earn a slightly higher interest rate on its short-term investment.

(d) The 'paper' is **tradeable**.

(These are among the advantages of dispensing with financial intermediaries, ie **financial disintermediation,** of which CP is an example.)

4.6 Syndicated credits

This is a facility where a borrower can borrow funds when required, but might in fact not take up the full amount of the facility. This differs from a loan, which involves an actual transaction for a specified sum for a particular period of time.

The **syndicated credit market** provides credit facilities at relatively high rates of interest. The market is frequently used by highly geared companies.

(a) Such a company might need such a facility if it is involved in a **takeover bid**, in which case it will use the standby credit to fund the acquisition if the bid is successful.

(b) The market is used in the re-financing of debts incurred in **past takeovers** in cases where the company has been unable to obtain alternative funds to pay off the debt.

(c) The market is also used for **government borrowings** and for project financing (eg Eurotunnel).

4.7 Multiple option facilities

Multiple option facilities (MOFs) comprise a variety of instruments through which companies can raise funds. Such instruments include **Note Issuance Facilities (NIFs)** and **Revolving Underwriting Facilities (RUFs)**.

In a typical MOF arrangement, the company may get a bank to put together **a panel of banks** who agree to provide an amount of 'standby' loans over a period of, say, five years. Another 'tender panel' of banks is set up and is invited to bid to provide loans when the company requires cash. The company is able to choose the lowest bid, or alternatively use the standby facility.

MOFs allow short-term loans (say, for three months) to be arranged in succession, effectively enabling **medium-term finance** to be **obtained**, if required, at competitive rates of interest. As implied by their name, MOFs allow the money required to be raised in various different forms, including foreign currency loans and bills of exchange.

Exam focus point

A very common mistake in exams is to assume that eurobonds are always denominated in euros.

4.8 Should a company borrow on the euromarkets or domestic markets?

The following factors are relevant to choosing between borrowing on euromarkets or domestic markets.

(a) **Spreads** between borrowing and lending rates are likely to be **lower on the euromarket**, because domestic banking systems are generally subject to tighter regulation and more stringent reserve requirements.

(b) **Euromarket loans** generally **require no security**, while borrowing on domestic markets is quite likely to involve fixed or floating charges on assets as security.

(c) Availability of euromarket funds is enhanced by the fact that euromarkets are **attractive to investors** as interest is paid gross without the deduction of withholding tax which occurs in many domestic markets.

(d) With interest normally at floating rates on euromarkets, **draw-down dates** can be **flexible**, although there may be early redemption penalties, and commitment fees to pay if the full amount of the loan is not drawn down.

(e) It is often easier for a large multinational to raise **very large sums** on the euromarkets than in a domestic financial market.

(f) Borrowing on domestic markets will mean that the **foreign exchange risk** cannot be reduced by **matching**. If the investment fails, the local liability will remain.

(g) The company may have **very limited experience** of **borrowing from overseas**. Its greater familiarity with the domestic market may mean it is easier and cheaper to raise finance locally and then transfer it overseas. However this will be problematic if **exchange controls** exist domestically.

(h) Borrowing in a currency that is attractive because **interest rates** are **lower** may be only temporarily beneficial. Interest rate differentials will mean that the currency appreciates, and ultimately the company suffer an exchange loss.

5 Lenders' assessment of creditworthiness 5/06

5.1 The factors that lenders will consider

FAST FORWARD

When lenders are assessing creditworthiness of borrowers, they will consider the trade-off between **risk and return**, although they should not lend if the borrower appears to lack the resources to repay the debt.

When an organisation is seeking loan finance, lenders will consider several factors. They will obviously be concerned with the **return** they receive, and ensuring that return is reasonable given the level of **risk** of default.

One way of remembering some of the main factors is the mnemonic PARTS.

- Purpose
- Amount
- Repayment
- Term
- Security

(a) **Purpose**

Loans to finance new businesses are likely to be risky. Lenders will be particularly careful to assess the business's **growth potential, strategy** and the abilities of **management** to put their plans into effect.

Borrowing to finance increases in working capital should normally be short-term and hence bank overdrafts be used; lenders will be very cautious of funding long-term substantial increases in working capital because of the scope offered for poor management.

(b) **Amount**

The lender will wish to make sure that the amount that is being requested is a reasonable estimate of the amount the borrower will need. The lender will be concerned if the borrower is not asking for **too much**, or **more than** is **needed** for the particular purpose. This consideration is linked in with the customer's wealth and ability to repay. The lender will also be concerned if the borrower appears to be asking for *less* than he or she really needs, and may need more later.

(c) **Repayment**

The lender will want to ensure that the **terms of repayment** are **clear** and that the borrower will be able to obtain **sufficient income** to make the necessary repayments. The lender will therefore scour the borrowers' accounts for signs of problems such as declining profits, excessive gearing or poor control over working capital.

(d) **Term**

Lenders will consider whether the **term of the loan** is **appropriate**, and in particular whether the term appears **consistent** with the timescale of the income stream that will be used to finance repayment.

(e) **Security**

Lenders may ask for security, and will be concerned that the security is adequate. However the likelihood that the advance will be repaid is the most important requirement for a loan. A lender should not lend money to a person or business who has not got the resources to repay it with interest, even if it also has security for the loan. Security for the loan gives the lender the right to take certain assets if the borrower defaults. Security is only a **safety net**.

Question

Choice of finance

Learning outcome: B(i)

What are the advantages and disadvantages of debt finance:

(a) To the company
(b) To the lender
(c) To the shareholder

Answer

(a) **The company**

The **advantages** of debt are:

(i) Debt has a **lower direct cost** than **equity finance**, for two reasons: it is less risky to the investor (see below), and interest, unlike dividends, is a tax-allowable expense.

(ii) **Issue costs of debt** are **cheaper** than **equity shares**, because there are no onerous prospectus requirements. Loans can normally be arranged more quickly than share issues.

(iii) There is **no dilution of ownership** if debt is issued. This may be important if control of the company is at stake.

The **disadvantages** are:

(i) Introducing debt into the capital structure causes an **increase in the cost of equity**, because of financial risk (see below).

(ii) Too much debt **increases the risk of bankruptcy** and can cause the company to incur significant costs in trying to avoid it, as well as increasing the costs of equity and debt.

(iii) Unlike equity, debt normally has to be **repaid** at the end of its term. This may cause problems if lenders are unwilling to renew the facility.

(iv) Assets of the company, or even personal assets of company directors, may need to be pledged as **security** for the loan. Other restrictive covenants may be written into loan agreements.

(v) **Interest rate risk**. For example, the company has borrowed at floating rate and interest rates rise.

(b) **The lender**

The **advantages** of lending are:

(i) It earns the lender **interest** (and frequently other charges). This provides a steady stream of predictable income, even if the company's profits are reduced, because interest must be paid before any dividends on shares are allowed.

(ii) It provides a **business contact** for the lender, which may allow the marketing of other services (eg insurance, foreign exchange, etc.)

The **disadvantages** are:

(i) The company may **default** on its interest or repayment.

(ii) There is **no extra benefit** if the company does well. Interest is not dependent on company profits.

(iii) **Interest rate risk**, for example the risk of lending at fixed interest when interest rates rise, may be significant.

(c) **The shareholder**

The **advantages** of the company borrowing are:

(i) The **cheap cost of debt finance** allows **returns** to shareholders to be **increased**. In particular the expectations of tax relief on debt interest can cause an increase in the value of the shares (the 'tax shield').

(ii) **Ownership** is not **diluted**.

The **disadvantages** are:

(i) The existence of debt in the capital structure makes equity returns **more volatile**. This is known as **financial risk** and it causes a compensating increase in the required return of shareholders.

(ii) Too much debt increases the **risk of bankruptcy** (see (i) above).

Chapter roundup

- Bank loans tend to be a **source** of **medium-term finance**, linked with the purchase of specific assets. Interest and repayments will be set in advance.
- The term **bonds** describes various forms of long-term debt a company may issue, such as loan stock, which may be **redeemable** or **irredeemable**. Bonds or loans come in various forms, including **floating rate loan notes**, **zero coupon bonds** and **convertible loan stock**.
- Charges (**fixed** or **floating**) may be given over debt.
- **Convertible securities** give investors the opportunity to turn their stock into shares at a later date if they wish and, because of this, they usually carry a lower rate of interest than a similar non-convertible security. For the companies issuing them, convertibles may be viewed as a delayed form of equity which does not immediately affect EPS.
- Multinational companies will have access to international debt, such as **Eurobonds**.
- When lenders are assessing creditworthiness of borrowers, they will consider the trade-off between **risk and return**, although they should not lend if the borrower appears to lack the resources to repay the debt.

Quick quiz

1 Which of the following comparisons between debentures and preference shares is not a true statement?

A Debentures are cheaper to service since interest is tax-deductible.
B Debentures are more attractive to investors because they are secured against assets.
C Debentures holders rank above preference shareholders in the event of a liquidation.
D Debentures are more similar to equity than preference shares.

2 Holders of debentures are long-term receivables of the company.

True ☐

False ☐

3 A company has 12% debentures in issue, which have a market value of £135 per £100 nominal value. What is:

(a) The coupon rate?
(b) The amount of interest payable per annum per £100 nominal?

4 An investor has the option of redeeming a company's 11% loan notes 2008/2010 at any date between 1 January 2008 and 31 December 2010 inclusive.

True ☐

False ☐

5 Convertible securities are fixed return securities that may be converted into zero coupon bonds/ordinary shares/warrants. (Delete as appropriate.)

6 Which of the following statements about convertible securities is false?

A They are fixed return securities.
B They must be converted into shares before the redemption date.
C The price at which they will be converted into shares is predetermined.
D Issue costs are lower than for equity.

7 Do borrowers benefit from floating rate debentures when interest rates are rising or falling?

8 What is the value of £100 12% debt redeemable in 3 years time at a premium of 20p per £ if the debtholder's required return is 10%?

9 What are the main factors lenders will consider when deciding whether to offer loan finance?

Answers to quick quiz

1 D

2 2 False. They are long-term payables of the company.

3 (a) 12%
(b) £12

4 False. The company will be able to choose the date of redemption.

5 Ordinary shares

6 B The holder has the option to convert, but he will only convert if it is advantageous for him to do so. If the share price falls, the notes may run their full term and need to be redeemed in the same way as other forms of debt.

7 Falling

8

Years			*Discount factor*	*Present value*
		£	10%	£
1 – 3	Interest	12	2.487	29.84
3	Redemption premium	120	0.751	90.12
				119.96

Value of debt = £119.96

9 **P**urpose
Amount
Repayment
Term
Security

Now try the questions below from the Exam Question Bank

Number	Level	Marks	Time
Q9	Examination	19	34 mins
Q10	Introductory	n/a	35 mins

7

Leasing

Introduction

In this chapter, we consider the option of **leasing** an asset.

As well as looking at the **advantages** and **disadvantages** of different types of lease compared with **other forms of credit finance**, we shall be discussing the tax and cash flow implications of leasing. You need to know how to determine whether an organisation should **lease** or **buy** an asset.

Topic list	Learning outcomes	Syllabus references	Ability required
1 Leasing as a source of finance	B(i)	B(2)	Evaluation
2 Lease or buy decisions	B(i)	B(4)	Evaluation

1 Leasing as a source of finance

FAST FORWARD

Leasing is a commonly used source of finance. Major types of leases are: **operating leases (lessor** responsible for maintaining asset), **finance leases (lessee** responsible for maintenance), and **sale and leaseback** arrangements.

1.1 The nature of leasing

Rather than buying an asset outright, using either available cash resources or borrowed funds, a business may lease an asset.

Key term

Leasing is a contract between lessor and lessee for hire of a specific asset selected from a manufacturer or vendor of such assets by the lessee.

(a) The **lessor** retains ownership of the asset.

(b) The **lessee** has possession and use of the asset on payment of specified rentals over a period.

(c) Many lessors are **financial intermediaries** such as banks and insurance companies.

(d) The **range of assets leased** is wide, including office equipment and computers, cars and commercial vehicles, aircraft, ships and buildings.

Key terms

Finance lease is a lease agreement that transfers substantially all the risks and rewards incidental to ownership of an asset from the lessor to the lessee.

Operating lease is a lease agreement other than a finance lease. The lessor retains most of the risk and rewards of ownership. *(OT 2005)*

1.2 Operating leases

Operating leases are rental agreements between the user of the leased asset (the lessee) and a provider of finance (the lessor) whereby:

(a) The **lessor supplies the equipment** to the lessee.

(b) The **lessor** is **responsible** for **servicing and maintaining the leased equipment.**

(c) The **period of the lease** is fairly **short**, **less** than the **expected economic life** of the asset, so that at the end of one lease agreement, the lessor can either lease the same equipment to someone else, and obtain a good rent for it, or sell the equipment second-hand.

With an operating lease, the lessor, often a finance house, purchases the equipment from the manufacturer and then leases it to the user (the lessee) for the agreed period.

1.3 Finance leases

Finance leases are lease agreements between a **lessor** and **lessee**, for most or all of the asset's expected useful life.

Suppose that a company decides to obtain a company car and to finance the acquisition by means of a finance lease. A **car dealer** will **supply the car**. A finance house will agree to act as lessor in a finance leasing arrangement, and so will purchase the car from the dealer and lease it to the company. The company will take possession of the car from the car dealer, and make regular payments (monthly, quarterly, six monthly or annually) to the finance house under the terms of the lease.

There are other important characteristics of a finance lease.

(a) The **lessee** is **responsible** for the **upkeep**, servicing and maintenance of the asset. For a car this would mean repairs and servicing, road tax insurance and garaging. The lessor is not involved in this at all.

(b) The **lease** has a **primary period**, which covers all or most of the useful economic life of the asset. At the end of this primary period, the lessor would not be able to lease the asset to someone else, because the asset would be worn out. The lessor must therefore ensure that the lease payments during the primary period pay for the full cost of the asset as well as providing the lessor with a suitable return on his investment.

(c) The lessee may be able to continue to lease the asset for an **indefinite secondary period**, in return for a very low nominal rent, sometimes called a 'peppercorn rent'. Alternatively, the lessee might be allowed to sell the asset on a lessor's behalf (since the lessor is the owner) and to keep most of the sale proceeds, paying only a small percentage (perhaps 10%) to the lessor.

1.4 Sale and leaseback arrangements

A company which owns its own premises can obtain finance by selling the property to an insurance company or pension fund for immediate cash and renting it back, usually for at least 50 years with rent reviews every few years.

A company would raise more cash from a **sale and leaseback agreement** than from a mortgage, but it should only make such an agreement if it cannot raise sufficient funds any other way. **Disadvantages** of sale and leaseback are as follows.

(a) The company **loses ownership** of a valuable asset which is almost certain to appreciate over time.

(b) The **future borrowing capacity** of the firm will be reduced, since the property if owned could be used to provide security for a loan.

(c) The company is **contractually committed** to occupying the property for many years ahead, and this can be restricting.

(d) The **real cost** is likely to be high, particularly as there will be frequent rent reviews.

1.5 Attractions of leasing

The attractions of leases to the supplier of the equipment, the lessee and the lessor are as follows.

(a) The **supplier** of the **equipment** is **paid in full** at the **beginning**. The equipment is sold to the lessor, and apart from obligations under guarantees or warranties, the supplier has no further financial concern about the asset.

(b) The **lessor invests finance** by **purchasing assets** from suppliers and makes a return out of the lease payments from the lessee. Provided that a lessor can find lessees willing to pay the amounts he wants to make his return, the lessor can make good profits. He will also get capital allowances on his purchase of the equipment.

(c) **Leasing** might be **attractive** to the **lessee**:

- If the lessee does not have enough cash to pay for the asset, and would have difficulty obtaining a bank loan to buy it, and so has to rent it in one way or another if he is to have the use of it at all

- As finance leases are **cheaper** than **bank loans**. Surveys suggest that this is a major reason why leases are used. The logic is that the lessor is prepared to **lend** at a **lower cost** because he possesses greater security i.e. the ownership of the asset
- As leases, once negotiated, are **legally binding** and **cannot be withdrawn** with immediate effect in the way an overdraft facility might be

The lessee may find the **tax relief** available advantageous.

Operating leases have these further advantages.

(a) The leased equipment does **not** have to be **shown** in the **lessee's published balance sheet**, and so the lessee's balance sheet shows no increase in its gearing ratio.

(b) The **equipment** is **leased** for a **shorter period** than its expected useful life. In the case of high-technology equipment, if the equipment becomes out of date before the end of its expected life, the lessee does not have to keep on using it, and it is the lessor who must bear the risk of having to sell obsolete equipment secondhand.

(c) The lessor deals with **servicing**, **maintenance** and **administration**.

Not surprisingly perhaps, a major growth area in operating leasing has been in computers and office equipment (such as photocopiers and fax machines) where technology is continually improving.

1.6 Hire purchase

Hire purchase is a vendor credit arrangement similar to leasing, with the exception that ownership of the goods passes to the hire purchase customer on payment of the final credit instalment, whereas a lessee never becomes the owner of the goods.

Key term

> **Hire purchase contract** is a contract for the hire of an asset that contains a provision giving the hirer an option to acquire title to the asset upon the fulfilment of agreed conditions. *(OT 2000)*

Hire purchase agreements nowadays usually involve a finance house.

- The supplier sells the goods to the finance house.
- The supplier delivers the goods to the customer who will eventually purchase them.
- The hire purchase arrangement exists between the finance house and the customer.

The finance house will nearly always insist that the hirer should pay a **deposit** towards the purchase price, perhaps as low as 10%, or as high as 33%.

The HP payments consist partly of 'capital' payments towards the purchase of the asset, and partly of interest charges. For example, if a company buys a car costing £10,000 under an HP agreement, the car supplier might provide HP finance over a three year period at an interest cost of 10%, and the HP payments might be, say, as follows.

	Capital element	*Interest element*	*Total HP payment*
	£	£	£
Year 0: down payment	2,540	0	2,540
Year 1	2,254	746	3,000
Year 2	2,479	521	3,000
Year 3	2,727	273	3,000
Total	10,000	1,540	11,540

The tax situation is that the buyer is likely to be able to claim for tax-allowable depreciation, and for the interest element of repayments, though not for the capital element.

Question

Lease v. loan

Learning outcome: B(i)

Explain the cash flow characteristics of a finance lease, and compare it with the use of a bank loan. Your answer should include some comment on the significance of a company's anticipated tax position on lease versus buy decisions.

Answer

A finance lease is an agreement between the user of the leased asset and a provider of finance that covers the majority of the asset's useful life. Key features of a finance lease are as follows.

(a) The provider of finance is usually a **third party finance house** and not the original provider of the equipment.

(b) The **lessee is responsible for the upkeep**, servicing and maintenance of the asset.

(c) The lease has a **primary period**, which covers all or most of the useful economic life of the asset. At the end of the primary period the lessor would not be able to lease the equipment to someone else because it would be worn out.

(d) It is common at the end of the primary period to allow the lessee to continue to lease the asset for an indefinite **secondary period**, in return for a very low nominal rent, sometimes known as a 'peppercorn' rent.

The cash flow implications of this form of lease are therefore as follows.

(a) **Regular payments** to the **lessor**, which comprise interest and principal. This can be very useful to the lessee from a cash flow management point of view.

(b) **Costs of maintenance** and so on, which may be less predictable in terms of both timing and amount.

(c) **Tax-allowable depreciation** cannot be claimed on the purchase cost of the equipment, but the lease payments are fully allowable for tax purposes. This may be of benefit to a company that is unable to make full use of its tax-allowable depreciation.

If the equipment is acquired using a medium term bank loan, the cash flow patterns would be similar to those that would arise using a finance lease. However, if the loan were subject to a variable rate of interest, this would introduce a further source of variability into the cash flows. The main difference between the two approaches would be that the company could claim tax-allowable depreciation on the purchase cost of the equipment. The interest element of the repayments would also be allowable against tax, but the repayments of principal would not.

2 Lease or buy decisions 5/05

FAST FORWARD

The decision whether to **lease or buy** an asset involves two steps.

- The **acquisition decision**: is the asset worth having? Test by discounting project cash flows at a suitable cost of capital.
- The **financing decision**: if the asset should be acquired, compare the cash flows of purchasing and leasing or HP arrangements. The cash flows can be discounted at an after-tax cost of borrowing.

2.1 Lease or buy calculations

There are several ways of evaluating a decision whether to lease an asset, or to purchase it by another means of finance. The **traditional method** is to take the view that a decision to lease is a financing decision, which can only be made after a decision to acquire the asset has already been taken. It is therefore necessary to make a two-stage decision, as follows.

Step 1 An **acquisition decision** is made on whether the asset is worth having. The present values of operational costs and benefits from using the asset are found to derive a net present value (NPV).

Step 2 A **financing decision** is then made if the acquisition is justified by a positive NPV. This is the decision on whether to **lease or buy**.

Knowledge brought forward from earlier studies

Again this topic requires you to use discounted cash flow and investment appraisal techniques that you encountered in your earlier studies. Quickly revise the basics in Chapter 18 if you're still not sure.

The traditional method is complicated by the need to choose a discount rate for each stage of the decision. In the case of a non-taxpaying organisation, the method is applied as follows.

Step 1 The cost of capital that should be applied to the cash flows for the acquisition decision is the cost of capital that the organisation would normally apply to its **project evaluations**.

Step 2 The cost of capital that should be applied to the **(differential) cash flows** for the **financing** decision is the **cost of borrowing**.

We assume that if the organisation decided to purchase the equipment, it would finance the purchase by borrowing funds (rather than out of retained funds).

We therefore compare the **cost of borrowing** with the **cost of leasing** (or hire purchase) by applying this cost of borrowing to the financing cash flows.

Exam focus point

The distinction between using the **cost of capital** to appraise the **investment** decision, and using the **cost of borrowing** to appraise the **finance** decision is important.

In the case of a tax-paying organisation, taxation should be allowed for in the cash flows, so that the traditional method would recommend:

(a) Discounting the **cash flows** of the **acquisition** decision at the firm's **after-tax cost of capital**
(b) Discounting the **cash flows** of the **financing** decision at the **after-tax cost of borrowing**

2.2 Example: lease or buy decisions (1)

Mallen and Mullins has decided to install a new milling machine. The machine costs £20,000 and it would have a useful life of five years with a trade-in value of £4,000 at the end of the fifth year. Additional cash profits from the machine would be £8,000 a year for five years. A decision has now to be taken on the method of financing the project.

(a) The company could purchase the machine for cash, using bank loan facilities on which the current rate of interest is 13% before tax.

(b) The company could lease the machine under an agreement which would entail payment of £4,800 at the end of each year for the next five years.

The company's weighted average cost of capital, normally used for project evaluating, is 12% after tax. The rate of tax is 30%. If the machine is purchased, the company will be able to claim an allowance of 100% in Year 1. Tax is payable with a year's delay.

Advise the management on whether to acquire the machine, on the most economical method of finance, and on any other matter which should be considered before finally deciding which method of finance should be adopted.

Solution

The traditional method begins with the acquisition decision. The cash flows of the project should be discounted at 12%.

Taxable profits and tax liability

Year	*Cash profits*	*Tax-allowable depreciation*	*Taxable profits/(losses)*	*Tax at 30%*
	£	£	£	£
1	8,000	20,000	(12,000)	3,600
2	8,000	–	8,000	(2,400)
3	8,000	–	8,000	(2,400)
4	8,000	–	8,000	(2,400)
5	8,000	–	8,000	(2,400)

NPV calculation for the acquisition decision

Year	*Equipment*	*Cash profits*	*Tax*	*Net cash flow*	*Discount factor*	*Present value*
	£	£	£	£	12%	£
0	(20,000)			(20,000)	1.000	(20,000)
1		8,000		8,000	0.893	7,144
2		8,000	3,600	11,600	0.797	9,245
3		8,000	(2,400)	5,600	0.712	3,987
4		8,000	(2,400)	5,600	0.636	3,562
5	4,000	8,000	(2,400)	9,600	0.567	5,443
6			(2,400)	(2,400)	0.507	(1,217)
					NPV	8,164

The net present value (NPV) is positive, and so we conclude that the machine should be acquired, regardless of the method used to finance the acquisition.

The second stage is the financing decision, and cash flows are discounted at the after-tax cost of borrowing, which is at 13% × 70% = 9.1%, say 9%. The only cash flows that we need to consider are those which will be affected by the choice of the method of financing. The operating savings of £8,000 a year, and the tax on these savings, can be ignored.

(a) The present value (PV) of purchase costs

Year	*Item*	*Cash flow*	*Discount factor*	*PV*
		£	9%	£
0	Equipment cost	(20,000)	1.000	(20,000)
5	Trade-in value	4,000	0.650	2,600
2	Tax savings, from allowances 30% × £20,000	6,000	0.842	5,052
			NPV of purchase	(12,348)

(b) The PV of leasing costs

It is assumed that the lease payments are fully tax-allowable.

Year	*Lease payment*	*Savings in tax (30%)*	*Discount factor*	*PV*
	£	£	9%	£
1-5	(4,800) pa		3.890	(18,672)
2-6		1,440 pa	3.569*	5,139
			NPV of leasing	(13,533)

*Discount factor 1–6 – Discount factor 1 = 4.486–0.917

The cheapest option would be to purchase the machine.

Other methods of making lease or buy decisions are as follows.

(a) **Compare the costs of leasing** with the **costs of purchase**, and select the cheaper method of financing; then calculate the NPV of the project on the assumption that the cheaper method of financing is used. In other words, make the financing decision first and the acquisition decision afterwards.

(b) Calculate an NPV for the project if the machine is **purchased**, and secondly if the machine is **leased**. Select the method of financing which gives the **higher NPV**, provided that the project is viable (that is, has a positive NPV). In other words, combine the acquisition and financing decisions together into a single-stage decision.

(c) (i) Carry out a single financing calculation with the payments for one method being negative and the receipts being positive, and vice versa for the other method. In the example given, for the outright purchase option.

Year	*Item*	*Cash flow*	*Discount factor*	*Present value*
		£	9%	£
0	Equipment cost	(20,000)	1.000	(20,000)
5	Trade-in value	4,000	0.650	2,600
2	Tax savings from allowances			
	30% × £20,000	6,000	0.842	5,052
1-5	Lease payments saved	4,800	3.890	18,672
2-6	Tax allowances foregone	(1,440)	3.569	(5,139)
				1,185

The positive NPV indicates that the purchasing decision is better, as the net savings from not leasing outweigh the net costs of purchasing.

(ii) The cost of finance at which the company will be **indifferent** between the leasing and purchasing can be calculated using an IRR **calculation**. We can use 9% as the first rate and let us use 12% as the second rate

Year	*Item*	*Cash flow*	*Discount factor*	*Present value*
		£	12%	£
0	Equipment cost	(20,000)	1.000	(20,000)
5	Trade-in value	4,000	0.567	2,268
2	Tax savings from allowances			
	30% × £20,000	6,000	0.797	4,782
1-5	Lease payments saved	4,800	3.605	17,304
2-6	Tax allowances foregone	(1,440)	3.218	(4,634)
				(280)

$$\text{IRR} = 9 + 3\left(\frac{1{,}185}{1{,}185-(-280)}\right) = 11.4\%$$

Thus at a cost of finance of 11.4%, the company will be indifferent whether it purchases or leases the asset.

Since **operating leases** are a form of renting, the only cash flows to consider for this type of leasing are the lease payments and the tax saved. Operating lease payments are like to be allowable expenses for tax purposes.

2.3 Evaluating a lease or buy decision

Lease or buy decisions are not purely a matter of calculations. We discussed above why leasing might be attractive to a business; the following issues are also relevant to a lease or buy decision.

(a) **Effect on cash flow**

The organisation's liquidity at the time the **decision** is made may be **important**. If the business is suffering cash-flow difficulties, lease payments may offer a smoother cash flow than one big lump sum.

(b) **Cost of capital**

The decision on whether to **obtain use** of the asset may be **dependent upon the appraisal method or cost of capital used**. A decision not to invest taken using the company's overall cost of capital may be reversed if a significantly lower cost of leasing is used in the cash flow.

(c) **Running expenses**

Lease or buy calculations normally assume that the **running costs** are the **same** under each alternative. This may not be so. **Expenses like maintenance and insurance** may differ between the alternatives.

(d) **Trade in value**

The organisation will gain the (uncertain) benefits of a **trade-in value** if it chooses the purchase option.

(e) **Effect on reported profits**

Annual profits are reported on an **accruals basis**, after the deduction of depreciation. The effect of the alternatives on reported profits should be considered since this could, if significant, affect **dividend policy** and the **valuation of shares**.

(f) **Alternative uses of funds**

Lease or buy decisions will not be taken in **isolation**. If the business has limited funds available, there may be **better uses** for those funds than obtaining the asset, even if the asset does yield net positive cash flows.

Exam focus point

Question 4 in May 2005 required calculations and discussions of a lease or buy decision.

2.4 The position of the lessor

Exam focus point

So far, we have looked at examples of leasing decisions from the viewpoint of the lessee. You might be asked to evaluate a leasing arrangement from the position of the lessor. This is rather like a mirror image of the lessee's position.

Assuming that it is purchasing the asset, the lessor will receive capital allowances on the expenditure, and the lease payments will be taxable income.

2.5 Example: lessor's position

Continuing the same case of Mallen and Mullins, suppose that the lessor's required rate of return is 12% after tax. The lessor's cash flows will be as follows.

	Cash flow	*Discount factor*	*PV*
Purchase costs (see above)	£	12%	£
Year 0	(20,000)	1.000	(20,000)
Year 5 trade-in	4,000	0.567	2,268
Tax savings			
Year 2	6,000	0.797	4,782
Lease payments: years 1-5	4,800	3.605	17,304
Tax on lease payments: years 2-6	(1,440)	3.218	(4,634)
NPV			(280)

Conclusion. The leasing payments proposed are not justifiable for the lessor if it seeks a required rate of return of 12%, since the resulting NPV is negative.

Question — Lease or buy

Learning outcome: B(i)

The management of a company has decided to acquire Machine X which costs £63,000 and has an operational life of four years. The expected scrap value would be zero. Tax is payable at 30% on operating cash flows one year in arrears. Capital allowances are available at 100% in Year 1.

Suppose that the company has the opportunity either to purchase the machine or to lease it under a finance lease arrangement, at an annual rent of £20,000 for four years, payable at the end of each year. The company can borrow to finance the acquisition at 10%. Should the company lease or buy the machine?

Answer

The financing decision will be appraised by discounting the relevant cash flows at the after-tax cost of borrowing, which is 10% × 70% = 7%.

(a) Purchase option

Year	*Item*	*Cash flow* £	*Discount factor* 7%	*Present value* £
0	Cost of machine	(63,000)	1.000	(63,000)
2	Tax saved from tax-allowable depreciation 30% × £63,000	18,900	0.873	16,500
				(46,500)

(b) Leasing option

It is assumed that the lease payments are tax-allowable in full.

Year	*Item*	*Cash flow* £	*Discount factor* 7%	*Present value* £
1-4	Lease costs	(20,000)	3.387	(67,740)
2-5	Tax savings on lease costs (× 30%)	6,000	3.165	18,990
				(48,750)

The purchase option is cheaper, using a cost of capital based on the after-tax cost of borrowing. On the assumption that investors would regard borrowing and leasing as equally risky finance options, the purchase option is recommended.

Chapter roundup

- **Leasing** is a commonly used source of finance. Major types of leases are **operating leases (lessor** responsible for maintaining asset), **finance leases (lessee** responsible for maintenance), and **sale and leaseback** arrangements.
- The decision whether to **lease or buy** an asset involves two steps.
  - The **acquisition decision**: is the asset worth having? Test by discounting project cash flows at a suitable cost of capital.
  - The **financing decision**: if the asset should be acquired, compare the cash flows of purchasing and leasing or HP arrangements. The cash flows can be discounted at an after-tax cost of borrowing.

Quick quiz

1 Operating leases and finance leases are distinguished for accounting purposes. Which of the following statements is not true of an operating lease?

A The lessor supplies the equipment to the lessee.
B The period of the lease is less than the expected economic life of the asset.
C The lessee is normally responsible for servicing and maintaining the leased equipment.
D The lessor retains most of the risks and rewards of ownership.

2 Who is responsible for the servicing of a leased asset in the case of:

(a) An operating lease?
(b) A finance lease?

The lessee or The lessor

3 What two steps in a lease or buy decision evaluation may be distinguished?

4 Which discount rate should be used at each stage (delete as applicable)?

	(a)	*Discount rate (b)*
Step 1		Pre-tax/after-tax cost of capital/cost of borrowing
Step 2		Pre-tax/after-tax cost of capital/ cost of borrowing

5 Why should operating leases be popular for users of high technology equipment?

6 Cemstone has decided to acquire a new grinding machine. It cannot afford to purchase the machine outright, and has therefore arranged to pay for it in regular instalments using a finance house. What type of arrangement is this?

A Finance lease
B Operating lease
C Lender credit
D Vendor credit

7 A hire purchase contract is a contract for the hire of an asset that contains a provision giving the hirer an option to acquire legal title to the asset upon the fulfilment of certain conditions stated in the contract.

True ☐

False ☐

8 .... credit occurs when the buyer borrows money and uses it to purchase goods outright.

Answers to quick quiz

1 C The lessor is normally responsible for maintaining the equipment.

2 (a) The lessor

(b) The lessee

3/4 ***Step 1***. The acquisition decision - discount at the firm's after-tax cost of capital

Step 2. The financing decision - discount at the after-tax cost of borrowing

5 Because such equipment may soon become obsolete.

6 D This is also known as hire purchase.

7 True

8 Lender credit

Now try the question below from the Exam Question Bank

Number	Level	Marks	Time
Q11	Introductory	n/a	30 mins

8

Securities markets and market efficiency

Introduction

The first few sections of this chapter give insights into the role of banks and money and capital markets in helping businesses. You need to be aware of the services businesses can use, and also what sources of finance are provided by different types of market.

Sections 5 and 6 of this chapter deal with the determination of share prices. As we shall see, there are various theories which seek to provide a rationale for share price movement. The most important of these is the **efficient market hypothesis**, which provides theoretical underpinning for how markets take into account new information. We mentioned in Chapter 4 that the efficient market hypothesis was a key factor that businesses have to consider when deciding on their financial strategies. In chapter 15 we shall see how the efficient market hypothesis impacts upon business valuations.

Topic list	Learning outcomes	Syllabus references	Ability required
1 Financial intermediation	B(i)	B(5)	Evaluation
2 Commercial and merchant banks	B(i)	B(5)	Evaluation
3 Money and capital markets	B(i)	B(5)	Evaluation
4 International money and capital markets	B(i)	B(5)	Evaluation
5 Share prices and investment returns	B(i)	B(5)	Evaluation
6 The efficient market hypothesis	B(i)	B(5)	Evaluation

1 Financial intermediation

FAST FORWARD

A **financial intermediary** links those with surplus funds (eg **lenders**) to those with funds deficits (eg potential **borrowers**) thus providing **aggregation** and **economies of scale**, **risk pooling** and **maturity transformation**.

1.1 Financial intermediaries

Key term

Financial intermediary is a party bringing together providers and users of finance, either as broker or as principal.

A **financial intermediary** is an institution which links lenders with borrowers, by obtaining deposits from lenders and then re-lending them to borrowers.

Not all intermediation takes place between savers and investors. Some institutions act mainly as intermediaries between other institutions. Almost all place part of their funds with other institutions, and a number (including finance houses, leasing companies and factoring companies) obtain most of their funds by borrowing from other institutions.

2 Commercial and merchant banks

FAST FORWARD

Commercial banks provide payments mechanisms and means of storing wealth. They also act as providers of funds.

Merchant banks (investment banks) provide various services, including business advice on mergers and takeovers.

2.1 Commercial banks

An important grouping of financial intermediaries is the **commercial banks**, which include both the retail banks, which include the well known 'High Street' banks, and the wholesale banks, which offer services mainly to larger customers, including large companies.

(a) They provide a **payments mechanism**: a way in which individuals, firms and government can make payments to each other.

(b) They provide a place for individuals, firms and government to **store their wealth**. Banks compete with other financial institutions to attract the funds of individuals and firms.

(c) They act as **providers of funds** by lending money in the form of loans or overdrafts.

2.2 Merchant banks

Merchant (or **investment**) banks engage in diverse activities, with individual banks having their specialised areas of expertise and interest. Merchant banking is perhaps best thought of in terms of its customers, who are generally corporate clients wanting particular financial services. The clearing banks carry out some merchant banking activities themselves.

2.3 The range of merchant banking activities

Merchant banking activities are various. The following list gives some examples.

- Involvement in the issue and underwriting of shares on the Stock Exchange
- Taking 'wholesale' deposits of funds, both in sterling and foreign currencies
- Large scale term lending to corporate borrowers
- Dealing in foreign exchange
- Dealing in the gold and silver bullion markets
- Handling Stock Exchange business on behalf of clients
- Managing investments on behalf of clients
- Advising business customers on takeovers and mergers
- Providing venture capital
- Share registration
- Dealing in stocks and shares as a market maker or stockbroker, through a subsidiary

3 Money and capital markets

FAST FORWARD

The **capital markets** and **money markets** are markets for long-term and short-term capital respectively.

3.1 Money and capital markets

The **capital markets**, being markets for long-term capital, are distinguished from the **money markets**, which are markets for

- Trading short-term financial instruments
- Short-term lending and borrowing.

3.2 Differences between loan terms

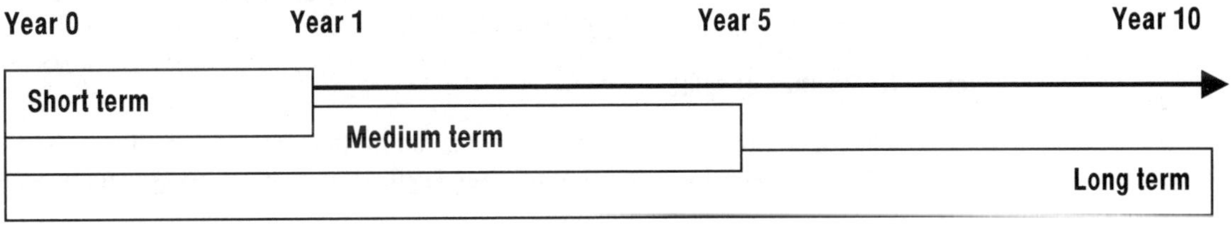

3.3 The money markets

Key term

Money market is a short-term wholesale market for securities maturing in one year, such as certificates of deposit, treasury bills and commercial paper. *(OT 2000)*

The money markets are operated by the banks and other financial institutions. Examples include the following.

MONEY MARKETS	
Primary or official	Approved institutions buy bills of exchange/other short-term instruments in daily trading with central bank
Interbank	Banks lend short-term funds to each other. Money brokers operate in the interbank market, acting as intermediaries between banks that wish to borrow and banks that wish to lend
Eurocurrency	Banks lend and borrow in foreign currencies

MONEY MARKETS	
Certificate of deposit	Trading in certificates of deposits, negotiable instruments issued by banks acknowledging a deposit of money
Local authority	Local authorities borrow short-term from banks/other investors
Finance house	Finance houses raise short-term loans
Inter-company	Direct short-term lending between companies, without financial intermediary

3.4 The capital markets

Capital markets are markets for trading in **long-term finance**, in the form of long-term financial instruments. In the UK, the principal capital markets are the **Stock Exchange 'main market'** (for companies with a full Stock Exchange listing) and the more loosely regulated 'second tier' **Alternative Investment Market (AIM)** which is also regulated by the Stock Exchange. Apart from regulating these two markets, the Stock Exchange is also the market for dealings in **government securities** (gilts).

The stock markets serve the following main purposes.

(a) **Primary markets**

As **primary markets** they enable organisations to **raise new finance**, by issuing new shares or new debentures. Capital markets make it easier for companies to raise new long-term finance than if they had to raise funds privately by contacting investors individually. In the UK, a company must have public company status (be a plc) to be allowed to raise finance from the public on a capital market.

(b) **Secondary markets**

As **secondary markets** they enable existing investors to sell their investments, should they wish to do so. The **marketability** of securities is a very important feature of the capital markets, because investors are more willing to buy stocks and shares if they know that they could sell them easily, should they wish to.

(c) **Realisation of value**

When a company comes to the stock market for the first time, and 'floats' its shares on the market, the **owners** of the company can **realise** some of the **value** of their shares in cash, because they will offer a proportion of their personally-held shares for sale to new investors.

(d) **Takeovers by share exchange**

When one company wants to take over another, it is common to do so by issuing shares to finance the takeover. Takeovers by means of a share exchange are only feasible if the shares that are offered can be readily traded on a stock market, and so have an identifiable market value.

3.5 Over-the-counter markets

Key term

The **over-the-counter (OTC) market** is securities trading carried on outside regulated exchanges. It allows tailormade transactions. *(OT 2000)*

Shares and other financial instruments are bought and sold outside the supervised and regulated official exchanges in the **'over-the-counter' (OTC) markets**. Shares are traded 'off the market' to reduce costs as well as to maintain secrecy.

3.6 Institutional investors

Key term

> **Institutional investors** are institutions which have large amounts of funds which they want to invest, and they will invest in stocks and shares or any other assets (such as gold or works of art) which offer satisfactory returns and security.

The institutional investors are now the biggest investors on many stock markets but they might also invest venture capital, or lend directly to companies.

3.7 Capital market participants

The various participants in the capital markets are summarised in the diagram below.

Capital markets

Demand for funds comes from ...		*INTERMEDIARIES*		Suppliers of funds
INDIVIDUALS (eg housing/consumer goods finance)	←	Banks	←	INDIVIDUALS (as savers and investors)
	←	Building societies	←	
FIRMS (share capital; loans)	←	Insurance companies and pension funds	←	
	←	Unit trust/investment trust companies	←	FIRMS (with long-term funds to invest)
	←	Stock exchanges	←	
GOVERNMENT (budget deficit)	←	Venture capital organisations	←	GOVERNMENT (budget surplus)

3.8 Venture capital **11/06**

Key term

> **Venture capital** is risk capital, normally provided in return for an equity stake.

Venture capital organisations have been operating for many years. There are now quite a large number of such organisations.

(a) The British Venture Capital Association is a regulatory body for all the institutions that have joined it as members.

(b) **Investors in Industry plc**, or the **3i group** as it is more commonly known, is the biggest and oldest of the venture capital organisations. It is involved in many venture capital schemes in Europe, Singapore, Japan and the US.

The supply of venture capital in the UK has grown in recent years, as governments have helped to create an environment which supports entrepreneurial business.

Like other venture capitalists, the 3i group wants to invest in companies that will be successful. The group's publicity material states that successful investments have certain common characteristics.

- Highly motivated individuals with a strong management team in place
- A well defined strategy
- A clearly defined target market
- Current turnover between $1m and $100m
- A proven ability to outperform your competitors
- Innovation

The types of venture that the 3i group might invest in include the following.

(a) **Business start-ups**. When a business has been set up by someone who has already put time and money into getting it started, the group may be willing to **provide finance** to enable it to get off the ground.

(b) **Business development**. The group may be willing to **provide development capital** for a company which wants to invest in new products or new markets or to make a business acquisition, and so which needs a major capital injection.

(c) **Management buyouts**. A management buyout is the **purchase** of all or parts of a **business** from its owners by its managers (see Chapter 16).

(d) Helping a company where one of its owners wants to **realise all or part of his investment**. The 3i group may be prepared to buy some of the company's equity.

When a company's directors look for help from a venture capital institution, they must recognise that:

(a) The institution will want an **equity stake** in the company.

(b) It will need convincing that the company can be successful (management buyouts of companies which already have a record of **successful trading** have been increasingly favoured by venture capitalists in recent years).

(c) It may want to have a **representative** appointed to the company's board, to look after its interests, or an **independent director** (the 3i group runs an Independent Director Scheme).

4 International money and capital markets

FAST FORWARD

International money and capital markets are available for larger companies wishing to raise larger amounts of finance.

4.1 Eurocurrency and Eurobond markets

As we have seen in earlier chapters, larger companies are able to borrow funds on the **eurocurrency markets** (which are international money markets) and on the markets for **eurobonds** (international capital markets).

Exam focus point

Don't suggest these international markets as possible sources of finance for a *smaller* business in an exam answer.

5 Share prices and investment returns

FAST FORWARD

Fundamental analysis is based on the theory that share prices can be derived from an analysis of **future dividends**.

Technical analysts or **chartists** work on the basis that past price patterns will be repeated.

Random walk theory is based on the idea that share prices will alter when **new information** becomes **available**.

5.1 Theories of share price behaviour

There are the following differing views about share price movements.

- **The fundamental analysis theory**
- **Technical analysis (chartist theory)**
- **Random walk theory**

These different theories about how share prices are reached in the market, especially fundamental analysis, have important consequences for financial management.

5.2 The fundamental analysis theory of share values 11/05

The fundamental theory of share values is based on the theory that the 'realistic' market price of a share can be derived from a **valuation of estimated future dividends** (the dividend valuation model). The value of a share will be the discounted present value of all future expected dividends on the share, discounted at the shareholders' cost of capital.

Key term

Fundamental analysis is the analysis of external and internal influences that directly affect the operations of a company with a view to assisting in investment decisions. Information accessed might include fiscal/monetary policy, financial statements, industry trends, competitor analysis, etc. *(OT 2005)*

(a) The formula below applies when the company is expected to pay constant dividends every year into the future, 'in perpetuity'.

Exam Formula

Ordinary (equity) share paying a constant annual dividend d in perpetuity, where P_0 is the ex-div value.

$$P_0 = \frac{d}{k_e}$$

where k_e is the shareholders' cost of capital (the required rate of return).

Similar formulae can be used to find the price of preference share capital and debt.

Exam Formulae

Irredeemable preferred share, paying a constant annual dividend, d in perpetuity, where P_0 is the ex-div value:

$$P_0 = \frac{d}{k_{pref}}$$

where k_{pref} is the preferred shareholders' cost of capital.

Irredeemable (undated) debt, paying annual after tax interest, i(1 – t) in perpetuity, where P_0 is the ex-interest value:

$$P_0 = \frac{i(1-t)}{k_d \text{ net}}$$

Or, without tax:

$$P_0 = \frac{i}{k_d}$$

Where k_d is the cost of debt.

(b) When the company is expected to pay a dividend which increases at a constant rate, g, every year into the future, the following **dividend growth model** may be used.

Exam Formula

Ordinary (equity) share paying an annual dividend d, growing in perpetuity at a constant rate g, where P_0 is the ex-div value.

$$P_0 = \frac{d_0(1+g)}{k_e - g} = \frac{d_1}{k_e - g}$$

where d_0 is the dividend in the current year (year 0) and so $d_0(1+g)$ is the expected future dividend in year 1 (d_1).

5.3 Example: constant dividend

Hocus expects to pay a constant dividend of £450,000 at the end of every year for ever (in perpetuity). Assuming that a dividend has just been paid, calculate what the market value of Hocus's shares ought to be if its shareholders' cost of capital is 15%.

Solution

$$P_0 = \frac{£450{,}000}{(1.15)} + \frac{£450{,}000}{(1.15)^2} + \frac{£450{,}000}{(1.15)^3} + \text{ .... and so on, in perpetuity.}$$

Exam Formulae

Present value of £1 per annum, payable or receivable in perpetuity, commencing in the year, discounted at r% per annum:

$$PV = \frac{1}{r}$$

Present value of £1 per annum, receivable or payable, commencing in one year, growing in perpetuity at a constant rate of g% per annum, discounted at r% per annum:

$$PV = \frac{1}{r-g}$$

Therefore, the present value of £450,000 a year at a rate of interest of 15%

is $£450{,}000 \times \frac{1}{0.15} = £3{,}000{,}000$.

The value of Hocus's shares will be £3,000,000.

5.4 Example: Market value of shares (1)

Fluff has a cost of equity of 8%, and its last dividend per share was 20p. If the company's dividends are growing at a rate of 4% per annum, calculate the market price per share.

Solution

$$P_0 = \frac{d_0(1+g)}{(k_e - g)}$$

$$= \frac{20(1+0.04)}{(0.08-0.04)}$$

$$= £5.20$$

5.5 Example: Market value of shares (2)

Little Tortoise has a cost of equity of 10%. The company is expecting to pay dividends of 40p per share for the next five years and then 60p per share in perpetuity. What is the market value of each share?

Solution

Year	*Dividend*	*Discount factor*	*Present value*
	£	10%	£
1-5	0.40	*3.791	1.52
6-onwards	0.60	**6.209	3.73
			5.25

* Annuity factor 10% Period 5

** Annuity factor in perpetuity – annuity factor 1-5 = 1/0.1 – 3.791

Market value of each share is £5.25.

Exam focus point

Question 1 in November 2005 required a calculation of a share price given a dividend forecast. You need to be able to do such calculations quickly.

5.6 Example: Market value of shares (3)

Pocus paid a dividend this year of £3,000,000. The company expects the dividend to rise by 2% a year in perpetuity. This expectation is shared by the investors in the stock market. The current return expected by investors from shares in the same industry as Pocus is 11%.

(a) What would you expect the total market value of the shares of Pocus to be?

(b) If it is now rumoured in the stock market that interest rates are about to rise and so shareholders will want to earn an extra 1% on their shares, what change would you expect in the value of the shares of Pocus?

(c) What conclusion do you draw from this example?

Solution

$$P_0 = \frac{d_0(1+g)}{k_e - g}$$

(a) Predicted share value (return of 11%) = $\frac{£3{,}000{,}000(1.02)}{(0.11-0.02)}$ = £34,000,000

(b) Predicted share value (return of 12%) = $\frac{£3{,}000{,}000(1.02)}{(0.12-0.02)}$ = £30,600,000

The value of the company's shares would fall by £3,400,000.

(c) When interest rates are expected to go up, there may well be a fall in share prices. Similarly, expectations of a fall in interest rates may well result in an increase in share prices. This is because the required return on shares is likely to move approximately in step with changes in rates of interest on other investments.

Question — Dividend policy

Learning outcome: B(i)

The management of Crocus are trying to decide on the dividend policy of the company.

There are two options that are being considered.

(a) The company could pay a constant annual dividend of 8p per share.

(b) The company could pay a dividend of 6p per share next year, and use the retained earnings to achieve an annual growth of 3% in dividends for each year after that.

The shareholders' cost of capital is thought to be 18%. Which dividend policy would maximise the wealth of shareholders, by maximising the share price?

Answer

(a) With a constant annual dividend

$$\text{Share price} = \frac{8p}{0.18} = 44.4p$$

(b) With dividend growth

$$\text{Share price} = \frac{6p(1.03)}{(0.18-0.03)} = \frac{6.18}{0.15} = 41.2p$$

The constant annual dividend would be preferable.

5.7 The importance of the fundamental theory of share values

In general terms, fundamental analysis seems to be valid. This means that if an investment analyst can foresee before anyone else that:

(a) A **company's future profits** and **dividends** are going to be different from what is currently expected, or

(b) **Shareholders' cost of capital** will **rise or fall** (for example in response to interest rate changes)

then the analyst will be able to predict a future share price movement, and so recommend clients to buy or sell the share before the price change occurs.

In practice however, share price movements are affected by day to day fluctuations, reflecting

- Supply and demand in a particular period
- Investor confidence
- Market interest rate movements

Investment analysts want to be able to predict these fluctuations in prices, but **fundamental** analysis might be inadequate as a technique. Some analysts, known as **chartists**, therefore rely on **technical** analysis of share price movements.

5.8 Charting or technical analysis

Chartists or **'technical analysts'** attempt to predict share price movements by assuming that past price patterns will be repeated. There is no real theoretical justification for this approach, but it can at times be spectacularly successful. Studies have suggested that the degree of success is greater than could be expected merely from chance.

Key term

Technical analysis is the analysis of past movements in the prices of financial instruments, currencies, commodities etc, with a view to, by applying analytical techniques, predicting future price movements.

(OT 2005)

Chartists do not attempt to predict every price change. They are primarily interested in trend reversals, for example when the price of a share has been rising for several months but suddenly starts to fall.

Moving averages help the chartist to examine overall trends. For example, he may calculate and plot moving averages of share prices for 20 days, 60 days and 240 days. The 20 day figures will give a reasonable representation of the actual movement in share prices after eliminating day to day fluctuations. The other two moving averages give a good idea of longer term trends.

One of the main problems with chartism is that it is **often difficult to see a new trend until after it has happened**. By the time the chartist has detected a signal, other chartists will have as well, and the resulting mass movement to buy or sell will push the price so as to eliminate any advantage.

With the use of sophisticated computer programs to simulate the work of a chartist, academic studies have found that the **results obtained were no better or worse** than those obtained from a simple 'buy and hold' strategy of a **well diversified portfolio of shares.**

This may be explained by research that has found that there are no regular patterns or cycles in share price movements over time – they follow a **random walk.**

5.9 Random walk theory

Random walk theory is consistent with the fundamental theory of share values. It accepts that a share should have an intrinsic price dependent on the fortunes of the company and the expectations of investors. One of its underlying assumptions is that **all relevant information about a company is available to all potential investors** who will act upon the information in a **rational** manner.

The key feature of random walk theory is that although share prices will have an **intrinsic or fundamental value**, this value will be altered as new information becomes available, and that the behaviour of investors is such that the actual share price will fluctuate from day to day around the intrinsic value.

5.9.1 Random walks and an efficient stock market

Research was carried out in the late 1960s to explain why share prices in the stock market display a random walk phenomenon. This research led to the development of the **efficient market hypothesis**. It can be shown that random movements in share prices will occur if the stock market operates 'efficiently' and makes information about companies, earnings, dividends and so on, freely (or cheaply) available to all customers in the market. In displaying efficiency, the stock market also lends support to the fundamental analysis theory of share prices.

6 The efficient market hypothesis 11/05

FAST FORWARD

The theory behind share price movements can be explained by the three forms of the **efficient markets hypothesis.**

- **Weak form efficiency** implies that prices reflect all relevant information about past price movements and their implications.
- **Semi-strong form efficiency** implies that prices reflect past price movements and publicly available knowledge.
- **Strong form efficiency** implies that prices reflect past price movements, publicly available knowledge and inside knowledge.

6.1 The definition of efficiency

Key term

Efficient market hypothesis is the hypothesis that the stock market responds immediately to all available information, with the effect that an individual investor cannot, in the long run, expect to obtain greater than average returns from a diversified portfolio of shares. *(OT 2005)*

It has been argued that the UK and US stock markets are efficient capital markets, that is, markets in which:

(a) The prices of securities bought and sold **reflect all the relevant information** which is available to the buyers and sellers, ie share prices change quickly to reflect all new information about future prospects

(b) No individual dominates the market

(c) **Transaction costs** of buying and selling are not so high as to discourage trading significantly

If the stock market is efficient at processing information, share prices should vary in a rational way.

(a) If a company makes an **investment** with a **positive net present value** (NPV), shareholders will get to know about it and the **market price** of its shares **will rise** in anticipation of future dividend increases.

(b) If a company makes a **bad investment** shareholders will find out and so the **price** of its shares will **fall**.

(c) If **interest rates rise**, shareholders will want a **higher return** from their investments, so **market prices** will **fall**.

6.2 Types of efficiency

Different types of efficiency can be distinguished in the context of the operation of financial markets.

TYPES OF EFFICIENCY	
Allocative	Direction of funds towards firms making best use of them
Operational	Minimisation of transaction costs such as commissions, interest rate margins and loan arrangement fees.
Information processing	Reflects ability of stock market to absorb information, achieved when market prices of all securities reflect all available information. It has three forms: • Weak • Semi-strong • Strong

6.2.1 Weak form tests and weak form efficiency

The weak form hypothesis suggests that share prices take into account all relevant information about past price movements and their implications. Share prices do **not** change **in anticipation** of new information being announced. Share prices will move up and down without a predictable pattern, and past price movements are unlikely to be repeated.

6.2.2 Semi-strong form tests and semi-strong form efficiency

Semi-strong form tests attempt to show that the stock market displays semi-strong efficiency, by which we mean that current share prices reflect both:

- All **relevant information** about past **price movements** and their implications, and
- All **knowledge** which is available **publicly**

Tests to prove semi-strong efficiency have concentrated on the ability of the market to **anticipate share price changes** before new information is formally announced.

For example, if two companies plan a merger, share prices of the two companies will inevitably change once the merger plans are formally announced. The market would show semi-strong efficiency, however, if it were able to **anticipate** such an announcement, so that share prices of the companies concerned would change in advance of the merger plans being confirmed.

Semi-strong efficiency will mean that investors will not gain an advantage through studying company accounts or economic forecasts, since share prices will have already taken account of this information.

Research in both the UK and the USA has suggested that market prices anticipate mergers several months before they are formally announced, and the conclusion drawn is that the stock markets in these countries **do** exhibit semi-strong efficiency.

6.2.3 Strong form tests and strong form efficiency

A strong form test of market efficiency attempts to prove that the stock market displays a strong form of efficiency, by which we mean that share prices reflect all information available:

- From past price changes
- From public knowledge or anticipation
- From specialists' or experts' insider knowledge (eg investment managers)

In theory an expert, such as an investment manager, should be able to use his privileged access to additional information about companies to earn a higher rate of return than an ordinary investor. Unit trusts should in theory therefore perform better than the average investor. Research has suggested, however, that this expert skill does not exist.

6.3 Implications of efficient market hypothesis for the financial manager

If the markets are quite strongly efficient, the main consequence for financial managers will be that they simply need to **concentrate** on **maximising the net present value** of the **company's investments** in order to maximise the wealth of shareholders. Managers need not worry, for example, about the effect on share prices of financial results in the published accounts because investors will make **allowances** for **low profits** or **dividends** in the current year if higher profits or dividends are expected in the future. A company's real financial position will be reflected in its share price.

If the market is strongly efficient, there is little point in financial managers attempting strategies that attempt to mislead the markets and they need to realise what will cause prices to move in practice.

(a) There is no point for example in trying to identify a correct date when **shares** should be **issued**, since share prices will always reflect the true worth of the company – they will not be over or under valued at any point in time.

(b) The market will identify any attempts to **window dress the accounts** and put an optimistic spin on the figures. Directors should therefore focus on projects which earn high long-term net present values, even if their short-term rate of return is poor.

(c) The market will decide what **level of return** it requires for the risk involved in making an investment in the company. It is pointless for the company to try to change the market's view by issuing different types of capital instruments.

(d) **Large quantities of new shares** can be sold **without depressing the share price**. Directors may believe that the increase in the number of shares will lower the price, but studies suggest that this won't be the case if investors believe that the new shares will **generate a return** that is at least as high as the return on existing funds.

(e) Directors should take **signals from price movements** seriously. If directors are seeking to acquire another company, and on the day the acquisition is announced the share price falls drastically, this will clearly indicate the market's view of the merger.

Similarly if the company is looking to expand, the directors will be wasting their time if they seek as **takeover targets** companies whose shares are undervalued, since the market will fairly value all companies' shares.

Only if the market is semi-strongly efficient and the financial managers possess **inside information** that would significantly alter the price of the company's shares if released to the market could they perhaps gain an advantage. Attempts to take account of this inside information may breach insider dealing laws, however managers may seek to keep the share price artificially high by withholding unfavourable information from the public domain.

Exam focus point

Question 1 in November 2005 required an explanation of the influences over movements in share prices.

6.4 How efficient are stock markets in reality?

Evidence so far collected suggests that stock markets show efficiency that is at least weak form, but tending more towards a semi-strong form. In other words, current share prices reflect all or most publicly available information about companies and their securities.

6.5 Example: efficient market hypothesis

Company X has 3,000,000 shares in issue and company Y 8,000,000.

(a) On day 1, the market value per share is £3 for X and £6 for Y.

(b) On day 2, the management of Y decide, at a private meeting, to make a takeover bid for X at a price of £5 per share. The takeover will produce large operating savings with a present value of £8,000,000.

(c) On day 5, Y publicly announces an unconditional offer to purchase all shares of X at a price of £5 per share with settlement on day 20. Details of the large savings are not announced and are not public knowledge.

(d) On day 10, Y announces details of the savings which will be derived from the takeover.

Ignoring tax and the time value of money between day 1 and 20, and assuming the details given are the only factors having an impact on the share price of X and Y, determine the day 2, day 5 and day 10 share price of X and Y if the market is:

(a) Semi-strong form efficient
(b) Strong form efficient

in each of the following *separate* circumstances.

(a) The purchase consideration is cash as specified above.
(b) The purchase consideration, decided on day 2 and publicly announced on day 5, is five newly issued shares of Y for six shares of X.

Solution

(a) **Semi-strong form efficient market (i) cash offer**

With a semi-strong form of market efficiency, shareholders know all the relevant historical data and publicly available current information.

(i) Day 1 Value of X shares: £3 each, £9,000,000 in total.
Value of Y shares: £6 each, £48,000,000 in total.

(ii) Day 2 The decision at the **private** meeting does not reach the market, and so share prices are unchanged.

(iii) Day 5 The takeover bid is announced, but no information is available yet about the savings.

(1) The value of X shares will rise to their takeover bid price of £5 each, £15,000,000 in total.

(2) The value of Y shares will be as follows.

	£
Previous value (8,000,000 × £6)	48,000,000
Add value of X shares to be acquired, at previous market worth (3,000,000 × £3)	9,000,000
	57,000,000
Less purchase consideration for X shares	15,000,000
New value of Y shares	42,000,000
Price per share	£5.25

The share price of Y shares will fall on the announcement of the takeover.

(iv) Day 10 The market learns of the potential savings of £8,000,000 (present value) and the price of Y shares will rise accordingly to:

$$\frac{£42,000,000 + £8,000,000}{8,000,000 \text{ shares}} = £6.25 \text{ per share.}$$

The share price of X shares will remain the same as before, £5 per share.

Semi-strong form efficient market (ii) share exchange offer

(I) The share price will not change until the takeover is announced on day 5, when the value of the combined company will be perceived by the market to be (48 + 9) £57,000,000.

The number of shares in the enlarged company Y would be as follows.

Current	8,000,000
Shares issued to former X shareholders (3,000,000 × 5/6)	2,500,000
	10,500,000

The value per share in Y would change to reflect what the market expects the value of the enlarged company to be.

$$\frac{£57,000,000}{10,500,000} = £5.43 \text{ per share}$$

The value per share in X would reflect this same price, adjusted for the share exchange terms.

$$\frac{5}{6} \text{ of } £5.43 = £4.52$$

(ii) Day 10 The value of the enlarged company would now be seen by the market to have risen by £8,000,000 to £65,000,000 and the value of Y shares would rise to:

$$\frac{£65,000,000}{10,500,000} = £6.19 \text{ per share}$$

The value per X share would be:

$$\frac{5}{6} \text{ of } £6.19 = £5.16$$

(b) **Strong form efficient market (i) cash offer**

In a strong form efficient market, the market would become aware of **all** the relevant information when the private meeting takes place. The value per share would change as early as **day 2** to:

(i) X: £5
(ii) Y: £6.25

The share prices would then remain unchanged until day 20.

Strong form efficient market (ii) share exchange offer

In the same way, for the same reason, the value per share would change **on day 2** to:

(i) X: £5.16
(ii) Y: £6.19

and remain unchanged thereafter until day 20.

The different characteristics of a semi-strong form and a strong form efficient market thus affect the timing of share price movements, in cases where the relevant information becomes available to the market eventually. The difference between the two forms of market efficiency concerns when the share prices change, not by how much prices eventually change.

You should notice, however, that in neither case would the share prices remain unchanged until day 20. In a **weak form** efficient market, the price of Y's shares would not reflect the expected savings until after the savings had been achieved and reported, so that the takeover bid would result in a fall in the value of Y's shares for a considerable time to come.

Exam focus point

> Examiners' reports suggest that discussion on the efficient markets' hypothesis are often general, and not applied to the company described in the question.

6.6 Explaining share price movements

Various types of anomaly appear to support the views that irrationality often drives the stock market, including the following.

(a) **Seasonal month-of-the-year effects**, day-of-the-week effects and also hour-of-the-day effects seem to occur, so that share prices might tend to rise or fall at a particular time of the year, week or day.

(b) There may be a **short-run overreaction** to recent events.

(c) **Individual shares** or **shares in small companies** may be **neglected**.

Question **Market efficiency**

Learning outcome B(i)

Briefly describe the main forms of market efficiency.

Answer

It is often argued that the UK and US stock markets are **efficient capital markets**, in which:

(a) The prices at which securities are traded **reflect all the relevant information** that is available to buyers and sellers, meaning that prices change quickly to reflect all new information about future prospects.

(b) **No individual dominates** the market.

(c) **Transaction costs are not so high** as to impact significantly on the level of trading activity.

If the market is efficient, then share prices should vary in a rational way.

The main forms of market efficiency are usually defined in relation to the varying degrees of efficiency with which the market processes information, and are as follows.

Weak form. This form of the hypothesis contends that share prices reflect all relevant information about past price movements. Share prices do not change in anticipation of new information being announced. Since new information arrives unexpectedly, it follows that share prices should be expected to change in a random manner and therefore that definable trends in share prices should not exist.

Semi-strong form. This form of the hypothesis contends that share prices reflect both **all relevant information** about past price movements and their implications, and all knowledge that is **publicly available**. This means that it will be expected that share prices can anticipate the formal announcement of new information. For example, if two companies plan a merger, their share prices will inevitably change once the merger plans are formally announced.

The market would show semi-strong efficiency if it were able to anticipate such an announcement, so that share prices of the two companies would change in advance of the merger plans being confirmed. Research in the UK and the US suggests that this does happen in practice, with the conclusion being drawn that the stock markets in these countries do demonstrate semi-strong form efficiency.

Strong form. If the market displays strong form efficiency, it would react in both the ways described above, but in addition, prices would also reflect **information** from **insider knowledge** available only to experts such as investment managers. If this is the case, then it would follow that managers should not need to worry overmuch about the presentation of information in one year's accounts provided that they are taking decisions aimed at maximising the net worth of the firm in the long term. This does not seem to be borne out by the short-term nature of much decision making in quoted companies. In addition, an expert such as an investment manager should be able to use his privileged access to additional information about companies to earn a higher rate of return than an ordinary investor. However, if unit trust results do out-perform the market, the excess returns would seem to be absorbed by management charges, since there is no evidence that such funds consistently beat the market.

Exam focus point

Bear the efficient markets hypothesis in mind when discussing how a company's value might be affected by the financing or investment decisions it takes. Knowledge of **what** and **when** information will be incorporated into a quoted share price is likely to influence how and when information regarding financial management decisions is made public.

In particular, since current share prices can be crucial to the success or otherwise of takeover **bids and new share issues**, it will be important to be aware of how the market is likely to react to varying levels of information released. The market may not react predictably, nor in a way a business wants it to, if it does not have full information.

Chapter roundup

- A **financial intermediary** links those with surplus funds (eg **lenders**) to those with funds deficits (eg potential **borrowers**) thus providing **aggregation** and **economies of scale**, **risk pooling** and **maturity transformation**.
- **Commercial banks** provide payments mechanisms and means of storing wealth. They also act as providers of funds.
- **Merchant banks (investment banks)** provide various services, including business advice on mergers and takeovers.
- The **capital markets** and **money markets** are markets for long-term and short-term capital respectively.
- **International money and capital markets** are available for larger companies wishing to raise larger amounts of finance.
- **Fundamental analysis** is based on the theory that share prices can be derived from an analysis of **future dividends**.
- **Technical analysts** or **chartists** work on the basis that past price patterns will be repeated.
- **Random walk theory** is based on the idea that share prices will alter when **new information** becomes **available**.
- The theory behind share price movements can be explained by the three forms of the **efficient markets hypothesis.**
  - **Weak form efficiency** implies that prices reflect all relevant information about past price movements and their implications.
  - **Semi-strong form efficiency** implies that prices reflect past price movements and publicly available knowledge.
  - **Strong form efficiency** implies that prices reflect past price movements, publicly available knowledge and inside knowledge.

Quick quiz

1 Which of the following activities would **not** normally be undertaken by a merchant bank?

A Handling Stock Exchange business on behalf of clients
B Providing mortgage finance to individuals
C Acting as trustees
D Dealing in the gold and silver bullion markets

2 For short-term borrowing, a company will go to the **money markets/capital markets**? (Which?)

3 (a) From which does the **demand** for capital markets funds come: Individuals/Firms/Government? (Delete any that do not apply).

(b) From which does the **supply** of capital market funds come: Individuals/Firms/Government? (Delete any that do not apply).

4 Identify five types of capital market intermediaries.

5 What types of venture do venture capitalists typically invest in?

6 Which theory of share price behaviour does the following statement describe?

'The analysis of external and internal influences upon the operations of a company with a view to assisting in investment decisions.'

A Technical analysis
B Random walk theory
C Fundamental analysis theory
D Chartism

7 What is meant by 'efficiency', in the context of the efficient market hypothesis?

8 The different 'forms' of the efficient market hypothesis state that share prices reflect *which* types of information? Tick all that apply.

		Form of EMH	
	Weak	*Semi-strong*	*Strong*
No information	☐	☐	☐
All information in past share price record	☐	☐	☐
All other publicly available information	☐	☐	☐
Specialists' and experts' 'insider' knowledge	☐	☐	☐

9 Which theory makes which assertions?

(a)	Chartism	(i)	A share price can be expected to fluctuate around its 'intrinsic' value.
(b)	Random walk theory	(ii)	Past share price patterns tend to be repeated.
(c)	Fundamental analysis theory	(iii)	The value of a share is the discounted present value of all future expected dividends on the share, discounted at the shareholders' cost of capital.

Answers to quick quiz

1 B Merchant banks normally act for corporate clients, and not for individuals.

2 Money markets.

3 (a) and (b): You should have deleted none.

4 Any five of:

(a) Banks
(b) Building societies
(c) Insurance companies
(d) Pension funds
(e) Unit trust companies
(f) Investment trusts
(g) Stock Exchanges
(h) Venture capital organisations

5 (a) Business start-ups
(b) Business development capital
(c) Management buyouts
(d) Helping an owner to realise capital

6 C Fundamental analysis theory

7 Efficiency in processing information in the pricing of stocks and shares

8

	Form of EMH		
	Weak	*Semi-strong*	*Strong*
No information	☐	☐	☐
All information in past share price record	✓	✓	✓
All other publicly available information	☐	✓	✓
Specialists' and experts' 'insider' knowledge	☐	☐	✓

9 (a) (ii)
(b) (i)
(c) (iii)

Now try the question below from the Exam Question Bank

Number	Level	Marks	Time
Q12	Examination	25	45 mins

9

The cost of capital

Introduction

In this chapter we examine the concept of the **cost of capital**, which can be used as a **discount rate** in evaluating the investments of an organisation.

We base cost of equity calculations on the **dividend valuation model**, which we covered briefly in Chapter 8. In Chapters 11 and 12, we shall be looking at a way of establishing the cost of equity that takes risk into account: the **capital asset pricing model**.

Don't neglect the **cost of debt** though as this often causes students problems, in particular the distinction between the cost of irredeemable and cost of redeemable debt.

In the exam you may be asked to calculate the weighted average cost of capital and its component costs, either as a separate sub-question, or as part of a larger question, most likely an investment appraisal. Remember that questions won't just involve calculations; you may be asked to discuss the problems with the methods of calculation you've used or the relevance of the costs of capital to investment decisions.

You need to understand the effect on the costs of capital of a change in the **financing mix** of a company. We cover this effect in this chapter, and also in Chapter 15 in the context of company valuation.

Calculation of the cost of capital is a fundamental technique in this paper.

Topic list	Learning outcomes	Syllabus references	Ability required
1 Investment decisions, financing and the cost of capital	B(i)	B(9)	Evaluation
2 The cost of equity	B(i)	B(6)	Evaluation
3 The cost of debt	B(i)	B(8)	Evaluation
4 Special problems	B(i)	B(6),(8)	Evaluation
5 The weighted average cost of capital	B(i)	B(9)	Evaluation
6 Effect of gearing on cost of capital	B(i)	B(9)	Evaluation

1 Investment decisions, financing and the cost of capital

FAST FORWARD

The **cost of capital** is the rate of return that the enterprise must pay to satisfy the providers of funds, and it reflects the riskiness of the funding transaction.

1.1 The cost of capital

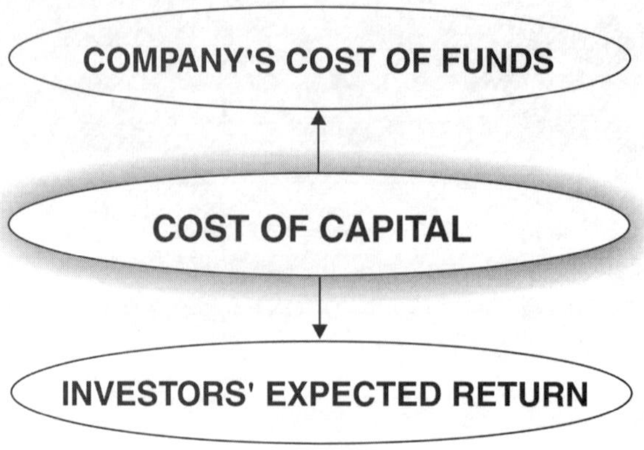

It is thus the **minimum return** that a company should make on its own investments, to earn the cash flows out of which investors can be paid their return.

Key term

Cost of capital is the minimum acceptable return on an investment, generally computed as a discount rate for use in investment appraisal exercises. The computation of the optimal cost of capital can be complex, and many ways of determining this opportunity cost have been suggested. *(OT 2005)*

1.2 The cost of capital as an opportunity cost of finance

The cost of capital, however it is measured, is an **opportunity cost of finance,** because it is the minimum return that investors require. If they do not get this return, they will transfer some or all of their investment somewhere else. Here are two examples.

(a) If a bank offers to lend money to a company, the interest rate it charges is the **yield** that the bank wants to receive from **investing** in the company, because it can get just as good a return from lending the money to someone else. In other words, the interest rate is the **opportunity cost** of lending for the bank.

(b) When shareholders invest in a company, the returns that they can expect must be sufficient to persuade them not to sell some or all of their shares and invest the money somewhere else. The yield on the shares is therefore the **opportunity cost** to the shareholders of not investing somewhere else.

1.3 The cost of capital and risk

The cost of capital has three elements.

Risk-free rate of return +
Premium for business risk +
Premium for financial risk

COST OF CAPITAL

(a) **Risk-free rate of return**

This is the return which would be required from an investment if it were completely free from risk. Typically, a risk-free yield would be the **yield on government securities**.

(b) **Premium for business risk**

This is an increase in the required rate of return due to the existence of **uncertainty about** the future and about a **firm's business prospects**. The actual returns from an investment may not be as high as they are expected to be. Business risk will be higher for some firms than for others, and some types of project undertaken by a firm may be more risky than other types of project that it undertakes.

(c) **Premium for financial risk**

This relates to the danger of high debt levels (high gearing). For ordinary shareholders, financial risk is evident in the variability of earnings after deducting payments to holders of debt capital. The higher the gearing of a company's capital structure, the greater will be the financial risk to ordinary shareholders, and this should be reflected in a higher risk premium and therefore a higher cost of capital.

Because different companies are in different types of business (varying **business risk**) and have different capital structures (varying **financial risk**) the cost of capital applied to one company may differ radically from the cost of capital of another.

2 The cost of equity

FAST FORWARD

The **dividend valuation model** can be used to estimate a **cost of equity**, on the assumption that the market value of shares is directly related to the expected future dividends from the shares.

2.1 The cost of ordinary share capital

New funds from equity shareholders are obtained either from **new issues of shares** or from **retained earnings**. Both of these sources of funds have a cost.

(a) Shareholders will **not** be prepared to **provide funds** for a **new issue** of **shares** unless the return on their investment is sufficiently attractive.

(b) Retained earnings also have a cost. This is an **opportunity cost**, the dividend forgone by shareholders.

2.2 The dividend valuation model

Key terms

Cum dividend or **cum div** means the purchaser of shares is entitled to receive the next dividend payment.

Ex dividend or **ex div** means that the purchaser of shares is not entitled to receive the next dividend payment

If we begin by ignoring share issue costs, the cost of equity, both for new issues and retained earnings, could be estimated by means of a **dividend valuation model**, on the assumption that the market value of shares is directly related to expected future dividends on the shares.

If the future dividend per share is expected to be **constant** in amount, then the **ex dividend** share price will be calculated by the formula:

$$P_0 = \frac{d}{(1+k_e)} + \frac{d}{(1+k_e)^2} + \frac{d}{(1+k_e)^3} + \ldots\ldots = \frac{d}{k_e}, \text{ so } k_e = \frac{d}{P_0}$$

where k_e is the shareholders' cost of capital

d is the annual dividend per share, starting at year 1 and then continuing annually in perpetuity.

P_0 is the ex-dividend share price (the price of a share where the share's new owner is **not** entitled to the dividend that is soon to be paid).

Exam Formula

Cost of ordinary (equity) share capital, paying an annual dividend d in perpetuity, and having a current ex div price P_0:

$$k_e = \frac{d}{P_0}$$

We shall look at the dividend valuation model again in Chapter 15, in the context of valuation of shares.

2.3 Example: Dividend valuation model

Cygnus has a dividend cover ratio of 4.0 times and expects zero growth in dividends. The company has one million £1 ordinary shares in issue and the market capitalisation (value) of the company is £50 million. After-tax profits for next year are expected to be £20 million.

What is the expected rate of return from the ordinary shares?

Solution

Total dividends = 20 million/4 = £5 million.

k_e = 5/50 = 10%.

2.4 Share issue costs and the cost of equity

The issue of shares, whether to the general public or as a rights issue, costs money and these costs should be considered in investment appraisal. Two approaches have been suggested.

(a) One approach is to **deduct issue costs** as a year 0 cash outflow of the project or projects for which the share capital is being raised. The issue costs would not affect the cost of equity capital.

(b) An alternative approach you might come across is to **calculate the cost of new equity** with the formula:

$$k_e = \frac{d}{P_0 - X}$$

where X represents the issue costs. Thus, if the issue price of a share is £2.50, issue costs are 20p per share, and new shareholders expect constant annual dividends of 46p, the cost of new equity would be:

$$\frac{46}{(250 - 20)} = 0.2 = 20\%$$

Approach (a) is recommended.

2.5 The dividend growth model

Shareholders will normally expect dividends to increase year by year and not to remain constant in perpetuity. The **fundamental theory of share values** states that the market price of a share is the present value of the discounted future cash flows of revenues from the share, so the market value given an expected constant annual growth in dividends would be:

$$P_0 = \frac{d_0(1+g)}{(1+k_e)} + \frac{d_0(1+g)^2}{(1+k_e)^2} + ...$$

where P_0 is the current market price (ex div)
d_0 is the current net dividend
k_e is the shareholders' cost of capital
g is the expected annual growth in dividend payments

and both k_e and g are expressed as proportions.

The **rate of growth in dividends** is sometimes expressed, theoretically, as:

$g = bR$

where g is the annual growth rate in dividends
b is the proportion of profits that are retained
R is the rate of return on new investments

This is **Gordan's growth model**

This formula assumes a **constant growth rate** in dividends, but it could easily be adapted for uneven growth. Capital growth through increases in the share price will arise from changed expectations about future dividend growth, or changes in the required return.

It is often convenient to assume a constant expected dividend growth rate in perpetuity. The formula above then simplifies to:

$$P_0 = \frac{d_0(1+g)}{(k_e - g)}$$

Re-arranging this, we get a formula for the ordinary shareholders' cost of capital.

Exam Formula

Cost of ordinary (equity) share capital, having a current ex div price, P_0, having just paid a dividend, d_0, with the dividend growing in perpetuity by a constant g% per annum:

$$k_e = \frac{d_0(1+g)}{P_0} + g, \text{ or } k_e = \frac{d_1}{P_0} + g$$

where d_1 is the dividend in year 1, so that:

$d_1 = d_0(1+g)$

Question

Cost of equity

Learning outcome: B(i)

A share has a current market value of 96p, and the last dividend was 12p. If the expected annual growth rate of dividends is 4%, calculate the cost of equity capital.

Answer

Cost of capital $= \frac{12(1+0.04)}{96} + 0.04$

$= 0.13 + 0.04$
$= 0.17$
$= 17\%$

Exam focus point

If an examination question requires you to calculate a cost of equity using the growth model, it is likely that you will be expected to predict the future growth rate from an analysis of the growth in dividends over the past few years.

2.6 Example: cost of capital (1)

The dividends and earnings of Hall Shores over the last five years have been as follows.

Year	*Dividends*	*Earnings*
	£	£
20X1	150,000	400,000
20X2	192,000	510,000
20X3	206,000	550,000
20X4	245,000	650,000
20X5	262,350	700,000

The company is financed entirely by equity and there are 1,000,000 shares in issue, each with a market value of £3.35 ex div.

(a) What is the cost of equity?

(b) What implications does dividend growth appear to have for earnings retentions?

Solution

The dividend growth model will be used.

(a) Dividends have risen from £150,000 in 20X1 to £262,350 in 20X5. The increase represents four years growth. (Check that you can see that there are four years growth, and not five years growth, in the table.) The average growth rate, g, may be calculated as follows.

$$\text{Dividend in 20X1} \times (1 + g)^4 = \text{Dividend in 20X5}$$

$$(1+g)^4 = \frac{\text{Dividend in 20X5}}{\text{Dividend in 20X1}}$$

$$= \frac{£262{,}350}{£150{,}000}$$

$$= 1.749$$

$$1 + g = \sqrt[4]{1.749} = 1.15$$

$$g = 0.15, \text{ ie } 15\%$$

The growth rate over the last four years is assumed to be expected by shareholders into the indefinite future, so the cost of equity, K_e, is:

$$\frac{d_0(1+g)}{P_0} + g = \frac{0.26235\,(1.15)}{3.35} + 0.15 = 0.24, \text{ ie } 24\%$$

(b) Retained profits will earn a certain rate of return and so growth will come from the yield on the retained funds.

Assume g = bR

where b = proportion of profits retained for reinvestment

R = yield on new investments (this is often taken to be the accounting rate of return:

$$\frac{\text{Profits}}{\text{Investment}} \text{ or } \frac{\text{Profits after taxation and preference dividends}}{\text{Equity}}$$

In our example, if we applied this assumption the future annual growth rate would be 15% if bR continued to be 15%. If the rate of return on new investments averages 24% (the cost of equity) and if the proportion of earnings retained is 62.5% (which it has been, approximately, in the period 20X1 – 20X5) then g = bR = 62.5% × 24% = 15%.

In chapters 11 and 12 we shall examine an alternative method of calculating the cost of equity, the **capital asset pricing model**, based on the risks a company faces and how its returns move in relation to stock market returns.

Question

Growth rate

Learning outcome: B(i)

The following figures have been extracted from the accounts of Mezzo:

Year	*Dividends*	*Earnings*
	€	€
20X1	100,000	350,000
20X2	125,000	400,000
20X3	125,000	370,000
20X4	160,000	450,000
20X5	200,000	550,000

You have been asked to calculate the cost of equity for the company. What growth rate would you use in the calculations?

Answer

Let 'g' = rate of growth in dividends.

Dividend in 20X1 × $(1 + g)^4$ = Dividend in 20X5

$(1 + g)^4$ = Dividend in 20X5 ÷ Dividend in 20X1

$(1 + g)^4$ = 200,000 ÷ 100,000

$(1 + g)^4$ = 2.0

$1 + g = \sqrt[4]{2}$

$1 + g = 1.19$

$g = 19\%$

2.7 Cost of preference shares

For preference shares the future cash flows are the dividend payments in perpetuity so that:

$$P_0 = \frac{d}{(1+k_{pref})} + \frac{d}{(1+k_{pref})^2} + \frac{d}{(1+k_{pref})^3} + \ldots.$$

where P_0 is the current market price of preference share capital after payment of the current dividend

d is the dividend received

k_{pref} is the cost of preference share capital

$$\frac{d}{(1+k_{pref})} + \frac{d}{(1+k_{pref})^2} + \frac{d}{(1+k_{pref})^3} \ldots..$$

simplifies to $\frac{d}{k_{pref}}$

Exam Formula

The cost of preference shares, can be calculated as $k_{pref} = \frac{d}{P_0}$.

Exam focus point

Don't forget that tax relief is **not given** for preference share dividends.

When calculating the weighted average cost of capital (see section 5), the cost of preferred shares is a separate component and should not be combined with the cost of debt or the cost of equity.

3 The cost of debt

FAST FORWARD

The **cost of debt** is the return an enterprise must pay to its lenders.

- For **irredeemable debt**, this is the (post-tax) interest as a percentage of the ex interest market value of the loan stock (or preferred shares).
- For **redeemable debt**, the cost is given by the internal rate of return of the cash flows involved.

3.1 The cost of debt capital

The cost of debt capital estimated above represents:

(a) The cost of **continuing to use the finance** rather than redeem the securities at their current market price.

(b) The cost of raising **additional fixed interest capital** if we assume that the cost of the additional capital would be equal to the cost of that already issued. If a company has not already issued any fixed interest capital, it may estimate the cost of doing so by making a similar calculation for another company which is judged to be similar as regards risk.

Exam focus point

Remember that different types of debt have different costs. The cost of a loan note will not be the same as the cost of a bank loan.

3.2 Irredeemable debt capital

Using the same logic as for preferred shares:

Cost of irredeemable debt capital, paying interest i in perpetuity, and having a current ex-div price P_0:

$$k_d = \frac{i}{P_0}$$

3.3 Example: cost of capital (1)

Lepus has issued loan notes of £100 nominal value with annual interest of 9% per year, based on the nominal value. The current market price of the loan notes is £90. What is the cost of the loan notes?

Solution

k_d = 9/90 =10%

3.4 Non-annual interest

If interest on loan capital is paid other than annually,

$$\text{Cost of loan capital} = \left(1+\frac{\text{Interest}}{\text{Ex interest price}}\right)^n - 1$$

where n = number of times interest is paid per year

3.5 Example: cost of capital (2)

Henryted has 12% irredeemable debentures in issue with a nominal value of £100. The market price is £95 ex interest. Calculate the cost of capital if interest is paid half-yearly.

Solution

If interest is 12% annually, therefore 6% is payable half-yearly.

$$\text{Cost of loan capital} = \left(1+\frac{6}{95}\right)^2 - 1 = 13.0\%$$

3.6 Redeemable debt capital

If the debt is **redeemable** then in the year of redemption the interest payment will be received by the holder as well as the amount payable on redemption, so:

$$P_0 = \frac{i}{(1+k_{d\,net})} + \frac{i}{(1+k_{d\,net})^2} + \ldots.. + \frac{i+p_n}{(1+k_{d\,net})^n}$$

where p_n = the amount payable on redemption in year n.

The above equation cannot be simplified, so 'r' will have to be calculated by trial and error, as an **internal rate of return (IRR)**.

The best trial and error figure to start with in calculating the cost of redeemable debt is to take the cost of debt capital as if it were irredeemable and then add the annualised capital profit that will be made from the present time to the time of redemption.

With **convertible** stock, the redemption **payment** is the market value of the shares into which the debt is to be converted.

3.7 Example: cost of capital (3)

Owen Allot has in issue 10% loan notes of a nominal value of £100. The market price is £90 ex interest. Calculate the cost of this capital if the debenture is:

(a) Irredeemable
(b) Redeemable at par after 10 years

Ignore taxation.

Solution

(a) **The cost of irredeemable debt capital** is $\frac{i}{P_0} = \frac{\pounds 10}{\pounds 90} \times 100\% = 11.1\%$

(b) **The cost of redeemable debt capital**. The capital profit that will be made from now to the date of redemption is £10 (£100 – £90). This profit will be made over a period of ten years which gives an annualised profit of £1 which is about 1% of current market value. The best trial and error figure to try first is therefore 12%.

Year		*Cash flow*	*Discount factor*	*PV*	*Discount factor*	*PV*
		£	12%	£	11%	£
0	Market value	(90)	1.000	(90.00)	1.000	(90.00)
1-10	Interest	10	5.650	56.50	5.889	58.89
10	Capital repayment	100	0.322	32.20	0.352	35.20
				(1.30)		+4.09

The approximate cost of redeemable debt capital is, therefore:

$$(11 + \frac{4.09}{(4.09 - -1.30)} \times 1) = 11.76\%$$

3.8 Debt capital and taxation

The interest on debt capital is likely to be an allowable deduction for purposes of taxation and so the cost of debt capital and the cost of share capital are not properly comparable costs. This tax relief on interest must be recognised in computations. The after-tax cost of irredeemable debt capital is:

$$k_{d\ net} = \frac{i(1-t)}{P_0}$$

where $k_{d\ net}$ is the cost of debt capital

i is the annual interest payment

P_0 is the current market price of the debt capital ex interest (that is, after payment of the current interest)

t is the rate of corporation tax

Exam formula

Cost of irredeemable debt capital, paying annual net interest $i(1 - t)$, and having a current ex-interest price P_0:

$$k_{d\ net} = \frac{i(1-t)}{P_0}$$

Therefore if a company pays £10,000 a year interest on irredeemable debt with a nominal value of £100,000 and a market price of £80,000, and the rate of tax is 30%, the cost of the debt would be:

$$\frac{10{,}000}{80{,}000}(1 - 0.30) = 0.0875 = 8.75\%$$

The higher the rate of tax is, the greater the tax benefits in having debt finance will be compared with equity finance. In the example above, if the rate of tax had been 50%, the cost of debt would have been, after tax:

$$\frac{10{,}000}{80{,}000}(1 - 0.50) = 0.0625 = 6.25$$

Exam focus point

Students often don't remember that debt attracts tax relief in most jurisdictions.

In the case of **redeemable debt**, the capital repayment is not allowable for tax. To calculate the cost of the debt capital to include in the weighted average cost of capital, it is necessary to calculate an internal rate of return which takes account of tax relief on the interest.

3.9 Example: cost of capital (4)

(a) A company has outstanding £660,000 of 8% loan notes on which the interest is payable annually on 31 December. The notes are due for redemption at par on 1 January 20X6. The market price of the stock at 28 December 20X2 was 103 cum interest. Ignoring any question of personal taxation, what do you estimate to be the current market rate of interest?

(b) If a new expectation emerged that the market rate of interest would rise to 12% during 20X3 and 20X4 what effect might this have in theory on the market price at 28 December 20X2?

(c) If the effective rate of tax was 30% what would be the percentage cost to the company of loan notes in (a) above? Tax is paid each 31 December on profits earned in the year ended on the previous 31 December.

Solution

(a) The current market rate of interest is found by calculating the pre-tax internal rate of return of the cash flows shown in the table below. We must subtract the current interest (of 8% per £100) from the current market price, and use this 'ex interest' market value. A discount rate of 10% is chosen for a trial-and-error start to the calculation.

Item and date		*Year*	*Cash flow*	*Discount factor*	*Present value*
			£	10%	£
Market value (ex int)	28.12.X2	0	(95)	1.000	(95.0)
Interest	31.12.X3	1	8	0.909	7.3
Interest	31.12.X4	2	8	0.826	6.6
Interest	31.12.X5	3	8	0.751	6.0
Redemption	1.1.X6	3	100	0.751	75.1
NPV					0.0

By coincidence, the market rate of interest is 10% since the NPV of the cash flows above is zero.

(b) If the market rate of interest is expected to rise in 20X3 and 20X4 it is probable that the market price in December 20X2 will fall to reflect the new rates obtainable. The probable market price would be the discounted value of all future cash flows up to 20X6, at a discount rate of 12%.

Item and date		*Year*	*Cash flow*	*Discount factor*	*Present value*
			£	12%	£
Interest	31.12.X2	0	8	1.000	8.0
Interest	31.12.X3	1	8	0.893	7.1
Interest	31.12.X4	2	8	0.797	6.4
Interest	31.12.X5	3	8	0.712	5.7
Redemption	1.1.X6	3	100	0.712	71.2
NPV					98.4

The estimated market price would be £98.4 per cent **cum** interest.

(c) Again we must deduct the current interest payable and use ex interest figures.

At a market value of 103

Item and date		*Year*	*Cash flow ex int*	*PV 5%*	*PV 8%*
			£	£	£
Market value		0	(95.0)	(95.0)	(95.0)
Interest	31.12.X3	1	8.0	7.6	7.4
Tax saved	31.12.X4	2	(2.4)	(2.2)	(2.1)
Interest	31.12.X4	2	8.0	7.3	6.9
Tax saved	31.12.X5	3	(2.4)	(2.1)	(2.0)
Interest	31.12.X5	3	8.0	6.9	6.4
Tax saved	31.12.X6	4	(2.4)	(2.0)	(1.8)
Redemption	1. 1.X6	3	100.0	86.4	79.4
NPV				6.9	(0.8)

The estimated cost of capital is: $5\% + (\frac{6.9}{(6.9 - -0.8)} \times 3\%) = 7.7\%$

Exam focus point

Make sure that you know the difference in methods for calculating the cost of irredeemable **and** redeemable debt, as this is often an weakness in exams.

3.10 The cost of floating rate debt

If a firm has variable or **'floating rate' debt**, then the cost of an equivalent fixed interest debt should be substituted. 'Equivalent' usually means fixed interest debt with a similar term to maturity in a firm of similar standing, although if the cost of capital is to be used for project appraisal purposes, there is an argument for using debt of the same duration as the project under consideration.

3.11 The cost of short-term funds

The cost of short-term funds such as bank loans and overdrafts is the current interest being charged on such funds.

4 Special problems

FAST FORWARD

There may be problems calculating the cost of sources of finance of organisations that are **not listed** on a stock exchange.

4.1 Private companies and the cost of equity

The cost of capital cannot be calculated from market values for **private companies** in the way that has been described so far, because the shares in a private company do not have a quoted market price. Since private companies do not have a cost of equity that can be readily estimated, it follows that a big problem for private companies which want to use DCF for evaluating investment projects is how to select a cost of capital for a discount rate.

The following approaches are possible:

(a) **Estimate** the **cost of capital** for similar public companies, but then add a **further premium** for additional business and financial risk

(b) Build up a cost of capital by adding **estimated premiums** for **business risk** and **financial risk** to the risk-free rate of return.

4.2 Government organisations and the cost of capital

The same problem faces government organisations. Government organisations do not have a market value, and most of them do not pay interest on much or all of the finance they receive. Government activities do not involve business risk, and there is no financial risk either for the investor, which is mainly the government itself. It is therefore impossible to calculate a cost of capital for government organisations. The problem is overcome in their case by using a target 'real' rate of return set by the Treasury.

4.3 The cost of equity capital: gross dividend or net dividend yield?

We have seen that the cost of equity is calculated on the basis of net dividends (perhaps with dividend growth). This selection of net dividends rather than gross dividends for the cost of equity requires some explanation. The net dividend is the appropriate choice because the **cost of capital** is used as the **discount rate** for the evaluation of capital projects by a company, and the company must have sufficient profits from its investments to pay shareholders the net dividends they require out of after-tax profits.

5 The weighted average cost of capital 11/05

FAST FORWARD

The **weighted average cost of capital** can be used to evaluate a business's investment projects if:

- The project is small relative to the business.
- The existing capital structure will be maintained (same financial risk).
- The project has the same business risk as the business.

The weighted average cost of capital is influenced by the **risk-free rate of return**, and the need to provide for extra return to compensate for the business and financial risks the business faces.

5.1 Computing a discount rate

We have looked at the costs of individual sources of capital for a company. But how does this help us to work out the cost of capital as a whole, or the discount rate to apply in DCF investment appraisals?

In many cases it will be difficult to associate a particular project with a particular form of finance. A company's funds may be viewed as a **pool of resources**. Money is withdrawn from this pool of funds to invest in new projects and added to the pool as new finance is raised or profits are retained. Under these circumstances it might seem appropriate to use an average cost of capital as the discount rate.

The correct cost of capital to use in investment appraisal is the **marginal cost of the funds** raised (or earnings retained) to finance the investment. The weighted average cost of capital (WACC) might be considered the most **reliable guide** to the **marginal cost of capital**, but only on the assumption that the company continues to invest in the future, in projects of a standard level of business risk, by raising funds in the same proportions as its existing capital structure.

Key term

Weighted average cost of capital is the average cost of the company's finance (equity, debentures, bank loans) weighted according to the proportion each element bears to the total pool of capital. Weighting is usually based on market valuations, current yields and costs after tax. *(OT 2005)*

5.2 General formula for the WACC

A general formula for the weighted average cost of capital (WACC) k_0 is as follows.

Exam formula

$$k_0 = k_e\left(\frac{V_E}{V_E + V_D}\right) + k_d\left(\frac{V_D}{V_E + V_D}\right)$$

where k_e is the cost of equity
k_d is the cost of debt
V_E is the market value of equity in the firm
V_D is the market value of debt in the firm

Preference shares can be added in if necessary as in the example below.

5.3 Example: weighted average cost of capital

An entity has the following information in its balance sheet.

	$'000
Ordinary shares of 50¢	2,500
8% preference shares of $1 each	1,500
12% unsecured loan notes	1,000

The ordinary shares are currently quoted at 130¢ each, the loan notes are trading at $72 per $100 nominal and the preference shares at 52¢ each. The ordinary dividend of 15¢ has just been paid with an expected growth rate of 10%. Corporation tax is currently 30%.

Calculate the weighted average cost of capital for this entity.

Solution

Market values:

		$'000
Equity (V_E):	$\frac{2,500}{0.5} \times 1.30$	6,500
Preference shares (V_P):	$1,500 \times 0.52$	780
Loan notes (V_D):	$1,000 \times 0.72$	720
		8,000

Cost of equity:

$$k_e = \frac{d_0(1+g)}{P_0} + g = \frac{0.15(1+0.1)}{1.3} + 0.1 = 0.2269 = 22.69\%$$

Cost of preference shares:

$$k_p = \frac{d}{P_0} = \frac{0.08}{0.52} = 0.1538 = 15.38\%$$

Cost of loan notes:

$$k_d = \frac{i(1-t)}{P_0} = \frac{0.12(1-0.3)}{0.72} = 0.1167 = 11.67\%$$

Weighted average cost of capital:

$$k_o = k_e\left(\frac{V_E}{V_E + V_P + V_D}\right) + k_p\left(\frac{V_P}{V_E + V_P + V_D}\right) + k_e\left(\frac{V_D}{V_E + V_P + V_D}\right)$$

$$V_E + V_P + V_D = 8{,}000$$

$$k_o = \left(22.69\% \times \frac{6{,}500}{8{,}000}\right) + \left(15.38\% \times \frac{780}{8{,}000}\right) + \left(11.67\% \times \frac{720}{8{,}000}\right)$$

$$= 18.43\% + 1.5\% + 1.05\% = 20.98\%$$

5.4 Weighting

Two methods of weighting could be used.

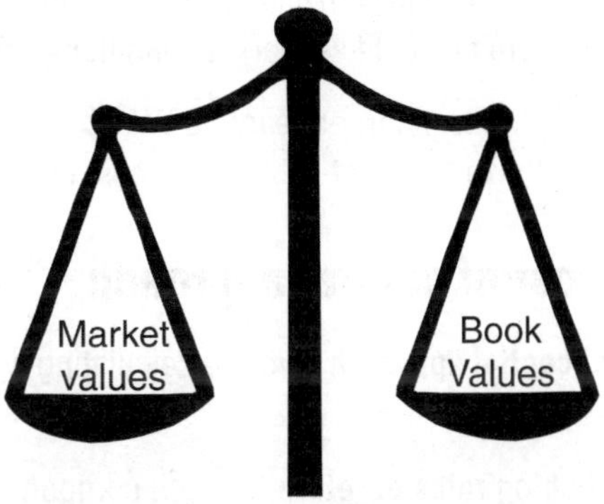

Although book values are often easier to obtain they are of doubtful economic significance. It is, therefore, more meaningful to use market values when data are available. For unquoted companies estimates of market values are likely to be extremely subjective and consequently book values may be used. When using market values it is not possible to split the equity value between share capital and reserves and only one cost of equity can be used. This removes the need to estimate a separate cost of retained earnings.

Exam focus point

Always use market values in an exam question unless you are told otherwise.

Question 4 of November 2005 required a calculation of the market value of equity using the capitalisation of earnings at the cost of capital.

5.5 Using the WACC in investment appraisal

The weighted average cost of capital can be used in investment appraisal if we make the following assumptions.

(a) New investments must be **financed** by **new sources of funds**: retained earnings, new share issues, new loans and so on.

(b) The cost of capital to be applied to project evaluation must **reflect** the **marginal cost** of new capital.

(c) The weighted average cost of capital **reflects** the **company's long-term future capital structure**, and capital costs. If this were not so, the current weighted average cost would become irrelevant because eventually it would not relate to any actual cost of capital.

5.6 Arguments against using the WACC

The arguments against using the WACC as the cost of capital for investment appraisal (as follows) are based on criticisms of the assumptions that are used to justify use of the WACC.

(a) New investments undertaken by a company might have different **business risk** characteristics from the company's existing operations. As a consequence, the return required by investors might go up (or down) if the investments are undertaken, because their business risk is perceived to be higher (or lower).

(b) The finance that is raised to fund a new investment might substantially change the capital structure and the perceived **financial risk** of investing in the company. Depending on whether the project is financed by equity or by debt capital, the perceived financial risk of the entire company might change. This must be taken into account when appraising investments.

(c) Many companies raise **floating rate** debt capital as well as fixed interest debt capital. With floating rate debt capital, the interest rate is variable, and is altered every three or six months or so in line with changes in current market interest rates. The cost of debt capital will therefore fluctuate as market conditions vary.

Floating rate debt is difficult to incorporate into a WACC computation, and the best that can be done is to substitute an 'equivalent' fixed interest debt capital cost in place of the floating rate debt cost.

5.7 Marginal cost of capital approach

The **marginal cost of capital** approach involves calculating a marginal cut-off rate for acceptable investment projects by:

(a) **Establishing rates of return** for each component of capital structure, except retained earnings, based on its value if it were to be raised under current market conditions

(b) **Relating dividends or interest** to these values to obtain a marginal cost for each component

(c) **Applying the marginal cost** to each component depending on its proportionate weight within the capital structure and adding the resultant costs to give a weighted average

It can be argued that the current weighted average cost of capital should be used to evaluate projects, where a company's capital structure changes only very slowly over time; then the marginal cost of new capital should be roughly equal to the weighted average cost of current capital.

Where gearing levels fluctuate significantly, or the finance for new project carries a significantly different level of risks to that of the existing company, there is good reason to seek an alternative marginal cost of capital.

5.8 Example: Marginal cost of capital

Georgebear has the following capital structure:

Source	*After tax cost*	*Market value*	*After tax cost × Market value*
	%	£m	
Equity	12	10	1.2
Preference	10	2	0.2
Existing loan notes	7.5	8	0.6
New loan notes		20	2.0

Weighted average cost of capital $= \dfrac{2 \times 100\%}{20}$

$= 10\%$

Georgebear's directors have decided to embark on major capital expenditure, which will be financed by a major issue of funds. The estimated project cost is £3,000,000, 1/3 of which will be financed by equity, 2/3 of which will be financed by loan notes. As a result of undertaking the project, the cost of equity (existing and new shares) will rise from 12% to 14%. The cost of preference shares and the cost of existing loan notes will remain the same, while the after tax cost of the new loan notes will be 9%.

Required

Calculate the company's new weighted average cost of capital, and its marginal cost of capital.

Solution

New weighted average cost of capital

Source	*After tax cost*	*Market value*	*After tax cost × Market value*
	%	£m	
Equity	14	11	1.54
Preference	10	2	0.20
Existing loan notes	7.5	8	0.60
New loan notes	9	2	0.18
		23	2.5

$$\text{WACC} = \frac{2.52 \times 100\%}{23}$$

$$= 11.0\%$$

$$\text{Marginal cost of capital} = \frac{(2.52 - 2.0) \times 100\%}{23 - 20}$$

$$= 17.3\%$$

6 Effect of gearing on cost of capital

FAST FORWARD

The **traditional theory of cost of capital** suggests that WACC is influenced by gearing; **Modigliani and Miller** disagree.

6.1 Effect of gearing

There are two main theories about the effect of changes in gearing on the weighted average cost of capital (WACC) and share values. These are the '**traditional**' **view**, and the **net operating income approach** (Modigliani and Miller).

The assumptions on which these theories are based are as follows:

(a) The company **pays out** all its **earnings** as **dividends.**

(b) The **gearing** of the company **can be changed immediately** by issuing debt to repurchase shares, or by issuing shares to repurchase debt. There are no transaction costs for issues.

(c) The earnings of the company are **expected to remain constant in perpetuity** and all investors share the same expectations about these future earnings.

(d) **Business risk** is also **constant**, regardless of how the company invests its funds.

(e) **Taxation**, for the time being, is **ignored**.

6.2 The traditional view of WACC

FAST FORWARD

Under the **traditional theory of cost of capital**, the cost declines initially and then rises as gearing increases. The **optimal capital structure** will be the point at which WACC is lowest.

The **traditional view** is as follows:

(a) As the **level of gearing increases**, the **cost of debt** remains **unchanged** up to a certain level of gearing. Beyond this level, the cost of debt will increase.

(b) The **cost of equity** rises as the level of **gearing increases.**

(c) The **weighted average cost of capital** does **not remain constant**, but rather falls initially as the proportion of debt capital increases, and then begins to increase as the rising cost of equity (and possibly of debt) becomes more significant.

(d) The **optimum level of gearing** is where the **company's weighted average cost of capital is minimised**.

The traditional view about the cost of capital is illustrated in the following figure. It shows that the weighted average cost of capital will be minimised at a particular level of gearing P.

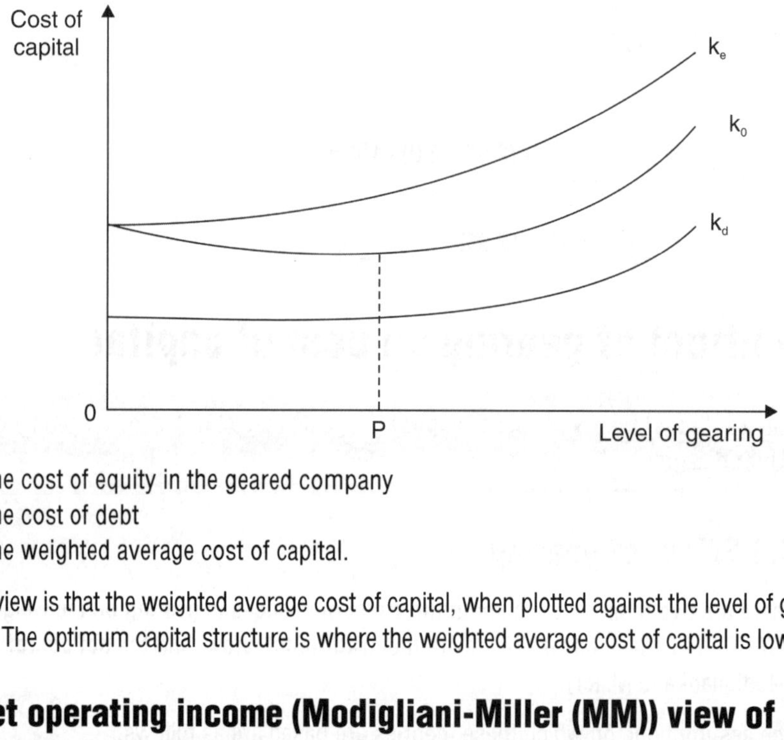

where k_e is the cost of equity in the geared company
k_d is the cost of debt
k_0 is the weighted average cost of capital.

The traditional view is that the weighted average cost of capital, when plotted against the level of gearing, is saucer shaped. The optimum capital structure is where the weighted average cost of capital is lowest, at point P.

6.3 The net operating income (Modigliani-Miller (MM)) view of WACC

FAST FORWARD

Modigliani and Miller stated that, in the absence of tax, a company's **capital structure** would have **no impact** upon its WACC.

The net operating income approach takes a different view of the effect of gearing on WACC. In their 1958 theory, Modigliani and Miller (MM) proposed that the total market value of a company, in the absence of tax, will be determined only by two factors:

- The **total earnings** of the company
- The **level of operating (business) risk** attached to those earnings

The total market value would be computed by discounting the total earnings at a rate that is appropriate to the level of operating risk. This rate would represent the WACC of the company.

Thus Modigliani and Miller concluded that **the capital structure of a company would have no effect on its overall value or WACC**.

6.3.1 Assumptions of net operating income approach

Modigliani and Miller made various assumptions in arriving at this conclusion, including:

(a) A **perfect capital market** exists, in which investors have the same information, upon which they act rationally, to arrive at the same expectations about future earnings and risks.

(b) There are no **tax or transaction costs**.

(c) **Debt is risk-free** and freely available at the same cost to investors and companies alike.

Modigliani and Miller justified their approach by the use of **arbitrage**.

Key term

Arbitrage is the simultaneous purchase and sale of a security in different markets, with the aim of making a risk-free profit through the exploitation of any price difference between the markets. *(OT 2005)*

Arbitrage can be used to show that once all opportunities for profit have been exploited, the market values of two companies with the same earnings in equivalent business risk classes will have moved to an equal value.

Exam focus point

The proof of Modigliani and Miller's theory by arbitrage is not examinable.

If Modigliani and Miller's theory holds, it implies:

(a) The **cost of debt remains unchanged** as the level of gearing increases.

(b) The **cost of equity rises** in such a way as to keep the **weighted average cost of capital constant**.

This would be represented on a graph as shown below.

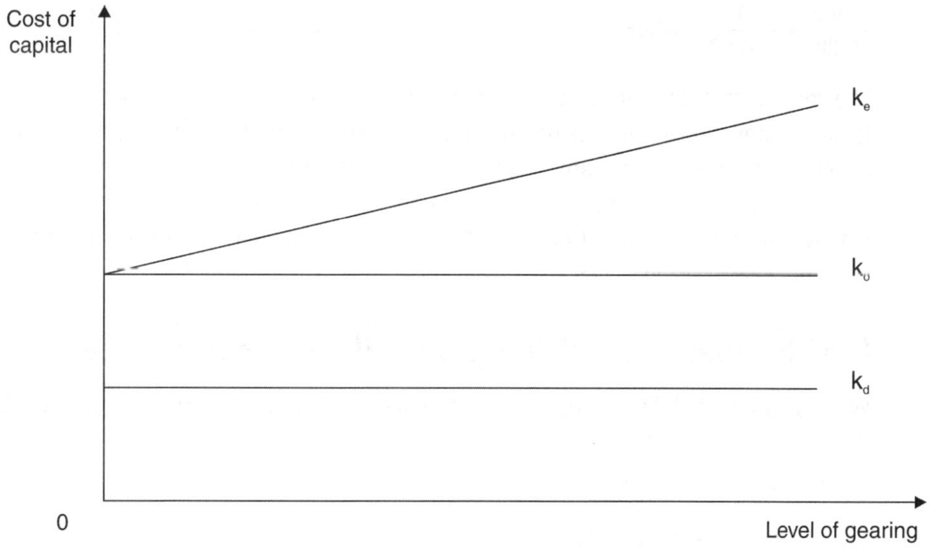

6.4 Example: net operating income approach

A company has £5,000 of debt at 10% interest, and earns £5,000 a year before interest is paid. There are 2,250 issued shares, and the weighted average cost of capital of the company is 20%.

The market value of the company should be as follows.

Earnings	£5,000
Weighted average cost of capital	0.2
	£
Market value of the company (£5,000 ÷ 0.2)	25,000
Less market value of debt	5,000
Market value of equity	20,000

The cost of equity is therefore $\frac{5{,}000 - 500}{20{,}000} = \frac{4{,}500}{20{,}000} = 22.5\%$

and the market value per share is $\frac{4{,}500}{2{,}250} \times \frac{1}{0.225} = £8.89$

Suppose that the level of gearing is increased by issuing £5,000 more of debt at 10% interest to repurchase 562 shares (at a market value of £8.89 per share) leaving 1,688 shares in issue.

The weighted average cost of capital will, according to the net operating income approach, remain unchanged at 20%. The market value of the company should still therefore be £25,000.

Earnings	£5,000
Weighted average cost of capital	0.2
	£
Market value of the company	25,000
Less market value of debt	10,000
Market value of equity	15,000

Annual dividends will now be £5,000 – £1,000 interest = £4,000.

The cost of equity has risen to $\frac{4{,}000}{15{,}000}$ = 26.667% and the market value per share is still:

$$\frac{4{,}000}{1{,}688} \times \frac{1}{0.2667} = £8.89$$

The conclusion of the net operating income approach is that the level of gearing is a matter of indifference to an investor, because it does not affect the market value of the company, nor of an individual share. This is because as the level of gearing rises, so does the cost of equity in such a way as to keep both the weighted average cost of capital and the market value of the shares constant. Although, in our example, the dividend per share rises from £2 to £2.37, the increase in the cost of equity is such that the market value per share remains at £8.89.

6.5 The Modigliani-Miller propositions, ignoring taxes

We can now set out the propositions of Modigliani and Miller, ignoring tax relief on the interest charged on debt capital.

The following symbols will be used.

V_u = the market value of an ungeared (all equity) company

V_D = the market value of the debt capital in a geared company which is similar in every respect to the ungeared company (same profits before interest and same business risk) except for its capital structure. The debt capital is assumed, for simplicity, to be irredeemable.

V_E = the market value of the equity in the geared company

k_{eu} = the cost of equity in an ungeared company

k_{eg} = the cost of equity in the geared company

k_d = the cost of debt capital

The total market value of the geared company V_g is then equal to $(V_E + V_D)$.

6.5.1 The total market value of a company and the WACC (ignoring taxation)

MM suggested that the total market value of any company is independent of its capital structure, and is given by discounting its expected return at the appropriate rate. The value of a geared company is therefore as follows.

$$V_g = V_u$$

$$V_g = \frac{\text{Profit before interest}}{\text{WACC } (k_0 = k_{eu})}$$

$$V_u = V_g = \frac{\text{Earnings in an ungeared company}}{k_{eu}}$$

Note that since WACC (k_0) is unaltered by gearing, $k_0 = k_{eu}$ under this theory.

6.5.2 The cost of equity in a geared company (ignoring taxation)

MM went on to argue that the **expected return on a share** in a **geared company** equals the expected cost of equity in a similar but ungeared company, plus a premium related to financial risk.

The **premium for financial risk** can be calculated as the debt/equity ratio multiplied by the difference between the cost of equity for an ungeared company and the risk-free cost of debt capital.

Exam Formula

$$k_{eg} = k_0 + [(k_0 - k_d) \times \frac{V_D}{V_E}]$$

Note the following points.

(a) The part of the formula to the right of the plus sign is the value of the premium for financial risk.

(b) The formula requires the debt ratio (debt: equity) to be used rather than the more common debt: (debt + equity).

(c) Market values are used, not book values.

6.6 Example: MM, ignoring taxation (1)

The cost of equity in Minehead, an all equity company, is 15%. The WACC is therefore also 15%.

Another company, Dunster, is identical in every respect to the first, except that it is geared, with a debt: equity ratio of 1:4. The cost of debt capital is 5% and this is a risk-free cost of debt. What is Dunster's WACC?

Solution

k_{eg} = 15% + ((15 – 5)% × ¼) = 17.5%.

	Weighting	*Cost*	*Product*
Equity	80%	17.5%	14%
Debt	20%	5.0%	1%
		WACC =	15%

The WACC in the geared company is the same as in the ungeared company.

6.7 Example: MM, ignoring taxation (2)

Loesch is an all equity company and its cost of equity is 12%.

Berelco is similar in all respects to Loesch, except that it is a geared company, financed by £1,000,000 of 3% debentures (current market price £50 per cent) and 1,000,000 ordinary shares (current market price £1.50 ex div).

What is Berelco's cost of equity and weighted average cost of capital?

Solution

$$k_d = 3\% \times \frac{100}{50} = 6\%$$

$$k_{eg} = 12\% + [(12\% - 6\%) \times \frac{500}{1{,}500}] = 14\%$$

	Market value		*Cost*		
	£'000				£'000
Equity	1,500	×	0.14	=	210
Debt	500	×	0.06	=	30
	2,000				240

$$WACC = \frac{240}{2{,}000} = 0.12 = 12\%$$

This is the same as Loesch's WACC. As gearing is introduced, the cost of equity rises, but in such a way that the WACC does not change.

6.8 Weaknesses in MM theory

MM theory has been criticised on three main grounds.

(a) The **risks** for the investor may **differ** between **personal gearing** and **corporate gearing**, and the **cost** of borrowing for an **individual** is likely to be **higher** than the cost of borrowing for a company. MM's arbitrage 'proof' depends upon the assumptions that assume that the risk and cost is the same for personal and corporate borrowers.

(b) **Transaction costs** will restrict the arbitrage process.

(c) MM theory initially ignored **tax implications** (discussed below).

Further weaknesses in the MM theory are as follows.

(a) In practice, it may be **impossible to identify firms** with **identical business risk** and **operating characteristics**.

(b) Some **earnings may be retained** and so the simplifying assumption of paying out all earnings as dividends would not apply.

(c) Investors are **assumed to act rationally** which may not be the case in practice.

MM have acknowledged that **when the level of gearing becomes high**, **the cost of debt will rise**. They argue, however, that this does not affect the weighted average cost of capital because the cost of equity falls at the same time as risk-seeking investors are attracted to buying shares in the company.

When a company's gearing reaches very high levels, it may be perceived as being in danger of insolvency, and its market value will be very low (instead of being very high, as MM would predict). MM ignored the possibility of **bankruptcy**, and so their theory may not be valid at very high levels of gearing.

6.9 Modigliani-Miller theory adjusted for taxation

Exam focus point

> Remember, follow any assumptions about taxation given in questions carefully. Tax rates assumed will not necessarily be those that currently apply in the real world.

Allowing for taxation reduces the cost of debt capital by multiplying it by a factor $(1 - T_c)$ where T_c is the rate of tax (assuming the debt to be irredeemable). So far, our analysis of MM theory has ignored the tax relief on debt interest, which makes debt capital cheaper to a company, and therefore reduces the weighted average cost of capital where a company has debt in its capital structure.

MM modified their theory to admit that tax relief on interest payments does lower the weighted average cost of capital. They claimed that the weighted average cost of capital will continue to fall, up to gearing of 100%.

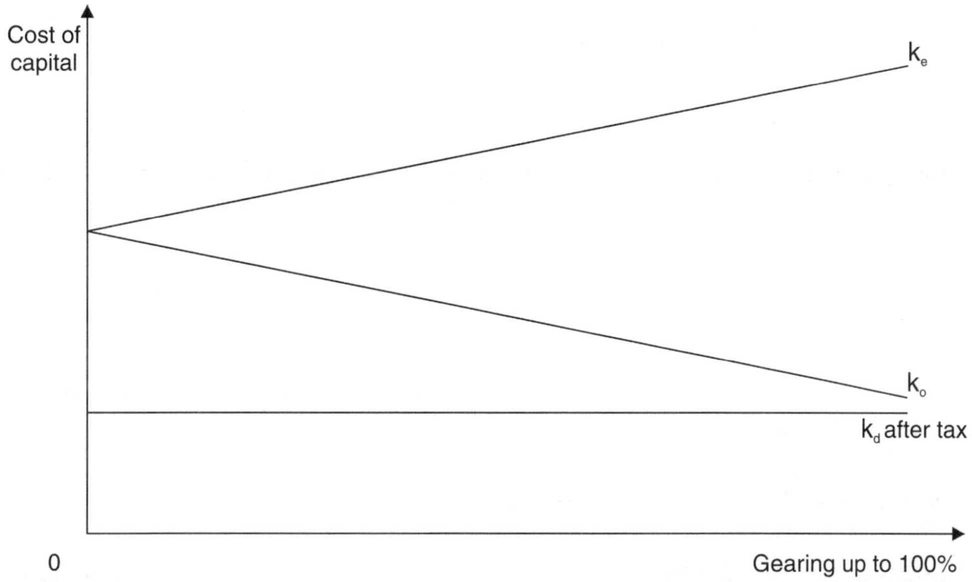

6.10 Adjustment to the MM cost of equity formula to allow for taxes

The formula for the cost of equity in a geared company becomes:

Exam Formula

$$k_{eg} = k_{eu} + [k_{eu} - k_d] \frac{V_D (1 - t)}{V_E}$$

where t is the corporation tax rate and k_d is the pre-tax (gross) cost of debt capital.

The financial risk premium is adjusted by a factor of $(1 - t)$.

6.11 The adjusted cost of capital

From this formula we can derive the following formula:

Exam Formula

$$r^* = r(1 - T^*L) \text{ or } k_{adj} = k_{eu}(1 - tL)$$

where r^* is the weighted average cost of capital of a geared company

r is the cost of equity and the WACC of a similar ungeared company

T^* is the tax saving due to interest payments expressed as a decimal, usually equal to the tax rate (t)

L is equivalent to $\frac{V_D}{V_D + V_E}$

6.11.1 Usefulness of adjusted cost of capital

This adjusted cost of capital is an **opportunity cost**, reflecting the **financing side-effects of projects** undertaken. The formula works exactly for any project that is expected to generate a level cash flow in perpetuity and to support permanent debt. The formula also works as a reasonable approximation for projects with limited lives or irregular cash flow streams.

6.12 Example (continued)

Thus, assuming a corporation tax rate of 30%, Dunster's cost of equity, using the information above, would be:

$$15\% + (1 - 0.30)\ [(15\% - 5\%) \times {}^{1}/_{4}] = 16.75\%$$

and its WACC would be:

$$15\% \left[1 - \frac{0.30 \times 1}{(1+4)}\right] = 15\% \times 0.94 = 14.1\%$$

This is below the ungeared company's WACC which is 15%. So higher gearing reduces the WACC.

Question WACC

Learning outcome: B(i)

Apply the formulae given above to find the cost of equity and WACC for Berelco, using the information given. The tax rate is 30%.

Answer

Berelco's cost of equity would be:

$$12\% + [(12 - 6)\% \times \frac{500(1 - 0.30)}{1{,}500}] = 13.4\%$$

and its WACC would be:

$$12\% \left[1 - \frac{0.30 \times 500}{1{,}500 + 500}\right] = 12\% \times 0.925 = 11.1\%$$

This is below Loesch's WACC of 12%.

6.13 Is there an optimum level of gearing?

We have now seen that MM modified their theory to say that when taxation is taken into account, the WACC will continue to fall as the level of gearing increases. The arbitrage process still operates, although the actions of investors will be influenced by their personal rates of taxation.

MM argued that since WACC falls as gearing rises, and the value of a company should rise as its WACC falls, **the value of a geared company will always be greater than its ungeared counterpart**, but only by the amount of the debt-associated tax saving of the geared company, assuming a permanent change in gearing.

Exam Formula

$$V_g = V_u + TB_c$$

where V_u is the value of the ungeared company, V_g is the value of the similar (equivalent) geared company, and TB_c total tax benefit.

The additional amount of value in the geared company, TB_c , is known as the value of the **'tax shield'** on debt.

We shall look further at this equation in Chapter 15.

6.14 Empirical testing and conclusion

It might be imagined that empirical testing should have been carried out by now either to prove or to disprove MM theory. Given, however, that MM accept that the weighted average cost of capital declines after allowing for tax, and that traditional theorists argue in favour of a flattish bottom to the weighted average cost of capital curve, it is very difficult to prove that one theory is preferable to the other.

Question — WACC and gearing

Learning outcome: B(i)

The cost of equity in an ungeared company is 18%. The cost of risk free debt capital is 8%.

(a) What is the cost of equity in a similar geared company, according to MM, which is 75% equity financed and 25% debt financed, assuming corporation tax at a rate of 30%?

(b) What is the WACC of the geared company, allowing for taxation?

Answer

(a) $k_{eg} = 18\% + \left[(18-8)\%\times\frac{25(1-0.30)}{75}\right] = 20.333\%$

(b) $r^* = r\left[1-\frac{T^*\times V_D}{(V_E+V_D)}\right] = 18\%\left[1-\frac{25\times 0.30}{(75+25)}\right]$

$= 18\% \times 0.925 = 16.7\%$

TOPCIMA link

In the TOPCIMA exam, you may be told the business's capital structure is to be maintained or have to consider the potential impact on capital structure of various proposals.

Question — WACC

Learning outcome B(i)

(a) What is meant by the 'weighted average cost of capital' of a company? Why do many companies use it as a discount rate in investment appraisal?

(b) Explain how this cost of capital is calculated and discuss the components required. (Detailed mathematical calculations are not required.)

Answer

(a) The **weighted average cost of capital** (WACC) is the **average cost** of the different elements within the capital structure of a company, using weightings based on the market values of each of the different elements.

In many cases it will be difficult to associate a particular project with a particular form of finance. A company's funds may be viewed as a pool of resources. Money is withdrawn from this pool of funds to invest in new projects and added to the pool as new finance is raised or profits are retained. Under these circumstances it might seem appropriate to use an average cost of capital as a discount rate.

The correct cost of capital to use in investment appraisal is the **marginal cost** of the funds raised (or earnings retained) to finance the investment. The WACC might be considered the most reliable guide to the marginal cost of capital, but only on the assumption that the company continues to invest in the future, in projects of a standard level of business risk, by raising funds in the same proportions as its existing capital structure.

(b) The WACC can be expressed using the formula:

$$\text{WACC} = k_e\left(\frac{V_E}{V_E + V_D}\right) + k_d\left(\frac{V_D}{V_E + V_D}\right)$$

where k_e = cost of equity
k_d = cost of debt
V_E = market value of equity in the firm
V_D = market value of debt in the firm

The cost of capital is the **cost of funds** that a company raises and uses, and the return that investors expect to be paid for putting funds into the company. It is therefore the minimum return that a company should make on its own investments to earn the cash flows out of which investors can be paid their return.

New equity funds are obtained from new issues of shares and from retained earnings. The costs of these funds are effectively the rate of return required by shareholders. In the case of retained earnings, the cost is the opportunity cost of the dividend forgone by the shareholders.

The cost of equity, both for new issues and retained earnings, is often estimated using the **dividend valuation model**, on the assumption that the market value of shares is directly related to expected future dividends on the shares.

Estimating the cost of **fixed interest** or fixed dividend capital is much easier than estimating the cost of ordinary share capital because the interest received by the holder of the security is fixed by contract and will not fluctuate.

The cost of debt capital already issued is the **rate of interest** (the internal rate of return) which equates the current market price with the discounted future cash receipts from the security.

Since the interest on debt capital is an allowable deduction for tax purposes, this should be taken into account in computing the cost of debt capital so as to make it properly comparable with the cost of equity.

If a firm has floating rate debt, the cost of an equivalent fixed interest debt should be substituted. This means debt with a similar term to maturity in a firm of similar standing. The cost of short-term funds such as bank loans and overdrafts is the current rate of interest being charged on such funds.

Weightings should be based on market values where possible because they have greater economic significance than book values.

Chapter roundup

- The **cost of capital** is the rate of return that the enterprise must pay to satisfy the providers of funds, and it reflects the riskiness of the funding transaction.
- The **dividend valuation model** can be used to estimate a cost of equity, on the assumption that the market value of shares is directly related to the expected future dividends on the shares.
- The **cost of debt** is the return an enterprise must pay to its lenders.
  - For **irredeemable debt**, this is the (post-tax) interest as a percentage of the ex interest market value of the loan stock (or preference shares).
  - For **redeemable debt**, the cost is given by the internal rate of return of the cash flows involved.
- There may be problems calculating the cost of sources of finance for organisations that are **not listed** on a stock exchange.
- The **weighted average cost of capital** can be used to evaluate a business's investment projects if:
  - The project is small relative to the business.
  - The existing capital structure will be maintained (same financial risk).
  - The project has the same business risk as the business.
- The weighted average cost of capital is influenced by the **risk-free rate of return**, and the need to provide for extra return to compensate for the business and financial risks the organisation faces.
- The **traditional theory of cost of capital** suggests that WACC is influenced by gearing; **Modigliani and Miller** disagree.
- Under the **traditional theory of cost of capital**, the cost declines initially and then rises as gearing increases. The **optimal capital structure** will be the point at which WACC is lowest.
- Modigliani and Miller stated that, in the absence of tax, a company's **capital structure** would have **no impact** upon its WACC.

Quick quiz

1 The cost of capital has three elements. Which of the following is not one of these elements?

A The market rate of return
B The premium for business risk
C The premium for financial risk
D The risk-free rate of return

2 'The minimum acceptable return on an investment, generally computed as a hurdle rate for use in investment appraisal exercises' *(CIMA Official Terminology)*. What does this define?

3 A share has a current market value of 120c and the last dividend was 10c. If the expected annual growth rate of dividends is 5%, calculate the cost of equity capital.

4 Explain how gearing affects the risk borne by ordinary shareholders.

5 Identify the variables k_e, d_1, P_0 and g in the following dividend valuation model formula.

$$k_e = \frac{d_1}{P_0} + g$$

6 Identify the variables k_e, k_d, V_E and V_D in the following weighted average cost of capital formula.

$$k_0 = k_e\left(\frac{V_E}{V_E + V_D}\right) + k_d\left(\frac{V_D}{V_E + V_D}\right)$$

7 When calculating the weighted average cost of capital, which of the following is the preferred method of weighting?

A Book values of debt and equity
B Average levels of the market values of debt and equity (ignoring reserves) over five years
C Current market values of debt and equity (ignoring reserves)
D Current market values of debt and equity (plus reserves)

8 What is the cost of $1 irredeemable debt capital paying an annual rate of interest of 7%, and having a current market price of $1.50?

Answers to quick quiz

1 A The market rate of return

2 The cost of capital

3 $\frac{10(1+0.05)}{120} + 0.05 = 13.75\%$

4 If gearing is higher, the variability of earnings after deducting payments to holders of debt capital is higher. If the rate of return exceeds the rate of interest paid on debt, this works to ordinary shareholders' advantage. If it does not, ordinary shareholders' returns are reduced by gearing.

5 k_e is the shareholders' cost of capital
d_1 is the dividend in year 1
P_0 is the current market price (ex div)
g is the expected annual growth in dividend payments

6 k_e is the cost of equity
k_d is the cost of debt
V_E is the market value of equity in the firm
V_D is the market value of debt in the firm

7 C Current market values of debt and equity (ignoring reserves)

8 Cost of debt = $\frac{0.07}{1.50}$ = 4.67%

Now try the questions below from the Exam Question Bank

Number	Level	Marks	Time
Q13	Examination	25	45 mins
Q14	Examination	20	36 mins

10

The capital structure decision

Introduction

This chapter looks at the question of what a company's **financial structure** should be. Choosing the best possible capital structure is a key strategic decision. However we shall see that companies often face a conflict between choosing the structure that is most **suitable** in an ideal world, and a structure that is **acceptable** to stakeholders and is **feasible** in terms of the sources of finance available. Section 1 of this chapter covers how companies can determine what structure is suitable, whilst Section 2 covers stakeholder attitudes and other possible restrictions.

The capital structure chosen will have a major effect on investor ratios and hence on how stock markets judge the company. In Section 3 we examine how gearing impacts upon the key ratios that you will have encountered in previous studies.

Topic list	Learning outcomes	Syllabus references	Ability required
1 The gearing decision	B(i)	B(10)	Evaluation
2 Restrictions on capital structure	B(i)	B(10)	Evaluation
3 Effects of capital structure on ratios	B(i)	B(11)	Evaluation

1 The gearing decision 5/05, 11/05

FAST FORWARD

Gearing must be considered when deciding how to finance a business.

Factors determining the **suitability** of capital structure include the **stability** of the company's situation, matching of assets and funds, **impact on shareholders**, the possibility of **international finance** and the **cost** and **flexibility** of sources available.

1.1 Principles of capital structure

Key term

Capital structure refers to the way in which an organisation is financed, by a combination of long-term capital (ordinary shares and reserves, preferred shares, loan notes, bank loans, convertible loan stock and so on) and short-term liabilities, such as a bank overdraft and trade payables. The mix of finance can be measured by **gearing** ratios.

The assets of a business must be financed somehow. When a business is growing, the additional assets must be financed by additional capital.

However using debt to finance the business creates financial risk. **Financial risk** can be seen from different points of view.

(a) **The company as a whole**

If a company builds up debts that it cannot pay when they fall due, it will be forced into liquidation.

(b) **Lenders**

If a company cannot pay its debts, the company will go into liquidation owing lenders money that they are unlikely to recover in full. Lenders will probably want a **higher interest yield** to compensate them for higher financial risk and gearing.

(c) **Ordinary shareholders**

A company will not make any distributable profits unless it is able to earn enough profit from operations to pay all its interest charges, and then tax. The lower the profits or the higher the interest-bearing debts, the less there will be, if there is anything at all, for shareholders.

Ordinary shareholders will probably want a **bigger expected return** from their shares to compensate them for a **higher financial risk**. The market value of shares will therefore depend on gearing, because of this premium for financial risk that shareholders will want to earn.

In this section we shall examine how a business can decide what a suitable capital structure might be.

1.2 Company circumstances

One determinant of how suitable the gearing mix is is the stability of the company. It may seem obvious, but it is worth stressing that debt financing will be more appropriate when:

- The company is in a **healthy competitive position**
- **Cash flows** and **earnings** are stable
- **Profit margins** are **reasonable**
- The **bulk of the company's assets** are **tangible.**
- The **liquidity** and **cash flow position** is **strong**
- The **debt-equity ratio** is low
- **Share prices** are **low**

1.3 Matching assets with funds

As a general rule, **assets which yield profits over a long period of time should be financed** by **long-term funds**.

In this way, the returns made by the asset will be sufficient to pay either the interest cost of the loans raised to buy it, or dividends on its equity funding.

If, however a long-term asset is financed by short-term funds, the company cannot be certain that when the loan becomes repayable, it will have enough cash (from profits) to repay it.

A company would not normally finance all of its short-term assets with short-term liabilities, but instead finance **short-term assets partly with short-term funding** and **partly with long-term funding**. We shall look at this further in Section 4.

1.4 Long-term capital requirements for replacement and growth

A distinction can be made between long-term capital that is needed to finance the replacement of worn-out assets, and capital that is needed to finance growth.

Aims	Main funding sources
Maintenance of current level of operations	Internal sources
Growth	External finance

1.5 Signalling

Some investors may see the issue of debt capital as a sign that the directors are confident enough of the future cash flows of the business to be prepared to commit the company to making **regular interest payments** to **lenders.** However this depends on the view that market efficiency is not very high. The argument would be that an efficient market would have sufficient information to be able to make its own mind up about the debt issue, without needing to take the directors' views into account.

1.6 Clientele effect

When considering whether to change gearing significantly, directors may take into account changes in the profile of shareholders. If gearing does change significantly, the company may adjust to a **new risk-return trade-off** that is unsuitable for many shareholders. These shareholders will look to sell their shares, whilst other investors, who are now attracted by the new gearing levels, will look to buy shares.

1.7 Domestic and international borrowing 11/06

If the company is receiving income in a foreign currency or has a long-term investment overseas, it can try to limit the **risk** of adverse exchange rate movements by **matching**. It can take out a long-term loan and use the foreign currency receipts to repay the loan. Similarly it can try to **match its foreign assets** (property, plant etc) by a **long-term loan** in the foreign currency. However if the asset ultimately generates home currency receipts, there will be a long-term currency risk.

In addition foreign loans may carry a lower **interest rate**, but the principle of **interest rate parity** suggests that the foreign currency will ultimately strengthen, and hence loan repayments will become more expensive.

Exam focus point

In November 2006, the compulsory question required a discussion of the comparative advantages of Euro denominated and US dollar denominated borrowing for a multinational organisation. The examiners were concerned that knowledge was not applied to the scenario provided.

1.8 Cost and flexibility

Interest rates on longer-term debt may be higher than interest rates on shorter-term debt. However **issue costs** or **arrangement fees** will be **higher** for shorter-term debt as it has to be renewed more frequently.

A business may also find itself locked into **longer-term debt**, with adverse interest rates and large penalties if it repays the debt early. Both **inflation** and **uncertainty** about future interest rate changes are reasons why companies are unwilling to borrow long-term at high rates of interest and investors are unwilling to lend long-term when they think that interest yields might go even higher.

1.9 Optimal capital structure and the cost of capital

FAST FORWARD

Some commentators believe that an **optimal mix of finance** exists at which the company's **cost of capital** will be minimised.

When we consider the capital structure decision, the question arises of whether there is an optimal mix of capital and debt which a company should try to achieve. Remember that under one view (the traditional view) there is an optimal capital mix at which the **average cost of capital**, weighted according to the different forms of capital employed, is **minimised**.

However, the alternative view of **Modigliani and Miller** is that the firm's overall **weighted average cost of capital** is **not influenced** by changes in its **capital structure**. Their argument is that the issue of debt causes the cost of equity to rise in such a way that the benefits of debt on returns are exactly offset. Investors themselves adjust their level of personal gearing and thus the level of corporate gearing becomes irrelevant.

2 Restrictions on capital structure

2.1 Acceptability of capital structure

FAST FORWARD

The **acceptability** of **gearing** will depend on director-shareholder attitudes to **risk**, also the **degree of control** they are willing to sacrifice, and the **costs** and **commitments** required for extra funding.

2.1.1 Risk attitudes

The choice of capital structure will not only depend on company circumstances, but the **attitudes** that directors and owners have towards the **principal risks**. This will include the risks that are specific to the business, more general economic risks, and also the risks of raising finance. It could for example adversely affect the company's reputation if it made a rights issue that was not fully subscribed.

Owner-director attitudes to risk may also differ. Owners will be concerned about the combination of **risk and return**. Directors may be concerned with the **risk** to their **income** and **job security**, but on the other hand significant profit incentives in their remuneration packages may encourage them to take more risks than the owners deem desirable.

2.1.2 Loss of control

The directors and shareholders may be unwilling to accept the **conditions** and the **loss of control** that obtaining extra finance will mean. Control may be diminished whether equity or loan funding is sought:

(a) **Issuing shares** to outsiders may **dilute** the **control** of the existing shareholders and directors, and the company will be subject to greater regulatory control if it obtains a stock market listing.

(b) The price of additional debt finance may be **security** restricting disposal of the assets secured and **covenants** that limit the company's rights to **dispose of assets** in general or to pay dividends.

2.1.3 Costs

The directors may consider that the **extra interest costs** the company is committed to are too high. On the other hand the effective cost of debt might be cheaper than the cost of equity, particularly if tax relief can be obtained.

2.1.4 Commitments

The interest and repayment schedules that the company is required to meet may be considered **too tight.** The collateral loan providers require may also be too much, particularly if the directors are themselves required to provide **personal guarantees.**

2.1.5 Present sources of finance

Perhaps it's easy to find reasons why new sources of finance may not be desirable, but equally they may be considered more acceptable than drawing on current sources. For example shareholders may be **unwilling to contribute further funds** in a rights issue; the business may wish to improve its relations with its suppliers, and one condition may be lessening its reliance on trade credit.

2.2 Feasibility of capital structure

FAST FORWARD

The mix of finance chosen must be **feasible;** companies may face **restrictions** in the finance available, and will not be able to commit to repaying too much at any one time.

Even if directors and shareholders are happy with the implications of obtaining significant extra finance, the company may not be able to obtain that finance.

2.2.1 Lenders' attitudes

Whether lenders are prepared to lend the company any money will depend on the factors we described in Chapter 6. The company's circumstances, particularly as they affect the company's ability to generate **cash** and **security** for the loan, will obviously be significant.

2.2.2 Availability of share capital

If the **stock market** is **depressed**, it may be difficult to raise cash through share issues, so major amounts will have to be borrowed.

2.2.3 Future trends

Likely **future trends** of **fund availability** will be significant if a business is likely to require a number of injections of funds over the next few years.

2.2.4 Restrictions in loan agreements

Restrictions written into agreements on current loans may prohibit a business from taking out **further loans**, or may require that its gearing does **not exceed specified limits.**

2.2.5 Maturity dates

If a business already has significant debt repayable in a few years' time, because of **cash flow restrictions** it may not be able to take out further debt repayable around the same time.

2.3 Position of small and medium-sized enterprises

The options open to small and medium-sized enterprises (SMEs) may be particularly limited. They face **competition** for funds, as investors have opportunities to invest in all sizes of organisation, also overseas and in government debt. In this competition they are handicapped by the problem of uncertainty.

(a) Whatever the details provided to potential investors, SMEs have **neither** the **business** history **nor larger track record** that larger organisations possess.

(b) Larger enterprises are subject by law to **more public scrutiny**; their accounts have to contain more detail and be audited, they receive more press coverage and so on.

(c) Because of the uncertainties involved, banks often use **credit scoring** systems to **control exposure.**

(d) **The costs of monitoring** small businesses may be **excessive for banks**, particularly if they are **facing difficult conditions themselves**.

(e) Banks face **regulatory pressures** with regulators classifying **lending to the small business sector** as being a **higher risk investment**.

A common problem is often that banks will be **unwilling** to increase **loan funding** without an increase in **security given** (which the owners may be unwilling or unable to give), or an increase in **equity funding** (which may be difficult to obtain).

Certain trends in various countries may be more helpful for small businesses.

(a) The **development of the non-bank sector**, with some organisations specialising in lending to small businesses.

(b) Banks may be more **amenable** to **granting certain types of finance**, for example long-term loans or more specialist schemes such as the securitisation of assets.

Exam focus point

> Make sure that your financing recommendations are suitable for the type of entity in the scenario and not just a 'brain-dump' of types of finance.

3 Effect of capital structure on ratios

FAST FORWARD

> **Financial gearing** and **operating** or **operational gearing** need to be distinguished.
>
> - **Financial gearing** measures the relationship between **shareholders' funds** and **prior charge capital**.
> - **Operating gearing** measures the relationship between **contribution** and **profit before interest and tax**.
>
> If a company can generate returns on capital in excess of the interest payable on debt, financial gearing will raise the EPS. Gearing will, however, also increase **the variability of returns** for shareholders and increase the chance of corporate **failure**.

3.1 Gearing 5/05, 11/05

In Chapter 3, we revised gearing briefly. You should remember that the financial risk of a company's capital structure can be measured by a **gearing ratio**, a **debt ratio** or **debt/equity ratio** and by the **interest cover**. A gearing ratio should not be given without stating how it has been defined.

Exam focus point

> You need to be able to explain and calculate the level of financial gearing using alternative measures. The question may specify how gearing should be calculated eg debt to total value of entity using market values in Question 4, November 2005.

Financial gearing measures the relationship between shareholders' capital plus reserves, and either prior charge capital or borrowings or both.

Commonly used measures of financial gearing are based on the balance sheet values of the fixed interest and equity capital. They include:

Formulae to learn

$$\frac{\text{Prior charge capital}}{\text{Equity capital (including reserves)}}$$

and $\dfrac{\text{Prior charge capital}}{\text{Total capital employed *}}$

* Either including or excluding minority interests, deferred tax and deferred income.

With the first definition above, a company is low geared if the gearing ratio is less than 100%, highly geared if the ratio is over 100% and neutrally geared if it is exactly 100%. With the second definition, a company is neutrally geared if the ratio is 50%, low geared below that, and highly geared above that.

Question — Gearing

Learning outcome: B(i)

From the following balance sheet, compute the company's financial gearing ratio.

	£'000	£'000	£'000
Non-current assets			12,400
Current assets		1,000	
Payables: amounts falling due within one year			
Loans	120		
Bank overdraft	260		
Trade payables	430		
Bills of exchange	70		
		880	
Net current assets			120
Total assets less current liabilities			12,520
Payables: amounts falling due after more than one year			
Loan notes		4,700	
Bank loans		500	
			(5,200)
Provisions for liabilities and charges: deferred taxation			(300)
Deferred Income			(250)
			6,770

Capital and reserves	
Called up share capital	
Ordinary shares	1,500
Preferred shares	500
	2,000
Share premium account	760
Revaluation reserve	1,200
Accumulated profits	2,810
	6,770

Answer

Prior charge capital	£'000
Preferred shares	500
Loan notes	4,700
Long-term bank loans	500
Prior charge capital, ignoring short-term debt	5,700
Short-term loans	120
Overdraft	260
Prior charge capital, including short-term interest bearing debt	6,080

Either figure, £6,080,000 or £5,700,000, could be used. If gearing is calculated with capital employed in the denominator, and capital employed is non-current assets plus **net** current assets, it would be better to exclude short-term interest bearing debt from prior charge capital. This is because short-term debt is set off against current assets in arriving at the figure for net current assets.

Equity = 1,500 + 760 + 1,200 + 2,810 = £6,270,000

The gearing ratio can be calculated in any of the following ways.

(a) $\frac{\text{Prior charge capital}}{\text{Equity}} \times 100\% = \frac{6{,}080}{6{,}270} \times 100\% = 97\%$

(b) $\frac{\text{Prior charge capital}}{\text{Equity plus prior charge capital}} \times 100\% = \frac{6{,}080}{(6{,}080 + 6{,}270)} \times 100\% = 49.2\%$

(c) $\frac{\text{Prior charge capital}}{\text{Total capital employed}} \times 100\% = \frac{5{,}700}{12{,}520} \times 100\% = 45.5\%$

3.1.1 Gearing ratios based on market values

An alternative method of calculating a gearing ratio is one based on **market values**:

Formula to learn

$$\frac{\text{Market value of debt (including preference shares)}}{\text{Market value of equity + Market value of debt}}$$

The advantage of this method is that potential investors in a company are able to judge the further debt capacity of the company more clearly by **reference** to **market values** than they could by looking at balance sheet values.

The disadvantage of a gearing ratio based on market values is that it **disregards** the **value** of the company's **assets**, which might be used to secure further loans. A gearing ratio based on balance sheet values arguably gives a better indication of the security for lenders of fixed interest capital.

3.1.2 Changing financial gearing

Financial gearing is an attempt to quantify the **degree of risk** involved in holding equity shares in a company, both in terms of the company's ability to remain in business and in terms of expected ordinary dividends from the company.

The more geared the company is, the **greater the risk** that little (if anything) will be available to distribute by way of dividend to the ordinary shareholders. The more geared the company, the greater the percentage change in profit available for ordinary shareholders for any given percentage change in profit before interest and tax.

This means that there will be greater **volatility** of amounts available for ordinary shareholders, and presumably therefore greater volatility in dividends paid to those shareholders, where a company is highly geared. That is the risk. You may do extremely well or extremely badly without a particularly large movement in the profit from operations of the company.

Gearing ultimately measures the company's ability to **remain in business**. A highly geared company has a large amount of interest to pay annually. If those borrowings are 'secured' in any way (and loan notes in particular are secured), then the holders of the debt are perfectly entitled to force the company to realise assets to pay their interest if funds are not available from other sources. Clearly, the more highly geared a company, the more likely this is to occur when and if profits fall.

3.1.3 Operating gearing

Financial risk, as we have seen, can be measured by financial gearing. **Business risk** refers to the risk of making only low profits, or even losses, due to the nature of the business that the company is involved in. One way of measuring business risk is by calculating a company's **operating gearing** or 'operational gearing'.

Formula to learn

$$\textbf{Operating gearing or leverage} = \frac{\text{Contribution}}{\text{Profit before interest and tax (PBIT)}}$$

Contribution is sales minus variable cost of sales.

The significance of operating gearing is as follows.

(a) **If contribution is high but PBIT is low**, fixed costs will be high, and only just covered by contribution. Business risk, as measured by operating gearing, will be high.

(b) **If contribution is not much bigger than PBIT**, fixed costs will be low, and fairly easily covered. Business risk, as measured by operating gearing, will be low.

3.2 Interest cover

Like gearing, **interest cover** is a measure of financial risk which is designed to show the risks in terms of profit rather than in terms of capital values.

Formula to learn

$$\textbf{Interest cover} = \frac{\text{Profit before interest and tax (incl. int receivable)}}{\text{Interest payable}} \text{ or}$$

$$\textbf{Finance cost cover} = \frac{\text{Profit from operations}}{\text{Finance costs}}$$

The reciprocal of this, the interest to profit ratio, is also sometimes used. As a general guide, an interest cover of **less than three times** is considered low, indicating that profitability is too low given the gearing of the company.

3.3 The debt ratio (debt/equity ratio) and net debt

Another measure of financial risk is the **debt ratio.**

Debt ratio = Total debts : Total assets

Debt/equity ratio = Debt : Equity

Debt does not include long-term provisions and liabilities such as deferred taxation.

There is no firm rule on the maximum safe debt ratio, but as a general guide, you might regard 50% as a safe limit to debt.

A variation on the debt ratio is **net debt**.

Formula to learn

Net debt = Total overdrafts and borrowings – Cash balances

If a business is doing well, it should be able to reduce net debt levels each year, indicating a fall in financial risk levels. It will be particularly important to reduce net debt levels if interest rates are high and the business has a significant amount of floating rate finance.

3.4 Earnings per share

Remember the definition of earnings per share.

Key term

Basic **earnings per share** should be calculated by dividing the net profit or loss for the period attributable to ordinary shareholders by the weighted average number of ordinary shares outstanding during the period.

One measure of gearing uses earnings per share.

$$\text{Financial gearing at a given level of sales} = \frac{\%\ \text{change in earnings per share}}{\%\ \text{change in profits before interest and tax}}$$

The relationship between these two figures can be used to evaluate alternative financing plans by examining their effect on earnings per share over a range of PBIT levels. Its objective is to determine the PBIT indifference points amongst the various alternative financing plans. The indifference points between any two methods of financing can be determined by solving for PBIT the following equation:

$$\frac{(\text{PBIT} - \text{I})(1-\text{t})}{\text{S1}} = \frac{(\text{PBIT} - \text{I})(1-\text{t})}{\text{S2}}$$

where t = tax rate, I = interest payable, S1 and S2 = number of shares after financing for plans 1 and 2

3.5 Example: PBIT and EPS

Edted Company has 10,000 m €1 shares in issue and wants to raise €5,000 m to fund an investment by either:

(a) Selling 2,500 m shares at €2 each or

(b) Issuing €5,000 m 10% loan stock at par

The income tax rate is 40%.

In order to calculate the indifference point between issuing equity shares and issuing debt, we use the above equation.

$$\frac{(\text{PBIT} - 0)(1-0.4)}{12{,}500} = \frac{(\text{PBIT} - 500)(1-0.4)}{10{,}000}$$

$$10{,}000 \times 0.6 \times \text{PBIT} = 12{,}500 \times 0.6 \times (\text{PBIT} - 500)$$

$$6{,}000\ \text{PBIT} = 7{,}500\ \text{PBIT} - 3{,}750{,}000$$

1,500 PBIT = 3,750,000

PBIT = 2,500

We can prove this calculation as follows

	Issues Equity	*Issues Debt*
	€m	€m
PBIT	2,500	2,500
Interest		(500)
PBIT	2,500	2,000
Tax	(1,000)	(800)
Earnings after tax	1,500	1,200
Number of shares	12,500	10,000
Earnings per share	€0.12	€0.12

At a level of PBIT above €2,500 million, it will be better to issue debt, as every € extra of earnings will be distributed between fewer shareholders. At a level of PBIT below €2,500 million, it will be better to issue equity, as the loss of each € will be by more shareholders.

The company's attitude will depend on what levels of earnings it expects and also the **variability** of **possible earnings** limits. Variations from what is expected will have a greater impact on earnings per share if the company chooses debt finance.

3.6 Price-earnings ratio

You will remember that the price-earnings ratio is calculated in the following way:

Key term

Price earnings (P/E) ratio = $\frac{\text{Market price per share}}{\text{Earnings per share}}$

and that the **value of the P/E ratio** reflects the market's appraisal of the share's future prospects. If earnings per share falls because of an increased burden arising from increased gearing, an increased P/E ratio will mean that the share price has not fallen as much as earnings, indicating the market views positively the projects that the increased gearing will fund.

3.7 Dividend cover

You will recall that the **dividend cover** is the number of times the actual dividend could be paid out of current profits.

Key term

Dividend cover = $\frac{\text{Earnings per share}}{\text{Dividend per share}}$

To judge the effect of increased gearing on dividend cover, you should consider changes in the dividend levels and changes in dividend cover. If earnings decrease because of an increased burden of interest payments, then:

(a) The directors may decide to make **corresponding reductions in dividend** to maintain levels of dividend cover.

(b) Alternatively the directions may choose to maintain dividend levels, in which case **dividend cover** will **fall.** This will indicate to shareholders an **increased risk** that the company will not be able to maintain the same dividend payments in future years, should earnings fall.

3.8 Dividend yield

Remember that the dividend yield is calculated as follows:

Key term

Dividend yield = $\frac{\text{Gross dividend per share}}{\text{Market price per share}} \times 100\%$

The gross dividend is the dividend paid plus the appropriate tax credit. The (net) dividend yield (using the dividend per share net of taxes deducted at source) can also be used.

We have discussed how increased gearing might affect dividends and dividend cover. However with dividend yield, we are also looking at the effect on the **market price of shares**. If the additional debt finance is expected to be used to generate good returns in the long-term, it is possible that the dividend yield might fall significantly in the short-term because of a fall in short-term dividends, but also an increase in the market price reflecting market expectations of enhanced long-term returns. How shareholders view this movement will depend on their preference between short-term and long-term returns.

Question — Gearing

Learning outcome: B(i)

A summarised balance sheet of Rufus is as follows.

	£m
Assets less current liabilities	150
Debt capital	(70)
	80
Share capital (20 million shares of £1)	20
Reserves	60
	80

The company's profits in the year just ended are as follows.

	£m
Profit from operations	21.0
Interest	6.0
Profit before tax	15.0
Taxation at 30%	4.5
Profit after tax (earnings)	10.5
Dividends	6.5
Retained profits	4.0

The company is now considering an investment of £25 million. This will add £5 million each year to profits before interest and tax.

(a) There are two ways of financing this investment. One would be to borrow £25 million at a cost of 8% per annum in interest. The other would be to raise the money by means of a 1 for 4 rights issue.

(b) Whichever financing method is used, the company will increase dividends per share next year from 32.5p to 35p.

(c) The company does not intend to allow its gearing level, measured as debt finance as a proportion of equity capital plus debt finance, to exceed 55% as at the end of any financial year. In addition, the company will not accept any dilution in earnings per share.

Assume that the rate of taxation will remain at 30% and that debt interest costs will be £6 million plus the interest cost of any new debt capital.

Required

(a) Produce a profit forecast for next year, assuming that the new project is undertaken and is financed (i) by debt capital or (ii) by a rights issue.

(b) Calculate the earnings per share next year, with each financing method.

(c) Calculate the effect on gearing as at the end of next year, with each financing method.

(d) Explain whether either or both methods of funding would be acceptable.

Answer

Current earnings per share are £10.5 million/20 million shares = 52.5 pence.

If the project is financed by £25 million of debt at 8%, interest charges will rise by £2 million. If the project is financed by a 1 for 4 rights issue, there will be 25 million shares in issue.

	Finance with debt	*Finance with rights issue*
	£m	£m
Profit before interest and tax (+ 5.0)	26.00	26.00
Interest	8.00	6.00
	18.00	20.00
Taxation (30%)	5.40	6.00
Profit after tax	12.60	14.00
Dividends (35p per share)	7.00	8.75
Retained profits	5.60	5.25
Earnings (profits after tax)	£12.6 m	£14.0 m
Number of shares	20 million	25 million
Earnings per share	63 p	56 p

The projected balance sheet as at the end of the year will be:

	Finance with debt	*Finance with rights issue*
	£m	£m
Assets less current liabilities	180.6	180.25
(150 + new capital 25 + retained profits)		
Debt capital	(95.0)	(70.00)
	85.6	110.25
Share capital	20.0	25.00
Reserves	65.6	* 85.25
	85.6	110.25

* The rights issue raises £25 million, of which £5 million is represented in the balance sheet by share capital and the remaining £20 million by share premium. The reserves are therefore the current amount (£60 million) plus the share premium of £20 million plus accumulated profits of £5.25 million.

	Finance with debt	*Finance with rights issue*
Debt capital	95.0	70.0
Debt capital plus equity finance	(95.0 + 85.6)	(70.0 + 110.25)
Gearing	53%	39%

Either financing method would be acceptable, since the company's requirements for no dilution in EPS would be met with a rights issue as well as by borrowing, and the company's requirement for the gearing level to remain below 55% is (just) met even if the company were to borrow the money.

Chapter roundup

- **Gearing** must be considered when deciding how to finance a business.
- Factors determining the **suitability** of capital structure include the **stability** of the company's situation, matching of assets and funds, **impact on shareholders**, the possibility of **international finance** and the **cost** and **flexibility** of sources available.
- Some commentators believe that an **optimal mix of finance** exists at which the company's **cost of capital** will be minimised.
- The **acceptability** of **gearing** will depend on director-shareholder attitudes to **risk**, also the **degree of control** they are willing to sacrifice, and the **costs** and **commitments** required for extra funding.
- The mix of finance chosen must be **feasible;** companies may face **restrictions** in the finance available, and will not be able to commit to repaying too much at any one time.
- **Financial gearing** and **operating** or **operational gearing** need to be distinguished.
  - **Financial gearing** measures the relationship between **shareholders' funds** and **prior charge capital**.
  - **Operating gearing** measures the relationship between **contribution** and **profit before interest and tax**.
- If a company can generate returns on capital in excess of the interest payable on debt, financial gearing will raise the EPS. Gearing will, however, also increase **the variability of returns** for shareholders and increase the chance of corporate **failure**.

Quick quiz

1 Fill in the blanks.

$$\text{.................................... gearing} = \frac{\text{Prior charge capital}}{\text{Total capital employed}}$$

$$\text{.................................... gearing} = \frac{\text{Contribution}}{\text{Profit before interest and tax}}$$

2 Fill in the blank.

Interest cover = ...

3 What type of policy is characterised by all non-current assets and permanent current assets being financed by long-term funding?

4 Puppy has decided to calculate its gearing ratio according to the formula:

prior charge capital: equity capital (incl reserves)

At what level would it be neutrally geared?

5 Are preference shares prior charge or equity capital?

6 Why should a long-term asset not be financed by short-term loans?

7 What condition has to be fulfilled for increased financial gearing to result in increased earnings per share?

8 What is the debt ratio?

9 What is meant by matching?

Answers to quick quiz

1 Financial gearing = $\frac{\text{Prior charge capital}}{\text{Total capital employed}}$

Operating gearing = $\frac{\text{Contribution}}{\text{Profit before interest and tax}}$

2 Interest cover = $\frac{\text{Profit before interest and tax}}{\text{Interest paid}}$

3 Conservative

4 Gearing is neutral where Debt = Equity, 100% on the basis of this calculation

5 Prior charge capital

6 When the loan becomes repayable, the company cannot be certain that it will have generated enough profits to repay the loan.

7 The extra earnings generated by the investment must exceed the interest payable on the extra debt used to finance the investment.

8 Total debt: Total assets

9 Matching is where assets which yield profits over a long period of time are financed by long-term funds. It is also where foreign assets are financed by a long-term loan in the foreign currency.

Now try the question below from the Exam Question Bank

Number	Level	Marks	Time
Q15	Introductory	25	45 mins

11

Portfolios and diversification

Introduction

CIMA Paper P3 is all about approaching risk and devising control strategy. However as we have already seen, risk is a very important topic in financial strategy as well.

In this chapter we consider one approach for dealing with risk, diversification and portfolio theory. Diversification, spreading investments in order to reduce risk, has some benefits for the financial manager, although as we shall see in Section 2 its benefits can be exaggerated.

However portfolio theory does enable us to calculate beta factors, which are a measure of the premium investors are prepared to accept in return for bearing a certain level of portfolio risk. Beta factors are the basis of the **CAPM** approach to calculating cost of capital and making investment decisions under risk, which we turn to in the next chapter.

Topic list	Learning outcomes	Syllabus references	Ability required
1 Portfolios and portfolio theory	B (i)	B (7)	Evaluation
2 Portfolio theory and financial management	B (i)	B (7)	Evaluation
3 Investors' preferences	B (i)	B (7)	Evaluation

1 Portfolios and portfolio theory

FAST FORWARD

Portfolio theory takes account of the fact that many investors have a range of investments that are unlikely all to change values in step. The investor should be concerned with his or her overall position, not with the performance of individual investments.

1.1 Portfolio theory

A **portfolio** is the collection of different investments that make up an investor's total holding. A portfolio might be:

- The investments in stocks and shares of an investor
- The investments in capital projects of a company

Portfolio theory, which originates from the work of Markowitz, is concerned with establishing guidelines for building up a portfolio of stocks and shares, or a portfolio of projects. The same theory applies to both stock market investors and to companies with capital projects to invest in.

1.2 Factors in the choice of investments

There are five major factors to be considered when any investor chooses investments.

CHOOSING INVESTMENTS	
Security	Investments at least maintaining their capital value
Liquidity	If investments are with short-term funds, should be convertible back into cash at short notice
Return	Make highest return compatible with safety
Spreading risks	Spreading investments over several types of security, so losses on some offset by gains on others
Growth prospects	Most profitable investments are in businesses with good growth prospects

1.3 Portfolios: expected return and risk

When an investor has a portfolio of securities, he will expect the portfolio to provide a certain return on his investment.

The **expected return of a portfolio** will be a weighted average of the expected returns of the investments in the portfolio, weighted by the proportion of total funds invested in each.

The **risk** in an investment, or in a portfolio of investments, is the risk that the actual return will not be the same as the expected return. The actual return may be higher, but it may be lower. A prudent investor will want to avoid too much risk, and will hope that the actual returns from his portfolio are much the same as what he expected them to be.

The risk of a security, and the risk of a portfolio, can be measured as the standard deviation of expected returns, given estimated probabilities of actual returns.

1.4 Example: portfolios (1)

Suppose that the return from an investment has the following probability distribution.

Return	*Probability*	*Expected value*
x	p	px
%		
8	0.2	1.6
10	0.2	2.0
12	0.5	6.0
14	0.1	1.4
		11.0

The expected return is 11%, and the standard deviation of the expected return is as follows. The symbol $\bar{x}$ refers to the expected value of the return, 11%.

Return			
x	$x - \bar{x}$	p	$p(x - \bar{x})^2$
%	%		
8	–3	0.2	1.8
10	–1	0.2	0.2
12	1	0.5	0.5
14	3	0.1	0.9
		Variance	3.4

Standard deviation $= \sqrt{3.4} = 1.84\%$

Thus, the expected return is 11% with a standard deviation of 1.84%.

The risk of an investment might be high or low, depending on the nature of the investment.

(a) Low risk investments usually give low returns.

(b) High risk investments might give high returns, but with more risk of disappointing results.

So how does holding a **portfolio of investments** affect expected returns and investment risk?

1.5 Correlation between investments

FAST FORWARD

Correlation measures the degree to which the returns on investments vary with each other.

Portfolio theory states that individual investments cannot be viewed simply in terms of their risk and return. The relationship between the return from one investment and the return from other investments is just as important.

The relationship between investments can be one of three types.

(a) **Positive correlation**

When there is positive correlation between investments, if one investment does well (or badly) it is likely that the other will perform likewise. Thus if you buy shares in one company making umbrellas and in another which sells raincoats you would expect both companies to do badly in dry weather.

(b) **Negative correlation**

If one investment does well the other will do badly, and vice versa. Thus if you hold shares in one company making umbrellas and in another which sells ice cream, the weather will affect the companies differently.

(c) **No correlation**

The performance of one investment will be independent of how the other performs. If you hold shares in a mining company and in a leisure company, it is likely that there would be no relationship between the profits and returns from each.

This relationship between the returns from different investments is measured by the correlation coefficient. A figure close to +1 indicates high positive correlation, and a figure close to –1 indicates high negative correlation. A figure of 0 indicates no correlation.

If investments show high negative correlation, then by combining them in a portfolio overall risk would be reduced. Risk will also be reduced by combining in a portfolio investments which have no significant correlation.

2 Portfolio theory and financial management

FAST FORWARD

Both individuals and firms diversify their investments. Individuals have **portfolios of shares** and firms have **portfolios of business operations** and **investments. Diversification** is equally an important consideration for the financial manager in making investment decisions.

Reasons why companies should not diversify too far include their **lack of expertise** and **unfamiliarity with markets**. In particular diversification by investors is more efficient than diversification by companies.

2.1 Should companies try to diversify?

Our discussion of portfolio theory has concentrated mainly on portfolios of stocks and shares. Investors can reduce their investment risk by diversifying, but what about individual companies choosing a range of businesses or projects to invest in?

You can probably think of examples of large companies today which concentrate mainly on a single industry or product range (for example, British Telecom) and **conglomerates** which are **widely diversified** (for example, the so-called 'guns-to-buns' Tomkins group).

Key term

Conglomerate is an entity comprising a number of dissimilar businesses. *(OT 2005)*

2.1.1 Disadvantages of diversification

(a) A company may employ people with particular skills, and it will get the best out of its employees by allowing them to stick to doing **what they are good at**. A manager with expert knowledge of the electronics business, for example, might not be any good at managing a retailing business.

(b) When companies try to grow, they will often find the **best opportunities** to make extra profits in **industries or markets** with which they are **familiar.**

(c) Conglomerates are vulnerable to takeover bids where the buyer plans to **'unbundle'** the **companies** in the group and **sell them off individually** at a profit. Conglomerates' returns will often be mediocre rather than high, and so the stock market will value the shares on a fairly low P/E ratio, making them vulnerable to acquirers. Separate companies within the group would be valued according to their individual performance and prospects, often at P/E ratios that are much higher than for the conglomerate as a whole.

(d) A company can reduce its investment risk by diversifying and **lower investment risk** would **protect the company's shareholders**; however, a shareholder does not need the company to reduce investment risk on his behalf. Investors can probably **reduce investment risk more efficiently** than companies. They have a wider range of investment opportunities. Investments with uncorrelated or negatively correlated returns will be easier to identify. Estimates of beta factors will be more reliable for quoted companies' shares than for companies' capital expenditure projects.

2.2 Limitations of portfolio analysis for the financial manager

Portfolio analysis offers a way in which the financial manager can deal with risk by diversifying through the investment decisions which are made by the firm. However, portfolio theory applied to the selection of investment proposals has a number of limitations.

(a) In practice, it may require guesswork to **estimate probabilities** of different outcomes, for example when a new product is to be developed. In other cases, such as machine replacement, sufficient information may however be available to make relatively good probability estimates.

(b) It will be difficult in practical cases to know what are **shareholders' preferences** between risk and return and therefore to reflect these preferences in decision-making.

(c) The '**agency problem**' in management's relationship to the company is relevant. Managers have the security of their jobs to consider, while the shareholder can easily buy and sell securities. It is arguable that managers are as a result more risk-averse than shareholders, and this may distort managers' investment decisions.

(d) Projects may be of such a size that they are not **easy to divide** in accordance with recommended diversification principles.

(e) The theory assumes that there are **constant returns** to scale, in other words that the percentage returns provided by a project are the same however much is invested in it. In practice, there may be economies of scale to be gained from making a larger investment in a single project.

(f) **Other aspects** of risk **not covered** by the theory may need to be considered, eg bankruptcy costs.

Exam focus point

Despite its limitations, portfolio theory does provide a means of understanding how businesses deal with financial risk.

3 Investors' preferences

FAST FORWARD

The interaction of **investors' preferences, efficient portfolios** and the **returns from risk-free investments** provides the **basis for calculating beta factors**.

3.1 Choosing a portfolio

Investors must choose a portfolio which gives them a satisfactory balance between:

- The **expected returns** from the **portfolio**, and
- The **risk** that **actual returns** from the **portfolio** will be **higher or lower** than expected

Some portfolios will be more risky than others.

3.1.1 Indifference curves

Traditional investment theory suggests that rational investors wish to maximise return and minimise risk. Thus if two portfolios have the same element of risk, the investor will choose the one yielding the higher return. Similarly, if two portfolios offer the same return the investor will select the portfolio with the lesser risk. This is illustrated by Figure 1.

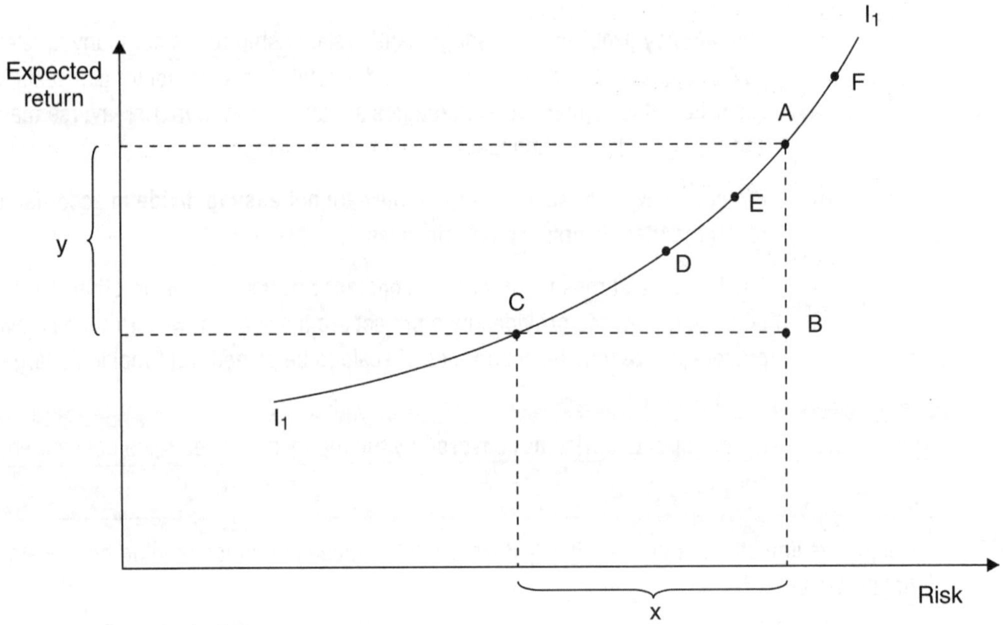

Figure 1 An investor's indifference curve

Portfolio A will be **preferred** to portfolio B because it offers a higher expected return for the same level of risk. Similarly, portfolio C will be preferred to portfolio B because it offers the same expected return for lower risk. But whether an investor chooses portfolio A or portfolio C will depend on the individual's attitude to risk: whether he wishes to accept a greater risk for a greater expected return.

The curve I_1 is an **investor's indifference curve**. The investor will have no preference between any portfolios which give a mix of risk and expected return which lies on the curve.

Thus, to the investor the portfolios A, C, D, E and F are all just as good as each other, and all of them are better than portfolio B.

An investor would prefer combinations of return and risk on indifference curve A to those on curve B (Figure 2) because curve A offers higher returns for the same degree of risk (and less risk for the same expected returns).

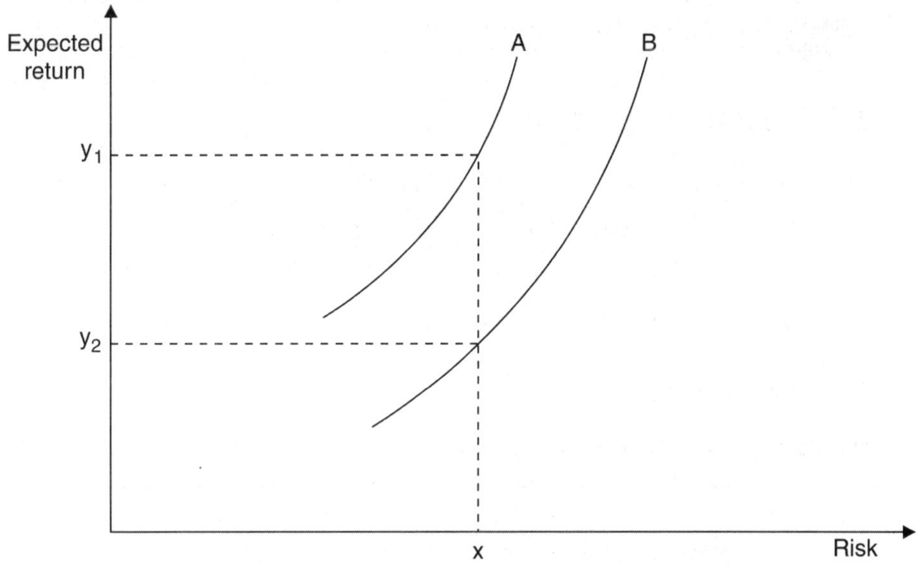

Figure 2 Indifference curves compared

3.2 Efficient portfolios

Suppose we draw a graph (Figure 3) to show the expected return and the risk of the many possible portfolios of investments.

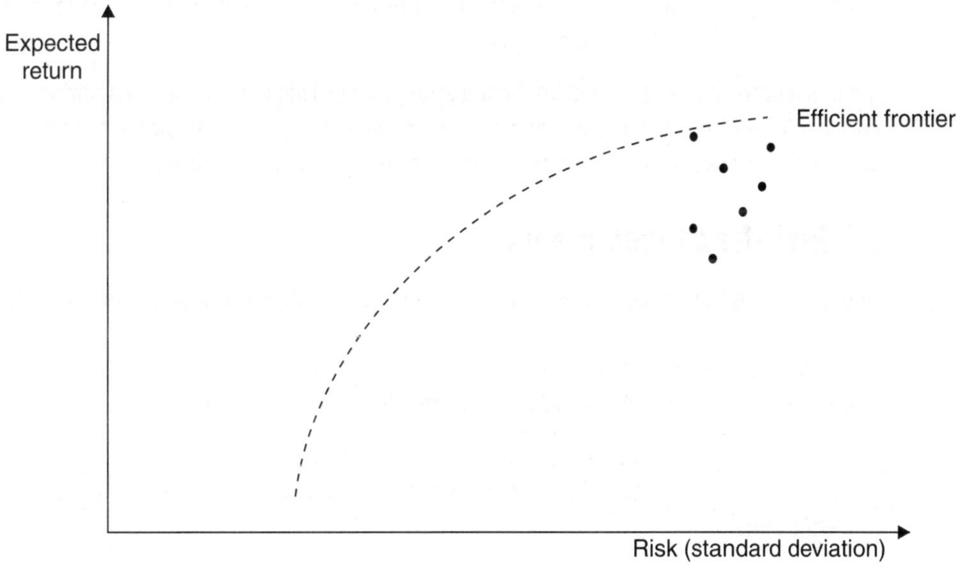

Figure 3 The efficient frontier of available investment portfolios

In this graph, there are some portfolios which would not be as good as others. However, there are other portfolios which are neither better nor worse than each other, because they have either a higher expected return but a higher risk, or a lower expected return but a lower risk. These portfolios lie along the so-called 'efficient frontier' of portfolios which is shown as a dotted line in Figure 3. Portfolios on this efficient frontier are called 'efficient' portfolios.

We can now place an investor's indifference curves on the same graph as the efficient frontier, as in Figure 4.

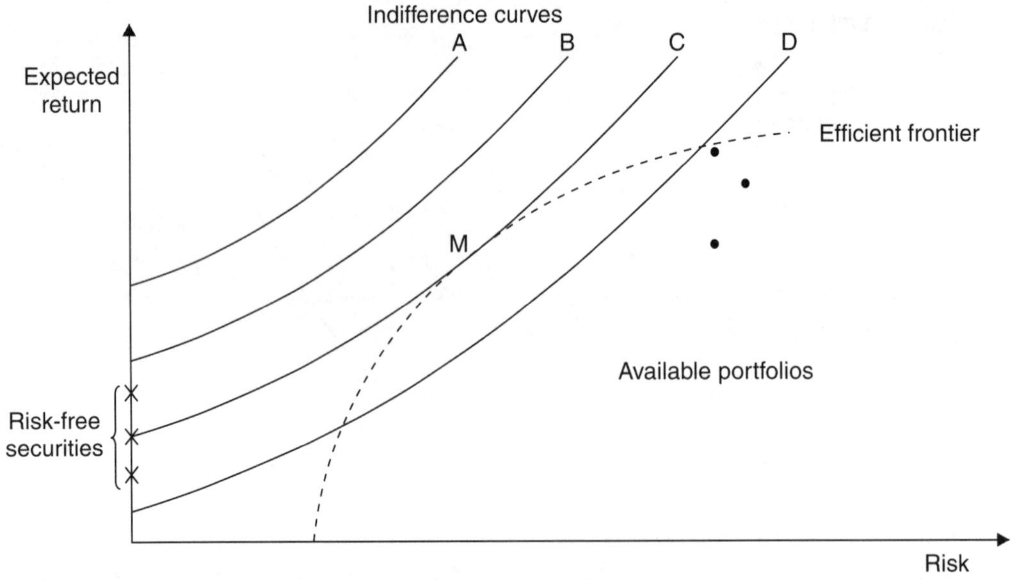

Figure 4 The optimum portfolio (ignoring risk-free securities)

An investor would prefer a portfolio of investments on indifference curve A to a portfolio on curve B, which in turn is preferable to a portfolio on curve C which in turn is preferable to curve D. No portfolio exists, however, which is on curve A or curve B.

The optimum portfolio (or portfolios) to select is one where an indifference curve touches the efficient frontier of portfolios at a **tangent**. In Figure 4, this is the portfolio marked M, where indifference curve C touches the efficient frontier at a tangent. Any portfolio on an indifference curve to the right of curve C, such as one on curve D, would be worse than M.

The efficient frontier is a curved line, not a straight line. This is because the additional return for accepting a greater level of risk will not be constant. The curve eventually levels off because a point will be reached where no more return can be offered to an investor for accepting more risk.

3.3 Risk-free investments

All the portfolios under consideration carry some degree of risk. But some investments are risk-free. It is unlikely that most governments would default on any payment of interest and capital on its stocks. Thus government stocks can be taken to be risk-free investments. If we introduce a risk-free investment into the analysis we can see that the old efficient frontier is superseded (Figure 5).

The straight line XZME is drawn at a tangent to the efficient frontier and cuts the y axis at the point of the risk-free investment's return. The line (known as the 'capital market line' (CML)) becomes the new efficient frontier.

Portfolio M is the same as in Figure 4. It is the **efficient portfolio** which will appeal to the investor most, ignoring risk-free investments. Portfolio Z is a mixture of the investments in portfolio M and risk-free investments. Investors will prefer portfolio Z to portfolio P because a higher return is obtained for the same level of risk. The only portfolio consisting entirely of **risky investments** a rational investor should want to hold is portfolio M. All other risky portfolios are inefficient (because they are below the capital market line).

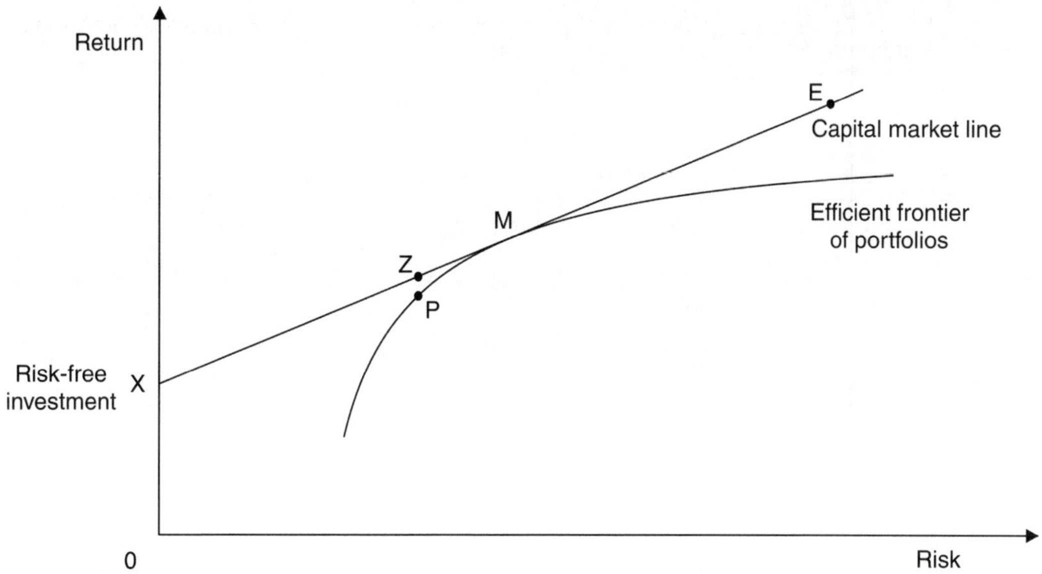

Figure 5 The capital market line

One portfolio on the capital market line is as attractive as another to a rational investor. One investor may wish to hold portfolio Z consisting partly of risk-free investments, partly of portfolio M. Another investor may wish to hold portfolio E, which entails putting all his funds in portfolio M and borrowing money at the risk-free rate to acquire more of portfolio M.

3.4 The market portfolio

We have said that investors will only want to hold one portfolio of risky investments: portfolio M. Therefore:

- Since all investors wish to hold portfolio M, and
- All shares quoted on the Stock Exchange must be held by investors, it follows that
- All shares quoted on the Stock Exchange must be in portfolio M

Thus **portfolio M is the market portfolio** and each investor's portfolio will contain a proportion of it. However, in practice, investors **might** be able to build up a small portfolio that 'beats the market' or might have a portfolio which performs worse than the market average.

3.5 The return on the market portfolio M

The expected returns from portfolio M will be higher than the return from risk-free investments because the investors expect a greater return for accepting a degree of investment risk. The size of the risk premium will increase as the risk of the market portfolio increases. We can show this with an analysis of the capital market line (CML) as in Figure 6.

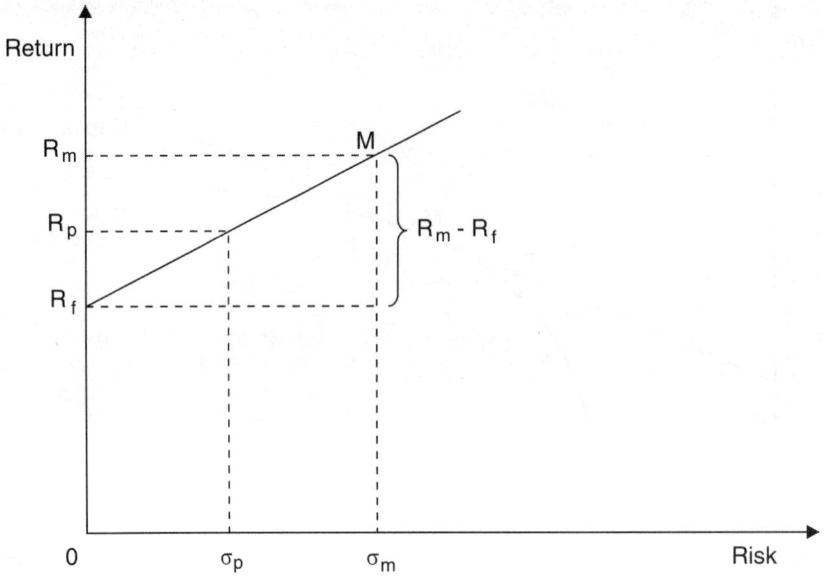

R_m = return from portfolio M
R_f = risk-free return
σ_m = risk of the portfolio M

Let R_f = the risk-free rate of return

R_m = the return on market portfolio M

R_p = the return on portfolio P, which is a mixture of investments in portfolio M and risk-free investments

σ_m = the risk (standard deviation) of returns in portfolio M

σ_p = the risk (standard deviation) of returns in portfolio P

The gradient of the CML can be expressed as: $\frac{R_m - R_f}{\sigma_m}$

This represents the extent to which the required returns from a portfolio should exceed the risk-free rate of return, to compensate investors for risk.

3.6 The beta factor

The equation of the CML can be expressed as: $R_p = R_f + \left(\frac{R_m - R_f}{\sigma_m}\right)\sigma_p$

where $\left(\frac{R_m - R_f}{\sigma_m}\right)\sigma_p$ is the risk premium that the investor should require as compensation for accepting portfolio risk σ_p.

The risk premium can be arranged into:

$$\frac{\sigma_p}{\sigma_m}(R_m - R_f)$$

The expression $\frac{\sigma_p}{\sigma_m}$ is referred to as a **beta factor**, so that an investor's required return from a portfolio can be stated as:

Formula to learn

$$R_p = R_f + (R_m - R_f)\,\beta$$

The beta factor (β) can therefore be used to measure the extent to which a portfolio's return (or indeed an individual investment's return) should **exceed** the **risk-free rate of return**. This risk premium will include both a business risk and a financial risk element in it. This equation forms the basis of the **capital asset pricing model (CAPM)**, which we shall look at in the next chapter.

Question

Portfolio theory

Learning outcome: B(i)

What are the practical implications of portfolio theory to a fund manager and to the projects manager of a company?

Answer

The practical implications of portfolio theory to a fund manager are highly significant, and are increasingly put into practice as competition for investment funds becomes keener.

Portfolio theory suggests that fund managers should **diversify** the risk-bearing part of their holdings. When taken in conjunction with the efficient market hypothesis, portfolio theory suggests that investors cannot consistently achieve a better risk return trade-off than that offered by the stock market index (eg the FTSE index for London shares). To satisfy the demand for diversified portfolios, index tracking funds are now available. These are popular in UK and US but are of less relevance in less efficient stock markets.

At first sight it may appear that the projects manager of a company should seek to diversify the company's business into as many different fields as possible, in order to reduce the company's risk. However, the manager should realise that investment decisions are made on behalf of shareholders, who are able to **diversify** their **overall portfolios** by buying shares in many different companies. For such shareholders the **overall risk** of any individual company is irrelevant. What matters is the **incremental risk** that an individual project adds to the market portfolio.

Chapter roundup

- **Portfolio theory** takes account of the fact that many investors have a range of investments that are unlikely all to change values in step. The investor should be concerned with his or her overall position, not with the performance of individual investments.
- **Correlation** measures the degree to which the returns on investments vary with each other.
- Both individuals and firms diversify their investments. Individuals have **portfolios of shares** and firms have **portfolios of business operations** and **investments**. **Diversification** is equally an important consideration for the financial manager in making investment decisions.
- Reasons why companies should not diversify too far include their **lack of expertise** and **unfamiliarity with markets**. In particular diversification by investors is more efficient than diversification by companies.
- The interaction of **investors' preferences**, **efficient portfolios** and the **returns from risk-free investments** provides the **basis for calculating beta factors**.

Quick quiz

1 Which of the following factors is the least important when choosing investments to include in a portfolio?

A Security of returns
B Liquidity of investments
C Expected returns
D Geographical location

2 Match each of A, B, C and D to its equivalent: one of 1, 2, 3 or 4.

A	the expected return of a portfolio	1	the correlation coefficient of expected returns
B	the risk of a portfolio	2	the beta factor
C	relationship between returns from different investments	3	a weighted average of expected returns on portfolio investments
D	extent to which return exceeds the risk-free rate of return	4	the standard deviation of expected returns

3 Give an example of a risk-free security.

4 What do the initials 'CAPM' stand for?

5 Which of the following is an argument in favour of diversification by a company?

A Employees of the company are likely to possess specialised skills.
B Investors can probably reduce investment risk more efficiently than companies.
C Conglomerates are vulnerable to takeover bids with the purpose of 'unbundling'.
D The risk of variable profits may be reduced.

6 Negative correlation is where the performance of the investment is independent of how the other performs.

True ☐

False ☐

7 What is the significance of the equation $\frac{R_m - R_f}{\sigma_m}$?

8 .... is an entity comprising a number of dissimilar businesses.

Answers to quick quiz

1 D This will only be relevant if it impacts on one of the other primary factors, such as security or the expected level of returns.

2 A3; B4; C1; D2

3 Government stocks are generally considered to be virtually risk-free.

4 Capital asset pricing model

5 D The risk of variable profits may be reduced.

6 False; no correlation is the situation where performance is independent.

7 The equation is the gradient of the capital market line, the extent to which the required returns from a portfolio should exceed the risk-free rate of return.

8 Conglomerate

Now try the question below from the Exam Question Bank

Number	Level	Marks	Time
Q16	Introductory	n/a	25 mins

12

The capital asset pricing model

Introduction

The **Capital Asset Pricing Model** (CAPM) brings together aspects of topics already raised in earlier chapters: **portfolio theory**, the **cost of capital** and **gearing**. You need to be comfortable with using the CAPM equation $k_e = R_f + (R_m - R_f)\beta$, and also to be able to explain how CAPM can be used when organisations make investments, and what its limitations are. The concepts of systematic and unsystematic risk are particularly important, also the relationship between risk, uncertainty and reward.

In Section 4 we shall examine briefly the arbitrage pricing model, an alternative to the capital asset pricing model.

The last section of this chapter deals with the technique of manipulating beta factors to deal with changes in the risks organisations face. This is an important technique for exam purposes.

Topic list	Learning outcomes	Syllabus references	Ability required
1 Risk and the CAPM	B(i)	B(6), (7)	Evaluation
2 CAPM and portfolio management	B(i)	B(6)	Evaluation
3 CAPM and investment	B(i)	B(6)	Evaluation
4 The arbitrage pricing model	B(i)	B(6)	Evaluation
5 CAPM and MM combined – geared betas	B(i)	B(6)	Evaluation

1 Risk and the CAPM

FAST FORWARD

The CAPM is based on a comparison of the **systematic risk** of **individual investments** with the **risks of all shares** in the **market**.

1.1 Uses of the capital asset pricing model (CAPM)

(a) Trying to **establish** the **'correct' equilibrium market value** of a company's shares

(b) Trying to **establish** the **cost of a company's equity** (and the company's average cost of capital), taking account of the risk characteristics of a company's investments, both business and financial risk

The capital asset pricing model (CAPM) provides an approach to establishing a cost of equity capital which is an alternative to the dividend valuation model which we looked at earlier.

1.2 Systematic risk and unsystematic risk

FAST FORWARD

The **risk** involved in holding securities (shares) divides into **risk specific** to the company (unsystematic) and risk due to **variations** in **market activity** (systematic).

Unsystematic or business risk can be diversified away, while **systematic or market risk** cannot. Investors may mix a diversified market portfolio with risk-free assets to achieve a preferred mix of risk and return.

Whenever an investor invests in some shares, or a company invests in a new project, there will be some risk involved. The actual return on the investment might be better or worse than that hoped for. To some extent, risk is unavoidable (unless the investor settles for risk-free securities such as gilts).

Provided that the investor **diversifies** his investments in a suitably wide portfolio, the investments which perform well and those which perform badly should tend to cancel each other out, and much risk can be diversified away. In the same way, a company which invests in a number of projects will find that some do well and some do badly, but taking the whole portfolio of investments, average returns should turn out much as expected.

Risks that can be diversified away are referred to as **unsystematic risk**. But there is another sort of risk too. Some investments are by their very nature more risky than others. This has nothing to do with chance variations up or down in actual returns compared with what an investor should expect. This **inherent risk** – the **systematic risk** or **market risk** – cannot be diversified away (see Figure 1).

Key terms

Market or **systematic risk** is risk that cannot be diversified away. **Non-systematic** or **unsystematic risk** applies to a single investment or class of investments, and can be reduced or eliminated by diversification. *(OT 2005)*

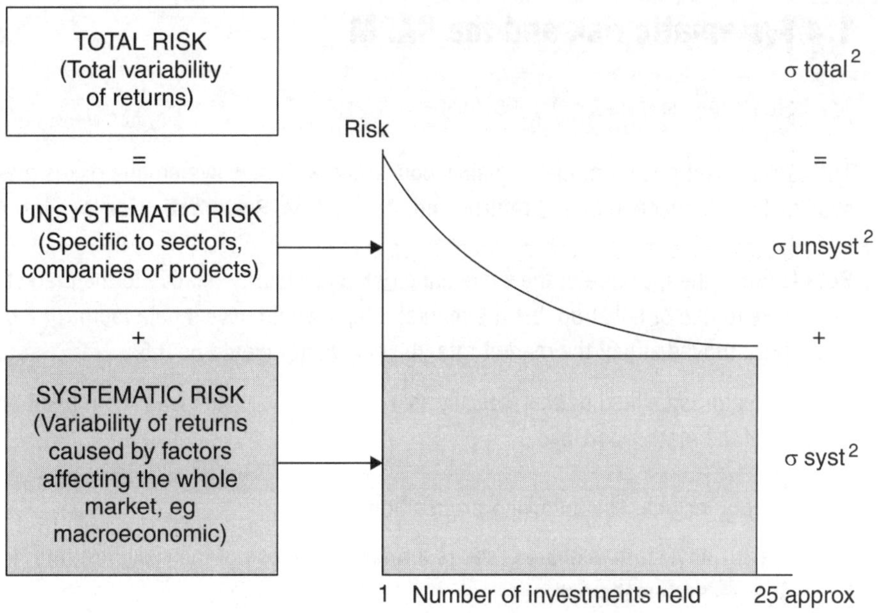

Figure 1

In return for accepting systematic risk, a **risk-averse investor** will expect to **earn a return** which is **higher** than the return on a risk-free investment.

The amount of systematic risk in an investment varies between different types of investment.

Exam focus point

Common errors on this topic in exams include:

- Assuming risk-averse investors wish to eliminate risk. Risk-averse investors are prepared to accept risk, in exchange for higher returns
- Failing to link the risks of an investment with its returns
- Mixing up systematic and unsystematic risk

1.3 Systematic risk and unsystematic risk: implications for investments

The implications of systematic risk and unsystematic risk are as follows.

(a) If an investor wants to **avoid risk** altogether, he must **invest entirely** in **risk-free securities**.

(b) If an investor **holds shares in just a few companies**, there will be **some unsystematic risk** as well as systematic risk in his portfolio, because he will not have spread his risk enough to diversify away the unsystematic risk. To eliminate unsystematic risk, he must build up a well diversified portfolio of investments.

(c) If an investor holds a **balanced portfolio** of all the stocks and shares on the stock market, he will incur systematic risk which is exactly equal to the average systematic risk in the stock market as a whole.

(d) **Shares in individual companies** will have **different systematic risk characteristics** to this market average. Some shares will be less risky and some will be more risky than the stock market average. Similarly, some investments will be more risky and some will be less risky than a company's 'average' investments.

1.4 Systematic risk and the CAPM

FAST FORWARD

The **beta factor** measures a share's volatility in terms of market risk.

The capital asset pricing model is mainly concerned with how systematic risk is measured, and how systematic risk affects required returns and share prices. **Systematic risk** is measured using **beta factors**.

Key term

Beta factor is the measure of the systematic risk of a security relative to the market portfolio. If a share price were to rise or fall at double the market rate, it would have a beta factor of 2.0. Conversely, if the share price moved at half the market rate, the beta factor would be 0.5.

The beta factor is defined mathematically as a share's covariance with the market portfolio divided by the variance of the market portfolio. *(OT 2005)*

CAPM theory includes the following propositions.

(a) Investors in shares require a **return** in **excess of the risk-free rate**, to compensate them for systematic risk.

(b) Investors should **not require** a **premium** for **unsystematic risk**, because this can be diversified away by holding a wide portfolio of investments.

(c) Because systematic risk varies between companies, investors will require a **higher return** from shares in those companies where the systematic risk is bigger.

The same propositions can be applied to capital investments by companies.

(a) Companies will want a **return on a project** to **exceed** the **risk-free rate**, to compensate them for systematic risk.

(b) **Unsystematic risk** can be **diversified away**, and so a premium for unsystematic risk should not be required.

(c) Companies should want a **bigger return** on projects where **systematic risk is greater**.

1.5 Market risk and returns

Market risk (systematic risk) is the average risk of the market as a whole. Taking all the shares on a stock market together, the total expected returns from the market will vary because of systematic risk. The market as a whole might do well or it might do badly.

1.6 Risk and returns from an individual security

In the same way, an individual security may offer prospects of a return of x%, but with some risk (business risk and financial risk) attached. The return (the x%) that investors will require from the individual security will be higher or lower than the market return, depending on whether the security's systematic risk is greater or less than the market average. A major **assumption in CAPM** is that there is a linear relationship between the return obtained from an individual security and the average return from all securities in the market.

1.7 Example: CAPM (1)

The following information is available about the performance of an individual company's shares and the stock market as a whole.

	Individual company	*Stock market as a whole*
Price at start of period	105.0	480.0
Price at end of period	110.0	490.0
Dividend during period	7.6	39.2

The expected return on the company's shares R_j and the expected return on the 'market portfolio' of shares R_m may be calculated as:

$$\frac{\text{Capital gain (or loss)} + \text{dividend}}{\text{Price at start of period}}$$

$$R_j = \frac{(110-105)+7.6}{105} = 0.12 \qquad R_m = \frac{(490-480)+39.2}{480} = 0.1025$$

A statistical analysis of 'historic' returns from a security and from the 'average' market may suggest that a linear relationship can be assumed to exist between them. A series of comparative figures could be prepared (month by month) of the return from a company's shares and the average return of the market as a whole. The results could be drawn on a scattergraph and a 'line of best fit' drawn (using linear regression techniques) as shown in Figure 2.

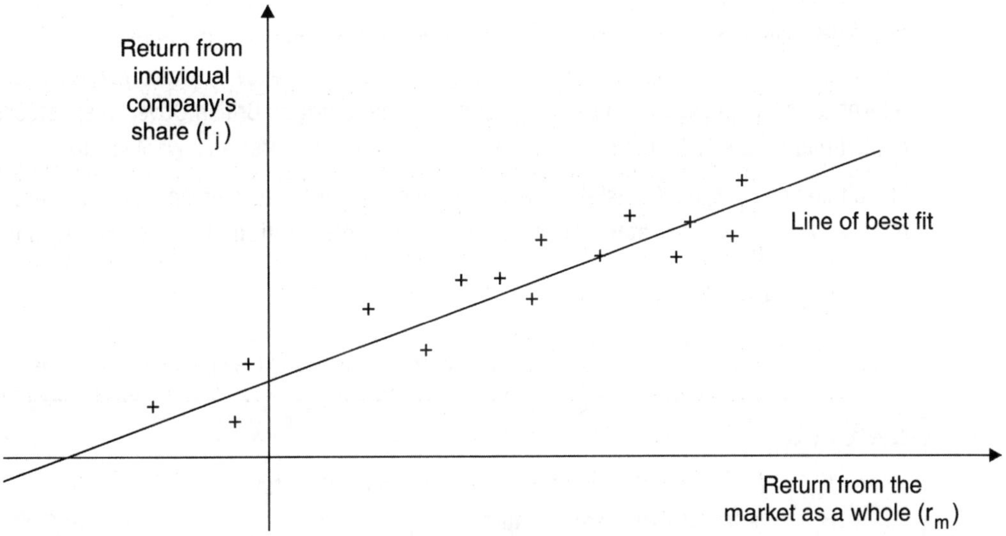

Figure 2

This analysis would show three things.

(a) The **return from** the **security** and the **return from** the **market** as a whole **will tend to rise or fall together**.

(b) The **return from the security** may be **higher or lower** than the **market return**. This is because the systematic risk of the individual security differs from that of the market as a whole.

(c) The scattergraph may **not give a good line of best fit**, unless a large number of data items are plotted, because actual returns are affected by unsystematic risk as well as by systematic risk.

Note that returns can be negative. A share price fall represents a capital loss, which is a negative return.

The conclusion from this analysis is that individual securities will be either more or less risky than the market average in a fairly predictable way. The measure of this relationship between market returns and an individual security's returns, reflecting differences in systematic risk characteristics, can be developed into a beta factor for the individual security.

1.8 The beta factor and the market risk premium

Key term

Market risk premium is the difference between the expected rate of return on a market portfolio and the risk-free rate of return over the same period. *(OT 2005)*

Suppose that returns on shares in XYZ plc tend to vary twice as much as returns from the market as a whole, so that if market returns went up 3%, say, returns on XYZ plc shares would be expected to go up by 6% and if market returns fell by 3%, returns on XYZ plc shares would be expected to fall by 6%. The beta factor of XYZ plc shares would be 2.0.

Thus if the average market return rises by, say, 2%, the return from a share with a beta factor of 0.8 should rise by 1.6% in response to the **same conditions** which have caused the market return to change. The **actual return** from the share might rise by, say, 2.5%, or even fall by, say, 1%, but the difference between the actual change and a change of 1.6% due to general market factors would be attributed to unsystematic risk factors unique to the company or its industry.

It is an essential principle of CAPM theory that **unsystematic** risk can be **cancelled** out by diversification.

1.9 Excess returns over returns on risk-free investments

The CAPM also makes use of the principle that **returns on shares** in the **market** as a whole are expected to be higher than the returns on risk-free investments. The difference between market returns and risk-free returns is called an **excess return**. For example, if the return on British Government stocks is 9% and market returns are 13%, the **excess** return on the market's shares as a whole is 4%.

The difference between the risk-free return and the expected return on an individual security can be measured as the **excess return for the market as a whole multiplied** by **the security's beta factor**.

1.10 The CAPM formula

The capital asset pricing model is a statement of the principles explained above. It can be stated as follows.

Exam Formula

$$k_e = R_f + (R_m - R_f)\beta$$

where k_e is the cost of equity capital – expected equity return
R_f is the risk-free rate of return
R_m is the return from the market as a whole
β is the beta factor of the individual security

1.11 Example: CAPM (1)

Shares in Louie and Dewie have a beta of 0.9. The expected returns to the market are 10% and the risk-free rate of return is 4%. What is the expected rate of return of ordinary shares in Louie and Dewie?

Solution

$$k_e = R_f + [R_m - R_f]\ \beta$$

$$= 4 + (10 - 4)\ 0.9$$

$$= 9.4\%$$

1.12 Example: CAPM (2)

Investors have an expected rate of return of 8% from ordinary shares in Algol, which have a beta of 1.2. The expected returns to the market are 7%.

What will be the expected rate of return from ordinary shares in Rigel, which have a beta of 1.8?

Solution

Algol $k_e = R_f + \beta[R_m - R_f]\ \beta$

$8 = R_f + 1.2(7 - R_f)$

$8 = R_f + 8.4 - 1.2\ R_f$

$0.2\ R_f = 0.4$

$R_f = 2$

Rigel $k_e = 2 + (7 - 2)\ 1.8$

$= 11\%$

Key terms

Capital asset pricing model (CAPM) is a theory which predicts that the expected risk premium for an individual stock will be proportional to its beta, such that:

Expected risk premium on a stock = beta × expected risk premium in the market.

Risk premium is defined as the expected incremental return for making a risky investment rather than a safe one. *(OT 2005)*

Exam focus point

A common mistake when using the formula is to take (Rm – Rf) to the power of Beta, rather than multiplying it by the Beta factor.

Question

Returns

Learning outcome: B(i)

The risk-free rate of return is 7%. The average market return is 11%.

(a) What will be the return expected from a share whose β factor is 0.9?

(b) What would be the share's expected value if it is expected to earn an annual dividend of 5.3p, with no capital growth?

Answer

(a) 7% + (11% – 7%) × 0.9 = 10.6%

(b) $\dfrac{5.3\text{p}}{10.6\%} = 50$ pence

1.13 Problems with applying the CAPM in practice

FAST FORWARD

Problems of CAPM include **unrealistic assumptions** and the **required estimates being difficult to make.**

(a) The need to **determine** the **excess return** ($R_m - R_f$). Expected, rather than historical, returns should be used, although historical returns are often used in practice.

(b) The need to **determine** the **risk-free rate.** A risk-free investment might be a government security. However, interest rates vary with the term of the lending.

(c) **Errors** in the **statistical analysis used** to calculate β values. Betas may also **change over** time.

(d) The CAPM is also **unable to forecast accurately returns** for companies with **low price/earnings** ratios and to take account of seasonal 'month-of-the-year' effects and 'day-of-the-week' effects that appear to influence returns on shares.

Question

Beta factor

Learning outcome: B(i)

(a) What does beta measure, and what do betas of 0.5, 1 and 1.5 mean?
(b) What factors determine the level of beta which a company may have?

Answer

(a) **Beta measures** the systematic risk of a risky investment such as a share in a company. The total risk of the share can be sub-divided into two parts, known as **systematic (or market) risk** and **unsystematic (or unique) risk**. The systematic risk depends on the sensitivity of the return of the share to general economic and market factors such as periods of boom and recession. The capital asset pricing model shows how the return which investors expect from shares should depend only on systematic risk, not on unsystematic risk, which can be eliminated by holding a well-diversified portfolio.

Beta is calibrated such that the average risk of stock market investments has a **beta of 1**. Thus shares with betas of 0.5 or 1.5 would have half or 1½ times the average sensitivity to market variations respectively.

This is reflected by higher volatility of share prices for shares with a beta of 1.5 than for those with a beta of 0.5. For example, a 10% increase in general stock market prices would be expected to be reflected as a 5% increase for a share with a beta of 0.5 and a 15% increase for a share with a beta of 1.5, with a similar effect for price reductions.

(b) The beta of a company will be the **weighted average** of the beta of its shares and the beta of its debt. The beta of debt is very low, but not zero, because corporate debt bears default risk, which in turn is dependent on the volatility of the company's cash flows.

Factors determining the beta of a company's equity shares include:

(i) **Sensitivity** of the company's **cash flows** to economic factors, as stated above. For example sales of new cars are more sensitive than sales of basic foods and necessities.

(ii) The company's **operating gearing**. A high level of fixed costs in the company's cost structure will cause high variations in operating profit compared with variations in sales.

(iii) The company's **financial gearing**. High borrowing and interest costs will cause high variations in equity earnings compared with variations in operating profit, increasing the equity beta as equity returns become more variable in relation to the market as a whole. This effect will be countered by the low beta of debt when computing the weighted average beta of the whole company.

1.14 Dividend growth model and CAPM

The two models will not necessarily give the same cost of equity and you may have to calculate the cost of equity using either, or both, models.

1.14.1 Example : Dividend growth model and CAPM

The following data relates to the ordinary shares of Stilton.

Current market price, 31 December 20X1	250p
Dividend per share, 20X1	3p
Expected growth rate in dividends and earnings	10% pa
Average market return	8%
Risk-free rate of return	5%
Beta factor of Stilton equity shares	1.40

(a) What is the estimated cost of equity using the dividend growth model?

(b) What is the estimated cost of equity using the capital asset pricing model?

Solution

(a) $k_e = \dfrac{d(1+g)}{MV} + g$

$= \dfrac{3(1.10)}{250} + 0.10$

$= 0.1132$ or 11.32%

(b) $k_e = 5 + (8 - 5)\,1.40 = 9.2\%$

1.15 Alpha values

FAST FORWARD

The **alpha value** is a measure of a share's **abnormal return.**

Key term

A share's **alpha value** is a measure of its abnormal return, which is the amount by which the share's returns are currently above or below the required return, given the level of systematic risk.

The alpha value can be seen as a measure of how wrong the CAPM is.
Alpha values:

(a) **Reflect only temporary, abnormal returns**, if CAPM is a realistic model

(b) **Can be positive or negative**

(c) Over time, will **tend towards zero** for any individual share, and for a well-diversified portfolio taken as a whole will be 0

(d) May exist due to the **inaccuracies and limitations of the CAPM**

Exam focus point

In the exam you may be asked to compare the required return (calculated by CAPM) with the expected current return of the portfolio, and hence calculate the alpha value.

If the **alpha value** is **positive**, investors who don't hold shares will be tempted to buy them (to take advantage of the abnormal return), and investors who do hold shares will want to hold on to them so share prices will rise. If the **alpha value** is **negative**, investors won't want to buy shares, and current holders will want to sell them, so share prices will fall.

Exam focus point

In the exam you may need to identify which share has the largest alpha value and hence is the most attractive investment.

1.15.1 Example: Alpha values

ABC's shares have a beta value of 1.2 and an alpha value of +2%. The market return is 10% and the risk-free rate of return is 6%. What is the current return?

Solution

Required return = 6 + (10 – 6) 1.2 = 10.8%

Current return = required return ± alpha value
= 10.8 + 2 = 12.8%

2 CAPM and portfolio management

FAST FORWARD

The **expected return** of a portfolio of shares can be calculated by calculating the weighted beta of the portfolio and using CAPM.

2.1 Beta factors of portfolio

Just as an individual security has a beta factor, so too does a portfolio of securities.

(a) A **portfolio** consisting of **all the securities** on the stock market (in the same proportions as the market as a whole), **excluding risk-free securities**, will have an expected return equal to the expected return for the market as a whole, and so will have a **beta factor of 1**.

(b) A portfolio consisting entirely of **risk-free securities** will have a **beta factor of 0**.

(c) The **beta factor** of an **investor's portfolio** is the **weighted average** of the **beta factors** of the **securities in the portfolio**.

2.2 Example: CAPM

A portfolio consisting of five securities could have its beta factor computed as follows.

Security	*Percentage of portfolio*	*Beta factor of security*	*Weighted beta factor*
A plc	20%	0.90	0.180
B plc	10%	1.25	0.125
C plc	15%	1.10	0.165
D plc	20%	1.15	0.230
E plc	35%	0.70	0.245
	100%	Portfolio beta	0.945

If the risk-free rate of return is 12% and the average market return is 20%, the expected return from the portfolio would be 12% + (20 – 12) × 0.945% = 19.56%

The calculation could have been made as follows.

Security	*Beta factor*	*Expected return*	*Weighting* %	*Weighted return* %
A plc	0.90	19.2	20	3.84
B plc	1.25	22.0	10	2.20
C plc	1.10	20.8	15	3.12
D plc	1.15	21.2	20	4.24
E plc	0.70	17.6	35	6.16
			100	19.56

Exam focus point

Possible mistakes here include calculating the required rate of return for individual shares without calculating the average for the portfolio, and calculating a simple average rather than a weighted average.

2.3 CAPM and portfolio management

Practical implications of CAPM theory for an investor are as follows.

(a) He should decide what **beta factor** he would like to have for his portfolio. He might prefer a portfolio beta factor of greater than 1, in order to expect above-average returns when market returns exceed the risk-free rate, but he would then expect to lose heavily if market returns fall. On the other hand, he might prefer a portfolio beta factor of 1 or even less.

(b) He should seek to invest in shares with **low beta factors** in a bear market, when **average market returns** are **falling**. He should then also sell shares with high beta factors.

(c) He should seek to **invest in shares** with **high beta factors** in a **bull market**, when average market returns are rising.

An investor can measure the beta factor of his portfolio by obtaining information about the beta factors of individual securities. These are obtainable from a variety of investment analysts.

2.4 Limitations of the CAPM for the selection of a portfolio of securities

Under the CAPM, the return required from a security is related to its systematic risk rather than its total risk. If we relax some of the assumptions upon which the model is based, as follows, then the **total risk** may be important.

(a) The model assumes that the costs of insolvency are zero, or in other words, that all assets can be sold at going concern prices. In practice, the costs of insolvency cannot be ignored. Furthermore, the risk of insolvency is related to a firm's total risk rather than just its systematic risk.

(b) The model assumes that the **investment market** is **efficient**. If it is not, this will limit the extent to which investors are able to eliminate unsystematic risk.

(c) The model also assumes that portfolios are **well diversified** and so need only be concerned with systematic risk. However, this is not necessarily the case, and undiversified or partly diversified shareholders should also be concerned with unsystematic risk.

3 CAPM and investment

FAST FORWARD

CAPM can be used to produce a **cost of capital** for an **investment project**, based on the systematic risk of that investment.

3.1 The use of the CAPM for capital investment decisions

The CAPM produces a required return based on the expected return of the market (R_m), the risk-free interest rate (R_f) and the variability of project returns relative to the market returns (β). Its main advantage when used for investment appraisal is that it produces a discount rate which is based on the **systematic** risk of the individual investment. It can be used to **compare projects of all different risk classes** and is therefore superior to an NPV approach which uses only one discount rate for all projects, regardless of their risk.

The model was developed with respect to securities; by applying it to an investment within the firm, the company is assuming that the shareholder wishes investments to be evaluated as if they were securities in the capital market and thus assumes that all shareholders will hold **diversified portfolios** and will not look to the company to achieve diversification for them.

3.2 Example: required return

Panda is all-equity financed. It wishes to invest in a project with an estimated beta of 1.5. The project has significantly different business risk characteristics from Panda's current operations. The project requires an outlay of £10,000 and will generate expected returns of £12,000.

The market rate of return is 12% and the risk-free rate of return is 6%.

Required

Estimate the minimum return that Panda will require from the project and assess whether the project is worthwhile, based on the figures you are given.

Solution

We do not need to know Panda's current weighted average cost of capital, as the new project has different business characteristics from its current operations. Instead we use the capital asset pricing model so that;

$$\text{Required return} = 6 + 1.5(12 - 6)$$
$$= 15\%$$

$$\text{Expected return} = \frac{12{,}000 - 10{,}000}{10{,}000}$$

$$= 20\%$$

Thus the project is worthwhile, as expected return exceeds required return.

3.3 Limitations of using CAPM in investment decisions

The greatest practical problems with the use of the CAPM in capital investment decisions are as follows.

(a) It is **hard to estimate** returns on projects under different economic environments, market returns under different economic environments and the probabilities of the various environments.

(b) The CAPM is really just a **single period model**. Few investment projects last for one year only and to extend the use of the return estimated from the model to more than one time period would require both project performance relative to the market and the economic environment to be reasonably stable.

In theory, it should be possible to apply the CAPM for each time period, thus arriving at successive discount rates, one for each year of the project's life. In practice, this would exacerbate the estimation problems mentioned above and also make the discounting process much more cumbersome.

(c) It may be **hard to determine the risk-free rate of return**. Government securities are usually taken to be risk-free, but the return on these securities varies according to their term to maturity.

Some experts have argued that betas calculated using complicated statistical techniques often overestimate high betas, and underestimate low betas, particularly for small companies. Sometimes equations are used to adjust betas calculated statistically, such as:

Adjusted β = 0.5 (statistically calculated Beta) + 0.5

This sort of equation increases Betas that are less than 1 and lowers Betas higher than one.

4 The arbitrage pricing model

FAST FORWARD

In the future the **arbitrage pricing model** could replace the CAPM as a tool for analysing the determination of risk and returns.

4.1 CAPM and APM

Exam focus point

What is important here is to be aware that there are other models apart from the CAPM, and to know the benefits and limitations of the arbitrage pricing model (APM) relative to the CAPM.

The CAPM is seen as a useful analytical tool by financial managers as well as by financial analysts. However, critics suggest that the relationship between risk and return is more complex than is assumed in the CAPM. One model which could replace the CAPM in the future is the **arbitrage pricing model (APM)**.

4.2 Factors influencing APM

Unlike the CAPM, which analyses the returns on a share as a function of a single factor – the return on the market portfolio – the APM assumes that the return on each security is based on a number of independent factors. The required return on an asset is shown as:

$E(k_e) = r_f + \lambda\beta_1 + \lambda_2\beta_2 + \dots \lambda_n\beta_n$

where $E(k_e)$ is the required return on an asset

r_f is the risk-free rate of return

λ is the 'market price' for each risk factor ie the difference between the actual and expected value of each factor

β is the sensitivity of the asset's returns to changes in the value of each factor

Key term

Arbitrage pricing theory is a model which assumes that the return on a security is based on a number of independent factors, to each of which a particular risk premium is attached.

Factor analysis is used to ascertain the factors to which security returns are sensitive. Four key factors identified by researchers have been:

- Unanticipated inflation
- Changes in the expected level of industrial production
- Changes in the risk premium on bonds (debentures)
- Unanticipated changes in the term structure of interest rates

4.3 APM in practice

With the APM, the CAPM's problem of identifying the market portfolio is avoided, but this is replaced with the problem of identifying the macroeconomic factors and their risk sensitivities. As with the CAPM, the available empirical evidence is inconclusive and neither proves nor disproves the theory of the APM. Both the CAPM and the APM do however provide a means of analysing how risk and return may be determined in conditions of competition and uncertainty.

5 CAPM and MM combined – geared betas 11/05

FAST FORWARD

When an investment has differing business and finance risks from the existing business, **geared betas** may be used to obtain an appropriate required return.

Geared betas are calculated by:

– Ungearing industry betas
– Converting ungeared betas back into a geared beta that reflects the company's own gearing ratio

5.1 Beta values and the effect of gearing

The gearing of a company will affect the risk of its equity. If a company is geared and its **financial risk is therefore higher** than the risk of an all-equity company, then the β value of the geared company's equity will be higher than the β value of a similar ungeared company's equity.

The CAPM is consistent with the propositions of Modigliani and Miller. MM argue that as gearing rises, the cost of equity rises to compensate shareholders for the extra financial risk of investing in a geared company. This financial risk is an aspect of systematic risk, and ought to be reflected in a company's beta factor.

5.2 Geared betas and ungeared betas

The connection between MM theory and the CAPM means that it is possible to establish a mathematical relationship between the β value of an ungeared company and the β value of a similar, but geared, company. The β value of a geared company will be higher than the β value of a company identical in every respect except that it is all-equity financed. This is because of the extra financial risk. The mathematical relationship between the 'ungeared' (or asset) and 'geared' betas is as follows.

$$\beta_u = \beta_g \frac{V_E}{V_E + V_D(1-t)} + \beta_d \frac{V_D(1-t)}{V_E + V_D(1-t)}$$

where β_u is the beta factor of an ungeared company: the ungeared beta
β_g is the beta factor of equity in a similar, but geared company: the geared beta
β_d is the beta factor of debt in the geared company
V_D is the market value of the debt capital in the geared company
V_E is the market value of the equity capital in the geared company
t is the rate of corporate tax

Debt is often assumed to be risk-free and its beta (β_d) is then taken as zero, in which case the formula above reduces to the following form.

Exam Formulae

$$\beta_u = \beta_g \times \frac{V_E}{V_E + V_D(1-t)} \quad \text{or, without tax,} \quad \beta_u = \beta_g \times \frac{V_E}{V_E + V_D}$$

Exam focus point

You will need to be able to ungear and regear a beta in order to calculate a value for a company.

5.3 Example: CAPM and geared betas

Two companies are identical in every respect except for their capital structure. Their market values are in equilibrium, as follows.

	Geared	*Ungeared*
	£'000	£'000
Annual profit before interest and tax	1,000	1,000
Less interest (4,000 × 8%)	320	0
	680	1,000
Less tax at 30%	204	300
Profit after tax = dividends	476	700
Market value of equity	3,900	6,600
Market value of debt	4,180	0
Total market value of company	8,080	6,600

The total value of Geared is higher than the total value of Ungeared, which is consistent with MM.

All profits after tax are paid out as dividends, and so there is no dividend growth. The beta value of Ungeared has been calculated as 1.0. The debt capital of Geared can be regarded as risk-free.

Calculate:

(a) The cost of equity in Geared
(b) The market return R_m
(c) The beta value of Geared

Solution

(a) Since its market value (MV) is in equilibrium, the cost of equity in Geared can be calculated as:

$$\frac{d}{MV} = \frac{476}{3,900} = 12.20\%$$

(b) The beta value of Ungeared is 1.0, which means that the expected returns from Ungeared are exactly the same as the market returns, and R_m = 700/6,600 = 10.6%.

(c) $$\beta_g = \beta_u \times \frac{V_E + V_D(1-t)}{V_E}$$

$$= 1.0 \times \frac{3,900 + (4,180 \times 0.70)}{3,900} = 1.75$$

The beta of Geared, as we should expect, is higher than the beta of Ungeared.

5.4 Using the geared and ungeared beta formula to estimate a beta factor

Another way of estimating a beta factor for a company's equity is to use data about the returns of other quoted companies which have similar operating characteristics: that is, to use the beta values of other companies' equity to estimate a beta value for the company under consideration. The beta values estimated for the firm under consideration must be **adjusted to allow for differences in gearing** from the firms whose equity beta values are known. The formula for geared and ungeared beta values can be applied.

If a company plans to invest in a project which involves diversification into a new business, the investment will involve a different level of systematic risk from that applying to the company's existing business. A discount rate should be calculated which is specific to the project, and which takes account of both the project's systematic risk and the company's gearing level. The discount rate can be found using the CAPM.

Step 1 Get an estimate of the systematic risk characteristics of the project's operating cash flows by obtaining published beta values for companies in the industry into which the company is planning to diversify.

Step 2 Adjust these beta values to allow for the company's capital gearing level. This adjustment is done in two stages.

Step 2A Convert the beta values of other companies in the industry to ungeared betas, using the formula:

$$\beta_u = \beta_g \frac{V_E}{V_E + V_D(1-t)}$$

Step 2B Having obtained an ungeared beta value β_u, convert it back to a geared beta β_g, which reflects the company's own gearing ratio, using the formula:

$$\beta_g = \beta_u \frac{V_E + V_D(1-t)}{V_E}$$

Step 3 Having estimated a project-specific geared beta, use the CAPM to estimate:

Step 3A A project-specific cost of equity, and

Step 3B A project-specific cost of capital, based on a weighting of this cost of equity and the cost of the company's debt capital

5.5 Example: Gearing and ungearing betas

A company's debt:equity ratio, by market values, is 2:5. The corporate debt, which is assumed to be risk-free, yields 11% before tax. The beta value of the company's equity is currently 1.1. The average returns on stock market equity are 16%.

The company is now proposing to invest in a project which would involve diversification into a new industry, and the following information is available about this industry.

(a) Average beta coefficient of equity capital = 1.59
(b) Average debt:equity ratio in the industry = 1:2 (by market value).

The rate of corporation tax is 30%. What would be a suitable cost of capital to apply to the project?

Solution

Step 1 The beta value for the industry is 1.59.

Step 2A Convert the geared beta value for the industry to an ungeared beta for the industry.

$$\beta_u = 1.59 \left(\frac{2}{2+(1(1-0.30))} \right) = 1.18$$

Step 2B Convert this ungeared industry beta back into a geared beta, which reflects the company's own gearing level of 2:5.

$$\beta_g = 1.18 \left(\frac{5+(2(1-0.30))}{5} \right) = 1.51$$

Step 3A This is a project-specific beta for the firm's equity capital, and so using the CAPM, we can estimate the project-specific cost of equity as:

$$k_{eg} = 11\% + (16\% - 11\%)\ 1.51 = 18.55\%$$

Step 3B The project will presumably be financed in a gearing ratio of 2:5 debt to equity, and so the project-specific cost of capital ought to be:

$$[\frac{5}{7} \times 18.55\%\,] + [\,\frac{2}{7} \times 70\% \times 11\%\,] = 15.45\%$$

Question

Ungeared and geared betas

Learning outcome: B (i)

Two companies are identical in every respect except for their capital structure. XY has a debt: equity ratio of 1:3, and its equity has a β value of 1.20. PQ has a debt:equity ratio of 2:3. Corporation tax is at 30%. Estimate a β value for PQ's equity.

Answer

Estimate an ungeared beta from XY data.

$$\beta_a = 1.20 \frac{3}{3+(1(1-0.30))} = 0.973$$

Estimate a geared beta for PQ using this ungeared beta.

$$\beta_e = 0.973\ \frac{3+(2(1-0.30))}{3} = 1.427$$

Exam focus point

Question 3 in November 2005 required candidates to de-gear and re-gear a beta and calculate a range of values for a given entity. This was generally poorly attempted with many not realising the approach that was required.

5.6 Weaknesses in the formula

The problems with using the geared and ungeared beta formula for calculating a firm's equity beta from data about other firms are as follows.

(a) It is **difficult to identify other firms** with **identical operating characteristics**.

(b) **Estimates of beta values** from **share price information are not wholly accurate**. They are based on statistical analysis of historical data, and as the previous example shows, estimates using one firm's data will differ from estimates using another firm's data. The beta values for Crispy estimated from Snapp, Crackle and Popper are all different.

(c) There may be **differences in beta values** between firms caused by:

   (i) Different cost structures (eg, the ratio of fixed costs to variable costs)
   (ii) Size differences between firms
   (iii) Debt capital not being risk-free

(d) If the firm for which an equity beta is being estimated has **opportunities for growth** that are recognised by investors, and which will affect its equity beta, estimates of the equity beta based on other firms' data will be inaccurate, because the opportunities for growth will not be allowed for.

Perhaps the most significant simplifying assumption is that to link MM theory to the CAPM, it must be assumed that the **cost of debt** is a **risk-free rate of return**. This could obviously be unrealistic. Companies may default on interest payments or capital repayments on their loans. It has been estimated that corporate debt has a beta value of 0.2 or 0.3.

The consequence of making the assumption that debt is risk-free is that the formulae tend to **overstate** the financial risk in a geared company and to **understate** the business risk in geared and ungeared companies by a compensating amount. In other words, β_u will be slightly higher and β_g will be slightly lower than the formulae suggest.

Question — Gearing and ungearing betas

Learning outcome: B(i)

Backwoods is a major international company with its head office in the UK, wanting to raise €150 million to establish a new production plant in the eastern region of Germany. Backwoods evaluates its investments using NPV, but is not sure what cost of capital to use in the discounting process for this project evaluation.

The company is also proposing to increase its equity finance in the near future for UK expansion, resulting overall in little change in the company's market-weighted capital gearing.

The summarised financial data for the company before the expansion are shown below.

Income statement for the year ended 31 December 20X1

	£m
Revenue	1,984
Gross profit	432
Profit after tax	81
Dividends	37
Retained earnings	44

Balance sheet as at 31 December 20X1

	£m
Non-current assets	846
Working capital	350
	1,196
Medium term and long term loans (see note below)	210
	986
Shareholders' funds	
Issued ordinary shares of £0.50 each nominal value	225
Reserves	761
	986

Note on borrowings

These include £75m 14% fixed rate bonds due to mature in five years time and redeemable at par. The current market price of these bonds is £120.00 and they have a cost of debt of 9%. Other medium and long-term loans are floating rate UK bank loans at LIBOR plus 1%, with a cost of debt of 7%.

Company rate of tax may be assumed to be at the rate of 30%. The company's ordinary shares are currently trading at 376 pence.

The equity beta of Backwoods is estimated to be 1.18. The systematic risk of debt may be assumed to be zero. The risk free rate is 7.75% and market return 14.5%.

The estimated equity beta of the main German competitor in the same industry as the new proposed plant in the eastern region of Germany is 1.5, and the competitor's capital gearing is 35% equity and 65% debt by book values, and 60% equity and 40% debt by market values.

Required

Estimate the cost of capital that the company should use as the discount rate for its proposed investment in eastern Germany. State clearly any assumptions that you make.

Answer

The discount rate that should be used is the weighted average cost of capital (WACC), with weightings based on market values. The cost of capital should take into account the systematic risk of the new investment, and therefore it will not be appropriate to use the company's existing equity beta. Instead, the estimated equity beta of the main German competitor in the same industry as the new proposed plant will be ungeared, and then the capital structure of Backwoods applied to find the WACC to be used for the discount rate.

Since the systematic risk of debt can be assumed to be zero, the German equity beta can be 'ungeared' using the following expression.

$$\beta_u = \beta_g \frac{V_E}{V_E + V_D(1-t)}$$

where: β_u = asset beta
β_g = equity beta
V_E = proportion of equity in capital structure
V_D = proportion of debt in capital structure
t = tax rate

For the German company:

$$\beta_u = 1.5\left(\frac{60}{60+40(1-0.30)}\right) = 1.023$$

The next step is to calculate the debt and equity of Backwoods based on market values.

		£m
Equity	450m shares at 376p	1,692.0
Debt: bank loans	(210 – 75)	135.0
Debt: bonds	(75 million × 1.20)	90.0
Total debt		225.0
Total market value		1,917.0

The beta can now be re-geared

$$\beta_g = \frac{1.023(1{,}692 + 225\,(1-0.3))}{1{,}692} = 1.118$$

This can now be substituted into the capital asset pricing model (CAPM) to find the cost of equity.

$k_e = R_f + [R_m - R_f]\beta$

where: k_e = cost of equity
R_f = risk free rate of return
R_m = market rate of return
k_e = 7.75% + (14.5% – 7.75%) × 1.118 = 15.30%

The WACC can now be calculated:

$$\left[15.3 \times \frac{1{,}692}{1{,}917}\right] + \left[7 \times \frac{135}{1{,}917}\right] + \left[9 \times \frac{90}{1{,}917}\right] = 14.4\%$$

NB You have been given both costs of debt. In the exam you may well be asked to calculate the cost of debt.

Chapter roundup

- The CAPM is based on a comparison of the **systematic risk** of **individual investments** with the **risks of all shares** in the **market**.
- The **risk** involved in holding securities (shares) divides into **risk specific** to the company (unsystematic) and risk due to **variations** in **market activity** (systematic).
- **Unsystematic or business risk** can be diversified away, while **systematic or market risk** cannot. Investors may mix a diversified market portfolio with risk-free assets to achieve a preferred mix of risk and return.
- The **beta factor** measures a share's volatility in terms of market risk.
- Problems of CAPM include **unrealistic assumptions** and the **required estimates being difficult to make**.
- The **alpha value** is a measure of a share's abnormal return.
- The **expected return** of a portfolio of shares can be calculated by calculating the weighted beta of the portfolio and using CAPM.
- CAPM can be used to produce a **cost of capital** for an **investment project**, based on the systematic risk of that investment.
- In the future the **arbitrage pricing model** could replace the CAPM as a tool for analysing the determination of risk and returns.
- When an investment has differing business and finance risks from the existing business, **geared betas** may be used to obtain an appropriate required return.
- Geared betas are calculated by:
  - Ungearing industry betas
  - Converting ungeared betas back into a geared beta that reflects the company's own gearing ratio

Quick quiz

1 Which of the following risks can be eliminated by diversification?

A Inherent risk
B Systematic risk
C Market risk
D Unsystematic risk

2 Systematic risk is the risk arising from variability in returns caused by factors affecting the whole market.

True ☐

False ☐

3 An investor can virtually eliminate unsystematic risk by building up a well diversified portfolio of investments.

True ☐

False ☐

4 Unsystematic risk is measured by beta factors.

True ☐

False ☐

5 A portfolio consisting entirely of risk-free securities will have a beta factor of (tick one box):

–1 ☐

0 ☐

1 ☐

6 What are the main problems in using geared and ungeared Betas to calculate a firm's equity beta?

7 The risk free rate of return is 8%. Average market return is 14%. A share's beta factor is 0.5. What will be its expected return?

8 Which model assumes that the return on a security is based on a number of independent factors, to each of which a risk premium is attached?

9 What does the alpha value measure?

Answers to quick quiz

1 D Unsystematic risk is risk that is specific to sectors, companies or projects. Systematic risk (also known as inherent risk or market risk) affects the whole market and therefore cannot be reduced by diversification.

2 True

3 True

4 False. Beta factors measure systematic risk.

5 Zero

6
(a) It is difficult to identify other firms with identical operating characteristics.
(b) Estimates of beta values from share price information are not wholly accurate.
(c) There may be firm-specific causes of differences in beta values.
(d) The market may recognise opportunities for future growth for some firms but not others.

7 Expected return = 8 + (14 – 8)0.5 = 11%

8 Arbitrage pricing theory

9 The abnormal return which is the amount by which the share's returns are currently above or below the required return, given the level of systematic risk.

Now try the question below from the Exam Question Bank

Number	Level	Marks	Time
Q17	Examination	25	45 mins

13

The finance function

Introduction

In the last two chapters of Part B we consider the roles of the departments principally responsible for financial management, the finance function and the treasury function. In many organisations, there will only be a single function. However in larger organisations the responsibilities will be split broadly so that the **finance function** will be responsible for most of the operational issues, and the **treasury function** will be responsible for higher level strategic development plus operational issues involving special skills such as dealing with derivatives.

In the first section of this chapter we deal with the work of the finance function, and also provide indications of how its **performance** is **measured**. One of the most important roles of the finance function is maintaining good relations with stakeholders, for example auditors and investors, and we consider this aspect of their work in Section 2. The last section deals with how the role of the finance function is changing in the light of commercial and regulatory pressures.

Topic list	Learning outcomes	Syllabus references	Ability required
1 The role of the finance function	B(ii)	B(12)	Evaluation
2 Relationships with stakeholders	B(ii)	B(12)	Evaluation
3 Changes in the finance function	B(ii)	B(12)	Evaluation

1 The role of the finance function 11/06

FAST FORWARD

- The finance or financial control function's traditional role has been based on **recording, reporting** and **control of information**.
- Means of appraising this function include assessing the **reliability** of data and the **speed and efficiency** with which it is produced, and a wider scope **balanced scorecard** approach.

1.1 Financial control and treasury

Although an organisation may operate a single finance function covering all its financial activities, within this function a distinction can be made between financial control activities and treasury activities. Financial control activities have traditionally been focused on **recording** and **reporting results**. They have included:

- Preparation and monitoring of budgets
- Preparation of monthly, quarterly and annual accounts
- Co-ordination and management of associated functions such as payroll and internal audit

We shall discuss the function of the treasury department in the next chapter, but broadly the treasury department is responsible for determining **financial objectives and strategy**, and is also principally concerned with **managing funding, cash and investment**.

Clearly the two roles have many links. Treasury will use the detailed information prepared by the financial control function, and will in turn set down the parameters, (major assumptions, cost of capital) that the financial control function will use in its detailed calculations.

Exam focus point

The compulsory question in November 2006 required a discussion of the differing roles and responsibilities of the treasury and finance departments in relation to evaluating and implementing a project.

1.2 Assessment of the financial control function

There has been increasing emphasis over the last few years on assessment of the contribution made by financial control. Traditional measures of success have included the following.

1.2.1 Reliable information

A recent survey suggested that about four fifths of chief finance officers rate **reliability of information** as their highest priority. Its importance has been enhanced by the recent financial scandals and the requirement of the American Sarbanes-Oxley legislation for chief finance officers to sign off personally their company's accounts.

As well as fulfilling legal requirements, finance departments must have regard for the information required by different **stakeholders**, the information that is **relevant** to their needs.

Organisations will need to develop processes to ensure that information is reliable. For the finance function this means playing a key role in the development of technology that will **ensure information is reliable**, being available to answer queries and resolve problems and **educating** other staff to make sure that they are aware of the information needed, the accounting policies used by the company and the legal framework.

1.2.2 Flexibility

A very important aspect of the finance function's work is how it copes with **new developments**. A key task currently is to cope with the introduction of **international financial reporting standards**, which we discussed in detail in Chapter 4. As well as coping with the technical issues, the finance function also plays a vital role in **educating investors** on the language of the new standards and their impact upon the key performance indicators.

The management accounting function also needs to be flexible in **its response to users' requests** for information and reports.

1.2.3 Speed of reporting

The Sarbanes-Oxley legislation has also resulted in tighter reporting deadlines, with companies listed in the USA being required to file quarterly accounts in 35 days rather than 45 days, and annual reports in 60 rather than 90 days. An EU draft directive specifies 60 days for quarterly reports with further reductions towards 35 days.

In addition surveys suggest a possible link between market valuation and speed of reporting, with larger investors in particular viewing shorter reporting times as a sign that the company is well managed.

1.2.4 Efficiency

Pressure on the finance function to reduce costs and make greater use of resources, in particular speeding up basic processing functions, has greatly increased over the last few years. We shall see in Section 3 that this has led to pressure to **outsource** the basic functions, and let the financial control function concentrate on more 'exciting' work.

Measures of efficiency include:

- The number of transactions processed per transaction processing employee
- The cost of transactions processed as a percentage of revenue per transaction
- The time taken at period-ends to report results

1.3 Balanced scorecard approach

As well as the traditional measures discussed above, many organisations have used a balanced scorecard approach to judge the work of the finance function, focusing not just on **traditional financial measures**, but other measures of concern to stakeholders. Whilst many traditional measures focus purely on outcomes, balanced scorecard measures often go a stage back and measure the **factors** that will result in satisfactory outcomes.

1.3.1 Value enhancements

Success here is measured by enhancements of the **value drivers** of the finance function. Indicators of success might include the **level of integration of planning processes**, the **frequency of forecasts**, the **average preparation times** for key elements of the business planning process and the **percentage of finance function time** spent in **decision support activities**.

1.3.2 Customer satisfaction

This important element focuses on how much **support** the finance function provides to internal operations, suppliers and customers. Measures aim to assess the strength of relationships between the finance function and other stakeholders and whether the finance function is viewed as delivering the right mixture and quality of transaction processing, risk management and decision support.

Measures include how much **time** is spent with other stakeholders, the proportion of the finance staff who have had experience of operations and the percentage of transactions processed with errors. Regular **satisfaction surveys** are also important.

1.3.3 Internal processes measures

These focus on the processes that the finance function must carry out efficiently and effectively in order to report accurately and give customer satisfaction. Traditional efficiency measures are useful here, also **activity-based measures** and benchmarking (discussed further below).

1.3.4 Learning and growth

These measures concentrate on the organisation's ability to adapt to change and also the development of finance staff's **skills and competencies**. Possible measures include turnover of finance staff, what percentage of staff have a recognised financial qualification (what percentage of staff are CIMA qualified?) and amount of time that finance employees spend in internal training.

1.4 Benchmarking the finance function

One method of measuring the success of the finance function is to benchmark against finance functions elsewhere. With a large group, comparisons can be made of different finance functions within the same group. Alternatively there are organisations who will bring finance directors together to compare best practice, or who offer databases of other departments.

Most benchmarking exercises have suggested that too much time is spent on transaction processing and not enough time on value added activities. This has influenced the way the role of the finance function is developing (which we discuss further in Section 3).

Problems with using benchmarking include the **money and time involved**. If the exercise is to be effective, data has to be collected for an organisation's own finance function as well as obtained for others.

2 Relationships with stakeholders

FAST FORWARD

The most important aspect of establishing good relationships with stakeholders is to establish **what information** they require and **when** they need it. **Active co-operation** is particularly beneficial in relationships with financiers and external auditors.

2.1 Relationships with internal stakeholders

The most important part of the finance function's role in connection with internal stakeholders is making sure **information** goes to managers and staff who most **need it**. Finance staff need a good understanding of the structure of the organisation and the information requirements of different roles. For example senior managers will need information about value drivers and free cash flow. Other staff will require the insights provided by activity-based or value added measures.

We shall see in Section 3 that criticisms that the finance function has not been providing the information required have led to changes in the role of the function.

2.2 Relationships with business advisers

It is important to establish at the start of a relationship with business advisers the **purposes of the relationship** and the **services provided**. This will involve establishing the obligations on both sides, and also the **information** that will be required from the finance function and other organisation, the **level of detail** required and **when** the information will need to be made available.

2.3 Relationships with auditors

The considerations that apply to relationships with business advisers also apply of course to relationships with auditors. The finance function will, of course, have a lot of dealing with auditors.

For any organisation certain straightforward steps can be taken to smooth the progress of external audit and (hopefully) minimise its costs. These include agreeing in advance with the auditor **what information** the auditor will need and making it available. The auditors will be looking for a **clear audit trail** with the figures in the accounts backed up by schedules that clearly show how each figure was calculated. Equally important is making sure that **staff will be available** when required to answer auditor questions.

The relationship between finance staff with **internal audit responsibilities** and the **external auditors** will be particularly significant. Links can be strengthened in various ways.

(a) Both internal and external auditors can benefit if both adopt as far as possible a **common methodology**. However this will not work for all audit areas, because of differences in the scope of the work of internal and external auditors. For areas where the methodology is different the approaches need to be **understood** by both sides.

(b) **Joint training** on general audit techniques can help improve links.

(c) **Joint planning** of audit work is very important. At a basic level this means **exchanging copies of plans**.

A potentially more valuable approach would be **holding meetings together** and issuing a single plan covering both internal and external work. This is most likely to happen where the aims of both are similar, for example in the audit of government bodies when both external and internal auditors are assessing value for money.

(d) **Other means of assistance** include an exchange of resources, for example interrogation software or audit programmes.

2.4 Relationships with investors

The finance function plays a key role in providing information to investors that will enable them to take the active role in corporate governance recommended by the corporate governance reports of various countries.

(a) **Large investors** will be most concerned to see that the business has delivered the results projected and made good use of resources, in particular cash.

(b) **Smaller investors** will wish to be sure that the information they have received is accurate and complete, and there is evidence of appropriate financial controls and prudent financial management.

2.5 Relationships with financiers

When an organisation is seeking finance from its bank, the finance function will have to provide the detailed financial information that **explains why** the money is needed and **demonstrates to the bank** that the **money** is **safe**.

When preparing this information, the finance team need to appreciate that the bank is working on the basis of limited information about management and possibly also market prospects. This uncertainty can be reduced by giving the bank **as much information as possible** at the outset, and **keeping the bank informed** of the position during the term of the lending. The stronger the flow of information, the better the relationship is likely to be with the bank. The marketing literature of banks emphasises their experience in helping businesses in difficulties continue trading.

Supplying detailed information to bank also helps businesses gain access to a range of banking services, enabling them for example to assess their own performance.

Case Study

Lloyds TSB states that its managers can use the information readily available in annual accounts and management records to help businesses identify and set priorities for action. In particular they can use this information to benchmark performance in key areas against best practice within the sector and compared with other similar-sized companies.

3 Changes in the finance function

FAST FORWARD

The finance function has faced pressures to become **more actively involved** in business operations, although recent corporate scandals have underlined the importance of the finance function's role in control systems.

3.1 Changes in the role of finance

As indicated above, the proportion of time spent by the finance function on its traditional role of transaction processing as opposed to more proactive business partnership or decision support roles has been challenged by many organisations over recent years.

3.1.1 Criticisms of traditional role

Some of the pressure on the finance function to refocus its role has come from technological developments that mean that information is more widely available and routine account and budget preparation has been **automated**.

The finance function has also been frequently criticised for having too much of an **audit and control mentality** and being too interested in **analysing past performance**. Operational managers criticise the finance function for displaying limited commercial understanding and limited interaction with the business. Managers claim that they are forced to use other sources of information and do not see the finance function as adding value. They want the finance function to be sufficiently close to the business to be able to anticipate and interpret information requirements.

3.1.2 The finance function as business partner

Many finance functions have therefore re-focused their roles as business partners, adopting a more **commercial, action-orientated approach**. This means gaining broad knowledge of the business, participating as full members of operational teams and bringing financial expertise to the management process. They are expected to **integrate management accounting information** with **strategic management accounting data**.

Important areas where the finance function's role has developed have included:

- Providing more useful information on business units, projects, products and customers
- Supplying business cases for new investments
- Giving support in helping operational managers understand the information provided
- Collaborating in strategic planning and budgeting
- Designing information systems that provide greater support for operational managers

One example of where finance functions have been expected to assume a more active role is **investment appraisal**. Accountants are now often required to do more than state that the proposal does not meet financial criteria; they are expected to help develop and refine proposals.

Question

Sales support

Learning outcome: B(ii)

In what ways can the finance function support the sales function?

Answer

Support could be provided in the following ways (this is not a definitive list):

(a) Profitability analysis on sales and discount decisions

(b) Developing finance deals for customers, such as leasing arrangements

(c) Planning and analysis of the costs and revenue outcomes of sales promotions and advertising campaigns

(d) Providing facilities for customers to review products, services and prices

(e) Setting up deals with other suppliers to provide facilities to simplify customer purchasing

(f) Developing product and service deals assisting the customer to improve processes and review their costs

(g) Building relationships and sharing information with customers, and assisting their financial planning

(h) Dealing with sales administration to enable sales to spend more time with customers

3.1.3 Problems with the business partner model

Over the last couple of years the business partner model has in turn faced criticism, due primarily to Enron and other financial scandals. Critics have questioned the **identification** of the finance function with **operational viewpoints** and the **loss of independence** of the finance function that has arisen from finance staff reporting to, and being accountable to, operational managers.

Critics also claim that the finance function has become too greatly diverted from delivering basic controls and safeguards and functions, providing prudent financial management and ensuring the **true and fair view** is given. The finance function has, critics suggest, lost sight of its role in governance and failed to protect shareholder and public interest.

3.1.4 Independent business partner

A new independent business partner model has therefore emerged, not losing sight of co-operation with operational managers, but also having at its heart **strict controls**, **safeguarding of assets** and **effective reporting**.

The independent business partner model stresses that the finance function should seek to **add** value, but its role is not to **create** value. The creation of strategy, ideas and opportunities is the responsibility of the operational departments. Finance's role is to **assess** and **validate** these ideas, taking a commercial view, but also ensuring that business plans and strategy are rigorously reviewed and challenged if necessary.

Finance must also **review actual performance** rigorously and be prepared to challenge better than expected as well as worse than expected performance in order to minimise the risks of understatement.

Case Study

One prompt towards the finance function re-focusing on controls and risks to the business has been the Turnbull report, published in the UK in 1999.

'Effective financial controls, including the maintenance of proper accounting records, are an important element of internal control. They help ensure that the company is not unnecessarily exposed to financial risks and that the financial information used within the business and for publication is reliable. They also contribute to the safeguarding of assets, including the prevention and detection of fraud.'

Turnbull goes on to emphasise the key aspects of an internal control system, all of which are relevant to the finance function's work.

'An internal control system encompasses the policies, processes, tasks, behaviours and other aspects of a company, that, taken together,

- Facilitate its effective and efficient operation by enabling it to respond appropriately to significant business, operational, financial compliance and other risks to achieving the company's objectives. This includes the safeguarding of assets from inappropriate use or from loss and fraud, and ensuring that liabilities are identified and managed.
- Help ensure the quality of internal and external reporting. This requires the maintenance of proper records and processes that generate a flow of timely, relevant and reliable information from within and without the organisation
- Help ensure compliance with applicable laws and regulations, and also with internal policies in respect to the conduct of business.'

The main change of emphasis in the finance function's role is its increased involvement in risk management. Turnbull underlines that in order to create shareholder value, a company needs to **manage the risks** it faces and **communicate** to the **capital markets** how it is carrying out this task.

The board's role in risk management is fundamental. Members need to receive and review regular reports on internal control that review the **significant risks** and **how effective internal controls** are in managing the significant risks. The finance function and internal audit will have a major role in preparing these reports, which will cover:

(a) The **nature and extent** of the **risks** facing the organisation

(b) The **extent and categories** of **risk** that have been identified as acceptable for the organisation to bear

(c) The **likelihood** of those **risks** materialising

(d) The ability of the company to **reduce the incidence and impact** of the risks that do materialise

(e) The **costs of** operating particular controls, compared with the **benefits** obtained from managing the related risks

3.2 Outsourcing and shared servicing

FAST FORWARD

Basic processing tasks are now often **outsourced** or **concentrated** in **shared service centres**.

3.2.1 Outsourcing the finance function

Even if the finance function has to re-focus towards its more traditional roles, there will still be strong pressures to **outsource basic transaction processing functions**, payroll and expense management.

Case Study

In May 2003 kitchen manufacturer Magnet outsourced accounts payable, credit control, general accounting, reporting and auditing to Liberata in a seven year deal. However Magnet retained its management accounting function. Marc Bertand, the HR director at Magnet, commented 'Our management accountants produce the monthly figures and forecasts, three-month flashes and financial strategy. This is the sort of thing you need to keep close to the business.'

What Magnet did is typical of many organisations, according to a survey carried out by Accenture. Over 85% of senior executives won't outsource budgeting and forecasting and will also retain policy, strategy, tax planning, merger and acquisition support and economic and financial analysis.

Exam focus point

You will have covered outsourcing in other papers, and knowledge from these papers may be relevant.

3.2.2 Shared servicing

An alternative to outsourcing is shared servicing, where shared service centres consolidate the **transaction-processing activities** of many operations within a company. Shared service centres are meant to achieve significant cost reductions whilst improving service levels through the use of standardised technology and processes and service level agreements.

Chapter roundup

- The finance or financial control function's traditional role has been based on **recording**, **reporting** and **control of information**.
- Means of appraising this function include assessing the **reliability** of data and the **speed and efficiency** with which it is produced, and a wider scope **balanced scorecard** approach.
- The most important aspect of establishing good relationships with stakeholders is to establish **what information** they require and **when** they need it. **Active co-operation** is particularly beneficial in relationships with financiers and external auditors.
- The finance function has faced pressures to become **more actively involved** in business operations although recent corporate scandals have underlined the importance of the finance function's role in control systems.
- Basic processing tasks are now often **outsourced** or **concentrated** in **shared service centres**.

Quick quiz

1 Assuming an organisation has separate financial control and treasury functions, which is more likely to be responsible for currency management?

2 Which function is more likely to be responsible for preparation of quarterly accounts?

3 Name four measures that have traditionally been used to assess the work of the finance function.

4 Which of the following measures might be used to assess the work of the finance function using a balanced scorecard approach?

A Value enhancements
B Customer satisfaction
C Profits from investments
D Learning and growth

5 Name four ways in which internal and external audit can co-operate.

6 The independent partner model of the finance function sees creation of value as a key part of the finance function's role.

True ☐

False ☐

7 Fill in the gaps in this extract from the Turnbull report.

'Effective financial controls, including the maintenance of .... are an important element of internal control. They help ensure that the company is not unnecessarily exposed to .... and that the financial information used within the business and for publication is .... They also contribute to the safeguarding of assets, including the prevention and detection of ....'

8 What is the main role of shared service centres in the context of the finance function?

Answers to quick quiz

1 Treasury function

2 Financial control function

3
- Reliability of information
- Dealing with current developments
- Speed of reporting
- Efficiency

4 All of them apart from C, which is most likely to be used to assess the treasury function's work.

5
- Common methodology
- Joint training
- Joint planning
- Exchange of resources

6 False. The independent business partner model sees adding (not creating) value as an important part of the finance function's role.

7 'Effective financial controls, including the maintenance of **proper accounting records**, are an important element of internal control. They help ensure that the company is not unnecessarily exposed to **financial risks** and that the financial information used within the business and for publication is **reliable**. They also contribute to the safeguarding of assets, including the prevention and detection of **fraud**.'

8 Shared service centres are generally used to carry out basic processing activities for many different operations.

Now try the question below from the Exam Question Bank

Number	Level	Marks	Time
Q18	Introductory	n/a	25 mins

14

The treasury function

Introduction

In this chapter, we discuss the work of the **treasury function**, which in larger companies will form a separate department.

The key decisions relating to the treasury department – centralised or decentralised, cost centre or profit centre – are good territory for a discussion question in the exam.

Topic list	Learning outcomes	Syllabus references	Ability required
1 Treasury departments	B(iii)	B(13)	Analysis
2 Centralised or decentralised cash management?	B(iii)	B(13)	Analysis
3 The treasury department as cost centre or profit centre	B(iii)	B(14)	Analysis
4 Current developments in the treasury function	B(iii)	B(13)	Analysis

1 Treasury departments **11/06**

FAST FORWARD

Treasury management in a modern enterprise covers a number of areas including **liquidity management**, **funding management**, **currency management** and **corporate finance**.

1.1 Treasury management

Large companies rely heavily for both long-term and short-term funds on the financial and currency markets. To manage cash (funds) and currency efficiently, many large companies have set up a separate **treasury department**.

Key term

The Association of Corporate Treasurers' definition of **treasury management** is 'the corporate handling of all financial matters, the generation of external and internal funds for business, the management of currencies and cash flows, and the complex strategies, policies and procedures of corporate finance'.

A treasury department, even in a large company, is likely to be quite small, with perhaps a staff of three to six qualified accountants, bankers or corporate treasurers working under a Treasurer, who is responsible to the Finance Director. In some cases, where the company or organisation handles very large amounts of cash or foreign currency dealings, and often has large cash surpluses, the treasury department might be larger.

1.2 The role of the treasurer

The diagrams below are based on the **Association of Corporate Treasurers'** list of experience it requires from its student members before they are eligible for full membership of the Association. Required experience gives a good indication of the roles of treasury departments.

(a) **Corporate financial objectives**

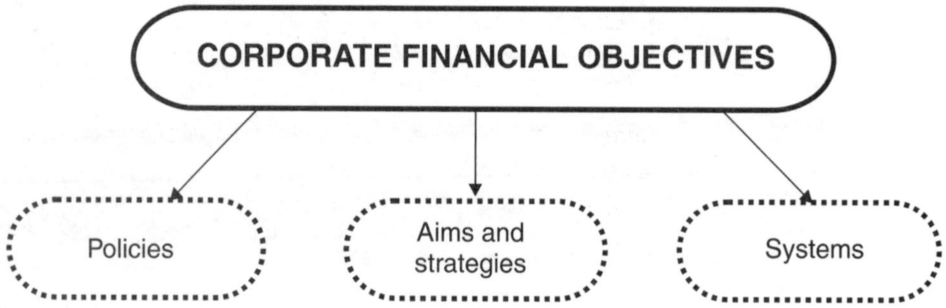

(b) **Liquidity management**: making sure the company has the liquid funds it needs, and invests any surplus funds, even for very short terms.

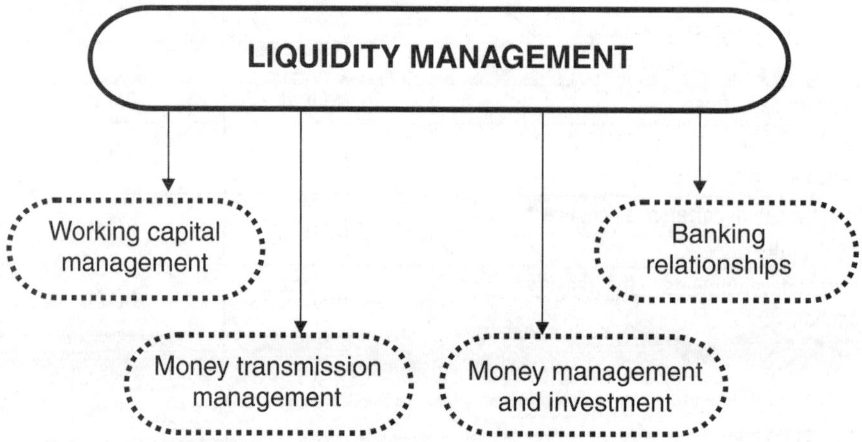

(c) **Funding management**

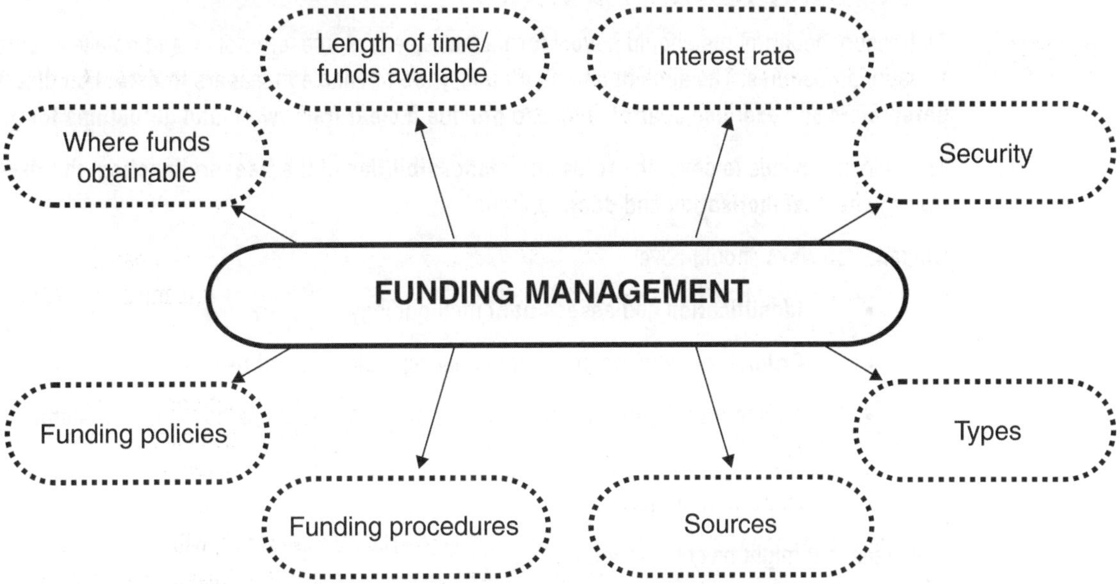

Funding management is concerned with all forms of borrowing, and alternative sources of funds, such as leasing and factoring.

(d) **Currency management**

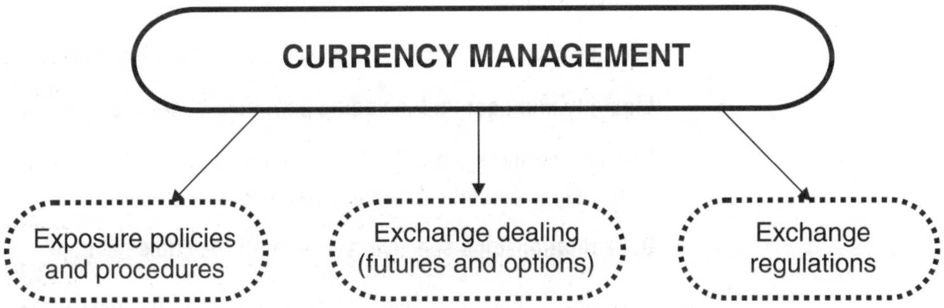

Currency dealings can save or cost a company considerable amounts of money, and the success or shortcomings of the corporate treasurer can have a significant impact on the income statement of a company which is heavily involved in foreign trade.

(e) **Corporate finance**

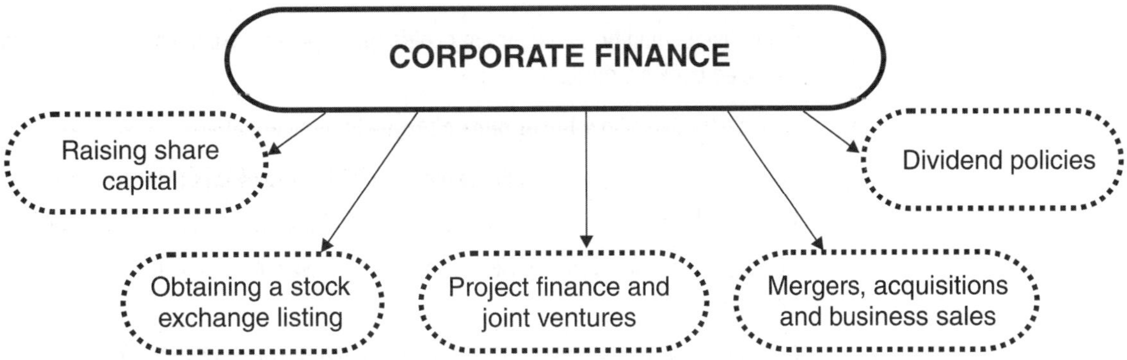

The treasury department has a role in all levels of decision-making within the company. It is involved with **strategic** decisions such as dividend policy or the raising of capital, **tactical** decisions such as risk management, and **operational** decisions such as the investment of surplus funds.

1.3 Treasury policy

All treasury departments should have a formal statement of treasury policy and detailed guidance on treasury procedures. The aims of a treasury policy are to enable managers to **establish direction**, **specify parameters** and **exercise control**, and also **provide a clear framework and guidelines for decisions**.

The guidance needs to cover the **roles** and **responsibilities** of the **treasury function**, the **risks** requiring management, **authorisation** and **dealing** limits.

Guidance on **risks** should cover:

- **Identification** and **assessment** methodology
- **Criteria** including tolerable and unacceptable levels of risk
- **Management guidelines**, covering risk elimination, risk control, risk retention and risk transfer
- **Reporting guidelines**

The areas that might be covered include:

- **Counterparty exposure** including limits for each counterparty and monitoring of exposures in relation to the limits
- **Currency and interest rate risk** such as hedging methods, authorised instruments and exposure limits
- **Funding risk** including limits and targets for different sources of funding
- **Liquidity management** including permitted banks, netting and inter-group procedures
- **Investment management** covering sources of funds, authorised counterparties and instruments, and inter-company funding
- **Bank relationships** specifying criteria for the choice of bank

The guidance must also include guidance on **measurement** of **treasury performance**. Measurement must cover both the **management of risk** and the **financial contribution** the department makes.

1.4 Advantages of a separate treasury department

Advantages of having a treasury function which is **separate from the financial control function** are as follows.

(a) Centralised liquidity management avoids mixing cash surpluses and overdrafts in different localised bank accounts.

(b) Bulk cash flows allow **lower bank charges** to be negotiated.

(c) Larger volumes of cash can be invested, giving **better short-term investment opportunities**.

(d) Borrowing can be agreed in bulk, probably at **lower interest rates** than for smaller borrowings.

(e) Currency risk management should be improved, through **matching of cash flows in different subsidiaries**. There should be less need to use expensive hedging instruments such as option contracts.

(f) A specialist department can employ staff with a **greater level of expertise** than would be possible in a local, more broadly based, finance department.

(g) The company will be able to benefit from the use of **specialised cash management software**.

(h) Access to treasury expertise should **improve the quality of strategic planning and decision making**.

Case Study

Treasury management can be a very significant function with public bodies such as local authorities.

The Argyll and Bute council in Scotland's treasury strategy for 2004 highlighted the following areas:

- Treasury limits in force limiting the treasury risk and activities of the council; £40 million short-term borrowing and 25% maximum proportion of interest on borrowing subject to variable rate interest.
- Borrowings strategy; because of expected favourable and stable short-term rates, the council will borrow as much as possible short-term at variable rates to minimise borrowing costs or make short-term savings in order to meet budgetary constraints.
- Investments strategy; the basic principles are security of principal and access to funds as needed. Surplus cash flows are generally lodged with bankers. Substantial surpluses might be placed in short-term business deposit accounts with approved institutions, subject to liaison with the council's treasury advisers.
- Extent of debt repayment opportunities. Debt repayment would occur when fixed interest rates are anticipated to be at their peak, or when there appear to be anomalies with the yield curve. The aim will be to enhance the balance of the long-term portfolio.
- Retention of set aside capital receipts. Scottish councils are required to set aside 75% of receipts generated by the Housing Revenue Account for either the redemption of external debt or to use monies to finance new capital expenditure as an alternative to new borrowing.
- Extraordinary activities. The treasury department was also involved in a feasibility study for housing stock transfer and negotiations over the financing of a public-private partnership school buildings project.

1.5 Outsourcing

Because of the specialist nature of treasury management, a number of businesses **outsource** the function to specialist institutions. The company receives the benefit of the **expertise** of the staff of the institution, who may be able to fill resource or skills gaps from which the internal team is suffering. Outsourcing operational functions may enable the internal team to concentrate on **strategic functions**. It may also give the organisation access to better systems solutions. The specialists can deal on a large scale and pass some of the benefit on in the form of fees that are lower than the cost of setting up an internal function would be.

However whether the **same level of service** could be guaranteed from the external institution as from an internal department is perhaps questionable. The external institution may not have as much knowledge of the needs of the business that an internal department would have.

If treasury activities are to be outsourced, **contract documentation** needs to be clear and **management** and **reporting** procedures must be established.

Other mechanisms may achieve the cost savings of outsourcing, but be more responsive to an organisation's needs. These include **shared service centres** (separate legal entities owned by the organisation and acting as independent service providers), which can be used to obtain economies of scale by concentrating dispersed units into one location. These may not necessarily be located near head office; in fact many are located where they can obtain tax advantages.

2 Centralised or decentralised cash management?

FAST FORWARD

Centralising the treasury management function allows businesses to **employ experts**, **deal in bulk cash flows** and hence take **advantage of lower bank charges** and **avoid a mix of surpluses and deficits**. **Decentralised** cash management can be **more responsive to local needs** however.

2.1 The centralisation decision

A large company may have a number of subsidiaries and divisions. In the case of a multinational, these will be located in different countries. It will be necessary to decide whether the treasury function should be centralised.

With **centralised cash management**, the central Treasury department effectively acts as the bank to the group. The central Treasury has the job of ensuring that individual operating units have all the funds they need at the right time.

2.2 Advantages of a specialist centralised treasury department

(a) **Centralised liquidity management** avoids having a mix of cash surpluses and overdrafts in different local bank accounts and facilitates bulk cash flows, so that lower bank charges can be negotiated.

(b) Larger volumes of cash are available to invest, giving better **short-term investment opportunities** (for example, money market deposits, high interest accounts and Certificates of Deposit).

(c) Any borrowing can be arranged **in bulk**, at lower interest rates than for smaller borrowings, and perhaps on the eurocurrency or eurobond markets.

(d) **Foreign currency risk management** is likely to be improved in a group of companies. A central treasury department can match foreign currency income earned by one subsidiary with expenditure in the same currency by another subsidiary. In this way, the risk of losses on adverse exchange rate changes can be avoided without the expense of forward exchange contracts or other 'hedging' (risk-reducing) methods.

(e) A specialist treasury department will employ **experts** with knowledge of dealing in futures, eurocurrency markets, taxation, transfer prices and so on. Localised departments would not have such expertise.

(f) The centralised pool of **funds required for precautionary purposes** will be smaller than the sum of separate precautionary balances which would need to be held under decentralised treasury arrangements.

(g) Through having a separate **profit centre**, attention will be focused on the contribution to group profit performance that can be achieved by good cash, funding, investment and foreign currency management.

(h) Centralisation provides a means of exercising **better control** through use of **standardised procedures** and **risk monitoring**, Standardised practices and performance measures can also create productivity benefits.

2.3 Possible advantages of decentralised cash management

(a) Sources of finance can be **diversified** and can be **matched with local assets**.

(b) Greater **autonomy** can be given to subsidiaries and divisions because of the closer relationships they will have with the decentralised cash management function.

(c) The decentralised Treasury function may be able to be **more responsive** to the needs of individual operating units.

However, since cash balances will not be aggregated at group level, there will be **more limited opportunities to invest** such balances on a short-term basis.

2.4 Centralised cash management in the multinational firm

If cash management within a **multinational firm** is centralised, each subsidiary holds only the minimum cash balance required for transaction purposes. All excess funds will be remitted to the central Treasury department.

Funds held in the central pool of funds can be returned quickly to the local subsidiary by telegraphic transfer or by means of worldwide bank credit facilities. The firm's bank can instruct its branch office in the country in which the subsidiary is located to advance funds to the subsidiary.

Exam focus point

Always read the question very carefully and make sure you answer the specific question. Don't be tempted to answer the discussion question that you wanted rather than what is required!

Question — Treasury centralisation

Learning outcome: B(iii)

Touten is a US registered multinational company with subsidiaries in 14 countries in Europe, Asia and Africa. The subsidiaries have traditionally been allowed a large amount of autonomy, but Touten is now proposing to centralise most of the group treasury management operations.

Required

Acting as a consultant to Touten prepare a memo suitable for distribution from the group finance director to the senior management of each of the subsidiaries explaining:

(a) The potential benefits of treasury centralisation; and

(b) How the company proposes to minimise any potential problems for the subsidiaries that might arise as a result of treasury centralisation

Answer

MEMORANDUM

To: Directors of all foreign subsidiaries
From: Group Finance Director
Date: 1 July 20X0

Centralisation of treasury management operations

At its last meeting, the board of directors of Touten made the decision to centralise group treasury management operations. A further memo giving detailed plans will be circulated shortly, but my objective in this memo is to outline the potential benefits of treasury centralisation and how any potential problems arising at subsidiaries can be minimised. Most of you will be familiar with the basic arguments, which we have been discussing informally for some time.

What it means

Centralisation of treasury management means that most decisions on borrowing, investment of cash surpluses, currency management and financial risk management will be taken by an enhanced central treasury team, based at head office, instead of by subsidiaries directly. In addition we propose to set most transfer prices for inter-company goods and services centrally.

The potential benefits

The main benefits are:

(a) **Cost savings** resulting from reduction of unnecessary banking charges
(b) **Reduction of the group's total taxation charge**
(c) **Enhanced control over financial risk**

Reduction in banking charges will result from:

(a) **Netting off inter-company debts before settlement**. At the moment we are spending too much on foreign exchange commission by settling inter-company debts in a wide range of currencies through the banking system.

(b) **Knowledge of total group currency exposure from transactions**. Amounts receivable in one subsidiary can hedge payables in another, eliminating unnecessary hedging by subsidiaries.

(c) **Knowledge of the group's total cash resources and borrowing requirement**. This will reduce the incidence of one company lending cash while a fellow subsidiary borrows at a higher interest rate and will also eliminate unnecessary interest rate hedging. It will also facilitate higher deposit rates and lower borrowing rates.

Reduction in the group's tax charge will be made possible by a comprehensive centrally-set **transfer pricing policy**.

Enhanced control over financial risks will be possible because we will be able to develop a central team of specialists who will have a clear-cut strategy on hedging and risk management. Many of you have requested help in this area.

This team will be able to ensure that decisions are taken in line with **group strategy** and will also be able to provide you with enhanced financial information to assist you with your own decision making.

Potential problems for subsidiaries and their solution

Our group culture is one of **decentralisation** and **enablement of management at individual subsidiary level**. There is no intention to change this culture. Rather, it is hoped that releasing you from specialist treasury decisions will enable you to devote more time to developing your own business units.

The system can only work properly, however, if **information exchange** between head office and subsidiaries is swift and efficient. Enhanced computer systems are to be provided at all centres to assist you with daily reports. It is also important that you keep head office informed of all local conditions that could be beneficial to the treasury function, such as the availability of local subsidised loans, as well as potential local risks such as the threat of exchange control restrictions.

You will find that movements in your cash balances will be affected by **group policy**, as well as reported profitability. Any adjustments made by head office will be eliminated when preparing the performance reports for your own business units and we will ensure that joint venture partners are not penalised by group policy.

Please contact me with any further comments that you may have on our new treasury policy.

3 The treasury department as cost centre or profit centre

FAST FORWARD

The treasury department is usually run as a **cost centre** if its main focus is to keep costs within budgeted spending targets. It may be run as a **profit centre** if there is a high level of foreign exchange transactions, or the business wishes to make speculative profits.

3.1 Treasury department as cost centre

A treasury department might be managed either as a **cost centre** or as a **profit centre**. For a group of companies, this decision may need to be made for treasury departments in separate subsidiaries as well as for the central corporate treasury department.

In a cost centre, managers have an incentive only to **keep the costs** of the department within **budgeted spending targets**. The cost centre approach implies that the treasury is there to perform a service of a certain standard to other departments in the enterprise. The treasury is treated much like any other service department.

3.2 Treasury department as profit centre

However, some companies (including BP, for example) are able to make significant profits from their treasury activities. Treating the treasury department as a profit centre recognises the fact that treasury activities such as speculation may earn **revenues** for the company, and may as a result make treasury staff more motivated. It also means that treasury departments have to operate with a greater degree of commercial awareness, in for example the management of working capital.

Question — Profit centre

Learning outcome: B(iii)

Suppose that your company is considering plans to establish its treasury function as a profit centre. Before reading the next paragraph, see if you can think of how the following issues are of potential importance to these plans.

(a) How can we ensure that high quality treasury staff can be recruited?

(b) How might costly errors and overexposure to risk be prevented?

(c) Why will the treasury team need extensive market information to be successful?

(d) Could there be a danger that attitudes to risk in the treasury team will differ from those of the Board? If so, how?

(e) What is the relevance of internal charges?

(f) What problems could there be in evaluating performance of the treasury team?

If a profit centre approach is being considered, the following issues should be addressed.

(a) **Competence of staff**

Local managers may not have sufficient expertise in the area of treasury management to carry out speculative treasury operations competently. Mistakes in this specialised field may be costly. It may only be appropriate to operate a larger **centralised** treasury as a profit centre, and additional specialist staff demanding high salaries may need to be recruited.

(b) **Controls**

Adequate controls must be in place to prevent costly errors and overexposure to risks such as foreign exchange risks. It is possible to enter into a very large foreign exchange deal over the telephone.

(c) **Information**

A treasury team which trades in futures and options or in currencies is competing with other traders employed by major financial institutions who may have better knowledge of the market because of the large number of customers they deal with. In order to compete effectively, the team needs to have detailed and up-to-date market information.

(d) **Attitudes to risk**

The more aggressive approach to risk-taking which is characteristic of treasury professionals may be difficult to reconcile with the more measured approach to risk which may prevail within the board of directors. The recognition of treasury operations as profit making activities may not fit well with the main business operations of the company.

(e) **Internal charges**

If the department is to be a true profit centre, then market prices should be charged for its services to other departments. It may be difficult to put realistic prices on some services, such as arrangement of finance or general financial advice.

(f) **Performance evaluation**

Even with a profit centre approach, it may be difficult to measure the success of a treasury team for the reason that successful treasury activities sometimes involve **avoiding** the incurring of costs, for example when a currency devalues. For example, a treasury team which hedges a future foreign currency receipt over a period when the domestic currency undergoes devaluation (as sterling did in 1992 when it left the European exchange rate mechanism) may avoid a substantial loss for the company.

4 Current developments in the treasury function

FAST FORWARD

Globalisation, **information technology** and **pressures to add value** are significant catalysts for changes in the role of the treasury function.

4.1 The changing role of the treasury function

A predictable consequence of the wide-ranging scope of the treasurer's role is that it is constantly evolving. Partly this is in response to changes in the financial world such as the development of **different types** of **capital instruments**. It is also due to a changing emphasis on the relative importance of different aspects of the treasury role.

4.2 Globalisation

Globalisation requires treasury to monitor continuously market conditions, currency rates and political conditions. Another important aspect currently as we saw in Chapter 4 are developments in international rules and convergence of international accounting standards.

Globalisation is a clear impetus towards further centralisation and concentration on **control frameworks**, **decision support** and **improved business performance**. However its implications need to be considered carefully.

Involvement of **regional and local personnel** has to be built into the system, drawing on their knowledge of local financial management requirements and operations. Regional personnel may be used for operational tasks such as credit control or payroll, but they will be subject to liquidity management guidelines decided centrally.

The needs of the regions also need to be considered when **banking relationships** are assessed. Businesses will be concerned about whether their banks have the ability to provide global treasury services. However the services of the global bank(s) chosen need to be matched with regional needs. In addition although globalisation may make it desirable to concentrate on banks who can provide the necessary services and cost savings, using fewer banks goes against risk management principles of diversifying the number and nature of banking partners.

4.3 Risk prevention

We have already stressed that **risk control** is an integral part of the treasury management function. More accurate forecasting techniques are being used to help other departments mitigate and avoid risks.

4.4 Working capital management

Many businesses are placing increased emphasis on constant working capital improvement to minimise funding requirements. This means greater treasury involvement in **supplier and inventory management**.

4.5 Tax management

Consequences of global developments such as European Union harmonisation need to be considered carefully. However in many businesses limitation of tax liabilities must be seen in the context of optimum liquidity management.

4.6 Information and technology management

Careful management is needed of all the information sources that are relevant for the business including the internet, wire services and mass communication media. Optimum use of technology is a key part of information management and as well as choosing the right supplier, treasury departments need to monitor technological developments that could enhance their operations.

Enterprise resource planning procedures offer common technology throughout the organisation. These have obvious advantages for the treasury function, since they offer integration with the rest of the business and the chance to obtain timely and accurate reports. However implementation of these systems has proved problematic, with different software versions being used in different places and specialist systems evolving for certain functions, defeating the whole object of having an integrated system

Technology can also be used to provide a **common information base** that the service providers to the treasury function can use.

4.7 Relationship management

The wider scope of treasury's role implies strengthening of relations with other functions, and co-operation in tasks such as establishment of terms and payment methods for customers.

4.8 Co-operation between treasuries

Treasury functions of different organisations sometimes pass aspects of their operations to a **single independent supplier**. This enables the organisations to share processes, information and knowledge. Treasury functions also co-operate together in payment systems harmonisation, supplying information to rating agencies, and presenting a common front to suppliers and regulators.

Exam focus point

As with financial control, knowledge of recent developments may earn you marks in a discussion.

Chapter roundup

- **Treasury management** in a modern enterprise covers a number of areas including **liquidity management**, **funding management**, **currency management** and **corporate finance**.
- **Centralising** the treasury management function allows businesses to **employ experts**, **deal in bulk cash flows** and hence take **advantage of lower bank charges** and avoid a mix of surpluses and deficits. **Decentralised** cash management can be **more responsive to local needs** however.
- The treasury department is usually run as a **cost centre** if its main focus is to keep costs within budgeted spending targets. It may be run as a **profit centre** if there is a high level of foreign exchange transactions, or the business wishes to make speculative profits.
- **Globalisation, information technology** and **pressures to add value** are significant catalysts for changes in the role of the treasury function.

Quick quiz

1 Which of the following functions is the **least likely** to be carried out by a treasury department?

A Negotiating arrangements with bankers
B Dealing in foreign exchange
C Preparing the corporate budget and business plan
D Involvement in business acquisitions and sales

2 **Fill in the blanks** in the statement below, using the words in the box. (Words may be used more than once.)

- Treasury management may be defined as 'the corporate handling of all (1) .... matters, the generation of external and internal (2) .... for business, the management of (3) .... and cash flow, and the complex strategies, policies and procedures of (4) ....
- A treasury department may be managed either as a (5) .... centre or a (6) .... centre.
- A (7) .... treasury department has the role of ensuring that individual operating units have all the funds they need at the right time.
- Futures and options might be employed in (8) .... risk management.
- Acquisitions and sales of businesses fall within the area of (9) ....
- Money transmission management is an aspect of (10) .... management.

• Corporate finance	• Centralised	• Profit	• Financial
• Liquidity	• Cost	• Currency/ies	• Funds

3 Why might a treasurer choose *not* to 'hedge' against the risk of a foreign exchange movement?

4 What are the main things a treasurer needs to know to carry out funding management effectively?

5 What are the main general elements that guidance on risks should cover?

6 What should be the main benefit of enterprise resource planning systems?

7 Give three possible advantages of decentralisation of the treasury function.

8 What is a shared service centre in the context of treasury management?

Answers to quick quiz

1 C While the treasury department will be involved in the preparation of the cash budget, it is unlikely to have a major role in the wider budgeting and planning process.

2 (1) Financial (2) Funds (3) Currencies (4) Corporate finance (5) Cost (6) Profit (7) Centralised (8) Currency (9) Corporate finance (10) Liquidity

3 Because they think it likely that a profit will be made in refraining from hedging the risk.

4
- Where funds are obtainable
- For how long
- At what interest rate
- Whether security will be required
- Whether interest rates would be fixed or variable

5
- Identification and assessment methodology
- Criteria including tolerable and unacceptable levels of risk
- Management guidelines, covering risk elimination, risk control, risk retention and risk transfer
- Reporting guidelines

6 The use of common technology throughout the organisation, improving the quality and timing of the information received by the treasury function.

7
- Diversification of sources of finance and matching with local assets
- Greater autonomy for subsidiaries and divisions
- Greater responsiveness to the needs of individual operating units

8 A separate legal entity owned by the organisation that acts as an independent provider of treasury services, and is often located to gain tax advantages.

Now try the question below from the Exam Question Bank

Number	Level	Marks	Time
Q19	Introductory	n/a	20 mins

Part C
Business valuations and acquisitions

15

Valuation techniques

Introduction

In Part C we shall be concentrating on **methods of calculating the valuations** of organisations of different types. We shall cover the **main methods of valuation** in this chapter, and demonstrate how **market efficiency** and **changing capital structure** impact upon valuation. The most important use of valuation techniques is in a merger or acquisition situation, and therefore Chapter 16 concentrates on these.

Because valuation will be examined frequently, this chapter is one of the most important in the Text. You need to be able to use a range of measures in practical situations, also to discuss why they show different values and which measure is the most useful.

Topic list	Learning outcomes	Syllabus references	Ability required
1 Reasons for share valuations	C(i)	C(1),(2)	Application
2 Asset valuation bases	C(i)	C(1),(2)	Application
3 Earnings valuation bases	C(i)	C(1),(2)	Application
4 Dividend valuation bases	C(i)	C(1),(2), (5)	Application
5 Cash flow valuation methods	C(i)	C(1),(2)	Application
6 Other valuation bases	C(i)	C(1),(2)	Application
7 Share valuation and market efficiency	C(i)	C(4)	Application
8 Share valuation and change in capital structure	C(i)	C(6)	Application
9 Intangible assets and intellectual capital	C(ii)	C(7)	Application

1 Reasons for share valuations

FAST FORWARD

There are a number of different ways of **putting a value on a business**, or on shares in an unquoted company. It makes sense to use **several methods** of valuation, and to compare the values they produce.

1.1 When valuations are required

Given quoted share prices on the Stock Exchange, why devise techniques for estimating the value of a share? A share valuation will be necessary:

(a) For **quoted companies**, when there is a takeover bid and the offer price is an estimated 'fair value' in excess of the current market price of the shares

Key term

A **takeover** is the acquisition by a company of a controlling interest in the voting share capital of another company, usually achieved by the purchase of a majority of the voting shares. *(OT 2005)*

(b) For **unquoted companies**, when:

- (i) The company wishes to 'go public' and must fix an issue price for its shares
- (ii) There is a scheme of merger
- (iii) Shares are sold
- (iv) Shares need to be valued for the purposes of taxation
- (v) Shares are pledged as collateral for a loan

(c) For **subsidiary companies**, when the group's holding company is negotiating the sale of the subsidiary to a management buyout team or to an external buyer

(d) For **any company**, where a shareholder wishes to dispose of his or her holding. Some of the valuation methods we describe will be most appropriate if a large or controlling interest is being sold. However even a small shareholding may be a significant disposal, if the purchasers can increase their holding to a controlling interest as a result of the acquisition

(e) For **any company**, when the company is being broken up in a liquidation situation or the company needs to obtain additional finance, or re-finance current debt

1.2 Stakeholder concerns

Exam focus point

Remember that valuation should never be a purely mechanical exercise. When discussing how realistic your valuation methods are, you should bear in mind the impact of shareholders on the valuation process.

1.2.1 Legal issues

In a number of situations, stakeholders will be given important legal rights. As we shall see in Chapter 16, in merger and acquisition situations shareholders have rights to be treated fairly by the directors of the companies that are joining together. Governments may also be interested if the merger leads to an organisation that is considered to be too large or dominant in its markets.

Insolvency legislation will give creditor stakeholders prior rights to receive the proceeds of dissolution, and may give them rights to object to arrangements designed to avoid insolvency.

1.2.2 Other situations

In certain circumstances the attitude of stakeholders other than shareholders will significantly influence valuation. A good example is a takeover situation where the acquiring company is paying for the skills and expertise of its target's employees. If key employees are unhappy with the takeover, and decide to leave, then the valuation of the target will be impaired.

1.3 General factors affecting valuation

As well as the calculations, buyers and sellers will also take into account the **industry situation**, the **fixed and human assets** of the company, and a number of factors relating to **shareholdings**:

- The **size** of shareholding to be acquired
- The **distribution** of other shareholdings
- The **rights** related to the shares
- Any **restrictions** on transfers

Exam focus point

In an exam question as well as in practice, it is unlikely that one method would be used in isolation. Several valuations might be made, each using a different technique or different assumptions. The valuations could then be compared, and a final price reached as a compromise between the different values. Remember that some methods may be more appropriate for valuing a small parcel of shares, others for valuing a whole company.

2 Asset valuation bases 5/05, 11/05, 11/06

FAST FORWARD

The **net assets valuation** method can be used as one of many valuation methods, or to provide a lower limit for the value of a company. By itself it is unlikely to produce the most realistic value.

2.1 The net assets method of share valuation

Using this method of valuation, the value of a share in a particular class is equal to the **net tangible assets attributable to that class,** divided by the **number of shares in the class. Intangible assets** (including goodwill) should be excluded, unless they have a market value (for example patents and copyrights, which could be sold).

(a) **Goodwill**, if shown in the accounts, is unlikely to be shown at a true figure for purposes of valuation, and the value of goodwill should be reflected in another method of valuation (for example the earnings basis, the dividend yield basis or the super-profits method).

(b) **Development expenditure**, if shown in the accounts, would also have a value which is related to future profits rather than to the worth of the company's physical assets.

The valuation of intangible assets in general, and intellectual capital in particular, is discussed at the end of thls chapter.

2.2 Example: net assets method of share valuation

The summary balance sheet of Cactus is as follows.

	£	£	£
Non-current assets			
Land and buildings			160,000
Plant and machinery			80,000
Motor vehicles			20,000
			260,000
Goodwill			20,000
Current assets			
Inventory		80,000	
Receivables		60,000	
Short-term investments		15,000	
Cash		5,000	
		160,000	
Current liabilities			
Payables	60,000		
Taxation	20,000		
Proposed ordinary dividend	20,000		
		(100,000)	
			60,000
			340,000
12% loan notes			(60,000)
Deferred taxation			(10,000)
			270,000
Ordinary shares of £1			80,000
Reserves			140,000
			220,000
4.9% preference shares of £1			50,000
			270,000

What is the value of an ordinary share using the net assets basis of valuation?

Solution

If the figures given for asset values are not questioned, the valuation would be as follows.

	£	£
Total value of assets less current liabilities		340,000
Less intangible asset (goodwill)		20,000
Total value of assets less current liabilities		320,000
Less: preference shares	50,000	
loan notes	60,000	
deferred taxation	10,000	
		120,000
Net asset value of equity		200,000
Number of ordinary shares		80,000
Value per share		£2.50

2.3 Choice of valuation bases

The difficulty in an asset valuation method is establishing the **asset values** to use. Values ought to be realistic. The figure attached to an individual asset may vary considerably depending on whether it is valued on a **going concern** or a **break-up** basis.

Possibilities include:

- **Historic basis** – unlikely to give a realistic value as it is dependent upon the business's depreciation and amortisation policy
- **Replacement basis** – if the assets are to be used on an on-going basis
- **Realisable basis** – if the assets are to be sold, or the business as a whole broken up. This won't be relevant if a minority shareholder is selling his stake, as the assets will continue in the business's use

The following list should give you some idea of the factors that must be considered.

(a) Do the assets need **professional valuation?** If so, how much will this cost?

(b) Have the **liabilities** been accurately quantified, for example deferred taxation? Are there any contingent liabilities? Will any balancing tax charges arise on disposal?

(c) How have the **current assets** been valued? Are all receivables collectable? Is all inventory realisable? Can all the assets be physically located and brought into a saleable condition? This may be difficult in certain circumstances where the assets are situated abroad.

(d) Can any **hidden liabilities** be accurately assessed? Would there be redundancy payments and closure costs?

(e) Is there an **available market** in which the assets can be realised (on a break-up basis)? If so, do the balance sheet values truly reflect these break-up values?

(f) Are there any **prior charges** on the assets?

(g) Does the business have a regular **revaluation and replacement** policy? What are the bases of the valuation? As a broad rule, valuations will be more useful the better they estimate the **future cash flows** that are derived from the asset.

(h) Are there factors that might indicate that the **going concern valuation** of the business **as a whole** is **significantly higher** than the valuation of the individual assets?

(i) What shareholdings are being sold? If a minority interest is being disposed of, realisable value is of limited relevance as the assets will not be sold.

Exam focus point

In November 2005, the examiner expected candidates to recognise that net asset values would be increased by directors' estimates of retained earnings for the current year.

2.4 Use of net asset basis

The net assets basis of valuation might be used in the following circumstances.

(a) **As a measure of the 'security' in a share value**. A share might be valued using an earnings basis. This valuation might be **higher or lower than the net asset value per share**. If the earnings basis is higher, then if the company went into liquidation, the investor could not expect to receive the full value of his shares when the underlying assets were realised.

The **asset backing** for shares thus provides a measure of the **possible loss** if the company fails to make the expected earnings or dividend payments. Valuable tangible assets may be a good reason for acquiring a company, especially freehold property which might be expected to increase in value over time.

(b) **As a measure of comparison in a scheme of merger**

Key term

A **merger** is essentially a business combination of two or more companies, of which none obtains control over any other.

For example, if company A, which has a low asset backing, is planning a merger with company B, which has a high asset backing, the shareholders of B might consider that their shares' value ought to reflect this. It might therefore be agreed that a something should be added to the value of the company B shares to allow for this difference in asset backing.

(c) As a **'floor value'** for a business that is up for sale – shareholders will be reluctant to sell for less than the NAV. However, if the sale is essential for cash flow purposes or to realign with corporate strategy, even the asset value may not be realised.

For these reasons, it is always advisable to calculate the net assets per share.

3 Earnings valuation bases 5/05, 11/05, 5/06, 11/06

FAST FORWARD

P/E ratios are used when a large block of shares, or a whole business, is being valued. This method can be problematic when quoted companies' P/E ratios are used to value unquoted companies.

3.1 The P/E ratio (earnings) method of valuation

This is a common method of valuing a **controlling interest** in a company, where the owner can decide on **dividend** and **retentions policy**. The P/E ratio relates earnings per share to a share's value.

Since P/E ratio = $\dfrac{\text{Market value}}{\text{EPS}}$,

then market value per share = EPS × P/E ratio

Exam focus point

Remember that earnings per share (EPS) = $\dfrac{\text{Profit /loss attributable to ordinary shareholders}}{\text{Weighted average number of ordinary shares}}$

Examiners have commented in the past that students often calculate earnings per share incorrectly.

Case Study

You will find frequent references to the P/E ratio in the financial press. For example, the *Guardian* newspaper recently reported:

City speculators were keeping a close watch on waste management company Shanks Group yesterday as rumours of corporate activity resurfaced.

In a weak market, Shanks gained 2.25p to 120p, supported by talk of predatory interest from European utility groups RWE and Suez – the owner of Europe's biggest waste company, Sita.

As the last quoted player in a rapidly consolidating industry there is no doubt that Shanks – trading on a price-earnings ratio of 13 – is vulnerable to an approach, particularly given its sizeable presence in the UK.

According to stockbroker Panmure, which yesterday raised its rating on Shanks to 'buy', the company's domestic divisions are showing signs of recovery after a tough 18 months.

The P/E ratio produces an **earnings-based** valuation of shares by deciding a suitable P/E ratio and multiplying this by the EPS for the shares which are being valued.

Market valuation or capitalisation = P/E ratio × Earnings per share

The EPS could be a historical EPS or a prospective future EPS. For a given EPS figure, a higher P/E ratio will result in a higher price.

3.2 Significance of high P/E ratio

A high P/E ratio may indicate:

(a) **Expectations that the EPS will grow rapidly**

A **high price is being paid for future profit prospects**. Many small but successful and fast-growing companies are valued on the stock market on a high P/E ratio. Some stocks (for example those of some internet companies in the late 1990s) have reached high valuations before making any profits at all, on the strength of expected future earnings.

Case Study

By April 1999, the internet 'portal' company 'Yahoo!', with only very limited assets, commanded a higher stock market value than Boeing the aircraft manufacturer. Amazon.com, the online bookseller, was valued at $20 billion but had yet to make a profit. eBay, the internet auctioneer was valued at 2,000 times prospective earnings.

Press comment at the time suggested that private investors, many of them trading through the internet, were mainly responsible for the volatility in internet stocks. These were 'momentum investors' who seemed to care little about the economic fundamentals underlying a business. If enough people pile in to buy stocks whose prices seem to rise inexorably, the prices are driven even higher perhaps until the 'bubble' bursts, and investors panic and sell *en masse*, when the price drops again sharply.

This was indeed seen to happen in the latter half of 2000 when high tech stocks dropped on average by 25% in the space of 6 weeks and many weaker dot.com companies died a death.

(b) **Security of earnings**

A well-established low-risk company would be valued on a higher P/E ratio than a similar company whose earnings are subject to greater uncertainty.

(c) **Status**

If a quoted company (the predator) made a share-for-share takeover bid for an unquoted company (the target), it would normally expect its own shares to be valued on a higher P/E ratio than the target company's shares. This is because a quoted company ought to be a lower-risk company; but in addition, there is an advantage in having shares which are quoted on a stock market: the shares can be readily sold. The P/E ratio of an unquoted company's shares might be around 50% to 60% of the P/E ratio of a similar public company with a full Stock Exchange listing.

3.2.1 Problems with using P/E ratios

However using the price-earnings ratios of quoted companies to value unquoted companies may be problematic.

- Finding a quoted company with a **similar range of activities** may be difficult. Quoted companies are often **diversified**.

- A **single year's P/E ratio** may not be a good basis, if earnings are volatile, or the quoted company's share price is at an abnormal level, due for example to the expectation of a takeover bid
- If a P/E ratio trend is used, then **historical data** will be being used to value how the unquoted company will do in the future.
- The quoted company may have a **different capital structure** to the unquoted company.

Case Study

Some sample P/E ratios taken from the Financial Times on 3 April 2007:

Market indices

FTSE 100	12.52
FTSE all-share	13.51

Industry sector averages (main market)

Chemicals	21.39
Construction and materials	19.88
Food producers	10.96
General retailers	22.30
Health care equipment and services	34.48
Mobile telecommunications	24.71
Software and computer services	27.99

3.3 Example: earnings method of valuation

Spider is considering the takeover of an unquoted company, Fly. Spider's shares are quoted on the Stock Exchange at a price of £3.20 and since the most recent published EPS of the company is 20p, the company's P/E ratio is 16. Fly is a company with 100,000 shares and current earnings of £50,000, 50p per share. How might Spider decide on an offer price?

Solution

The decision about the offer price is likely to be preceded by the estimation of a 'reasonable' P/E ratio in the light of the particular circumstances.

(a) If Fly is in the **same industry** as Spider, its P/E ratio ought to be lower, because of its lower status as an unquoted company.

(b) If Fly is in a **different industry**, a suitable P/E ratio might be based on the P/E ratio that is typical for quoted companies in that industry.

(c) If Fly is thought to be **growing fast**, so that its EPS will rise rapidly in the years to come, the P/E ratio that should be used for the share valuation will be higher than if only small EPS growth is expected.

(d) If the acquisition of Fly would **contribute substantially to Spider's own profitability and growth**, or to any other strategic objective that Spider has, then Spider should be willing to offer a higher P/E ratio valuation, in order to secure acceptance of the offer by Fly's shareholders.

Of course, the P/E ratio on which Spider bases its offer will probably be lower than the P/E ratio that Fly's shareholders think their shares ought to be valued on. Some haggling over the price might be necessary.

Spider might decide that Fly's shares ought to be valued on a P/E ratio of 60% × 16 = 9.6, that is, at 9.6 × 50p = £4.80 each.

Fly's shareholders might reject this offer, and suggest a valuation based on a P/E ratio of, say, 12.5, that is, 12.5 × 50p = £6.25.

Spider's management might then come back with a revised offer, say valuation on a P/E ratio of 10.5, that is, 10.5 × 50p = £5.25.

The haggling will go on until the negotiations either break down or succeed in arriving at an agreed price.

3.4 Guidelines for a P/E ratio-based valuation

When a company is thinking of acquiring an **unquoted** company in a takeover, the final offer price will be agreed by **negotiation**, but a list of some of the factors affecting the valuer's choice of P/E ratio is given below.

(a) General **economic** and **financial** conditions.

(b) The type of **industry** and the prospects of that industry. Use of current P/E ratios may give an unrealistically low valuation if these ratios are being affected by a lack of confidence throughout the industry.

(c) The **size** of the undertaking and its **status** within its industry. If an unquoted company's earnings are growing annually and are currently around £300,000 or so, then it could probably get a quote in its own right on the Alternative Investment Market, and a higher P/E ratio should therefore be used when valuing its shares.

(d) **Marketability**. The market in shares which do not have a Stock Exchange quotation is always a restricted one and a higher yield is therefore required.

Exam focus point

For examination purposes, you should normally **take a figure around one half to two thirds** of the industry average when valuing an unquoted company.

(e) The **diversity** of shareholdings and the **financial status** of any principal shareholders.

(f) The **reliability** of profit estimates and the past profit record. Use of profits and P/E ratios over time may give a more reliable valuation, especially if they are being compared with industry levels over that time.

(g) **Asset backing** and **liquidity**.

(h) The **nature of the assets**, for example whether some of the non-current assets are of a highly specialised nature, and so have only a small break-up value.

(i) **Gearing**. A relatively high gearing ratio will generally mean greater financial risk for ordinary shareholders and call for a higher rate of return on equity.

(j) The extent to which the business is dependent on the **technical skills** of one or more individuals.

(k) The predator may need to be particularly careful when valuing an unlisted company of using a P/E ratio of a **'similar' listed company**. The predator should obtain reasonable evidence that the listed company does have the same risk and growth characteristics, and has similar policies on significant areas such as directors' remuneration.

3.4.1 Use of predator's P/E ratios

A predator company may sometimes use their higher P/E ratio to value a target company. This assumes that the predator **can improve the target's business**, which may be a dangerous assumption to make. The predator's intentions will also be important; the choice of P/E ratio may depend on whether the predator envisages demerging some of the target's operations, or retaining them all. It may be better to use an adjusted industry P/E ratio, or some other method.

3.4.2 Use of forecast earnings

When one company is thinking about taking over another, it should look at the target company's **forecast earnings**, not just its historical results.

Forecasts of **earnings growth** should only be used if:

(a) There are good reasons to believe that earnings growth will be achieved

(b) A reasonable estimate of growth can be made

(c) Forecasts supplied by the target company's directors are made in good faith and using reasonable assumptions and fair accounting policies

Question

Valuations

Learning outcome: C(i)

Flycatcher wishes to make a takeover bid for the shares of an unquoted company, Mayfly. The earnings of Mayfly over the past five years have been as follows.

20X0	£50,000	20X3	£71,000
20X1	£72,000	20X4	£75,000
20X2	£68,000		

The average P/E ratio of quoted companies in the industry in which Mayfly operates is 10. Quoted companies which are similar in many respects to Mayfly are:

(a) Bumblebee, which has a P/E ratio of 15, but is a company with very good growth prospects

(b) Wasp, which has had a poor profit record for several years, and has a P/E ratio of 7

What would be a suitable range of valuations for the shares of Mayfly?

Answer

(a) **Earnings**. Average earnings over the last five years have been £67,200, and over the last four years £71,500. There might appear to be some growth prospects, but estimates of future earnings are uncertain.

A low estimate of earnings in 20X5 would be, perhaps, £71,500.

A high estimate of earnings might be £75,000 or more. This solution will use the most recent earnings figure of £75,000 as the high estimate.

(b) **P/E ratio**. A P/E ratio of 15 (Bumblebee's) would be much too high for Mayfly, because the growth of Mayfly earnings is not as certain, and Mayfly is an unquoted company.

On the other hand, Mayfly's expectations of earnings are probably better than those of Wasp. A suitable P/E ratio might be based on the industry's average, 10; but since Mayfly is an unquoted company and therefore more risky, a lower P/E ratio might be more appropriate: perhaps 60% to 70% of 10 = 6 or 7, or conceivably even as low as 50% of 10 = 5.

The valuation of Mayfly's shares might therefore range between:

high P/E ratio and high earnings: 7 × £75,000 = £525,000; and

low P/E ratio and low earnings: 5 × £71,500 = £357,500.

3.5 The earnings yield valuation method

FAST FORWARD

Other earnings' methods include the **earnings yield valuation method** and the **accounting rate of return method**.

$$\text{Earnings yield (EY)} = \frac{\text{EPS}}{\text{Market price per share}} \times 100\%$$

This method is effectively a variation on the P/E method (the EY being the reciprocal of the P/E ratio), using an appropriate earnings yield effectively as a discount rate to value the earnings:

$$\text{Market value} = \frac{\text{Earnings}}{\text{EY}}$$

Exactly the same guidelines apply to this method as for the P/E method. Note that where **high growth** is envisaged, **the EY will be low,** as current earnings will be low relative to a market price that has built in future earnings growth. A stable earnings yield may suggest a company with low risk characteristics.

3.6 The accounting rate of return (ARR) method of share valuation

This method considers the **accounting** rate of return which will be required from the company whose shares are to be valued. It is therefore distinct from the P/E ratio method, which is concerned with the **market** rate of return required.

The following formula should be used.

$$\text{Value} = \frac{\text{Estimated future profits}}{\text{Required return on capital employed}}$$

For a takeover bid valuation, it will often be necessary to adjust the profits figure to allow for **expected changes** after the takeover. Those arising in an examination question might include:

(a) New levels of directors' remuneration

(b) New levels of interest charges (perhaps because the predator company will be able to replace existing loans with new loans at a lower rate of interest, or because the previous owners had lent the company money at non-commercial rates)

(c) A charge for notional rent where it is intended to sell existing properties or where the rate of return used is based on the results of similar companies that do not own their own properties

(d) The effects of product rationalisation and improved management

Note that such adjustments can also apply to earnings used in a P/E valuation approach.

3.7 Example: ARR method of share valuation

Chambers is considering acquiring Hall. At present Hall is earning, on average, £480,000 after tax. The directors of Chambers feel that after reorganisation, this figure could be increased to £600,000. All the companies in the Chambers group are expected to yield a post-tax accounting return of 15% on capital employed. What should Hall be valued at?

Solution

$$\text{Valuation} = \frac{£600,000}{15\%} = £4,000,000$$

This figure is the maximum that Chambers should be prepared to pay. The first offer would probably be much lower.

An ARR valuation might be used in a takeover when the acquiring company is trying to assess the **maximum amount it can afford to pay**.

4 Dividend valuation bases 11/05, 11/06

FAST FORWARD

Dividend yield and valuation methods are more relevant to small shareholdings. **Earnings' valuation methods** may be preferable if dividends are irregular.

4.1 The dividend yield method of share valuation

The **dividend yield method** of share valuation is suitable for the valuation of **small shareholdings in unquoted companies**. It is based on the principle that small shareholders are mainly interested in **dividends**, since they cannot control decisions affecting the company's profits and earnings. A suitable offer price would therefore be one which compensates them for the future dividends they will be giving up if they sell their shares.

This approach is similar to that of the earnings yield methods – a 'suitable dividend yield is applied as a discount rate to the expected level of dividend:

$$\text{Dividend yield} = \frac{\text{Dividend per share}}{\text{Market price per share}} \times 100\% \text{ and thus}$$

$$\text{Market price} = \frac{\text{Dividend}}{\text{Dividend yield}}$$

This method has the same problems as those of the earning based methods – the determination of a **'suitable' dividend yield**, and the appropriate level of **sustainable dividend** to use. Again, note that the dividend yield will be lower the higher the level of growth envisaged in the market price.

4.2 Using the dividend valuation model

The dividend valuation model is based on the theory that an equilibrium price for any share (or bond) on a stock market is:

- The **future expected stream of income** from the security
- **Discounted** at a suitable **cost of capital**

Equilibrium market price is thus a **present value** of a **future expected income stream**. The annual income stream for a share is the expected dividend every year in perpetuity.

The basic dividend-based formula for the market value of shares is expressed in the **dividend valuation model** as follows:

$$\text{MV (ex div)} = \frac{d}{1+k_e} + \frac{d}{(1+k_e)^2} + \frac{d}{(1+k_e)^3} + \ldots = \frac{d}{k_e}$$

where MV = ex dividend market value of the shares
d = constant annual dividend
k_e = shareholders' required rate of return

4.3 The dividend growth model

Using the **dividend growth model** we have:

$$P_0 = \frac{d_0(1+g)}{(1+k_e)} + \frac{d_0(1+g)^2}{(1+k_e)^2} + \ldots = \frac{d_0(1+g)}{(k_e - g)}$$

where d_0 = Current year's dividend
g = Growth rate in earnings and dividends
$d_0(1+g)$ = Expected dividend in one year's time
P_0 = Market value excluding any dividend currently payable

4.4 Example: dividend growth

(a) If a company has a payout ratio of 40%, and retains the rest for investing in projects which yield 15%, the annual rate of growth in dividends could be estimated as 15% × 60% = 9%.

(b) If a company pays out 80% of its profits as dividends, and retains the rest for reinvestment at 15%, the current dividend would be twice as big as in (a), but annual dividend growth would be only 15% × 20% = 3%.

4.5 Example: dividend growth model

Tantrum has achieved earnings of $800,000 this year. The company intends to pursue a policy of financing all its investment opportunities out of retained earnings. There are considerable investment opportunities, which are expected to be available indefinitely. However, if Tantrum does not exploit any of the available opportunities, its annual earnings will remain at $800,000 in perpetuity. The following figures are available.

Proportion of earnings retained	*Growth rate in earnings*	*Required return on all investments by shareholders*
%	%	%
0	0	14
25	5	15
40	7	16

The rate of return required by shareholders would rise if earnings are retained, because of the risk associated with the new investments. What is the optimum retentions policy for Tantrum? The full dividend payment for this year will be paid in the near future in any case.

Solution

Since $P_0 \text{ (MV ex div)} = \dfrac{D(1+g)}{(r-g)}$

$$\text{MV cum div} = \frac{D(1+g)}{(r-g)} + D$$

We are trying to maximise the value of shareholder wealth, which is currently represented by the cum div market value, since a dividend will soon be paid.

(a) If retentions are 0%:

$$\text{MV cum div} = \frac{800{,}000}{0.14} + 800{,}000 = \$6{,}514{,}286$$

(b) If retentions are 25%, the current dividend will be $600,000 and:

$$\text{MV cum div} = \frac{600{,}000(1.05)}{(0.15-0.05)} + 600{,}000 = \$6{,}900{,}000$$

(c) If retentions are 40%, the current dividend will be $480,000 and:

$$\text{MV cum div} = \frac{480{,}000(1.07)}{(0.16 - 0.07)} + 480{,}000 = \$6{,}186{,}667$$

The best policy (out of the three for which figures are provided) would be to retain 25% of earnings.

4.6 Assumptions of dividend models

The dividend models are underpinned by a number of assumptions that you should bear in mind.

(a) Investors act **rationally** and **monolithically** and have **perfect information** available. The model fails to take into account the **different expectations** or **different marginal costs of capital of** shareholders, nor how much they are motivated by dividends vs future capital appreciation on their shares.

(b) The d_0 figure used does **not vary significantly** from the **trend or risk of dividends**. If d_0 does appear to be a rogue figure, it may be better to use an adjusted trend figure, calculated on the basis of the past few years' dividends.

(c) The **estimates** of future dividends and prices used, and also the cost of capital are **reasonable**. As with other methods, it may be difficult to make a confident estimate of the cost of capital. Dividend estimates may be made from historical trends that may not be a good guide for a future if for example there is a takeover, or derived from uncertain forecasts about future earnings, which assumes that there are **enough profitable projects** in the future to **maintain dividend levels**.

(d) Investors' attitudes to receiving different cash flows at different times can be modelled using **discounted cashflow arithmetic.**

(e) Directors use dividends to **signal** the strength of the company's position (however companies that pay zero dividends do not have zero share values).

(f) Dividends either show **no growth** or **constant growth**. If the growth rate is calculated using g=bR, then the model assumes that b and R are constant

(g) **Other influences** on share prices are **ignored**.

(h) The company's **earnings** will **increase** sufficiently to maintain dividend growth levels.

(i) The **discount rate** used exceeds the **dividend growth rate**.

(j) **Tax and issue expenses** are ignored.

Question — DVM

Learning outcome: C(i)

Target paid a dividend of £250,000 this year. The current return to shareholders of companies in the same industry as Target is 12%, although it is expected that an additional risk premium of 2% will be applicable to Target, being a smaller and unquoted company. Compute the expected valuation of Target, if:

(a) The current level of dividend is expected to continue into the foreseeable future, or
(b) The dividend is expected to grow at a rate of 4% pa into the foreseeable future

Answer

k_e = 12% + 2% = 14% (0.14) d_0 = £250,000 g (in (b)) = 4% or 0.04

(a) $P_0 = \frac{d_0}{k_e} = \frac{£250,000}{0.14} = £1,785,714$

(b) $P_0 = \frac{d_0(1+g)}{k_e - g} = \frac{£250,000(1.04)}{0.14 - 0.04} = £2,600,000$

5 Cash flow valuation methods 11/06

FAST FORWARD

Cash flow **DCF valuation** may be used to value a company. **Free cash flows** are a development of the DCF method. **Shareholder value analysis** focuses on the key decisions affecting value and risk.

5.1 The discounted future cash flows method of share valuation

This method of share valuation may be appropriate when one company intends to buy the assets of another company and to make further investments in order to improve cash flows in the future.

We shall be looking at the discounted cash flow method (DCF) of investment appraisal in Chapter 18 and you may wish to refresh your memory of your earlier studies.

5.2 Example: discounted future cash flows method of share valuation

Diversification wishes to make a bid for Tadpole. Tadpole makes after-tax profits of £40,000 a year. Diversification believes that if further money is spent on additional investments, the after-tax cash flows (ignoring the purchase consideration) could be as follows.

Year	*Cash flow (net of tax)*
	£
0	(100,000)
1	(80,000)
2	60,000
3	100,000
4	150,000
5	150,000

The after-tax cost of capital of Diversification is 15% and the company expects all its investments to pay back, in discounted terms, within five years. What is the maximum price that the company should be willing to pay for the shares of Tadpole?

Solution

The maximum price is one which would make the return from the total investment exactly 15% over five years, so that the NPV at 15% would be 0.

Year	*Cash flows ignoring purchase consideration* £	*Discount factor (from tables)* 15%	*Present value* £
0	(100,000)	1.000	(100,000)
1	(80,000)	0.870	(69,600)
2	60,000	0.756	45,360
3	100,000	0.658	65,800
4	150,000	0.572	85,800
5	150,000	0.497	74,550
Maximum purchase price			101,910

Exam focus point

You may also need to calculate the value of cash flows in perpetuity using the formula given to you in the exam.

5.3 Selection of an appropriate cost of capital

In the above example, Diversification used its own cost of capital to discount the cash flows of Tadpole. There are a number of reasons why this may not be appropriate.

(a) The **business risk** of the new investment may not match that of the investing company. If Tadpole is in a completely different line of business from Diversification, its cash flows are likely to be subject to differing degrees of risk, and this should be taken into account when valuing them.

(b) The **method of finance** of the new investment may not match the current debt/equity mix of the investing company, which may have an effect on the cost of capital to be used.

5.4 Free cash flow

Under NPV

Valuation of a new company = Cash subscribed/paid for investment + NPV of proposed activities

The **present value** of future **free cash flows model** (also known as the **surplus project cash flow model**) focuses on the strategic need of companies to reinvest in new plant to maintain or increase current operating cash flows. This investment expenditure does not generally equal the depreciation charge in the accounts. Free cash flow takes into account this difference.

In the free flow cash flow model:

Operating free cash flow	=	Revenues
	–	Operating costs
	+	Depreciation
	–	Debt repayments and lease obligations
	–	Working capital increases
	–	Taxes
	–	Replacement capital expenditure

Using this model, the value of a company is the **sum** of **future discounted free cash flows**.

You may see other definitions of free cash flow used by different companies.

The advantage of including strategic value as well as existing project value in the definition of free cash flow is that **strategic value** can often be a significant element of **company value**.

Free cash flows can also be used as an element in ratio calculations. For example, the dividend cover ratio can be adjusted to take account of free cash flow.

$$\text{Dividend cover} = \frac{\text{Free cash flow}}{\text{Dividends paid}}$$

thus emphasising the importance of having cash available to pay dividends.

Possible disadvantages are that free cashflows may **fluctuate significantly** and will depend considerably on the company's **capital replacement policy**.

Free cash flow is also an important element in shareholder value analysis.

5.5 Shareholder value analysis

Shareholder value analysis (SVA) was developed during the 1980s from the work of Rappaport and focuses on value creation using the net present value (NPV) approach. Thus, SVA assumes that **the value of a business is the net present value of its future cash flows, discounted at the appropriate cost of capital.** Many leading companies (including, for example, Pepsi, Quaker and Disney) have used SVA as a way of linking management strategy and decisions to the creation of value for shareholders.

Key term

Shareholder value analysis is an approach to financial management which focuses on the creation of economic value for shareholders, as measured by share price performance and flow of dividends.

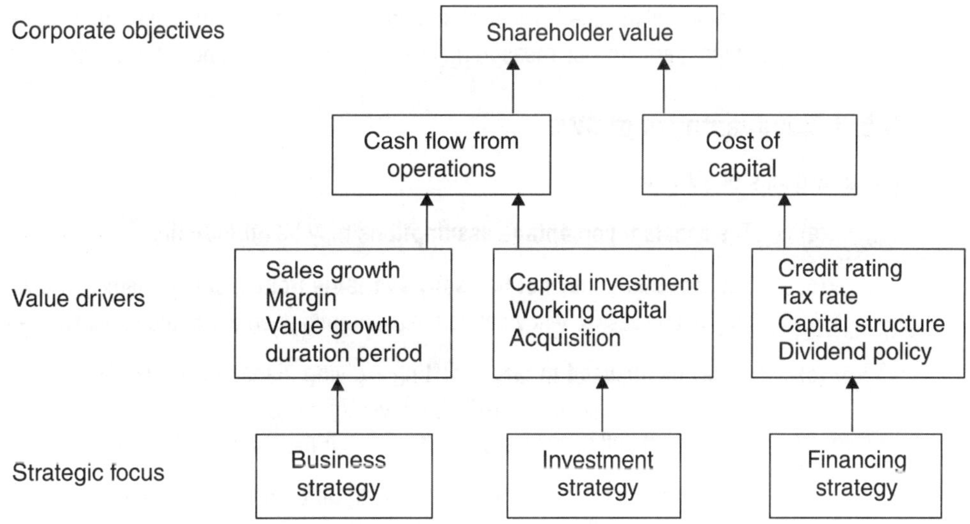

SVA takes the following approach.

(a) Key decisions with implications for cash flow and risk are specified. These may be **strategic**, **operational**, **related to investment** or **financial**.

(b) **Value drivers** are identified as the factors having the greatest impact on shareholder value, and management attention is focused on the decisions which influence the value drivers.

Value drivers are identified as being fundamental to the determination of value:

- Sales growth rate
- Operating profit margin
- Tax rate
- Fixed capital investment
- Working capital investment
- The planning horizon
- The required rate of return

The model assumes a constant percentage rate of sales growth and a constant operating profit margin. Tax is assumed to be a constant percentage of operating profit. Finally, fixed and working capital investments are assumed to be a constant percentage of changes in sales.

5.5.1 Calculating shareholder value

Using the free cash flows, corporate value is then computed at a rate reflecting the company's risk. A question covering this area may well indicate the rate that you should use to discount free cash flows. If you are not told the rate to use, the rate you should use should reflect the company's **risk**. This may be the weighted average cost of capital, but the WACC should not be used if interest has been included in the calculation of free cash flows. After tax cost of equity (ungeared) should be used if interest has been included in the free cash flow calculation, or if debt is assumed to be risk-free.

5.5.2 Advantages of SVA

This approach is:

- **Inclusive of the cost of capital** and **risk**
- **Not sensitive** to the choice of **accounting policies**
- Relatively **simple to apply**
- **Consistent with the concept of share valuation by DCF**
- A spur to management awareness of the **key long-term value variables (**drivers)

Sevren suggests that it should lead to the establishment of a value management system aimed at maximising long-term shareholder value added. The system should include strategic assessment, long-term planning, operational planning, performance measurement and management, and incentive compensation.

5.5.3 Disadvantages of SVA

The drawbacks of SVA include:

(a) The **constant percentage assumptions** may be **unrealistic**.

(b) The **input data** may **not** be **easily available** from current systems, particularly to outsiders. It may not be easy to test whether the assumptions on which the forecasts are based are realistic.

(c) It may be **misused in target setting** – giving managers a 12-month target cash flow may discourage longer term profitable investment. On the other hand a longer-term target may be very difficult to set because of uncertainties over future cash flows.

(d) Other models have been suggested with different value drivers; Copeland, Koller and Murrin suggested that there are three value drivers, **return on invested capital, cash flow** and **economic profit or economic value added**.

5.6 Economic value added

Economic value added is closely associated with SVA and gives the economic value or profit added per year. It can be used as a means of **measuring managerial performance,** by assessing the net present value of revenues (profits) less resources used (capital employed). It is **not** a measure of share valuation.

Economic value added	=	**NOPAT – (cost of capital × capital employed)**
where NOPAT	=	Net operating profit after tax adjusted for non-cash expenses (see below)
(cost of capital × capital employed)	=	imputed charge for the capital consumed, the cost of capital being the weighted average cost of capital for the firm's **target capital structure**

Adjustments may be needed to the profit figures in the accounts to arrive at NOPAT.

(a) **Interest** and **tax relief on interest** should be excluded from NOPAT, as they are taken into account in the imputed capital charge.

(b) **Investing cash flows** should be excluded from NOPAT **but** allowed for in **capital employed.** These include **goodwill, research and development** and **advertising**, and other expenditure designed to build the business up over the next few years. The amount added to capital employed should be a figure that reflects the expenditure that has affected profit this year, say the research and development charge for the last four years or goodwill that has previously been written off. (In some calculations a small charge for research and development is included in the income statement to reflect the economic depreciation of the capitalised value.)

(c) **Lease charges** should be excluded from NOPAT but added in as part of capital employed.

(d) The **depreciation** figure in the accounts can be used as an approximation for economic depreciation.

Economic depreciation = the fall in asset value due to wear and tear and obsolescence

If a separate figure is calculated for economic depreciation, accounting depreciation should be excluded from NOPAT.

5.6.1 Advantages of EVA

The economic value added approach focuses on long-term net present value. By including a financing element, it brings home to managers the costs of capital used, emphasising the importance of careful investment and control of working capital.

5.6.2 Disadvantages of EVA

EVA may cause managers to avoid projects with poor initial returns or large initial expenditure (for example on research and development) if they are primarily being judged on short-term performance.

The economic value added approach also suffers from the usual problems of being based on historical accounting figures that can be distorted. There may be other value drivers that are important, such as non-capitalised goodwill.

5.7 Market value added

Market value added (MVA) is the difference between:

(a) The **contribution** put into the business by investors (the purchase price of their shares **and** the re-investment of profits that would otherwise have been distributed)

(b) The increase in **current market value of their shares** resulting from the contribution

The MVA figure tends to correspond closely to the difference between the market value of equity and the book value of equity. To assess whether MVA is reasonable, you need to assess what Economic value added will be for several years into the future; this may not be easy. Market value added also does not adjust for size differences for comparisons.

5.8 Drawbacks of cash flow methods

Whichever method is used, cash flow methods suffer from the following general drawbacks.

(a) As we have seen above, selection of an **appropriate cost of capital** may prove difficult.

(b) **Estimating future cash flows**, particularly of companies that are being acquired, may be **very difficult**.

(c) Cash flows are most appropriate for valuing **controlling interests**, which might have a significant influence on whether expected cash flows are attained.

6 Other valuation bases

FAST FORWARD

The super-profits method uses **excess profits** to **value goodwill. Earn-out arrangements** are where the buyer of a business agrees to pay the seller an additional amount of consideration if the acquired company achieves a certain level of profitability.

6.1 The super-profits method of share valuation

This method, which is rather out of fashion at present, starts by applying a 'fair return' to the net tangible assets and comparing the result with the expected profits. Any excess of profits **(the super-profits)** is used to calculate goodwill. The goodwill is normally taken as a fixed number of years super-profits. The goodwill is then added to the value of the target company's tangible assets to arrive at a value for the business.

6.2 Example: super-profits method of share valuation

Light has net tangible assets of £120,000 and present earnings of £20,000. Doppler wants to take over Light and considers that a fair return for this type of industry is 12%, and decides to value Light taking goodwill at three years super-profits.

	£
Actual profits	20,000
Less fair return on net tangible assets: 12% × £120,000	14,400
Super-profits	5,600
Goodwill: 3 × £5,600	£16,800
Value of Light: £120,000 + £16,800	£136,800

The principal drawbacks to this valuation method are as follows.

(a) The rate of return required is **chosen subjectively**.

(b) The number of years purchase of super-profits is **arbitrary**. In the example above, goodwill was valued at three years of super-profits, but it could have been, for example, two years or four years of super-profits.

6.3 Earn-out arrangements

Earn-out arrangements were discussed in Chapter 3, whereby the buyer of a business agrees to pay the seller an additional amount of consideration if the acquired company achieves a certain level of performance.

For example, the consideration may be structured as follows.

(a) An initial amount payable at the time of acquisition

(b) A guaranteed minimum amount of deferred consideration, payable in, say, three years time

(c) An additional amount of deferred consideration, payable if a specified target performance is achieved over the next three years.

The total of the **initial and guaranteed deferred consideration** amounts may be based upon an **assets based approach to valuation**, or on an earnings basis, using, for example, the average level of expected profits over a given future period.

The **additional amount of deferred consideration** might be payable if the acquired company's **average profits or revenues** over the next three years exceeds a certain amount.

This method would only be appropriate if the acquired company was to be **run independently** of the **buyer's company**, at least for the period upon which the contingent consideration is based. If the acquired business were to be immediately integrated within the buyer's, it would be difficult to identify separately the relevant sales or profits.

Under these types of arrangement, then, the **overall valuation** of the business will have a **variable element**. The buyer will need to estimate the minimum, maximum and expected total amounts they may have to pay, with corresponding probabilities relating to the likelihood of the business reaching the specified targets. In particular, they will have to ensure that they could, if necessary, afford to pay the maximum amount, regardless of how unlikely that is to arise.

Question — Valuation methods

Learning outcome: C(i)

Profed provides a tuition service to professional students. This includes courses of lectures provided on their own premises and provision of study material for home study. Most of the lecturers are qualified professionals with many years' experience in both their profession and tuition. Study materials are written and word processed in-house, but sent out to an external printers.

The business was started fifteen years ago, and now employs around 40 full-time lecturers, 10 authors and 20 support staff. Freelance lecturers and authors are employed from time to time in times of peak demand.

The shareholders of Profed mainly comprise the original founders of the business who would now like to realise their investment. In order to arrive at an estimate of what they believe the business is worth, they have identified a long-established quoted company, City Tutors, who have a similar business, although they also publish texts for external sale to universities, colleges etc.

Summary financial statistics for the two companies for the most recent financial year are as follows.

	Profed	*City Tutors*
Issued shares (million)	4	10
Net asset values (£m)	7.2	15
Earnings per share (pence)	35	20
Dividend per share (pence)	20	18
Debt: equity ratio	1:7	1:65
Share price (pence)		362
Expected rate of growth in earnings/dividends	9% pa	7.5% pa

Notes

1 The net assets of Profed are the net book values of tangible non-current assets plus net working capital. However:

- A recent valuation of the buildings was £1.5m above book value.
- Inventory includes past editions of text books which have a realisable value of £100,000 below their cost.
- Due to a dispute with one of their clients, an additional allowance for bad debts of £750,000 could prudently be made.

2 Growth rates should be assumed to be constant per annum; Profed's earnings growth rate estimate was provided by the marketing manager, based on expected growth in sales adjusted by normal profit margins. City Tutors' growth rates were gleaned from press reports.

3 Profed uses a discount rate of 15% to appraise its investments, and has done for many years.

Required

(a) Compute a range of valuations for the business of Profed, using the information available and stating any assumptions made.

(b) Comment upon the strengths and weaknesses of the methods you used in (a) and their suitability for valuing Profed.

Answer

(a) The information provided allows us to value Profed on three bases: net assets, P/E ratio and dividend valuation

All three will be computed, even though their validity may be questioned in part (b) of the answer.

Assets based

	£'000
Net assets at book value	7,200
Add: increased valuation of buildings	1,500
Less: decreased value of inventory and receivables	(850)
Net asset value of equity	7,850
Value per share	£1.96

P/E ratio

	Profed	*City Tutors*
Issued shares (million)	4	10
Share price (pence)		362
Market value (£m)		36.2
Earnings per shares (pence)	35	20
P/E ratio (share price ÷ EPS)		18.1

The P/E for a similar quoted company is 18.1. This will take account of factors such as marketability of shares, status of company, growth potential that will differ from those for Profed. Profed's growth rate has been estimated as higher than that of City Tutors, possibly because it is a younger, developing company, although the basis for the estimate may be questionable.

All other things being equal, the P/E ratio for an unquoted company should be taken as between one half to two thirds of that of an equivalent quoted company. Being generous, in view of the possible higher growth prospects of Profed, we might estimate an appropriate P/E ratio of around 12, assuming Profed is to remain a private company.

This will value Profed at 12 × £0.35 = £4.20 per share, a total valuation of £16.8m.

Dividend valuation model

The dividend valuation method gives the share price as

$$\frac{\text{Next year's dividend}}{\text{Cost of equity} - \text{growth rate}}$$

which assumes dividends being paid into perpetuity, and growth at a constant rate.

For Profed, next year's dividend = £0.20 × 1.09 = £0.218 per share

Whilst we are given a discount rate of 15% as being traditionally used by the directors of Profed for investment appraisal, there appears to be no rational basis for this. We can instead use the information for City Courses to estimate a cost of equity for Profed. This is assuming the business risks to be similar, and ignoring the small difference in their gearing ratio.

Again, from the DVM, cost of equity = $\frac{\text{next year's dividend}}{\text{market price}}$ + growth rate

For City Tutors, cost of equity = $\frac{£0.18 \times 1.075}{£3.62} + 0.075 = 12.84\%$

Using, say, 13% as a cost of equity for Profed:

Share price = $\frac{£0.218}{0.13 - 0.09} = £5.45$

valuing the whole of the share capital at £21.8 million

Range for valuation

The three methods used have thus come up with a range of value of Profed as follows.

	Value per share	*Total valuation*
	£	£m
Net assets	1.96	7.9
P/E ratio	4.20	16.8
Dividend valuation	5.45	21.8

(b) **Comment on relative merits of the methods used, and their suitability**

Asset based valuation

Valuing a company on the **basis of its asset values** alone is rarely appropriate if it is to be sold on a going concern basis. Exceptions would include property Investment companies and investment trusts, the market values of the assets of which will bear a close relationship to their earning capacities.

Profed is typical of a lot of service companies, a large part of whose value lies in the **skill, knowledge and reputation of its personnel**. This is not reflected in the net asset values, and renders this method quite inappropriate. A potential purchaser of Profed will generally value its intangible assets such as knowledge, expertise, customer/supplier relationships, brands etc more highly than those that can be measured in accounting terms.

Knowledge of the net asset value (NAV) of a company will, however, be important as a **floor value** for a company in financial difficulties or subject to a takeover bid. Shareholders will be reluctant to sell for less than the net asset value even if future prospects are poor.

P/E ratio valuation

The P/E ratio measures the **multiple of the current year's earnings** that is reflected in the **market price** of a share. It is thus a method that reflects the earnings potential of a company from a market point of view. Provided the marketing is efficient, it is likely to give the most meaningful basis for valuation.

One of the first things to say is that the market price of a share at any point in time is determined by supply and demand forces prevalent during small transactions, and will be dependent upon a lot of factors in addition to a realistic appraisal of future prospects. A downturn in the market, economies and political changes can all affect the day-to-day price of a share, and thus its prevailing P/E ratio. it is not known whether the share price given for City Tutors was taken on one particular day, or was some sort of average over a period. The latter would perhaps give a sounder basis from which to compute an applicable P/E ratio.

Even if the P/E ratio of City Tutors can be taken to be **indicative of its true worth**, using it as a basis to value a smaller, unquoted company in the same industry can be problematic.

The status and marketability of shares in a quoted company have tangible effects on value but these are difficult to measure.

The P/E ratio will also be affected by **growth prospects** – the higher the growth expected, the higher the ratio. The growth rate incorporated by the shareholders of City Tutors is probably based on a more rational approach than that used by Profed.

If the growth prospects of Profed, as would be perceived by the market, did not coincide with those of **Profed management** it is difficult to see how the P/E ratio should be adjusted for relative levels of growth.

In the valuation in (a) a crude adjustment has been made to City Tutors' P/E ratio to arrive at a ratio to use to value Profed's earnings. This can result in a very inaccurate result if account has not been taken of all the differences involved.

Dividend based valuation

The dividend valuation model (DVM) is a **cash flow based approach**, which valued the dividends that the shareholders expect to receive from the company by discounting them at their required rate of return. It is perhaps more appropriate for valuing a minority shareholding where the holder has no influence over the level of dividends to be paid than for valuing a whole company, where the total cash flows will be of greater relevance.

The practical problems with the dividend valuation model lie mainly in its **assumptions**. Even accepting that the required 'perfect capital market' assumptions may be satisfied to some extent, in reality, the formula used in (a) assumes constant growth rates and constant required rates of return in perpetuity.

Determination of an **appropriate cost of equity** is particularly difficult for a unquoted company, and the use of an 'equivalent' quoted company's data carries the same drawbacks as discussed above. Similar problems arise in estimating future growth rates, and the results from the model are highly sensitive to changes in both these inputs.

It is also highly dependent upon the **current year's dividend** being a representative base from which to start.

The dividend valuation model valuation provided in (a) results in a higher valuation than that under the P/E ratio approach. Reasons for this may be:

- The **share price** for City Courses may be currently **depressed below its normal level**, resulting in an inappropriately low P/E ratio.
- The **adjustment** to get to an **appropriate P/E ratio** for Profed may have been too harsh, particularly in light of its apparently better growth prospects.

- The **cost of equity** used in the dividend valuation model was that of City Courses. The validity of this will largely depend upon the relative levels of risk of the two companies. Although they both operate the same type of business, the fact that City Courses sells its material externally means it is perhaps less reliant on a fixed customer base.
- Even if business risks and gearing risk may be thought to be comparable a prospective buyer of Profed may consider investment in a **younger, unquoted company** to carry **greater personal risk**. His required return may thus be higher than that envisaged in the dividend valuation model, reducing the valuation.

Exam focus point

In a business valuation question, there is no one 'correct' answer. You need to be able to present a well reasoned report that takes into account a number of different view points whilst making reasonable assumptions.

TOPCIMA link

As well as assessing valuation issues in the TOPCIMA exam, you may also have to consider whether a premium should be paid to secure a particularly desirable acquisition.

7 Share valuation and market efficiency

FAST FORWARD

The reliability of the various methods used to value shares may be affected by the **level of market efficiency**.

7.1 Impact of market efficiency

In Chapter 7 we discussed the significance of market efficiency and in this section we examine how market efficiency impacts upon the company valuation process.

7.1.1 Availability of information

The different methods we have discussed above are built upon different levels of efficiency. Broadly speaking, methods based on **historical or current position** require the market to have a **lower** degree of efficiency than methods that are based on **future cash flows** or **dividend flows**. This implies that directors must concern themselves with how much detail needs to be given out for the markets to value shares fairly. Of course this can work both ways, and directors may wish to suppress information that the market has not been able to anticipate and that would lower the share price if the market knew of it.

7.1.2 Investors' needs

Arguably as well the valuation methods depend on a fully functional market for shares wlth ready availability of buyers and sellers. The number of investors may though be affected by the **levels of market efficiency**, as investors will prefer a market where shares are priced on a rational basis.

7.1.3 Mergers and takeovers

Market efficiency is particularly important when companies are considering making an offer for another company. If the market is fairly efficient, the target's shares will be valued at a **fair price**; hence any premium offered on those shares has to be justified in terms of post-acquisition gains or savings. However if the market is **very efficient**, arguably it will anticipate that a merger will take place and these gains will be realised. There is some evidence from the major stock exchanges that mergers are anticipated some months in advance. The more this happens, and the more likely benefits from anticipated mergers are factored into the share price, the less a premium is likely to be value for money for an acquiror.

8 Share valuation and change in capital structure

FAST FORWARD

The **traditional view of gearing** states that **market value** should be **maximised** at the optimum capital structure, where cost of capital is minimised. **Modigliani and Miller** state that in a world with taxes, market value should continue to rise as gearing rises, because tax benefits arise from interest paid.

8.1 Effect of gearing

In Chapter 9 on the cost of capital we detailed the different viewpoints concerning the effect of capital structure on the cost of capital. In this section we look in greater detail on how capital structure impacts upon the valuation of companies.

8.2 Traditional approach

Remember that the traditional view was that the optimum level of gearing is where the company's weighted average cost of capital is minimised and therefore the company's total market value is maximised.

8.2.1 Example: traditional approach

Gearing has the following capital structure (no tax):

		Constant annual payments to investors	*Market value*
		£m	£m
Equity	dividends	27	150
Debt	interest	3	30
		30	180

The current cost of equity is thus $k_e = \frac{d_0}{P_0} = \frac{27}{150} = 18\%$

The current cost of debt is thus $k_d = \frac{i}{P_0} = \frac{3}{30} = 10\%$

Thus the WACC is $\frac{150}{180} \times 18\% + \frac{30}{180} \times 10\% = 16.67\%$

Note that in the case of constant dividends and interest, the WACC can be computed as

$$\text{WACC} = \frac{\text{Total payments to investors}}{\text{Total MV}} = \frac{£30\text{m}}{£180\text{m}} = 16.67\%$$

Conversely, discounting the total payments to investors by the WACC in perpetuity can derive the total MV:

$$\text{Total MV} = \frac{\text{Total payments to investors}}{\text{WACC}} = \frac{£30\text{m}}{0.1667} = £180\text{m}$$

Current gearing level, equity:debt, is 150:30 or 5:1

Now suppose the gearing is to be increased to (1) 3:1 or (2) 3:2 by the repurchase of shares, funded by new debt. It is estimated that the cost of equity will rise to compensate for the increase in gearing risk, by (1) 0.75% and (2) 3%, and that the cost of debt will rise, in the case of (2) only, by 0.5%.

What are the effects on WACC and total MV of each change?

New WACC under (1): $\frac{3}{4} \times 18.75\% + \frac{1}{4} \times 10\% = 16.56\%$

and, since total payments to investors will be unchanged,

Total MV under (1) $= \frac{£30m}{0.1656} = £181.16m$

New WACC under (2): $\frac{3}{5} \times 21\% + \frac{2}{5} \times 10.5\% = 16.8\%$

Total MV under (2) $= \frac{£30m}{0.168} = £178.57m$

Method (1), with the lower increase in gearing, had a small associated increase in the cost of equity, and the WACC went down – the impact of more cheaper debt outweighed the effect of the increased cost of equity. This led to a rise in the total MV.

Under Method (2), with the percentage of total capital represented by debt more than doubling, there was a much higher increase in the cost of equity, accompanied by an increase in the cost of debt. Despite the much higher proportion of cheap debt, the WACC went up, and the total MV fell.

Question — Change in capital structure

Learning outcome: C(i)

AB has a WACC of 16%. It is financed partly by equity (cost 18%) and partly by debt capital (cost 10%). The company is considering a new project which would cost £5,000,000 and would yield annual profits of £850,000 before interest charges. It would be financed by a loan at 10%. As a consequence of the higher gearing, the cost of equity would rise to 20%. The company pays out all profits as dividends, which are currently £2,250,000 a year.

(a) What would be the effect on the value of equity of undertaking the project?

(b) To what extent can you analyse the increase or decrease in equity value into two causes, the NPV of the project at the current WACC and the effect of the method of financing?

Ignore taxation. The traditional view of WACC and gearing is assumed in this exercise.

Answer

(a)

	£
Current profits and dividends	2,250,000
Increase in profits and dividends	
(£850,000 less extra interest 10% × £5,000,000)	350,000
New dividends, if project is undertaken	2,600,000
New cost of equity	20%
	£
New MV of equity	13,000,000
Current MV of equity	
(£2,250,000 ÷ 0.18)	12,500,000
Increase in shareholder wealth from project	500,000

(b) (i) NPV of project if financed at current WACC = $\frac{£850,000}{0.16} - £5,000,000 = +£312,500$

(ii) The effect of financing on share values must be to increase the MV of equity by the remaining £187,500, which indicates that the effect of financing the project in the manner proposed will be to increase the company's gearing, but to reduce its WACC.

8.3 Net operating income approach

We saw earlier in this text that Modigliani and Miller stated in their basic theory that the level of gearing would not affect the value of shares in a tax-less world. However if taxation was introduced, the weighted average cost of capital will continue to fall as gearing increased.

You will remember that Modigliani and Miller argued that since WACC falls as gearing rises, and the value of a company should rise as its WACC falls, **the value of a geared company will always be greater than its ungeared counterpart**, but only by the amount of the debt-associated tax saving of the geared company, assuming a permanent change in gearing.

Exam Formula

$V_g = V_u + TB_c$

You will remember that the additional amount of value in the geared company, TB_c is known as the value of the '**tax shield**' on debt.

However, the positive tax effects of debt finance will be exhausted where there is insufficient tax liability to use the tax relief which is available. This is known as **tax shield exhaustion**.

8.3.1 Example: MM, with taxes

Notnil and Newbegin are companies in the same industry. They have the same business risk and operating characteristics, but Notnil is a geared company whereas Newbegin is all equity financed. Notnil earns three times as much profit before interest as Newbegin. Both companies pursue a policy of paying out all their earnings each year as dividends.

The market value of each company is currently as follows.

		Notnil		*Newbegin*
		£m		£m
Equity	(10m shares)	36	(20m shares)	15
Debt	(£12m of 12% loan stock)	14		
		50		15

The annual profit before interest of Notnil is £3,000,000 and that of Newbegin is £1,000,000. The rate of tax is 30%. It is thought that the current market value per ordinary share in Newbegin is at the equilibrium level, and that the market value of Notnil's debt capital is also at its equilibrium level. There is some doubt, however, about whether the value of Notnil's shares is at its equilibrium level.

Apply the MM formula to establish the equilibrium price of Notnil's shares.

Solution

$V_g = V_u + TB_c$

V_u = the market value of an equivalent ungeared company. Equivalence is in both size and risk of earnings. Since Notnil earnings (before interest) are three times the size of Newbegin's, V_u is three times the value of Newbegin's equity:

3 × £15,000,000 = £45,000,000.

TB_c = £14,000,000 × 30% = £4,200,000

V_g = £45,000,000 + £4,200,000 = £49,200,000.

Since the market value of debt in Notnil is £14,000,000, it follows that the market value of Notnil's equity should be £49,200,000 – £14,000,000 = £35,200,000.

$$\text{Value per share} = \frac{£35,200,000}{10,000,000} = £3.52 \text{ per share}$$

Since the current share price is £3.60 per share, MM would argue that the shares in Notnil are currently over-valued by the market, by £800,000 in total or 8p per share. MM argue that this discrepancy would be rapidly removed by the process of arbitrage until the equity value of Notnil was as predicted by their model.

Question — WACC and MM theory

Learning outcome: C(i)

CD and YZ are identical in every respect except for their gearing. The market value of each company is as follows.

	CD		*YZ*
	£m		£m
Equity (5m shares)	?	(8m shares)	24
Debt (£20m of 5% loan stock)	10		
	?		24

According to MM theory, what is the value of CD shares, given a corporation tax rate of 30%?

Answer

Value of CD in total $V_g = V_u + TB_c$ where V_u is the value of YZ.

V_g = £24,000,000 + £10,000,000 × 30% = £27,000,000.

CD's equity is valued at £27,000,000 – debt of £10,000,000 = £17,000,000, or £3.40 per share.

9 Intangible assets and intellectual capital 11/06

FAST FORWARD

The valuation of **intangible assets** and **intellectual capital** presents special problems. Various methods can be used to value them including the relief from royalties, premium profits and capitalisation of earnings methods.

9.1 Valuation of intangibles

The asset based valuation method discussed earlier specifically excluded most intangible assets from the computation. This rendered this method unsuitable for the valuation of most established businesses, particularly those in the service industry. Here we consider the various types of intangible assets that a business may benefit from and how they might be valued.

9.1.1 Intangible assets and goodwill

Key terms

Intangible assets are identifiable non-monetary assets without physical substance which must be controlled by the entity as the result of past events and from which the entity expects a flow of future economic benefits. *(IAS 38)*

Goodwill (acquired)is future economic benefits arising from assets that are not capable of being individually identified and separately recognised. *(IFRS 3)*

The above definition of intangible assets distinguishes:

(a) Intangible assets from tangible assets, by the phrase 'do not have physical substance'.

(b) Intangible assets from goodwill, by the word 'identifiable', an identifiable asset is legally defined as one that can be disposed of separately without disposing of a business of the entity.

The strict accounting distinctions do not need to concern us here. We are interested in any element of business that may have some value.

Certain intangible assets can be recorded at their **historical cost**. Examples include patents and trademarks being recorded at **registration value** and franchises being recorded at **contract cost**. However over time these historical values may become poor reflections of the assets' value in use or of their market value.

9.1.2 Intellectual capital

Key term

Intellectual capital is knowledge which can be used to create value. Intellectual capital includes:

(a) **Human resources**: the collective skills, experience and knowledge of employees

(b) **Intellectual assets**: knowledge which is defined and codified such as a drawing, computer program or collection of data

(c) **Intellectual property**: intellectual assets which can be legally protected, such as patents and copyrights *(OT 2005)*

As the demand for knowledge-based products grows with the changing structure of the global economy, knowledge plays an expanding role in achieving competitive advantage. Employees may thus be extremely valuable to a business, and they should be included in a full assets based valuation.

The principles of valuation discussed below should be taken as applying to all assets, resources or property that are defined as intangible assets or intellectual capital, which will include:

- Patents, trademarks and copyrights
- Franchises and licensing agreements
- Research and development
- Brands
- Technology, management and consulting processes
- Know-how, education, vocational qualification
- Customer loyalty
- Distribution channels
- Management philosophy

9.2 Measurement of intangible assets of an enterprise

The expanding intellectual capital of firms accentuates the need for methods of valuation for comparative purposes, for example when an acquisition or buy-out is being considered.

Ramona Dzinkowski (*The measurement and management of intellectual capital*, Management Accounting) identifies the following three indicators, which are derived from audited financial statements and are independent of the definitions of intellectual capital adopted by the firm.

- **Market-to-book values**
- **Tobin's 'q'**
- **Calculated intangible value**

9.2.1 Market-to-book values

This method represents the value of a firm's intellectual capital as **the difference between the book value of tangible assets and the market value of the firm**. Thus, if a company's market value is £8 million and its book value is £5 million, the £3 million difference is taken to represent the value of the firm's intangible (or intellectual) assets.

Although obviously **simple**, this method's simplicity merely serves to indicate that it fails to take account of **real world complexities.** There may be imperfections in the market valuation, and book values are subject to accounting standards which reflect historic cost and amortisation policies rather than true market values of tangible non-current assets.

In addition, the accounting valuation does not attempt to value a company as a whole, but rather as a sum of separate asset values computed under particular accounting conventions. The market, on the other hand, values the entire company as a going concern, following its defined strategy.

9.2.2 Tobin's 'q'

The Nobel prize-winning economist James Tobin developed the 'q' method initially as a way of predicting investment behaviour.

'q' is the ratio of the **market capitalisation of the firm** (share price × number of shares) to the **replacement cost** of its assets.

If the replacement cost of assets is **lower** than the market capitalisation, **q is greater than unity** and the company is enjoying higher than average returns on its investment ('monopoly rents'). Technology and so called 'human-capital' assets are likely to lead to high q values.

Tobin's 'q' is affected by the same variables influencing market capitalisation as the market-to-book method. In common with that method, it is used most appropriately to make comparisons of the value of intangible assets of companies within an industry which serve the same markets and have similar tangible non-current assets. As such, these methods could serve as performance benchmarks by which to appraise management or corporate strategy.

9.2.3 Calculated intangible values

NCI Research has developed the method of **calculated intangible value (CIV)** for calculating the fair market value of a firm's intangible assets. CIV calculates an 'excess return' on tangible assets. This figure is then used in determining the proportion of return attributable to intangible assets.

A step-by-step approach would be as follows.

Step 1 Calculate average pre-tax earnings over a time period.

Step 2 Calculate average year end tangible assets over the time period using balance sheet figures.

Step 3 Divide earnings by average assets to get the return on assets.

Step 4 Find the industry's return on assets.

Step 5 Multiply the industry's return on asset percentage by the entity's average tangible asset. Subtract this from the entity's pre-tax earnings to calculate the excess return.

Step 6 Calculate the average tax rate over the time period and multiply this by the excess return. Subtract this from the excess return to give the after-tax premium attributable to intangible assets.

Step 7 Calculate the NPV of the premium by dividing it by the entity's cost of capital.

Exam focus point

> This is the method used to value intellectual capital in the examiners' answer to Question 2 in November 2006. You would have however have been given credit for any valid attempt to place a value on intellectual capital. Very few candidates made a serious attempt at the valuation.

Whilst this seemingly straightforward approach, using readily available information, seems attractive, it does have two problems.

(a) It uses average industry ROA as a basis for computing excess returns, which may be distorted by extreme values.

(b) The choice of discount rate to apply to the excess returns to value the intangible asset needs to be made with care. To ensure comparability between companies and industries, some sort of average cost of capital should perhaps be applied. This again has the potential problems of distortion.

9.2.4 Valuation indicators

Some approaches assess the valuation of intellectual capital on the basis of a series of indicators. Skandia AFS developed an intellectual capital report based on a number of different indicators grouped according to their primary focus.

(a) **Financial focus**. Indicators such as: revenue per employee, revenue from new customers/total revenue.

(b) **Customer focus**. Indicators such as: market share, satisfied customer index, annual sales per customer, average time from customer contact to sales response.

(c) **Process focus**. Indicators such as: administrative expense/total revenue, IT expense per employee, cost of administrative error/management revenues.

(d) **Renewal and development focus**. Indicators such as: training expense per employee, R&D expense/administrative expense, educational expense per customer.

(e) **Human focus**. Indicators such as: IT literacy of staff, motivation index, annual turnover of full-time permanent employees.

9.3 Valuation of individual intangible assets

9.3.1 Relief from royalties method

This method involves trying to determine:

(a) The value obtainable from licensing out the right to exploit the intangible asset to a third party, or

(b) The royalties that the owner of the intangible asset is relieved from paying through being the owner rather than the licensee

A **notional royalty rate** is estimated as a percentage of revenue expected to be generated by the intangible asset. The estimated royalty stream can then be **capitalised**, for example by discounting at a risk-free market rate, to find an estimated market value.

This relatively simple valuation method is easiest to apply if the intangible asset is already subject to licensing agreements. If they are not, the valuer might reach an appropriate figure from other comparable licensing arrangements.

9.3.2 Premium profits method

The premium profits method is often used for **brands**. It bases the valuation on capitalisation of the **extra profits generated** by the brand or other intangible asset in excess of profits made by businesses lacking the intangible asset or brand.

The premium profits specifically attributable to the brand or other intangible asset may be estimated (for example) by comparing the price of branded products and unbranded products. The estimated premium profits can then be capitalised by discounting at a risk-adjusted market rate.

9.3.3 Capitalisation of earnings method

With the capitalised earnings method, the **maintainable earnings accruing to the intangible asset** are estimated. An **earnings multiple** is then applied to the earnings, taking account of expected risks and rewards, including the prospects for future earnings growth and the risks involved. This method of valuation is often used to value **publishing titles**.

9.3.4 Comparison with market transactions method

This method looks at **actual market transactions** in similar intangible assets. A multiple of revenue or earnings from the intangible asset might then be derived from a similar market transaction. A problem with this method is that many **intangible assets are unique** and it may therefore be difficult to identify 'similar' market transactions, although this might be done by examining acquisitions and disposals of businesses that include similar intangible assets.

The method might be used alongside other valuation methods, to provide a comparison.

Chapter roundup

- There are a number of different ways of **putting a value on a business**, or on shares in an unquoted company. It makes sense to use **several methods** of valuation, and to compare the values they produce.
- The **net assets valuation** method can be used as one of many valuation methods, or to provide a lower limit for the value of a company. By itself it is unlikely to produce the most realistic value.
- **P/E ratios** are used when a large block of shares, or a whole business, is being valued. This method can be problematic when quoted companies' P/E ratios are used to value unquoted companies.
- Other earnings' methods include the **earnings yield valuation method** and the **accounting rate of return method**.
- **Dividend yield and valuation methods** are more relevant to small shareholdings. **Earnings' valuation methods** may be preferable if dividends are irregular.
- Cash flow **DCF valuation** may be used to value a company. **Free cash flows** are a development of the DCF method. **Shareholder value analysis** focuses on the key decisions affecting value and risk.
- The super-profits method uses **excess profits** to **value goodwill**. **Earn-out arrangements** are where the buyer of a business agrees to pay the seller an additional amount of consideration if the acquired company achieves a certain level of profitability.
- The reliability of the various methods used to value shares may be affected by the level of **market efficiency**.
- The **traditional view** of gearing states that **market value** should be **maximised** at the optimum capital structure, where cost of capital is minimised. **Modigliani and Miller** state that in a world with taxes, market value should continue to rise as gearing rises, because tax benefits arise from interest paid.
- The valuation of **intangible assets** and **intellectual capital** presents special problems. Various methods can be used to value them including the relief from royalties, premium profits and capitalisation of earnings methods.

Quick quiz

1 Give four circumstances in which the shares of an unquoted company might need to be valued.

2 How is the P/E ratio related to EPS?

3 What is meant by 'multiples' in the context of share valuation?

4 Value = Estimated future profits/Required return on capital employed. What is the name of this valuation model?

5 Suggest two circumstances in which net assets might be used as a basis for valuation of a company.

6 There is one correct value for a business

True ☐

False ☐

7 Give six examples of types of intangible assets.

8 Identify three methods of valuing the intellectual capital of a business.

9 Identify four methods of valuing individual intangible assets.

Answers to quick quiz

1 (a) Setting an issue price if the company is floating its shares
(b) When shares are sold
(c) For tax purposes
(d) When shares are pledged as collateral for a loan

2 P/E ratio = Share price/EPS

3 The P/E ratio: the multiple of earnings at which a company's shares are traded

4 Accounting rate of return method

5 (a) As a measure of asset backing
(b) For comparison, in a scheme of merger

6 False. In a business valuation, there is no one correct answer. A range of valuations should be calculated.

7 Patents; trade marks; brands; copyrights; franchises; research and development

8 Market-to-book values; Tobin's q; calculated intangible value

9 Relief from royalties; premium profits; capitalisation of earnings; comparison with market transactions

Now try the question below from the Exam Question Bank

Number	Level	Marks	Time
Q20	Introductory	n/a	30 mins

16

Amalgamations and restructuring

Introduction

In this chapter, we are concerned with the issues of **business combinations** and **restructuring** from the point of view of financial management and financial strategy.

Questions in this area are likely to involve some calculations so you will need to bring in your knowledge of company valuation. However, questions will not be purely numerical. Topics you might be asked to discuss include why companies might choose to make an offer in a particular form, takeover tactics, the effect on shareholders, the different types of consideration and what happens after the takeover. Question on the subjects discussed in this chapter will be **regularly** set in the compulsory section of this paper.

Topic list	Learning outcomes	Syllabus references	Ability required
1 Mergers and takeovers (acquisitions)	C(iii)	C(8)	Evaluation
2 Trends in takeover activity	C(iii)	C(8)	Evaluation
3 The conduct of a takeover	C(iii)	C(8)	Evaluation
4 Payment methods	C(iv)	C(9)	Evaluation
5 Valuation of mergers and takeovers	C(iii), (v)	C(3), (9)	Evaluation
6 Regulation of takeovers	C(vii)	C(11)	Analysis
7 Post-acquisition integration	C(vi)	C(10)	Evaluation
8 Impact of mergers and takeovers on stakeholders	C(iii)	C(3)	Evaluation
9 Demergers and other forms of divestment	C(viii)	C(13)	Evaluation
10 Management buyouts (MBOs)	C(viii)	C(12)	Evaluation

1 Mergers and takeovers (acquisitions)

FAST FORWARD

Takeovers often target companies that are good **strategic fits** with the acquiring companies, often to acquire a new product range or to develop a presence in a new market. **Mergers** have been more common in industries with low growth and returns.

1.1 Definition of mergers and takeovers

Key terms

Takeover: the **acquisition** by a company of a controlling interest in the voting share capital of another company, usually achieved by the purchase of a majority of the voting shares. *(OT 2005)*

Reverse takeover: when the smaller company takes over the larger one, so that the predator company has to increase its equity by over 100% to complete the takeover.

Merger: a business combination that results in the creation of a new reporting entity formed from the combining parties, in which the shareholders of the combining entities come together in a partnership for the mutual sharing of the risks and benefits of the combined entity, and in which no party to the combination in substance obtains control over any other, or is otherwise seen to be dominant, whether by virtue of the proportion of its shareholders' rights in the combined entity, the influence of its directors or otherwise. *(FRS 6) (OT 2005)*

Horizontal integration is characterised by a firm adding new products to its existing market, or new markets to its existing products.

Vertical integration, or vertical diversification, occurs when a company becomes either its own supplier of raw materials or components (ie **backward** vertical integration) or its own distributor or sales agent (ie **forward** vertical integration).

Concentric diversification occurs when a company seeks to add new products that have technological and/or marketing synergies with the existing product line. These products will normally appeal to new classes of customer.

Conglomerate diversification consists of making entirely new products for new classes of customers. These new products have no relationship to the company's current technology, products or markets.

The distinction between mergers and takeovers (acquisitions) is not always clear, for example when a large company 'merges' with another smaller company. The methods used for mergers are often the same as the methods used to make takeovers. In practice, the number of genuine mergers is small relative to the number of takeovers.

Exam focus point

Business amalgamations (mergers and takeovers) are likely to be a key topic for exam questions in *Financial Strategy* and the TOPCIMA exams.

Mergers or acquisitions should be undertaken to make profits **in the long term** as well as in the short term.

(a) **Acquisitions** may provide a means of entering a market at a **lower cost** than would be incurred if the company tried to develop its own resources, or a means of acquiring the business of a competitor. Acquisitions or mergers which might reduce or eliminate competition in a market may be prohibited by competition authorities.

(b) **Mergers** have tended to be more common in industries with a history of little growth and low returns. Highly profitable companies tend to seek acquisitions rather than mergers.

1.2 Reasons for mergers and takeovers

Key terms

Synergy is where the present value of the combined enterprise is greater than the sum of the net present value of the individual firms.

When two or more companies join together, there should be a **'synergistic'** effect. Synergy can be described as the **2 + 2 = 5** effect, whereby a group after a takeover achieves combined results that reflect a better rate of return than was being achieved by the same resources used in two separate operations before the takeover.

The main reasons why one company may wish to acquire the shares or the business of another may be categorised as follows.

REASONS FOR MERGERS AND TAKEOVERS	
Operating economies	Elimination of duplicate facilities and many other ways
Management acquisition	Acquisition of competent and go-ahead team to compensate for lack of internal management abilities
Diversification	Securing long-term future by spreading risk through diversification
Asset backing	Company with high earnings:assets ratios reducing risk through acquiring company with substantial assets
Quality of earnings	Reducing risk by acquiring company with less risky earnings
Finance and liquidity	Improve liquidity/ability to raise finance through acquisition of more stable company
Growth	Cheaper way of growing than internal expansion
Tax factors	Tax-efficient way of transferring cash out of corporate sector. In some jurisdictions, means of utilising tax losses by setting them against profits of acquired companies
Defensive merger	Stop competitors obtaining advantage
Strategic opportunities	Acquiring a company that provides a strategic fit (see below)

1.3 A strategic approach to takeovers

A strategic approach to takeovers would imply that acquisitions are only made after a full analysis of the underlying strengths of the acquirer company, and identification of candidates' **'strategic fit' with its existing activities**. Possible strategic reasons for a takeover are matched with suggested ways of achieving the aim in the following list from a publication of 3i (Investors in Industry), which specialises in offering advice on takeovers.

Strategic opportunities	
Where you are	**How to get to where you want to be**
Growing steadily but in a mature market with limited growth prospects	Acquire a company in a younger market with a higher growth rate
Marketing an incomplete product range, or having the potential to sell other products or services to your existing customers	Acquire a company with a complementary product range
Operating at maximum productive capacity	Acquire a company making similar products operating substantially below capacity

Strategic opportunities	
Where you are	**How to get to where you want to be**
Under-utilising management resources	Acquire a company into which your talents can extend
Needing more control of suppliers or customers	Acquire a company which is, or gives access to, a significant customer or supplier
Lacking key clients in a targeted sector	Acquire a company with the right customer profile
Preparing for flotation but needing to improve your balance sheet	Acquire a suitable company which will enhance earnings per share
Needing to increase market share	Acquire an important competitor
Needing to widen your capability	Acquire a company with the key talents and/or technology

1.4 Factors in a takeover decision

Several factors will need to be considered before deciding to try to take over a target business. These include the following.

Price factors

(a) What would the **cost** of acquisition be?

(b) Would the acquisition be **worth** the price?

(c) Alternatively, factors (a) and (b) above could be expressed in terms of:

What is the **highest price** that it would be worth paying to acquire the business?

The value of a business could be assessed in terms of:

- Its earnings
- Its assets
- Its prospects for sales and earnings growth
- How it would contribute to the strategy of the 'predator' company

The valuation of companies was covered in the previous chapter of this Study Text.

Other factors

(d) Would the takeover be regarded as **desirable** by the predator company's shareholders and (in the case of quoted companies) the stock market in general?

(e) Are the owners of the target company **amenable** to a takeover bid? Or would they be likely to adopt defensive tactics to resist a bid?

(f) What form would the **purchase consideration take?** An acquisition is accomplished by buying the shares of a target company. The purchase consideration might be cash, but the purchasing company might issue new shares (or loan stock) and exchange them for shares in the company taken over. If purchase is by means of a share exchange, the former shareholders in the company taken over will acquire an interest in the new, enlarged company.

(g) How would the takeover be **reflected in the published accounts** of the predator company?

(h) Would there be any **other potential problems** arising from the proposed takeover, such as future dividend policy and service contracts for key personnel?

TOPCIMA link

A takeover is a possible TOPCIMA exam scenario.

2 Trends in takeover activity

FAST FORWARD

The incidence of takeovers may depend on the state of the **equity markets, capital structures, regulations** and **government attitudes.**

2.1 UK takeover activity

There was a boom in takeover activity around the world in the second half of the 1980s. As the increased level of expenditure on acquisitions took place at the same time as a surge in capital expenditure by industrial and commercial companies (ICCs), it appears that the increase in takeover activity must partly reflect a desire of companies to expand.

A surge in takeover activity in the mid 1990s included, for example, the £8.9 billion takeover of Wellcome by Glaxo, Europe's largest ever takeover by that time.

More recently in 2006, P&O were taken over by Dubai Ports and Abbey National were taken over by Banko Santander, indicating the multi-national nature of takeover activity.

2.2 International takeovers

Acquisition is one of the chief ways of carrying out **foreign direct investment** (FDI). Over the past fifteen years or so, approximately half of the UK's FDI was in the form of acquisition of share and loan capital overseas, of which a substantial proportion was related to takeovers.

Takeover transactions conducted by UK companies in the **European Union** (EU) have on average been much smaller (at around £10 million on average) than for takeovers in the USA in past years. However, the Single European Act and financial deregulation are factors contributing to a growth in importance in UK takeovers in the rest of the EU.

2.3 Takeovers in the UK compared with other European countries

Distinctive features of the UK takeover boom have been the frequency of **hostile bids** (relative to other EU countries) and the greater emphasis **on equity finance** than in the USA. Hostile bids involve payment of a substantial premium over the pre-bid share price of the target firm and are therefore only feasible if the profitability of the joint assets can be improved to compensate for this premium.

It has been suggested that UK companies are more vulnerable to takeover than their counterparts in other European countries. There are a number of reasons why this should be so.

(a) The equity markets in Britain are more highly developed than in other European countries and a greater proportion of companies are either quoted or are subsidiaries of quoted firms with publicly traded shares. Thus **access to ownership in Britain is easier.**

(b) In addition, the capital structure of British firms is generally different to their European counterparts. In European firms there is frequently a large class of shares that do not have voting rights, unlike the ordinary shares that make up the major part of the equity for most UK companies. Thus in **Europe there is a greater division between ownership and control,** and access to the controlling shares is harder to obtain.

(c) It has been argued that it is **easier to build a stake in a UK** firm due to the '3% rule' whereby a shareholder does not have to declare an interest until he holds 3% of the shares or 10% of any particular class of share. This is enhanced by the rule that a full bid need not be triggered until he owns 30%. It is difficult for a firm to mount a defence until a bid is declared, by which time the bidder already has a strong hand.

(d) Government attitudes to the issues of ownership and control are also different to those in many other European countries. The prevalent **non-interventionist policies** mean that the government holds much fewer stakes and controlling interests in companies than say in France, and the 'national interest' lobby in the UK is also weaker.

(e) Reporting requirements in the UK have been generally more rigorous than in Continental Europe. Annual reports contain more information and are more transparent than those of comparable European firms, and thus it is **easier for a predator to obtain a meaningful preliminary valuation of a potential target.**

3 The conduct of a takeover

FAST FORWARD

A takeover may be **resisted** by the target company, if its directors believe that the terms are poor or there are no obvious advantages. Possible **defensive tactics** include issuing a forecast of attractive future profits, lobbying or finding a white knight (a company that would make a welcome takeover bid).

3.1 Will the bidding company's shareholders approve of a takeover?

When a company is planning a takeover bid for another company, its board of directors should give some thought to **how its own shareholders might react** to the bid. A company does not have to ask its shareholders for their approval of every takeover.

(a) When a large takeover is planned by a listed company involving **the issue of a substantial number of new shares by the predator company** (to pay for the takeover), Stock Exchange rules may require the company to obtain the formal approval of its shareholders to the takeover bid at a general meeting (probably an extraordinary general meeting, called specifically to approve the takeover bid).

(b) If shareholders, and the stock market in general, think the takeover is not a good one the **market value of the company's shares is likely to fall**. The company's directors have a responsibility to protect their shareholders' interests, and are accountable to them at the annual general meeting of the company.

A takeover bid might seem **unattractive** to shareholders of the bidding company because:

(a) It might **reduce the EPS** of their company.

(b) The **target company** is in a risky industry, or is in danger of going into liquidation.

(c) It might **reduce the net asset backing** per share of the company, because the target company will probably be bought at a price which is well in excess of its net asset value.

3.2 Will a takeover bid be resisted by the target company?

Quite often, a takeover bid will be resisted. Resistance comes from the target company's board of directors, who adopt defensive tactics, and ultimately the target company's shareholders, who can refuse to sell their shares to the bidding company.

Resistance can be overcome by offering a higher price.

(a) In cases where an **unquoted** company is the target company, if resistance to a takeover cannot be overcome, the takeover will not take place, and negotiations would simply break down.

(b) Where the target company is a **quoted company**, the situation is different. The target company will have many shareholders, some of whom will want to accept the offer for their shares, and some of whom will not. In addition, the target company's board of directors might resist a takeover, even though their shareholders might want to accept the offer.

Because there are likely to be major **differences of opinion** about whether to accept a takeover bid or not, companies in most jurisdictions are subject to formal rules for the conduct of takeover bids. These and other regulatory issues are covered later in the chapter.

Exam focus point

Detailed knowledge of the City Code will not be tested in your examination, but you should be aware of its implications.

3.3 Contesting an offer

The directors of a target company must **act in the interests of their shareholders, employees and creditors**. They may decide to contest an offer on several grounds.

(a) The offer may be **unacceptable** because the **terms are poor**. Rejection of the offer may lead to an improved bid.

(b) The merger or takeover may have **no obvious advantage**.

(c) **Employees** may be **strongly opposed** to the bid.

(d) The **founder members of the business** may oppose the bid, and appeal to the loyalty of other shareholders.

When a company receives a takeover bid which the board of directors considers unwelcome, the directors must act quickly to fight off the bid.

3.4 Defensive tactics

The steps that might be taken to **thwart a bid** or **make it seem less attractive** include:

(a) **Revaluing assets** or **issuing a forecast of attractive future profits and dividends** to persuade shareholders that to sell their shares would be unwise, that the offer price is too low, and that it would be better for them to retain their shares.

(b) **Lobbying** to have the offer referred to the competition authorities

(c) Launching an **advertising campaign** against the takeover bid (one technique is to attack the accounts of the predator company)

(d) Finding a **'white knight'**, a company which will make a welcome takeover bid (see below)

(e) Making a **counter-bid** for the predator company (this can only be done if the companies are of reasonably similar size)

(f) Arranging a **management buyout**

(g) Introducing a **'poison-pill'** anti-takeover device (see below)

(h) Introducing a '**shark repellent**' – changing the company's constitution to require a large majority to approve the takeover

Case Study

In November 2006, Japanese firm Nissin, the maker of Cup Noodle, intervened to prevent smaller rival Myojo from being swallowed up by a US hedge fund. Nissin launched a friendly 37 billion yen bid for Myojo after the US hedge fund had offered 29 billion yen. Myojo's president said: 'Now we'll be able to develop the business without outside pressure.

In 2005 Sina-Corp, the US listed firm behind China's biggest internet portal, adopted a shareholder rights plan to guard against a possible takeover. The plan would give shareholders the right to buy Sina shares at half price and would be triggered if one person or group acquired more than 20% of the shares. Sina is listed on New York's Nasdaq technology exchange where poison pills are commonly used to protect companies from hostile takeovers.

3.5 Costs of contested takeover bids

Takeover bids, when contested, can be very expensive, involving:

- Costs of professional services, eg merchant bank and public relations agency
- Advertising costs
- Underwriting costs
- Interest costs
- Possible capital loss on buying/selling the target company's shares

3.6 Gaining the consent of the target company shareholders

A takeover bid will only succeed if the predator company can persuade enough shareholders in the target company to sell their shares. Shareholders will only do this if they are dissatisfied with the performance of their company and its shares, or they are attracted by a high offer and the chance to make a good capital gain.

4 Payment methods 5/05, 11/05

FAST FORWARD

Payment can be in the form of **cash**, a **share exchange** or **convertible loan stock**. The choice will depend on available cash, desired levels of gearing, shareholders' taxation position and changes in control.

4.1 Methods of payment

The terms of a takeover will involve a purchase of the shares of the target company for **cash** or for **'paper'** (shares, or possibly loan stock). A purchase of a target company's shares with shares of the predator company is referred to as a **share exchange**.

4.2 Cash purchases

If the purchase consideration is in **cash**, the shareholders of the target company will simply be bought out. For example, suppose that there are two companies.

	Big	*Small*
Net assets (book value)	£1,500,000	£200,000
Number of shares	100,000	10,000
Earnings	£2,000,000	£40,000

Big negotiates a takeover of Small for £400,000 in cash.

As a result, Big will end up with:

(a) Net assets (book value) of

£1,500,000 + £200,000 – £400,000 cash = £1,300,000

(b) 100,000 shares (no change)

(c) Expected earnings of £2,040,000, minus the loss of interest (net of tax) which would have been obtained from the investment of the £400,000 in cash which was given up to acquire Small

Exam focus point

You may be asked in the exam about the consequences of using different finance sources to support a cash offer.

4.3 Purchases by share exchange 5/06

One company can acquire another company by **issuing shares** to pay for the acquisition. The new shares might be issued:

(a) **In exchange** for shares in the target company. Thus, if A acquires B, A might issue shares which it gives to B's shareholders in exchange for their shares. The B shareholders therefore become new shareholders of A. This is a takeover for a 'paper' consideration. Paper offers will often be accompanied by a **cash alternative.**

(b) **To raise cash** on the stock market, which will then be used to buy the target company's shares. To the target company shareholders, this is a cash bid.

Sometimes, a company might acquire another in a share exchange, but the shares are then **sold immediately** on a stock market to raise cash for the seller.

Whatever the detailed arrangements of a takeover with paper, the end result will be an **increase in the issued share capital of the predator company**.

4.3.1 Example: Share consideration (1)

Arcturus has agreed to acquire all the ordinary shares in Mira and has also agreed a share-for-share exchange as the form of consideration. The following information is available.

	Arcturus	*Mira*
	£m	£m
Operating profit	100	20
Net profit before taxation	80	14
Net profit after taxation	60	10
Share capital – £0.50 ordinary shares	£20m	£5m
Price/earnings ratio	10	12

The agreed share price for Mira will result in its shareholders receiving a premium of 25% on the current share price.

How many new shares must Arcturus issue to purchase the shares in Mira?

Solution

Market value Arcturus (10 × £60m)	= £600m
Value per share (£600m/40m)	= £15 per share
Market value Mira (12 × £10m)	= £120m
Value of bid (£120m × 1.25)	= £150m
Number of shares issued (£150m/£15)	= 10 million shares

4.3.2 Example: Share consideration (2)

Demeter wishes to take over Semele. The following information relates to the two companies:

	Number of ordinary shares in issue	*Market price per ordinary share*
Demeter	20 million	£10.00
Semele	6 million	£3.00

The market price of each company's shares is regarded as an accurate reflection of their intrinsic value.

The takeover is expected to lead to research and development savings after taxation that have a present value of £12 million. The bid offer consists of one share in Demeter for every three shares held in Semele, plus £1.00 in cash for every three shares held in Semele.

By how much would the wealth of a shareholder who owns 3,000 shares in Semele increase if the takeover was successful?

Solution

Number of shares to be issued	=	6m × 1/3 = 2 million
Total number of shares in issue after takeover	=	20m + 2m = 22 million
Cash payment	=	£2 million
Value of combined company after takeover	=	£200m + 18m + 12m – 2m
	=	£228 million
Value of 1,000 shares after takeover	=	£228m × 1,000/22,000,000 = £10,364

	£
Share value	10,364
Cash	1,000
	11,364
Value of 3,000 shares before take over (3,000 × £3)	9,000
	2,364

4.3.3 Example: Share consideration (3)

X and Y are both listed companies.

	X plc	*Y plc*
Profit before tax for the year just ended	£4m	£3.5m
Profit after tax for the year just ended	£2.75m	£2.4m
Number of shares	10m	5m
P/E ratio (current)	12	10

X has made an offer to acquire all the share capital of Y. The offer price is 5 new shares in X for every 3 shares in Y.

What is the premium in % in the price offered to the shareholders of Y?

Solution

EPS, X = (£2.75 million/10 million shares) = £0.275
Share price, X = £0.275 × 12 = £3.30
EPS, Y = (£2.4 million/5 million shares) = £0.48
Share price, Y = £0.48 × 10 = £4.80

Offer = 5 shares in X, value 5 × £3.30, £16.50, for 3 shares in Y
Current market value of 3 shares in Y = 3 × £4.80 = £14.40

The premium in the offer price is therefore (£16.50 – £14.40)/ £14.40 = 14.6%

4.4 Use of loan notes

Alternative forms of paper consideration, including debentures, loan notes and preference shares, are not so commonly used, due to:

- Difficulties in **establishing a rate of return** that is attractive to target shareholders
- The **effects on the gearing levels** of the acquiring company
- The **change in the structure of the target shareholders'** portfolios
- The **securities being potentially less marketable**, and lacking voting rights

Issuing **convertible loan notes** will overcome some of these drawbacks, by offering the target shareholders the option of partaking in the future profits of the company if they wish.

4.4.1 Example: Loan consideration

Trim offers to buy 100% of the equity shares of Slim from its three owners. The purchase price will be £7 million, made up of 1.5 million new shares of Trim and £2 million in 10% loan notes. The annual profits before tax of Slim have been £1 million for each of the past three years, after making suitable adjustments for directors' salaries and differences in accounting policies, and this level of profits is expected to continue after the takeover by Trim.

Trim has announced its intention of paying a dividend of £0.12 per share next year.

Assuming no synergy as the result of the acquisition, by how much will the earnings of Trim be expected to increase next year, when the profits of Slim are taken into account? Company tax is 30%.

Solution

	£'000	£'000
Slim profit before tax		1,000
Less: tax (30%)		300
		700
Interest on loan notes	200	
Less: tax reduction	60	
Net increase in interest		140
Increase in profit after tax for Trim		560

4.5 The choice between a cash offer and a paper offer

The choice between cash and paper offers (or a combination of both) will depend on how the different methods are viewed by the company and its existing shareholders, and on the attitudes of the shareholders of the target company. The factors that the directors of the bidding company must consider include the following.

COMPANY AND ITS EXISTING SHAREHOLDERS	
Dilution of EPS	Fall in EPS attributable to existing shareholders may occur if purchase consideration is in equity shares
Cost to the company	Use of loan stock to back cash offer will attract tax relief on interest and have lower cost than equity. Convertible loan stock can have lower interest rate than ordinary stock
Gearing	Highly geared company may not be able to issue further loan stock to obtain cash for cash offer
Control	Control could change considerably if large number of new shares issued
Authorised share capital increase	May be required if consideration is in form of shares. This will involve calling a general meeting to pass the necessary resolution
Borrowing limits increase	General meeting resolution also required if borrowing limits have to change
Taxation	If consideration is cash, many investors may suffer immediate liability to tax on capital gain
Income	If consideration is not cash, arrangement must mean existing income is maintained, or be compensated by suitable capital gain or reasonable growth expectations

COMPANY AND ITS EXISTING SHAREHOLDERS	
Future investments	Shareholders who want to retain stake in target business may prefer shares
Share price	If consideration is shares, recipients will want to be sure that the shares retain their values

4.6 Mezzanine finance and takeover bids

When the purchase consideration in a takeover bid is cash, the cash must be obtained somehow by the bidding company, in order to pay for the shares that it buys. Occasionally, the company will have sufficient cash in hand to pay for the target company's shares. More frequently, the cash will have to be raised, possibly from existing shareholders, by means of **a rights issue** or, more probably, by **borrowing from** banks or other financial institutions.

When cash for a takeover is raised by borrowing, the loans would normally be **medium-term** and **secured**.

However, there have been many takeover bids, with a **cash purchase option** for the target company's shareholders, where the bidding company has arranged loans that:

(a) Are **short-to-medium term**

(b) Are **unsecured** (that is, 'junior' debt, low in the priority list for repayment in the event of liquidation of the borrower)

(c) Because they are unsecured, **attract a much higher rate of interest** than secured debt (typically 4% or 5% above LIBOR)

(d) Often, give the lender the option to **exchange the loan** for shares after the takeover

This type of borrowing is called **mezzanine finance** (because it lies between equity and debt financing) – a form of finance which is also often used in **management buyouts** (which are discussed later in this chapter).

4.7 Earn-out arrangements

The purchase consideration may not all be paid at the time of acquisition. Part of it may be deferred, payable upon the target company reaching certain performance targets. You should refer back to Chapter 15 for an illustration of their application.

Exam focus point

In the exam, you could well get a question where the cash v shares decision is finely balanced, and financing the cash offer may be the critical issue.

5 Valuation of mergers and takeovers

FAST FORWARD

Shareholders of both the companies involved in a merger will be sensitive to the effect of the merger on **share prices** and **earnings per share**.

5.1 The market values of the companies' shares during a takeover bid

Market share prices can be very important during a takeover bid. Suppose that Velvet decides to make a takeover bid for the shares of Noggin. Noggin shares are currently quoted on the market at £2 each. Velvet shares are quoted at £4.50 and Velvet offers one of its shares for every two shares in Noggin, thus making an offer at current market values worth £2.25 per share in Noggin. This is only the value of the bid so long as Velvet's shares remain valued at £4.50. If their value falls, the bid will become less attractive.

Companies that make takeover bids with a share exchange offer are thus always concerned that the market value of their shares should not fall during the takeover negotiations, before the target company's shareholders have decided whether to accept the bid.

Case Study

In November 2000, **PricewaterhouseCoopers (PwC)**, the accountancy group, were about three days away from signing a $18bn deal with computer group Hewlett-Packard (HP) to sell HP PwC's consultancy division. Then HP announced that it had missed Wall Street earnings estimate by a wide margin, its share price dropped by nearly 13%, to $34.13, taking the share price down to a level 45% below that at which the talks had started. The bid, unsurprisingly, failed. With HP trading at well below its year-high price of $78, the acquisition would have been a pricey one.

If the market price of the target company's shares rises above the offer price during the course of a takeover bid, the bid price will seem too low, and the takeover is then likely to fail, with shareholders in the target company refusing to sell their shares to the bidder.

5.2 EPS before and after a takeover

If one company acquires another by issuing shares, its EPS will go up or down according to the P/E ratio at which the target company has been bought.

(a) If the **target company's shares** are bought at a **higher P/E ratio** than the predator company's shares, the **predator company's shareholders** will suffer a **fall in EPS**.

(b) If the **target company's shares** are **valued at a lower P/E ratio**, the **predator company's shareholders** will benefit from a **rise in EPS**.

5.3 Example: mergers and takeovers (1)

Giant takes over Tiddler by offering two shares in Giant for one share in Tiddler. Details about each company are as follows.

	Giant	*Tiddler*
Number of shares	2,800,000	100,000
Market value per share	£4	–
Annual earnings	£560,000	£50,000
EPS	20p	50p
P/E ratio	20	

By offering two shares in Giant worth £4 each for one share in Tiddler, the valuation placed on each Tiddler share is £8, and with Tiddler's EPS of 50p, this implies that Tiddler would be acquired on a P/E ratio of 16. This is lower than the P/E ratio of Giant, which is 20.

If the acquisition produces no synergy, and there is no growth in the earnings of either Giant or its new subsidiary Tiddler, then the EPS of Giant would still be higher than before, because Tiddler was bought on a lower P/E ratio. The combined group's results would be as follows.

	Giant group
Number of shares (2,800,000 + 200,000)	3,000,000
Annual earnings (560,000 + 50,000)	610,000
EPS	20.33p

If the P/E ratio is still 20, the market value per share would be £4.07, which is 7p more than the pre-takeover price.

The process of buying a company with a higher EPS in order to boost your own EPS is known as **bootstrapping**. Whether the stock market is fooled by this process is debatable. The P/E ratio is likely to fall after the takeover in the absence of synergistic or other gains.

5.4 Example: mergers and takeovers (2)

Redwood agrees to acquire the shares of Hawthorn in a share exchange arrangement. The agreed P/E ratio for Hawthorn's shares is 15.

	Redwood	*Hawthorn*
Number of shares	3,000,000	100,000
Market price per share	£2	–
Earnings	£600,000	£120,000
P/E ratio	10	

The EPS of Hawthorn is £1.20, and so the agreed price per share will be £1.20 × 15 = £18. In a share exchange agreement, Redwood would have to issue nine new shares (valued at £2 each) to acquire each share in Hawthorn, and so a total of 900,000 new shares must be issued to complete the takeover.

After the takeover, the enlarged company would have 3,900,000 shares in issue and, assuming no earnings growth, total earnings of £720,000. This would give an EPS of:

$$\frac{£720,000}{3,900,000} = 18.5p$$

The pre-takeover EPS of Redwood was 20p, and so the EPS would fall. This is because Hawthorne has been bought on a higher P/E ratio (15 compared with Redwood's 10).

5.5 Buying companies on a higher P/E ratio, but with profit growth

Buying companies on a higher P/E ratio will result in a fall in EPS unless there is profit growth to offset this fall. For example, suppose that Starving acquires Bigmeal, by offering two shares in Starving for three shares in Bigmeal. Details of each company are as follows.

	Starving	*Bigmeal*
Number of shares	5,000,000	3,000,000
Value per share	£6	£4
Annual earnings		
Current	£2,000,000	£600,000
Next year	£2,200,000	£950,000
EPS	40p	20p
P/E ratio	15	20

Starving is acquiring Bigmeal on a higher P/E ratio, and it is only the profit growth in the acquired subsidiary that gives the enlarged Starving group its growth in EPS.

	Starving group
Number of shares (5,000,000 + 2,000,000)	7,000,000
Earnings	
If no profit growth (2,000,000 + 600,000) £2,600,000	EPS would have been 37.24p
With profit growth (2,200,000 + 950,000) £3,150,000	EPS will be 45p

If an acquisition strategy involves buying companies on a higher P/E ratio, it is therefore essential for continuing EPS growth that the acquired companies offer prospects of strong profit growth.

5.6 Further points to consider: net assets per share and the quality of earnings

You might think that dilution of earnings must be avoided at all cost. However, there are three cases where a dilution of earnings might be accepted on an acquisition if there were other advantages to be gained.

(a) **Earnings growth** may hide the dilution in EPS as above.

(b) A company might be willing to accept earnings dilution if the **quality of the acquired company's earnings** is superior to that of the acquiring company.

(c) A trading company with high earnings, but with few assets, may want to increase its assets base by acquiring a company which is strong in assets but weak in earnings so that assets and earnings get more into line with each other. In this case, **dilution in earnings is compensated for by an increase in net asset backing.**

5.7 Example: mergers and takeovers (3)

Intangible has an issued capital of 2,000,000 £1 ordinary shares. Net assets (excluding goodwill) are £2,500,000 and annual earnings average £1,500,000. The company is valued by the stock market on a P/E ratio of 8. Tangible has an issued capital of 1,000,000 ordinary shares. Net assets (excluding goodwill) are £3,500,000 and annual earnings average £400,000. The shareholders of Tangible accept an all-equity offer from Intangible valuing each share in Tangible at £4. Calculate Intangible's earnings and assets per share before and after the acquisition of Tangible.

Solution

(a) Before the acquisition of Tangible, the position is as follows.

$$\text{Earnings per share (EPS)} = \frac{£1{,}500{,}000}{2{,}000{,}000} = 75\text{p}$$

$$\text{Assets per share (APS)} = \frac{£2{,}500{,}000}{2{,}000{,}000} = £1.25$$

(b) Tangible's EPS figure is 40p (£400,000 ÷ 1,000,000), and the company is being bought on a multiple of 10 at £4 per share. As the takeover consideration is being satisfied by shares, Intangible's earnings will be diluted because Intangible is valuing Tangible on a higher multiple of earnings than itself. Intangible will have to issue 666,667 shares valued at £6 each (earnings of 75p per share at a multiple of 8) to satisfy the £4,000,000 consideration. The results for Intangible will be as follows.

$$\text{EPS} = \frac{£1{,}900{,}000}{2{,}666{,}667} = 71.25\text{p (3.75p lower than the previous 75p)}$$

$$\text{APS} = \frac{£6{,}000{,}000}{2{,}666{,}667} = £2.25 \text{ (£1 higher than the previous £1.25)}$$

If Intangible is still valued on the stock market on a P/E ratio of 8, the share price should fall by approximately 30p (8 × 3.75p, the fall in EPS) but because the asset backing has been increased substantially the company will probably now be valued on a higher P/E ratio than 8.

The shareholders in Tangible would receive 666,667 shares in Intangible in exchange for their current 1,000,000 shares, that is, two shares in Intangible for every three shares currently held.

(a)	Earnings	£
	Three shares in Tangible earn (3 × 40p)	1.200
	Two shares in Intangible will earn (2 × 71.25p)	1.425
	Increase in earnings, per three shares held in Tangible	0.225

(b)	Assets	£
	Three shares in Tangible have an asset backing of (3 × £3.5)	10.50
	Two shares in Intangible will have an asset backing of (2 × £2.25)	4.50
	Loss in asset backing, per three shares held in Tangible	6.00

The shareholders in Tangible would be trading asset backing for an increase in earnings.

5.8 Valuation using post-merger dividends or cash flows

An alternative method to using the P/E ratios, is to consider the dividends or cash flows of the merged company. Reliable cash flow estimates should take into account the effects of the merger such as economies of scale and greater combined power.

5.8.1 Dividend method

The steps are as follows:

- Estimate the **initial dividends** of the **combined company** and the **dividend growth rate**
- Estimate the **new cost of capital**; if the cost of the two old companies differs significantly, some sort of weighted average method will be required
- Calculate the **value of the combined company** using the dividend valuation model
- Compare the **value of the combined company** with the **pre-merger value** of the acquiror. The excess is the value of the target

In practice, the level of dividends and dividend cover expected by shareholders in both companies may create difficulties before the merger or takeover is agreed

5.8.2 Cash flow method

The steps here are as follows.

- Estimate the **cash flows of the combined company**, including the acquired's, the acquiror's and the additional cash flows arising from the beneficial effects of the merger
- Estimate the **new cost of capital** as above
- Calculate the **net present value** of the combined cash flows
- Compare the **value of the combined cash flows** with the acquiror's cash flows if no merger took place. The excess is the value of the target.

Question — Bid terms

Learning outcome: C(v)

Themis is a fast-growing business which operates a chain of motels situated in motorway service stations throughout the UK. The company is committed to an aggressive strategy of expansion through acquisition and has recently made a bid for the shares of Arethusa that operates a chain of restaurants also situated in motorway service stations throughout the UK. Themis has offered 1 share for every 3 shares held in Arethusa. The following financial data concerning each company is available.

Income statements for the year ended 31 May 20X9

	Themis	*Arethusa*
	£m	£m
Revenue	564	242
Profit from operations	181	41
Finance costs	9	2
Net profit before taxation	172	39
Taxation	45	11
Net profit after taxation	127	28
Dividends	16	24
Accumulated profits	111	4

Balance sheet as at 31 May 20X9

	Themis	*Arethusa*
	£m	£m
Non-current assets	261	117
Net current assets	82	45
	343	162
Less: payables due beyond one year	62	6
	281	156
Capital and reserves		
Ordinary share capital	150	50
Accumulated profits	131	106
	281	156

The ordinary share capital of Themis consists of £0.50 shares and the ordinary share capital of Arethusa consists of £1 shares. The board of directors of Themis believes there is a strong synergy between the two businesses which will lead to an increase in after-tax profits of £15m per year following acquisition.

Share prices for each company in recent years have been as follows:

Year ended 31 May	*20X6*	*20X7*	*20X8*	*20X9 (ie present)*
	£	£	£	£
Themis	3.50	4.80	6.90	9.30
Arethusa	2.40	3.20	3.40	2.90

A shareholder in Arethusa has expressed concern over the bid. He points out that, following acquisition, the annual dividends are likely to be lower as Themis normally pays small dividends. As the shareholder relies on dividend income to cover his living expenses, he is concerned that he will be worse off following acquisition of Arethusa. He also believes that the price offered for the shares of Arethusa is too low.

Required

(a) Calculate:

(i) The total value of the proposed bid

(ii) The earnings per share of Themis following the successful takeover of Arethusa

(iii) The share price of Themis following the takeover, assuming the price-earnings ratio of the company is maintained and the synergy achieved.

(b) Discuss the bid from the viewpoint of the shareholders of Arethusa and include in your discussion the shareholder's concerns mentioned above.

Answer

(a) (i) *Number of shares in Arethusa: 50 million*

Themis shares issued to acquire Arethusa (1 for 3): 50 million/3 = 16,666,667

Value of the bid, at £9.30 per Themis share = 16,666,667 × £9.30 = £155 million.

(ii)

	£m
After-tax profits:	
Themis	127
Arethusa	28
Increase due to synergy	15
Earnings of combined group	170

Number of Themis shares in issue

Prior to takeover (150 m × £1/50p)	300,000,000
Issued to finance takeover	16,666,667
	316,666,667

EPS after the takeover = £170 million/316,666,667 shares = 53.7p per share, say 54p per share.

(iii) EPS of Themis before the takeover = £127 million/300 million share = 42.3p

P/E ratio of Themis before the takeover = £9.30/£0.423 = 21.99, say 22.

Share price of Themis after the takeover = 54p × 22 = £11.88.

(b) Arethusa shareholders are being offered shares in Themis, currently valued at £9.30 each, in exchange for every three shares they hold in Arethusa, currently valued at (3 × £2.90) £8.70. The offer price represents a **premium** to the current market price of Arethusa shares of just £0.60 per £8.70 of shares, which is about 5%. This **bid premium** seems very low.

The **current share price of Themis** is £9.30, having risen from £6.90 last year. The possibility that the share price will remain at this level (a P/E ratio of 22), or might even rise after the takeover, should be questioned. A fall in the Themis share price of about 5% or more (to less than £8.70) would mean that Arethusa shareholders would suffer a loss by agreeing to the takeover offer.

In contrast, the **current EPS of Arethusa** is (£28 million/50 million shares) 56p and the P/E ratio is therefore just 5.2 (£2.90/56p). There is a very **large difference** between the **P/E ratios** at which the two companies are currently valued, adding weight to the concern that either Themis shares are currently over-valued or Arethusa shares are under-valued by the market.

On the other hand, Arethusa shareholders might take the view that shares in Themis are likely to **rise still further** in value after the takeover. Accepting the offer from Themis would therefore enable them to make a further capital gain after the takeover has occurred.

Arethusa shareholders might want to invest in a company with a **high dividend payout policy**, and so would not want to hold on to their Themis shares after a takeover. If so, they should sell their Themis shares and invest in a different company. Concerns about dividend policy should not affect the response of Arethusa shareholders to the takeover offer.

Question — Post-merger valuation

Learning outcome: C(v)

Nyasa is committed to increasing its earnings per share through a policy of acquisition. The company has acquired several businesses in the past five years and is now considering the acquisition of Turkana. Financial information relating to Nyasa and Turkana is as follows:

Abbreviated income statements for the year ended 30 April 20X1

	Nyasa	*Turkana*
	£m	£m
Revenue	120.4	80.9
Profit from operations	15.8	8.4
Finance costs	9.5	3.8
Profit before taxation	6.3	4.6
Taxation	2.1	1.6
Profit after taxation	4.2	3.0

Balance sheets as at 30 April 20X1

	Nyasa	*Turkana*
	£m	£m
Non-current assets	50.5	28.6
Net current assets	12.4	8.2
	62.9	36.8
Less Payables due beyond one year	4.6	3.1
	58.3	33.7
Capital and reserves		
£1 Ordinary shares	40.0	12.0
Reserves	18.3	21.7
	58.3	33.7
Price earnings ratio prior to bid	18	14

Nyasa has offered the shareholders of Turkana four shares in Nyasa for every three shares held. After-tax savings in overheads of £1.5m per annum are expected from the acquisition of Turkana.

Required

(a) Calculate:

(i) The total value of the proposed bid

(ii) The earnings per share for Nyasa following the successful takeover of Turkana

(iii) The share price of Nyasa following the takeover, assuming that the price earnings ratio is maintained and the savings achieved

(b) Calculate the effect of the proposed acquisition from the perspective of a shareholder who holds 3,000 ordinary shares in:

(i) Nyasa, and
(ii) Turkana.

Comment on your results.

Answer

(a) *Workings*

$$\text{Nyasa current EPS} = \frac{\text{Total earnings}}{\text{Number of shares}} = \frac{£4.2\text{ million}}{40\text{ million}} = 10.5\text{p}$$

P/E ratio = 18

Current market price of Nyasa shares = 18 × 10.5p = 189p.

$$\text{Turkana current EPS} = \frac{£3.0\text{ million}}{12\text{ million shares}} = 25\text{p}$$

P/E ratio = 14

Current price of Turkana shares = 14 × 25p = 350p.

(i) The bid price is 4 Nyasa shares for every 3 Turkana shares.

This values 3 Turkana shares at (4 × 189p) = 756p.

Bid value per Turkana share = 756p/3 = 252p per share.

The total value of the proposed bid, given 12 million Turkana shares:

= 12 million × 252p = £30.24 million.

The bid, if successful, would result in the issue of (12 million × 4/3) 16 million new Nyasa shares.

(ii) Total earnings after takeover

	£m
Nyasa earnings	4.2
Turkana earnings	3.0
Savings from the acquisition	1.5
	8.7
Number of shares (40 million + 16 million)	56m

EPS following the takeover: £8.7 million/56 million = £0.155, ie 15.5p.

(iii) Share price of Nyasa after the takeover, assuming a P/E ratio of 18:

15.5p × 18 = £2.79

(b) *Holder of 3,000 shares in Nyasa*

	£
Value of shares before the takeover (× £1.89)	5,670
Value of shares after the takeover (× £2.79)	8,370
Increase in value of investment	2,700

Holder of 3,000 shares in Turkana

	£
Value of 3,000 shares before the takeover (3,000 × £3.50)	10,500
Value of shares after the takeover (4,000 × £2.79)	11,160
Increase in value of investment	660

The takeover would **increase the total value** of the **equity shares** of the companies, on the assumption that a P/E ratio of 18 can be maintained. There are two reasons for this increase in value.

(i) The earnings of Turkana will be re-rated from a P/E of 14 to a P/E of 18.
(ii) There will be savings of £1.5 million, adding (× 18) £27 million to equity values.

Under the terms of the current bid, Nyasa shareholders would enjoy an **increase in the value of their investment** by (£2,700/£5,670) almost 50%. Turkana shareholders would also expect some increase in the value of their investment but only by (£660/£10,500) about 6%. Most of the increase in the equity valuation arising from the acquisition would therefore be enjoyed by the Nyasa shareholders.

The estimated increase in the equity valuation is dependent on the assumption of savings of £1.5 million and the assumption that a **P/E ratio of 18** will be **maintained**. If these assumptions turn out to be over-optimistic, the value of Nyasa shares after the takeover will be lower than £2.79, and there would be a serious risk that the value of the investment of Turkana shareholders would fall as a result of the takeover.

The offer from Nyasa is therefore too low, and the directors of Turkana would recommend rejection of the bid on these grounds.

6 Regulation of takeovers

FAST FORWARD

Directors of companies of any size must treat all shareholders **fairly** and give them **sufficient information** about the takeover. Larger mergers will be of interest to the competition authorities.

6.1 Takeover regulation

The UK's City Code on Takeovers and Mergers contains good examples of the principles that companies are expected to follow in most of the stock markets round the world. The Code has no statutory backing, although it is administered and enforced by the Takeover panel. When it is adopted, the EU's thirteenth company law directive will supersede the City Code and will mean that a statutory approach is adopted.

6.2 The City Code: general principles

The City Code is divided into general principles and detailed rules which must be observed by persons involved in a merger or takeover transaction. The general principles include the following.

(a) 'All shareholders of the same class of an offeree company must be **treated similarly** by an offeror.' In other words, a company making a takeover bid cannot offer one set of purchase terms to some shareholders in the target company, and a different set of terms to other shareholders holding shares of the same class in that company.

(b) 'During the course of a takeover, or when such is in contemplation, neither the offeror nor the offeree company ...may **furnish information** to **some shareholders** which is **not made available** to all shareholders.'

(c) 'Shareholders must be given **sufficient information** and **advice to enable them to reach a properly informed decision** and must have sufficient time to do so. No relevant information should be withheld from them.'

(d) Directors of a target company are **not permitted** to **frustrate a takeover bid**, nor to prevent the shareholders from having a chance to decide for themselves.

(e) 'Rights of control must be **exercised in good faith** and the oppression of a minority is wholly unacceptable.' For example, a holding company cannot take decisions about a takeover bid for one of its subsidiaries in such a way that minority shareholders would be unfairly treated.

(f) 'Where **control of a company is acquired** ... a **general offer** to all other shareholders is **normally required**.' Control is defined as a 'holding, or aggregate holdings, of shares carrying 30% of the voting rights of a company, irrespective of whether that holding or holdings gives *de facto* control'.

6.3 The City Code: rules

In addition to its general principles, the City Code also contains a number of detailed rules, which are intended to govern the conduct of the parties in a takeover bid. These rules relate to matters such as:

(a) How the approach to the target company should be made by the predator company

(b) The announcement of a takeover bid

(c) The obligation of the target company board to seek independent advice (eg from a merchant bank)

(d) Conduct during the offer

(e) A time barrier to re-bidding if an offer fails

6.4 Competition legislation

The government, through legislation, can significantly influence the nature of relationships between a firm and members of its micro environment. Legislation can be used, for example, to control the price at which goals or services are sold to customers, or to allow a supplier access to a market which economic and technical barriers had previously excluded it.

A good example of competition regulation is the UK's **Competition Act 1998**. The Act prohibits:

(a) Certain agreements or concerted practices which have as their object or effect the **prevention, restriction** or **distortion** of **competition** within the United Kingdom

(b) The **abuse** of a **dominant position** in a market if it may affect trade within the United Kingdom

Case Study

In December 2006, an acquisition of Marine Harvest by Pan Fish was given the go-ahead by the Competition Commission. Pan Fish would then control around 65% of the Scottish salmon farming industry.

The Office of Fair Trading referred the merger to the Competition Commission because the move could increase salmon prices and have an impact on the Scottish salmon market.

The amalgamation had already been approved in Norway, Canada and Spain. The Competition Commission concluded that the acquisition may not be expected to result in a substantial lessening of competition in the market for the supply of European farmed Atlantic salmon in the UK.

In contrast, in July 2001 the UK's Competition Commission reported on the proposed acquisition of the Abbey National plc banking group by Lloyds TSB, one of the 'big four' clearing banks in the UK.

The Commission observed that there was overlap in the following categories of product market:

(a) Markets for financial products sold to personal customers
(b) Markets for financial products sold to small and medium-sized enterprises
(c) Markets for financial products sold to larger firms
(d) Wholesale banking

The Competition Commission was most concerned with the effect on the markets in (a) and (b) as it believed there was sufficient competition in the other markets.

The Commission saw the personal sector as characterised by customers with little power who were unwilling to switch banks, and high barriers to entry. It was therefore concerned about the removal of a long-established rival to the traditional banks, fearing it would lead to higher fees and overdraft rates and lower interest on deposit accounts, also the loss of an incentive to innovate. The picture was similar in the small and medium-sized enterprises, as Abbey National had the potential to become a player of increasing importance over the next few years.

The Commission considered various alternatives to prohibition of the merger. It concluded that divestment of branches or businesses would not be effective; there would be little demand for the businesses that could be divested, and divestment of branches would have to be substantial and would not necessarily have the desired consequence of improving competition. Undertakings by Lloyds would represent an interference in the operation of market forces and would be difficult to police. Improving customer awareness of the terms of products would probably be ineffective.

The Commission therefore concluded that the merger should be prohibited.

7 Post-acquisition integration 5/05, 5/06

FAST FORWARD

Many takeovers fail to achieve their full potential because of lack of attention paid to **post-acquisition integration**. A clear programme should be in place, designed to re-define objectives and strategy, and take appropriate care of the human element.

7.1 Problems of integration

Failures of takeovers often result from **inadequate integration** of the companies after the takeover has taken place. There is a tendency for senior management to devote their energies to the next acquisition rather than to the newly-acquired firm. The particular approach adopted will depend upon the **culture** of the organisation as well as the **nature** of the company acquired and **how it fits** into the amalgamated organisation (eg horizontally, vertically, or as part of a diversified conglomerate).

7.2 Drucker's Golden Rules

P F Drucker has suggested Five Golden Rules for the process of post-acquisition integration.

Rule 1	There should be a 'common core of unity' shared by the acquiror and acquiree. The ties should involve overlapping characteristics such as shared technology and markets, and not just financial links.
Rule 2	The acquiror should ask 'What can we offer them?' as well as 'What's in it for us?'
Rule 3	The acquiror should treat the products, markets and customers of the acquired company with respect, and not disparagingly.
Rule 4	The acquiring company should provide top management with relevant skills for the acquired company within a year.
Rule 5	Cross-company promotions of staff should occur within one year.

7.3 Jones's Integration Sequence

C S Jones has proposed a five-step 'integration sequence'.

Step 1 **Decide on and communicate initial reporting relationships**

This will reduce uncertainty. The issue of whether to impose relationships at the beginning, although these may be subject to change, or to wait for the organisation structure to become more established (see Step 5 below) needs to be addressed.

Step 2 **Achieve rapid control of key factors**

This will require access to the right accurate information. Control of information channels needs to be gained without dampening motivation. Note that it may have been poor financial controls which led to the demise of the acquiree company.

Step 3 **Resource audit**

Both physical and human assets are examined in order to get a clear picture. This includes examining the roles of each of the main stakeholders (staff, customers and suppliers) and evaluating the products sold.

Step 4 **Re-define corporate objectives and to develop strategic plans**

These should harmonise with those of the acquiror company as appropriate, depending on the degree of autonomy managers are to have to develop their own systems of management control.

Step 5 **Revise the organisational structure**

Successful post-acquisition integration requires careful management of the 'human factor' to avoid loss of motivation. Employees in the acquired company will want to know how they and their company are to fit into the structure and strategy of the amalgamated enterprise. Morale can, hopefully, be preserved by **reducing uncertainty** and by providing appropriate performance incentives, staff benefits and career prospects. If redundancies are felt to be necessary, voluntary redundancies should be offered first.

7.4 Service contracts for key personnel

When the target company employs certain key personnel, on whom the success of the company has been based, the predator company might want to ensure that these key people do not leave as soon as the takeover occurs. To do this, it might be necessary to insist as a condition of the offer that the key people should agree to sign **service contracts**, tying them to the company for a certain time (perhaps three years). Service contracts would have to be attractive to the employees concerned, perhaps through offering a high salary or other benefits such as share options in the predator company. Where key personnel are shareholders, they might be bound not to sell shares for a period.

7.5 Merging systems

The degree to which the information, control and reporting systems of the two companies involved in a takeover are merged will depend to some extent upon the **degree of integration** envisaged. There are two extremes of integration:

(a) **Complete absorption of the target firm**, where the cultures, operational procedures and organisational structures of the two firms are to be fused together. This approach is most suitable where significant cost reductions are expected to be achieved through economies of scale, and/or combining marketing and distribution effort can enhance revenues.

(b) **The preservation approach**, where the target company is to become an independent subsidiary of the holding company. This would be most beneficial for the merger of companies with very different products, markets and cultures.

In the circumstances of a complete absorption, the two companies will become one, and thus a **common operational system** must be developed. The acquiring company's management should not impose immediately their own systems upon the target company's operations, assuming them to be superior. This is likely to **alienate** acquired employees.

It is probably best to **use the system already in place**, in the acquired company, initially supplemented by requests for additional reports felt to be immediately necessary for adequate information and control flows between the two management bodies. As the integration process proceeds, the best aspects of each of the companies' systems will be identified and a **common system developed.**

Where the two companies are to operate independently, it is likely that some changes will be needed to financial control procedures to get the two group companies in line. Essentially, however, the target company's management may **continue with their own cultures, operations and systems.**

Exam focus point

Question 1 in May 2006 required a discussion of post-merger value enhancing strategies. Such a discussion must involve more than just a list of bullet points and must be relevant to the entities involved.

7.6 Failure of mergers and takeovers

The aim of any takeover will be to **generate value for the acquiring shareholders.** Where this does not happen, there may be a number of reasons, including **a strategic plan that fails to produce the benefits expected,** or **over-optimism** about future market conditions, operating synergies and the amount of time and money required to make the merger work.

A third recurring reasons for failure is **poor integration management**, in particular:

(a) **Inflexibility** in the application of integration plans drawn up prior to the event. Once the takeover has happened, management must be prepared to adapt plans in the light of changed circumstances or inaccurate prior information.

(b) **Poor man management**, with lack of communication of goals and future prospects of employees, and failure to recognise and deal with the uncertainty and anxiety invariably felt by them.

A survey carried out in 1992, through the interviewing of senior executives of the UK's top 100 companies covering 50 deals, revealed some common factors contributing to the failure of mergers. In order of decreasing rate of incidence:

- Cultural differences and poor attitude of target management
- Little or no post-acquisition planning
- Lack of knowledge of industry or target company
- Poor management and poor practices in target company
- Little or no experience of acquisitions

8 Impact of mergers and takeovers on stakeholders

FAST FORWARD

Don't forget that **managers, employees** and **financial institutions** are key stakeholders in mergers as well as shareholders.

8.1 To what extent do the stakeholders in a merger or takeover benefit from it?

The following comments are based upon extensive empirical research.

(a) **Acquiring company shareholders**

At least half of mergers studied have shown a decline in profitability compared with industry averages. Returns to equity can often be poor relative to the market in the early years, particularly for equity-financed bids and first time players. Costs of mergers frequently outweigh the gains.

(b) **Target company shareholders**

In the majority of cases, it is the target shareholders who benefit most from a takeover. Bidding companies invariable have to offer a significant premium over the market price prevailing prior to the bid in order to achieve the purchase.

(c) **Acquiring company management**

The management of the newly enlarged organisation will often enjoy increased status and influence, as well as increased salary and benefits.

(d) **Target company management**

Whilst some key personnel may be kept on for some time after the takeover, a significant number of managers will find themselves out of a job. However, a 'golden handshake' and the prospect of equally remunerative employment elsewhere may lessen the blow of this somewhat.

(e) **Other employees**

Commonly the economy of scale cost savings anticipated in a merger will be largely achieved by the loss of jobs, as duplicated service operations are eliminated and loss-making divisions closed down. However, in some instances, the increased competitive strength of the newly enlarged enterprise can led to expansion of operations and the need for an increased workforce.

(f) **Financial institutions**

These are perhaps the outright winners. The more complex the deal, the longer the battle, and the more legal and financial problems encountered, the greater their fee income, regardless of the end result.

Exam focus point

Remember, you may well get a compulsory question on mergers and takeovers, and it will be a wide-ranging question if it is worth 50 marks.

Question — Mega-mergers

Learning outcome: C(iii)

There have been a number of proposed and actual mega-mergers throughout the world over recent years sectors as financial services, oil, pharmaceuticals and automobiles.

(a) Discuss the main reasons for these mergers. Include in your answer the main advantages for the companies concerned.

(b) Discuss the main problems arising from these mergers. Discuss from the point of view of the companies concerned and evaluate their effects on the national economies.

Answer

There are a variety of factors that have contributed to the recent rise in mega-mergers.

(a) (i) The increasing **level of deregulation** in the financial markets has made it easier to organise the finance for large deals.

(ii) The increasing trend towards **globalisation** of both operations and financing has made the concept of the 'mega-company' more attractive.

(iii) There is some evidence that there has been a trend towards getting bigger becoming a **defence** against being taken over, as the number of key players in the different market sectors has gradually declined.

(iv) In some sectors, for example vehicle manufacturing, there is a trend towards bigger companies, as the market becomes **increasingly concentrated** in the hands of a declining number of large producers such as Ford and General Motors.

(v) Large corporations see the opportunity for achieving **significant economies of scale** and thereby becoming more competitive. These economies are no longer primarily in the field of operations, but rather in the overhead areas such as head office costs, research and IT.

(vi) In some sectors, takeover activity is still driven through the opportunity to achieve **operating economies**.

(vii) Sometimes, a merger may be the **quickest and cheapest way** of **achieving the growth in earnings** that is demanded by investors, and the increasing size of leading companies means that some of these mergers will fall into the 'mega-merger' category.

(b) (i) The creation of very large companies may lead to unforeseen **diseconomies of scale**. For example, there may be problems of communication and control within the organisation which mean that large and costly new IT solutions are required that were not originally envisaged.

(ii) There is an increasing climate of **job uncertainty** within the companies concerned as staff anticipate possible redundancies as part of a post-merger rationalisation. This may translate into a reduced level of commitment to the new organisation, a higher level of staff turnover with a loss of key staff, and a corresponding decline in performance.

(iii) The **cultures** of the two organisations may be so different as to make integration very difficult. This is less important where a small company is taken over by a large one since in this situation there will be a greater expectation of change. In the mega-merger, change will be required by all staff within both companies, and if the cultural divergence is too great, this may be difficult to achieve successfully. If such integration is not achieved, then the merger is less likely to succeed operationally and financially.

(iv) Very large organisations may **lose their flexibility** and ability to provide a good quality of local **customer service**, as managers become increasingly distanced from their customers. This in turn may mean that they lose some of their competitive advantage.

(v) If the merger is international, and if the parties do not enter it on equal terms, this may mean that the country of the weaker party shows some of the features of a **'branch plant economy'**. In the branch plant economy, it is the operations in countries that are not the 'home' country of the group that are likely to experience cutbacks first.

(vi) Another effect of these mergers is that the national economy will become more **dependent on global economic conditions**. In times of general economic growth, this will be beneficial since it is likely that there will be a flow of investment into the country's economy. However, it will also mean that the economy will become more sensitive to changes in economic conditions elsewhere that are outside its direct control.

9 Demergers and other forms of divestment

9.1 Divestment

Key term

A **divestment** is disposal of part of its activities by an entity. *(OT 2005)*

FAST FORWARD

Divestments can take a number of forms.

Mergers and takeovers are not inevitably good strategy for a business. In some circumstances, strategies of **internal growth**, no growth or even some form of **divestment** might be preferable.

Businesses must though have regard for the impact on:

- The **performance** of the company
- **Workforce morale** and performance
- **Stock market reaction** – the market dislikes uncertainty so must be given as much information as soon as possible

9.2 Demergers

FAST FORWARD

A **demerger** is the splitting up of corporate bodies into two or more separate bodies, to ensure share prices reflect the true value of underlying operations.

A **demerger** is the opposite of a merger. It is the **splitting up of a corporate body into two or more separate and independent bodies.** For example, the ABC Group might demerge by splitting into two independently operating companies AB and C. Existing shareholders are given a stake in each of the new separate companies.

Demerging, in its strictest sense, stops short of selling out, but is an attempt to ensure that share prices reflect the true value of the underlying operations. In large diversified conglomerates, such as those built up by Lord Hanson in the 1980s and early 1990s, so many different businesses are combined into one organisation that it becomes difficult for analysts to understand them fully. In addition, a management running ten businesses instead of two could be seen to lose some focus.

The potential disadvantages with demergers are as follows.

(a) **Economies of scale may be lost**, where the demerged parts of the business had operations in common to which economies of scale applied.

(b) The smaller companies which result from the demerger will have **lower revenue, profits and status** than the group before the demerger.

(c) There may be **higher overhead costs** as a percentage of **revenue**, resulting from (b).

(d) The ability to **raise extra finance**, especially debt finance, to support new investments and expansion may be **reduced**.

(e) **Vulnerability** to takeover may be **increased**.

9.3 Sell-offs

FAST FORWARD

A **sell-off** is the sale of part of a company to a third party, generally for cash.

A **sell-off** is a form of **divestment** involving the sale of part of a company to a third party, usually another company. Generally, cash will be received in exchange.

A company may carry out a sell-off for one of the following reasons.

(a) As **part of its strategic planning**, it has decided to restructure, concentrating management effort on particular parts of the business. Control problems may be reduced if peripheral activities are sold off.

(b) It **wishes to sell off a part of its business** which makes losses, and so to improve the company's future reported consolidated profit performance. This may be in the form of a management buy-out (MBO) – see below.

(c) In order to **protect the rest of the business from takeover**, it may choose to sell a part of the business which is particularly attractive to a buyer.

(d) The company may be **short of cash**.

(e) A subsidiary with **high risk** in its operating cash flows could be **sold**, so as to reduce the business risk of the group as a whole.

(f) A **subsidiary** could be **sold at a profit**. Some companies have specialised in taking over large groups of companies, and then selling off parts of the newly-acquired groups, so that the proceeds of sales more than pay for the original takeovers.

A sell-off may however **disrupt** the rest of the organisation, especially if key players within the organisation disappear as a result.

Case Study

The *Financial Times* 26 April 2002 reported that the parent company of Burger King restaurants, Diageo, had put the chain up for sale. In the late 1990s Burger King had not grown as fast as its principal rival, McDonalds, and suffered management and investment problems. It has also suffered problems in relationships with franchisees.

Diageo decided to concentrate on becoming a pure premium drinks business and separate off the Burger King chain. A new chief executive, John Dasburg, was appointed to Burger King and money spent on developing new products and installing drive-through technology. The results were a small increase in sales but an initial decrease in operating profits because of the heavy level of investment. However if the investments had paid off, payments could have risen rapidly.

The investment required meant that bidders needed to team up to provide a reasonable offer. The main distinguishing feature of bids was likely to be finance structure, particularly the possible securitisation of royalty and rental revenues. The successful bidder would also require the support of the franchisees.

The chain was eventually sold to a US investment consortium at the end of 2002. However the deal was about one-third less than the original price that the group had agreed to pay earlier in the year. The difference was due to weakening sales in Burger King during the second half of 2002 owing to an industry price war. Although Diageo investors welcomed this deal, they remained concerned about Diageo's declining position in its liquor business. However Burger King's management and franchisees, who had been distracted by the negotiations, were able to focus once more on improving its business.

9.4 Liquidations

The extreme form of a sell-off is where the entire business is sold off in a **liquidation**. In a voluntary dissolution, the shareholders might decide to close the whole business, sell off all the assets and distribute net funds raised to shareholders.

TOPCIMA link

You may have to consider the desirability of a sell-off in order to raise funds for an acquisition.

9.5 Spin-offs

FAST FORWARD

A **spin-off** is the creation of a new company, where the shareholders of the original company own the shares.

In a **spin-off**, a new company is created whose shares are owned by the shareholders of the original company which is making the distribution of assets. There is no change in the ownership of assets, as the shareholders own the same proportion of shares in the new company as they did in the old company. Assets of the part of the business to be separated off are transferred into the new company, which will usually have different management from the old company. In more complex cases, a spin-off may involve the original company being split into a number of separate companies.

For a number of possible reasons such as those set out below, a spin-off appears generally to meet with favour from stock market investors.

(a) The change may make a **merger or takeover** of some part of the business **easier** in the future, or may protect parts of the business from predators.

(b) There may be **improved efficiency** and **more streamlined management** within the new structure.

(c) It may be **easier** to **see the value of the separated parts** of the business now that they are no longer hidden within a conglomerate.

(d) The **requirements** of **regulatory agencies** might be **met more easily** within the new structure, for example if the agency is able to exercise price control over a particular part of the business which was previously hidden within the conglomerate structure.

(e) After the spin-off, shareholders have the **opportunity to adjust the proportions** of their **holdings** between the different companies created.

Case Study

In January 2007 the US-based Altria Group announced that Kraft, the world's second largest food and drinks firm was to be spun off into a separate business. Altria hoped that spinning-off would allow managers to focus more on their specific company and make more acquisitions.

9.6 Going private

FAST FORWARD

A company **goes private** when a small group of individuals buys all the company's shares. Going private may **decrease costs** and make the company **less vulnerable** to hostile takeover bids.

A public company **'goes private'** when a **small group of individuals**, possibly including existing shareholders and/or managers and with or without support from a financial institution, **buys all of the company's shares.** This form of restructuring is relatively common in the USA and may involve the shares in the company ceasing to be listed on a stock exchange.

Advantages in going private could include the following.

(a) The costs of meeting listing requirements can be saved.

(b) The company is protected from volatility in share prices which financial problems may create.

(c) The company will be less vulnerable to hostile takeover bids.

(d) Management can concentrate on the long-term needs of the business rather than the short-term expectations of shareholders.

(e) Shareholders are likely to be closer to management in a private company, reducing costs arising from the separation of ownership and control (the 'agency problem').

Case Study

The San Francisco Business Times reported in March 2003 that several companies were considering going private, particularly young companies with shares under pressure in public markets. Tighter scrutiny of public company finances, together with new federal disclosure laws, had added to the cost of financing through public equity markets. Going private would allow greater flexibility to restructure operations, and a potential increase in value for those companies whose cash at bank or non-current assets were worth far more than the depressed stock market value.

10 Management buyouts (MBOs)

FAST FORWARD

A **management buy-out** is the purchase of all or part of the business by its managers. Management buy-outs can be the best way of maintaining links with a subsidiary, and can ensure the co-operation of management. The main complication with **management buy-outs** is obtaining the consent of all parties involved. Venture capital may be an important source of financial backing.

10.1 Buyouts

Key term

> A **management buy-out** is the purchase of a business from its existing owners by members of the management team, generally in association with a financing institution. *(OT 2005)*

A **management buyout** is the purchase of all or part of a business from its owners by its managers. For example, the directors of a subsidiary company in a group might buy the company from the holding company, with the intention of running it as proprietors of a separate business entity.

(a) **To the managers,** the buyout would be a method of setting up in business for themselves.

(b) **To the group**, the buyout would be a method of **divestment**, selling off the subsidiary as a going concern.

A large organisation's board of directors may agree to a management buyout of a subsidiary for any of a number of different reasons.

(a) The **subsidiary** may be **peripheral** to the group's mainstream activities, and no longer fit in with the group's overall strategy.

(b) The group may wish to **sell off a loss-making subsidiary**, and a management team may think that it can restore the subsidiary's fortunes.

(c) The parent company may need to **raise cash quickly**.

(d) The subsidiary may be part of a **group that has just been taken over** and the new parent company may wish to sell off parts of the group it has just acquired.

(e) The **best offer price** might come from a **small management group** wanting to arrange a buyout.

(f) When a group has taken the decision to sell a subsidiary, it will probably **get better co-operation** from the management and employees of the subsidiary if the sale is a management buyout.

A private company's shareholders might agree to sell out to a management team because they need cash, they want to retire, or the business is not profitable enough for them.

10.2 The parties to a buyout

There are usually three parties to a management buyout.

(a) A **management team** wanting to make a buyout. This team ought to have the skills and ability to convince financial backers that it is worth supporting.

(b) **Directors** of a group of companies.

(c) **Financial backers** of the buyout team, who will usually want an equity stake in the bought-out business, because of the **venture capital risk** they are taking. Often, several financial backers provide the venture capital for a single buyout.

10.3 The role of the venture capitalist **11/06**

Venture capitalists are far more inclined to fund MBOs, management buy-ins (MBI) and corporate expansion projects than the more risky and relatively costly early stage investments such as start-ups. The minimum investment considered will normally be around £100,000, with average investment of £1m-£2m.

Whilst the return required on venture capital for the high-risk, early stage investments may be as high as 80%, where the funding is for a well established business with sound management, it is more commonly around the 25-30% mark. Whilst this may be achieved by the successful investments, of course there will be many more that fail, and the overall returns on venture capital funds averages out at around 10-15%.

For MBOs and MBIs the venture capitalist will not necessarily provide the majority of the finance. A £50m buy-out may be funded by, say, £15m venture capital, £20m debt finance and £15m mezzanine debt.

Venture capital funds may require:

- A 20-30% shareholding
- Special rights to appoint a number of directors
- The company to seek their prior approval for new issues or acquisitions

10.3.1 Exit strategies

Venture capitalists generally like to have a predetermined **target exit date,** the point at which they can recoup some or all of their investment in an MBO. At the outset, they will wish to establish various **exit routes**, the possibilities including:

- The sale of shares following a **flotation** on a recognised stock exchange
- The **sale** of the company to another firm
- The **repurchase** of the venture capitalist's shares by the company or its owners
- The sales of the venture capitalist's shares to an **institution** such as an investment trust

Exam focus point

Question 3 in November 2006 required an evaluation of exit strategies available to a venture capitalist.

10.4 Business angel financing

Business angel financing can be an important initial source of business finance. Business angels are wealthy individuals or groups of individuals who invest directly in small businesses.

The main problems with business angel financing are that it is **informal in terms of a market** and can be **difficult to set up**. However informality can be a strength. There may be less need to provide business angels with detailed information about the company, since business angels generally have prior knowledge of the industry.

Surveys suggest that business angels are often more patient than providers of other sources of finance. However the **money available** from **individual business** angels may be **limited**, and **large sums** may only be **available** from a **consortium of business angels**.

10.5 The appraisal of proposed buyouts

10.5.1 How likely is a management buyout to succeed?

Management-owned companies seem to achieve better performance probably because of:

- A **favourable buyout price** having been **achieved**
- **Personal motivation and determination**
- **Quicker decision making** and so **more flexibility**
- **Keener decisions** and action on pricing and debt collection
- **Savings in overheads**, eg in contributions to a large head office

However, many management buyouts, once they occur, begin with some redundancies to cut running costs.

10.5.2 How should an institutional investor evaluate a buyout?

An institutional investor (such as a venture capitalist) should evaluate a buyout before deciding whether or not to finance. Aspects of any buyout that ought to be checked are as follows.

(a) Does the management team have the **full range of management skills** that are needed (for example a technical expert and a finance director)? Does it have the right blend of experience? Does it have the commitment?

(b) Why is the **company for sale**? The possible reasons for buyouts have already been listed. If the reason is that the parent company wants to get rid of a loss-making subsidiary, what evidence is there to suggest that the company can be made profitable after a buyout?

(c) What are the **projected profits and cash flows of the business**? The prospective returns must justify the risks involved.

(d) What is **being bought**? The buyout team might be buying the shares of the company, or only selected assets of the company. Are the assets that are being acquired sufficient for the task? Will more assets have to be bought? When will the existing assets need replacing? How much extra finance would be needed for these asset purchases? Can the company be operated profitably?

(e) What is **the price**? Is the price right or is it too high?

(f) What **financial contribution** can be made by members of the management team themselves?

(g) What are the **exit routes** and when might they be taken?

10.6 Financial arrangements in buyouts

10.6.1 Equity finance

Typically, the **buyout team** will have a **minority** of the equity in the bought-out company, with the **various financial backers** holding a **majority** of the shares between them. A buyout might have several financial backers, each providing finance in exchange for some equity.

Investors of venture capital usually want the **managers to be financially committed**. Individual managers could borrow personally from a bank, say £20,000 to £50,000.

The suppliers of equity finance might insist on investing part of their capital in the form of **redeemable convertible preference shares**. These often have voting rights should the preference dividend fall in arrears, giving increased influence over the company's affairs. They are issued in a redeemable form to give some hope of taking out part of the investment if it does not develop satisfactorily, and in convertible form for the opposite reason: to allow an increased stake in the equity of a successful company.

10.6.2 Debt finance

Possible debt finance includes secured loans from banks or other sources. These are likely to require a **priority charge** over all the assets involved in the MBO and the share capital, and regular provision of financial information. **Mezzanine finance** (discussed earlier) is also a possibility.

10.7 Problems with buyouts

A common problem with management buyouts is that the managers have little or no experience in **financial management** or **financial accounting**. Managers will also be required to take tough decisions. A good way of approaching the problem is **scenario analysis** addressing the effect of taking a major decision in isolation. However, the results may be painful, including the ditching of long established products.

Other problems are:

(a) Tax and legal complications

(b) Difficulties in deciding on a fair price to be paid

(c) Convincing employees of the need to change working practices or to accept redundancy

(d) Inadequate resources to finance the maintenance and replacement of tangible non-current assets

(e) The maintenance of employees' employment or pension rights

(f) Accepting the board representation requirement that many sources of funds will insist upon

(g) The loss of key employees if the company moves geographically, or wage rates are decreased too far, or employment conditions are unacceptable in other ways

(h) Maintaining continuity of relationships with suppliers and customers

(i) Lack of time to make decisions

10.8 Buy-ins

'Buy-in' is a term used when a team of **outside managers**, as opposed to managers who are already running the business, mount a takeover bid and then run the business themselves. A management buy-in might occur when a business venture is running into trouble, and a group of outside managers see an opportunity to take over the business and restore its profitability.

TOPCIMA link

The issues discussed in this chapter may be very important when you come to take the TOPCIMA exam. You may be asked to consider various options including mergers, strategic alliances (and doing nothing).

Chapter roundup

- **Takeovers** often target companies that are good **strategic fits** with the acquiring companies, often to acquire a new product range or to develop a presence in a new market. **Mergers** have been more common in industries with low growth and returns.
- The incidence of takeovers may depend on the state of the **equity markets**, **capital structures**, **regulations** and **government attitudes**.
- A takeover may be **resisted** by the target company, if its directors believe that the terms are poor or there are no obvious advantages. Possible **defensive tactics** include issuing a forecast of attractive future profits, lobbying or finding a white knight (a company that would make a welcome takeover bid).
- Payment can be in the form of **cash**, a **share exchange** or **convertible loan stock**. The choice will depend on available cash, desired levels of gearing, shareholders' taxation position and changes in control.
- Shareholders of both the companies involved in a merger will be sensitive to the effect of the merger on **share prices** and **earnings per share**.
- Directors of companies of any size must treat all shareholders **fairly** and give them **sufficient information** about the takeover. Larger mergers will be of interest to the competition authorities.
- Many takeovers fail to achieve their full potential because of lack of attention paid to **post-acquisition integration**. A clear programme should be in place, designed to re-define objectives and strategy, and take appropriate care of the human element.
- Don't forget that **managers**, **employees** and **financial institutions** are key stakeholders in mergers as well as shareholders.
- **Divestments** can take a number of forms.
- A **demerger** is the splitting up of corporate bodies into two or more separate bodies, to ensure share prices reflect the true value of underlying operations.
- A **sell-off** is the sale of part of a company to a third party, generally for cash.
- A **spin-off** is the creation of a new company, where the shareholders of the original company own the shares.
- A company **goes private** when a small group of individuals buys all the company's shares. Going private may **decrease costs** and make the company **less vulnerable** to hostile takeover bids.
- A **management buy-out** is the purchase of all or part of the business by its managers. Management buy-outs can be the best way of maintaining links with a subsidiary, and can ensure the co-operation of management. The main complication with **management buy-outs** is obtaining the consent of all parties involved. Venture capital may be an important source of financial backing.

Quick quiz

1 **Fill in the blank.**

.... is 'the acquisition by a company of a controlling interest in the voting share capital of another company, usually achieved by the purchase of a majority of the voting shares.' (CIMA Official Terminology)

2 What is meant by a 'white knight'?

3 What is a 'poison pill' in the context of takeovers and mergers?

4 A smaller company takes over a larger one, so that the smaller company must increase its voting equity by over 100% to complete the takeover. What is this process called?

5 What is the name of the arrangement where part of the purchase consideration is only paid when the target company reaches certain performance targets?

6 What are Drucker's five golden rules for post-acquisition integration?

7 If the target company's shares are valued at a lower P/E ratio, the predator company's shareholders will suffer a fall in EPS.

True ☐

False ☐

8 Why might management owned companies achieve improved performance?

9 What are the main exit routes for a venture capitalist?

Answers to quick quiz

1 A takeover

2 A company which will make a welcome takeover bid

3 An anti-takeover device

4 A reverse takeover

5 An earn-out arrangement

6 (1) Common sense of unity shared by acquiror and acquiree

(2) Acquiror should ask 'what can we offer them'?

(3) Acquiror should treat products, markets and customers of acquired company with respect

(4) Acquiring company should provide top management with relevant skills for managing acquired company within one year

(5) Cross-company promotions of staff within one year

7 False. The predator company's shareholders will benefit from a rise in earnings per share.

8 (a) Personal motivation and determination
(b) Quicker and more flexible decision making
(c) Keener decisions, eg on pricing
(d) Overhead savings

9
- The sale of shares following a **flotation** on a recognised stock exchange
- The **sale** of the company to another firm
- The **repurchase** of the venture capitalist's shares by the company or its owners
- The sales of the venture capitalist's shares to an **institution** such as an investment trust

Now try the questions below from the Exam Question Bank

Number	Level	Marks	Time
Q21	Introductory	–	30 mins
Q22	Examination	20	36 mins
Q23	Examination	25	45 mins
Q24	Examination	20	36 mins
Q25	Examination	25	45 mins
Q26	Examination	50	90 mins
Q27	Examination	25	45 mins

Part D
Investment decisions and project control

17

Elements of investment appraisal

Introduction

In the last Part of this Text, we examine investment decisions, in particular investments in specific projects. In Chapter 17 we deal with various general issues connected with investment appraisal including what is **relevant to** that **appraisal** in terms of costs, benefits and risks. We also examine how customer **requirements will influence investment in new products and services**, and look at important issues when an organisation is investing in information technology, or is looking to invest abroad.

In Chapters 18 and 19 we shall cover **various techniques** for **appraising investments**. Much of Chapter 18, dealing with the basic techniques should be revision, but you should take it seriously, as these techniques will be important in this paper. You may well need to use them when answering the compulsory question. Chapter 19 covers more complicated techniques including ways of linking investments with the methods used to finance them. Chapter 20 deals with how investments are controlled; careful management is necessary from the time the need to invest is first considered up until the post-audit review.

Topic list	Learning outcomes	Syllabus references	Ability required
1 Relevant costs of investments	D(i)	D(1)	Analysis
2 Relevant benefits of investments	D(i)	D(1)	Analysis
3 Risks of investments	D(i)	D(1)	Analysis
4 Customer requirements and design of products and services	D(i)	D(2)	Analysis
5 IT investment	D(i)	D(3)	Analysis
6 International investment	D(i)	D(1)	Analysis

1 Relevant costs of investments 5/05

FAST FORWARD

Relevant costs of investment appraisal include opportunity costs, working capital costs and wider costs such as infrastructure and human development costs. **Non-relevant costs** include past costs and committed costs.

1.1 Relevant cash flows in investment appraisals

The cash flows that should be considered in investment appraisals are those which arise as a **consequence** of the investment decision under evaluation. Any costs incurred in the **past**, or any **committed costs** which will be **incurred regardless** of whether or not an investment is undertaken, are **not relevant cash flows**. They have occurred, or will occur, whatever investment decision is taken. This includes **centrally-allocated overheads** that are not a consequence of undertaking the project.

Exam focus point

Examiners often complain that students often include non-relevant costs in investment appraisals.

The **annual profits** from a project can be calculated as the **incremental contribution** earned **minus any incremental fixed costs** which are additional cash items of expenditure (that is, ignoring depreciation and so on).

There are, however, other cash flows to consider. These might include the following.

1.2 Opportunity costs

These are the costs incurred or revenues lost from diverting existing resources from their best use.

1.2.1 Example: opportunity costs

If a salesman, who is paid an annual salary of £30,000, is diverted to work on a new project and as a result existing sales of £50,000 are lost, the opportunity cost to the new project will be the £50,000 of lost sales. The salesman's salary of £30,000 is **not** an opportunity cost since it will be incurred however the salesman's time is spent.

1.3 Tax

The extra **taxation** that will be payable on extra profits, or the reductions in tax arising from capital allowances or operating losses in any year. We shall consider the effect of taxation in the next chapter.

1.4 Residual value

The **residual value or disposal value of equipment at the end of its life, or its disposal cost**.

1.5 Working capital

If a company invests £20,000 in working capital and earns cash profits of £50,000, the net cash receipts will be £30,000. Working capital will be released again at the end of a project's life, and so there will be a cash inflow arising out of the eventual realisation into cash of the project's inventory and receivables in the final year of the project.

1.5.1 Example: Working capital

Fluffyted has £40,000 in working capital at the start of a three-year project , £50,000 at the end of year 1, £20,000 at the end of year 2 and the remaining working capital was repaid at the end of year 3. What entries are shown for working capital in the NPV calculation?

Solution

Year		£
0	Initial working capital	(40,000)
1	Increase in working capital	(10,000)
2	Decrease in working capital	30,000
3	Repayment of working capital	20,000

1.6 Finance-related cash flows

Finance-related cash flows are normally **excluded** from project appraisal exercises because the discounting process takes account of the time value of money, that is the opportunity cost of investing the money in the project.

(a) If you included the cash inflow from, say, a loan, then the cash outflows of the interest payments and the loan repayment would also have to be included.

(b) These flows would all be discounted at the cost of capital, (which we assume is the same as the cost of the loan) and they would reduce to a zero net present value. They would therefore have had no effect on the NPV and are thus deemed irrelevant to the appraisal.

Finance-related cash flows are **only relevant if they incur a different rate of interest from that which is being used as the discount rate**. For example, a company may be offered a loan at a preferential rate below that which it uses for its discount rate, and so the inclusion and discounting of the loan's cash flows produces a differential NPV.

Dividend payments should also be **ignored** as they represent a distribution of the benefits of the project, rather than a **cash flow** influencing its appraisal.

1.7 Other relevant costs

The syllabus of this paper emphasises the need for you to take a wide view of the relevant costs of investment projects. Costs that will often need to be considered include:

- **Infrastructure costs**
- **Marketing costs** may be substantial, particularly of course if the investment is in a new product or service (something we shall consider further in Section 4). They will include the costs of market research, promotion and branding and the organisation of new distribution channels
- **Human resource costs** including training costs and the costs of reorganisation arising from investments

We shall consider information technology investments in Section 5, and this will include examples of several types of cost that are not just relevant to IT investments, but are also relevant to other sorts of investments.

Exam focus point

Identifying relevant costs was a very significant element in Question 5 of the May 2005 exam. A new angle in this question was the calculation of a breakeven figure, the calculations for which you have covered in Managerial level studies.

Question — Relevant costs

Learning outcome: D(i)

Itervero, a small engineering company, operates a job order costing system. It has been invited to tender for a comparatively large job which is outside the range of its normal activities and, since there is surplus capacity, the management are keen to quote as low a price as possible. It is decided that the opportunity should be treated in isolation without any regard to the possibility of its leading to further work of a similar nature (although such a possibility does exist). A low price will not have any repercussions on Itervero's regular work.

Staff of the Estimating Department have spent 100 hours on work in connection with the quotation and they have incurred travelling expenses of £550 in connection with a visits to the prospective customer's factory overseas.

The following cost estimate has been prepared on the basis of their study.

INQUIRY 205H/81
COST ESTIMATE

	£	£
Direct materials and components		
2,000 units of A at £25 a unit		50,000
200 units of B at £10 a unit		2,000
Other material and components to be bought in (specified)		12,500
		64,500
Direct labour		
700 hours of skilled labour at £3.50 an hour	2,450	
1,500 hours of unskilled labour at £2 an hour	3,000	
		5,450
Overhead		
Department P: 200 hours at £25 an hour	5,000	
Department Q: 400 hours at £20 an hour	8,000	
		13,000
Estimating department		
100 hours at £5 an hour	500	
Travelling expenses	550	
		1,050
Planning department		
300 hours at £5 an hour		1,500
		85,500

The following information is also available.

Material A. This is a regular inventory item. The inventory holding is more than sufficient for this job. The material currently held has an average cost of £25 a unit but the current replacement cost is £20 unit.

Material B. An inventory of 4,000 of B is currently held in the stores. This material is slow moving and the inventory is the residue of a batch bought seven years ago at a cost of £10 a unit. B currently costs £24 a unit but the resale value is only £18 a unit. A foreman has pointed out that B could be used as a substitute for another type of regularly used raw material which costs £20 a unit.

Direct Labour. The workforce is paid on a time basis. The company has a policy of avoiding redundancies and this means that skilled workers are frequently moved to jobs which do not make proper use of their skills. The wages included in the cost estimate are for the mix of labour which the job ideally requires. It seems likely, if the job is obtained, that most of the 2,200 hours of direct labour will be performed by skilled staff receiving £3.50 an hour.

Overhead department P. Department P is the one department of Itervero that is working at full capacity. The department is treated as a profit centre and it uses a transfer price of £25 an hour for charging out its processing time to other departments.

This charge is calculated as follows.

	£
Estimated variable cost per machine hour	10
Fixed department overhead	8
Department profit	7
	25

Department P's facilities are frequently hired out to other firms and a charge of £30 an hour is made. There is a steady demand from outside customers for the use of these facilities.

Overhead department Q. Department Q uses a transfer price of £20 for charging out machine processing time to other departments. This charge is calculated as follows.

	£
Estimated variable cost per machine hour	8
Fixed department overhead	9
Department profit	3
	20

Estimating department. The estimating department charges out its time to specific jobs using a rate of £5 an hour. The average wage rate within the department is £2.50 an hour but the higher rate is justified as being necessary to cover departmental overheads and the work done on unsuccessful quotations.

Planning department. This department also uses a charging out rate which is intended to cover all department costs.

Required

Restate the cost estimate by using an opportunity cost approach. Make any assumptions that you deem to be necessary and briefly justify each of the figures that you give.

Answer

The way to approach this question is to determine whether materials A and B, direct labour and overhead in departments P and Q are relevant costs. If in doubt about the relevant amount of a cost, ask yourself the following question: 'How much cash would I save (or how much extra cash would I receive), now or in the future, by not going ahead with this project?'

	£
Direct Materials and Components	
2,000 units of A at £20 a unit (current cost standard item)	40,000
200 units of B at £20 (since it can be used elsewhere the opportunity cost is the current cost of the substitute materials)	4,000
Other specific material and components bought in	12,500
	56,500
Direct Labour	
Direct labour is effectively a fixed cost and since there is no suggestion that additional labour would have to be employed there is no opportunity cost	0
Overhead	
Department P (lost opportunity cost of £30 an hour)	
200 hours at £30	6,000
Department Q (the variable cost of £8)	
400 hours at £8	3,200
	65,700

The costs of the estimating and planning department have already been incurred. They are sunk costs and should be ignored.

2 Relevant benefits of investments

FAST FORWARD

Relevant benefits from investments include not only **increased cash flows**, but also **savings** and **better relationships** with **customers and employees.**

2.1 Types of benefit

The benefits from a proposed investment must also be evaluated. These might consist of benefits of several types.

(a) **Savings** because assets used currently will no longer be used. The savings should include:

- Savings in **staff costs**.
- Savings in **other operating costs**, such as consumable materials.

(b) Extra **savings** or revenue benefits because of the improvements or enhancements that the investment **might** bring:

- **More sales revenue** and so additional contribution
- **More efficient system operation**
- Further savings in **staff time**, resulting perhaps in reduced future staff growth

(c) Possibly, some one-off revenue benefits from the **sale of assets** that are currently in use, but which will no longer be required

Some benefits might be **intangible**, or impossible to give a money value to.

(a) Greater **customer satisfaction**, arising from a more prompt service (eg because of a computerised sales and delivery service)

(b) Improved **staff morale** from working with higher-quality assets

(c) **Better decision making** may result from better information systems

3 Risks of investments 11/05

FAST FORWARD

There are a number of **risks** involved in making investments, and businesses may use techniques such as expected values and best-worst outcomes to estimate their impact.

3.1 Types of risk

Risk relates to uncertainty about the future. Any forward looking investment strategy is risky, because events might not turn out as anticipated.

Exam focus point

You will consider risk in detail in Paper P3 *Management Accounting Risk and Control Strategy*. You should use relevant knowledge from that paper, particularly in discussions about the desirability of particular investments. Remember always not just to consider the risks an organisation faces, but also the organisation's **attitude** to risk. Don't forget to question the validity of cost and revenue estimates if appropriate.

The risks relating to a new investment may include the following.

(a) **Physical risk**, such as fire, earthquakes, computer failure.

(b) **Economic risk**. The strategy might be based on assumptions as to the economy which might turn out to be wrong.

(c) **Financial risk** relates to the method of financing of the investment, and the quality of the cash flows.

(d) **Business risk**. This risk relates to commercial and industry factors. There is the possibility that the strategy will fail because of new technology, competitors, customer reaction, operational failures.

(e) **Political or country risk**. This includes nationalisation, sanctions, civil war, political instability, if these have an impact on the business.

(f) **Exchange risk**. Changes in exchange rates affect the value of a transaction in a foreign currency.

(g) **Information risk**. The data may not be reliable.

Case Study

The *Financial Times* reported an interesting aspect of the takeover of *Safeway* by *Wm Morrison Supermarkets.*

'Integrating the faltering Safeway with Wm Morrison Supermarkets (like-for-like sales over Christmas up by more than 10 per cent) is going to be quite a headache. And that makes the news that the group has failed to find a role for the two Safeway board members that it had agreed to take on very worrying.

'Lawrence Christensen may be staying on for three months. But that will make little difference in the three year integration process. Sir Ken and Bob Stott, one of his two managing directors, had always made big play of the fact that Mr Christensen and his colleague Jack Sinclair were going to join. It was usually the first thing they mentioned when asked about the integration risk.

'Apparently the two men felt there was not enough of a role for them. For that read that Morrison's current board members were not prepared to give up any of their responsibilities.

'It certainly increases the risk profile of the deal. It makes it more important then ever that Sir Ken gets quickly on with his much-promised (but yet-to-be-delivered) appointment of two non-executive directors.'

Martin Dickson, *Financial Times*, 20 January 2004

3.2 Risk appraisal in investment evaluation

Some investment strategies will be **more risky** than others. One of the problems arising when evaluating alternative strategies is the reliability of the data used. Since the figures are compiled on estimates of the future, there must be considerable uncertainty about the final accuracy of the figures. Business planners frequently use the following.

(a) **Operational research** techniques to measure the degree of uncertainty involved
(b) **Probability theory** to express the likelihood of a forecast result occurring

Risk can be quantified in **statistical terms** by for example **expected values**. The impact of risk can also be assessed as we saw in Chapter 3, by sensitivity analysis, asking **what if questions**. By changing the value of different variables in the model, a number of different **scenarios** for the future will be produced.

3.2.1 Dealing with risk

Sensitivity analysis would show which were the **key variables**. If an investment involves an **unacceptable amount of risk** it should be eliminated from further consideration. However, the risk of an **individual**

strategy should also be considered in the context of the **overall 'portfolio' of investment strategies** and products adopted by the company.

Once it has identified the most important risks and critical variables, the business has a choice.

(a) **Apply the most stringent controls** to the most critical variables
(b) **Alter the plans** so that the most critical variables are no longer as critical
(c) When different planning options are available, **choose a lower-risk plan**

4 Customer requirements and design of products and services 5/06

FAST FORWARD

New product investment is often necessary if competitive position is to be maintained. A rigorous process of product development should ensure that new products are **viable** and will be **popular with customers**.

4.1 What is a product?

Key term

A **product** is something that **satisfies a set of wants** that customers have.

A product is a **bundle of benefits**: things that the customer values. A product satisfies needs and wants because it possesses the following attributes.

(a) **Tangible attributes**

- Availability and delivery
- Performance
- Price
- Design

(b) **Intangible attributes**

- Image
- Perceived value

A product has a tangible **price** (you hand over your hard earned money), but you obtain the **value** that you perceive the product to have. You may get satisfaction from paying a very high price, because this says something about your status in life.

When developing new products, businesses need to focus on these attributes, constantly asking themselves the question: 'What is the buyer really buying?'

4.2 New product investment

New products can open up an **entirely new market**, **replace an existing product**, or **broaden significantly** the **market** for an **existing product.**

4.2.1 Reasons for developing new products

There are a number of reasons why a company may consider extending its product mix with the introduction of new products.

(a) To meet the **changing needs/wants of customers**: a new product may meet a new need (eg for environmentally friendly alternatives) or meet an existing need more effectively (eg digital cameras). Needs may change due to technological breakthroughs resulting in higher customer expectations or because of wider changes in society

(b) To **pace (or outpace) competitors**: responding to innovations and market trends before or shortly after competitors, so as not to miss marketing opportunities.

(c) To respond to **environmental threats and opportunities**: capitalising on opportunities presented by new technology, say (digital cameras), or other products (accessories and supplies for digital cameras); minimising the effects of threats such as environmental impacts (developing 'green' alternatives) or safety concerns (developing new safety features).

(d) To **extend the product portfolio** as part of a product development or diversification growth strategy. New products can bring new customers to the brand, enable cross-selling of products in the mix and so on.

(e) To **extend the life of a product**, by modifying it to maintain interest, simulate re-purchase (because it is 'new and improved') and/or target as yet unreached market segments.

(f) To **refresh the product portfolio**. Some products may become obsolete and need updating. Others will simply be deleted, and the company will need to replace them in the product mix in order to maintain brand presence and profitability.

4.2.2 Sources for new products

- Licensing (eg Formica, Monopoly)
- Acquisition (buy the organisation making it)
- Internal product development (your own Research and Development team)
- Customers (listen to and observe them, analyse and research – eg the Walkman)
- External inventors (Trevor Baylis and the wind-up radio)
- Competition (Dyson's bag-less vacuum cleaners, now copied by other manufacturers)
- Patent agents
- Academic institutions (eg the pharmaceutical industry funds higher education research)

4.3 Development of new products

New products should only be taken to advanced development if there is evidence of:

- Adequate demand
- Compatibility with existing marketing ability
- Compatibility with existing production ability

The stages of new product (or service) development are as follows.

Stage 1 Initial assessment

Stage 2 Business analysis

Stage 3 Product design

Stage 4 Early testing

Stage 5 Final testing

Stage 6 Product launch

Stage 1 **Initial assessment**

The concept for the new product could be **tested on potential customers** to obtain their reactions.

Stage 2 **Business analysis**

A thorough **business analysis** is required for each product idea, projecting future sales and revenues, giving a description of the product so as to provide costs of production, providing estimates of sales promotion and advertising costs, the resources required, profits and return on investment. Other factors such as **the product life cycle**, **legal restrictions**, **competitors' reaction** etc, must also be evaluated.

Stage 3 **Product development and design**

A good **design** is a very important way of making products distinctive. Some businesses have a reputation for designing good products, whilst the products others produce are difficult to use and appear dull. Good design is however more than a stylish appearance. It will take into account customer comments in producing products that are **easy to use**. Products should also be safe, inexpensive to use and service, and easy to produce and distribute. Good design not only draws attention to the company's products, it also **improves performance** and **cuts production costs.**

Other important aspects of product development include what **features** to offer. Features can be used to **differentiate** products from the competition. Businesses should therefore use the feedback channels they have with customers to determine what features customers like, what other features they would like added (and how much extra they would be prepared to pay!)

Branding is another form of product differentiation. **Brand identity** conveys a lot of information very quickly and concisely. This helps customers readily to identify and select the goods or services and so helps to create a **customer loyalty** to the brand. It is, therefore, a means of increasing or maintaining sales.

Quality will be an important consideration. Customers do not necessarily want the best quality of goods, and there may be potential in a market dominated by established brand names for a lower quality article. Customers do want the highest quality level available for the cheapest price.

Stage 4 **Early testing**

Money is invested to produce a **working prototype** of the product which can be tried by customers. This stage ensures that the product can be produced in sufficient quantities at the right price.

Stage 5 **Final testing**

The purpose of **test marketing** is to **obtain information** about how consumers react to the product. Will they buy it, and if so, will they buy it again? With this information an **estimate of total market demand** for the product can be made.

A test market involves testing a new consumer product in selected areas which are thought to be 'representative' of the total market. In the selected areas, the firm will attempt to distribute the product through the same types of sales outlets it plans to use in the full market launch, and also to use the intended advertising and promotion plans.

Stage 6 **Product launch**

Finally the product is developed for **full launch**. This involves ensuring that the product is in the right place at the right time, and that customers know about it.

Exam focus point

Question 4 in May 2006 required candidates to comment on how to determine customer requirements and an appropriate product design.

4.4 Services

FAST FORWARD

Special considerations apply to the **design of services** because of their **intangible** nature and the direct contact with consumers.

Key term

Definitions of **services** include:

'... those separately identifiable but intangible activities that provide want-satisfaction, and that are not, of necessity, tied to, or inextricable from, the sale of a product or another service. To produce a service may or may not require the use of tangible goods or assets. However, where such use is required, there is no transfer of title (permanent ownership) to these tangible goods.'

(Donald Cowell, *The Marketing of Services*)

'... any activity of benefit that one party can offer to another that is essentially intangible and does not result in the ownership of anything. Its production may or may not be tied to a physical product.'

(P Kotler, *Social Marketing*)

4.4.1 Characteristics of services

The following characteristics of services distinguish them from goods.

- **Intangibility**: services cannot be touched
- **Inseparability**: services cannot be separated from the provider
- **Heterogeneity** (or 'sameness'): the standard of service will vary with each delivery
- **Perishability**: services cannot be stored
- **Ownership**: service purchase does not transfer ownership of property

These characteristics mean that as well as the development considerations outlined above, there are a number of additional factors that need to be taken into account when designing services. Major design considerations in high– and low-contact service systems are as follows.

Decision	High-contact system	Low-contact system
Facility location	Operations must be near the customer	Operations may be placed near supply, transportation or labour
Facility layout	Facility should accommodate the customer's physical and psychological needs and expectations	Facility should enhance production
Product design	Environment as well as the physical product define the nature of the service	Customer is not in the service environment so the product can be defined by fewer attributes
Process design	Stages of production process have a direct immediate effect on the customer	Customer is not involved in majority of processing steps
Scheduling	Customer is in the production schedule and must be accommodated	Customer is concerned mainly with completion dates
Production planning	Orders cannot be stored, so smoothing production flow results in a loss of business	Both backlogging and smoothing are possible

Decision	High-contact system	Low-contact system
Worker skills	Direct work force comprises a major part of the service	Direct work force need only have technical skills
Quality control	Quality standards are often in the eye of the beholder and hence variable	Quality standards are generally measurable and hence fixed
Time standards	Service time depends on customer needs, and therefore time standards are inherently loose	Work is performed on customer surrogates (eg forms) and time standards can be tight
Wage payment	Variable output requires time-based wage systems	'Fixable' output permits output-based wage systems
Capacity planning	To avoid lost sales, capacity must be set to match peak demand	Storable output permits setting capacity at some average demand level
Forecasting	Forecasts are short term, time-oriented	Forecasts are long term, output-oriented

(Richard B Chase, 'Where does the customer fit into a service operation?', *Harvard Business Review*, November-December 1978)

5 IT investment

FAST FORWARD

Investment in information technology must be **viewed** in the context of a business's overall strategic aims.

The **costs** of information technology may be analysed in different ways, but include equipment costs, installation costs, development costs, personnel costs and running costs. **Benefits** are usually more intangible and qualitative.

5.1 The case for IT investment

IT investments can be amongst the most difficult to appraise. We shall examine the relevant costs and benefits of IT investments below, but these are often difficult to quantify.

What is most important with information technology investments is that investments are linked in with the business's **strategic, operational and control** needs. A strong business case needs to be made for investment in IT. Adopting a general framework for business case development enables comparisons between competing investment opportunities to be made more easily.

Stage 1 **Where are we now?**

A business case starts by establishing **what the current position is**. The person (or people) responsible for authorising the investment will use this information to develop an understanding as to why the new information system is being proposed.

Stage 2 **Where do we want to be?**

This stage involves devising a statement of where the organisation would like to be (**the desired position**), and a justification (maybe a cost-benefit analysis) showing why the position described is desirable. The statement may be broken down into more detailed objectives for the investment.

Stage 3 **How are we going to get there?**

This stage focuses on the actual work that needs to be undertaken to move from the current position to the desired position. In an information system installation for example this would include work breakdown and network analysis.

A clear plan of exactly **what is involved in the project** should be developed.

Stage 4 **Overall justification** This stage focuses on the information most relevant to making a decision on **whether to proceed** with, or reject, the investment.

Cost-benefit analysis is a key part of a business case justification, and organisations will use the appraisal techniques such as net present value and internal rate of return that we shall look at in the next chapter.

Cost-benefit analysis of **information systems** is complicated by the fact that many of the system cost elements are poorly defined and that benefits can often be highly **qualitative** and **subjective** in nature. An added complication is that the benefits or returns are not certain – there is a **risk** that the benefit will not eventuate

5.2 The costs of a proposed system

The costs of a new system will include costs in a number of different categories.

Cost	Example
Hardware costs	• Computers and peripherals
Installation costs	• New buildings (if necessary) • The computer room (wiring, air-conditioning if necessary) • Desks, security systems etc
Development costs	• Costs of measuring and analysing the existing system • Costs of looking at the new system. • Software/consultancy work • Systems analysis • Programming. • Changeover costs, particularly file conversion, may be very considerable.
Personnel costs	• Staff training • Staff recruitment/relocation • Staff salaries and pensions • Redundancy payments • Overheads
Operating costs	• Consumable materials (tapes, disks, stationery etc) • Maintenance • Accommodation costs • Heating/power/insurance/telephone • Standby arrangements, in case the system breaks down
Intangible costs	Some costs are **harder to quantify**. • 'Learning curve' – staff will work slower until they become familiar with the new system • Staff morale may suffer from the enforced changes • Investment opportunities forsaken – the opportunity cost • Incompatibility with other systems may mean an unforeseen change is required elsewhere in the organisation

Exam focus point

Remember that many of these costs will also be relevant for investments other than information technology investments.

Question

Costs of IT system

Learning outcome: D(i)

Draw up a table with three headings: capital cost items, one-off revenue cost items and regular annual costs. Identify at least three items to be included under each heading, regarding the costs of IT systems.

Answer

Capital cost items	'One-off ' revenue cost items	Regular annual costs
Hardware purchase costs	Consultancy fees	Operating staff salaries/wages
Software purchase costs	Systems analysts' and programmers' salaries	Data transmission costs
Purchase of accommodation (if needed)	Costs of testing the system (staff costs, consumables)	Consumable materials
Installation costs (new desks, cables, physical storage etc)	Costs of converting the files for the new system	Power
	Staff recruitment fees	Maintenance costs
		Cost of standby arrangements
		Ongoing staff training

5.3 The benefits of a proposed system

The benefits from a proposed new system must also be evaluated. These consist of direct and indirect or intangible benefits.

5.3.1 Direct benefits

These include the sorts of benefits discussed in Section 2 such as:

(a) **Savings** because the old system is no longer operating.

(b) **Efficiency savings**

(c) **Extra cost savings or revenue benefits** because of the improvements or enhancements that the new system should bring. These include more sales revenue. There may also be operational efficiencies such as better inventory control and so fewer inventory losses from obsolescence and deterioration, reduced bad debts from a new receivables system or increased capacity utilisation. Cost savings may also derive from **better IT security and hence fewer losses.**

(d) Possibly, **some one-off revenue benefits** from the sale of equipment which the new system does not require. However, computer equipment depreciates very quickly. It is also possible that the new system will use **less office space**, possibly providing an opportunity to sell or rent the spare space.

5.3.2 Intangible benefits

Many of the benefits are **intangible**, or impossible to give a money value to.

- Improved **staff morale** from working with a more efficient system
- **Better management information**

- Automating routine decisions and tasks should provide **more time for planning**
- More informed **decision making**
- Further savings in staff time
- Benefits accruing from gaining **competitive advantage** through better quality and enhanced products
- Greater **customer satisfaction** and **loyalty**, arising from better customer service and equity
- **Better relationships** with **other supply chain participants**

The fact that so many of the benefits a new information system provides are intangible means that it is difficult to construct a meaningful cost benefit analysis. There are three possible approaches to dealing with this problem.

Approach	Comment
Calculate a value for the benefits	We could estimate the worth of each of the intangible benefits and allocate an appropriate cash value. The problem with this approach is that realistically it is nothing more than **guesswork**.
Ignore the 'too intangible' benefits	Allocate a value to those intangible benefits we are able to estimate a realistic value for. Ignore the other intangible benefits. This approach will significantly **undervalue** the system.
Adopt a qualitative approach	Find a reasonable non-financial way of stating intangible benefits. For example customer satisfaction ratings could be established through questionnaires – as could staff time savings and staff morale. Market share could be used to assess competitive advantage. The problems with this approach are: • Much of the information would only be available **after** the system had been implemented • Determining **appropriate measures** • **Isolating the effect** of the information system from other factors

6 International investment 11/05, 11/06

FAST FORWARD

Foreign direct investment (FDI) will generally be undertaken if exporting is more costly than overseas production.

6.1 Reasons for undertaking FDI

Key term

Foreign direct investment (FDI) is the establishment of new overseas facilities or the expansion of existing overseas facilities, by an investor. FDI may be *inward* (domestic investment by overseas companies) or *outward* (overseas investment by domestic companies). *(OT 2000)*

FDI provides an alternative to growth restricted to a firm's domestic market. A firm might develop **horizontally** in different countries, replicating its existing operations on a global basis. **Vertical** integration might have an international dimension through FDI to acquire raw material or component sources overseas (**backwards**

integration) or to establish final production and distribution in other countries (**forward integration**). **Diversification** might alternatively provide the impetus to developing international interests.

FDI is likely to take place in the context of a **worldwide corporate strategy** which takes account of relative costs and revenues, tax considerations and **process specialisation** (specialisation of processes within particular production facilities). For example, some motor vehicle manufacturers locate labour-intensive processes in lower wage countries, leaving the final stage of the production process to be located nearer the intended market.

6.2 Forms of overseas operations

Different forms of expansion overseas are available to meet various strategic objectives.

(a) Firms may expand by means of new **'start-up' investments**, for example the setting up of an **overseas subsidiary** to operate a manufacturing plant. This does allow flexibility, although it may be slow to achieve, expensive to maintain and slow to yield satisfactory results.

(b) A firm might **take over or merge with established firms abroad**. This provides a means of **purchasing market information**, **market share** and **distribution channels**. However, the better acquisitions will only be available at a premium.

(c) A **joint venture** with a local overseas partner might be entered into.

6.3 Joint ventures

Key term

Joint venture is a contractual arrangement whereby two or more parties undertake an economic activity which is subject to joint control. *(IAS 31)*

The two distinct types of joint venture are **industrial co-operation (contractual)**, and **joint-equity**. A contractual joint venture is for a fixed period and the duties and responsibility of the parties are contractually defined. A joint-equity venture involves investment, is of no fixed duration and continually evolves. It may be the best route in countries where full foreign ownership is discouraged.

There is a growing trend towards a contractual form of joint venture as a consequence of the **high research and development costs** and the **'critical mass'** necessary to take advantage of economies of scale in industries such as automobile engineering.

6.4 Foreign subsidiaries

The basic structure of many multinationals consists of a parent company (a holding company) with subsidiaries in several countries. The subsidiaries may be wholly owned or just partly owned, and some may be owned through other subsidiaries.

6.4.1 The purpose of setting up subsidiaries abroad

The following are some reasons why a parent company might want to set up subsidiary companies in other countries.

- The location of markets
- The need for a sales organisation
- The opportunity to produce goods more cheaply
- The need to avoid import controls
- The need to obtain access to raw materials
- The availability of grants and tax concessions

6.4.2 Extracting profits

Whatever the reason for setting up subsidiaries abroad, the aim is to **increase the profits** of the **multinational's parent company**. However there are different approaches to increasing profits that the multinational might take.

(a) At one extreme, the **parent company** might **choose** to get **as much money** as it can **from the subsidiary**, and as quickly as it can. This would involve the transfer of all or most of the subsidiary's profits to the parent company.

(b) At the other extreme, the parent company might **encourage** a **foreign subsidiary** to **develop its business gradually**, to achieve long-term growth in sales and profits. To encourage growth, the subsidiary would be allowed to retain a large proportion of its profits, instead of remitting the profits to the parent company. A further consequence is that the economy of the country in which the subsidiary operates should be improved, with higher output adding to the country's gross domestic product and increasing employment.

6.4.3 Obtaining cash returns from an overseas subsidiary

If a subsidiary earns a profit, but then retains and reinvests the profits, the parent company will not get any cash at all. Various ways of obtaining a cash return are as follows.

(a) The subsidiary could make a profit and pay a **dividend** out of profits.

(b) The parent company could sell goods or services to the subsidiary and obtain payment. The amount of this payment will depend on the volume of sales and also on the **transfer price** for the sales.

(c) A parent company which grants a subsidiary the right to make goods protected by patents can charge a **royalty** on any goods that the subsidiary sells. The size of any royalty can be adjusted to suit the wishes of the parent company's management.

(d) If the parent company makes a **loan** to a subsidiary, it can set the interest rate high or low, thereby affecting the profits of both companies. A high rate of interest on a loan, for example, would improve the parent company's profits to the detriment of the subsidiary's profits.

(e) **Management charges** may be levied by the parent company for costs incurred in the management of international operations.

When the subsidiary is in a country where there are exchange control regulations, the parent company may have difficulty getting cash from the subsidiary.

6.4.4 Transfer pricing

When a foreign subsidiary makes a profit from goods/services supplied by its parent company, the profit will be included in the total profits of the multinational group. The management of the parent company must decide, however how the total profit of the group should be **divided** between the parent company and each of its subsidiaries, which is likely to depend on the **transfer prices** adopted.

6.4.5 Example: Transfer pricing

(a) Suppose that a US parent company ships some goods to a UK subsidiary. The goods cost US$40,000 to make, and they are sold in the UK by the subsidiary for £50,000, which is the equivalent, say, of US$75,000. The US multinational group will make a total profit of US$35,000. So how much profit from the US$35,000 has been earned by the US parent company, and how much has been earned by the UK subsidiary?

The answer depends on the transfer price at which the US parent sells the goods to its UK subsidiary.

(i) If the transfer price is US$45,000, the US parent company would make a profit of $5,000, leaving a profit of $30,000 for the UK subsidiary.

(ii) If the transfer price is US$70,000, the US parent company would make a profit of $30,000, leaving only a $5,000 profit for the UK subsidiary.

(b) The same choice of how to share total profits can be made in fixing a transfer price for goods made by a subsidiary and sold to the parent company or to another subsidiary.

Case Study

In its 2003 annual report, **Tate and Lyle** disclosed 17 joint ventures which were located in countries such as Colombia, the Czech Republic, Hungary, Mexico, Spain and Turkey. Examples of the activities of these joint ventures include the sourcing of molasses through purchase contracts, the operation of sugar beet processing plants and the manufacture of cereal sweeteners.

6.5 Alternatives to FDI

Exporting and **licensing** stand as alternatives to FDI.

(a) **Exporting** may be direct selling by the firm's own export division into the overseas markets, or it may be indirect through agents, distributors, trading companies and various other such channels. Exporting may be unattractive because of tariffs, quotas or other import restrictions in overseas markets, and local production may be the only feasible option in the case of bulky products such as cement and flat glass.

(b) **Licensing** involves conferring rights to make use of the licensor company's production process on producers located in the overseas market in return for royalty payments. Licensing can allow fairly rapid penetration of overseas markets and has the advantage that substantial financial resources will not be required. Many multinationals use a combination of various methods of servicing international markets, depending on the particular circumstances.

6.6 Countertrade

Countertrade is a general term used to describe a variety of commercial arrangements for reciprocal international trade or barter between companies or other organisations (eg state controlled organisations) in two or more countries.

Key term

Countertrade is a form of trading activity based on other than an arm's-length goods for cash exchange. Types of countertrade include:

- **Barter**: the direct exchange of goods and services between two parties without the use of money
- **Counterpurchase**: a trading agreement in which the primary contract vendor agrees to make purchases of an agreed percentage of the primary contract value, from the primary contract purchaser, through a linked counterpurchase contract
- **Offsets**: a trading agreement in which the purchaser becomes involved in the production process, often acquiring technology supplied by the vendor

(OT 2005)

Countertrade is **costly for the exporter**; it creates lengthy and cumbersome **administrative problems**, just to set up a countertrade arrangement. It is fraught with **uncertainty**, and deals can easily collapse or go wrong. Small and medium-sized firms might be unable and unwilling to accept the costs and administrative burdens of exporting by means of countertrade arrangements. However, in some situations, countertrade might be the **only way of securing export orders.**

6.7 The risks of multinationals 11/06

Multinational companies, like any other companies, must accept the normal risks of business. However, compared with companies that trade entirely within one country, and even with companies that export from their base in one country, multinationals face additional risks, some of which we have already examined in earlier chapters.

The risks include the following.

(a) **Foreign exchange risks**

As we have already seen, any company that exports or imports faces the risk of **higher costs** or **lower revenues** because of adverse movements in foreign exchange rates. Multinationals that trade between one country and another therefore face this risk. A company that owns assets in different countries (subsidiaries abroad) faces the risk of accounting losses due to adverse movements in exchange rates causing a fall in the value of those assets, as expressed in domestic currency.

(b) **Political risks and country risks**

A multinational can face risks of **economic** or **political measures** being taken by governments, affecting the operations of its subsidiaries abroad. An example was the import restrictions imposed by the USA on the British cashmere industry during 1999, in retaliation for EU restrictions on banana imports.

(c) **Geographical separation**

The **geographical separation** of the **parent company** from its subsidiaries adds to the problems of management control of the group of companies as a whole.

(d) **Litigation risk**

The risk of litigation varies in different countries and to minimise this risk, attention should be paid to **legislation** and **regulations** covering the products sold in different countries. Care should be taken to comply with contract terms.

(e) **Risk of loss of goods in transit**

It may be possible to **insure** against this risk.

Exam focus point

Question 1 in November 2006 required a discussion on external constraints affecting an investment decision by a multi-national company.

6.8 Tax implications of international investment

FAST FORWARD

Taxation issues can influence the manner in which the foreign investment is set up and returns received by the parent company (eg by **transfer pricing).**

If a company makes investments abroad it will be liable to income tax on the profits made, the taxable amount being before the deduction of any foreign taxes. The profits may be any of the following.

- **Profits of an overseas branch** or agency
- **Income from foreign securities**, for example debentures in overseas companies
- **Dividends from overseas subsidiaries**
- **Gains** made on disposals of foreign assets

In many instances, a company will be potentially subject to overseas taxes as well as to local income tax on the same profits. There are however various ways that this may be avoided partly or wholly.

6.9 Double taxation relief (DTR) 11/05

Key term

> A **double taxation agreement** is an agreement between two countries intended to avoid the double taxation of income which would otherwise be subject to taxation in both. *(OT 2005)*

Typical provisions of double taxation agreements based on the OECD Model Agreement are as follows.

(a) **Total exemption from tax** is given in the country where income arises in the hands of, for example:

(i) Visiting diplomats
(ii) Teachers on exchange programmes

(b) **Preferential rates of withholding tax** are applied to, for example, payments of rent, interest and dividends. The usual rate is frequently replaced by 15% or less.

(c) DTR is given to taxpayers in their **country of residence** by way of a credit for tax suffered in the country where income arises. This may be in the form of relief for withholding tax only or, given a holding of specified size in a foreign company, for the underlying tax on the profits out of which dividends are paid.

(d) There are **exchange of information** clauses so that tax evaders can be chased internationally.

(e) There are **rules to determine** a person's residence and to prevent dual residence (tie-breaker clauses).

(f) There are **clauses** which render certain profits taxable in only one rather than both of the contracting states.

(g) There is a **non-discrimination clause** so that a country does not tax foreigners more heavily than its own nationals.

6.9.1 Example: Double taxation relief

Suppose the tax rate on profits in the Federal West Asian Republic is 20%, the UK company tax is 30%, and there is a double taxation agreement between the two countries. A subsidiary of a UK firm operating in the Federal West Asian Republic earns the equivalent of £1 million in profit, and therefore pays £200,000 in tax on profits. When the profits are remitted to the UK, the UK parent can claim a credit of £200,000 against the full UK tax charge of £300,000, and hence will only pay £100,000.

Exam focus point

> The compulsory question in November 2005 required double taxation relief to be incorporated into an NPV calculation.

6.10 Other ways of minimising taxation

6.10.1 Controlled foreign companies (CFCs)

A company may choose to trade abroad through an investment in a local company. Providing there are no exchange control problems and cash flow requirements do not call for the repatriation of all profits, there may be a **tax benefit** in **accumulating income** in a foreign company whose effective tax rate is lower than that of the investing company.

6.10.2 The migration of companies

If the overseas profits of a resident company are chargeable to company tax whereas the overseas profits of a company resident elsewhere are not, companies might wish to **transfer their residence** in order to avoid paying company tax in their country of origin.

6.10.3 Sales at artificial transfer prices

Where sales are made to a **non-resident fellow group company** at an undervalue, or purchases are made from such a company at an overvalue, the tax authorities may substitute a market price in computing the profits chargeable to tax.

6.10.4 Trading abroad

It may be possible to design a bona fide group structure with the result that tax can be minimised by controlling the timing and amounts of dividends paid by the foreign subsidiary.

If an overseas operation is expected to make losses at first and then become profitable, it may be sensible to start with a **branch** and then transfer the trade to a **subsidiary**. Provided all the assets (or all except cash) are transferred, and the consideration is in the form of shares, **gains** on **the transfers of assets** can be deducted from the value of the shares instead of being immediately taxable in the investing company's country. Where the overseas country is a member state of the European Union, an alternative is to allow the gains to be taxable but to claim **relief** for **tax** which would have been payable overseas but for the EU Mergers Directive (which gives certain reliefs from tax).

Exam focus point

In the exam you may be asked about the issue of using an international structure to improve a company's position, by taking advantage of double tax arrangements, transfer pricing and location in countries with favourable tax regimes.

Chapter roundup

- **Relevant costs** of investment appraisal include opportunity costs, working costs and wider costs such as infrastructure and human development costs. **Non-relevant costs** include past costs and committed costs.
- **Relevant benefits** from investments include not only **increased cash flows**, but also **savings** and **better relationships** with **customers and employees**.
- There are a number of **risks** involved in making investments, and businesses may use techniques such as expected values and best-worst outcomes to estimate their impact.
- **New product investment** is often necessary if competitive position is to be maintained. A rigorous process of product development should ensure that new products are **viable** and will be **popular with customers**.
- Special considerations apply to the **design of services** because of their **intangible** nature and the direct contact with consumers.
- **Investment in information technology** must be **viewed** in the context of a business's overall strategic aims.
- The **costs** of information technology may be analysed in different ways, but include equipment costs, installation costs, development costs, personnel costs and running costs. **Benefits** are usually more intangible and qualitative.
- **Foreign direct investment (FDI)** will generally be undertaken if exporting is more costly than overseas production.
- **Taxation issues** can influence the manner in which the foreign investment is set up and returns received by the parent company (eg by transfer pricing).

Quick quiz

1 If a machine with annual running costs of $100,000, was diverted from producing output selling for $50,000 to producing a special order worth $70,000, what would be the relevant costs of what has happened?

A $170,000
B $100,000
C $50,000
D $20,000

2 The financial benefits of a new investment consist of the increased sales revenues it generates.

True ☐

False ☐

3 Give five examples of the risks organisations face when they make investments.

4 What are the six stages involved in new product development?

5 What do the following terms mean in the context of services?

- Intangibility
- Inseparability
- Heterogeneity
- Perishability
- Ownership

6 What are the main categories of cost that will be incurred by a new computer system?

7 What is a double taxation agreement?

8 **Fill in the blank.**

.... are 'funds affected by government regulations restricting flows of money out of a country.'

9 **Fill in the blank.**

.... is 'a form of trading activity based on other than an arm's-length goods for cash exchange'. (OT 2005)

Answers to quick quiz

1 C $50,000, the opportunity cost of the lost sales revenue. A and B are wrong because they include the $100,000 running costs which would be incurred anyway are not relevant. In the absence of any further information, $20,000 (D) would be the net benefit ($70,000 – $50,000).

2 False. Financial benefits could also include the savings from not operating existing assets any more, and also proceeds from the disposal of old assets.

3
- Physical
- Economic
- Financial
- Business
- Political
- Exchange
- Information

4

Stage 1	Initial assessment
Stage 2	Business analysis
Stage 3	Product design
Stage 4	Early testing
Stage 5	Final testing
Stage 6	Product launch

5
- Intangibility: services cannot be touched
- Inseparability: services cannot be separated from the provider
- Heterogeneity (or 'sameness'): the standard of service will vary with each delivery
- Perishability: services cannot be stored
- Ownership: service purchase does not transfer ownership of property

6
- Hardware
- Installation
- Development
- Personnel
- Operating
- Intangible

7 An agreement between countries to avoid or minimise double taxation on profits earned abroad which are also taxable in the investor's home country

8 Blocked funds

9 Countertrade

Now try the questions below from the Exam Question Bank

Number	Level	Marks	Time
Q28	Introductory	n/a	35 mins
Q29	Examination	15	27 mins

18

Investment appraisal methods

Introduction

Having discussed influences on investment appraisal in this chapter, we go through the principles of appraising investments numerically. Although you may feel that these topics are familiar, it is worth working through the examples again to confirm that you do understand them. Examiners' reports often highlight basic errors of principle in answers to investment appraisal questions. It is likely that NPV calculations will be set somewhere on virtually every paper, often in the compulsory question.

Pay careful attention to the complications in international investment appraisals, as many of the questions you see will have a significant international dimension.

Topic list	Learning outcomes	Syllabus references	Ability required
1 Capital investment appraisal	D(ii)	D(4), (5)	Evaluation
2 The use of appraisal methods in practice	D(ii)	D(4)	Evaluation
3 Allowing for inflation in DCF	D(ii)	D(4)	Evaluation
4 Allowing for taxation in DCF	D(ii)	D(6)	Evaluation
5 International investment appraisal	D(ii)	D(4), (6)	Evaluation

1 Capital investment appraisal

FAST FORWARD

The **payback method** of project appraisal and the **ARR/ROCE/ROI method** of project appraisal are popular appraisal techniques despite their limitations.

There are two methods of using **discounted cash flow** to appraise investment projects, the NPV method and the IRR/DCF yield method.

The **NPV method** of project appraisal is to accept projects with a positive NPV.

The **IRR method** of project appraisal is to accept projects whose IRR (the rate at which the NPV is zero) exceeds a target rate of return. The IRR is estimated either from a graph or using interpolation. The formula to apply is $IRR = A + \frac{N_A}{N_A - N_B}(B - A)$

1.1 Capital investment evaluation 11/05

Key term

Capital investment appraisal: the application of a set of methodologies (generally based on the discounting of projected cash flows) whose purpose is to give guidance to managers with respect to decisions as to how best to commit long-term investment funds. *(OT 2000)*

The principal methods of evaluating capital projects are as follows.

(a) The return on investment method, or accounting rate of return method

(b) The payback method

(c) Discounted cash flow (DCF):

- The net present value method (NPV)
- The internal rate of return method (IRR)

Of these, DCF should be by far the most important, although (a) and (b) are used more in practice by small and medium-sized firms.

The principles and mechanics of these methods were covered in your studies for *Management Accounting Decision Making* paper. Before we go on to look at the more advanced aspects, and their application to international investment appraisal, we briefly revise the main points here, followed by some questions for you to brush up your knowledge.

Exam focus point

In November 2005, students had difficulty differentiating profit from cash flow. It is essential that you are confident with the methods covered here.

Knowledge brought forward from Management Accounting: Decision Management

The accounting rate of return (ARR) method of investment appraisal

- This method uses **financial accounting based figures** in arriving at a rate of return on a project, which is compared with a target rate of return to decide on its acceptability.
- There are various **definitions** of the ARR, the most common of which is

$$ARR = \frac{\text{Estimated average annual profits, after depreciation, before interest and tax}}{\text{Average book value of capital employed}} \times 100\%$$

- The main disadvantages of the ARR are that it uses **subjective accounting profits** rather than cash flows; it does not take account of the **timing** of flows, and it can be computed under **various definitions**, which makes comparisons difficult

The payback method of investment appraisal

- The **payback period** is the time required for the cash inflows from a capital investment project to equal the cash outflows. Either payback periods of different projects are compared, or the period is measured against an 'acceptable' period.
- The payback should not be used as the sole appraisal method, as it ignores the cash flows after the payback period, but may be used as a **first screening method**, particularly when applied to risky projects.
- The payback period may be estimated by computing the **accumulated cash inflows** year by year until the initial capital investment is covered.
- The **discounted payback period** is a modification of payback; the future cash flows are discounted when the period is calculated.

Discounted cash flow (DCF) methods of investment appraisal

- **DCF** is an appraisal technique which uses **cash flows,** takes account of both the **time value** of money and also the **total profitability** over a project's life, and is thus a method superior to both the ARR and payback methods.
- The time value of money (why £1 now is worth more than £1 in the future) arises from considerations of **investment opportunities, risk** and **inflation.**
- **Basic discounting** of cash flows using an appropriate opportunity cost of capital principally takes account of the first of these considerations.
- The cash flows used in DCF methods are those that are **relevant** – the **changes** in **future cash flows** of the business that will arise as a result of undertaking the project.
- The **NPV** approach applies a **specific discount rate** to the cash flows of the project to arrive at an **absolute** measure, the NPV, which, if positive, implies the project is acceptable.
- The **IRR** approach is to calculate the **discount rate at which the NPV of the project would be zero,** indicating the maximum cost of capital at which the project would be viable. Provided the investing business's cost of capital is less than this, the project may be accepted.
- The IRR is found approximately by using interpolation, using the results from NPV computations at two different discount rates:

  $$IRR = A + \frac{N_A}{N_A - N_B}(B - A)$$ where A = lower discount rate used with NPV = N_A

  B = higher discount rate used with NPV = N_B

Exam formulae

Future value S, of a sum X, invested for n periods, compounded at r% interest $S = X(1+r)^n$

Present value of £1 payable or receivable in n years, discounted at r% per annum:

$$PV = \frac{1}{(1+r)^n}$$

Present value of an annuity of £1 per annum, receivable or payable in n years, discounted at r% per annum

$$PV = \frac{1}{r}\left[1 - \frac{1}{(1+r)^n}\right]$$

Question — Accounting rate of return

Learning outcome: D(ii)

A company has a target accounting rate of return of 20% (using the definition given above), and is now considering the following project.

Capital cost of asset	£80,000
Estimated life	4 years

Estimated profit before depreciation

	£
Year 1	20,000
Year 2	25,000
Year 3	35,000
Year 4	25,000

The capital asset would be depreciated by 25% of its cost each year, and will have no residual value. Should the project be undertaken?

Answer

	£
Total profit before depreciation over four years	105,000
Total profit after depreciation over four years	25,000
Average annual profit after depreciation	6,250
Original cost of investment	80,000
Average net book value over the four year period $\frac{(80{,}000+0)}{2}$	40,000

The average ARR is $6{,}250 \div 40{,}000 = 15.625\%$.

The project would not be undertaken because it would fail to yield the target return of 20%.

Question — Net present value

Learning outcome: D(ii)

What are the net present values of the following?

(a) £5,000 payable in 2 years' time, cost of capital 17%

(b) £5,000 payable in 3 years' time, cost of capital 8.5%

(c) £5,000 payable each year for five years beginning in a year's time, cost of capital 16%
(d) £5,000 payable each year for five years beginning in two year's time, cost of capital 16%
(e) £5,000 payable each year for five years beginning today, cost of capital 16%
(f) £5,000 payable each year for five years beginning in a year's time, cost of capital 16.5%

Answer

(a) £5,000 × 17% year 2 discount factor = £5,000 × 0.731 = £3,655

(b) £5,000 × 8.5% year 3 discount factor = £5,000 × $\frac{1}{(1.085)^3}$ = £3,915

(c) £5,000 × 16% year 5 cumulative discount factor = 5,000 × 3.274 = £16,370

(d) £5,000 × (16% year 6 cdf – year 1 cdf) = 5,000 × (3.685 – 0.862) = £14,115

(e) £5,000 × (1 + 16% year 4 cdf) = 5,000 × (1 + 2.798) = £18,990

(f) £5,000 × 16.5% cdf = 5,000 × $\frac{(1-(1+0.165)^{-5})}{0.165}$ = £16,182

Question — Purchase of material

Learning outcome: D(ii)

LCH Inc manufactures product X which it sells for $5 a unit. Variable costs of production are currently $3 a unit, and fixed costs 50c a unit. A new machine is available which would cost $90,000 but which could be used to make product X for a variable cost of only $2.50 a unit. Fixed costs, however, would increase by $7,500 a year as a direct result of purchasing the machine. The machine would have an expected life of four years and a resale value after that time of $10,000. Sales of product X are estimated to be 75,000 units a year. If LCH expects to earn at least 12% a year from its investments, should the machine be purchased? (Ignore taxation.)

Answer

Savings are 75,000 × $(3.00 – 2.50) = $37,500 a year.

Additional costs are $7,500 a year.

Net cash savings are therefore $30,000 a year.

It is assumed that the machine will be sold for $10,000 at the end of year 4.

Year	*Cash flow*	*PV factor*		*PV of cash flow*
	$	12%		$
0	(90,000)	1.000		(90,000)
1	30,000	0.893		26,790
2	30,000	0.797		23,910
3	30,000	0.712		21,360
4	40,000	0.636		25,440
			NPV	+7,500

The NPV is positive and so the project is expected to earn more than 12% a year and is therefore acceptable.

1.2 The timing of cash flows: conventions used in DCF

The following guidelines may be applied unless a question indicates that they should not be.

(a) A cash outlay to be incurred at the beginning of an investment project, that is now, occurs in year 0. The present value of $1 in year 0 is $1.

(b) A cash outlay, saving or inflow which occurs during the course of a time period (say, one year) is assumed to occur all at once at the end of the time period. Therefore receipts of $10,000 during the first year are taken to occur at the end of that year. That point in time is called 'year 1'.

(c) A cash outlay, saving or inflow which occurs at the beginning of a time period (say at the beginning of the second year) is taken to occur at the end of the previous year. Therefore a cash outlay of $5,000 at the beginning of the second year is taken to occur at year 1.

Question — ROI

Learning outcome: D(ii)

A company is trying to decide whether to buy a machine for $80,000 which will save $20,000 a year for five years and which will have a resale value of $10,000 at the end of year 5. What would the IRR of the investment project be?

Answer

The return on investment is $\dfrac{20{,}000 - \text{depreciation of } 14{,}000}{\frac{1}{2} \text{ of } (80{,}000 + 10{,}000)} = \dfrac{6{,}000}{45{,}000} = 13.3\%$

Two thirds of this is 8.9% and so we can start by trying 9%.

The IRR is the rate for the cost of capital at which the NPV = 0.

Year	*Cash flow*	*PV factor*	*PV of cash flow*
	$	9%	$
0	(80,000)	1.000	(80,000)
1–5	20,000	3.890	77,800
5	10,000	0.650	6,500
		NPV	4,300

This is fairly close to zero. It is also positive, which means that the IRR is more than 9%. We will try 12% next.

Year	*Cash flow*	*PV factor*	*PV of cash flow*
	$	12%	$
0	(80,000)	1.000	(80,000)
1–5	20,000	3.605	72,100
5	10,000	0.567	5,670
		NPV	(2,230)

This is fairly close to zero and negative. The IRR is therefore greater than 9% but less than 12%. We shall now use the two NPV values to estimate the IRR, using the formula given above.

Internal rate of return = $9 + \left[\dfrac{4{,}300}{4{,}300 - -2{,}230} \times (12-9)\right] = 10.98\%, \text{say } 11\%$

BPP LEARNING MEDIA

Exam focus point

> Don't forget the simpler methods of appraising investments (payback and accounting rate of return) as these are likely to be examined.

1.3 Working capital

As we have seen, **increases** in working capital **reduce** the net cash flow of the period to which they relate. So for example, if a project lasts for five years with a £20,000 working capital requirement at the end of year 1, rising to £30,000 at the end of year 2, the DCF calculation will show £20,000 as a year 1 cash outflow and £10,000 (30,000 – £20,000) as a year 2 cash outflow.

Working capital is assumed to be **recovered** at the end of the project. In our example, this will be shown by a £30,000 cash inflow at year 5.

Exam focus point

> In November 2005, there was a loss on realisation of working capital at the end of the project. Make sure you read the question carefully so that such details are not over–looked.

Question — Net present value

Learning outcome D(ii)

Elsie is considering the manufacture of a new product which would involve the use of both a new machine (costing £150,000) and an existing machine, which cost £80,000 two years ago and has a current net book value of £60,000. There is sufficient capacity on this machine, which has so far been under-used.

Annual sales of the product would be 5,000 units, selling at £32 a unit. Unit costs would be as follows.

	£
Direct labour (4 hours at £2)	8
Direct materials	7
Fixed costs including depreciation	9
	24

The project would have a five year life, after which the new machine would have a net residual value of £10,000. Because direct labour is continually in short supply, labour resources would have to be diverted from other work which currently earns a contribution of £1.50 per direct labour hour. The fixed overhead absorption rate would be £2.25 an hour (£9 a unit) but actual expenditure on fixed overhead would not alter.

Working capital requirements would be £10,000 in the first year, rising to £15,000 in the second year and remaining at this level until the end of the project, when it will all be recovered. The company's cost of capital is 20%. Ignore taxation.

Is the project worthwhile?

Answer

Working		£
Years 1-5	Contribution from new product	
	5,000 × £(32 – 15)	85,000
	Less contribution forgone	
	5,000 × (4 × £1.50)	30,000
		55,000

Year	Equipment £	Working capital £	Contribution £	Net cash flow £	Discount factor 20%	PV of net cash flow £
0	(150,000)	(10,000)		(160,000)	1.000	(160,000)
1		(5,000)		(5,000)	0.833	(4,165)
1–5			55,000	55,000	2.991	164,505
5	10,000	15,000		25,000	0.402	10,050
					NPV =	10,390

The NPV is positive and the project is worthwhile, although there is not much margin for error. Some risk analysis of the project is recommended.

Note. The discount factor 2.991 applied to the annual contribution is an example of an **annuity factor**, which can be used for a series of equal annual cash flows starting at time 0. Annuity factors may be found from the table or from the formula (viii), both given in the Appendix at the end of this text.

1.4 Other formulae 5/05

You may also find the following formulae useful.

(a) For **non-annual cash flows**, the period interest rate r is related to the annual interest rate R by the following formula.

$r = \sqrt[n]{1+R} - 1$

where n is the number of periods per annum.

For example, if the annual interest rate is 18%, the monthly interest rate $r = \sqrt[12]{1.18} - 1 = 0.0139$, ie 1.39%.

Question — Short-term investment

Learning outcome: D(ii)

Calculate the net present value of the following short-duration investment

Cost ($2,000,000)

Revenues

2 months $700,000
4 months $300,000
6 months $1,000,000
One year $250,000

The company's annual cost of capital is 16%

Answer

Two months

Interest rate $= \sqrt[6]{1+0.16} - 1 = 2.50\%$

Discount factor $= \dfrac{1}{1.025} = 0.976$

Four months

Interest rate $= \sqrt[3]{1+0.16} - 1 = 5.07\%$

Discount factor $= \frac{1}{1.0507} = 0.952$

Six months

Interest rate $= \sqrt[2]{1+0.16} - 1 = 7.70\%$

Discount factor $= \frac{1}{1.0770} = 0.928$

Time	*Cash flow*	*Discount factor*	*Present value*
	$	16%	$
0	(2,000,000)	1.000	(2,000,000)
2 months	700,000	0.976	683,200
4 months	300,000	0.952	285,600
6 months	1,000,0000	0.928	928,000
1	250,000	0.862	215,500
			112,300

(b) **Changes in interest rate** can be reflected as in the following example.

In years 1, 2 and 3, the interest rate is 10%, 12% and 14% respectively.

Then, Year 3 discount factor $= \frac{1}{(1+r_1)(1+r_2)(1+r_3)}$

$= \frac{1}{1.10 \times 1.12 \times 1.14} = 0.712$

1.5 NPV or IRR?

FAST FORWARD

When compared with the NPV method, the **IRR method** has a number of **disadvantages**.

- It **ignores** the **relative size** of investments.
- It is difficult to use if a project has **non-conventional cashflows** or when deciding between **mutually exclusive projects**.
- **Discount rates** that **differ** over the life of a project cannot be included in IRR calculations, although the **modified internal rate of return** (MIRR) method can incorporate them.

Given that there are two methods of using DCF, the NPV method and the IRR method, the relative merits of each method have to be considered. Which is better?

The **main advantage** of the **IRR** method is that the information it provides is more easily understood by managers, especially non-financial managers. For example, it is fairly easy to understand the meaning of the following statement.

'The project has an initial capital outlay of £100,000, and will earn a yield of 25%. This is in excess of the target yield of 15% for investments.'

It is not so easy to understand the meaning of this statement.

'The project will cost £100,000 and have an NPV of £30,000 when discounted at the minimum required rate of 15%.'

In other respects, the IRR method has serious disadvantages.

(a) It might be tempting to **confuse the IRR** and the **accounting ROCE**. The accounting ROCE and the IRR are two completely different measures. If managers were given information about both ROCE (or ROI) and IRR, it might be easy to get their meanings and significance mixed up.

(b) It ignores the relative size of investments. Both the following projects have an IRR of 18%.

	Project A	*Project B*
	€	€
Cost, year 0	350,000	35,000
Annual savings, years 1-6	100,000	10,000

Clearly, project A is bigger (ten times as big) and so more profitable but if the only information on which the projects were judged were to be their IRR of 18%, project B would seem just as beneficial as project A.

(c) If the cash flows from a project are **not conventional** (with an outflow at the beginning resulting in inflows over the life of a project) there may be more than one IRR. This could be very difficult for managers to interpret. For example, the following project has cash flows which are not conventional, and as a result has two IRRs of approximately 7% and 35%.

Year	*Project X*
	€'000
0	(1,900)
1	4,590
2	(2,735)

This deficiency can be overcome by using the modified internal rate of return. This method assumes that all cash flows after the initial investment can be reinvested at the cost of capital, and converts all the flows to a single cash inflow at the end of the project's life.

(d) The IRR method should not be used to select between mutually exclusive projects. This follows on from point (b) and it is the most significant and damaging criticism of the IRR method.

1.6 Example: mutually exclusive options

A company is considering two mutually exclusive options, option A and option B. The cash flows for each would be as follows.

Year		*Option A*	*Option B*
		£	£
0	Capital outlay	(10,200)	(35,250)
1	Net cash inflow	6,000	18,000
2	Net cash inflow	5,000	15,000
3	Net cash inflow	3,000	15,000

The company's cost of capital is 16%. Which option should be chosen?

Solution

The NPV of each project is calculated below.

		Option A		*Option B*	
Year	*Discount factor*	*Cashflow*	*Present value*	*Cashflow*	*Present value*
	16%	£	£	£	£
0	1.000	(10,200)	(10,200)	(35,250)	(35,250)
1	0.862	6,000	5,172	18,000	15,516
2	0.743	5,000	3,715	15,000	11,145
3	0.641	3,000	1,923	15,000	9,615
		NPV	+610		+1,026

However, the IRR of option A is 20% and the IRR of option B is only 18% (workings not shown). On a comparison of NPVs, option B would be preferred but, on a comparison of IRRs, option A would be preferred.

Option B should be chosen. This is because the differences in the cash flows between the two options, when discounted at the cost of capital of 16%, show that the present value of the incremental benefits from option B compared with option A exceed the PV of the incremental costs. This can be re-stated in the following ways.

(a) The NPV of the differential cash flows (option B cash flows minus option A cash flows) is positive, and so it is worth spending the extra capital to get the extra benefits.

(b) The IRR of the differential cash flows exceeds the cost of capital of 16%, and so it is worth spending the extra capital to get the extra benefits.

1.7 Reinvestment assumption

An assumption underlying the NPV method is that any net cash inflows generated during the life of the project will be reinvested elsewhere at the cost of capital (that is, the discount rate). The IRR method, on the other hand, assumes these **cash flows** can be **reinvested elsewhere** to earn a return equal to the IRR of the original project.

If the IRR is **considerably higher** than the **cost of capital** this is an unlikely assumption. If the assumption is not valid the IRR method overestimates the project's return.

1.8 Modified internal rate of return (MIRR) 11/06

The MIRR **overcomes the problem of the reinvestment assumption** and the fact that **changes in the cost of capital over the life of the project cannot be incorporated in the IRR method.**

Consider a project requiring an initial investment of $24,500, with cash inflows of $15,000 in years 1 and 2 and cash inflows of $3,000 in years 3 and 4. The cost of capital is 10%.

If we calculate the IRR:

Year	*Cash flow*	*Discount factor*	*Present value*	*Discount factor*	*Present value*
	$	10%	$	25%	$
0	(24,500)	1.000	(24,500)	1.000	(24,500)
1	15,000	0.909	13,635	0.800	12,000
2	15,000	0.826	12,390	0.640	9,600
3	3,000	0.751	2,253	0.512	1,536
4	3,000	0.683	2,049	0.410	1,230
			5,827		(134)

$$\text{IRR} = 10\% + \left[\frac{5{,}827}{5{,}827+134} \times (25\% - 10\%)\right] = 24.7\%$$

The MIRR is calculated on the basis of **investing the inflows** at the **cost of capital**.

The table below shows the **values of the inflows if they were immediately reinvested at 10%.** For example the $15,000 received at the end of year 1 could be reinvested for three years at 10% pa (multiply by 1.1 × 1.1 × 1.1 = 1.331).

Year	*Cash inflows*	*Interest rate multiplier*	*Amount when reinvested*
	$		$
1	15,000	1.331	19,965
2	15,000	1.21	18,150
3	3,000	1.1	3,300
4	3,000	1.0	3,000
			44,415

The **total cash outflow in year 0** ($24,500) is **compared with the possible inflow at year 4**, and the **resulting figure** of 24,500/44,415 = 0.552 is the **discount factor in year 4**. By **looking along the year 4 row** in present value tables you will see that this gives a **return of 16%**. This means that the $44,415 **received in year 4 is equivalent to $24,500 in year 0 if the discount rate is 16%.**

In theory the MIRR of 16% will be a **better measure** than the IRR of 24.7%.

1.8.1 Advantages of MIRR

MIRR has the advantage over IRR that it assumes the **reinvestment rate** is the **company's cost of capital**. IRR assumes that the reinvestment rate is the IRR itself, which is usually untrue.

In many cases where there is conflict between the NPV and IRR methods, the MIRR will give the same indication as NPV, which is the **correct theoretical method**. This helps when explaining the appraisal of a project to managers, who often find the concept of rate of return easier to understand than that of net present value.

1.8.2 Disadvantages of MIRR

However, MIRR, like all rate of return methods, suffers from the problem that it may lead an investor to reject a project which has a **lower rate of return** but, because of its size, generates a **larger increase in wealth**.

In the same way, a **high-return** project with a **short life** may be preferred over a **lower-return** project with a longer life.

Exam focus point

Question 4 in November 2006 involved a calculation of MIRR and a discussion of the appropriateness and advantages of its use. Candidates were generally unable to explain what the calculations meant so make sure you really understand any techniques you use.

1.9 Abandonment of investment

Net present value calculations can be used to assess whether it is worth abandoning a project, where costs are incurred after time 0. The possibility of abandoning a project can be dealt with in a more sophisticated way, using real options (covered in Chapter 19).

1.9.1 Example: the decision to abandon

Auckland decided in 20X0 to go ahead with a project, the projected costs and revenues of which were as follows.

	$'000
20X0	(200)
20X1	(1,200)
20X2	(1,100)
20X3	(1,300)
20X4	2,500
20X5	2,400

Auckland's cost of capital is 10%.

The actual expenditure in 20X1 was $2,400,000. As a result Auckland reassessed expenditure for 20X2 as $2,100,000 and expenditure in 20X3 as $1,900,000. It is now the end of 20X1.

On the basis of NPV calculations and using the information available at the time of decision, should Auckland have gone ahead with the project in 20X0?

Given the change in projected costs, should Auckland continue with the project?

Solution

(a)

Year		Discount factor 10%	Present value
	$'000		$'000
0(20X0)	(200)	1.000	(200)
1(20X1)	(1,200)	0.909	(1,091)
2(20X2)	(1,100)	0.826	(909)
3(20X3)	(1,300)	0.751	(976)
4(20X4)	2,500	0.683	1,708
5(20X5)	2,400	0.621	1,490
			22

On the basis of the NPV calculation, the decision to undertake the project in 20X0 was correct.

(b) As it is now the end of 20X1, the timeframe for the expenditure has changed.

Year		Discount factor10%	Present value
	$'000		$'000
1(20X2)	(2,100)	0.909	(1,909)
2(20X3)	(1,900)	0.826	(1,569)
3(20X4)	2,500	0.751	1,878
4(20X5)	2,400	0.683	1,639
			39

The project remains just about worthwhile with a small positive net present value.

Note that the actual expenditure for 20X1 was not brought into the calculation in (a) because information about it was not available at the time the appraisal should have been made, and was not brought into (b) because it is a sunk cost and thus not relevant.

However the evident limitations of Auckland's forecasting may mean that the directors abandon the project at the end of 20X1 because of the small size of the forecast positive net present value compared with the possible errors in forecasts. At any rate they would be well advised to undertake some sort of uncertainty or sensitivity analysis (discussed further in Chapter 19).

2 The use of appraisal methods in practice

FAST FORWARD

In practice many businesses use the simpler, easy to understand methods, although some are developing strategic investment appraisal techniques.

2.1 Capital investment evaluation methods

A survey of the use of capital investment evaluation methods in the UK carried out by RH Pike produced the following results on the frequency of use of different methods by 100 large UK firms.

Capital investment evaluation methods in 100 large UK firms: frequency of use

	Total	*Always*	*Mostly*	*Often*	*Rarely*
Firms using	%	%	%	%	%
Payback	94	62	14	12	6
Accounting rate of return	56	21	5	13	17
Internal rate of return	81	54	7	13	7
Net present value	74	33	14	16	11

(Source: Pike & Neale, *Corporate Finance and Investment*)

Almost two-thirds of the firms surveyed by Pike used three or more appraisal techniques, indicating that DCF techniques complement rather than replace more traditional approaches.

The following points are worth noting.

(a) The **payback method** is used in the great majority (94%) of companies surveyed. Although it remains a traditional 'rule-of-thumb method' with limited theoretical justification because it ignores the profile of cash flows and cash flows beyond the payback period, it will provide in practice a **fair approximation** to the **net present value** method.

(b) In spite of its theoretical limitations (notably, its failure to take account of the time value of money), the **ARR method** was used in half of the companies surveyed. This is perhaps to be expected, given the importance in practice of the rate of return on capital as a financial goal.

(c) The data shows a preference for the **IRR method** over the **NPV method**. It would appear that, in spite of theoretical reasons that favour NPV, the IRR method is preferred by managers as a convenient way of ranking projects in percentage terms.

2.2 Strategic investment appraisal

Strategic investment appraisal has been defined as 'linking corporate strategy to costs and benefits associated with AMT adoption by combining both formal and informal evaluation procedures.' Formal appraisal methods may be of limited practical use when considering the acquisition of AMT, because of the strategic (often non-quantifiable) issues involved.

Key term

> **Strategic investment appraisal** is a method of investment appraisal which allows the inclusion of both financial and non-financial factors. Project benefits are appraised in terms of their contribution to the strategies of the organisation, either by their financial contribution or, for non-financial benefits, by the use of index numbers or other means. *(OT 2005)*

Management accountants are beginning to accept the need for a more external orientation and a consideration of the longer-term effects in investment appraisal generally, particularly in those organisations which operate in rapidly changing markets with a high level of uncertainty. You should by now be aware of the importance of combining formal and informal procedures, as well as short-term and long-term considerations, in effective capital investment appraisal.

TOPCIMA link

> 10 – 15 marks may be available in the case study for an investment appraisal. The calculations you do will need to be used to justify recommendations and explain problems.

3 Allowing for inflation in DCF

FAST FORWARD

- (1+ money rate of return) = (1 + real rate of return) × (1 + rate of inflation)
- **Real cash flows** should be discounted at a **real discount rate**.
- **Money cash flows** should be discounted at a **money discount rate**.

3.1 Effects of inflation

In our revision of the DCF approach to investment appraisal so far we have not considered the effect of inflation. Inflation may affect both the cash flows of the project and the rate at which they are discounted – the higher the expected rate of inflation, the higher will be the required return to compensate.

The incorporation of inflation into DCF computations was covered in your earlier studies; we now briefly revise this.

Knowledge brought forward

DCF and inflation

- In an inflationary environment, cash flows in a project may be given in **money terms** (the actual cash that will arise) or **real terms** (in today's currency).
- Similarly, the required rate of return on an investment may be given as a *money* rate of return (including an allowance for a general rate of inflation) or as a **real** rate of return (the return required over and above inflation).

Exam Formula

The two rates of return and the inflation rate are linked by the equation:

1 + nominal (money) rate of return = (1 + real interest rate)(1 + inflation rate)

Knowledge brought forward (continued)

- If cash flows are given in money terms, the money rate should be used to discount them; if the flows are in real terms, the real rate of return may be used to discount them, although this may not always result in the same answer (see next point).
- If some of the cost or revenues relating to the project **inflate at rates different from the general rate of inflation**, it is **not** appropriate to discount real flows at the real rate. Instead, **money flows must be computed**, by applying the relevant rates of inflation to the real flows, which must then be discounted at the money required return.

Question

Effect of inflation

Learning outcome: D(ii)

Rice is considering a project which would cost £5,000 now. The annual benefits, for four years, would be a fixed income of £2,500 a year, plus other savings of £500 a year in year 1, rising by 5% each year because of inflation. Running costs will be £1,000 in the first year, but would increase at 10% each year because of inflating labour costs. The general rate of inflation is expected to be 7½% and the company's required money rate of return is 16%. Is the project worthwhile? (Ignore taxation.)

Answer

The cash flows at inflated values are as follows.

Year	*Fixed income*	*Other savings*	*Running costs*	*Net cash flow*
	£	£	£	£
1	2,500	500	1,000	2,000
2	2,500	525	1,100	1,925
3	2,500	551	1,210	1,841
4	2,500	579	1,331	1,748

The NPV of the project is as follows.

Year	*Cash flow*	*Discount factor*	*PV*
	£	16%	£
0	(5,000)	1.000	(5,000)
1	2,000	0.862	1,724
2	1,925	0.743	1,430
3	1,841	0.641	1,180
4	1,748	0.552	965
			+ 299

The NPV is positive and the project would appear to be worthwhile.

3.2 Expectations of inflation and the effects of inflation

When managers evaluate a particular project, or when shareholders evaluate their investments, they can only guess at what the rate of inflation is going to be. Their expectations will probably be wrong, at least to some extent, because it is extremely difficult to forecast the rate of inflation accurately. The only way in which uncertainty about inflation can be allowed for in project evaluation is by risk and uncertainty analysis.

We stated earlier that costs and benefits may rise at levels different from the general rate of inflation: inflation may be **general,** affecting prices of all kinds, or **specific** to particular prices. Generalised inflation has the following effects.

(a) Since **non-current assets, inventories** and **other working capital** will **increase in money value**, the same quantities of assets or working capital must be financed by **increasing amounts of capital**.

(b) Inflation means higher costs and higher selling prices. The effect of higher prices on demand is not necessarily easy to predict. A company that raises its prices by 10% because the general rate of inflation is running at 10% might suffer a serious fall in demand.

(c) Inflation, because it affects financing needs, is also likely to affect gearing, and so the cost of capital.

4 Allowing for taxation in DCF 11/05

FAST FORWARD

In investment appraisal, tax is often assumed to be payable **one year in arrears,** but you should read the question details carefully.

Tax allowable depreciation details should be checked in any question you attempt.

4.1 Effects of taxation

So far, in looking at project appraisal, we have also ignored **taxation**. However, payments of tax, or reductions of tax payments, are cash flows and ought to be considered in DCF analysis. Again the basics were covered in your previous studies, and you may only need to skim through the next few sections of text to remind yourself.

Exam focus point

The tax rules might be simplified for an examination question and, as mentioned earlier, you should read any question carefully to establish what tax rules and rates to use. In November 2005 the effect of a double tax treaty needed to be brought into an NPV calculation.

Typical assumptions which may be stated in questions are as follows.

(a) An assumption about the timing of payments will have to be made.

- Half the tax is **payable** in the **same year** in which the **profits are earned** and **half in the following year.** This reflects the fact that large companies have to pay tax **quarterly** in some regimes.
- Tax is payable in the **year following** the one in which the taxable profits are made. Thus, if a project increases taxable profits by $10,000 in year 2, there will be a tax payment, assuming tax at (say) 30%, of $3,000 in year 3.
- Tax is payable in the **same year** that the **profits arise.**

The question should make clear what assumptions you should use.

(b) Net cash flows from a project should be considered as the taxable profits arising from the project (unless an indication is given to the contrary).

4.2 Tax-allowable depreciation

Tax allowable depreciation is used to reduce taxable profits, and the consequent reduction in a tax payment should be treated as a cash saving arising from the acceptance of a project.

For example, suppose tax-allowable depreciation is allowed on the cost of **plant and machinery** at the rate of 25% on a **reducing balance** basis. Thus if a company purchases plant costing $80,000, the subsequent writing down allowances would be as follows.

Year		*Tax-allowable depreciation*	*Reducing balance*
		$	$
1	(25% of cost)	20,000	60,000
2	(25% of RB)	15,000	45,000
3	(25% of RB)	11,250	33,750
4	(25% of RB)	8,438	25,312

When the plant is eventually sold, the difference between the sale price and the reducing balance amount at the time of sale will be treated as:

(a) A taxable profit if the sale price exceeds the reducing balance, and
(b) A tax-allowable loss if the reducing balance exceeds the sale price

Exam focus point

Examination questions often assume that this loss will be available immediately, though in practice the balance less the sale price may continue to be written off at 25% a year as part of a pool balance.

The cash saving on the tax-allowable depreciation (or the cash payment for the charge) is calculated by multiplying the depreciation (or charge) by the tax rate.

Assumptions about tax-allowable depreciation could be simplified in an exam question. For example, you might be told that tax-allowable depreciation can be claimed at the rate of 25% of cost on a straight line basis (that is, over four years).

There are two possible assumptions about the time when tax-allowable depreciation start to be claimed.

(a) It can be assumed that the **first claim** occurs at the **start of the project** (at year 0).
(b) Alternatively it can be assumed that the **first claim** occurs **later in the first year**.

You should state clearly which assumption you have made. Assumption (b) is more prudent, but assumption (a) is also perfectly feasible. It is very likely, however that an examination question will indicate which of the two assumptions is required.

4.3 Example: taxation

A company is considering whether or not to purchase an item of machinery costing £40,000 in 20X5. It would have a life of four years, after which it would be sold for £5,000. The machinery would create annual cost savings of £14,000.

The machinery would attract tax-allowable depreciation of 25% on the reducing balance basis which could be claimed against taxable profits of the current year, which is soon to end. A balancing allowance or charge would arise on disposal. The tax rate is 30%. Tax is payable half in the current year, half one year in arrears. The after-tax cost of capital is 8%.

Should the machinery be purchased?

Solution

Tax-allowable depreciation is first claimed against year 0 profits.

Cost: £40,000

Year	*Tax-allowable depreciation*	*Reducing balance (RB)*	
	£	£	
(0) 20X5 (25% of cost)	10,000	30,000	(40,000 – 10,000)
(1) 20X6 (25% of RB)	7,500	22,500	(30,000 – 7,500)
(2) 20X7 (25% of RB)	5,625	16,875	(22,500 – 5,625)
(3) 20X8 (25% of RB)	4,219	12,656	(16,875 – 4,219)
(4) 20X9 (25% of RB)	3,164	9,492	(12,656 – 3,164)

	£
Sale proceeds, end of fourth year	5,000
Less reducing balance, end of fourth year	9,492
Balancing allowance	4,492

Having calculated the depreciation each year, the tax savings can be computed. The year of the cash flow is one year after the year for which the allowance is claimed.

Year of claim	*Tax-allowable depreciation*	*Tax saved*	*Year of tax payment/saving*
	£	£	(50% in each)
0	10,000	3,000	0/1
1	7,500	2,250	1/2
2	5,625	1,688	2/3
3	4,219	1,266	3/4
4	7,656	2,297	4/5
	35,000 *		

* Net cost £(40,000 – 5,000) = £35,000

These tax savings relate to tax-allowable depreciation. We must also calculate the extra tax payments on annual savings of £14,000.

The net cash flows and the NPV are now calculated as follows.

Year	*Equip-ment*	*Savings*	*Tax on savings*	*Tax saved on tax-allowable depreciation*	*Net cash flow*	*Discount factor*	*Present value of cash flow*
	£	£	£	£	£	8%	£
0	(40,000)			1,500	(38,500)	1.000	(38,500)
1		14,000	(2,100)	2,625	14,525	0.926	13,450
2		14,000	(4,200)	1,969	11,769	0.857	10,086
3		14,000	(4,200)	1,477	11,277	0.794	8,954
4	5,000	14,000	(4,200)	1,782	16,582	0.735	12,188
5			(2,100)	1,148	(952)	0.681	(648)
							5,530

The NPV is positive and so the purchase appears to be worthwhile.

4.3.1 An alternative and quicker method of calculating tax payments or savings

In the above example, the tax computations could have been combined, as follows.

Year	*0*	*1*	*2*	*3*	*4*
	£	£	£	£	£
Cost savings	0	14,000	14,000	14,000	14,000
Tax-allowable depreciation	10,000	7,500	5,625	4,219	7,656
Taxable profits	(10,000)	6,500	8,375	9,781	6,344
Tax at 30%	3,000	(1,950)	(2,512)	(2,934)	(1,903)

The net cash flows would then be as follows.

Year	*Equipment*	*Savings*	*Tax*	*Net cash flow*
	£	£	£	£
0	(40,000)		1,500	(38,500)
1		14,000	525	14,525
2		14,000	(2,231)	11,769
3		14,000	(2,723)	11,277
4	5,000	14,000	(2,418)	16,582
5			(952)	(952)

The net cash flows are exactly the same as calculated previously.

4.4 Taxation and DCF

The effect of taxation on capital budgeting is theoretically quite simple. Organisations must pay tax, and the effect of undertaking a project will be to increase or decrease tax payments each year. These incremental tax cash flows should be included in the cash flows of the project for discounting to arrive at the project's NPV.

When **taxation is ignored** in the DCF calculations, the discount rate will **reflect the pre-tax rate of return** required on capital investments. When taxation is included in the cash flows, a **post-tax required rate of return** should be used.

If there is inflation and tax in a question, remember that tax flows do not get inflated by an extra year even though they may be paid one year later.

Question

Effect of taxation

Learning outcome: D(iii)

A project requires an initial investment in machinery of $300,000. Additional cash inflows of $120,000 at current price levels are expected for three years, at the end of which time the machinery will be scrapped. The machinery will attract tax-allowable depreciation of 25% on the reducing balance basis, which can be claimed against taxable profits of the current year, which is soon to end. A balancing charge or allowance will arise on disposal.

The tax rate is 50% and tax is payable 50% in the current year, 50% one year in arrears. The pre-tax cost of capital is 22% and the rate of inflation is 10%. Assume that the project is 100% debt financed.

Required

Assess whether the project should be undertaken.

Answer

Post-tax: Year	*Purchase*	*Inflation factor*	*Cash flow after inflation*	*Tax on cash inflow*	*(W1-3) Tax saved on tax-allowable depreciation*	*Net cash flow*	*Discount factor*	*Present value*
	$		$	$	$	$	11%	$
0	(300,000)	1.000	(300,000)		18,750	(281,250)	1.000	(281,250)
1		1.100	132,000	(33,000)	32,813	131,813	0.901	118,764
2		1.210	145,200	(69,300)	24,609	100,509	0.812	81,613
3		1.331	159,720	(76,230)	42,187	125,677	0.731	91,870
4				(39,930)	31,640	(8,290)	0.659	(5,463)
							NPV =	5,534

The project should be undertaken at least from the financial viewpoint.

Workings

1 **Tax-allowable depreciation** (Initial cost $300,000)

Year		*Tax-allowable depreciation*	*Reducing balance (RB)*
		$	$
0	(25% at cost)	75,000	225,000
1	(25% of RB)	56,250	168,750
2	(25% of RB)	42,188	126,562
3	(25% of RB)	31,641	94,921

2 **Balancing allowance**

	$
Sale proceeds, end of third year	–
RB, end of third year	94,921
Balancing allowance	94,921

3 **Tax saved on tax-allowable depreciation**

Year of claim	*Tax-allowable depreciation claimed*	*Tax saved*	*Year of tax saving*
	$	$	
0	75,000	37,500	0/1
1	56,250	28,125	1/2
2	42,188	21,094	2/3
3	126,562	63,281	3/4
	300,000		

5 International investment appraisal 5/05, 11/05, 5/06, 11/06

FAST FORWARD

Complications in DCF appraisals of international investments include exchange rates, differing inflation rates, withholding taxes and restrictions on remittances.

5.1 Foreign project appraisal

International capital budgeting can be based on similar concepts to those used in the purely domestic case.

Before looking at the techniques of foreign project appraisal, we will first consider the most appropriate cost of capital to be used as a basis for the discount rate.

5.2 The international cost of capital

The **weighted average cost of capital** (WACC) of a firm is the weighted average of the costs to the firm of providing the returns **currently** required by its investors, the shareholders and debt holders. Whilst this is very often used as the discount rate for DCF appraisals of new projects, we have already noted that this may not always be appropriate.

It will be appropriate to adopt the firm's WACC as a discount rate if the following two conditions are satisfied.

(a) The **systematic risk** associated with the investment should be **similar** to that of the **firm's other investments**. In this context, we assume that the company's shareholders hold the shares within a well diversified portfolio.

(b) The **method of financing** of the project should **not affect the level of gearing** of the company.

An overseas project may alter the firm's total risk. **Political risk** and **currency risk**, both of which are **unsystematic**, are likely to increase. Total risk may be allowed for by:

(a) **Adjusting** the **discount rate** for **total risk**, or

(b) **Accounting for risk in projected cash flows**, using a discount rate adjusted for systematic business risk and financial risk as in the case of a domestic project

In practice, it is common for firms to add a **premium** to the discount rate to account for risk. In comparing different approaches to adjusting for risk, the different characteristics of the special risks involved in international investment should be noted.

(a) **Political risk** is generally the risk of an adverse outcome in the form of possible expropriation of assets resulting from currently unforeseen changes in the political climate. If political risk were to be adjusted for through the discount rate, all cash flows would be affected.

(b) **Currency risk** can have either favourable or adverse effects on the project cashflows. Instead of adjusting the discount rate, it is more appropriate to adjust for this 'two-way' risk by reflecting alternative outcomes in the cash flow forecasts themselves.

5.3 Effects of international portfolio diversification

As already discussed, internationalisation of a portfolio provides a means of reducing the risk of the portfolio. For a firm contemplating a foreign investment, the **degree** of **correlation** between returns on the stock markets of the two countries involved provides an indication of the level of systematic risk associated with the investment: the lower is the correlation coefficient, the lower is the likely level of **systematic risk**.

The possibility of lowering systematic risk through international investment suggests that a lower discount rate is appropriate for overseas investments. However, whether this is reasonable depends upon whether it is true that shareholders will accept a lower return on their equity in an internationally diversified firm for the reason that there is a **reduction in the domestic (home-country) systematic risk**. This is likely to be the case if the multinational firm is enabling shareholders to achieve international diversification that they would **not otherwise be able to achieve**, perhaps because of regulatory restrictions.

5.4 The techniques for foreign project appraisal

5/05, 11/05, 5/06, 11/06

Depending upon the information which is available, two alternative NPV methods are available. Both methods produce the NPV in domestic currency terms. For a UK company investing overseas, we can:

(a) **Convert the project cash flows** into **sterling** and then discount at a sterling discount rate to calculate the NPV in sterling terms, or

(b) **Discount the cash flows** in the **host country's currency** from the project at an adjusted discount rate for that currency and then convert the resulting NPV at the spot exchange rate.

The approach to be chosen will depend on the available information and the extent to which **forecasts are reliable.** Both approaches should give the same answer, provided that the approach used to predict future exchange rates (**interest rate parity or purchasing power parity**) holds true.

Exam focus point

Question 1 in the May 2005 exam required you to use both methods and compare the two. In November 2005 Question 1, it was much quicker to adjust the discount factor and then convert at the spot rate.

There are, however, some special considerations in the international case, including the following.

(a) For the purpose of assessing how expected **performance** compares with potential performance, it is necessary to **compare the project's net present value** with those of **similar host country projects**. This involves measuring the cash flows in terms of the **currency of the host country**.

(b) A foreign project also needs to be evaluated on its net present value in respect of the **funds which can be remitted to the parent**. The purpose of this second stage is to evaluate whether the cash flow remitted justifies the cash invested from the home country. As we discussed in the last chapter, the host country may place restrictions on the amounts that can be remitted.

(c) Cash flows from the subsidiary may come about through a variety of means, including **licensing fees** and **payments for imports** from the parent company.

(d) The possibility of **differing national rates of inflation** needs to be taken into account.

You may need to use these formulae.

Exam formulae

Adjusted discount rate to use in international capital budgeting

$$\frac{1+\text{annual discount rate C\$}}{1+\text{annual discount rate Euro}} = \frac{\text{Exchange rate in 12 months' time C\$/Euro}}{\text{Spot rate C\$/Euro}}$$

Interest rate parity (International Fisher Effect)

$$\text{Forward rate US\$/£} = \text{Spot rate US\$/£} \times \frac{1+\text{nominal US interest rate}}{1+\text{nominal UK interest rate}}$$

Purchasing power parity

$$\text{Forward rate US\$/£} = \text{Spot rate US\$/£} \times \frac{1+\text{US inflation rate}}{1+\text{UK inflation rate}}$$

Exam focus point

In November 2005, the examiner noted that the calculation of forward rates and conversion of $ to £ was surprisingly poor. Make sure you are confident with these calculations, they were also required in May and November 2006 papers.

5.5 Example: overseas investment appraisal

Bromwich, a UK company, is considering undertaking a new project in Horavia. This will require initial capital expenditure of H$1,250m, with no scrap value envisaged at the end of the five year lifespan of the project. There will also be an initial working capital requirement of H$500m, which will be recovered at the end of the project. Pre-tax net cash inflows of H$800m are expected to be generated each year from the project.

Company tax will be charged in Horavia at a rate of 40%, with depreciation on a straight-line basis being an allowable deduction for tax purposes. Horavian tax is paid at the end of the year following that in which the taxable profits arise.

There is a double taxation agreement between the UK and Horavia, which means that no UK tax will be payable on the project profits.

The current H$/£ spot rate is 336, and the Horavian dollar is expected to appreciate against the £ by 5% per year.

A project of similar risk recently undertaken by Bromwich in the UK had a required post-tax rate of return of 16%.

Should the Horavian project be undertaken?

Solution

Method 1 – conversion of flows into sterling and discounting at sterling discount rate

Time	*0*	*1*	*2*	*3*	*4*	*5*	*6*
H$m flows							
Capital	(1,750)					500	
Net cash inflows		800	800	800	800	800	
Taxation (W1)			(220)	(220)	(220)	(220)	(220)
	(1,750)	800	580	580	580	1,080	(220)
Exchange rate (W2)	336	319	303	288	274	260	247
£m flows	(5.21)	2.51	1.91	2.01	2.12	4.15	(0.89)
16% df	1	0.862	0.743	0.641	0.552	0.476	0.410
PV	(5.21)	2.16	1.42	1.29	1.17	1.98	(0.36)

NPV = £2.45m

Workings

1 *Taxation*

	H$m
Net cash inflow	800
Less: depreciation (1,250/5)	(250)
	550 @ 40% = H$220m

2 *Exchange rate*

Current spot = H$336/£. If the H$ is *appreciating* against the £, this means that the H$ is getting more valuable in terms of £, ie there will be more £ per H$ or *less H$ per £*.

Thus in one year's time the H$/£ rate will fall by 5%, to 95% × 336 = 319, etc.

Method 2 – discounting foreign cash flows at an adjusted discount rate

If we are to keep the cash flows in H$, and they need to be discounted at a rate that takes account of both the domestic discount rate (16%) and the rate at which the exchange rate is expected to decrease (5%). This is in fact an application of the **interest rate parity theorem.**

$$\frac{1+\text{Horavian interest rate}}{1+\text{UK interest rate}} = \frac{\text{Forward rate H\$/£}}{\text{Spot rate H\$/£}}$$

$$\frac{1+1_H}{1.16} = \frac{319}{336}$$

$1 + I_H = 1.10$

Thus the adjusted discount rate is 10%.

Discounting the H$ flows at this rate:

Time	*0*	*1*	*2*	*3*	*4*	*5*	*6*
H$m flows							
Capital	(1,750)	800	580	580	580	1,080	(220)
10% df	1	0.909	0.826	0.751	0.683	0.621	0.564
PV	(1,750)	727.1	479.1	435.6	396.1	670.7	(124.1)

NPV = H$834.6m

Translating this present value at the spot rate gives H$834.6/336 = £2.48m

This method is useful if the currency flows are annuities and the adjusted discount rate is a round number, as the computation can be reduced by the use of annuity tables.

Question — Establishment of foreign subsidiary

Learning outcome: D(ii)

Donegal is considering whether to establish a subsidiary in Ruritania, at a cost of Ruritanian $2,400,000. This would be represented by non-current assets of $2,000,000 and working capital of $400,000. The subsidiary would produce a product which would achieve annual sales of $1,600,000 and incur cash expenditures of $1,000,000 a year.

The company has a planning horizon of four years, at the end of which it expects the realisable value of the subsidiary's non-current assets to be $800,000. It expects also to be able to sell the rights to make the product for $500,000 at the end of four years.

It is the company's policy to remit the maximum funds possible to the parent company at the end of each year.

Tax is payable at the rate of 35% in Ruritania and is payable one year in arrears.

Tax allowable depreciation is at a rate of 25% on a straight line basis on all non-current assets.

Administration costs of £100,000 per annum will be incurred each year in the UK over the expected life of the project.

The UK taxation rate on taxable profits made in Ruritania and remitted to the UK, and on UK income and expenditure is 30%, payable one year in arrears.

The Ruritanian $:£ exchange rate is 5:1.

The company's cost of capital for the project is 10%.

Calculate the NPV of the project.

Answer

			Time			
$'000 cash flows	*0*	*1*	*2*	*3*	*4*	*5*
Sales receipts		1,600	1,600	1,600	1,600	
Costs		(1,000)	(1,000)	(1,000)	(1,000)	
Tax allowable depreciation (brought in to calculate taxable profit)		(500)	(500)	(500)	(500)	
$ taxable profit		100	100	100	100	
Taxation			(35)	(35)	(35)	(35)
Add back tax allowable depreciation (as not a cash flow)		500	500	500	500	
Capital expenditure	(2,000)					
Scrap value					800	
Tax on scrap value (W1)						(280)
Terminal value					500	
Tax on terminal value						(175)
Working capital	(400)				400	
	(2,400)	600	565	565	2,265	(490)
Exchange rates	5:1	5:1	5:1	5:1	5:1	5:1
£'000 cash flows						
From/(to) Ruritania	(480)	120	113	113	453	(98)
Additional UK tax (W2)			(6)	(6)	(6)	(84)
Additional UK expenses/income		(100)	(100)	(100)	(100)	
UK tax effect of UK expenses/income			30	30	30	30
Net sterling cash flows	(480)	20	37	37	377	(152)
UK discount factors	1	0.909	0.826	0.751	0.683	0.621
Present values	(480)	18	31	28	257	(94)

NPV = (£240,000), therefore the company should not proceed.

Working 1

Tax is payable on $800,000 as tax written down value = $2,000,000 – (4 × $500,000) = 0

Working 2

Years 1-3

$ taxable profit = $100,000
At 5:1 exchange rate = £20,000
Tax at 30% = £6,000

Year 4

$ taxable profit = $100,000 + $800,000 + $500,000
= $1,400,000

At 5:1 exchange rate = £280,000

Tax at 30% = £84,000

Assume tax is fully payable in both countries.

Chapter roundup

- The **payback method** of project appraisal and the **ARR/ROCE/ROI method** of project appraisal are popular appraisal techniques despite their limitations.
- There are two methods of using **discounted cash flow** to appraise investment projects, the NPV method and the IRR/DCF yield method.
- The **NPV method** of project appraisal is to accept projects with a positive NPV.
- The **IRR method** of project appraisal is to accept projects whose IRR (the rate at which the NPV is zero) exceeds a target rate of return. The IRR is estimated either from a graph or using interpolation. The formula to apply is $IRR = A + \frac{N_A}{N_A - N_B}(B - A)$.
- When compared with the NPV method, the **IRR method** has a number of **disadvantages**.
  - It **ignores** the **relative size** of investments.
  - It is difficult to use if a project has **non-conventional cashflows** or when deciding between **mutually exclusive projects**.
  - **Discount rates** that **differ** over the life of a project cannot be included in IRR calculations, although the **modified internal rate of return** (MIRR) method can incorporate them.
- In practice many businesses use the simpler, easy to understand methods, although some are developing strategic investment appraisal techniques.
- (1+ money rate of return) = (1 + real rate of return) × (1 + rate of inflation)
- **Real cash flows** should be discounted at a **real discount rate**.
- **Money cash flows** should be discounted at a **money discount rate**.
- In investment appraisal, tax is often assumed to be payable **one year in arrears,** but you should read the question details carefully.
- **Tax allowable depreciation** details should be checked in any question you attempt.
- **Complications in DCF appraisals of international investments include** exchange rates, differing inflation rates, withholding taxes and restrictions on remittances.

Quick quiz

1 **Fill in the blank.**

.... is 'the time required for the cash inflows from a capital investment project to equal the cash outflows.' *(OT 2005)*

2 **Fill in the blank.**

.... is 'a periodic payment continuing for a limitless period.' *(OT 2005)*

3 Match up each term with the appropriate definition.

Terms

(A) Net terminal value

(B) Net present value

(C) Present value

Definitions

(1) The value obtained by discounting all cash outflows and inflows of a capital investment project at a chosen target rate of return or cost of capital.

(2) The cash equivalent now of a sum of money receivable or payable at a stated future date, discounted at a specified rate of return.

(3) The cash surplus remaining at the end of a project after taking account of interest and capital repayments.

4 Group the following items that occur in investment appraisal question under the following headings.

☐ Include in investment appraisal ☐ Exclude from investment appraisal

- Depreciation
- Sunk costs
- Opportunity costs
- Allocated costs and revenues
- After tax incremental cash flows
- Effect of tax allowances
- Dividend/interest
- Working capital requirements

5 Which equation links the money rate of return and the real rate of return?

6 Are cash flows that are given in terms of today's pounds being given in money or real terms?

7 How should the domestic discount rate be adjusted if the foreign project flows are to be discounted?

8 On what assumption is the Modified Internal Rate of Return based?

Answers to quick quiz

1 The payback period

2 A perpetuity

3 (A) (3)
(B) (1)
(C) (2)

4

Include in **investment appraisal**	**Exclude** from **investment appraisal**
• Opportunity costs	• Depreciation
• After tax incremental cash flows	• Sunk costs
• Effect of tax allowances	• Allocated costs and revenues
• Working capital requirements	• Dividends/interest

5 1 + money (nominal) rate of return = (1 + real rate) (1 + inflation rate)

6 Real terms

7 1 + adjusted discount rate = (1 + domestic discount rate)(1 + expected rate at which foreign exchange rate is expected to change)

8 Cash inflows are invested at the cost of capital

Now try the questions below from the Exam Question Bank

Number	Level	Marks	Time
Q30	Introductory	n/a	35 mins
Q31	Introductory	n/a	35 mins

19

Applications of discounted cash flow

Introduction

In this chapter, we examine some further **applications of discounted cash flow (DCF)** techniques revised in the previous chapter. An enterprise may be faced with more investment opportunities than it can finance with the capital available, and we look first at how **capital rationing** may affect the investment decision.

We then examine various techniques that can be used to deal with complications in investment decisions. The **equivalent annual cost** method can be used when maintenance costs are an important element in an investment decision. **Real option theory** can be used to assist when organisations have to or can make further decisions after the initial investment decision. The **adjusted present value method** provides a better means of taking into account the effects of using loan finance than simple NPV analysis does. Sections 5-9 deal with various methods of accounting for, and dealing with, risk.

All of these techniques could be included by the examiner in order to make the investment appraisal question more demanding. In particular real options theory is being used more and more in practice, and thus could well be included as a part question in your exam.

Topic list	Learning outcomes	Syllabus references	Ability required
1 Capital rationing	D(v)	D(12)	Evaluation
2 The annualised cost of a capital item	D(ii)	D(4)	Evaluation
3 Capital investment real options	D(i), (ii)	D(9)	Evaluation
4 The adjusted present value method	D(i), (ii), (iii)	D(8)	Evaluation
5 Sensitivity analysis	D(i), (ii)	D(4)	Evaluation
6 Certainty equivalents	D(i), (ii)	D(7)	Evaluation
7 Probability analysis	D(i), (ii)	D(4)	Evaluation
8 Simulation models	D(i), (ii)	D(4)	Evaluation
9 Ways of reducing risk	D(i), (ii)	D(4)	Evaluation

1 Capital rationing 5/06

FAST FORWARD

Capital rationing may occur due to internal factors (**soft** capital rationing) or external factors (**hard** capital rationing).

When capital rationing occurs in a **single period, divisible** projects are ranked in terms of a **profitability index. Trial and error NPV calculations** should be used to rank **indivisible projects**.

1.1 Restrictions on investment

We saw in the last chapter that the decision rule with DCF techniques is to accept all projects which result in positive NPVs when discounted at the company's cost of capital. If an entity suffers **capital rationing**, it will not be able to enter into all projects with positive NPVs because there is not enough capital for all the investments.

Key term

Capital rationing is a restriction on an organisation's ability to invest capital funds, caused by an internal budget ceiling being imposed on such expenditure by management (**soft capital rationing**), or by external limitations being applied to the company, as when additional borrowed funds cannot be obtained (**hard capital rationing**). *(OT 2005)*

Exam focus point

Always read the question carefully and apply any discussion to the specific organisation. Question 5 in May 2006 concerned a public sector organisation which is subject to debate as to whether capital rationing techniques are appropriate.

Managers are therefore faced with the problem of deciding which projects to invest in. The decision technique to be applied will depend on the type of capital rationing. **Single period capital rationing** is where capital is limited for the current period only but will be freely available in the future. **Multi-period capital rationing** is where capital will be limited for several periods.

Exam focus point

Multi period capital rationing is excluded from your syllabus.

1.2 Divisible and non-divisible projects

Before we look at some examples of single period capital rationing we need to distinguish between divisible projects and non-divisible projects.

(a) **Divisible projects** are those which can be undertaken completely or in fractions. Suppose that project A is divisible and requires the investment of £15,000 to achieve an NPV of £4,000. £7,500 invested in project A will earn an NPV of ½ × £4,000 = £2,000.

(b) **Indivisible projects** are those which must be undertaken completely or not at all. It is not possible to invest in a fraction of the project.

You may also encounter **mutually exclusive** projects when one, and only one, of two or more choices of project can be undertaken.

1.3 Single period rationing with divisible projects

With **single period capital rationing**, investment funds are a limiting factor in the current period. The total return will be maximised if management follows the decision rule of maximising the return per unit of the limiting factor. They should therefore **select those projects whose cash inflows have the highest present value per £1 of capital invested.** In other words, rank the projects according to their **profitability index.**

Key term

Profitability index = $\frac{\text{Present value of cash inflow}}{\text{Initial investment}}$ *(OT 2005)*

Note that the same rankings will result from the use of the ratio of **net present value** of the project (ie after deducting the initial investment) to the initial investment, which may be referred to as the **benefit-cost ratio.**

Note that the use of the PI assumes a 'standard' project, with one initial outlay, followed by a series of inflows.

1.4 Example: single period rationing with divisible projects

Short O'Funds has capital of £130,000 available for investment in the forthcoming period, at a cost of capital of 20%. Capital will be freely available in the future. Details of six projects under consideration are as follows. All projects are independent and divisible. Which projects should be undertaken and what NPV will result?

Project	*Investment required*	*Present value of inflows at 20%*
	£'000	£'000
P	40	56.5
Q	50	67.0
R	30	48.8
S	45	59.0
T	15	22.4
U	20	30.8

Solution

The first step is to rank the projects according to the return achieved from the limiting factor of investment funds.

Project	*PV inflows*	*Investment*	*PV per £1 invested*	*Ranking*
	£'000	£'000	£	
P	56.5	40	1.41	4
Q	67.0	50	1.34	5
R	48.8	30	1.63	1
S	59.0	45	1.31	6
T	22.4	15	1.49	3
U	30.8	20	1.54	2

The available funds of £130,000 can now be allocated.

Project	*Investment*		*PV*
	£'000		£'000
R	30		48.8
U	20		30.8
T	15		22.4
P	40		56.5
Q (balance)	25	(1/2)	33.5
	130	Maximum PV =	192.0

Project S should not be undertaken and only half of project Q should be undertaken.

The resulting total NPV generated will be 192.0 – 130 = £62,000.

Note that the PI can be used as a project appraisal method in its own right. The decision rule to apply will be to accept all projects with a PI greater than one (in which case, PV inflows > initial investment, ie NPV > 0).

Exam focus point

Read the question carefully to determine when the capital restriction will occur. Question 5 in May 2006 stated that the capital restriction occurred in Year 1 but it gave Year 0 and Year 1 cash outflow information.

1.5 Advantages of the PI method

(a) Similar to the NPV method, usually **giving the same result** on **individual projects**
(b) Can be used to rank divisible projects in conditions of **capital rationing**

1.6 Disadvantages of the PI method

(a) PI indicates **relative returns** and is not an absolute measure

(b) The PI method may **rank projects incorrectly** (If cash is not rationed, it is preferable to look at the NPV, which is an absolute measure.)

(c) **Establishing** what is the **initial investment** may **not be straightforward** (The PI method works well only if the project has an outflow of cash at time 0, followed by cash inflows which may be at various times.)

1.7 Single period rationing with indivisible projects

If the projects are **not divisible** then the method shown in the last paragraph may not result in the optimal solution. Another complication which arises is that there is likely to be a small amount of **unused capital** with each combination of projects. The best way to deal with this situation is to use **trial and error** and test the NPV available from different combinations of projects. This can be a laborious process if there are a large number of projects available. We will continue with the previous example to demonstrate the technique.

1.8 Example: single period rationing with indivisible projects

Short O'Funds now discovers that funds in the forthcoming period are actually restricted to £95,000. The directors decide to consider projects P, Q and R only. They wish to invest only in whole projects, but surplus funds can be invested to earn 25% per annum in perpetuity. Which combination of projects will produce the highest NPV at a cost of capital of 20%?

Solution

The investment combinations we need to consider are the various possible pairs of projects P, Q and R **plus** the investment of the surplus at 25%. Dealing with the latter first:

The cumulative PV of £1 received per annum in perpetuity is £1/r. Therefore at a cost of capital of 20% the PV of the interest on £1 invested in perpetuity at 25% is $\frac{£1 \times 0.25}{0.20}$ = £1.25

The net present value per pound invested is £1.25 less the original investment of £1. Therefore the NPV per pound invested is £0.25. The NPVs from all possible combinations of investments can now be tested.

Projects	*Required investment*	*Funds remaining for external investment*		*NPV of external investment*		*NPV from projects*	*Total NPV*
	£'000	£'000		£'000		£'000	£'000
P and Q	90	5	(× 0.25)	1.25	(16.5 + 17.0)	33.5	34.75
P and R	70	25		6.25	(16.5 + 18.8)	35.3	41.55
Q and R	80	15		3.75	(17.0 + 18.8)	35.8	39.55

The highest NPV will be achieved by undertaking projects P and R and investing the unused funds of £25,000 externally.

Question

Capital rationing

Learning outcome: D(v)

Bijoux is choosing which investment to undertake during the coming year. The following table has been prepared, summarising the main features of available projects.

	Cash outlays		*Cash receipts*	
	Time 0	*Time 1*	*Time 1*	*Time 2*
Project	£'000	£'000	£'000	£'000
Diamond	24	60	24	96
Sapphire	48	42	48	66
Platinum	60	42	12	138
Emerald	48	18	12	90
Quartz	36	48	24	96

There will be no cash flows on any of the projects after time 2. All projects are regarded as being of equal risk. Bijoux uses only equity sources of finance at an estimated cost of 20% per annum.

The cash flows given above represent estimated results for maximum possible investment in each project; lower levels of investment may be undertaken, in which case all cash flows will be reduced in proportion.

Required

Prepare calculations to identify the optimal set of investment assuming that capital available is limited to £120,000 at time 0, and £240,000 at time 1; assume that the Platinum project and the Emerald project are mutually exclusive (*Hint:* firstly check in which years capital rationing occurs).

Answer

Optimal investments for Bijoux

First we need to determine in which year(s) capital is rationed, taking account of the fact that only one of the Platinum and Emerald projects will be undertaken.

Project	*Cash flows with Platinum*		*Cash flows with Emerald*	
	Time 0	*Time 1*	*Time 0*	*Time 1*
	£'000	£'000	£'000	£'000
Diamond	(24)	(36)	(24)	(36)
Sapphire	(48)	6	(48)	6
Platinum	(60)	(30)		
Emerald			(48)	(6)
Quartz	(36)	(24)	(36)	(24)
Total	(168)	(84)	(156)	(60)
Capital available	120	240	120	240

To rank the projects the basic PI as previously defined cannot be used as this would ignore outlays at time 1. One option would be to use a PI defined as $\frac{\text{PV of inflows}}{\text{PV of outlays}}$ but this is not entirely appropriate as capital is not rationed at Time 1.

An alternative, used here, is to use a PI defined as $\frac{\text{NPV project}}{\text{Initial capital invested}}$

It is therefore concluded that effective capital rationing exists only at Time 0 ie a single period of capital rationing situation.

Project	*Cash flows*			*PV of cash flows @ 20%*					*Rank*
	0)	*1*	*2*	*0*	*1*	*2*	*NPV*	*PI*	
	£'000	£'000	£'000	£'000	£'000	£'000	£'000		
Diamond	(24)	(36)	96	(24)	(30.0)	66.6	12.6	0.525	1
Sapphire	(48)	6	66	(48)	5.0	45.8	2.8	0.058	5
Platinum	(60)	(30)	138	(60)	(25.0)	95.8	10.8	0.180	4
Emerald	(48)	(6)	90	(48)	(5.0)	62.5	9.5	0.198	3
Quartz	(36)	(24)	96	(36)	(20.0)	66.6	10.6	0.294	2

In time 0 with only £100,000 available projects would be introduced in order of profitability as shown.

Platinum without Emerald

Project	*Proportion accepted*	*Funds used at Time 0*	*Total NPV*
	%	£'000	£'000
Diamond	100	24	12.6
Quartz	100	36	10.6
Platinum	100	60	10.8
Sapphire	Nil	Nil	Nil
Funds utilised and available		120	34.0

Emerald without Platinum

Project	*Proportion accepted*	*Funds used at Time 0*	*Total NPV*
	%	£'000	£'000
Diamond	100	24	12.6
Quartz	100	36	10.6
Emerald	100	48	9.5
Sapphire	25	12	0.7
Funds utilised and available		120	33.4

Platinum without Emerald is to be preferred as it yields a higher NPV.

Note. Platinum is selected in preference to Emerald even though it has a lower profitability index. This is because the choice is effectively between investing £60,000 in Platinum with an NPV of £10,800 (PI = 0.18) or a package containing a £48,000 investment in Emerald and a £12,000 investment in Sapphire with a combined NPV of £10,200. This package has a profitability index of only 0.17 and is therefore rejected.

1.9 Soft and hard capital rationing

Capital rationing may be necessary in a business due to **internal factors** (soft capital rationing) or **external factors** (hard capital rationing).

1.9.1 Soft capital rationing

Soft capital rationing may arise for one of the following reasons.

(a) Management may be **reluctant to issue additional share capital** because of concern that this may lead to outsiders gaining control of the business.

(b) Management may be **unwilling to issue additional share capital** if it will lead to a dilution of earnings per share.

(c) Management may **not want to raise additional debt capital** because they do not wish to be committed to large fixed interest payments.

(d) There may be a desire within the organisation to **limit investment** to a level that can be financed solely from retained earnings.

(e) **Capital expenditure budgets** may restrict spending.

Note that whenever an organisation adopts a policy that restricts funds available for investment, such a policy may be less than optimal as the organisation may reject projects with a positive net present value and forgo opportunities that would have enhanced the market value of the organisation.

1.9.2 Hard capital rationing

Hard capital rationing may arise for one of the following reasons.

(a) **Raising money through the stock market may not be possible** if share prices are depressed.

(b) There may be **restrictions on bank lending** due to government control.

(c) **Lending institutions** may consider an organisation to be too risky to be granted further loan facilities.

(d) The costs associated with making small issues of capital may be **too great**.

2 The annualised cost of a capital item

FAST FORWARD

When an asset is being replaced with an identical asset, the **equivalent annual cost** method can be used to determine the **optimum replacement cycle**.

2.1 Equivalent annual cost method

When an investment is being evaluated in terms of annual running costs, it may be appropriate to convert the capital cost into an annualised cost at the company's cost of capital. For example, when the capital expenditure is only a relatively small feature of a project and annual running costs are a much more significant item, annual profitability is the key factor in the decision.

Exam formula

$$\text{Equivalent annual cost} = \frac{\text{PV of costs over n years}}{\text{n year annuity factor}}$$

(a) **'PV of costs'** is the **purchase cost**, minus the present value of any subsequent disposal proceeds at the end of the item's life.

(b) The **n-year annuity factor is** at the company's cost of capital, for the number of years of the item's life.

Exam focus point

This was examined in November 2005 Paper 6 Business Strategy.

2.2 Example: annualised cost

A project is being considered which would involve a capital expenditure of £500,000 on equipment. The annual running costs and benefits would be as follows.

	£	£
Revenues		450,000
Costs		
Depreciation	100,000	
Other	300,000	
		400,000
Profit		50,000

The equipment would have a five year life, and no residual value, and would be financed by a loan at 12% interest per annum. Using annualised figures, assess whether the project is a worthwhile undertaking. Ignore risk and taxation.

Solution

The annualised capital cost of the equipment is as follows.

$$\frac{£500,000}{\text{PV of £1 per annum for yrs 1 to 5 at 12\%}} = \frac{£500,000}{3.605} = £138,696$$

Annual profit = £450,000 – £138,696 – £300,000 = £11,304

Depreciation is ignored because it is a notional cost and has already been taken into account in the annualised cost.

The project is a worthwhile undertaking, but only by about £11,000 a year for five years.

2.3 Equivalent annual cost and asset replacement

The annualised cost method can be used to assess when and how frequently an asset should be replaced with another asset.

The equivalent annual cost method is the quickest method to use in a period of no inflation.

Step 1 Calculate the **present value of costs** for each **replacement cycle** over **one cycle only**.

These costs are not comparable because they refer to different time periods, whereas replacement is continuous.

Step 2 **Turn the present value** of costs for each replacement cycle into an **equivalent annual cost** (an annuity).

The equivalent annual costs is calculated as follows.

$$\frac{\text{The PV of cost over one replacement cycle}}{\text{The cumulative present value factor for the number of years in the cycle}}$$

For example if there are three years in the cycle, the denominator will be the present value of an annuity for three years (eg at 10% would be 2.487).

2.4 Example: replacement of an identical asset

James operates a machine which has the following costs and resale values over its four year life.

Purchase cost: £25,000

	Year 1	*Year 2*	*Year 3*	*Year 4*
	£	£	£	£
Running costs (cash expenses)	7,500	10,000	12,500	15,000
Resale value (end of year)	15,000	10,000	7,500	2,500

The organisation's cost of capital is 10%. You are required to assess how frequently the asset should be replaced.

Solution

In our example:

Step 1 Calculate the present value of costs for each replacement cycle over one cycle.

	Replace every year		*Replace every 2 years*		*Replace every 3 years*		*Replace every 4 years*	
Year	*Cash flow* £	*PV at 10%* £	*Cash flow* £	*PV at 10%* £	*Cash flow* £	*PV at 10%* £	*Cash flow* £	*PV at 10%* £
0	(25,000)	(25,000)	(25,000)	(25,000)	(25,000)	(25,000)	(25,000)	(25,000)
1	7,500	6,818	(7,500)	(6,818)	(7,500)	(6,818)	(7,500)	(6,818)
2			0	0	(10,000)	(8,260)	(10,000)	(8,260)
3					(5,000)	(3,755)	(12,500)	(9,388)
4							(12,500)	(8,538)
PV of cost over one replacement cycle		(18,182)		(31,818)		(43,833)		(58,004)

Step 2 Calculate the equivalent annual cost.

We use a discount rate of 10%.

(a) Replacement every year:

$$\text{Equivalent annual cost} = \frac{£(18,182)}{0.909} = £(20,002)$$

(b) Replacement every two years:

$$\text{Equivalent annual cost} = \frac{£(31,818)}{1.736} = £(18,328)$$

(c) Replacement every three years:

$$\text{Equivalent annual cost} = \frac{£(43,833)}{2.487} = £(17,625)$$

(d) Replacement every four years:

$$\text{Equivalent annual cost} = \frac{£(58,004)}{3.170} = £(18,298)$$

The optimum replacement policy is the one with the lowest equivalent annual cost, every three years.

3 Capital investment real options 5/05

FAST FORWARD

Options theory can be applied to capital investments, and can be used when managers are deciding whether to **wait**, **abandon** a project or make **follow-on investments**.

3.1 Types of real option

The application of option theory in the appraisal of capital investments is a relatively new development. To give one type of example, a business decision may amount to paying a specified price now – say, to develop a new production system – which gives the business wider flexibility in the future. Such a decision gives the business more **options** to exploit wider follow-on opportunities.

Common types of 'real option' found in capital projects

- The **option to make follow-on investments**: this is equivalent to a **call option**
- The **option to abandon** a project: equivalent to a **put option**
- The **option to wait** before making an investment: equivalent to a **call option**

Each of these types of scenario is discussed further below.

Exam focus point

Students often confuse real options with currency and interest rate options (covered in the *Risk and Control Systems* paper).

3.2 The value of follow-on investments

The discounted cash flow technique was originally developed for holdings of stocks and shares before being developed as a technique for investment appraisal. An investor in stocks and shares is usually a passive holder of assets, with no real influence over the interest or dividends paid on the asset. The managers of a business enterprise do not however 'hold' investment projects passively. Investing in a particular project may lead to other possibilities or options which managers can take advantage of, and which will not have been reflected in a conventional NPV analysis.

3.3 Example: follow-on investments as options

Cornseed Publishing is a publisher of study guides in a sector of the professional training market. Over the last ten years, it has built up a share of approximately 30% of its target market. The directors of the company are now considering a project which would involve producing its study guides on CD-ROM, to be called *CD Guides*. The new CD-ROMs would not simply duplicate the material in the study guides as they would involve some interactive features. However it is thought that in the future, *CD Guides* might be developed into a more innovative fully interactive format – provisionally called *CD Tutor* – which makes fuller use of the advantages of the CD-ROM format, but this would take much more time and would require greater software know-how than is currently available. The *CD Guides* project would involve employing additional staff to develop the CD-ROM material. It is thought that Cornseed's competitors are probably considering similar CD-ROM projects.

One of the directors, Mark Cornseed, has questioned whether the project is worthwhile. It has been calculated, using the NPV method, that the *CD Guides* project as proposed has a negative net present value of £50,000. 'Why invest in a negative NPV project?', he asks. 'CD-ROMs which are not fully interactive are not likely to be a success. Just because our competitors are putting money into them doesn't mean we should make the same mistake.'

Another director, Julia Cornseed, points out that if the project does not go ahead, Cornseed may be missing out on the opportunity to develop *CD Tutor*. If the *CD Guides* are developed, she argues, with the added expertise gained Cornseed will be able to pursue this follow-on option. It will have a 'call' on this follow-on investment: the option to 'buy' it at a future date, or alternatively not to buy it. The only downside is that the company, assuming it allows the option to lapse, is committing itself to a project with a negative NPV of £50,000. The possible upside is that, if conditions seem right at a future date for the *CD Tutor* option to be taken up, this follow-on project could be a great success.

The problem which now must be faced is that of putting a value on the option. The Black-Scholes model (covered in detail in your P3 *Management Accounting Risk and Control Strategy* text) can be adapted to value these options. We could value the option in terms of:

(a) The **present value** of the **future benefit streams** of the follow-on project (counterpart to: the current value of the share in Black-Scholes)

(b) The **initial cost** of the **follow-on project** (counterpart to: the exercise price in Black-Scholes)

(c) The time **within** which the option must be exercised

(d) The **variability of expected project returns** (counterpart to: variability of the share price in Black-Scholes)

(e) The **risk-free rate of interest**

The formulae used to value options (such as the 'Black-Scholes model') are complex and you do not need to be able to use such formulae for the *Financial Strategy* exam. For our purposes, assume that a computer model shows that the follow-on investment *(CD Tutor)* has a value of £125,000. This reflects the fact that the project could be very profitable, but the company will not know if it is likely to be until the outcome of the *CD Guides* project is known. The *CD Guides* project carries an option value of £125,000 for an option 'premium' of £50,000 – the NPV of the initial project.

Quantifying the variables in valuing such investment options is not easy to do objectively. However, viewing strategic investment decisions from the 'options' perspective can offer insights to decision-makers. If the follow-on project is high-risk, this will **increase** the value of the call option. Analogously, the value of a share option is higher if the volatility of the share price is high.

3.4 The option to abandon

In the example above (Cornseed Publishing), we were looking at the valuation of an option to expand a business. Sometimes there is the converse problem – the **value of an option to abandon a project**.

It may be that a major capital investment cannot be abandoned. Once the initial investment is made, it may be impossible to do things differently. If the benefit streams from a project are highly uncertain, an **option to abandon the project** if things go wrong could be of **great value**.

The possibility of putting a value on the **'put' option of abandonment** highlights the value of **pursuing investments** which **offer flexibility**. For example, a company may face a choice between:

- Developing custom-designed plant to produce a single type of product, and
- Buying lower-technology machine tools to produce the same product

The NPV of Proposal (a) may be greater than the NPV for (b). But what if the product fails to sell? Abandonment in case (b) carries the value of a 'put' option, in that the company has the flexibility of using the low-technology equipment for other purposes.

3.5 The option to wait

A third type of option associated with investment decisions is the option to **'wait and see'** in the expectation of gaining more relevant information before making a decision. This might seem like a justification for indefinite procrastination. The point to note is that, if we can make reasonable estimates of the determinants of the value of the option, then this could aid our strategic decision-making. Investments are rarely 'now-or-never' opportunities. More usually, there is some time period over which a project can be postponed, which corresponds to the period in which the option to invest can be exercised. During this period, new market information could emerge.

Against this, we need to consider the cash inflows forgone in the period of postponement. Managers will need to balance this cost against the value of waiting.

Real options may be of particular importance in developing sectors such as the information technology sector where the emphasis is upon very rapid response to changes in the business environment, one opportunity often leads to another and the value of future opportunities is a significant part of a company's valuation. The main problem here is that indications of future opportunities, and hence company valuation, are very subjective.

3.6 Other options

Other real options include the following.

3.6.1 Staging options

This is the option to make **investments in phases**. Each stage can be seen as an option on the value of later stages by incurring the expenditure required to move to the next stage.

3.6.2 Growth options

Growth options are small investments that may lead **to bigger opportunities** such as new technology or access to different markets.

3.6.3 Scale options

Scale options are options to **expand or contract an investment** depending on how market conditions develop. Option cash flows may arise from the sale of redundant assets or exit costs from certain markets.

3.6.4 Switching options

Switching options involve **changing the inputs or outputs** in a production process, switching from the current to the cheapest input or the current to the most profitable output. The organisation has to consider valuing the flexibility to switch against the extra costs of switching.

4 The adjusted present value method 5/06

FAST FORWARD

The **APV** method suggests that it is possible to calculate an **adjusted** cost of capital for use in project appraisal, as well as indicating how the net present value of a project can be increased or decreased by project financing effects.

- Evaluate the project as if it was all equity financed
- Make adjustments to allow for the effects of the financing method

4.1 NPV and APV

We have seen that a company's gearing level has implications for both the value of its equity shares and its WACC. The viability of an investment project will depend partly on how the investment is financed, and how the method of finance affects gearing.

The net present value method of investment appraisal is to **discount** the **cash flows** of a project at a **cost of capital**. This cost of capital might be the WACC, but it could also be another cost of capital, perhaps one which allows for the risk characteristics of the individual project.

An alternative method of carrying out project appraisal is to use the **adjusted present value (APV) method**.

4.2 Carrying out an APV calculation

The APV method involves two stages.

Step 1 **Evaluate** the **project** first of all as if it was **all equity financed**, and so as if the company were an all equity company to find the 'base case NPV'

Step 2 **Make adjustments** to allow for the effects of the method of financing that has been used

4.3 Example: APV method

A company is considering a project that would cost £100,000 to be financed 50% by equity (cost 21.6%) and 50% by debt (pre-tax cost 12%). The financing method would maintain the company's WACC unchanged. The cash flows from the project would be £36,000 a year in perpetuity, before interest charges. Tax is at 30%.

Appraise the project using firstly the NPV method and secondly the APV method.

Solution

We can use the **NPV method** because the company's WACC will be unchanged.

	Cost	*Weighting*		*Product*
	%			%
Equity	21.6	0.5		10.8
Debt (70% of 12%)	8.4	0.5		4.2
			WACC	15.0

Annual cash flows in perpetuity from the project are as follows.

	£
Before tax	36,000
Less tax (30%)	10,800
After tax	25,200

NPV of project $= -£100{,}000 + (25{,}200 \div 0.15)$

$= -£100{,}000 + £168{,}000$

$= +£68{,}000$

Note that the tax relief that will be obtained on debt interest is taken account of **in the WACC *not* in the project cash flows.**

Since £100,000 of new investment is being created, the value of the company will increase by £100,000 + £68,000 = £168,000, of which 50% must be debt capital.

The company must raise 50% × £168,000 = £84,000 of 12% debt capital, and (the balance) £16,000 of equity. The NPV of the project will raise the value of this equity from £16,000 to £84,000 thus leaving the gearing ratio at 50:50.

The **APV approach** to this example is as follows.

(a) First, we need to know the **cost of equity in an equivalent ungeared company**. The MM formula we can use to establish this is as follows.

Exam Formula

Cost of ordinary (equity) share capital in a geared firm (with tax):

$$k_{eg} = k_{eu} + [k_{eu} - k_d]\frac{V_D(1-t)}{V_E}$$

Remember k_d is the **pre-tax** cost of debt. Using the information from the question;

$$21.6\% = k_{eu} + \left[(k_{eu} - 12\%) \times \frac{50 \times 0.7}{50}\right]$$

$$21.6\% = k_{eu} + 0.70k_{eu} - 8.4\%$$

$$1.70k_{eu} = 30\%$$

$$k_{eu} = 17.647\%$$

(b) Next, we calculate the **NPV of the project as if it were all equity financed**. The cost of equity would be 17.647%

$$NPV = \frac{£25,200}{0.17647} - £100,000 = +£42,800$$

(c) Next, we can use an MM formula for the relationship between the value of geared and ungeared companies, to establish **the effect of gearing on the value of the project**. £84,000 will be financed by debt.

V_g (APV) = $V_u + TB_C$

= +£42,800 + (£84,000 × 0.30)

= + £42,800 + £25,200

= £68,000

The value TB_c (value of debt × corporate tax rate) represents the **present value of the tax shield on debt interest,** that is the present value of the savings arising from tax relief on debt interest.

This can be proved as follows.

Annual interest charge = 12% of £84,000 = £10,080

Tax saving (30% × £10,080) = £3,024.00

Cost of debt (pre-tax) = 12%

PV of tax savings in perpetuity = $\frac{£3,024}{0.12}$ (by coincidence only this equals the project net of tax cash flows)

= £25,200

TB_c = £84,000 × 0.30 = £25,200 is a quicker way of deriving the same value. Note, however, this only works where the interest is payable in **perpetuity.** If not the PV of the tax shield will need to be computed by the 'long hand' method, above using an appropriate annuity factor.

Exam focus point

Make sure you use the cost of debt to discount the tax relief on interest costs and not the cost of equity.

4.4 Example: APV method and limited cash flows

Suppose in the above example the cash flows only lasted for five years, and tax was payable one year in arrears. Calculate the present value of the tax shield.

Solution

The tax saving will now only last for years 2 to 6. (Remember interest will be paid in years 1 to 5, but the tax benefits will be felt a year in arrears).

PV of tax savings = 3,024 × Annuity factor years 2 to 6
= 3,024 × (Annuity factors years 1 to 6 – Annuity factor year 1)
= 3,024 × (4.111 – 0.893)
= £9,731

The APV and NPV approaches produce the same conclusion.

4.5 APV and changes in gearing

However, the APV method can also be adapted to allow for financing which **changes the gearing structure** and the WACC.

In this respect, it is superior to the NPV method. Suppose, for example, that in the previous example, the **entire project were to be financed by debt**. The APV of the project would be calculated as follows.

(a) The NPV of project if all equity financed is:

$$\frac{£25{,}200}{0.17647} - £100{,}000 = +\ £42{,}800 \text{ (as before)}$$

(b) The adjustment to allow for the method of financing is the present value of the tax relief on debt interest in perpetuity.

$DT_c = £100{,}000 \times 0.30 = £30{,}000$

(c) APV = £42,800 + £30,000 = +£72,800

The project would increase the value of equity by £72,800.

Question — APV

Learning outcome: D(iii)

A project costing £100,000 is to be financed by £60,000 of irredeemable 12% loan stock and £40,000 of new equity. The project will yield an after-tax annual cash flow of £21,000 in perpetuity. If it were all equity financed, an appropriate cost of capital would be 15%. The tax rate is 30%. What is the project's APV?

Answer

	£
NPV if all equity financed: £21,000/0.15 – £100,000	40,000
PV of the tax shield: £60,000 × 12% × 30%/0.12	18,000
APV	58,000

4.6 Discounting tax relief at the risk-free rate

Often in exams you will be given the risk-free rate of return. As tax relief is allowed by the government and is almost certain, there is an argument for saying that **all tax relief** should be discounted at the **risk-free rate**. However there is the opposing argument that the **risk of the tax relief** is the same as the **risk of the debt** to which it relates, and therefore the tax relief should be discounted at the cost of debt. The risk-free rate would also not be used if the company was unlikely to be in a taxpaying position for some years.

In the exam we suggest that you make clear the reasons for choosing the discount rate that you have chosen to discount the tax relief, and add a comment that an alternative rate might be used.

4.7 Other elements in APV calculation

The tax shield may not be the only complication introduced into APV calculations.

4.7.1 Issue costs

The costs of issuing the finance needed for the project may also be brought into APV calculations.

4.7.2 Example: issue costs

Edted is about to start a project with an initial investment of £20 million, which will generate cash flow over four years. The project will be financed with a £10 million 10 year bank loan and a rights issue. Issue costs are 5% of the amount raised.

Calculate the issue costs that will be used in the APV calculation.

Solution

Issue costs will not equal 5% of £10 million (£20 million – £10 million). The £10 million will be the figure left after the issue costs have been paid. Therefore £10 million must be 95%, not 100% of the amount raised, and the

$$\text{Issue costs} = \frac{5}{95} \times £10 \text{ million} = £526{,}316$$

In the above example, the issue costs do not need to be discounted as they are assumed to be paid at time 0. The complication comes if issue costs are allowable for tax purposes.

4.7.3 Example: the tax implications of issue costs

Assume in the example above that issue costs are allowable for tax purposes, the tax is assumed to be 30% payable one year in arrears and the risk-free rate of return is assumed to be 8%.

Calculate the tax effect of the issuing costs to be included in the APV calculation.

Solution

$$\begin{aligned}\text{Tax effect} &= \text{Tax rate} \times \text{Issue costs} \times \text{Discount rate}\\ &= 0.3 \times 526{,}316 \times 0.926\\ &= £146{,}211\end{aligned}$$

4.7.4 Spare debt capacity

Projects may yield other incremental benefits, for example increased borrowing or debt capacity. These benefits should be included in the APV calculations, even if the debt capacity is utilised elsewhere.

4.7.5 Example: spare debt capacity

Continuing with the Edted example, suppose the project increased the borrowing capacity of the company by £6 million, at the risk-free rate of return of 8%. Calculate the effect on the APV calculation.

Solution

Remember that we are concerned with the incremental benefit which is the **tax shield effect** of the increased debt finance.

$$\begin{aligned}\text{Present value of tax shield effect} &= \text{Increased debt capacity} \times \text{Interest rate} \times \text{Tax rate} \times \text{Discount factor Years 2 to 5}\\ &= £6 \text{ million} \times 8\% \times 30\% \times 3.067\\ &= £441{,}648\end{aligned}$$

4.7.6 Subsidy

You may face a situation where a company can obtain finance at a lower interest rate than its normal cost of borrowing. In this situation you have to include in the APV calculation the tax shield effect of the cheaper finance and the effect of the saving in interest.

4.7.7 Example: subsidy

Gordonbear is about to start a project requiring £6 million of initial investment. The company normally borrows at 12% but a government loan will be available to finance all of the project at 10%. The risk-free rate of interest is 6%.

Tax is payable at 30% one year in arrears. The project is scheduled to last for four years.

Calculate the effect on the APV calculation if Gordonbear finances the project by means of the government loan.

Solution

(a) The tax shield is as follows.

We assume that the loan is for the duration of the project (four years) only.

Annual interest = £6 million × 10%
= £600,000

Tax relief = £600,000 × 0.3
= £180,000

This needs to be discounted over years 2 to 5 (remember the one year time lag). We do not however use the 10% to discount the loan and the tax effect; instead we assume that the government loan is risk-free and the tax effect is also risk-free. Hence we use the 6% factor in discounting.

NPV tax relief = £180,000 × Discount factor Years 2 to 5
= £180,000 × 3.269
= £588,420

(b) We also need to take into account the benefits of **being able** to pay a **lower interest rate**.

Benefits = £6 million × (12% – 10%) × 6% Discount factor Years 1 to 4
= £6 million × 2% × 3.465
= £415,800

(c) Total effect = £588,420 + £415,800 = £1,004,220.

4.8 The advantages and disadvantages of the APV method

The main advantages of the APV are as follows.

(a) APV can be used to **evaluate** all the **effects of financing** a product including:

- Tax shield
- Changing capital structure
- Any other relevant cost

(b) When using APV you do not have to adjust the WACC using assumptions of perpetual risk-free debt.

The main difficulties with the APV technique are:

(a) **Establishing** a **suitable cost of equity**, for the initial DCF computation as if the project were all-equity financed, and also establishing the all-equity β

(b) **Identifying all the costs** associated with the method of financing

(c) **Choosing the correct discount rates** used to discount the costs

Exam focus point

Always be prepared to discuss the limitations of a technique as in Question 4 in May 2006

5 Sensitivity analysis

FAST FORWARD

Sensitivity analysis assesses how responsive the project's NPV is to changes in the variables used to calculate that NPV.

5.1 Value of risks

In general, risky projects are those whose future cash flows, and hence the project returns, are likely to be variable. The greater the variability is, the greater the risk. The problem of risk is more acute with capital investment decisions than other decisions for the following reasons.

(a) **Estimates** of capital expenditure might be for **several years ahead**, such as for major construction projects. Actual costs may escalate well above budget as the work progresses.

(b) Estimates of **benefits** will be for **several years ahead**, sometimes 10, 15 or 20 years ahead or even longer, and such long-term estimates can at best be approximations.

5.2 Impact of uncertainty

The NPV could depend on a number of uncertain independent variables.

- Selling price
- Sales volume
- Cost of capital
- Initial cost
- Operating costs
- Benefits

Key term

Sensitivity analysis is one method of analysing the risk surrounding a capital expenditure project and enables an assessment to be made of how responsive the project's NPV is to changes in the variables that are used to calculate that NPV.

5.3 Sensitivity analysis

The basic approach of sensitivity analysis is to **calculate the project's NPV** under **alternative assumptions** to determine how sensitive it is to changing conditions. An indication is thus provided of those variables to which the NPV is most sensitive (**critical variables**) and the **extent** to which those variables **may change** before the investment results in a negative NPV.

Sensitivity analysis therefore provides an indication of why a project might fail. Management should review critical variables to assess whether or not there is a strong possibility of events occurring which will lead to a negative NPV. Management should also pay particular attention to controlling those variables to which the NPV is particularly sensitive, once the decision has been taken to accept the investment.

When carrying out sensitivity analysis, you may need to use your knowledge of **breakeven analysis** (cost-volume-profit analysis) from your earlier studies.

Knowledge brought forward from earlier studies

Cost-volume-profit (breakeven) analysis

- Contribution per unit = unit selling price – unit variable costs
- Profit = (sales volume × contribution per unit) – fixed costs
- Breakeven point = activity level at which there is neither profit nor loss

  $$= \frac{\text{total fixed costs}}{\text{contribution per unit}} = \frac{\text{contribution requ'd to breakeven}}{\text{contribution per unit}}$$

- Contribution/sales (C/S) ratio = profit/volume (P/V) ratio = (contribution/sales) × 100%
- Sales revenue at breakeven point = $\frac{\text{fixed costs}}{\text{C/S ratio}}$
- Margin of safety (in units) = budgeted sales units – breakeven sales units

  Margin of safety (as %) = $\frac{\text{budgeted sales} - \text{breakeven sales}}{\text{budgeted sales}} \times 100\%$

- Sales volume to achieve a target profit = $\frac{\text{fixed cost} + \text{target profit}}{\text{contribution per unit}}$

Example

Selling price = £15 per unit

Variable cost = £12 per unit

Fixed costs = £5,400 per annum

Budgeted annual sales = 3,000 units

Breakeven point in units = $\frac{£5,400}{£(15-12)}$ = 1,800 units

C/S ratio = (3/15) × 100% = 20%

Breakeven point in revenue = $\frac{£5,400}{0.2}$ = £27,000

Sales volume to achieve profit of £3,300 = $\frac{£(5,400+3,300)}{£3}$ = 2,900 units

Margin of safety (as a %) = $\frac{3,000-1,800}{3,000} \times 100\% = 40\%$

5.4 Example: sensitivity analysis

Kenney Ltd is considering a project with the following cash flows.

	Initial investment	*Variable costs*	*Cash inflows*	*Net cash flows*
	£'000	£'000	£'000	£'000
0	7,000			
1		(2,000)	6,500	4,500
2		(2,000)	6,500	4,500

(650,000 units at £10 per unit)

Required

Measure the sensitivity of the project to changes in variables.

Solution

The PVs of the cash flow are as follows.

Year	*Discount factor*	*PV of initial investment*	*PV of variable costs*	*PV of cash inflows*	*PV of net cash flow*
	8%	£'000	£'000	£'000	£'000
0	1.000	(7,000)			(7,000)
1	0.926		(1,852)	6,019	4,167
2	0.857		(1,714)	5,571	3,857
		(7,000)	(3,566)	11,590	1,024

The project has a positive NPV and would appear to be worthwhile. The changes in cash flows which would need to occur for the project to breakeven (and hence be on the point of being unacceptable) are as follows.

(a) **Initial investment.** The initial investment can rise by £1,024,000 before the investment breaks even. The initial investment may therefore increase by 1,024/7,000 = 15%.

(b) **Sales volume.** The present value of the cash inflows less the present value of the variable costs will have to fall to £7,000,000 for the NPV to be zero.

We need to find the net cash flows in actual values. As the cash flows are equal each year, cumulative discount tables can be used.

(i) The discount factor for 8% and year 2 is 1.783.

(ii) If the discount factor is divided into the required present value of £7,000,000 we get an annual cash flow of £3,925,968.

(iii) Given that the most likely net cash flow is £4,500,000, the net cash flow may decline by approximately £574,032 (4,500,000 – 3,925,968) each year before the NPV becomes zero.

(iv) Total sales revenue may therefore decline by £831,930 (assuming net cash flow is 69% (4,500/6,500) of sales) (therefore sales = 574,032 × 6,500/4,500). At a selling price of £10 per unit this represents 83,193 units.

(v) Alternatively we may state that sales volume may decline by 13% before the NPV becomes negative.

(c) **Selling price.** When sales volume is 650,000 units per annum, total sales revenue can fall to £5,925,968 (£(6,500,000 – 574,032) per annum before the NPV becomes negative. This represents a selling price of £9.12 per unit, which represents a 8.8% reduction in the selling price.

(d) **Variable costs.** The total variable cost can increase by £574,032, or £0.88 per unit. This represents an increase of 28.6%.

(e) **Cost of capital.** We need to calculate the IRR of the project. Let us try discount rates of 15% and 20%.

Year	*Net cash flow*	*Discount factor*	*PV*	*Discount factor*	*PV*
	£'000	15%	£'000	20%	£'000
0	(7,000)	0.870	(6,090)	0.833	(5,831)
1	4,500	0.756	3,402	0.694	3,123
2	4,500	0.658	2,961	0.579	2,606
		NPV =	273	NPV =	(102)

$$\text{IRR} = 0.15 + \left[\frac{273}{273+102} \times (0.20 - 0.15)\right] = 18.64\%$$

The cost of capital can therefore increase by 133% before the NPV becomes negative.

The elements to which the NPV appears to be most sensitive are the selling price followed by the sales volume. Management should thus pay particular attention to these factors so that they can be carefully monitored.

5.5 Weaknesses of this approach to sensitivity analysis

(a) The method requires that **changes** in each key variable are **isolated.** However management is more interested in the combination of the effects of changes in two or more key variables.

(b) Looking at factors in isolation is unrealistic since they are often **interdependent**.

(c) Sensitivity analysis does not examine the **probability** that any particular variation in costs or revenues might occur.

(d) **Critical factors** may be those over which managers have no control.

(e) In itself it does not provide a decision rule. Parameters defining **acceptability** must be laid down by managers.

Question

Sensitivity analysis

Nevers Ure Ltd has a cost of capital of 8% and is considering a project with the following 'most-likely' cash flows.

Year	*Purchase of plant*	*Running costs*	*Savings*
	£	£	£
0	(7,000)		
1		2,000	6,000
2		2,500	7,000

Required

Measure the sensitivity (in percentages) of the project to changes in the levels of expected costs and savings.

Answer

The PVs of the cash flows are as follows.

Year	*Discount factor*	*PV of plant cost*	*PV of running costs*	*PV of savings*	*PV of net cash flow*
	8%	£	£	£	£
0	1.000	(7,000)			(7,000)
1	0.926		(1,852)	5,556	3,704
2	0.857		(2,143)	5,999	3,856
		(7,000)	(3,995)	11,555	560

The project has a positive NPV and would appear to be worthwhile. The changes in cash flows which would need to occur for the project to break even (NPV = 0) are as follows

(a) Plant costs would need to increase by a PV of £560, that is by (560/7,000) × 100% = 8%
(b) Running costs would need to increase by a PV of £560, that is by (560/3,995) × 100% = 14%
(c) Savings would need to fall by a PV of £560, that is by (560/11,555) × 100% = 4.8%

6 Certainty equivalents

FAST FORWARD

Project cash flows are converted to equivalent riskless amounts under the **certainty equivalent approach**.

6.1 Using certainty equivalents

Another, simpler method of allowing for risk in investment appraisal is the **certainty equivalent approach**. By this method, the expected cash flows of the project are **converted to equivalent riskless amounts**. The greater the risk of an expected cash flow, the smaller the certainty equivalent value (for receipts) or the larger the certainty equivalent value (for payments). The disadvantage of the certainty equivalent approach is that the amount of the adjustment to each cash flow is decided subjectively by management.

Key term

Certainty equivalent method is an approach to dealing with risk in a capital budgeting context. It involves expressing risky future cash flows in terms of the certain cash flow which would be considered, by the decision-maker, as their equivalent, ie the decision-maker would be indifferent between the risky amount and the (lower) riskless amount considered to be its equivalent. *(OT 2005)*

As the cash flows are reduced to supposedly certain amounts they should then be discounted at a risk free rate.

6.2 Example: certainty equivalents

Dark Ages, whose cost of capital is 10%, is considering a project with the following expected cash flows.

Year	*Cash flow*	*Discount factor10%*	*Present value*
	£		£
0	(9,000)	1.000	(9,000)
1	7,000	0.909	6,363
2	5,000	0.826	4,130
3	5,000	0.751	3,755
		NPV	5,248

The project would seem to be worthwhile. However, because of the uncertainty about the future cash flows, the management decides to reduce them to certainty equivalents by taking only 70%, 60% and 50% of the years 1, 2 and 3 cash flows respectively. (Note that this method of risk adjustment allows for different risk factors in each year of the project.) Is the project worthwhile?

Solution

The risk-adjusted NPV of the project would be as follows.

Year	*Cash flow*	*Discount factor 10%*	*Present value*
	£		£
0	(9,000)	1.000	(9,000)
1	4,900	0.909	4,454
2	3,000	0.826	2,478
3	2,500	0.751	1,878
		NPV	(190)

The project is too risky and should be rejected although this has ignored any potential adjustment to the discount rate as a result of the 'certainty' of the cash flows.

OPCIMA ink

Consideration of investment options may be a significant part of the case study requirements.

7 Probability analysis

FAST FORWARD

A **probability analysis** of expected cash flows can often be estimated and used both to calculate an expected NPV and to measure risk. The standard deviation of the NPV can be calculated to assess risk when the construction of probability distributions is complicated.

7.1 Probability distribution

A **probability distribution** of **'expected cash flows'** can often be estimated, recognising there are several possible outcomes, not just one. This may be used to do the following.

Step 1 Calculate an expected value of the NPV

Step 2 Measure risk, for example in the following ways.

(a) By calculating the worst possible outcome and its probability
(b) By calculating the probability that the project will fail to achieve a positive NPV
(c) By calculating the standard deviation of the NPV

7.2 Example: probability estimates of cash flows

A company is considering a project involving the outlay of £300,000 which it estimates will generate cash flows over its two year life at the probabilities shown in the following table.

Cash flows for project

Year 1

Cash flow £	*Probability*
100,000	0.25
200,000	0.50
300,000	0.25
	1.00

Year 2

If cash flow in Year 1 is: £	*there is a probability of:*	*that the cash flow in Year 2 will be:* £
100,000	0.25	Nil
	0.50	100,000
	0.25	200,000
	1.00	
200,000	0.25	100,000
	0.50	200,000
	0.25	300,000
	1.00	
300,000	0.25	200,000
	0.50	300,000
	0.25	350,000
	1.00	

The company's investment criterion for this type of project is 10% DCF.

You are required to calculate the expected value (EV) of the project's NPV and the probability that the NPV will be negative.

Solution

Step 1 Calculate expected value of the NPV.

First we need to draw up a probability distribution of the expected cash flows. We begin by calculating the present values of the cash flows.

Year	*Cash flow*	*Discount factor*	*Present value*
	£'000	10%	£'000
1	100	0.909	90.9
1	200	0.909	181.8
1	300	0.909	272.7
2	100	0.826	82.6
2	200	0.826	165.2
2	300	0.826	247.8
2	350	0.826	289.1

Year 1 PV of cash flow	*Probability*	*Year 2 PV of cash flow*	*Probability*	*Joint probability*	*Total PV of cash inflows*	*EV of PV of cash inflows*
£'000		£'000			£'000	£'000
(a)	(b)	(c)	(d)	(b) × (d)	(a) + (c)	
90.9	0.25	0.0	0.25	0.0625	90.9	5.681
90.9	0.25	82.6	0.50	0.1250	173.5	21.688
90.9	0.25	165.2	0.25	0.0625	256.1	16.006
181.8	0.50	82.6	0.25	0.1250	264.4	33.050
181.8	0.50	165.2	0.50	0.2500	347.0	86.750
181.8	0.50	247.8	0.25	0.1250	429.6	53.700
272.7	0.25	165.2	0.25	0.0625	437.9	27.369
272.7	0.25	247.8	0.50	0.1250	520.5	65.063
272.7	0.25	289.1	0.25	0.0625	561.8	35.113
						344.420

	£
EV of PV of cash inflows	344,420
Less project cost	300,000
EV of NPV	44,420

Step 2 Measure risk.

Since the EV of the NPV is positive, the project should go ahead unless the risk is unacceptably high. The probability that the project will have a negative NPV is the probability that the total PV of cash inflows is less than £300,000. From the column headed 'Total PV of cash inflows', we can establish that this probability is 0.0625 + 0.125 + 0.0625 + 0.125 = 0.375 or 37.5%. This might be considered an unacceptably high risk.

7.3 The standard deviation of the NPV

The disadvantage of using the EV of NPV approach to assess the risk of the project is that the **construction** of the **probability distribution** can become **very complicated**. If we were considering a project over 4 years, each year having five different forecasted cash flows, there would be 625 (5^4) NPVs to calculate. To avoid all of these calculations, an indication of the risk may be obtained by calculating the **standard deviation** of the NPV.

7.4 Example: standard deviation of the net present value

Frame is considering which of two mutually exclusive projects, A or B, to undertake. There is some uncertainty about the running costs with each project, and a probability distribution of the NPV for each project has been estimated, as follows.

Project A	Project B		
NPV	*Probability*	*NPV*	*Probability*
£'000		£'000	
– 20	0.15	+ 5	0.2
+ 10	0.20	+ 15	0.3
+ 20	0.35	+ 20	0.4
+ 40	0.30	+ 25	0.1

You are required to decide which project should the company choose, if either.

Solution

We can begin by calculating the EV of the NPV for each project.

	Project A			*Project B*	
NPV	*Prob*	*EV*	*NPV*	*Prob*	*EV*
£'000		£'000	£'000		£'000
– 20	0.15	(3.0)	5	0.2	1.0
10	0.20	2.0	15	0.3	4.5
20	0.35	7.0	20	0.4	8.0
40	0.30	12.0	25	0.1	2.5
		18.0			16.0

Project A has a higher EV of NPV, but what about the risk of variation in the NPV above or below the EV? This can be measured by the standard deviation of the NPV.

The standard deviation of a project's NPV, s, can be calculated as:

$$s=\sqrt{\Sigma p(x-\bar{x})^2}$$

where $\bar{x}$ is the EV of the NPV.

	Project A, $\bar{x}$ = 18				*Project B, $\bar{x}$ = 16*		
x	*p*	*$x-\bar{x}$*	*$p(x-\bar{x})^2$*	*x*	*p*	*$x-\bar{x}$*	*$p(x-\bar{x})^2$*
£'000		£'000		£'000		£'000	
– 20	0.15	– 38	216.6	5	0.2	– 11	24.2
10	0.20	– 8	12.8	15	0.3	– 1	0.3
20	0.35	+ 2	1.4	20	0.4	+ 4	6.4
40	0.30	+ 22	145.2	25	0.1	+ 9	8.1
			376.0				39.0

Project A

$$s = \sqrt{376}$$
$$= 19.391$$
$$= £19,391$$

Project B

$$s = \sqrt{39.0}$$
$$= 6.245$$
$$= £6,245$$

Although Project A has a higher EV of NPV, it also has a higher standard deviation of NPV, and so has greater risk associated with it.

Which project should be selected? Clearly it depends on the attitude of the company's management to risk.

(a) If management are prepared to take the risk of a **low NPV** in the hope of a high NPV they will opt for project A.

(b) If management are **risk-averse**, they will opt for the less risky project B.

7.5 Problems with expected values

There are the following problems with using expected values in making investment decisions.

- An investment may be **one-off**, and 'expected' NPV may never actually occur.
- **Assigning probabilities** to events is highly **subjective**.
- Expected values **do not evaluate the range** of possible NPV outcomes.

7.6 Decision trees

You will remember from other studies that decision trees are used to model a finite number of possible outcomes where more than one variable that affects the ultimate outcome is uncertain. In addition the value of some variables may be dependent on the value of other variables.

8 Simulation models

FAST FORWARD

Simulation models can be used to assess products which have a large number of possible outcomes, or projects which have correlated cash flows.

8.1 Simulations

Simulation will overcome problems of having a very large number of possible outcomes, also the correlation of cash flows (a project which is successful in its early years is more likely to be successful in its later years).

8.2 Example: simulation model

The following probability estimates have been prepared for a proposed project.

	Year	*Probability*	£
Cost of equipment	0	1.00	(40,000)
Revenue each year	1-5	0.15	40,000
		0.40	50,000
		0.30	55,000
		0.15	60,000
Running costs each year	1-5	0.10	25,000
		0.25	30,000
		0.35	35,000
		0.30	40,000

The cost of capital is 12%. Assess how a simulation model might be used to assess the project's NPV.

Solution

A simulation model could be constructed by assigning a range of random number digits to each possible value for each of the uncertain variables. The random numbers must exactly match their respective probabilities. This is achieved by working upwards cumulatively from the lowest to the highest cash flow values and assigning numbers that will correspond to probability groupings as follows.

Revenue				*Running costs*		
		Random				*Random*
£	*Prob*	*numbers*		£	*Prob*	*numbers*
40,000	0.15	00 – 14	*	25,000	0.10	00 – 09
50,000	0.40	15 – 54	**	30,000	0.25	10 – 34
55,000	0.30	55 – 84	***	40,000	0.35	35 – 69
60,000	0.15	85 – 99		40,000	0.30	70 – 99

* Probability is 0.15 (15%). Random numbers are 15% of range 00 – 99.

** Probability is 0.40 (40%). Random numbers are 40% of range 00 – 99 but starting at 15.

*** Probability is 0.30 (30%). Random numbers are 30% of range 00 – 99 but starting at 55.

For revenue, the selection of a random number in the range 00 and 14 has a probability of 0.15. This probability represents revenue of £40,000. Numbers have been assigned to cash flows so that when numbers are selected at random, the cash flows have exactly the same probability of being selected as is indicated in their respective probability distribution above.

Random numbers would be generated, for example by a computer program, and these would be used to assign values to each of the uncertain variables.

For example, if random numbers 378420015689 were generated, the values assigned to the variables would be as follows.

	Revenue		*Costs*	
Calculation	*Random number*	*Value*	*Random number*	*Value*
		£		£
1	37	50,000	84	40,000
2	20	50,000	01	25,000
3	56	55,000	89	40,000

A computer would calculate the NPV may times over using the values established in this way with more random numbers, and the results would be analysed to provide the following.

(a) An **expected NPV** for the project

(b) A **statistical distribution** pattern for the possible variation in the NPV above or below this average

The decision whether to go ahead with the project would then be made on the basis of **expected return** and **risk**.

9 Ways of reducing risk

9.1 Risk reduction methods

FAST FORWARD

Other risk reduction methods include a maximum payback period and high discount rate.

Only if management know for certainty what is going to happen in the future can they appraise a project in the knowledge that there is no risk. However the future is uncertain by nature. There are, nevertheless, steps that management can take to reduce the riskiness of a project.

(a) A **maximum payback period** can be set to reflect the fact that risk increases the longer the time period under consideration.

(b) A **high discounting rate** can be used so that a cash flow which occurs quite some time in the future will have less effect on the decision.

(c) Projects with **low standard deviations** and **acceptable average predicted outcomes** can be selected. If a business is undertaking a range of projects, it should ensure that some are **low-risk (diversification)**.

(d) **Sensitivity analysis** can be used to determine the critical factors within the decision-making process. Management effort can then be directed to those factors which are critical to the success of a particular decision.

(e) To ensure that future events are no worse than predicted, **prudence**, **slack** and **overly pessimistic estimates** can be applied.

(f) **Certainly equivalents**

(g) **Probability analysis**

(h) **Use of simulations**

Chapter roundup

- **Capital rationing** may occur due to internal factors (**soft** capital rationing) or external factors (**hard** capital rationing).
- When capital rationing occurs in a **single period, divisible** projects are ranked in terms of a **profitability index. Trial and error NPV calculations** should be used to rank **indivisible projects**.
- When an asset is being replaced with an identical asset, the **equivalent annual cost** method can be used to determine the **optimum replacement cycle**.
- **Options theory** can be applied to capital investments, and can be used when managers are deciding whether to **wait**, **abandon** a project or make **follow-on investments**.
- The **APV** method suggests that it is possible to calculate an **adjusted** cost of capital for use in project appraisal, as well as indicating how the net present value of a project can be increased or decreased by project financing effects.
  - Evaluate the project as if it was all equity financed
  - Make adjustments to allow for the effects of the financing method
- **Sensitivity analysis** assesses how responsive the project's NPV is to changes in the variables used to calculate that NPV.
- Project cash flows are converted to equivalent riskless amounts under the **certainty equivalent approach.**
- A **probability analysis** of expected cash flows can often be estimated and used both to calculate an expected NPV and to measure risk. The standard deviation of the NPV can be calculated to assess risk when the construction of probability distributions is complicated.
- **Simulation models** can be used to assess products that have a large number of possible outcomes, or projects that have correlated cash flows.
- Other **risk reduction methods** include a **maximum payback period and high discount rate**.

Quick quiz

1 *Hard capital rationing* occurs when a restriction on an organisation's ability to invest capital funds is caused by an internal budget ceiling imposed by management.

True ☐

False ☐

2 According to *CIMA Official Terminology*,

$$\text{Profitability Index (PI)} = \frac{(1)}{(2)}$$

What are (1) and (2)?

3 $$\text{Equivalent annual cost} = \frac{\text{PV of costs over n years}}{\text{n year annuity factor}}$$

Explain briefly what is meant by:

(a) PV of costs
(b) n year annuity factor

4 Identify three common types of 'real option' found in relation to capital projects.

5 What is an indivisible project?

6 Give three reasons why hard capital rationing may occur.

7 What is the best way to find the optimal solution in a situation of single period rationing with indivisible projects?

8 What is the best way to find the optimal solution in a situation of single period rationing with divisible projects?

9 What are the difficulties involved in using the APV technique?

Answers to quick quiz

1 False. This describes *soft* capital rationing.

2 (1) Present value of cash inflows
(2) Initial investment

3 (a) The purchase cost, minus the present value of any subsequent disposal proceeds at the end of the item's life

(b) The annuity factor at the company's cost of capital, for the number of years of the item's life

4 (a) The option to make follow-on investments
(b) The option to abandon a project
(c) The option to wait before making an investment

5 A project that must be undertaken completely or not at all

6 Any *three* of:

(a) Raising money through the stock market may not be possible if share prices are depressed.
(b) There are restrictions on lending due to government control.
(c) Lending institutions may consider the organisation to be too risky.
(d) The costs associated with making small issues of capital may be too great.

7 Use trial and error and test the NPV available from different project combinations.

8 Rank the projects according to their profitability index.

9 (a) Establishing a suitable cost of equity, for the initial DCF computation as if the project were all-equity financed, and also establishing the all-equity β

(b) Identifying all the costs associated with the method of financing

(c) Choosing the correct discount rates used to discount the costs

Now try the questions below from the Exam Question Bank

Number	Level	Marks	Time
Q32	Examination	20	36 mins
Q33	Examination	12	22 mins

20

Investment and project control

Introduction

In this chapter we discuss how investments, particularly investment projects are controlled. The first section concentrates on the various phases of projects. Deciding and carrying out smaller investments, for example the purchase of a specific piece of plant and machinery will be a simple process, but certain key stages will be the same whatever the nature of the investment.

In the rest of the chapter we examine certain processes in more detail. Whatever the investment, it is vital that it is carefully assessed for feasibility and we look at feasibility studies in Section 2. Section 4 deals with the steps businesses can take if problems arise or changes have to be made to the initial specification for the investment. Section 5 deals with assessment of whether the investment was a success and the wider issues that a **post-completion audit** covers.

Topic list	Learning outcomes	Syllabus references	Ability required
1 Investments and projects	D(iv)	D(10)	Evaluation
2 Feasibility study	D(iv)	D(10)	Evaluation
3 Project control	D(iv)	D(10)	Evaluation
4 Dealing with problems	D(iv)	D(10)	Evaluation
5 Investment performance and post-completion audits	D(iv)	D(11)	Evaluation

1 Investments and projects

FAST FORWARD

Investments, particularly projects, need to be carefully planned and controlled. Managers must consider the **need** for investments, choose the **best option**, control **development and implementation** and review whether the investment has **fulfilled its aims**.

1.1 Investment cycle

The investment process can be summarised as a cycle as follows

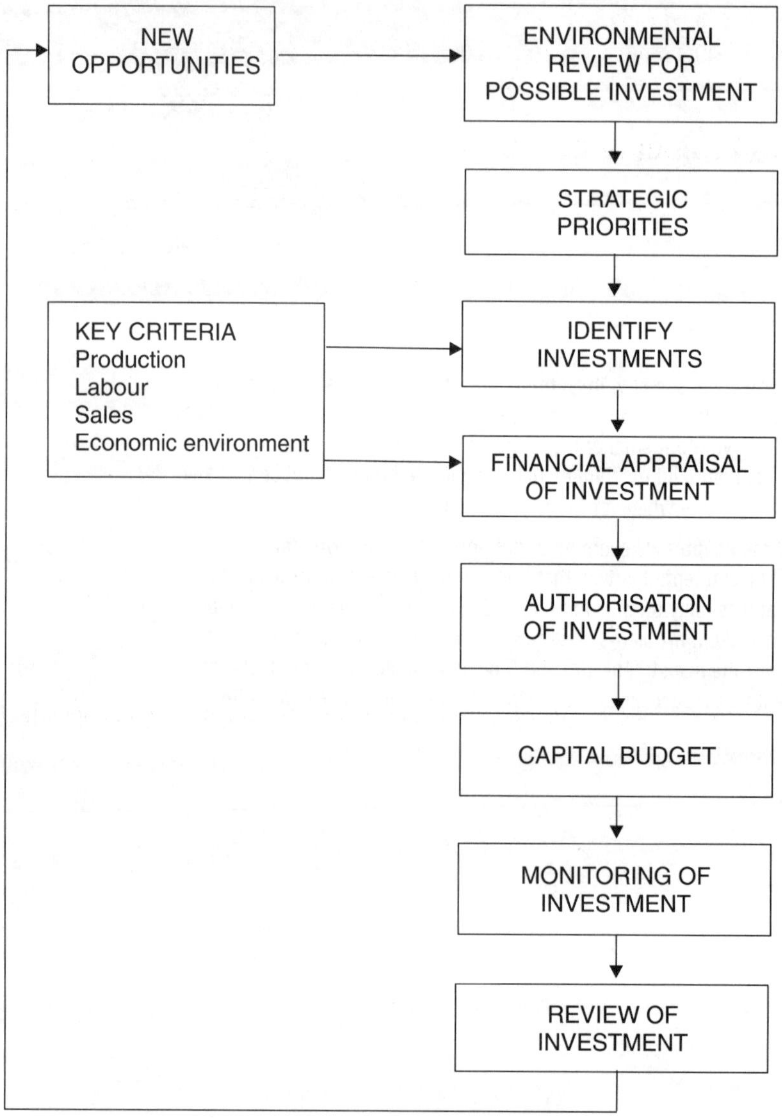

1.2 Nature of projects

A business may undertake major investments in different contexts. Some investments will be undertaken to enhance ongoing operations, and benefits and costs may be indefinite. Other investments may be specific projects.

Key term

Investment projects generally have the following characteristics:

(a) They have a defined beginning and end
(b) They have resources allocated to them, although often on a shared basis
(c) They are intended to be done only once
(d) They follow a plan towards a clear intended end-result
(e) They often cut across organisational and functional lines.

1.3 Project success factors

Projects, small or large, are prone to fail unless they are appropriately managed and some effort is applied to ensure that factors that might contribute to success are present. Here are some of the key factors.

- **Clearly defined mission and goals** effectively communicated to and understood by all participants
- **Top management support** that is visible is important in sending out the right messages regarding the importance of the project
- **Competent project manager** with the necessary skills
- **Competent team members** with the appropriate knowledge, skills and attitudes
- **Sufficient resources** in terms of finance, materials, people and processes
- **Excellent communication channels** to ensure information is shared and there are no misunderstandings
- **Clear client focus** so that all work is done bearing in mind the needs of internal and external customers

1.4 Project phases and stages

The phases of a project can be broken down into a number of stages. Again, the number of stages identified varies depending on type of project and the conventions of the organisation undertaking the project. Barnes *et al* (2002) has identified thirteen project stages. These are shown in the following diagram.

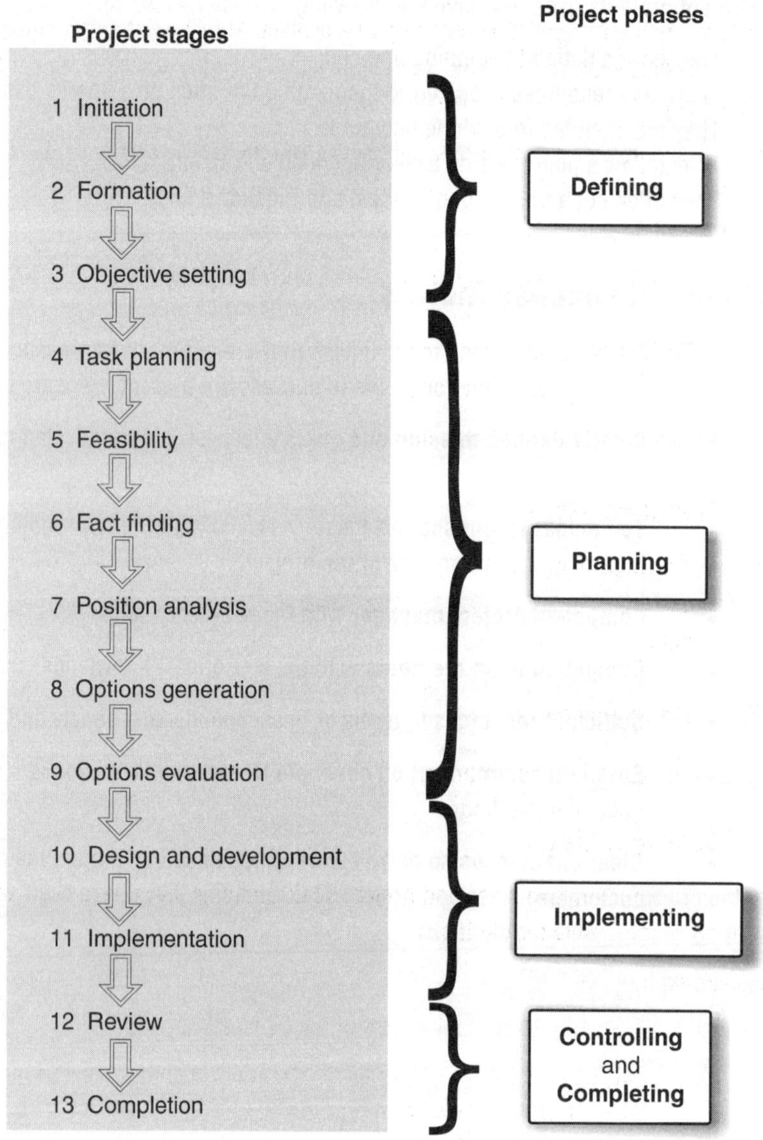

We now will look at each of these phases and stages.

1.5 Defining phase

The **defining phase** of a project is concerned with deciding whether a project should begin and committing to do so.

1.5.1 Initiation

Project initiation describes the beginning of a project. At this point certain management activities are required to ensure that the project is established with clear reference terms, an appropriate management structure and a carefully selected **project team**.

Projects originate from the **identification of a problem** or the **opportunity** to do something new. It is often not clear precisely what the problem is. The project team will have to study, discuss and **analyse** the problem, from a number of different aspects (eg technical, financial).

At the start of a project, documentation should be drawn up, setting out the **terms of reference** for the project.

1.5.2 Formation

The formation stage involves selecting the personnel who will be involved with the project, including a project manager and perhaps a project team.

1.5.3 Objective setting

Before specific objectives can be set it is necessary to establish more general **project goals**. Clear goals and objectives give team members **quantifiable targets** to aim for. This should improve motivation and performance, as attempting to achieve a challenging goal is more inspiring than simply being told 'do your best.'

1.6 Planning phase

The **planning phase** of a project aims to devise a workable scheme to accomplish the overall project goal.

1.6.1 Task planning

After the project team is in place and project goals and objectives have been set, the project should be broken down into **manageable tasks**.

Tasks should be:

(a) **Clear**. Eg 'Design the layout of the general sports halls.'

(b) **Self-contained**. No gaps in time should be apparent on work-units grouped together to form a task. All work-units within a task should be related.

1.6.2 Feasibility and fact finding

A more realistic judgement as to the **overall feasibility** of the project can now be made. Some large projects may involve a **pre-project feasibility study**, which establishes whether it is feasible to undertake the project at all. For complex projects, a detailed **feasibility study** may be required to establish if the project can be achieved within acceptable **cost and time constraints**.

We shall consider feasibility studies in more detail in Section 2.

1.6.3 Position analysis, options generation and options evaluation

Once the current situation has been clearly established, options can be generated for a range of projects or services, only one of which can be chosen.

Each course is analysed in terms of how well it would meet the project aims. A weighted scoring or ranking system may be useful here. Eventually the optimum course is chosen.

1.7 Implementing phase 5/06

The **implementing phase** is concerned with co-ordinating people and other resources to carry out the project plan.

1.7.1 Design and development

The design and development stage is where the actual product, service or process that will be the end result of the project is worked on. The activities carried out in this stage will vary greatly depending on the type of project. For example, in a software implementation, this is when the programming of the software would take place; in a construction project, the building design would be finalised.

We discussed the considerations that will impact upon design of products and services in Chapter 17. The main aim is to produce a design that will meet user requirements; for this to happen, the **design** has to be **tested** against what users want. Subsequent phases may have to be altered if the product design changes as a result of the testing process.

1.7.2 Implementation

After the process, service or product has been developed it will be **made available** or **installed** so it is available to be used.

Products can be launched globally, or on a country-by-country basis, depending on the markets involved. **Launch plans** may have to be **modified** if competitors change their response.

If the project involves a new system or process, a period of **parallel running** alongside the existing system or process may be carried out. This enables results to be checked, and any last-minute problems to be ironed out before the organisation is fully reliant on the new system or process. However implementation is not the time for adding new features or enhancements in response to user comments. Pressure for new features should have been dealt with earlier; if demand arises at this stage, there may need to be a follow-on project.

At this stage **communication** with **internal users** and **customers** is essential to ensure that they are happy and will start using what has been developed. Communication needs to be two-way, with those affected by the project being able to discuss their initial needs and requirements for ongoing support.

1.8 Controlling phase

The **controlling phase** is concerned with ensuring project objectives are met by monitoring and measuring progress and taking corrective action when necessary.

1.8.1 Review stage

Actual performance should be reviewed against the objectives identified in the project plan. If performance is not as expected, control action will be necessary.

1.9 Completing phase

Completion involves formalising acceptance of the project and bringing it to an orderly end.

1.9.1 Completion stage

Following installation and review there should be a review meeting to:

- Check that all products are complete and delivered
- Check the status of any outstanding requests for change
- Check all project issues have been cleared
- Approve the project completion report
- Arrange for a post completion audit (discussed later in this chapter)

2 Feasibility study

FAST FORWARD

A **feasibility study**, covering all aspects of a project's feasibility, and undertaken by a carefully selected team is a vital stage in assessing whether an investment is worthwhile. Feasibility studies are essential for investments and projects that are likely to be long and complicated.

2.1 Carrying out a feasibility study

If a major investment is to be successful, its feasibility needs to be carefully assessed before the organisation commits to it. A feasibility study should be carried out because a new investment:

- Might be complicated and costly
- Disrupt operations during development and implementation (eg staff and management time)
- Have far reaching consequences in a way an organisation conducts future business
- Impact on organisation strategy and structure

2.2 The feasibility study team

A feasibility study team might be appointed to carry out the study (although individuals might be given the task in the case of smaller projects).

(a) Members of the team should be drawn from the **departments affected by the investment**.

(b) At least one person must have relevant **detailed technical knowledge**, and one other person be able to assess the **organisational implications** of the new system.

(c) It is possible to hire **consultants** to carry out the feasibility study, but their **lack of knowledge about the organisation** may adversely affect the usefulness of their proposals.

(d) Before selecting the members of the study group, the steering committee must ensure that they possess **suitable personal qualities**, eg the ability to be **objectively critical**.

2.3 Conducting the feasibility study

2.3.1 Terms of reference

The terms of reference for a feasibility study group may be set out by a steering committee, the information director or the board of directors. They should include defining whether **additional investment** is required, **specifying targets**, **selecting possible options**, **assessing the options** for **feasibility** and **recommending the best option**.

2.3.2 Option evaluation

This stage involves suggesting a number of **options** for the new investment, evaluating them and recommending one for adoption. It concludes with a final **feasibility study report**.

Step 1 Create the **base constraints** in terms of expenditure, implementation and design time, and system requirements, which any system should satisfy.

Step 2 Create outlines of **options**, describing, in brief, each option.

Step 3 Assess the **impact** each proposal has on the operations of the relevant department and/or the organisation as a whole.

Step 4 **Review** these proposals with the people affected, who should indicate those options they favour for further analysis.

Question

Learning outcome: D(ii)

What are the base constraints likely to be for a computerised system?

Answer

The constraints will include:

- **Operations** (for example faster processing, larger volumes, greater security, greater accuracy, better quality)
- Information **output**
- **Volume of processing**
- **General system requirements** (eg accuracy, security and controls, audit trail, flexibility, adaptability)
- **Compatibility/integration** with existing systems

2.4 Key areas of feasibility

There are five key areas in which a project must be feasible if it is to be selected.

- Operational feasibility
- Technical feasibility
- Social feasibility
- Ecological feasibility
- Economic feasibility

2.4.1 Operational feasibility

Operational feasibility is a key concern. If an investment makes technical sense but **conflicts with the way the organisation does business**, the solution is not feasible. Thus an organisation might reject a solution because it forces a change in management responsibilities, status and chains of command, or does not suit regional reporting structures, or because the costs of redundancies, retraining and reorganisation are considered too high.

2.4.2 Technical feasibility

The requirements, as defined in the feasibility study, must be technically achievable. For a computer system for example, any proposed solution must be capable of being implemented using available hardware, software and other technology. Technical feasibility considerations could include the following.

- **Volume** of transactions that can be processed within a given time
- **Capacity** to hold files or records of a certain size
- **Response times** (how quickly the computer does what you ask it to)
- **Number of users** that can be supported without deterioration in the other criteria

2.4.3 Social feasibility

An assessment of social feasibility will address a number of areas, including the following.

- **Personnel** policies
- Redrawing of **job specifications**
- Threats to **industrial relations**
- Expected **skills requirements**
- **Motivation**

2.4.4 Ecological feasibility

Ecological feasibility relates to environmental considerations. A particular course of action may be rejected on the basis that it would cause too much damage to the environment. In some markets customers may prefer to purchase ecologically sound products. Ecological feasibility issues could include the following.

- What **waste** products are produced?
- How is waste **disposed** of?
- Is use of the product likely to damage the **environment**?
- Could the production process be '**cleaner**'?
- How much **energy** does the process consume?

2.4.5 Economic feasibility

Any project will have economic costs and economic benefits. Economic feasibility has three strands.

- The **benefits must justify the costs**.
- The project must be the **'best' option** from those under consideration for its particular purpose.
- The project must **compete with projects in other areas of the business** for funds. Even if it is projected to produce a positive return and satisfies all relevant criteria, it may not be chosen because other business needs are perceived as more important.

3 Project control 5/05, 5/06

FAST FORWARD

For projects to be successful, **standards** are required in a variety of areas.

3.1 Project organisation

Projects should have an **organisation chart** and **terms of reference** defining **objectives**, **timescales** and the roles of the **key individuals**, including taking steps to minimise the chances of loss of key individuals. The **resources** required need to be specified, and their availability confirmed.

Also in the initial stages, managers need to establish a **reporting structure**, so that project progress is regularly communicated to the right managers and staff.

3.2 Project monitoring

At the start of each project, an **overall project plan** needs to be produced to enable the business to monitor project delays. This should be supplemented by **detailed project plans and budgets** describing the tasks, resources and links. Techniques that you will have come across in your previous studies such as **Gantt charts** will be helpful here.

At the initial stage, the plan needs to highlight **resource and time constraints**, and also **project date constraints**.

Quality standards also need to be established before the project commences and ongoing quality control procedures defined.

Managers and **project monitoring committees** should be kept informed of progress, with achievements measured against the project's critical success factors being regularly reported. **Cost control systems** also need to be established that will monitor actual against planned expenditure.

3.3 Project risk management

At the initial stage, risks that could affect project implementation need to be carefully identified. Once this has happened, risks need to be **ranked** according to their **seriousness** and **likelihood**, and measures taken to transfer, minimise, accept or eliminate project risks. What happens to the risk will depend on the **severity** of the risk and the **cost** of management action.

The risk situation also needs to be reviewed every time key project decisions are taken,

4 Dealing with problems

FAST FORWARD

Organisations should consider carefully what they should do if investments slip **behind schedule** or **cost more** than budgeted. It may be necessary to **modify plans**, particularly if the investment is failing to fulfil the original objectives.

4.1 Significance of difficulties

An organisation could face serious problems if major investments are late, over budget or do not fulfil the objectives that they were meant to meet.

4.2 Types of difficulty

- The investment may be **poorly managed**; there may be conflict between managers and users, and there may be a lack of **monitoring and control**.
- **Deadlines** may be **unrealistic**.
- The **requirements** that the investment is designed to fulfil may change.
- The investment process may be poorly **timetabled** and **resourced**.
- There may be a **conflict** between time, cost and quality.

4.3 Dealing with slippage

When an investment has slipped behind schedule there are a range of options open to the project manager. Some of these options are summarised in the following table.

Action	Comment
Do nothing	After considering all options it may be decided that things should be allowed to continue as they are.
Add resources	It may be possible to recover some lost ground.
Work smarter	Consider whether the methods currently being used are the most suitable, and seek changes.
Replan	If the assumptions the original plan was based on have been proved invalid a more realistic plan should be devised.

Action	Comment
Reschedule	A complete replan may not be necessary – it may be possible to recover some time by changing the phasing of certain deliverables.
Introduce incentives	Incentives such as bonus payments could be linked to work deadlines and quality.

4.4 Change procedure

Some of the reactions to slippage discussed above would involve changes that would significantly affect the investment. Other possible causes of changes to the original investment plan include:

- The availability of new technology
- Changes in personnel
- A realisation that requirements were misunderstood
- Changes in the business environment
- New legislation eg Data protection

The **earlier** a change is made the **less expensive** it should prove. However, changes will cost time and money and should not be undertaken lightly.

When considering a change **an investigation** should be conducted to discover:

- The consequences of **not** implementing the proposed change
- The impact of the change on **time**, **cost** and **quality**
- The expected **costs and benefits** of the change
- The **risks** associated with the change, and with the status-quo

The process of ensuring that proper consideration is given to the impact of proposed changes is known as **change control**.

Changes will need to be implemented into the project plan and communicated to all stakeholders.

5 Investment performance and post-completion audits

FAST FORWARD

The **nature** of an investment or project will determine how its success is measured.

5.1 Reviewing investment performance

Performance reviews will vary in content from organisation to organisation, and from investment to investment. Organisations will need to consider carefully the following factors.

- **What is evaluated**
- Who decides **what constitutes performance** and whether it is **good or bad**
- Does the **investment** have a **single clear purpose**, or a number of different purposes which will complicate the targets that are set for it
- How important will **quantitative measures** be and how important will **qualitative measures** be

5.2 Assessment of investment

Financial measures are an important measure of many investments' success. Organisations will assess whether the investment is generating the **expected positive cash flows** and whether it is fulfilling other targets, for example a **payback period** of less than a certain number of years, or a target return on investment.

However other targets may also be important. This is particularly true in customer-focused organisations, where the financial success of an investment in generating extra revenues is likely to be viewed in the context of other significant indicators.

Customer rejects: total sales	Ratio monitors customer satisfaction, providing a check on the efficiency of quality control procedures
Deliveries late: Deliveries on schedule	Whether production efficiency and production scheduling have reached acceptable levels
Flexibility measures	Whether the investment has improved responsiveness to market needs
Number of people served and speed of service	Future sales may be lost if these are inadequate
Customer satisfaction	Expressed through questionnaires, surveys etc

With other investments, the key success indicators factors are likely to be direct **improvements in production**. Likely important measures here include:

- Number of customer complaints and warranty claims
- Rework
- Delivery time
- Non-productive hours
- Machine down time
- Stock-outs

Some investments will be undertaken to improve internal procedures, and will be assessed on the basis of whether they have fulfilled the needs that prompted the investment. The performance of a computer system for example will be evaluated on the basis of whether it meets the **basic needs** to **provide information** of the **required quality** (timely, accurate, relevant to business needs, clear etc), or improves **turnaround time** for information.

Question

Learning outcome: D(ii)

What performance measures are likely to be important in assessing the success of a new computerised sales processing system?

Answer

Important measures are likely to include the following.

(a) The **growth rates in file sizes** and the **number of transactions processed** by the system. Trends should be analysed and projected to assess whether there are likely to be problems with lengthy processing time or an inefficient file structure due to the volume of processing.

(b) The **clerical manpower** needs for the system, and deciding whether they are more or less than estimated.

(c) The identification of any **delays in processing** and an assessment of the consequences of any such delays.

(d) An assessment of the **efficiency of security procedures**, in terms of number of breaches, number of viruses encountered.

(e) A check of the **error rates** for input data. High error rates may indicate inefficient preparation of input documents, an inappropriate method of data capture or poor design of input media.

(f) An examination of whether output from the computer is being used to **good purpose**. (Is it used? Is it timely? Does it go to the right people?)

(g) **Operational running costs**, examined to discover any inefficient programs or processes. This examination may reveal excessive costs for certain items although in total, costs may be acceptable.

5.3 Post-completion audits 5/05

FAST FORWARD

A **post-completion audit** is designed to identify improvements not only over the remaining life of a specific project, but in the business's budgeting and management procedures.

A **post audit** or a **post-completion audit** is a review of the cash inflows to and outflows from a project after it has reached the end of its life, or at least some years after it began. As far as possible, the actual cash flows should be measured and compared with the estimates contained in the original capital expenditure appraisal. The manager responsible for the project should be asked to explain any significant variances.

Key term

A **post-completion audit** is an objective, independent assessment of the success of a capital project in relation to plan. Covers the whole life of the project and provides feedback to managers to aid the implementation and control of future projects.

5.3.1 Benefits of post-completion audits

Post completion audit checking cannot reverse the decision to make the capital expenditure, because the expenditure will already have taken place. However, it does have a certain control value.

(a) If a manager asks for and gets approval for a capital project, and knows that in due course the project will be subject to a post-completion audit, then the manager will be more likely to pay attention to the **benefits** and the **costs** than if no post audit were threatened.

(b) If the post audit takes place before the project life ends, and if it finds that the benefits have been less than expected because of management inefficiency, steps can be taken to **improve efficiency** and earn greater benefits over the remaining life of the project. Alternatively, the post -completion audit may highlight those projects which should be discontinued.

(c) A post-completion audit can help to identify managers who have been **good performers** and those who have been poor performers.

(d) A post-completion audit might **identify weaknesses** in the forecasting and estimating techniques used to evaluate projects, and so should help to improve the quality of forecasting for future investment decisions.

(e) A post-completion audit might reveal areas where **improvements** can be made in methods so as to achieve better results from capital investments in general.

(f) The **original estimates** may be **more realistic** if managers are aware that they will be monitored, but post-completion audits should not be unfairly critical.

It may be too expensive to post-completion audit all capital expenditure projects; therefore managers may need to select a sample for a post-completion audit. A reasonable guideline might be to audit all projects above a certain size, and a random sample of smaller projects.

5.3.2 Problems with post-completion audits

(a) There are **many uncontrollable factors** in long-term investments such as environmental changes. Since such factors are outside management control there may be little to gain by identifying the resulting variances.

(b) This means that it **may not be possible to identify separately the costs and benefits** of any particular project or, due to uncertainty, to identify the costs and benefits at all.

(c) Post-completion audit can be a **costly and time-consuming exercise**. Labour, which may be a scarce resource, is required to undertake the task.

(d) Applied punitively, post-completion audit exercises may lead to **managers becoming over cautious** and unnecessarily risk averse.

(e) The **strategic effects** of a **capital investment project** may take years to materialise and it may never be possible to identify or quantify them effectively.

Exam focus point

The benefits and limitations of post-audits often come up in exams, generally for as many as 6-8 comparatively easy marks.

Chapter roundup

- Investments, particularly projects, need to be carefully planned and controlled. Managers must consider the **need** for investments, choose the **best option**, control **development and implementation** and review whether the investment has **fulfilled its aims**.
- A **feasibility study**, covering all aspects of a project's feasibility, and undertaken by a carefully selected team is a vital stage in assessing whether an investment is worthwhile. Feasibility studies are essential for investments and projects that are likely to be long and complicated.
- For projects to be successful, **standards** are required in a variety of areas.
- Organisations should consider carefully what they should do if investments slip **behind schedule** or **cost more** than budgeted. It may be necessary to **modify plans**, particularly if the investment is failing to fulfil the original objectives.
- The **nature** of an investment or project will determine how its success is measured.
- A **post-completion audit** is designed to identify improvements not only over the remaining life of a specific project, but in the organisation's budgeting and management procedures.

Quick quiz

1 What are the four project phases identified by Barnes?

2 What are the thirteen project stages identified by Barnes?

3 Which of the following are key areas that a feasibility study should assess?

A Operational feasibility
B Technical feasibility
C Social feasibility
D Strategic feasibility
E Economic feasibility
F Ecological feasibility

4 What are the main elements in the option evaluation stage?

5 On what factors should a ranking of risks be based?

6 If an investment slips behind schedule, an organisation's best course of action may be to do nothing.

True ☐

False ☐

7 Give three indicators, other than increased sales revenues, that indicate that an investment has led to better products or a better service being offered to customers.

8 A .... is an objective and independent appraisal of the measure of success of a capital expenditure project in progressing the business as planned.

Answers to quick quiz

1
- Defining
- Planning
- Implementing
- Controlling and completing

2
- Initiation
- Formation
- Objective setting
- Task planning
- Feasibility
- Fact finding
- Position analysis
- Options generation
- Options evaluation
- Design and development
- Implementation
- Review
- Completion

3 A Operational, B Technical, C Social, E Economic, F Ecological. D Strategic concerns relate to whether a project is suitable.

4
- Create the base constraints
- Create outlines of options
- Assess the impact of each proposal
- Review proposals with people affected

5 The likelihood of their happening and the severity of their consequences

6 True

7
- Customer rejects:Total sales
- Deliveries late: Deliveries on schedule
- Flexibility measures
- Number of people served and speed of service
- Customer satisfaction

8 A **post-completion audit/post audit** is an objective and independent appraisal of the measure of success of a capital expenditure project in progressing the business as planned.

Now try the question below from the Exam Question Bank

Number	Level	Marks	Time
Q35	Introductory	n/a	35 mins

Appendix 1
International terminology

International Accounting Terminology and Formats

Terminology

Below is a short list of the most important terms you are likely to use or come across, together with their international equivalents.

UK term	International term
Profit and loss account	Income statement
Profit and loss reserve (in balance sheet)	Accumulated profits (or retained earnings)
Turnover	Revenue
Debtor account	Account receivable
Debtors (eg 'debtors have increased')	Receivables
Debtor	Customer
Creditor account	Account payable
Creditors (eg 'creditors have increased')	Payables
Creditor	Supplier
Debtors control account	Receivables control account
Creditors control account	Payables control account
Stock	Inventory
Fixed asset	Non-current asset (generally). Tangible fixed assets are also referred to as 'property, plant and equipment'.
Long-term liability	Non-current liability
Provision (eg for depreciation)	Allowance (You will sometimes see 'provision' used too.)
General ledger	Nominal ledger
VAT	Sales tax
Debentures	Loan notes
Preference shares/dividends	Preferred shares/dividends

Formats

In general the format for the income statement (international) is the same as the profit and loss account (UK) except for a couple of differences in terminology. Here is a simple example, with the differences highlighted.

CHEAPSTAKE
INCOME STATEMENT
FOR THE YEAR ENDED 31 DECEMBER 20X6

		$'000
= Turnover in UK	Revenue	9,000
	Cost of sales	4,529
	Gross profit	4,471
	Distribution expenses	918
	Administration expenses	1,598
= Operating profit in UK	Profit from operations	1,955
	Finance cost	50
	Profit before tax	1,905
= Tax/corporation tax in UK	Income tax expense	105
	Profit for the year	1,800

The format of the balance sheet is different from the UK. **Instead of having net assets (assets less liabilities) equal to capital and reserves, it has total assets in the top half equal to equity and liabilities in the bottom half.**

CHEAPSTAKE
BALANCE SHEET AS AT 31 DECEMBER 20X6

	$'000	$'000
ASSETS		
Non-current assets		
Tangible assets: property and plant		2,720
Intangible asset: goodwill		270
		2,990
Current assets		
Inventory	1,950	
Receivables	1,544	
Bank	200	
		3,694
		6,684
EQUITY AND LIABILITIES		
Capital and reserves		
$1 Ordinary shares		400
10% preferred shares		600
Revaluation reserve		350
Accumulated profits		2,274
		3,624
Non-current liabilities		
5% Loan notes	1,000	
Deferred tax	120	1,120
Current liabilities		1,940
		6,684

(As you can see, assets = capital plus liabilities, rather than assets less liabilities = capital.)

Appendix 2
Mathematical tables and exam formulae

PRESENT VALUE TABLE

Present value of 1.00 unit of currency ie $(1+r)^{-n}$ where r = interest rate, n = number of periods until payment or receipt.

Periods					Interest rates (r)					
(n)	1%	2%	3%	4%	5%	6%	7%	8%	9%	10%
1	0.990	0.980	0.971	0.962	0.952	0.943	0.935	0.926	0.917	0.909
2	0.980	0.961	0.943	0.925	0.907	0.890	0.873	0.857	0.842	0.826
3	0.971	0.942	0.915	0.889	0.864	0.840	0.816	0.794	0.772	0.751
4	0.961	0.924	0.888	0.855	0.823	0.792	0.763	0.735	0.708	0.683
5	0.951	0.906	0.863	0.822	0.784	0.747	0.713	0.681	0.650	0.621
6	0.942	0.888	0.837	0.790	0.746	0.705	0.666	0.630	0.596	0.564
7	0.933	0.871	0.813	0.760	0.711	0.665	0.623	0.583	0.547	0.513
8	0.923	0.853	0.789	0.731	0.677	0.627	0.582	0.540	0.502	0.467
9	0.914	0.837	0.766	0.703	0.645	0.592	0.544	0.500	0.460	0.424
10	0.905	0.820	0.744	0.676	0.614	0.558	0.508	0.463	0.422	0.386
11	0.896	0.804	0.722	0.650	0.585	0.527	0.475	0.429	0.388	0.350
12	0.887	0.788	0.701	0.625	0.557	0.497	0.444	0.397	0.356	0.319
13	0.879	0.773	0.681	0.601	0.530	0.469	0.415	0.368	0.326	0.290
14	0.870	0.758	0.661	0.577	0.505	0.442	0.388	0.340	0.299	0.263
15	0.861	0.743	0.642	0.555	0.481	0.417	0.362	0.315	0.275	0.239
16	0.853	0.728	0.623	0.534	0.458	0.394	0.339	0.292	0.252	0.218
17	0.844	0.714	0.605	0.513	0.436	0.371	0.317	0.270	0.231	0.198
18	0.836	0.700	0.587	0.494	0.416	0.350	0.296	0.250	0.212	0.180
19	0.828	0.686	0.570	0.475	0.396	0.331	0.277	0.232	0.194	0.164
20	0.820	0.673	0.554	0.456	0.377	0.312	0.258	0.215	0.178	0.149

Periods					Interest rates (r)					
(n)	11%	12%	13%	14%	15%	16%	17%	18%	19%	20%
1	0.901	0.893	0.885	0.877	0.870	0.862	0.855	0.847	0.840	0.833
2	0.812	0.797	0.783	0.769	0.756	0.743	0.731	0.718	0.706	0.694
3	0.731	0.712	0.693	0.675	0.658	0.641	0.624	0.609	0.593	0.579
4	0.659	0.636	0.613	0.592	0.572	0.552	0.534	0.516	0.499	0.482
5	0.593	0.567	0.543	0.519	0.497	0.476	0.456	0.437	0.419	0.402
6	0.535	0.507	0.480	0.456	0.432	0.410	0.390	0.370	0.352	0.335
7	0.482	0.452	0.425	0.400	0.376	0.354	0.333	0.314	0.296	0.279
8	0.434	0.404	0.376	0.351	0.327	0.305	0.285	0.266	0.249	0.233
9	0.391	0.361	0.333	0.308	0.284	0.263	0.243	0.225	0.209	0.194
10	0.352	0.322	0.295	0.270	0.247	0.227	0.208	0.191	0.176	0.162
11	0.317	0.287	0.261	0.237	0.215	0.195	0.178	0.162	0.148	0.135
12	0.286	0.257	0.231	0.208	0.187	0.168	0.152	0.137	0.124	0.112
13	0.258	0.229	0.204	0.182	0.163	0.145	0.130	0.116	0.104	0.093
14	0.232	0.205	0.181	0.160	0.141	0.125	0.111	0.099	0.088	0.078
15	0.209	0.183	0.160	0.140	0.123	0.108	0.095	0.084	0.074	0.065
16	0.188	0.163	0.141	0.123	0.107	0.093	0.081	0.071	0.062	0.054
17	0.170	0.146	0.125	0.108	0.093	0.080	0.069	0.060	0.052	0.045
18	0.153	0.130	0.111	0.095	0.081	0.069	0.059	0.051	0.044	0.038
19	0.138	0.116	0.098	0.083	0.070	0.060	0.051	0.043	0.037	0.031
20	0.124	0.104	0.087	0.073	0.061	0.051	0.043	0.037	0.031	0.026

CUMULATIVE PRESENT VALUE TABLE

This table shows the present value of 1.00 unit of currency per annum, receivable or payable at the end of each year for *n* years $\frac{1-(1+r)^{-n}}{r}$.

Periods (n)	Interest rates (r) 1%	2%	3%	4%	5%	6%	7%	8%	9%	10%
1	0.990	0.980	0.971	0.962	0.952	0.943	0.935	0.926	0.917	0.909
2	1.970	1.942	1.913	1.886	1.859	1.833	1.808	1.783	1.759	1.736
3	2.941	2.884	2.829	2.775	2.723	2.673	2.624	2.577	2.531	2.487
4	3.902	3.808	3.717	3.630	3.546	3.465	3.387	3.312	3.240	3.170
5	4.853	4.713	4.580	4.452	4.329	4.212	4.100	3.993	3.890	3.791
6	5.795	5.601	5.417	5.242	5.076	4.917	4.767	4.623	4.486	4.355
7	6.728	6.472	6.230	6.002	5.786	5.582	5.389	5.206	5.033	4.868
8	7.652	7.325	7.020	6.733	6.463	6.210	5.971	5.747	5.535	5.335
9	8.566	8.162	7.786	7.435	7.108	6.802	6.515	6.247	5.995	5.759
10	9.471	8.983	8.530	8.111	7.722	7.360	7.024	6.710	6.418	6.145
11	10.368	9.787	9.253	8.760	8.306	7.887	7.499	7.139	6.805	6.495
12	11.255	10.575	9.954	9.385	8.863	8.384	7.943	7.536	7.161	6.814
13	12.134	11.348	10.635	9.986	9.394	8.853	8.358	7.904	7.487	7.103
14	13.004	12.106	11.296	10.563	9.899	9.295	8.745	8.244	7.786	7.367
15	13.865	12.849	11.938	11.118	10.380	9.712	9.108	8.559	8.061	7.606
16	14.718	13.578	12.561	11.652	10.838	10.106	9.447	8.851	8.313	7.824
17	15.562	14.292	13.166	12.166	11.274	10.477	9.763	9.122	8.544	8.022
18	16.398	14.992	13.754	12.659	11.690	10.828	10.059	9.372	8.756	8.201
19	17.226	15.679	14.324	13.134	12.085	11.158	10.336	9.604	8.950	8.365
20	18.046	16.351	14.878	13.590	12.462	11.470	10.594	9.818	9.129	8.514

Periods (n)	Interest rates (r) 11%	12%	13%	14%	15%	16%	17%	18%	19%	20%
1	0.901	0.893	0.885	0.877	0.870	0.862	0.855	0.847	0.840	0.833
2	1.713	1.690	1.668	1.647	1.626	1.605	1.585	1.566	1.547	1.528
3	2.444	2.402	2.361	2.322	2.283	2.246	2.210	2.174	2.140	2.106
4	3.102	3.037	2.974	2.914	2.855	2.798	2.743	2.690	2.639	2.589
5	3.696	3.605	3.517	3.433	3.352	3.274	3.199	3.127	3.058	2.991
6	4.231	4.111	3.998	3.889	3.784	3.685	3.589	3.498	3.410	3.326
7	4.712	4.564	4.423	4.288	4.160	4.039	3.922	3.812	3.706	3.605
8	5.146	4.968	4.799	4.639	4.487	4.344	4.207	4.078	3.954	3.837
9	5.537	5.328	5.132	4.946	4.772	4.607	4.451	4.303	4.163	4.031
10	5.889	5.650	5.426	5.216	5.019	4.833	4.659	4.494	4.339	4.192
11	6.207	5.938	5.687	5.453	5.234	5.029	4.836	4.656	4.486	4.327
12	6.492	6.194	5.918	5.660	5.421	5.197	4.988	4.793	4.611	4.439
13	6.750	6.424	6.122	5.842	5.583	5.342	5.118	4.910	4.715	4.533
14	6.982	6.628	6.302	6.002	5.724	5.468	5.229	5.008	4.802	4.611
15	7.191	6.811	6.462	6.142	5.847	5.575	5.324	5.092	4.876	4.675
16	7.379	6.974	6.604	6.265	5.954	5.668	5.405	5.162	4.938	4.730
17	7.549	7.120	6.729	6.373	6.047	5.749	5.475	5.222	4.990	4.775
18	7.702	7.250	6.840	6.467	6.128	5.818	5.534	5.273	5.033	4.812
19	7.839	7.366	6.938	6.550	6.198	5.877	5.584	5.316	5.070	4.843
20	7.963	7.469	7.025	6.623	6.259	5.929	5.628	5.353	5.101	4.870

EXAM FORMULAE

Valuation models

(i) Irredeemable preference share, paying a constant annual dividend, d, in perpetuity, where P_0 is the ex-div value:

$$P_0 = \frac{d}{k_{pref}}$$

(ii) Ordinary (equity) share, paying a constant annual dividend, d, in perpetuity, where P_0 is the ex-div value:

$$P_0 = \frac{d}{k_e}$$

(iii) Ordinary (equity) share, paying an annual dividend, d, growing in perpetuity at a constant rate, g, where P_0 is the ex-div value:

$$P_0 = \frac{d_1}{k_e - g} \text{ or } P_0 = \frac{d_0[1+g]}{k_e - g}$$

(iv) Irredeemable (undated) bonds, paying annual after tax interest, i(1 – t), in perpetuity, where P_0 is the ex-interest value:

$$P_0 = \frac{i[1-t]}{k_{d\ net}}$$

or, without tax:

$$P_0 = \frac{i}{k_d}$$

(v) Total value of the geared firm, V_g (based on MM):

$$V_g = V_u + TB_c$$

(vi) Future value S, of a sum X, invested for n periods, compounded at r% interest:

$$S = X[1 + r]^n$$

(vii) Present value of 1.00 payable or receivable in n years, discounted at r% per annum:

$$PV = \frac{1}{[1+r]^n}$$

(viii) Present value of an annuity of 1.00 per annum, receivable or payable for n years, commencing in one year, discounted at r% per annum:

$$PV = \frac{1}{r}\left[1 - \frac{1}{[1+r]^n}\right]$$

(ix) Present value of 1.00 per annum, payable or receivable in perpetuity, commencing in one year, discounted at r% per annum:

$$PV = \frac{1}{r}$$

(x) Present value of 1.00 per annum, receivable or payable, commencing in one year, growing in perpetuity at a constant rate of g% per annum, discounted at r% per annum:

$$PV = \frac{1}{r-g}$$

Cost of capital

(i) Cost of irredeemable preference shares, paying an annual dividend d in perpetuity, and having a current ex-div price P_0:

$$k_{pref} = \frac{d}{P_0}$$

(ii) Cost of irredeemable bonds, paying annual net interest i(1 – t), and having a current ex-interest price P_0:

$$k_{d\ net} = \frac{i[1-t]}{P_0}$$

(iii) Cost of ordinary (equity) shares, paying an annual dividend d in perpetuity, and having a current ex div price P_0:

$$k_e = \frac{d}{P_0}$$

(iv) Cost of ordinary (equity) shares, having a current ex div price, P_0, having just paid a dividend, d_0, with the dividend growing in perpetuity by a constant g% per annum:

$$k_e = \frac{d_1}{P_0} + g \text{ or } k_e = \frac{d_0[1+g]}{P_0} + g$$

(v) Cost of ordinary (equity) shares, using the CAPM:

$$k_e = R_f + [R_m - R_f]\beta$$

(vi) Cost of ordinary (equity) shares in a geared firm, (no tax):

$$k_{eg} = k_0 + [k_0 - k_d]\frac{V_D}{V_E}$$

(vii) Cost of ordinary (equity) shares in a geared firm, (with tax):

$$k_{eg} = k_{eu} + [k_{eu} - k_d]\frac{V_D[1-t]}{V_E}$$

(viii) Weighted average cost of capital, k_0:

$$k_0 = k_{eg}\left[\frac{V_E}{V_E + V_D}\right] + k_d\left[\frac{V_D}{V_E + V_D}\right]$$

(ix) Adjusted cost of capital (MM formula)

$$k_{adj} = k_{eu}[1 - tL] \text{ or } r^* = r[1 - T^*L]$$

In the following formulae, β_u is used for an ungeared β, and β_g is used for a geared β:

(x) β_u from β_g, taking β_d as zero, (no tax):

$$\beta_u = \beta_g\left[\frac{V_E}{V_E + V_D}\right]$$

(xi) If β_d is not zero:

$$\beta_u = \beta_g \left[\frac{V_E}{V_E + V_D} \right] + \beta_d \left[\frac{V_D}{V_E + V_E} \right]$$

(xii) β_u from β_g, taking β_d as zero, (with tax):

$$\beta_u = \beta_g \left[\frac{V_E}{V_E + V_D[1 - t]} \right]$$

(xiii) Adjusted discount rate to use in international capital budgeting using interest rate parity:

$$\frac{1 + \text{annual discount rate C\$}}{1 + \text{annual discount rate Euro}} = \frac{\text{Exchange rate in 12 months time C\$/Euro}}{\text{Spot rate C\$/Euro}}$$

Other formulae

(i) Interest rate parity (International Fisher effect)

$$\text{Forward rate US\$/£} = \text{Spot US\$/£} \times \frac{1 + \text{nominal US interest rate}}{1 + \text{nominal UK interest rate}}$$

(ii) Purchasing power parity (Law of one price)

$$\text{Forward rate US\$/£} = \text{Spot US\$/£} \times \frac{1 + \text{US inflation rate}}{1 + \text{UK inflation rate}}$$

(iii) Link between nominal (money) and real interest rates

[1 + nominal (money) rate] = [1 + real interest rate][1 + inflation rate]

(iv) Equivalent annual cost

$$\text{Equivalent annual cost} = \frac{\text{PV of costs over n years}}{\text{n year annuity factor}}$$

(v) Theoretical ex-rights price

$$\text{TERP} = \frac{1}{N + 1}[(N \times \text{Cum rights price}) + \text{Issue price}]$$

(vi) Value of a right

$$\text{Value of a right} = \frac{\text{Rights on price} - \text{Issue price}}{N + 1}$$

or

$$\frac{\text{Theoretical ex rights price} - \text{Issue price}}{N}$$

where N = number of rights required to buy one share.

Exam question and answer bank

1 Earnings per share — 45 mins

Learning outcomes: A(i), (v)

(a) 'Financial managers need only concentrate on meeting the needs of shareholders by maximising earnings per share – no other group matters.'

Discuss. **(10 marks)**

(b) Many decisions in financial management are taken in a framework of conflicting stakeholder viewpoints. Identify the stakeholders and some of the financial management issues involved in the following situations.

(i) A private company converting into a public company.

(ii) A highly geared company, such as Eurotunnel, attempting to restructure its capital finance.

(iii) A large conglomerate 'spinning off' its numerous divisions by selling them, or setting them up as separate companies (eg Hanson).

(iv) Japanese car-makers, such as Nissan and Honda, building new car plants in other countries. **(15 marks)**

(Total = 25 marks)

2 Corporate governance — 30 mins

Learning outcome: A(iii)

You have recently joined ABC, a small textile company, as company secretary. Miss Grey, your predecessor as company secretary, was dismissed by the finance director who considered that she was incompetent.

ABC has its shares listed on the London Stock Exchange. There are six directors on the board of ABC – the executive chairman who is also the chief executive, the finance director and four other directors, each of whom is responsible for various geographical areas around the world. ABC is growing rapidly and the directors work long hours, often outside the United Kingdom, developing business abroad.

You notice when looking through the minutes of the board from the previous twelve months that the directors met formally on two occasions, the chairman and finance director having been delegated authority by the board to deal with any matters of importance between meetings.

You also notice from the minutes that few written reports are submitted to the board and that directors prefer to make oral reports on most matters.

The chairman is keen to add a non-executive director to the board and has decided to appoint a recently-retired executive director of the company who was very successful in winning business in the United Kingdom.

The chairman also intends to hire a firm of remuneration consultants to advise him on the level of salary he should set for himself and the other directors. To ensure a degree of stability in the company during the period of rapid growth, the chairman also has in mind increasing from one to two years the notice period specified in the service contracts of two of the company's executive directors.

You are aware of the principles of good governance and the Combined Code appended to the Stock Exchange listing rules.

Required

Write a memorandum to the chairman which identifies any concerns you may have about the governance arrangements in the company and the chairman's plans, describing the measures that should be taken by the company at its annual general meeting to ensure compliance with the Code.

3 Subsidiaries **35 mins**

Learning outcome: A(iv)

Your company has two subsidiaries, X and Y, both providing computer services, notably software development and implementation. The UK market for such services is said to be growing at about 20% a year. The business is seasonal, peaking between September and March.

You have available the comparative data shown in the Appendix to this question below. The holding company's policy is to leave the financing and management of subsidiaries entirely to the subsidiaries' directors.

Required

In the light of this information, compare and contrast the performance of the two subsidiaries.

It may be assumed that the difference in size of the two companies does not invalidate a comparison of the ratios provided.

Appendix

Data in this Appendix should be accepted as correct. Any apparent internal inconsistencies are due to rounding of the figures.

	X Ltd	*Y Ltd*
Revenue in most recent year (£'000)		
Home	2,856	6,080
Export	2,080	1,084
Total	4,936	7,164
Index of revenue 20X9 (20X6 = 100)		
Home	190%	235%
Export	220%	150%
Total	200%	220%
Operating profit 20X9 (£'000)	840	720
Operating capital employed 20X9 (£'000)	625	1,895

Ratio analysis		*X Ltd*			*Y Ltd*		
		20X9	*20X8*	*20X7*	*20X9*	*20X8*	*20X7*
Return on operating capital employed	%	134	142	47	38	40	52
Operating profit: Sales	%	17	16	6	10	8	5
Sales: Operating capital employed	×	8	9	8	4	5	10
Percentages to sales value:							
Cost of sales	%	65	67	71	49	49	51
Selling and distribution costs	%	12	11	15	15	16	19
Administration expenses	%	6	6	8	26	27	25
Number of employees		123	127	88	123	114	91
Sales per employee	£'000	40	37	31	58	52	47
Average remuneration per employee	£'000	13	13	12	16	4	13
Tangible non-current assets turnover rate	×	20	21	14	9	11	14
Additions, at cost	%	57	47	58	303	9	124
Percentage depreciated	%	45	36	20	41	60	72
Product development costs carried forward as a percentage of revenue	%	0	0	0	10	8	6
Receivables: Sales	%	18	18	22	61	41	39
Inventory: Sales	%	0	1	0	2	2	1
Cash: Sales	%	7	9	2	1	1	0
Trade payables: Sales	%	2	2	3	32	21	24
Trade payables: receivables	%	11	14	15	53	50	62
Current ratio (:1)		1.5	1.3	1.2	1.1	1.1	0.9
Liquid ratio (:1)		1.5	1.3	1.2	1.0	1.0	0.9
Liquid ratio excluding bank overdraft		0	0	0	1.4	1.5	1.2
Total debt : Total assets	%	61	71	109	75	72	84

4 ZX — 45 mins

Learning outcome: B(i)

ZX is a relatively small US-based company in the agricultural industry. It is highly mechanised and uses modern techniques and equipment. In the past, it has operated a very conservative policy in respect of the management of its working capital. Assume that you are a newly recruited management accountant. The finance director, who is responsible for both financial control and treasury functions, has asked you to review this policy.

You assemble the following information about the company's forecast end-of-year financial outcomes. The company's year end is in six months' time.

	US$'000
Receivables	2,500
Inventory	2,000
Cash at bank	500
Current assets	5,000
Non-current assets	1,250
Current liabilities	1,850
Forecast sales for the full year	8,000
Forecast operating profit (18% of sales)	1,440

You wish to evaluate the likely effect on the company if it introduced one or two alternative approaches to working capital management. The finance director suggests you adjust the figures in accordance with the following parameters.

	'Moderate' policy	'Aggressive' policy
Receivables and inventory	– 20%	– 30%
Cash	Reduce to $250,000	Reduce to $100,000
Non-current assets	No change	No change
Current liabilities	+10%	+20%
Forecast sales	+ 2%	+4%
Forecast profit	No change in percentage profit/sales	

Required

Write a report to the finance director that includes the following.

(a) A discussion of the main aspects to consider when determining policy in respect of the investment in, and financing of, working capital, in general and in the circumstances of ZX. **(10 marks)**

(b) Calculations of the return on net assets and the current ratio under each of three scenarios shown below.

- The company continues with its present policy.
- The company adopts the 'moderate' policy.
- The company adopts the 'aggressive' policy. **(8 marks)**

(c) A recommendation for the company of a proposed course of action. Your recommendation should be based on your evaluation as discussed above and on your opinion of what further action is necessary before a final decision can be taken. **(7 marks)**

(Total = 25 marks)

5 ABC — 20 mins

Learning outcome: A(ii)

The managing directors of three profitable listed companies discussed their company's dividend policies at a business lunch.

Company A has deliberately paid no dividends for the last five years.

Company B always pays a dividend of 50% of earnings after taxation.

Company C maintains a low but constant dividend per share (after adjusting for the general price index), and offers regular scrip issues and shareholder concessions.

Each managing director is convinced that his company's policy is maximising shareholder wealth.

Required

Discuss the advantages and disadvantages of the alternative dividend policies of the three, and the circumstances under which each managing director might be correct in his belief that his company's dividend policy is maximising shareholder wealth. State clearly any assumptions that you make.

6 Cuando — 36 mins

Learning outcome: A(ii)

Cuando is an on-line retailer of books, CDs and DVDs. The company was set up five years ago by a wealthy entrepreneur, David Nile, and has now grown to the point where the Board of Directors has decided that a listing should be sought on the local stock exchange. David Nile owns 80 per cent of the ordinary shares and has agreed to sell all of these as part of the public offering.

Recently, the Board of Directors began to debate the future dividend policy of the company, assuming that the stock exchange listing would be successful. However, there was a clear divergence of views. The Chairman felt that the current dividend policy was unacceptable and needed to be changed. He argued that the company had been investing heavily in its distribution methods and in advertising in the early years and that dividend policy had not been a pressing issue. However, the proposed listing must now lead to a reconsideration of the importance of dividends. The Chief Operating Officer, on the other hand, felt that the Chairman's concerns were unfounded as the pattern of dividends had no effect on shareholder wealth.

Information concerning the company since it was first set up is as follows:

Year ended 30 November	*Net profits after taxation*	*Ordinary dividends*	*Ordinary shares in issue*
	£000s	£000s	000s
20X0	650	320	800
20X1	520	150	1,000
20X2	760	480	1,000
20X3	1,240	600	1,500
20X4	1,450	540	1,500

Required

(a) Evaluate the views expressed by the Chief Operating Officer and by the Chairman. **(10 marks)**

(b) Analyse the dividend policy that has been pursued to date and discuss whether a change would be in the interests of shareholders. **(6 marks)**

(c) Discuss the key points that should be taken into account when establishing an appropriate dividend policy for the company. **(4 marks)**

(Total = 20 marks)

7 Astatine — 35 mins

Learning outcome: B(i)

The abridged balance sheet of Astatine as at 30 November 20X5 is as follows:

Balance sheet as at 30 November 20X5

	£m
Non-current assets	48
Current assets	66
	114
Less: amounts falling due within one year	43
	71
Less: amounts falling due beyond one year	30
	41
Capital and reserves	
Ordinary £1 shares	20
Accumulated profits	21
	41

The market value of the shares of the company is currently £3.46 per share.

'Now' is December 20X5.

At a recent meeting of the board of directors it was decided to reduce the gearing of the company by making a one for five rights issue at £2.50 per share and by using the proceeds of the share issue to repay some of the long-term lenders.

The directors also decided that, immediately following the rights issue, the company would make *either*:

(i) A one for four bonus issue; or
(ii) A one for one share split.

Required

(a) Prepare the balance sheet of the company after the rights issue.

(b) Separately prepare the balance sheet of the company after:

 (i) A bonus issue has been made, and
 (ii) A stock split has been made.

(c) Assuming no other factors affect the share price, calculate the likely value of a share in the company after the rights issue.

(d) Separately calculate the likely value of the shares after:

 (i) A bonus issue has been made, and
 (ii) A stock split has been made.

(e) Assuming a shareholder holding 1,000 shares in the company at 30 November 20X5 takes up the rights issue, calculate the effect on the shareholder's wealth after:

 (i) A bonus issue has been made, and
 (ii) A stock split has been made.

(f) Explain why the company may be considering either a bonus issue or share split.

8 Sagitta — 27 mins

Learning outcome: B(i)

Sagitta is a large UK fashion retailer that opened stores in India and China three years ago. This has proved to be less successful than expected and so the directors of the company have decided to withdraw from the overseas market and to concentrate on the UK market. To raise the finance necessary to close the overseas stores, the directors have also decided to make a one-for-five rights issue at a discount of 30% on the current market value. The most recent income statement of the business is as follows.

Income statement for the year ended 31 May 20X4

	£m
Sales	1,400.00
Net profit before interest and taxation	52.0
Interest payable	24.0
Net profit before taxation	28.0
Company tax	7.0
Net profit after taxation	21.0
Ordinary dividends payable	14.0
Accumulated profit	7.0

The capital and reserves of the business as at 31 May 20X4 are as follows.

	£m
£0.25 ordinary shares	60.0
Revaluation reserve	140.0
Accumulated profits	320.0
	520.0

The shares of the business are currently traded on the London Stock Exchange at a P/E ratio of 16 times. An investor owning 10,000 ordinary shares in the business has received information of the forthcoming rights issue but cannot decide whether to take up the rights issue, sell the rights or allow the rights offer to lapse.

Required

(a) Calculate the theoretical ex-rights price of an ordinary share in Sagitta. **(3 marks)**

(b) Calculate the price at which the rights in Sagitta are likely to be traded. **(3 marks)**

(c) Evaluate each of the options available to the investor with 10,000 ordinary shares. **(4 marks)**

(d) Discuss, from the viewpoint of the business, how critical the pricing of a rights issue is likely to be. **(5 marks)**

(Total = 15 marks)

9 Sundown Carehomes **34 mins**

Learning outcome: B(i)

Sundown Carehomes (Sundown) is planning to purchase for £1.6 million, a small private company, Thirdage. Originally Sundown suggested an all-share offer, but the owners of Thirdage insisted on payment in cash. Sundown are considering four ways to raise the money required;

(a) By making a '1 for 4' rights issue at £4. Sundown shares currently stand at £4.75.

(b) By issuing £1.6 million in 8% 20-year loan notes (maturing 20X0) at par.

(c) By issuing 20-year zero-coupon bonds with a redemption yield of 8% and repayable at par.

(d) By issuing £1.6 million in 6% 20-year convertible bonds, at par, with the option to convert into 5 shares at £20 per share on maturity of the bond in 20X0.

Current redemption yield of a 7% Government loan note maturing in 20X0 is 5%.

Required

(a) Explain what is meant by the phrase 'redemption yield of a 7% Government loan note'. **(3 marks)**

(b) Explain why Sundown Carehomes would issue bonds with a 8% redemption yield when yield on Government bonds is only 5%. **(3 marks)**

(c) Describe the features of a zero-coupon bond and explain why a company might issue such a bond and why investors might find it attractive. **(3 marks)**

(d) Calculate the theoretical share price immediately after making the proposed rights issue, if there is 100% take-up of the issue. **(3 marks)**

(e) Calculate the issue price of the zero coupon bond. **(3 marks)**

(f) Calculate the net present value of the convertibility option, assuming a discount rate of 8%, and explain what this tells you about expectations for Sundown's profitability or business performance. **(4 marks)**

(Total Marks = 19 marks)

10 PG — 35 mins

Learning outcome: B(i)

(a) PG has a paid-up ordinary share capital of £4,500,000 represented by 6 million shares of 75p each. It has no loan capital. Earnings after tax in the most recent year were £3,600,000. The P/E ratio of the company is 15.

The company is planning to make a large new investment which will cost £10,500,000, and is considering raising the necessary finance through a rights issue at 800p.

Required

(i) Calculate the current market price of PG's ordinary shares.

(ii) Calculate the theoretical ex-rights price, and state what factors in practice might invalidate your calculation.

(iii) Briefly explain what is meant by a deep-discounted rights issue, identifying the main reasons why a company might raise finance by this method.

(b) As an alternative to a rights issue, PG might raise the £10,500,000 required by means of an issue of convertible loan notes at par, with a coupon rate of 6%. The loan notes would be redeemable in seven years' time. Prior to redemption, the loan notes may be converted at a rate of 11 ordinary shares per £100 nominal.

Required

(i) Explain the term conversion premium and calculate the conversion premium at the date of issue implicit in the data given.

(ii) Identify the advantages to PG of issuing convertible loan notes instead of the rights issue to raise the necessary finance.

11 Ducey — 30 mins

Learning outcome: B(i)

Ducey has decided to acquire some new plant and machinery and is now considering whether to buy or to lease it. The machinery in question has a useful life of four years and is expected to have no residual value at the end of that time. It would cost £176,000 to buy which would be financed by borrowing. Alternatively it could be leased for four years at an annual rental of £55,000 payable annually in advance.

The tax rate is 30%. If purchased the machine would attract tax-allowable depreciation of 25% (reducing balance basis) per annum. A balancing allowance or charge would be made on disposal. If leased, the rental would be allowed fully against tax. Tax is paid (and allowances received) one year in arrears.

The before tax cost of borrowing to Ducey is estimated to be 19%.

Required

(a) Advise Ducey whether to buy or to lease the machine on the assumption that the company has sufficient taxable profits to fully absorb all tax allowances rising from the buy or lease decision.

(b) Advise Ducey whether to buy or to lease the machine on the basis that the company is in a permanent non-tax paying position.

(c) Describe briefly any other factors which the company should take into account when making the lease or buy decision.

12 Share values **45 mins**

Learning outcome: B(i)

(a) Describe the main forms of market efficiency and their impact upon the value of shares. **(9 marks)**

(b) Discuss the following in the context of the efficient markets hypothesis.

(i) The role of fundamental analysis
(ii) The purchase and sale of shares using 'insider information'
(iii) The popularity of index tracking funds which track stock market indices
(iv) The recent stock market volatility around the world, particularly in the Far East **(16 marks)**

(Total = 25 marks)

13 M and N **45 mins**

Learning outcome: B(i)

(a) Explain the Modigliani-Miller theory on the effect of gearing on the cost of capital to, and value of, the firm, in the absence of taxation. Explain how the theory is adjusted to take into account the effects of taxation. What are the principal weaknesses of this theory? **(10 marks)**

(b) M and N are two companies, operating in the same industry, which have reported identical net operating incomes. The stock market regards the net operating incomes of the two companies as being subject to the same degree of business risk.

M is financed entirely by equity, its share capital consisting of 20 million 50p shares with a market price of £4.80 per share (ex div). The cost of equity to M is estimated to be 18%. N is financed by a combination of £20,000,000 12% irredeemable debentures (market price £120) and 30 million £1 ordinary shares.

The risk free rate of interest is 10%. The market prices of M's shares and N's debentures are considered to be in equilibrium.

Required

Using (where appropriate) the Modigliani-Miller propositions, calculate:

(i) The equilibrium market price of N's shares
(ii) The equilibrium cost of equity of N
(iii) The weighted average cost of capital of N

Assume (i) no taxation; and (ii) corporation tax at 25%. (Make separate calculations for each assumption.)

Ignore dividends and accrued interest on the debentures. **(15 marks)**

(Total = 25 marks)

14 Serpens **36 mins**

Learning outcome: B(i)

Serpens has recently been listed on the London Stock Exchange. In the previous month, the company announced profits before interest and taxation of £0.5 million and the Board of Directors believes that this level of profits is unlikely to change in the foreseeable future. The dividend policy of the company is to distribute all available profits to shareholders. The company is financed entirely by equity shares but the

Board wishes to change its capital structure by issuing £3 million 5% debentures at par and using the proceeds to purchase and cancel some of the equity shares in issue.

Diphda operates within the same industry as Serpens and is considered to have the same level of business risk. It has a capital structure of 70% equity and 30% loan capital. The equity beta of Diphda is 1.4 and the loan capital is risk free. The after-tax, risk-free rate of return and returns to the market are 4% and 9% respectively. The rate of corporation tax is 20%.

Required

(a) Calculate the profits available for dividend for Serpens and the value of the company under:

(i) The current capital structure; and

(ii) The proposed capital structure. **(11 marks)**

(b) Discuss the arguments for and against the view that the capital structure of a company has no effect on the value of the company. **(9 marks)**

(Total = 20 marks)

15 ABC — 45 mins

Leaning outcome: B(i)

ABC is a large professional service company listed on a major international stock exchange. ABC has recently appointed a new Finance Director who is concerned about the financing of the company.

Forecast balance sheet at 31 May 20X4:

	$ million
Non-current assets	555
Current assets	195
	750
Issued share capital (per value 25 cents)	200
Reserves	250
	450
Debentures 7% annual coupon (nominal value) (redeemable 31 May 20X8 at par)	150
Bank loans	100
Current liabilities	50
	750

On 31 May 20X4, market values are $107 per cent ex interest for debentures and $0.75 ex dividend for each share. Interest on the bank loan is 5% per annum and the loans are not scheduled to be repaid before 31 May 20X7.

The following earnings and closing shareholder funds have been forecast for the next three years:

Year ending	*31 May 20X5*	*31 May 20X6*	*31 May 20X7*
	$ million	*$ million*	*$ million*
Earnings before interest and tax (EBIT)	58.0	50.0	54.0
Closing shareholder funds at year end	446.8	437.9	431.9

Debenture covenants

There are two covenants relating to the debentures, as follows:

> 'At no time will the debt ratio of prior charge capital/shareholders' funds exceed 60%, based upon book values.'

'The ratio of EBIT/total interest payable shall not fall below 3.5 times.'

Restructuring funding

The Finance director is concerned that the company is close to breaching debenture covenants and is considering ways of restructuring the company's funding to eliminate this risk.

Two alternatives are being considered.

One scheme is to redeem the debentures on 31 May 20X4 at market value, funded by a new bank loan. The company's bank has quoted an annual coupon of 5% for a loan maturing on 31 May 20X8.

An alternative scheme, being recommended by ABC's merchant bank, is a rights issue of 1 for 5 shares to raise $100 million of funds to repay the current bank loan.

Assume that tax is recoverable at 30% on interest payments at the time that the interest is paid and that all interest payments are made annually in arrears. Ignore any taxation implications of the redemption premium on the debenture.

Required:

(a) Calculate gearing and interest cover ratios for the years ending 31 May 20X5 to 31 May 20X7, and indicate whether ABC is likely to breach either of the two debenture covenants over the next three years. (Ignore any restructing funding proposals.) **(4 marks)**

(b) Calculate the cost of debt for the existing debenture based on the current market value on 31 May 20X4 and advise the Finance director whether or not it is likely to be cheaper to redeem the debenture with a bank loan. Identify what other factors would need to be taken into account when deciding whether to redeem the debenture with a bank loan. (No further calculations are required). **(10 marks)**

(c) Calculate the issue price and ex-rights price of the proposed rights issue. Discuss the advantages of the merchant bank's recommendation to repay the bank loan by raising new equity finance compared with the merits of redeeming the debentures by entering into a new bank loan.

(Note: No further gearing or interest cover calculations are required.) **(11 marks)**

(Total = 25 marks)

16 Risk reduction — 25 mins

Learning outcome: B(i)

(a) Explain the development of portfolio theory when more than two securities are available, including the availability of risk-free investments.

(b) Explain the practical implications of portfolio theory to a fund manager and to the projects manager of a company.

17 I — 45 mins

Learning outcome: B(i)

I is an all equity financed listed company. It develops customised software for clients which are mainly large civil engineering companies. Nearly all its shares are held by financial institutions.

I's chairman has been dissatisfied with the company's performance for some time. Some directors were also concerned about the way in which the company is perceived by financial markets. In response, the company recently appointed a new finance director who advocated using the capital asset pricing model as a means of evaluating risk and interpreting the stock market's reaction to the company.

The following initial information was put forward by the finance director for two rival companies operating in the same industry:

Company	*Beta*
A	0.7
B	1.4

The *finance director* notes that the risk-free rate is 5% each year and the expected rate of return on the market portfolio is 15% each year.

The *chairman* set out his concerns at a meeting of the board of directors: 'I fail to understand these calculations. A operates largely in overseas markets with all the risk which that involves, yet you seem to be arguing that it is a lower risk company than B, whose income is mainly derived from long-term contracts in our domestic UK building industry. I am very concerned that we can take too much notice of the stock market. Take last year for instance, we had to announce a loss and the share price went up.'

Required

(a) Calculate, using the capital asset pricing model, the required rate of return on equity of:

(i) A

(ii) B **(4 marks)**

(b) Calculate the beta of I, assuming its required annual rate of return on equity is 17% and the stock market uses the capital asset pricing model to calculate the beta, and explain the significance of the beta factor. **(6 marks)**

(c) As the new finance director, write a memorandum to the chairman which explains, in language understandable to a non-financial manager, the following:

(i) The assumptions and limitations of the capital asset pricing model; and

(ii) An explanation of why I's share price could rise following the announcement of a loss.

In so doing, discuss the observations and concerns expressed by the chairman. You may refer, where appropriate, to your calculations in (a) and (b) above. **(15 marks)**

(Total = 25 marks)

18 Ingredients and attributes — 25 mins

Learning outcome: B(ii)

Describe the ingredients and attributes of information which are important when planning the way information is presented by the finance function to decision makers in an organisation.

19 Treasury management — 20 mins

Learning outcome: B(iii)

Many large international organisations have a central treasury department, which might be a separate profit centre within the group. The responsibilities of this department will include the management of business risk and market risk for the group as a whole.

Required

(a) Describe the functions of a central treasury department.

(b) Describe the information that the treasury department needs, from inside and outside the organisation, to perform its function.

20 Perseus **30 mins**

Learning outcome: C(i)

Perseus is a wholly-owned subsidiary of Minos. Although the subsidiary has provided satisfactory levels of performance, Minos is considering the sale of the subsidiary to another conglomerate. Minos is experiencing trading problems in other parts of its operations and needs to sell Perseus in order to raise much-needed finance. The most recent balance sheet of Perseus is as follows:

Balance sheet as at 30 November 20X2

	£m	£m	£m
Non-current assets			
Freehold land and buildings at cost		58.5	
Less: Accumulated depreciation		10.2	
			48.3
Fixtures and fittings at cost		8.6	
Less: Accumulated depreciation		2.9	
			5.7
Motor vehicles at cost		3.2	
Less: Accumulated depreciation		1.4	
			1.8
			55.8
Current assets			
Inventory at cost	49.5		
Trade receivables	23.4		
Cash at bank	21.5		
		94.4	
Less: Payables: amounts falling due within one year			
Trade payables	25.9		
Tax	5.4		
		31.3	63.1
Loan notes			118.9
Less: payables: amounts falling due after one year			49.0
			69.9
Capital and reserves			
Ordinary £0.50 shares			25.0
Accumulated profits			44.9
			69.9

Extracts from the income statement for the year ended 30 November 20X2 are as follows:

	£m
Net profit after taxation	10.7
Dividend proposed and paid	3.3

The following details were taken from a financial newspaper concerning the shares of Tityus, a similar business operating in the same industry that is listed on the Stock Exchange.

20X1 – 20X2

High	*Low*	*Stock*	*Price*	*± or*	*Dividend (net)*	*Cover (times)*	*Yield (gross %)*	*P/E (times)*
640p	580p	Tityus	615p	+ 5p	12.0p	2.5	2.2	20.5

An independent valuer has recently estimated the current realisable value of the company's assets as follows:

	£m
Freehold land and buildings	104.2
Fixtures and fittings	3.5
Motor vehicles	0.4
Inventory	58.0

The balance sheet values of the remaining assets were considered to reflect their net realisable values.

Tax on dividends is at the lower rate of income tax of 10%.

Required

(a) Calculate the value per share of Perseus using the following valuation methods:

   (i) Net assets (liquidation) basis
   (ii) Dividend yield basis; and
   (iii) Price/earnings ratio basis

(b) Briefly evaluate the strengths and weaknesses of each of the share valuation methods set out in (a) above.

21 Hostile bids — 30 mins

Learning outcome: C(iii)

Recent articles in the financial press have suggested that hostile takeovers are often bad for the shareholders of the predator (bidding company) and good for shareholders of the target company.

Required

(a) With reference to agency theory or otherwise, explain why the above statements might be valid, and discuss the typical stages in a hostile bid.

(b) Describe and discuss three strategies that might be adopted by the board of a company to defend itself, when facing a hostile takeover approach.

22 Takeovers — 36 mins

Learning outcome: C(iii)

Despite substantial evidence, drawn from different countries and different time periods, that suggests the wealth of shareholders in a bidding company is unlikely to be increased as a result of taking over another company, takeovers remain an important part of the business landscape.

Required

(a) Explain, in economic terms, what a company, which is committed to increasing shareholder wealth, should look for when seeking to acquire another company. **(3 marks)**

(b) Describe four ways in which a takeover may lead to an increase in wealth for the bidding company's shareholders. **(8 marks)**

(c) Discuss four reasons why a takeover may fail to deliver an expected increase in wealth for the bidding company's shareholders. **(9 marks)**

(Total = 20 marks)

23 Gasco 45 mins

Learning outcome: C(iii)

Gasco, a public limited company with a market value of around £7 billion, is a major supplier of gas to both business and domestic customers. The company also provides maintenance contracts for both gas and central heating customers using the well-known brand name Gas For All. Customers can call emergency lines for assistance for any gas-related incident, such as a suspected leak. Gasco employs its own highly-trained workforce to deal with all such situations quickly and effectively. The company also operates a major new credit card, which has been extensively marketed and which gives users concessions, such as reductions in their gas bills.

Gasco has recently bid £1.1bn for CarCare, a long established mutual organisation (ie it is owned by its members) that is the country's leading motoring organisation. CarCare is financed primarily by an annual subscription to its 4.4 million members. In addition the organisation also obtains income from a range of other activities such as a high profile car insurance brokerage, a travel agency and assistance with all types of travel arrangements. Its main service to members is the provision of a roadside break-down service, which is now an extremely competitive market with many other companies involved. Although many of its competitors use local garages to deal with breakdowns, CarCare uses its own road patrols.

CarCare members have to approve the takeover, which once completed provided them each with a windfall of around £300 each.

Gasco intend to preserve the CarCare name which is extremely well-known by consumers.

Required

(a) Discuss the possible reasons why Gasco is seeking to buy CarCare. **(9 marks)**

(b) Discuss how the various stakeholders of CarCare might react to the takeover. **(8 marks)**

(c) Discuss the potential problems that may face Gasco in running CarCare now that the takeover has been achieved. **(8 marks)**

(Total = 25 marks)

24 Olivine 36 mins

Learning outcome: C(v)

Olivine is a holiday tour operator that is committed to a policy of expansion. The company has enjoyed record growth in recent years and is now seeking to acquire other companies in order to maintain its growth momentum. It has recently taken an interest in Halite, a charter airline business, as the Board of Directors of Olivine believes that there is a good strategic fit between the two companies. Both companies have the same level of risk. Abbreviated financial statements relating to each company are set out below.

Abbreviated income statement for the year ended 30 November 20X3

	Olivine	*Halite*
	£m	£m
Sales	182·6	75·2
Operating profit	43·6	21·4
Interest charges	12·3	10·2
Net profit before taxation	31·3	11·2
Company tax	6·3	1·6
Net profit after taxation	25·0	9·6
Dividends	6·0	4·0
Accumulated profits for the year	19·0	5·6

Summarised balance sheets as at 30 November 20X3

	Olivine	*Halite*
	£m	£m
Non-current assets	135·4	127·2
Net current assets	65·2	3·2
	200·6	130·4
Payables due after more than one year	120·5	104·8
	80·1	25·6
Capital and reserves		
£0·50 ordinary shares	20·0	8·0
Retained profit	60·1	17·6
	80·1	25·6
Price/earnings ratio before the bid	20	15

The Board of Directors of Olivine is considering making an offer to the shareholders of Halite of five shares in Olivine for every four shares held. It is believed that a rationalisation of administrative functions arising from the merger would reap after tax benefits of £2·4m.

Required

(a) Calculate:

(i) The total value of the proposed offer

(ii) The earnings per share of Olivine following the successful acquisition of Halite

(iii) The share price of Olivine following acquisition, assuming that the benefits of the acquisition are achieved and that the price/earnings ratio declines by 5%. **(10 marks)**

(b) Calculate the effect of the proposed takeover on the wealth of the shareholders of each company. **(5 marks)**

(c) Discuss your results in (a) and (b) above and state what recommendations, if any, you would make to the directors of Olivine. **(5 marks)**

(Total = 20 marks)

25 K and H — 45 mins

Learning outcomes: C(i), (iv), (v)

K wishes to acquire H. The directors of K are trying to justify the acquisition to the shareholders of both companies on the grounds that it will increase the wealth of all shareholders. The supporting financial evidence produced by K's directors is summarised below.

	K	*H*
	£'000	£'000
Operating profit	12,400	5,800
Less interest payable	4,431	2,200
Profit before tax	7,969	3,600
Less taxation	2,789	1,260
Earnings available to ordinary shareholders	5,180	2,340
Earnings per share (pre-acquisition)	14.80 pence	29.25 pence
Market price per share (pre-acquisition)	222 pence	322 pence
Estimated market price (post-acquisition)	240 pence	
Estimated equivalent value of one old H share (post-acquisition)		360 pence

Payment is to be made with K ordinary shares, at an exchange ratio of 3 K shares for every 2 H shares.

Required

(a) Demonstrate how the directors of K produced their estimates of post-acquisition value and, if you do not agree with these estimates, produce revised estimates of post-acquisition values. All calculations must be shown. State clearly any assumptions that you make. **(10 marks)**

(b) If the acquisition is contested by H, using K's estimate of its post-acquisition market price calculate the maximum price that K could offer without reducing the wealth of its existing shareholders. **(3 marks)**

(c) The board of directors of H later informally indicate that they are prepared to recommend to their shareholders a 2 for 1 share offer.

Further information regarding the effect of the acquisition on K is given below.

(i) The acquisition will result in an increase in the total pre-acquisition after tax operating cash flows of £2,750,000 a year indefinitely.

(ii) Rationalisation will allow machinery with a realisable value of £7,200,000 to be disposed of at the end of the next year.

(iii) Redundancy payments will total £3,500,000 immediately and £8,400,000 at the end of the next year.

(iv) K's cost of capital is estimated to be 14% a year.

All values are after any appropriate taxation. Assume that the pre-acquisition market values of K and H shares have not changed.

Recommend, using your own estimates of post-acquisition values, whether K should be prepared to make a 2 for 1 offer for the shares of H. **(6 marks)**

(d) Disregarding the information in (c) above and assuming no increase in the total post-acquisition earnings, evaluate whether this acquisition is likely to have any effect on the value of debt of K. **(6 Marks)**

(Total = 25 marks)

26 Intergrand — 90 mins

Learning outcomes: C(iii), (v)

(a) Discuss the advantages to a company of establishing an overseas operating subsidiary by:

either (i) Organic growth

or (ii) Acquisition **(10 marks)**

(b) The board of directors of Intergrand wishes to establish an operating subsidiary in Germany through the acquisition of an existing German company. Intergrand has undertaken research into a number of German quoted companies, and has decided to attempt to purchase Oberberg. Initial discussions suggest that the directors of Oberberg may be willing to recommend the sale of 100% of the company's equity to Intergrand for a total cash price of 115 million Euro, payable in full on acquisition.

Oberberg has provided the managers of Intergrand with internal management information regarding accounting/cash flow projections for the next four years.

The projects are in money/nominal terms.

Oberberg financial projections

Euro (million)

Year	*20X3*	*20X4*	*20X5*	*20X6*
Sales	38.2	41.2	44.0	49.0
Labour	11.0	12.1	13.0	14.1
Materials	8.3	8.7	9.0	9.4
Overheads	3.2	3.2	3.3	3.4
Interest	2.5	3.0	3.5	3.8
Tax allowable depreciation	6.3	5.8	5.6	5.2
	31.3	32.8	34.4	35.9
Taxable profit	6.9	8.4	9.6	13.1
Taxation (25%)	1.7	2.1	2.4	3.3
Incremental operating working capital	0.7	0.9	1.0	2.0
Replacement investment	4.2	4.2	4.2	4.2
Investment for expansion	–	–	9.0	–

Oberberg, pro forma summarised Income statement for the year ending 31 December 20X2

	Euro (million)
Sales	35.8
Operating expenses	21.1
Interest expense	3.4
Depreciation	6.2
	30.7
Taxable profit	5.1
Taxation (25%)	1.3
Profit after tax	3.8

Oberberg, pro forma summarised balance sheet as at 31 December 20X2

	Euro (million)
Non-current assets	73.2
Current assets	58.1
Current liabilities	(40.3)
	91.0
Financed by:	
Ordinary shares (100 Euro par value)	15.0
Reserves	28.0
Medium and long term bank loans	30.0
8% Bond 20X9 (par value 1,000 Euro)	18.0
	91.0

Notes

(i) The spot exchange rate between the Euro and pound is Euro 1.625/£.

(ii) Inflation is at 4% per year in the UK and 2% per year in the Euro bloc. This differential is expected to continue unless the UK joins the Euro bloc.

(iii) The market return is 11% and the risk free rate is 4%.

(iv) Oberberg's equity beta is estimated to be 1.4.

(v) Oberberg's 8% bond is currently priced at 1,230 Euro and its ordinary share price is 300 Euro.

(vi) Post-merger rationalisation will involve the sale of some non-current assets of Oberberg in 20X3 with an expected after tax market value of 8 million Euro.

(vii) Synergies in production and distribution are expected to yield 2 million Euro per annum before tax from 20X4 onwards.

(viii) £175,000 has already been spent researching into possible acquisition targets.

(ix) The purchase of Oberberg will provide publicity and exposure in Germany for the Intergrand name and brand. This extra publicity is believed to be the equivalent of Intergrand spending 1 million Euro per year on advertising in Germany.

(x) The weighted average cost of capital of Intergrand is 10%.

(xi) After tax cash flows of Oberberg after 20X6 are expected to grow at approximately 2% per year.

(xii) Oberberg does not plan to issue or redeem any equity or medium and long-term debt prior to 20X6.

(xiii) After tax redundancy costs as a result of the acquisition are expected to be 5 million Euro, payable almost immediately.

(xiv) Operating working capital comprises receivables and inventory less payables. It excludes short-term loans.

(xv) Current liabilities include negligible amounts of short-term loans.

(xvi) The corporate tax rate in Germany is 25% and in the UK 30%. A bilateral tax treaty exists between the two countries whereby tax paid in one country may be credited against any tax liability in the other country.

(xvii) If Intergrand acquires Oberberg existing exports to Germany yielding a pre-tax cash flow of £800,000 per annum will be lost. It is hoped that about half of these exports can be diverted to the French market.

Required

Intergrand has suggested that Oberberg should be valued based upon the expected present value (to infinity) of the operating free cash flows of Oberberg. These would be discounted at an all-equity rate and adjusted by the present value of all other relevant cash flows, discounted at an appropriate rate(s).

Acting as a consultant to Intergrand, prepare a report evaluating whether or not Intergrand should offer the 115 million Euro required to acquire Oberberg. Include in your report discussion of other commercial and business factors that Intergrand should consider prior to making a final decision.

Assume that it is now mid-December 20X2.

State clearly any other assumptions that you make. **(40 marks)**

Approximately 25 marks are available for calculations and 15 for discussion.

(Total = 50 marks)

27 Dalewater — 45 mins

Learning outcomes: C(iii), (viii)

Dalewater obtains water from a natural source in an area in the heart of England. The company bottles the water and sells it nationally to retailers and supermarkets. However, the company has performed poorly over the recent year. There have been problems in the bottling plant and some industrial unrest amongst employees. As a result, supplies to retailers have been interrupted. In addition, the marketing of the product has been criticised since it has involved the use of certain controversial celebrities who were not seen by some as appropriate role-models for the health claims of the product. The company's problems have culminated in a contamination in the latest batch of bottled water which has required a withdrawal of some bottles from the supermarket shelves. There are some lawsuits pending against the company as a result of people drinking the contaminated water.

Not surprisingly, all of this has had an impact on the share price of the company, which hit a new low in January 20X9 of 40p a share, valuing the company at £150 million.

Peakspring, a competitor company which also supplies bottled water to the retail trade, bid £0.50 a share for Dalewater in February after having bought 10% of the company's shares in the market. Dalewater advisors stated that they estimated the company's true value to be £0.70 a share as an operating company and £0.80 a share if it were wound up voluntarily.

To counter this offer, Dalewater offered to buy back 50% of the outstanding issued shares for £0.20 cash plus £0.50 worth of debentures per share. To finance this, Dalewater had to sell some land which the company owned but which it had never developed. The company also put in place a whole series of measures to improve the company's operations and market position. As a result the share price of Dalewater rose to £0.65. Peakspring decided not to increase its original offer and withdrew its bid, selling the shares it had bought.

Required

(a) Explain the circumstances that might produce a situation where a company like Dalewater is more valuable broken-up than being operated as a going concern. **(8 marks)**

(b) Discuss why Peakspring did not increase its bid to, say £0.70, and then break up the company. **(7 marks)**

(c) Discuss why Dalewater's share price rose by £0.25 during the time of this bid. **(5 marks)**

(d) If Peakspring's bid had succeeded, explain the implications to the company of making a cash offer for Dalewater as opposed to a share offer. **(5 marks)**

(Total = 25 marks)

28 Financial and non-financial appraisal — 35 mins

Learning outcome: D(i)

Two different organisations are considering investments.

- A private sector company is proposing to increase its production capacity by enlarging its factory.
- A government funded school intends to increase the range of its services by adding a new building to its present site.

The private sector organisation will obtain its funds for expansion from the capital market, while the school building project will be entirely funded by the government. The school has no power to make any charge for the services it provides.

Required

Discuss the financial and non-financial factors that should be taken into account in appraising the proposed developments for each of the organisations.

29 Shegdor — 27 mins

Learning outcomes: D(ii), (iii)

(a) Briefly discuss the possible objectives of transfer pricing strategies used by multinational companies. **(4 marks)**

Shegdor, a UK based multinational company, has subsidiaries in three countries – Umgaba, Mazila and Bettuna.

(i) The subsidiary in Umgaba manufactures specialist components, which may then be assembled and sold in either Mazila or Bettuna.

(ii) Production and sales volume may each be assumed to be 400,000 units per year no matter where the assembly and sales take place.

(iii) Manufacturing costs in Umgaba are $16 per unit and fixed costs (for the normal range of production) $1.8 million.

(iv) Assembly costs in Mazila are $9 per unit and in Bettuna $7.5 per unit. Fixed costs are $700,000 and $900,000 respectively.

(v) The unit sales price in Mazila is $40 and in Bettuna $37.

(vi) Corporate taxes on profits are at the rate of 40% in Umgaba, 25% in Mazila, 32% in Bettuna and 30% in the UK. No tax credits are available in these three countries for any losses made. Full credit is given by the UK tax authorities for tax paid overseas.

(vii) Tax allowable import duties of 10% are payable on all goods imported into Mazila.

(viii) A withholding tax of 15% is deducted from all dividends remitted from Umgaba.

(ix) Shegdor expects about 60% of profits from each subsidiary to be remitted direct to the UK each year.

(x) Cost and price data in all countries is shown in US dollars.

Required

(b) Evaluate and explain:

 (i) If the transfer price from Umgaba should be based upon fixed cost plus variable cost, or fixed cost plus variable cost plus a mark up of 30%.

 (ii) Whether assembly should take place in Mazila or Bettuna. **(8 marks)**

(c) Discuss upon the likely attitude of the governments of each of the four countries towards the transfer price and assembly location selected in (b)(i) and (b)(ii) above. **(3 marks)**

(Total = 15 marks)

30 Mezen — 35 mins

Learning outcomes: D(i), (ii)

Mezen is currently considering the launch of a new product. A market survey was recently commissioned to assess the likely demand for the product and this showed that the product has an expected life of four years. The survey cost £30,000 and this is due for payment in four months' time. On the basis of the survey information as well as internal management accounting information relating to costs, the assistant accountant prepared the following profit forecasts for the product.

Year	*1*	*2*	*3*	*4*
	£'000	£'000	£'000	£'000
Sales	180	200	160	120
Cost of sales	(115)	(140)	(110)	(85)
Gross profit	65	60	50	35
Variable overheads	(27)	(30)	(24)	(18)
Fixed overheads	(25)	(25)	(25)	(25)
Market survey written off	(30)	–	–	–
Net profit/(loss)	(17)	5	1	(8)

These profit forecasts were viewed with disappointment by the directors and there was a general feeling that the new product should not be launched. The Chief Executive pointed out that the product achieved profits in only two years of its four-year life and that over the four-year period as a whole, a net loss was expected. However, before a meeting that had been arranged to decide formally the future of the product, the following additional information became available:

(i) The new product will require the use of an existing machine. This has a written down value of £80,000 but could be sold for £70,000 immediately if the new product is not launched. If the product is launched, it will be sold at the end of the four-year period for £10,000.

(ii) Additional working capital of £20,000 will be required immediately and will be needed over the four-year period. It will be released at the end of the period.

(iii) The fixed overheads include a figure of £15,000 per year for depreciation of the machine and £5,000 per year for the re-allocation of existing overheads of the business.

The company has a cost of capital of 10%.

Ignore taxation.

Required

(a) Calculate the incremental cash flows arising from a decision to launch the product. **(9 marks)**

(b) Calculate the approximate internal rate of return of the product. **(4 marks)**

(c) Explain, with reasons, whether or not the product should be launched. **(2 marks)**

(d) Outline the strengths and weaknesses of the internal rate of return method as a basis for investment appraisal. **(5 marks)**

(Total = 20 marks)

31 DIN — 35 mins

Learning outcome: D(ii)

(a) Explain the difference between real rates of return and money rates of return and outline the circumstances in which the use of each would be appropriate when appraising capital projects under inflationary conditions

(b) DIN has just developed a new product to be called Rance and is now considering whether to put it into production. The following information is available.

(i) Costs incurred in the development of Rance amount to £480,000.

(ii) Production of Rance will require the purchase of new machinery at a cost of £2,400,000 payable immediately. This machinery is specific to the production of Rance and will be obsolete and valueless when that production ceases. The machinery has a production life of four years and a production capacity of 30,000 units per annum.

(iii) Production costs of Rance (at year 1 prices) are estimated as follows.

	£
Variable materials	8.00
Variable labour	12.00
Variable overheads	12.00

In addition, fixed production costs (at year 1 prices), including straight line depreciation on plant and machinery, will amount to £800,000 per annum.

(iv) The selling price of Rance will be £80.00 per unit (at year 1 prices). Demand is expected to be 25,000 units per annum for the next four years.

(v) The retail price index is expected to increase at 5% per annum for the next four years and the selling price of Rance is expected to increase at the same rate. Annual inflation rates for production costs are expected to be as follows.

	%
Variable materials	4
Variable labour	10
Variable overheads	4
Fixed costs	5

(vi) The company's weighted average cost of capital in money terms is expected to be 15%.

Required

Advise the directors of DIN whether it should produce Rance on the basis of the information above.

Notes

Unless otherwise specified all costs and revenues should be assumed to rise at the end of each year.

Ignore taxation.

32 Auriga — 36 mins

Learning outcome: D(ii)

Auriga (Healthcare) has invested £220,000 over the past two years in the development of a personal stress-monitoring device (PSMD). The device is designed for busy individuals wishing to check their stress levels. Market research that was commissioned earlier in the year at a cost of £45,000 suggests that the price for the PSMD should be £22 per unit and that the expected product life cycle of the device is four years.

In order to produce the device, the business must purchase immediately specialist machinery and equipment at a cost of £300,000. This machinery and equipment has an expected life of four years and will have no residual value at the end of this period. The machinery and equipment can produce a maximum of 15,000 PSMDs per year over four years. To ensure that the maximum output is achieved, the business will spend £50,000 a year in advertising the device over the next four years.

Based on the maximum output of 15,000 units per year, the PSMD has the following expected costs per unit (excluding the advertising costs above):

	Notes	£
Materials	(1)	6.50
Labour	(2)	5.50
Overheads	(3)	8.50
		20.50

Notes

(1) The materials figure above includes a charge of £2 for a polymer that is currently in stock and can be used for this project. Each PSMD requires 200 grams of the polymer and the charge is based on the original cost of £1 per 100 grams for the polymer. It is a material that is currently used in other areas of the business and the cost of replacing the polymer is £1.50 per 100 grams. The polymer could easily be sold at a price of £1.25 per 100 grams.

(2) The labour costs relate to payments made to employees that will be directly involved in producing the PSMD. These employees have no work at present and, if the PSMD is not produced, they will be made redundant immediately at a cost of £230,000. If, however, the PSMD is produced, the employees are likely to be found other work at the end of the four-year period and so no redundancy costs will be incurred.

(3) The figure includes a depreciation charge for the new machinery and equipment. The policy of the business is to depreciate non-current assets in equal instalments over their expected life. All other overheads included in the above figure are incurred in production of the new device.

(4) The business has a target capital structure of 50% equity and 50% loan capital. The market cost of equity is 12% and the market cost of loan capital is 8%. The PSMD project has the same level of risk as that of other projects undertaken and the level of investment required is very small compared to the size of the business. If the project is accepted, it will be financed entirely by equity.

Ignore taxation.

Required

(a) Calculate the net present value of the project. **(12 marks)**

(b) Calculate the required reduction in annual net cash flows from operations before the project becomes unprofitable. **(5 marks)**

(c) Discuss your findings in (a) and (b) above. **(3 marks)**

(Total = 20 marks)

33 Fund restrictions — 22 mins

Learning outcomes: D(ii), (iii)

A company can invest in the following four projects. The timing and amounts of the cash flows are shown below.

	T_0	t_1	t_2	*NPV (15%)*	*IRR*
	£'000	£'000	£'000	£'000	%
Project A	(150)	100	105	14.22	9
Project B	(200)	150	135	28.27	14
Project C		(175)	230	21.74	12
Project D	(300)	200	220	35.01	12

Required

(a) If the company has a present restriction of £450,000 for investment, calculate which projects it would invest in. Assume that all projects are divisible. **(5 marks)**

(b) If there are no fund restrictions and these four projects are mutually exclusive, explain with reasons which project the company should choose. **(2 marks)**

(c) Explain why capital rationing occurs. **(5 marks)**

(Total = 12 marks)

34 ANT **45 mins**

Learning outcomes: D(iii), (v)

ANT, a multi-product company, is considering four investment projects, details of which are given below.

Development costs already incurred on the projects are as follows.

A	*B*	*C*	*D*
£	£	£	£
100,000	75,000	80,000	60,000

Each project will require an immediate outlay on plant and machinery, the cost of which is estimated as follows.

A	*B*	*C*	*D*
£	£	£	£
2,100,000	1,400,000	2,400,000	600,000

In all four cases the plant and machinery has a useful life of five years at the end of which it will be valueless.

Unit sales per annum, for each project, are expected to be as follows.

A	*B*	*C*	*D*
150,000	75,000	80,000	120,000

Selling price and variable costs per unit for each project are estimated below.

	A	*B*	*C*	*D*
	£	£	£	£
Selling price	30.00	40.00	25.00	50.00
Materials	7.60	12.00	4.50	25.00
Labour	9.80	12.00	5.00	10.00
Variable overheads	6.00	7.00	2.50	10.50

The company charges depreciation on plant and machinery on a straight line basis over the useful life of the plant and machinery. Development costs of projects are written off in the year that they are incurred. The company apportions general administration costs to projects at a rate of 5% of selling price. None of the above projects will lead to any actual increase in the company's administration costs.

Working capital requirements for each project will amount to 20% of the expected annual sales value. In each case this investment will be made immediately and will be recovered in full when the projects end in five years time.

Funds available for investment are limited to £5,200,000. The company's cost of capital is estimated to be 18%.

Required

(a) Calculate the NPV of each project. **(12 marks)**

(b) Calculate the profitability index for each project and advise the company which of the new projects, if any, to undertake. You may assume that each of the projects can be undertaken on a reduced scale for a proportionate reduction in cash flows. Your advice should state clearly your order of preference for the four projects, what proportion you would take of any project that is scaled down, and the total NPV generated by your choice. **(5 marks)**

(c) Discuss the limitations of the profitability index as a means of dealing with capital rationing problems. **(8 marks)**

Ignore taxation. **(Total = 25 marks)**

35 Feasibility study **35 mins**

Learning outcome: D(iv)

An important step in the implementation of any computer system is the feasibility study. Senior staff in an organisation may be unconvinced of the value of the study.

Required

(a) Briefly explain what is meant by a computer feasibility study, and what such a study should achieve.

(b) Explain the importance of each of the main sections that should be contained in the feasibility study report.

(c) Identify three members of a 'typical' feasibility study team, and provide a one sentence description of their role.

(d) Discuss briefly on the suggestion that if a special purpose package is to be purchased, then there is no need for such a study.

(e) List four major factors which might justify the introduction of a computer system for production planning and scheduling in a manufacturing company.

1 Earnings per share

Top tips. You would not get a complete question on stakeholders, but might well need to bring them into discussions about the consequences of a merger or the results of an investment. You could take a less even-handed approach than we have in (a) provided you justified your arguments and gave some attention to opposing arguments. However if you take a fairly extreme position, you have to discuss the problems of doing so. On the one hand will government wish to intervene to prevent anti-social behaviour; on the other hand how do you measure success in fulfilling the requirements of stakeholders? What happens if those requirements conflict?

In (b) note how the interests of stakeholders who are **not directly involved** in decisions may be affected. Note also the potential **conflicts** – a sell-off may benefit shareholders but not employees. Instead of trying to avoid damaging stakeholder interests, a more practical solution may be to **compensate** them for damage incurred. Alternatively the damage may spur them to action – for example competitors damaged by a new car plant.

(a) **Profit maximisation**

One of the principles of the market economy is that if the owners of businesses attempt to achieve **maximum profitability** and **earnings** this will help to increase the wealth of society. As a result, it is usually assumed that a proper objective for private sector organisations is profit maximisation. This view is substantially correct. In general, the market economy has out-performed planned economies in most places in the world. Two key objectives of financial managers must therefore be the **effective management** of shareholders' funds and the provision of financial information which will help to increase shareholder wealth.

Problems with profit maximisation

However, profit-seeking organisations can also cause problems for society. For example, **monopolists** are able to earn large returns which are disproportionate to the benefits they bring to society. The **costs of pollution** fall on society rather than on the company which is causing it. A company may increase profitability by making some of its work-force redundant but the costs of unemployed people fall on society through the social security system.

The question that then follows is 'Should individual companies be concerned with these market imperfections?'

Government's role

There are two opposing viewpoints. On the one hand it can be argued that companies should only be concerned with **maximisation of shareholders' wealth**. It is the role of government to pick up the problems of market imperfections (eg by breaking up monopolies, by fining polluters and by paying social security benefits).

Stakeholder interests

An alternative viewpoint is that a company is a coalition of **different stakeholder** groups: shareholders, lenders, managers, employees, customers, suppliers, government and society as a whole. The objectives of all these groups, which are often in conflict, need to be considered by company managers when making decisions. From this viewpoint, financial managers cannot be content with meeting the needs of shareholders only.

Consideration of stakeholders

The truth is somewhere in between. The over-riding objective of companies is to create **long-term wealth for shareholders**. However this can only be done if we consider the likely behaviour of other stakeholders. For example, if we create extra short-term profits by cutting employee benefits or delaying payments to creditors there are likely to be **repercussions** which reduce longer term shareholder wealth. Or if we fail to motivate managers and employees adequately, the costs of the resulting inefficiencies will ultimately be borne by shareholders.

Conclusion

In summary, the financial manager is concerned with **managing the company's funds** on behalf of shareholders, and **producing information** which shows the likely effect of management decisions on shareholder wealth. However management decisions will be made after also considering other stakeholder groups and a good financial manager will be aware that financial information is only one input to the final decision.

(b)

Top tips. Only three of the situations need be addressed in your answer.

(i) **A private company converting into a public company**

When a private company converts into a public company, some of the existing shareholder/managers will sell their shares to outside investors. In addition, new shares may be issued. The **dilution of ownership** might cause loss of control by the existing management.

The stakeholders involved in potential conflicts are as follows.

(1) **Existing shareholder/managers**

They will want to sell some of their shareholding at as high a price as possible. This may motivate them to overstate their company's prospects. Those shareholder/managers who wish to retire from the business may be in conflict with those who wish to stay in control – the latter may oppose the conversion into a public company.

(2) **New outside shareholders**

Most of these will hold **minority stakes** in the company and will receive their rewards as **dividends only**. This may put them in conflict with the existing shareholder/ managers who receive rewards as salaries as well as dividends. On conversion to a public company there should be clear policies on dividends and directors' remuneration.

(3) **Employees, including managers who are not shareholders**

Part of the reason for the success of the company will be the efforts made by employees. They may feel that they should benefit when the company goes public. One way of organising this is to create **employee share options** or other bonus schemes.

(ii) **A highly geared company attempting to restructure its capital finance**

The major conflict here is between **shareholders** and **lenders**. If a company is very highly geared, the shareholders may be tempted to take very high risks. If the gamble fails, they have limited liability and can only lose the value of their shares. If they are lucky, they may make returns many times the value of their shares. The problem is that the shareholders are effectively gambling with money provided by lenders, but those lenders will get no extra return to compensate for the risk.

Removal of risk

In restructuring the company, something must be done either to shift risk away from the lenders or to reward the lenders for taking a risk.

Risk can be **shifted away** from lenders by taking **security** on previously unsecured loans or by **writing restrictive covenants** into loan agreements (eg the company agrees to set a ceiling to dividend pay-outs until gearing is reduced, and to confine its business to agreed activities).

Lenders can be **compensated** for taking risks by either negotiating increased interest rates or by the issue of 'sweeteners' with the loans, such as share warrants or the issue of convertible loan stock.

Other stakeholders

Other stakeholders who will be interested in the arrangements include **trade creditors** (who will be interested that loan creditors do not improve their position at the expense of themselves) and **managers**, who are likely to be more risk averse than shareholders if their livelihood depends on the company's continuing existence.

(iii) **A large conglomerate spinning off its divisions**

Large conglomerates may sometimes have a market capitalisation which is less than the total realisable value of the subsidiaries. This is referred to as '**conglomerate discount**'. It arises because more synergy could be found by the combination of the group's businesses with competitors than by running a diversified group where there is no obvious benefit from remaining together.

For many years, Hanson Trust was the exception to this situation, but subsequently it decided to break up the group.

The stakeholders involved in potential conflicts are as follows.

(1) **Shareholders**

They will see the chance of immediate gains in share price if subsidiaries are sold.

(2) **Subsidiary company directors and employees**

They may either gain opportunities (eg if their company becomes independent) or suffer the threat of job loss (eg if their company is sold to a competitor).

(iv) **Japanese car makers building new car plants in other countries**

The stakeholders involved in potential conflicts are as follows.

(1) **The shareholders and management of the Japanese company**

They will be able to gain from the combination of advanced technology with a cheaper workforce.

(2) **Local employees and managers engaged by the Japanese company**

They will gain **enhanced skills** and better **work prospects**.

(3) **The government of the local country, representing the tax payers**

The **reduction** in **unemployment** will ease the taxpayers' burden and increase the government's popularity (provided that subsidies offered by the government do not outweigh the benefits!)

(4) **Shareholders, managers and employees of local car-making firms**

These will be in **conflict** with the **other stakeholders** above as existing manufacturers lose market share.

(5) **Employees of car plants based in Japan**

These are likely to **lose work** if car-making is relocated to lower wage areas. They will need to compete on the basis of **higher efficiency**.

2 Corporate governance

Top tips. Although you would not get a full question on corporate governance, this question is a helpful reminder of important elements of the governance codes. You will be expected to recognise signs of questionable practice and bring them into your answer as appropriate. Don't worry though if you can't remember the detail - the principles are what are important.

In this question important principles include the board exercising **full control** and employing proper procedures (over the change in the secretaryship for example). The other major element which this question brings out is the **balance of power**, that is avoiding the situation where one individual dominates the company. The splitting of the lead roles, the involvement of non-executive directors and the use of board committees are all important checks.

MEMO

To: The Chairman – ABC
From: The Secretary
Date: 4 June 20X9
Subject: Corporate Governance

It is now some weeks since I was appointed company secretary. During this time I have been able to review the proceedings of the board especially bearing in mind the best modern practice as set out in the Combined Code.

From the outset I was guided by the fact that the company is **listed** on the London Stock Exchange and that its rapid growth will inevitably focus attention on aspects of its corporate governance.

The specific matters to which I would draw your immediate attention are as follows.

(a) **Secretary**

The Combined Code requires the directors to appoint a secretary who is both **capable** and **suitably qualified.** As this is an appointment by the board, it follows that the **dismissal** of the secretary must be **sanctioned** by the **board** and not by an individual. This ensures the independence of the secretary. In the case of my predecessor, I am concerned that Miss Grey was apparently dismissed by a single director. At this stage I would recommend that this dismissal receives ratification by the whole board.

(b) **Chairman/Chief Executive**

The Code stresses the crucial role of the chairman but emphasised that there should be a **clear division of responsibilities** at the head of the company, with no one person having complete power. Generally this would mean the posts of the chairman and chief executive being held by different people. If they are concentrated in one person as at present, the Code recommends that there should be a strong independent core of non-executive directors.

(c) **Board meetings**

It has long been recognised that the management of the company is vested in the board as a whole. Whilst the board does have the power to delegate any of its powers to a committee of directors on a day to day basis, the Code stresses the importance of the **board meeting** on a **regular basis** retaining full control over the business of the company. A frequency of twice a year is unlikely to be enough. However most companies do find that regular monthly meetings tend to be repetitious. A meeting every two months, say five or six a year allowing for holiday periods, is considered a useful period for meaningful review. Monthly reports can still be circulated to all directors to keep them up to date. A schedule of board meetings should be drawn up and agreed at the beginning of the year so that the directors can plan ahead.

It is essential that the board receives **written reports** on all important aspects of the company's operations including detailed financial information. Each director should receive the same information at the same time. This information should be included with the papers for the board meetings ideally sent out at least a week before the meeting. It is not good practice for reports, written or oral, to be presented at the meeting itself.

(d) **Non-executive directors**

The best modern practice requires that there be a sufficient contingent of **non-executive directors** on the board to exercise a strong independent judgement and to serve on key board committees. Non-executive directors should be drawn from outside the company. Whilst there is nothing to prevent a former executive director being appointed as a non-executive, this does not fulfil the requirement of true independence. I am sure that the Stock Market would expect this company to appoint at least two or possibly three independent directors.

(e) **Board committees**

I would recommend that the board set up three committees to facilitate good corporate governance. Each committee should be chaired by a non-executive director. They would also incorporate your other proposals as part of their remit. They would be:

(i) **Audit committee** to liaise with internal and external auditors and provide a forum for each to express their concerns. This committee should meet twice a year to review half yearly accounts and financial statements including the published report and accounts.

(ii) **Nominations committee** to meet periodically to recommend appointments to the board.

(iii) **Remuneration committee** to set levels of remuneration and benefits for the executive directors and review service agreements. There would be no obstacle to their working with outside remuneration consultants as proposed. Remuneration should be related to performance. The committee should consist of non-executive directors, as executive directors should not be involved in setting their own remuneration.

(f) **Service agreements**

Generally notice periods in **excess of one year** are not recommended and compensation payments should not be perceived as excessive.

Finally I think I should state that the company can only benefit from adopting the best modern practices of corporate governance, which, if adopted, can assist in its future expansion and success. A copy of the Combined Code is attached for your reference and I look forward to discussing the issues raised.

A Able

Secretary

3 Subsidiaries

Top tips. The very important point that current appearances might be deceptive is made first. The answer brings out other points you may need to consider when undertaking a financial analysis:

- Distortions built into various ratios, for example the effects of recent investments in assets
- Problems making comparisons, for example different classifications of costs
- Dubious accounting policies such as carrying forward product development costs
- The implications of involvements in different markets, particularly the overseas market
- Increased costs bringing, for example, more sales

The discussion on working capital suggests that Y may be suffering some of the signs of over-trading - remember the remedy is more long-term capital.

A conclusion is helpful here.

Profitability

X Ltd is the **more profitable** company, both in **absolute terms** and in **proportion to sales** and to **operating capital employed**. This may indicate that X Ltd is much better managed than Y Ltd, but this is not the only possibility, and a study of the other data shows that Y Ltd's profitability, while at present lower, may be more sustainable.

Asset usage

While Y appears to be making worse use of its assets than X, with **asset turnover ratios** lower than X's and falling, this seems to be largely because Y has recently acquired substantial new assets. It may be that within the next few years X will have to undertake a major renewals programme, with consequent adverse effects on its asset turnover ratios.

Sales

A higher percentage of Y's sales are to the home market, while it has still achieved fairly substantial export sales. This suggests that Y could have done better in **exploiting** the **export market**, but also that Y is less exposed than X to **exchange rate fluctuations** and the possible imposition of **trade barriers**. The prospects for the home market appear good, and should give scope for adequate growth. Y has achieved higher growth in total revenue than X over the past three years.

Y is making **sales per employee** about 50% higher than X, and has consistently done so over the past three years. X shows no sign of catching up, despite the fact that its total number of employees has recently fallen slightly. The modest rises in sales per employee over the past three years in both X and Y may be due largely to inflation.

Costs

Y seems to be significantly better than X at **controlling** the cost of sales (49% of sales in Y, and 65% in X), though X has made improvements over the past three years while there has been little change in Y. On the other hand, X's **administration expenses** have been only 6% of sales, while Y's have been 26% of sales. This contrast between the two types of cost suggests that different categorisations of costs may have been used. If we combine the cost of sales and administration expenses, then for X they total 71% of sales and for Y they total 75% of sales. There is thus little difference between the companies, though X has shown improved cost control while Y has not. X has also had **lower selling and distribution costs**.

One must however bear in mind that X will have had a lower depreciation element in its costs than Y, because Y has **recently invested substantially** in non-current assets. Y's costs will also be increased by its **higher salaries**, which may pay off in **better employee motivation** and hence higher sales per employee. On the other hand, Y's costs have been kept down by the carrying forward of an increasing amount of **product development costs**, an accounting policy which may well be imprudent.

Working capital management

In working capital management, X has the edge. Y has **very high receivables**, and these have recently risen sharply as a proportion of revenue. Y also carries rather more **inventory** than X, and has very little cash. While both companies have **tolerable current and liquid ratios**, X's are certainly safer. Y achieves a liquid ratio of 1:1 almost entirely by relying on its receivables. If it suffers substantial bad debts, or if the bank should become concerned and call in the overdraft, Y could suffer serious **liquidity problems**. It also depends heavily on **trade credit** to finance its receivables. While it is sensible to take advantage of trade credit offered, Y may depend too much on the continued goodwill of its **suppliers**. This may indicate the **need** for a fresh **injection of equity**.

Conclusion

On balance, X seems to be a sounder company than Y, with better financial management.

4 ZX

Top tips. The key point to emphasise is that holding too much working capital is expensive whereas holding too little can result in system breakdown. However, modern manufacturing techniques and re-engineering of business processes can help achieve the best of both worlds: low working capital *and* efficient production and sales systems.

The examiner highlighted an important point about many answers – that candidates discussed the procedures for managing working capital rather than concentrating on the higher level policy decisions that are more important at final level.

Points highlighted in the marking guide to (a) were the term of debt and safety inventory (each worth a couple of marks) and investment and financing (worth a mark), with other aspects accounting for the rest of the marks. In (b) you needed to show the effects on assets and liabilities, sales and profits, and current ratios and return on assets to score maximum marks. The marking guide suggested that there was time to carry out all those calculations. In (c) a couple of marks were available specifically for a recommendation, with the remaining marks being available for the effect on various stakeholders (staff, customers and suppliers) and possible disadvantages.

Examiner's comments. This question was popular and generally answered well. Good candidates scored well on the calculations, although the quality of discussion was often disappointing for final level. Where candidates did make mistakes in calculations, it was sometimes not possible to give them any credit as they failed to show workings.

To: Finance Director
From: Financial Manager
Date: 4 December 20X1
Subject: Working capital policy

(a) **Policy for investment and financing of working capital**

Choice of policies

The level of investment in working capital should be chosen after considering **manufacturing**, **marketing** and **financing factors** and other relevant stakeholder relationships. There is a range of possible investment policies, lying along a spectrum from conservative to aggressive.

Conservative policy

A conservative policy, such as we adopt at present, aims to **reduce the risk of system breakdown** by holding high levels of working capital. Thus customers are allowed **generous payment terms** to stimulate demand, **inventory** of finished goods is **high** to ensure availability for customers, and raw materials and work in progress are high to minimise the risk of running out of inventory and consequent downtime in the manufacturing process. Suppliers are paid promptly to ensure their goodwill, again to minimise the chance of stock-outs.

Effects of conservative policy

However, the cumulative effect on these policies can be that the firm carries a high burden of **unproductive assets**, resulting in a **financing cost** that can destroy profitability. A period of rapid expansion may also cause **severe cash flow problems** as working capital requirements outstrip available finance. Further problems may arise from inventory obsolescence and lack of flexibility to customer demands.

Aggressive working capital policy

An aggressive working capital investment policy aims to reduce this financing cost and increase profitability by **cutting inventory**, **speeding up collections from customers**, and **delaying payments to suppliers**. The potential disadvantage of this policy is an increase in the chances of **system breakdown** through **running out of inventory** or **loss of goodwill** with customers and suppliers. However, modern manufacturing techniques encourage inventory and work in progress reductions through just–in–time policies, flexible production facilities and improved quality management. Improved customer satisfaction through quality and effective response to customer demand can also enable the shortening of credit periods. Our **modern production facility** gives the company the potential to implement radical new management techniques, including those mentioned above, and to move along the working capital policy spectrum towards a more aggressive stance.

Short-term or long-term finance

Whatever the level of working capital in the business, there is a choice as to whether the investment is financed by short term or longer term funds. In this sense, a **conservative policy** would finance using **longer term loans or share capital** whereas an **aggressive policy** would finance using **shorter term measures** such as **bank overdraft**, **factoring of debts**, or **invoice discounting**. The advantage of short term finance is that it can be cheaper but its disadvantage is that it is more easily withdrawn in the event of a cash crisis.

(b) **Ratio analysis**

Policy:	*Conservative (present)*	*Change*	*Moderate*	*Change*	*Aggressive*
	$'000		$'000		$'000
Receivables	2,500	–20%	2,000	–30%	1,750
Inventory	2,000	–20%	1,600	–30%	1,400
Cash at bank	500		250		100
Current assets	5,000		3,850		3,250
Current liabilities	(1,850)	10%	(2,035)	20%	(2,220)
Net current assets	3,150		1,815		1,030
Non-current assets	1,250		1,250		1,250
Net assets	4,400		3,065		2,280
Forecast sales	8,000	2%	8,160	4%	8,320
Operating profit margin	18%		18%		18%
Forecast operating profit	1,440		1,469		1,498
Return on net assets	33%		48%		66%
Current ratio	2.70		1.89		1.46

Notes

- Return on net assets = operating profit / net assets.

- There is no logical reason why sales should increase as a result of a more aggressive working capital policy. The reasoning behind this assumption is unclear.

(c) **Recommended course of action**

The conclusion to be drawn from the figures in (b) above is that **substantial funds** can be released by moving from a conservative to an aggressive working capital position ($4.40m – $2.28m = $2.12m). These funds could be **repaid to shareholders**, **invested** or used to **reduce borrowings** depending on the company's situation.

Moderate working capital position

My first recommendation is that the company should attempt to move towards a moderate working capital position by **tightening up** its **debt collection procedures**, **buying inventory** in **smaller batches** and **negotiating longer credit periods** from suppliers. Our small size does not help us in this respect but, if achievable, this would result in a significant increase in return on net assets and an acceptable current ratio.

Use of modern techniques

However, further moves towards more aggressive working capital arrangements should be the outcome rather than the driver of policy changes. The key changes that need to be made in our firm are concerned with the adoption of **modern supply chain** and **manufacturing techniques**. These will enable us not only to reduce working capital while avoiding system breakdown but also to improve quality and flexibility and to increase customer demand. At the moment, we have modern equipment but are not taking full advantage of its potential. I therefore recommend that a **comprehensive study** of our **key business processes** is undertaken. I will be happy to evaluate the financial effects of the possible scenarios.

5 ABC

Top tips. The wisdom of the dividend policy each company adopts is somewhat dependent upon its current and future plans – whether in fact it can make 'better' use of the profits by re-investing them. The answer stresses the importance of stability in dividend payments – this is a very important 'real-world' issue. The scrip issues and other concessions by C are unlikely to be harmful, although their positive effect may not be very great.

The key element in the second part of the question is the **clientele effect**. You need to stress the importance of the shareholders' tax position here.

A's policy

Company A, which has deliberately avoided paying any dividends in the last five years, is pursuing a sensible policy for a rapidly growing company. All its post-tax profits are being **reinvested** in the company's business. By adopting this strategy, Company A reduces to a minimum its need to raise new capital from the market. **Issue costs** are **reduced** or **eliminated** and the company has **greater** flexibility in its investment programme since decision taking is not dependent on gaining market approval. Furthermore, since the company is probably investing heavily its taxation liability may well be small.

B's policy

At first sight the policy pursued by Company B, of distributing 50% of post-tax profits, appears to offer the shareholders **predictability**. In fact, however, with changes in the company's operating profits and in the tax regime, the post-tax earnings may fluctuate considerably. **Reducing** the **dividend** of a quoted company normally causes its **share price** to **fall sharply**, since the market takes this as casting considerable doubt on its future earnings potential. But, the more **mature** and **predictable** that Company B's business is, the **greater the merit** in its **dividend policy**. A mature business usually needs less new capital investment than a growing one and so a higher level of dividend is justified. Distributing profits allows shareholders to make some adjustment to the risk and return profile of their portfolios without incurring the transaction costs of buying and selling.

C's policy

Company C's policy falls between those of A and B in that a dividend is paid, albeit a small one. The **predictability** of the dividend will be welcomed by shareholders, since it allows them to make their financial plans with more certainty than would otherwise be possible. It also gives C part of A's advantage; **retained earnings** can be used as the principal source of investment capital. To the extent that they are relevant at all, **scrip issues** are likely to increase a company's market value, since they are often made to increase the **marketability** of the shares. Shareholder concessions are simply a means of attracting the 'small' shareholder who can benefit from them personally, and have no impact on dividend policy.

Effect on shareholders

In addition to looking at the cash flows of each company, we must also consider the impact of these dividend policies on the after tax wealth of shareholders. Shareholders can be divided into groups or '**clienteles**'. Different clienteles may be attracted to invest in each of the three firms, depending on their tax situation. It is worth noting that one clientele is as good as another in terms of the valuation it implies for the firm.

Company A would be particularly attractive to individuals who do not require an income stream from their investment and prefer to obtain a **return** through **capital growth**. Company B's clientele prefer a much higher proportion of their return to be in the form of **income**, although it would not be income on which they rely since it may be very variable from year to year. **Tax exempt funds**, such as pension funds, are indifferent between returns in the form of income or capital and might well invest in B since they need a flow of income to meet their day to day obligations. A large, diversified portfolio would reduce the effect of variability in the dividend. Company C is more likely to appeal to the **private investor** since most of the return is in the form of capital growth and there are shareholder concessions too.

So, each company may maximise the wealth of its shareholders. If the theorists are right, A, B and C all **maximise shareholder wealth** because the value of the companies is unaffected by dividend policy. Alternatively, each company's group of shareholders may favour their company's policy (and so their wealth is maximised) because the dividend policy is appropriate to their tax position and so maximises their post-tax returns.

6 Cuando

Top tips. In May 2005 one of the questions involved a discussion of different views being expressed by different directors, so this is likely to be a common situation in the exam. Answers on dividend policy should mix the theory (M&M) with the practical arguments against M&M. This question requires some planning so that you don't repeat in part (c) what you said in part (a). Note that part (a) takes into account the position of the main shareholder; spread of shareholdings will be a significant issue in many dividend questions.

(a) **Chairman's views**

At present the company has only one major shareholder, David Nile, who owns 80% of the shares. The extent to which Mr Nile has been involved in the management of the company is not clear, but it seems likely that he has been **involved in and has approved** previous decisions regarding dividends, probably in response to the investment needs of the company, and perhaps with an eye to his own individual tax position at different times. The **Chairman** is therefore surely correct to point out that the company has not needed to worry about the signals sent by its dividend policy in the past because it has been retaining profits as needed to develop the business.

Chief Operating Officer's views

The **Chief Operating Officer** says that the pattern of dividends has no effect on shareholder wealth, presumably following the theory put forward by Modigliani and Miller (MM) that dividend policy is irrelevant to shareholders because they can make their own adjustments (buying or selling shares) to achieve the level of income they require from their investments.

This may have been true in the case of David Nile, who probably began with a 100% stake and may since have sold 20% of his shares. But on the other hand to retain this stake he must have invested more money in the company in the meantime (in 20X3), given the increase in share capital from 800,000 shares to 1.5 million, so the argument does not really make sense.

Arguments against MM

In any case, there are strong arguments against MM's view that dividend policy is irrelevant as a means of affecting shareholder's wealth.

(i) **Differing rates of taxation on dividends** and **capital gains** can create a preference for a high dividend or one for high earnings retention.

(ii) Due to imperfect markets and the possible difficulties of selling shares easily at a fair price, shareholders might need **high dividends** in order to have funds to invest in opportunities outside the company.

(iii) **Markets are not perfect**. Because of **transaction costs** on the sale of shares, investors who want some cash from their investments should prefer to receive dividends rather than to sell some of their shares to get the cash they want.

(iv) **Information available** to shareholders is **imperfect**, and they are not aware of the future investment plans and expected profits of their company. Even if management were to provide them with profit forecasts, these forecasts would not necessarily be accurate or believable.

(v) As a consequence of imperfect information, companies are normally **expected at least to maintain the same level of dividends** from one year to the next. They are expected to pay a constant dividend or an increased dividend, but not a lower dividend than the year before. Failure to maintain the dividend level would undermine investors' confidence in the future.

(vi) Perhaps the strongest argument against the MM view is that shareholders will tend to prefer a **current dividend** to future capital gains (or deferred dividends) because the future is more uncertain.

Dividend policy in practice

In practice, dividend policy is significant to shareholders and the **Chairman's** view that a listing, putting all of the shares into public hands, will make dividend policy a **more pressing issue** is exactly in line with conventional thinking about dividend policy.

Unexpected changes in dividend payments will have an **effect on the share price**, and to avoid upsetting the market, a company might try to apply a policy of a consistent payout ratio (ratio of dividends to distributable profits for the year).

Companies will often also **'smooth' dividend payments**, ignoring 'temporary' fluctuations in annual profitability. Shareholders might therefore expect to receive dividends from a company that grow each year.

Market expectations can therefore be **a major factor in the formulation of dividend policy**, and listed companies are likely to be extremely reluctant to permit the kind of fluctuations in dividend level that have occurred in the case of Cuando in the past.

(b) The figures that are available can be analysed as follows.

	Net profits	*Annual growth*	*Dividends*	*Shares in issue*	*Earnings per share*	*Dividends per share*	*Dividend payout ratio*
	£000	%	£000	000	£	£	%
20X0	650	–	320	800	0.81	0.40	49.23
20X1	520	(20.00)	150	1,000	0.52	0.15	28.85
20X2	760	46.15	480	1,000	0.76	0.48	63.16
20X3	1,240	63.16	600	1,500	0.83	0.40	48.39
20X4	1,450	16.94	540	1,500	0.97	0.36	37.24

Cuando's earnings have increased steadily apart from a dip in its second year. However, without more detailed information no clear pattern to the growth can be discerned. Most growth was achieved in 20X3.

Earnings per share are typically around 80p with a dividend payout ratio of around 50% of this, but there is no consistent pattern at all. A higher than usual dividend was paid in 20X2, presumably to compensate shareholders for the much smaller dividend in 20X1, but in the following year, 20X3 (when the most spectacular growth occurred), the dividend fell back again to its 20X0 level. Despite the rise in earnings per share in 20X4 the dividend per share fell once more.

As mentioned in part (a) this policy has presumably been acceptable to the one major shareholder, but when his shares are sold to the public a change seems very desirable on the grounds that shareholders typically expect consistency, at the very least, and prefer steady growth to wild fluctuations for no apparent reason.

(c) Besides matters already mentioned in this answer there are a number of other factors that affect dividend policy, including the following.

(i) The purpose of retaining profits should usually be to **invest in new projects**, in order to develop and grow the business. Unless there are profitable investments available to invest in, there should be no reason to retain the profits instead of paying them out as dividends.

(ii) Companies are **prevented by law from distributing dividends in excess of the distributable reserves** of the company. Broadly speaking, distributable profits are accumulated profits. A loss-making company might therefore find its ability to pay dividends is restricted.

(iii) Dividends have to be **paid in cash** (given that scrip dividends are uncommon). In order to make a dividend payment, a company must therefore **have sufficient free cash flow** to afford to make the payment. It is quite possible for a company to make profits but have insufficient cash to pay a suitable dividend.

(iv) The board of directors might want to use dividend policy to provide signals to the market about **expectations for future profits and growth**. An increase in dividends could be used to signal optimism about the future. If the signal is well-received, the share price could be boosted.

7 Astatine

> **Top tips.** Calculations of the effect on the balance sheet and theoretical ex-rights price are likely to be set frequently. The calculations emphasise that the bonus issue and stock split have no effect on share valuation.

(a) *The balance sheet of Astatine after the rights issue and repayment of long-term loans*

	£m
Non-current assets	48
Current assets	66
	114
Amounts falling due within one year	43
	71
Amounts falling due after more than one year	20
	51
Ordinary shares of £1 (£20 million + 4 million × £1)	24
Share premium (4 million × £1.50)	6
Accumulated profits	21
	51

(b) *The amended balance sheets after a bonus issue and a stock split respectively would be as follows.*

	Bonus issue	*Stock split*
	£m	£m
Non-current assets		48
Current assets		66
		114
Amounts falling due within one year		43
		71
Amounts falling due after more than one year		20
		51
Ordinary shares of £1 (24 million × 5/4)	30	
Ordinary shares of 50p		24
Share premium		6
Accumulated profits	21	21
	51	51

> **Top tips.** It is assumed in this solution that the share premium would be used to make the bonus issue. It would also be correct to use the accumulated profit for the bonus issue, reducing the retained profit to £15 million, and retaining the share premium of £6 million.

(c) Theoretical value per share = $\frac{((5 \times 3.46) + 2.50)}{6}$ = £3.30

Alternative working

	£
Value of five existing shares at £3.46	17.30
Rights issue: value of one new share	2.50
Theoretical value of six shares	19.80

Theoretical value per share after the rights issue $\frac{£19.80}{6}$ = £3.30

The total market value of the company's equity would be (24 million shares × £3.30) = £79.2 million.

(d) (i) *Value per share after the bonus issue:*

Market value of equity / Number of shares	£79.2m / 30m
Value per share	£2.64

(ii) *Value per share after the stock split*

Market value of equity / Number of shares at 50p	£79.2m / 48m
Value per share	£1.65

(e)

Value of investment after the rights issue	(1,200 shares × £3.30)	£3,960
Value of investment after the bonus issue	((1,200 + 300 shares) × £2.64)	£3,960
Value of investment after the stock split	(1,200 × (2 shares at £1.65))	£3,960

There is no effect on shareholder wealth as a result of either a bonus issue or a stock split.

(f) **Increasing liquidity**

A **bonus issue** and **stock split** would both have the effect of increasing the number of shares in issue. A company might want to do this if it considers the current share price to be at a high level, that could deter liquidity in the shares on the stock market. A bonus issue or a stock split would reduce the share price to a more 'normal' level. For example, if shares are currently valued at £10 each, a one-for-four bonus issue should have the effect of reducing the share price to £8 each, and so perhaps make them more marketable. A stock split will usually reduce the share price by more than a bonus issue.

Signalling

A bonus issue or stock split might also be a way of **signalling to the stock market** that the company is buoyant about its expectations for future profits and earnings growth. Although the share price will be reduced in the short term, the signal would be that the company fully expects the share price to rise again to former levels at some time in the not-too-distant future.

Share premium

Making a bonus issue is one way that a company may be able by law to make use of its **share premium account**. A bonus issue is therefore a means of converting a non-distributable share premium into share capital.

Confidence boost

When a company makes use of distributable profits to make a bonus issue, it will convert distributable profits into **non-distributable long-term equity capital**. The result will be an increase in the long-term equity capital of the company. This could give creditors and lenders greater confidence in the company and its creditworthiness.

8 Sagitta

Top tips. Remember in (b) that the value of rights is **not** the cost of the rights share. (c) emphasises that taking up and selling the rights should have identical effects.

Examiner's comments. This was a popular question with some candidates achieving very high marks in parts (a) and (b). Part (c), however, which required an evaluation of options available to a holder of 10,000 shares in the company, was generally less well done. Too many candidates failed to make the point that the wealth of the shareholder would be unaffected, whether the rights were taken up or sold, but would be reduced if the rights were allowed to lapse.

The final part of the question on the importance of the pricing of the rights issue was less well-answered with few managing to make the point that so long as the issue price is below the market value the price is not critical.

(a) **Theoretical ex-rights price**

Current total market value $= £21\text{m} \times 16$
$= £336\text{m}$

Market value per share $= £336\text{m}/(60\text{m} \times 4)$
$= £1.40$

Rights issue price $= £1.40 \times 0.70$
$= £0.98$

$$\text{Theoretical ex –rights price} = \frac{((5 \times 1.40) + 0.98)}{6} = £1.33$$

Alternative working

	£
5 shares @ £1.40	7.00
1 share @ £0.98	0.98
6 shares	7.98

Theoretical ex-rights price = £7.98/6
= £1.33

(b) **Rights price**

	£
Theoretical ex-rights price	1.33
Cost of rights share	0.98
Value of rights	0.35

(c) **Take up rights issue**

	£
Value of shares after rights issue (10,000 × 6/5 × £1.33)	15,960
Cost of rights (2,000 × £0.98)	(1,960)
	14,000

(d) **Sell rights**

	£
Value of shares (10,000 × £1.33)	13,300
Sale of rights (2,000 × £0.35)	700
	14,000

Allow rights offer to lapse

	£
Value of shares (10,000 × £1.33)	13,300

If the investor either takes up the rights issue or sells his rights then his wealth will remain the same. The difference is that if he takes up the rights issue he will maintain his relative shareholding but if he sells his rights his percentage shareholding will fall, although he will gain £700 in cash.

However if the investor allows the rights to lapse his wealth will decrease by £700.

(d) Sagitta clearly needs to raise £47.04 million which is why it was decided to make a 1 for 5 rights issue of 48 million additional shares at a price of £0.98. Provided that this amount is raised it could have been done (for example) by issuing 96 million new shares as a two for five rights issue with the issue price at £0.49 per share.

The **price of the issue** and the **number of shares should not be important** in a competitive market as the value of the business will not change and nor will the shareholders' percentage shareholding.

However the critical factor about the **price of the rights issue** is that it **must be below the market value** at the time of the rights issue. If the rights issue price is higher than the market value then there is no incentive to shareholders to purchase the additional shares and the rights issue will fail. As far as the business is concerned the details of the rights issue including the price must be determined a considerable time before the rights issue actually takes place, therefore there is always the risk that the share price might fall in the intervening period.

9 Sundown Carehomes

Top tips. The question is made easier to answer because it is broken down into short sections which can be answered independently. The last section is puzzling, as the conversion terms described in the question appear dubious.

(a) The **redemption yield** is the true annual return received by an investor in the bond, taking into account both the interest received (in this case 7% before tax -referred to as the 'interest yield') and the gain or loss in capital value of the bond over the period to redemption.

The **gain or loss in capital value** arises because the current market value of the bond will be **dependent on its interest yield** compared with the market interest rate, and can be above or below par. For example, a 7% bond will sell at *above par* if the market interest rate is only 5%. If the bond is held to redemption, it will *redeemed at par value*, creating a capital loss, which will bring the redemption yield down to approximately 5%.

(b) Any public company suffers a **risk of bankruptcy** and/or default on its interest payments. In normal circumstances this **default risk is higher** than that of the national government. Because investors require compensation for risk, the company must offer to pay a higher interest rate than that paid by the government. Furthermore, the company will not be able to obtain the economies of scale on loan issue costs which are available to the government.

(c) A **zero coupon bond** pays **no interest**. If it is to be redeemed at par, it must be issued at a **large discount on par value**, giving the investor a return which consists entirely of the capital gain between redemption value and issue price.

A company would find such a **zero interest bond attractive** if it needs to finance a project through a start-up period of several years in which all cash generated is needed for reinvestment. The bond would be suitable provided that by the redemption date sufficient cash or refinancing is available to pay the lenders a much larger sum than was originally borrowed.

Investors who **prefer to make capital gains** rather than receive interest would find this **type of bond attractive**, because it has growth characteristics without the risk of equity shares. Although investors may prefer capital gains for tax reasons, any advantage depends on the tax rules of the country concerned.

(d) For every 4 shares at £4.75, one new share is issued at £4.00. The theoretical ex-rights price will therefore be $(4 \times £4.75) + £4.00 / 5 = £4.60$.

(e) The zero coupon bond must show an 8% return over 20 years. If redemption is at £100, the issue price should be $£100/1.08^{20} = £100 \times 0.215 = £21.50$.

This means the company must issue £7.44m nominal of bonds in order to raise £1.6m.

(f) Assuming the **convertible bond's par value** is £100, and it is issued at par, there is no gain on conversion in 20 years' time, which means there is no advantage to investing in it; 5 shares at £20 each are worth only £100. The NPV will be heavily negative, as follows:

Year	*Cash flow*	*Discount factor*	*Present Value*
	£	8%	£
0	(100)	1.000	(100.0)
1 - 20	6	9.818	58.9
20	100	0.215	21.5
			(19.6)

The company's shares are projected to rise from £4.75 to £20 in 20 years, from which the expected average annual return is calculated as $£4.75 \times (1 + r)^{20} = £20$.

Thus $1/(1 + r)^{20} = 4.75/20 = 0.2375$, from which r is approximately 7%, representing poor business performance from Sundown.

10 PG

Top tips. Be warned if you got (a) (i) wrong that manipulation of the earnings and price formulae may come up in this paper. (a)(ii) brings out the limitations of the theoretical ex rights price calculation. Actual price movements depend on the state of the market, the degree of market efficiency and, very importantly, the risk profile.

In (b) (ii) you are only asked about the advantages of issuing convertible loan stock; the principal feature is short-term benefits from being able to raise funds at limited cost, with possible adverse consequences (dilution of earnings, change in control) only happening long-term.

(a) (i) The **current market price** can be found by multiplying the earnings per share (EPS) by the price/earnings (P/E) ratio.

EPS is £3.6/6m = 60p per share
P/E ratio is 15
Market price of shares is 15 × 60p = **£9.00 per share**

(ii) In order to raise £10,500,000 at a price of 800 pence, the company will need to issue an additional 1,312,500 (£10,500,000/£8.00) shares.

Following the investment, the total number of shares in issue will be 7,312,500 (6,000,000 + 1,312,500).

At this point, the total value of the company will be:

(6m × £9) + £10,500,000 = £64,500,000

The **theoretical ex-rights price** will therefore be £64.5m/7.3125m = **£8.82**.

Problems with calculations

(1) The **costs of arranging the issue** have not been included in the calculations.

(2) The **market view** of the **quality of the new investment** will affect the actual price of the company's shares.

(3) If the **issue** is **not fully subscribed** and a significant number of shares remain with the underwriters, this will **depress the share price**.

(4) The effect of the new investment on the **risk profile** of the company and the expected **future dividend stream** could also cause the share price to differ from that predicted.

(5) The price of the shares depends not only on the financial performance of the company, but also on the **overall level of demand** in the stock market. If the market moves significantly following the announcement of the issue, this will affect the actual price at which the shares are traded.

(iii) **Features of deep discounted rights issue**

In a **deep-discounted** rights issue, the new shares are priced at a **large discount** to the current market price of the shares. The purpose of this is to ensure that the issue is well subscribed and that shares are not left with the underwriters, and thus this form of issue pricing is attractive when the stock market is particularly volatile. However, the shares cannot be issued at a price which is below their nominal value.

Disadvantage of deep discounted rights issue

The main drawback to this approach is that a **larger number of shares** will need to be **issued** in order to raise the required amount of finance, and this will lead to a larger dilution of earnings per share and dividends per share.

(b) (i) **Conversion premium**

The **conversion premium** is the **difference** between the **issue value** of the **notes** and the **conversion value** as at the date of issue. In other words it is the measure of the additional expense involved in buying shares via the convertible notes as compared with buying the shares on the open market immediately.

In this case, £100 loan notes can be converted into 11 ordinary shares. The **effective price** of these shares is therefore £9.09 per share.

The **current market price** of the shares is £9.00. The **conversion premium** is therefore £9.09 – £9.00 = **9 pence**. This can also be expressed in percentage terms as **1%** (0.09/9).

(ii) **Advantages of issuing convertible loan notes**

(1) **Convertibles** should be **cheaper than equity** because they offer greater security to the investor. This may make them particularly attractive in fast growing but high-risk companies.

(2) **Issue costs** are **lower** for loan notes than for equity.

(3) **Interest** on the **loan notes** is **tax deductible**, unlike dividends on ordinary shares.

(4) There is **no immediate change** in the **existing structure** of control, although this will change over time as conversion rights are exercised.

(5) There is no **immediate dilution** in **earnings** and **dividends per share**.

11 Ducey

Top tips. In part (a) it is helpful to show clearly how the tax allowable depreciation has been calculated and how they have been allocated over time. In part (b) state clearly the clear assumptions surrounding your choice of interest rate for evaluating the financing alternatives.

(a) First calculate the NPV cost of the plant if it is acquired using a bank loan. The discount rate to be used will be 13%, this being the approximate after-tax cost of the bank loan (19% × 70%).

Tax-allowable depreciation will be claimed as follows.

All figures £'000

Year	*Basis of claim*		*Value (× 30%)*	*Claimed in year*
1	176 × 25%	= 44.00	13.2	2
2	(176 – 44) × 25%	= 33.00	9.9	3
3	(176 – 44 – 33) × 25%	= 24.75	7.425	4
4	Balance	= 74.25	22.275	5

The NPV cost of the project can now be calculated.

Year	*Plant*	*Tax*	*Cash flow*	*Disc factor*	*NPV*
	£	£	£		£
0	(176.00)		(176.00)	1.000	(176.00)
1			0	0.885	0.00
2		13.2	13.2	0.783	10.34
3		9.9	9.9	0.693	6.86
4		7.425	7.425	0.613	4.55
5		22.275	22.275	0.543	12.10
NPV cost of purchase					(142.15)

The NPV cost of leasing the plant can be calculated using the discount rate of 13%.

Year	*Lease*	*Tax relief*	*Cash flow*	*Disc factor*	*NPV*
	£	£	£		£
0	(55.00)		(55.00)	1.000	(55.00)
1	(55.00)	16.5	(38.5)	0.885	(34.07)
2	(55.00)	16.5	(38.5)	0.783	(30.15)
3	(55.00)	16.5	(38.5)	0.693	(26.68)
4		16.5	16.5	0.613	10.11
NPV cost of leasing					(135.79)

The NPV cost of leasing is lower than buying outright using a bank loan and is therefore financially more advantageous to Ducey.

(b) If the company is in a permanent non-tax paying situation, then the alternative sources of finance can be evaluated on the basis of their **direct NPV costs** excluding tax allowances.

The NPV cost of purchase in year 0 is £176,000.

The NPV cost of leasing can be found by multiplying the annual rental payments in years 1 to 3 by the value of a three year annuity at 19%, and adding this to the year 0 PV of £55,000. Since the company is not paying tax, it will be unable to receive the tax benefits of any interest payments and therefore the before tax cost of borrowing (ie 19%) will be used to evaluate the lease:

NPV = £55,000 + (2.140 × £55,000) = £172,700.

Leasing is still therefore more financially advantageous than outright purchase.

(c) Other factors to be considered when the company is making the lease or buy decision include the following.

(i) **Running expenses**

It is assumed in the calculations that these are the same under the two financing alternatives. However in practice, items such as insurance, maintenance etc may vary.

(ii) **Current liquidity**

The effect of taking out and servicing an immediate loan of £176,000 on the overall liquidity and borrowing capacity must be considered.

(iii) **Accuracy of estimates**

The company must be certain that the life of the machine has been estimated correctly at four years. If there is a possibility that the life could be shorter than this then the alternatives should be re-evaluated.

(iv) **Effect on reported profits**

The effect of the alternatives on the reported profits should be taken into account, since this in turn could affect the dividend policy and therefore the valuation of the company's shares.

(v) **Change in interest rate**

The calculations assume that the interest rate will be fixed for the life of the machine. If the rate changes then this will have financial implications which should be evaluated.

12 Share values

Top tips. In (a) start off with the assumptions and then explain about each type of efficiency, clearly differentiating them on the basis of what information affects movements.
When discussing the issues in part (b) you should consider them in relation to the efficient market hypothesis, and not simply write as much as possible about the given topic. You need to bring timescale into your answer; does the efficient market hypothesis hold true in the long-term?

(a) It is often argued that the UK and US stock markets are **efficient capital markets**, in which:

(i) The prices at which securities are traded reflect all the relevant information that is available to buyers and sellers, meaning that prices change quickly to reflect all new information about future prospects.

(ii) **No individual dominates** the market.

(iii) **Transaction costs** are **not so high** as to impact significantly on the level of trading activity.

If the market is **efficient**, then share prices should vary in a rational way.

The main forms of market efficiency are usually defined in relation to the varying degrees of efficiency with which the market processes information, and are as follows.

Weak form

This form of the hypothesis contends that share prices only change when **new information** about a company and its profits have become available. Share prices do not change in anticipation of new information being announced. Since new information arrives unexpectedly, it follows that share prices should be expected to change in a random manner and therefore that definable trends in share prices should not exist, as share prices take into account all information available about past price movements.

Semi-strong form

This form of the hypothesis contends that **share prices reflect** both **all relevant information** about past price movements and their implications, and **all knowledge** that is **publicly available**. This means that it will be expected that share prices can anticipate the formal announcement of new information. For example, if two companies plan a merger, their share prices will inevitably change once the merger plans are formally announced.

The market would show semi-strong efficiency if it were able to **anticipate** such an **announcement**, so that share prices of the two companies would change in advance of the merger plans being confirmed. Research in the UK and the US suggests that this does happen in practice, with the conclusion being drawn that the stock markets in these countries do demonstrate semi-strong form efficiency.

Strong form

If the market displays strong form efficiency, it would react in both the ways described above, but in addition, prices would also reflect information from **insider knowledge** available only to experts such as investment managers. If this is the case, then it would follow that managers should not need to worry overmuch about the presentation of information in one year's accounts provided that they are taking decisions aimed at **maximising the net worth** of the firm in the long term.

This hypothesis does not seem to be borne out by the short-term nature of much decision making in quoted companies. In addition, an expert such as an investment manager should be able to use his **privileged access** to additional information about companies to earn a **higher rate of return** than an ordinary investor. However, if unit trust results do out-perform the market, the excess returns would seem to be absorbed by management charges, since there is no evidence that such funds to consistently beat the market.

(b) (i) **Fundamental analysis**

The fundamental theory of share values is based on the theory that the '**realistic**' market price of a share can be derived from a **valuation of estimated future** dividends. If this theory is correct, the price of any share will be predictable, provided that all investors have the same information about a company's expected future profits and dividends, and a known cost of capital. The evidence supports the theory in general terms, and thus supports the **efficient markets hypothesis** in relating the price of the shares to available information. However, in practice, share price movements are also affected by day to day fluctuations reflecting supply and demand, confidence, interest rate movements etc.

(ii) **Insider dealing**

It is illegal to deal in shares on the basis of privileged information that has been obtained by virtue of working for the company or for one of its professional advisers. Since the shares would be traded on the basis of information that is not available to the market, the occurrence of this practice could be described as demonstrating an '**extra-strong form**' of

market efficiency. The expectation would be that the individual would be able to make excess profits as a result of the use of privileged information.

The Stock Exchange maintains a surveillance group whose purpose is to scrutinise all unusual transactions. This group is effectively using the **efficient markets hypothesis** to help it to define what is a 'normal' transaction and therefore to identify cases where excess profits have been made on the basis of insider information.

(iii) **Index tracking funds**

The development of index tracking funds recognises the implications of the **semi-strong form** of the efficient markets hypothesis. It accepts the fact that it should not be possible to outperform the market on a consistent basis, and offers individuals the opportunity to allow their investment to **'track'** one or other of the **market indices**, such as the FTSE 100 index. This allows the investor to take some of the excess risk out of equity investment by **linking returns** to the **overall performance** of the market, which in the long-term has significantly out-performed many other investment sectors.

(iv) **Volatility**

Recent stock market volatility began with the exposure of fundamental weaknesses in some of the most strongly growing Far Eastern economies. The falls in the prices of share therefore reflect the fact that prospects for companies operating in those economies are no longer as good as they were believed to be a year ago. The market is therefore **responding** to **new information** that affects the prices of shares in a way that is consistent with the efficient markets hypothesis.

However, it could be argued that the falls in the value of shares are **out of proportion** to the actual likely downturn in results, and in this the situation is similar to the price crash of the 1987 when share prices suddenly fell by up to 40% on the world markets. The falls on the Far Eastern markets also generated nervousness in the European and US markets, with price falls being experienced there, although of a lower magnitude. In the short-term therefore, the markets tend to **over-react** to **significant changes** in information, but it still appears that the relationships underlying the fundamental theory of share values and the efficient markets hypothesis do hold good in the **longer term**.

13 M and N

Top tips. (a) is a thorough test of your understanding of Modigliani and Miller. Drawing graphs is not compulsory, but if you can do so neatly, it can save you time.

(b) (i) is about using the right equations. You may have found (b) (ii) complicated as you needed as a first stage to use the WACC to find the cost of equity of N and hence to find the level of dividends using the dividend valuation model. When you take tax into account, the situation is reversed – you use the level of dividend augmented by the tax shield in the dividend valuation model to find the new cost of equity.

(a) **Modigliani and Miller's theory** of capital structure differs from the traditional view in its assumptions about shareholder behaviour. As a consequence they questioned the view that there is an optimal level of gearing that reduces the cost of capital and maximises the total market value of the firm. They showed that it is the **income generated** from the business activities of the firm which determines value and not the way in which this income is allocated between the providers of capital. If the shares of two firms with different levels of gearing but the same level of business risk are traded at different prices, then **shareholders** will **switch** their **investment** from the **overvalued** to the **undervalued firm**. At the same time they will **adjust** their **level of personal borrowing** through the market in order to maintain their overall level of business risk at the same level. This process which is called arbitrage will result in the firms having the same equilibrium total value.

The implications of the theory for the firm's **cost of capital** and **total market value** at different levels of gearing can best be illustrated graphically.

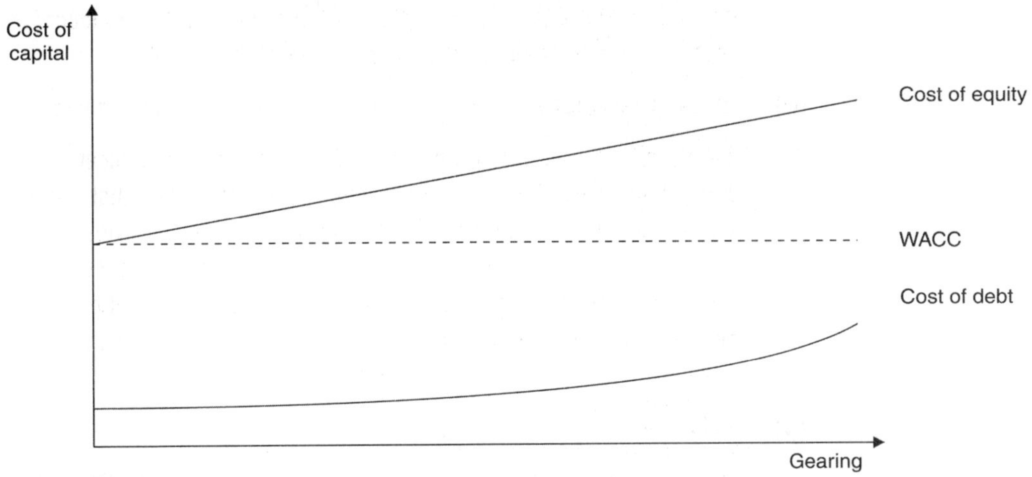

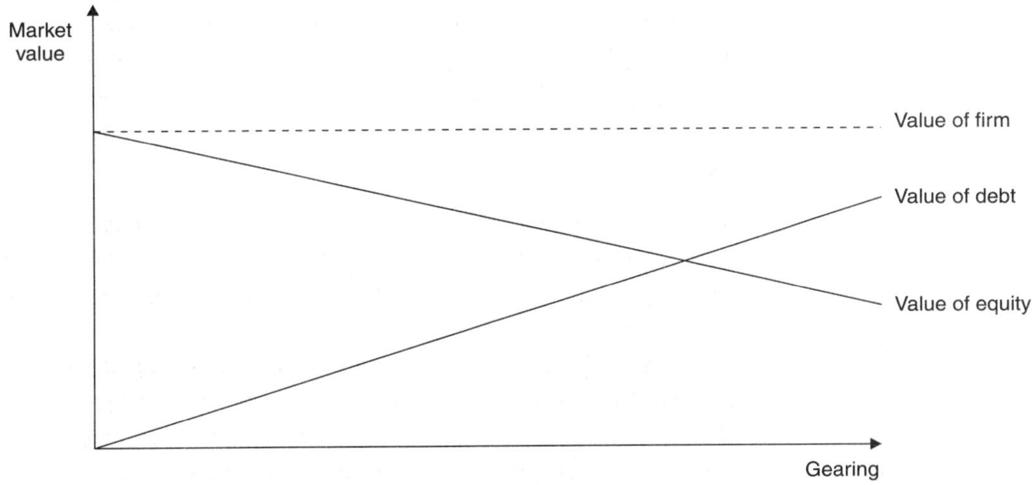

When **taxation is introduced** into the **model**, the total market value of the firm is no longer independent of its capital structure. This is because **interest on debt** is **allowable against tax**. The market value of the firm now increases with gearing, the amount of the increase being equal to the present value of the tax shield on the interest payments. This also means that the WACC declines as the gearing increases.

Weaknesses

The main weaknesses of the theory arise from its simplifying assumptions.

(i) In defining the arbitrage process it is assumed that **personal borrowing** is a **perfect substitute** for **corporate borrowing**. This is unlikely to be true in practice since the private investor does not have the protection of limited liability and cannot usually negotiate such good rates as the corporate borrower.

(ii) It is assumed that **all earnings** are **paid** out as **dividend**. In practice a variable proportion of carnings is normally retained.

(iii) It is extremely difficult to identify firms with identical business risk and operating profiles.

(iv) It is assumed that **investors' only criteria** are **risk and return**. In practice, investors will also be concerned with other factors such as the ethical stance of the company, and they do not have perfect information about the market.

The theory begins to break down at very high levels of gearing since firms in this situation are normally heading for bankruptcy. For all these reasons, it has not been possible for the theory to be fully proved empirically.

(b) (i) Since the companies are identical in every respect apart from their level of gearing, in the absence of taxation their total market value will be equal.

The total market value of M = 20m shares × £4.80 = £96m

The total market value of N is therefore also £96m. The total market value of a geared company is given by:

$MV_p = V_E + V_D$

where MV_p = market value of the company
V_E = market value of equity
V_E = market value of debt

In the case of N, V_D = £20m × 120% = £24m. The market value of the equity can now be found:

£96m = V_E + £24m
E = £72m

There are 30m shares in issue. The equilibrium share price will therefore be £72m/30m = £2.40 per share

If the rate of corporation tax is 25%, the total value of the company will be increased by the tax shield on the interest payments:

$V_g = V_u + TB_c$

where V_g = market value of the geared company
V_u = market value of the ungeared company
TB_c = value of tax shield

In this case:

V_g= £96m + (£24m × 0.25) = £102m

Of this, £78m (£102m – £24m) is attributable to equity. The theoretical equilibrium share price will therefore be £78m/30m = £2.60 per share.

(ii) Since the companies are identical in every respect, in the absence of taxation they will have the same WACC.

In the case of M which is totally equity financed, the WACC will be the same as the cost of equity, ie 18%. The WACC for N will also therefore be 18%. The cost of debt is 10% (12%/120%). The market values of debt and equity are known and therefore the cost of equity can be found using the expression:

$$WACC = k_e \times \frac{V_E}{V_E + V_D} + k_d \times \frac{V_D}{V_E + V_D}$$

where: k_e = cost of equity
k_d = cost of debt
$V_E/(V_E+V_D)$ = 72m/96m = 75%
$V_D/(V_E+V_D)$ = 24m/96m = 25%
18% = (k_e × 75%) + (10% × 25%)
k_e = (18% – (10% × 25%))/75% = 20.67%

If **taxation** is to be taken into account, it has been shown that the total market value of the company will rise due to the PV of the tax shield on the debt interest. This increase in value will accrue to the ordinary shareholders. The level of dividends in the absence of tax can be calculated using the dividend valuation model:

$k_e = d/p_0$

where: k_e = cost of equity
d = annual level of dividends
p_0 = market value of equity
20.67% = d/£72m
d = £14.8824m

The annual value of the **tax shield** on the **debt interest** is £0.6m (£20m × 12% × 25%). The dividend valuation model can now be used again to find the cost of equity if this amount is added to the dividend total:

$$k_e = \frac{£14.8824m + £0.6m}{£78.0m} = 19.85\%$$

(iii) In the absence of taxation, the WACC of N will be identical to that of M, ie 18%. If taxation is to be taken into account, then the WACC can be found using the expression:

$$WACC = k_e \times \frac{V_E}{V_E + V_D} + k_d(1-T_c) \times \frac{V_D}{V_E + V_D}$$

$$WACC = \frac{19.85\% \times 78}{78+24} + \frac{10\%(1-0.25) \times 24}{78+24} = 16.94\%$$

14 Serpens

Top tips. The key stages are:

1 Ungearing the equity beta to produce an asset beta for Serpens (an all-equity company).

2 Substituting this asset beta in the CAPM calculations.

As Serpens is all equity there is no need to regear.

In (b) any discussion on Modigliani-MIller should include discussion of the effect of tax.

Examiner's comments. The first part of the question requiring calculations of an asset beta and the value of a company using the MM propositions concerning the value of a geared company were poorly answered and marks were generally low.

However, in the second part of the question many candidates had no difficulty in discussing the arguments for and against the view that capital structure has no effect on the value of a company, incorporating the traditional and MM views.

(a) (i) **Current capital structure**

Profits available for dividend

	£
Profit before interest and tax	500,000
Corporation tax	(100,000)
Profit available for dividend	400,000

Value of the company

We need to determine the asset beta of Serpens by ungearing the equity beta of Diphda.

$$\beta_g = \beta_u\left[\frac{V_E + V_D(1-t)}{V_E}\right]$$

where β_g = equity beta
β_u = asset beta
V_E = proportion of equity in capital structure
V_D = proportion of debt in capital structure
t = corporation tax rate
1.4 = β_u ((70 + 30(1 – 0.2))/70)
1.4 = $\beta_u \times 1.34$
β_u = 1.04

Alternative working

$$\beta_u = \beta_g\left[\frac{V_E}{V_E + V_D(1-t)}\right]$$

$$= 1.4\ \frac{70}{70+30(1-0.2)}$$

$$= 1.04$$

The cost of equity of Serpens can now be found using the CAPM

k_e = 4% + 1.04 (9% – 4%)
= 9.2%

P_o = D_1/k_e
= 400,000/0.092
= £4,347,826

(ii) **Proposed capital structure**

Profits available for dividend

	£
Profit before interest and tax	500,000
Interest (3,000,000 × 5%)	(150,000)
Profit after interest	350,000
Corporation tax (20% × 350,000)	(70,000)
Profit available for dividend	280,000

Value of the company

MM's proposition can be used for this:

$Vg = Vu + TB_c$

where Vg = market value of the geared company
Vu = market value of the ungeared company
TB_c = tax benefit
Vg = 4,347,286 + (3,000,000 × 0.20)
= 4,947,286

(b) **MM view**

Modigliani and Miller (MM) were the first to suggest that the capital structure of a company has no effect on the value of the company. They argued that as cheaper debt capital is introduced into a company's capital structure this should serve to **lower the weighted average cost of capital** (WACC). However, the equity shareholders would require an **increase in their rate of return as debt capital** was introduced in order to compensate for their perceived additional risk. This increase in required return for the equity shareholders precisely cancels the benefit of the cheaper debt finance meaning that, as more and more debt is introduced, the WACC remains constant, as does the market value of the company.

Traditionalist view

This view of MM was directly opposed to that of the traditionalists. Their argument was that as additional, cheaper debt finance was introduced into the capital structure, initially the equity shareholders would not perceive there to be significant additional risk and therefore would require **no additional return on equity** or only a small increase in their cost of equity. The effect of the cheaper debt and little or no increase in the cost of equity would mean that the WACC would fall and therefore the market value of the company increase. However after a certain point, as even more debt capital is introduced the equity shareholders would require a **significant increase in their return** and from this point on, as more debt capital is introduced, the WACC would increase and the market value of the company would fall. There is therefore an optimal capital structure, where the WACC is at its lowest and the value of the company at its highest.

MM and tax

Returning to MM, their initial proposition was based upon a number of **restrictive assumptions** including perfect capital markets, no transaction costs, no bankruptcy costs and no corporation tax. In their second proposition MM recognised the **existence** of **corporation tax** and the fact that debt interest, as a tax allowable expense, was an additional benefit to the equity shareholders. Consequently they argued that as more debt is introduced into the capital structure the **benefit of the tax relief on the debt** will **increase the market value** of the company. Therefore even MM eventually recognised that the capital structure of a company does in fact have an effect on the value of the company.

15 ABC

> **Top tips.** This is a question from the old syllabus Paper 4 Finance exam so is not at strategic level. It does however provide excellent practise at some very important calculations. You will need to be completely comfortable with, and quick at, these types of calculations in your exam.

(a) **Gearing ratios**

$$\text{Gearing} = \frac{\text{Prior charge capital}}{\text{Shareholders' funds}}$$

20X5 $\frac{250}{446.8} = 56\%$

20X6 $\frac{250}{437.9} = 57.1\%$

20X7 $\frac{250}{431.9} = 57.9\%$

These are slightly below the covenant level of 60% and therefore appear acceptable. However, it would only take a fall of $5 million per annum in shareholder funds for gearing to rise to an unacceptable level.

Interest cover		$m
Interest on debentures =	7% × $150m=	10.5
Interest on bank loans =	5% × $100m=	5.0
Total interest		15.5

20X5 $\frac{58}{15.5} = 3.74$ times

20X6 $\frac{50}{15.5} = 3.23$ times

20X7 $\frac{54}{15.5} = 3.48$ times

The covenant for EBIT/total interest is 3.5 times so interest cover falls below acceptable limits in 20X6 and 20X7.

There is a significant risk that ABC will breach the debenture covenants so urgent action is required to obtain alternative finance or restructure the business to improve gearing and interest cover.

(b) **Cost of debt for existing debenture**

Year		*Cash flow*	*Discount factor*	*PV*	*Discount factor*	*PV*
		$m	*3%*		*4%*	
0	Market value	(107.00)	1.000	(107.00)	1.000	(107.00)
1 – 4	Interest (after tax)	4.90	3.717	18.21	3.630	17.79
4	Capital repayment	100.00	0.888	88.80	0.855	85.50
				0.01		(3.71)

After tax cost of debt = 3.00%

Pre-tax cost of debt $= \frac{3.00}{1-0.3} = 4.29\%$

Cost of debt for a 5% pre-tax bank loan

Year		*Cash flow*	*Discount factor*	*PV*	*Discount factor*	*PV*
		$m	*3%*		*4%*	
0	Loan	(107.00)	1.000	(107.00)	1.000	(107.00)
1 – 4	Interest (after tax)	3.745*	3.717	13.92	3.630	13.59
4	Loan repayment	107.00	0.888	95.02	0.855	91.49
				1.94		(1.92)

*107 × 0.05 = 5.35 × (1 – 0.3) = 3.745

After tax cost of debt $= 3 + \frac{1.94}{1.94 + 1.92} = 3.5\%$

Pre-tax cost of debt $= \frac{3.5}{1-0.3} = 5\%$

The debenture is therefore cheaper than the proposed replacement bank loan.

Other factors to consider

(i) The identity of the debenture holders and whether the debenture covenant could be renegotiated.

(ii) The security or loan covenants that may be required by the bank and whether these are any more flexible than the current debenture covenant.

(iii) The possibility of reducing the interest charge by offering non-current assets as security. The balance sheet contains a high level of non-current assets.

(iv) Alternative and cheaper sources of finance may be available.

(v) Planned dividend payouts are in excess of earnings which could be a serious concern for providers of finance.

(c) **Issue price of proposed rights issue**

Current number of shares $=\frac{200}{0.25}=800$ million

Number of new shares to be issued $=\frac{800}{5}=160$ million

\$100 million is needed so the issue price $=\frac{100}{160}=\$0.625$ per share

	\$
5 shares @ \$0.75	3.750
1 share @ 0.625	0.625
	4.375

$\frac{4.375}{6}=\$0.73$

Alternative solution

$$\text{Ex}-\text{rights price}=\frac{(\text{N x cum}-\text{rights price})+\text{issue price}}{\text{N}+1}$$

$$=\frac{(5\,\text{x}\,0.75)+0.625}{6}$$

$$=\$0.73 \text{ per share}$$

Advantages of new equity finance

- Avoidance of the redemption premium costs
- Improved gearing and interest cover
- Dividends are more flexible than loan interest as they do not have to be paid when profits are low
- It is a permanent form of finance and will not need to be restructured after four years
- It provides a good foundation for raising future debt finance

Advantages of the bank loan:

- Loan interest tends to be cheaper as it is tax deductible and constant unlike dividends where growth is expected
- The high value of non-current assets on the balance sheet could be used as security for a bank loan
- Debt can be repaid and is therefore more flexible than equity finance
- It is easier to arrange and administer and there is less risk involved.

16 Risk reduction

Top tips. You may be asked for a few marks to explain the importance of portfolio theory and the subject matter of this question is fairly typical. The last point about individuals being better able than companies to diversify is important, and you should bear it in mind when considering acquisitions of companies in different sectors.

(a) **Assumptions of portfolio theory**

In portfolio theory, investors are assumed to be **profit maximising** and **risk averse**. This means that they will trade off portfolio return against risk such that an 'efficient portfolio' will have the highest possible return for any given risk level and the lowest risk for any given return.

Two security portfolio

Investigation of the two-security portfolio reveals that, for two risky investments, only **some proportional combinations** will be efficient. The remaining possible combinations can be 'eliminated', that is they will be considered unattractive by investors.

As more risky investments are added to the portfolio, it is found that only a relatively **small proportion** of possible combinations are **efficient**. Portfolio theory shows how these efficient portfolios lie on part of the boundary of the set of all possible portfolios.

Investigation of a two-security portfolio consisting of a risk free investment and a risky investment shows that in this case there are **no inefficient portfolios** resulting from different proportional combinations. The set of possible portfolios simply gives a straight line trade-off between return and risk.

Optimal combination

Combining the effects described in the two preceding paragraphs, it is found that the optimal investment combination is a mix of **risk free investments** with an **efficient portfolio** of **risky securities.** When this is done, it becomes apparent that the best portfolio of risky securities would be one that consisted in theory of all possible investments. This is known as the market portfolio and is approximated by a diversified share portfolio of twenty or more shares.

Portfolio theory therefore arrives at the conclusion that all investors should split their funds between risk free investments (eg bank deposits, Treasury bills) and a diversified portfolio of risky investments (eg shares). The proportion invested in each category is, however, a personal choice for each investor and depends on their individual attitude to risk.

(b) The practical implications of portfolio theory to a fund manager are highly significant, and are increasingly put into practice as competition for investment funds becomes keener.

Diversification by companies

Portfolio theory suggests that fund managers should **diversify the risk-bearing part** of their holdings into at least twenty different shares or securities. When taken in conjunction with the efficient market hypothesis, portfolio theory suggests that investors cannot consistently achieve a better risk return trade-off than that offered by the stock market index (eg the FTSE index for London shares). To satisfy the demand for diversified portfolios, index tracking funds are now available. These are popular in UK and US but are of less relevance in less efficient stock markets.

Diversification by individuals

At first sight it may appear that the projects manager of a company should seek to diversify the company's business into as many different fields as possible, in order to reduce the company's risk. However, the manager should realise that investment decisions are made on behalf of shareholders, who are able to **diversify their overall portfolios** by buying shares in many different companies. For such shareholders the overall risk of any individual company is irrelevant. What matters is the incremental risk that an individual project adds to the market portfolio.

17 I

Top tips. Although this looks like a question on the CAPM, the final part of the question requires a discussion of the efficient markets hypothesis, so you should be confident in both these areas. Note the requirement for the discussion in (c) to be comprehensible to a non-financial manager. Discussion of the assumptions and limitations of CAPM carried most marks in (c), although to score heavily the efficient markets hypothesis and the chairman's assertions also needed to be discussed, and the calculations carried out in (a) and (b) used in support.

Examiner's comments. The main weakness in this question was discussion of the efficient markets hypothesis; the key point here was the market's expectations re the company's loss.

(a) The required rate of return on equity can be found using the capital asset pricing model:

$k_e = R_f + [R_m - R_f]\,\beta$

A $k_e = 5\% + 0.7(15\% - 5\%)$
$= \mathbf{12\%}$

B $k_e = 5\% + 1.4(15\% - 5\%)$
$= \mathbf{19\%}$

(b) The beta for I can be found using the same expression:

$17\% = 5\% + \beta(15\% - 5\%)$

$$\beta = \frac{(17\% - 5\%)}{(15\% - 5\%)}$$

The beta factor = 1.2

The **beta factor** is a measure of the volatility of the return on a share relative to the stock market. If for example a share price moved at three times the market rate, its beta factor would be 3.0. The beta factor indicates the level of **systematic risk**, the risk of making an investment that cannot be diversified away. It is used in the capital asset pricing model to determine the level of return required by investors; the higher the level of systematic risk, the higher the required level of return.

(c) To: The Chairman
From: Finance Director
Date: 20 November 20X1
Subject: The Capital Asset Pricing Model (CAPM) and stock market reactions

(i) **Assumptions and limitations of CAPM**

Diversification

Under the CAPM, the return required from a security is **related** to its **systematic risk** rather than its total risk. Only the risks that **cannot** be **eliminated** by diversification are **relevant.** The assumption is that investors will hold a **fully diversified portfolio** and therefore deal with the unsystematic risk themselves. However, in practice, markets are **not totally efficient** and investors do not all hold fully diversified portfolios. This means that total risk is relevant to investment decisions, and that therefore the relevance of the CAPM may be limited.

Excess return

In practice, it is difficult to determine the excess return ($R_m - R_f$). **Expected rather than historical returns** should be used, although historical returns are used in practice.

Risk-free rate

It is similarly difficult to **determine the risk-free rate**. A risk-free investment might be a government security; however, interest rates vary with the term of the debt.

Risk aversion

Shareholders are risk averse, and therefore **demand higher returns** in compensation for increased levels of risk.

Beta factors

Beta factors based on historical data may be a **poor basis** for future **decision making**, since evidence suggests that beta values fluctuate over time.

Unusual circumstances

The CAPM is **unable** to **forecast accurately returns for companies** with **low price/earnings ratios**, and to take account of **seasonal 'month-of-the-year' effects** and **'day-of-the-week'** effects that appear to influence returns on shares.

Possible reasons for the apparent discrepancy in betas for A and B

The Chairman has expressed the view that A is a higher risk company than B because it operates in overseas markets. This factor gives rise to its **lower beta value**. Its returns are likely to have a **lower correlation** with those of the UK stock market as a whole, and therefore it has a **lower level of systematic risk**. It is also possible that the **level of total risk** faced by A is lower because it is **better diversified** than B.

Efficient markets hypothesis

The way in which the stock market responds to information released by a company can be understood with reference to the **efficient markets hypothesis** (EMH). It is generally accepted that the UK stock market demonstrates a **semi-strong form** of **market efficiency**. This means that share prices **respond immediately** to all **publicly available information**, but not to information available only to insiders.

Implications of efficient markets hypothesis

- It is **not possible** consistently to **beat the market** (on a risk-adjusted basis) without the use of inside information.
- **Past share prices** are **not** a **predictor** of future share prices.
- The price of a share reflects **market expectations** of future performance.
- Investors behave **rationally** and are not deceived by manipulation of accounting figures.

(ii) **I's position**

This can help to explain the situation of I. The effect of an announcement of either profit or loss on the share price will not depend simply on the **magnitude** of the profit or loss, but in the relationship between the **announcement** and what the **market was expecting**. In this case, the company announced a loss and the share price rose. The market might have been expecting the **loss** to be **much larger** than it actually was, and the share price therefore adjusted in response to what was effectively good news. Alternatively, it could be that investors looked not simply at the loss, but at the **future prospects** of the company and decided that these were better than had been expected. The share price would then rise accordingly.

18 Ingredients and attributes

Top tips. A good general question on what the finance function provides. In the exam you may be asked about relations with, and information provided to, specific stakeholders, and you should bear these qualities in mind.

In planning the presentation of information to managers there are several attributes and ingredients which are significant.

(a) **Relevance**

Relevance is an important ingredient of information since the usefulness of information is dependent upon how strongly related it is to the problems or issues being considered. In planning a presentation or report it is important to consider whether the information actually focuses on the concerns addressed.

(b) **Accuracy**

Accuracy is another critical ingredient of information. Inaccurate information is useless. In many cases it is not possible to obtain entirely accurate information but information should be as accurate as is economically and organisationally practical.

(c) **Timeliness**

The **timeliness** of the information delivered is also an important ingredient since decision makers want the most up-to-date information available. The timing of presentations or reports must therefore take the decision-making process into account.

(i) If decisions are made **periodically**, the information system's activities should be timed to the decision cycle. For example, many organisations make regular decisions weekly, monthly, quarterly or on some other fixed term, and so information systems should be designed to provide the latest information in time for each decision. The system designer could also use the regularity of the decision for planning the data collection, processing and output activities.

(ii) **Irregular** or **infrequent** presentations or reports are much less easy to plan for since they lack predictability. In these cases an on-line or demand-driven system is most appropriate, possibly an **exception reporting** approach. The system would monitor the organisation's operations and whenever unusual or notable situations are detected the system would automatically generate reports to alert management. Systems designers need to plan information delivery so that decision makers receive it at the appropriate times.

(d) **Completeness**

Information should also be **complete**. This attribute describes the **fullness** of the information delivered by the system. Information which only applies to part of a problem is often insufficient and can sometimes be quite misleading.

For example, many companies set prices for their products based upon their costs (a cost plus mark-up) without knowing or having good information about the effects this price may have on consumers or competitors. But **having full and accurate information about costs does not imply**

that decision makers have complete information about the real problem of setting an appropriate price for their product.

Where possible a system designer should provide as full and complete information as possible, although design should be driven by user needs rather than the system specialist's notions of what is important.

(e) **Well-presented**

The information should be **effectively communicated** to the decision makers. They should **not be overwhelmed by detail or volume.** The information should be **summarised** or **aggregated** so that it is appropriate for the problems considered without being excessive. Information should also be produced in the **most useful mode**: for example, graphics can often allow managers to identify important information which would otherwise be unclear. Information should be **tailored to the needs of its recipients**, communicated in an **effective format**, and **delivered to the correct people** within the organisation.

(f) **Cost effective**

A final attribute of information is that it should be **cost effective**. Some **balance** must be made between the **costs** of acquiring, processing and analysing data and the **benefits** of so doing. There are **diminishing returns** on information so that the costs of obtaining additional data increase disproportionately while the benefits of having it tend to decrease more and more rapidly. No organisation can support an information system which costs more than the benefits it delivers.

19 Treasury management

Top tips. A few easy marks may be available for discussing the role of the treasury function. (b) looks at the role from another angle.

(a) **Management of cash**

A central treasury department will normally have the responsibility for the **management of the group's cash flows** and borrowings. Subsidiaries with surplus cash will be required to submit the cash to the treasury department, and subsidiaries needing cash will borrow it from the treasury department, not from an external bank.

Borrowing

A central treasury will also be given the **responsibility for borrowing** on behalf of the group. If a subsidiary needs capital to invest, the treasury department will borrow the money required, and lend it on to the subsidiary. The subsidiary will be responsible for **paying interest** and **repaying the capital** to the treasury department, which will in turn be responsible for the interest and capital payments to the original lenders.

Risk management

Another function of the treasury department will be to **manage the financial risk** of the group, such as currency risk and interest rate risk. Within broad guidelines, the treasurer might have authority to decide on the balance between fixed rate and floating rate borrowing, and to use swaps to adjust the balance. The department would also be responsible for arranging forward exchange contracts and other hedging transactions.

Taxation

The central treasury department could also be responsible for the **tax affairs** of the group, and an objective would be to minimise the overall tax bill. To accomplish this effectively, the treasury must have **authority to manage transfer prices** between subsidiaries in the group, as a means of transferring profits from high-tax countries to lower-tax countries.

(b) The treasury function needs information from within and from outside the organisation to carry out its tasks.

(i) From each subsidiary within the group, it will need **figures for future cash receipts and payments**, making a distinction between definite amounts and estimates of future amounts. This information about cash flows will be used to **forecast the cash flows of the group**, and identify any future borrowing needs, particularly short-term and medium-term requirements. Figures should be provided regularly, possibly on a daily basis.

(ii) Information will also be required about **capital expenditure requirements**, so that long-term capital can be made available to fund it.

(iii) Subsidiary finance managers should be encouraged to **submit information** to the **treasury department** about local market and business conditions, such as prospects for a change in the value of the local currency, or a change in interest rates.

(iv) From outside the group, the treasury will need a **range of information** about current market prices, such as exchange rates and interest rates, and about which banks are offering those prices. Large treasury departments will have a link to one or more information systems such as Reuters and Bloomberg.

(v) The treasury department should be alert to any **favourable market opportunities** for raising new debt capital. The treasurer should maintain regular contact with several banks, and expect to be kept informed of opportunities as they arise.

(vi) Where the treasury is responsible for the group's tax affairs, information will also be needed about **tax regulations** in each country where the group operates, and changes in those regulations.

20 Perseus

Top tips. If you struggled on either part of this question, you should go back over the material again, as valuation will occur in practically every sitting, often in the compulsory question. Remember that the examiner will never just want you to carry out valuation calculations. You should **always** comment on the methods you use, even if you are not explicitly asked to in the question as you are here.

(a) (i) **Net assets basis**

	£m
Freehold land and building	104.2
Fixtures and fittings	3.5
Motor vehicles	0.4
Inventory	58.0
Trade receivables	23.4
Cash	21.5
Trade payables	(25.9)
Tax	(5.4)
Loan notes	(49.0)
Net assets	130.7

$$\text{Value per share} = \frac{£130.7\text{m}}{50\text{m}}$$

$$= £2.61 \text{ per share}$$

(ii) **Dividend yield basis**

$$\text{Dividend per share in Perseus (gross)} = \frac{£3.3\text{m} \times 10/9}{50\text{m}}$$

$$= 7.33 \text{ pence}$$

It is assumed that this dividend will remain constant in future years.

Gross dividend yield of Tityus = 2.2%

Adjust upwards for lesser marketability/greater risk of an unlisted company - say 2.6%*

$$\text{Value per share in Perseus} = \frac{\text{Dividend per share}}{\text{Dividend yield}} = \frac{0.073}{0.026}$$

$$= £2.81 \text{ per share}$$

*(Alternatively, since this is a very arbitrary adjustment, it would be acceptable to use the unadjusted yield to get a value of £3.22, then add a note to acknowledge that this is likely to be an over-valuation.)

(iii) **Price/earnings ratio basis**

$$\text{Earnings per share of Perseus} = \frac{£10.7\text{m}}{50\text{m}}$$

$$= 21.4 \text{ pence}$$

P/E ratio of Tityus = 20.5

Adjust downwards for lesser marketability/ greater risk of an unlisted company - say 15**

Value per share in Perseus = £0.214 × 15
= £3.21

**(A similar note to that at the end of (ii) applies here, with an unadjusted value of £4.39)

(b) **Net assets basis**

The **net assets (liquidation)** basis is a method of valuation that can be used if the company is to be liquidated and the individual assets sold off to pay the shareholders. If the company is a going concern then the actual business **should be worth** a lot more than the break up value of the assets, due to the future earnings and cash flows of the business and unrecorded assets such as goodwill. Therefore if the business is to be sold as a going concern then the net asset value is far too low a value. However it can be used as a bottom line figure to give an indication of the absolute lowest figure that could be accepted from a bidder.

Dividend yield basis

The **dividend yield method** of valuation is a conceptually sounder method of valuation for a business that is being valued as a going concern. The dividend valuation model is used to find the **present value of future dividends** based on the shareholders' required dividend yield.

However there are a number of problems with this method. Firstly **a suitable dividend yield** has to be determined. It is possible, as above, to use the published dividend yield of a similar listed company; however when valuing the shares of a private company the dividend yield must be adjusted upwards to reflect the lack of marketability of private company shares and the increased perceived risk compared to a listed company. This adjustment is arbitrary. In addition, the published dividend yield will incorporate an **expected level of growth** (the higher the growth the lower the yield) which may not match growth expectations in the company to be valued.

Secondly a **suitable dividend figure** must be used. This could be the latest year's dividend, an average of a number of past years or an estimate of the actual future dividends.

There is a further problem with the use of the dividend yield for the valuation of an entire company. The dividend yield method is suitable for the **valuation of a small holding** in a company but if the entire company is to be purchased then the new owners may have an entirely different dividend policy and therefore it is the earnings of the company rather than the dividends which are of importance.

Price/earnings method

The price/earnings method of valuation is therefore a good method to use for the purchase of an entire company as it is based upon the last reported earnings of the company.

Again however there are problems with **determining an appropriate price/earnings ratio** and sustainable earnings. The price/earnings ratio of a similar listed company can be used but as with the dividend yield this must be adjusted to reflect the **lack of marketability**, increased risk and difference in growth expectations. This time however the adjustment should be downwards and is again an arbitrary one. The earnings figure that is used could be the current earnings figure, an average of a number of years past earnings or the future earnings that the purchaser expects from the company.

21 Hostile bids

Top tips. Part (a) is actually two questions in one and difficult to cover in its entirety. Don't spend too long discussing each stage of a hostile bid. In part (b) we have shown the most common defences. Several others are acceptable (e.g. make a counter-bid, find a 'White Knight', etc., but beware of concentrating on potentially illegal defences (e.g. poison pills, purchase of own shares, etc.). Part (c) is a common question.

(a) **Lack of power of shareholders**

Shareholders in a listed company usually **lack individual control** because of the **small size of their shareholdings** and rely on their agents, the directors, to run the company on their behalf. It is the **directors' duty,** under company law, to act in the **shareholders' best interests** when making decisions. However, this does not always happen and cases when directors act on their own behalf, to improve their own wealth or prestige or to protect their position, are well documented in literature on agency theory.

Unfortunately, shareholders' **remedies against ineffective or inefficient directors** are limited because they cannot interfere in the day-to-day decision making. The choice is usually one of removing directors by special resolution or submitting to a takeover bid by a more effective management team. Potential and actual takeover bids therefore have an important role in securing shareholders' returns.

Hostile bids

A takeover bid will be hostile when the **target company's directors disagree** with **the predator's bid**. Even if their hostility is to protect their own position, their defensive actions will be designed to secure the approval of their shareholders and will benefit the shareholders directly, for example by improving cash distributions, and indirectly by encouraging a higher bid price from the predator.

Impact of hostile bids

Hostile bids are not always good for the predator company, however. Research shows that the **price paid for the target company** in a hostile bid situation is often too high, resulting in a shift in wealth from the bidding company's shareholders to the those in the target company. This is particularly likely if the target company can find an alternative 'suitor' and effectively put itself up for auction. Problems of managing a new acquisition which was hostile to the takeover will also result in additional costs.

Typical stages in a hostile bid are:

(i) There may be **unofficial discussions** between the directors of the two companies. Absolute secrecy must be maintained until an official bid is made.

(ii) The bidding company's directors make a **firm offer,** addressed to the directors of the target company, for the shares of the target company.

(iii) The shareholders of both companies must **immediately be informed** by press notice.

(iv) Within a limited number of days, a **formal offer** is **then made** by the bidding company to the shareholders of the target company.

(v) **Directors of the target company circulate their views** on the bid and defence against the bid to their shareholders.

(vi) The **bidding company may revise its bid**, or the target company may make a counter-bid, or another party may make an offer for the target company.

(vii) **Shareholders of the target company vote** on **whether to accept the bid**. If more than 50% agree, the offer is accepted.

(b) When defending itself against a hostile takeover bid, the board of directors must comply with the relevant law or code (in UK this is the City Code on Takeovers and Mergers) which will have as its overriding principle the need for the directors to act in the best interest of shareholders at all times.

Among the legal strategies that the Board may adopt are:

(i) **Improve asset utilisation**

This may be achieved by **taking cash off low-interest deposit** accounts; by **selling redundant non-current assets** such as under-utilised property; by **rationalising operations** to make full use of business assets; or by improving efficiency of working capital management (eg reducing stockholdings and speeding up receivable collections). In each case the cash released can be returned to shareholders as dividends or by buying back shares. The effect may be to boost share price and persuade shareholders to vote against the bid.

(ii) **Release information on the company's prospects**

Information on new investment projects may have been kept secret in order to protect new developments from competition. Release of **beneficial information concerning improved future cash flows** may boost the share price and prevent the bid from succeeding.

(iii) **Present a rational argument against the bidding company's plans**

Documents **justifying the company's existing management and strategy** and criticising the bidding company's plans are an important part of the defence procedures when a hostile bid is received. Any such documents must be prepared with the utmost care, however (in the UK the City Code requires the same standard of care as for a share issue prospectus).

22 Takeovers

Top tips. This question discusses the issues that may well be raised in the latter half of compulsory question 1. (b) illustrates why companies are acquired. (c) what can go wrong. Together they constitute a checklist of the sorts of issues to look out for in a takeover question.

Examiner's comments. This question required candidates to consider various aspects of company takeovers. This narrative question was very popular and, on the whole, answers were of a reasonable standard. The first section required candidates to identify what a company seeking to acquire another company should look for when assessing suitable targets. This part was not always answered well with many candidates missing the basic point that a takeover will only make economic sense if the value of the combined business exceeds the value of each business when taken separately.

The second section was answered rather better with most candidates gaining marks for identifying ways in which a takeover may benefit the shareholders of a bidding company. The final section, requiring candidates to discuss reasons why a takeover may fail to deliver an expected increase in wealth, was also answered reasonably well.

(a) Shareholder wealth in a company can be expressed as the present value of the future cash flows of the business. Therefore if a takeover of another company is to increase shareholder wealth then the present value of the combined entity must exceed the sum of the present values of the two individual businesses.

PV combined business > PV bidding company + PV target company

(b) In order for a takeover to lead to an increase in wealth for the bidding company's shareholders there must be gains that would not have arisen if the two companies had not combined.

Economies of scale

When two businesses combine this creates a **larger business** which can **lead to economies of scale**. For example there could be direct cost savings by eliminating duplication of costs, or market power could be exerted by the larger entity in order for example to gain lower purchase prices for buying larger quantities.

Complementary resources

One company may decide to buy another company as a method of directly acquiring resources the other company may have. For example a manufacturing company may acquire a company with a strong research and development division which will eventually improve the bidding company's products.

Competition

The motivation for a bidding company to acquire a competitor may be in order to eliminate that market competition and improve market share. This in turn might mean that the combined entity is in more of a position to influence prices and increase profits. However as this will not always benefit the final consumer such an acquisition may not be allowed by government.

Undervalued shares

In some circumstances, due to market imperfections, the shares in the target company may be undervalued and therefore the bidding company is effectively buying a bargain.

Underutilisation of resources

The target company may have been chosen due to a perception by the bidding company management that the resources of the target are being underutilised and by introducing a new management team additional profits can be earned.

(c) In other cases although the bidding company management might have expectations of an increase in wealth for its shareholders this may not always transpire.

Paying too high a price

In a takeover bid, particularly a contested one, it is entirely possible that the bidding company may pay a **higher price for the target company shares** than they are worth. This is often the case as it is common for a **premium** to be offered to the target company shareholders in order to persuade them to sell their shares. If the premium is greater than the benefits from the takeover then this will be a direct transfer of wealth from the bidding company shareholders to the target company shareholders.

Integration of the businesses

After a takeover it is often **hard to integrate the two businesses** to such an extent that any anticipated benefits can be realised. This may be due to **differences in culture, management style or operational or organisational matters**. The problem is particularly highlighted where the bidding company tries to impose its own systems, culture and management on the target company.

Unforeseen problems

Despite thorough investigation and due diligence procedures being carried out during a takeover bid it is entirely possible after the combination to **discover problems** in the target company which were not evident before the bid and which will eliminate any anticipated increases in wealth.

Management problems

In some cases the management of the bidding company **lose motivation** after a takeover and assume that the benefits foreseen will just happen without additional effort on their behalf. This is rarely the case and continued management effort and motivation will be required in order to achieve the desired results.

23 Gasco

Top tips. This case study is a welcome change to most 'general questions' on mergers and takeovers as it provides a lot of detail for use as illustrations of synergy, stakeholder expectations and post-merger problems. You should state the general principles involved and illustrate them with examples drawn from the question.

Examiner's comments. Generally answers were good, with most students making the most of the opportunity to apply stakeholder and takeover theory to a specific situation.

(a) There is frequently a mix of good and bad reasons behind a takeover bid. Amongst the good reasons, the most significant is the possibility of creating **synergy,** which means that the value of cash flows from the combined business is higher than the value of cash flows from the two individual businesses. Although CarCare and Gasco are in different market sectors, there are a number of areas which may generate synergy.

(i) **Elimination of duplicated resources**. The most obvious areas are the marketing systems, the call centre systems and local offices and training facilities for mobile repair/emergency staff. Head office overheads may also be reduced.

(ii) **Cross-selling**. Opportunities exist to cross-sell products to customers on the other company's database.

(iii) **Building a critical mass** for non-core business. This might apply to the financial services areas of both businesses. The credit card and insurance businesses may gain from a combined brand name.

(iv) **Reduction in the risk of the company's cash flow profile**. CarCare receives membership subscriptions in advance, whereas Gasco's customers will pay mainly in arrears. The combined cash flows will be perceived as less risky by shareholders and lenders.

(v) The takeover of CarCare will **abolish its mutual status** and will allow equity funds for expansion to be raised more easily, by share issues made by the parent company, reducing the cost of capital.

Amongst the many possible bad reasons for takeover are:

(i) The directors of Gasco **seeking the prestige** of a larger company
(ii) Diversification with **no real strategic objective**
(iii) Gasco using up surplus cash**, again with no strategic objective**

(b) **Stakeholders**

The major stakeholders of CarCare are its members, who are both owners and customers, its directors and employees, and its creditors. Competitors will also be highly interested in the takeover.

Members

The members will have **mixed reactions.** The replacement of mutual status with marketable equity shares or cash will give them an immediate **'windfall' gain,** which many will welcome. However, the cost of this is **lost influence** on the future direction of CarCare. As customers, many may fear a reduction in the quality of service, particularly in the light of increased competition in the market and the fact that GasCo has to demonstrate that it is making a **return on its investment**. Others may disagree, on the basis that Gasco will be able to raise money for expansion, modernisation and improvements more easily than CarCare could as a mutual organisation.

CarCare's directors have a duty to ensure that they act in the **best interest** of **members.** However they will also be concerned about their own positions after the takeover and will wish to seek suitable positions in the new company's management structure. Some may fear loss of their jobs.

Employees

Employees will have **mixed reactions** depending on whether they are likely to be presented with additional opportunities or loss of status or redundancy. There is likely to be some **rationalisation** of the workforce except for those with highly specific skills, and for those who remain there may also be the threat of relocation. Employees will be seeking answers to these questions before the takeover happens, but are unlikely to receive comprehensive answers.

Creditors

Creditors, including bankers, will probably be **happy** with the **merger** provided that Gasco has no financial problems.

Competitors

Some competitors will fear that they will **lose market share** if the takeover enables new finance for expansion, improvement and marketing of CarCare. Others will be more optimistic, believing that CarCare will become less sensitive to the needs of customers.

(c) Gasco may face a number of problems after the takeover has been achieved.

(i) Former members of Gasco who did not agree with the takeover, and who may have been actively resisting it, may decide to **change their service provider** to another organisation. The parent company will have to be pro-active in giving confidence to all its CarCare customers.

(ii) The two organisations probably had **different management styles**, Gasco being a stock exchange quoted company with a clear need for financial results and CarCare being more orientated to serving its customers and acting as a pressure group to represent their needs. Conflicts may arise between directors, managers and employees of CarCare after the takeover as a result of an enforced change in management style from Gasco.

(iii) Actual and feared redundancies, relocations, changes in work practice, training methods and other problems may **demotivate CarCare employees,** causing resistance and a drop in productivity. In this respect, delays in information provision and decision making can make the situation worse.

(iv) **Competitors may take advantage** of reorganisation problems at CarCare in order to gain market share.

24 Olivine

Top tips. Our answer to part (a)(ii) assumes that the administrative savings have been achieved. Otherwise the answer to (a)(ii) is £(25 + 9.6)m/60m = 57.7 pence per share, and subsequent answers also change.

Examiner's comments. The calculations in the first two parts of the question were generally well answered but the final part which required discussion of the calculations was not particularly well done. The terms of the proposed takeover favoured the target company's shareholders and candidates should have identified the need to achieve a more equitable outcome between the two shareholder groups by changing the offer price.

(a) (i) **The total value of the share offer**

Earnings per share = £25m/40m = £0.625

P/E ratio = 20

Share price = 20 × £0.625 = £12.50 per share

Share offer = 5 shares × (16m shares/4) = 20m shares issued

Value of share offer = £12.50 × 20 million = £250 million

(ii) **Olivine earnings per share**

Earnings = £25m + £9.6m + £2.4m = £37.0m

Number of shares = 40m + 20m = 60 million

Earnings per share = £37.0m/60m = 61.7 pence per share

(iii) **Share price of Olivine**

Earnings per share (part ii) = 61.7 pence per share

Price earnings ratio = 20 × (100 – 5)% = 19

Share price = 19 × £0.617 = £11.72 per share

(b) Effect on wealth of shareholders

Olivine shareholders

Original holding = 40m shares @ £12.50 per share = £500m

New share price = £11.72

New share value = 40m shares @ £11.72 = £468.8m

Loss in shareholder wealth = £500m – £468.8m = £31.2m or 6.24%

Halite shareholders

Original earnings per share = £9.6m/16m shares = £0.60

Price/earnings ratio = 15

Share price = 15 × £0.60 = £9.00 per share

Original holding = 16m shares @ £9.00 = £144m

New holding = 20m shares @ £11.72 = £234.4m

Gain in shareholder wealth = £234.4m – £144m = £90.4m or 62.78%

(c) The market capitalisation of the separate businesses is (40m × £12.50) + (16m × £9.00) = £644m. When combined the market capitalisation will be 60m × £11.72 = £703.2m so there are benefits to be gained in overall terms.

Effect on share price

The **total share value** of Halite prior to the acquisition is £144 million. However the intended share issue by Olivine of 20 million shares has a value at Olivine's current share price of £250 million. The issue of so many shares to achieve this premium means that there is a small reduction in the size of the earnings per share of Olivine even when the earnings of Halite and the benefits of the acquisition are taken into account. This reduction in earnings per share together with a 5% reduction in the price/earnings ratio of Olivine after the acquisition would lead to a reduction in Olivine's share price from £12.50 per share before the acquisition to £11.72 per share after the acquisition. The estimate of the revised P/E ratio is possibly too high and needs further scrutiny.

This reduction in share value for Olivine shareholders would **result in a loss in shareholder value** from the acquisition of £31.2 million (6.24%). In contrast the generous premium being considered for the shares of Halite would lead to an increase in the value of the shares held by former Halite plc shareholders of £90.4 million (62.78%).

Beneficiaries of offer

If the proposed offer is made all of the benefit of the acquisition will accrue to the Halite plc shareholders and the Olivine shareholders will suffer a loss in share value. However, the dividend per share for Halite shareholders is likely to be lower in the future than it is at present.

The directors of Olivine might wish to consider a less generous offer than the current premium of £106 million (£250m – £144m) on the purchase of Halite. For example a share for share exchange would value the offer at £200 million (16 million shares @ £12.50 per share) thereby still providing a substantial premium to the Halite shareholders but with no loss to the Olivine shareholders.

25 K and H

Top tips. The stages used in (a) are:

- Calculate combined earnings
- Calculate earnings per share
- Calculate p/e ratio using share price given in the question

and then comment on the lack of realism, suggesting a better method.

Note in (b) that the 240p estimate is an assumption which should be questioned.

In (c) you have to find out what the excess (premium) on acquisition is, and compare it with the change in earnings that will result from the acquisition. The key to (d) is explaining the significance of the enhancement in size.

(a)

	K	*H*
Earnings	£5,180,000	£2,340,000
EPS	14.8p	29.25p
Number of shares	35,000,000	8,000,000

An offer of three shares in K for two shares in H would result in the equity of K increasing to 47,000,000 shares.

In order to establish how the estimated post-acquisition market price of K was reached, we must look at **P/E ratios**.

	K	*H*
Pre-acquisition price	222	322
EPS	14.8	29.25
P/E ratio, pre-acquisition	15	11

The post-acquisition earnings, assuming no synergy or growth, would be (5,180 + 2,340) £7,520,000 or (÷ 47 million shares) 16p a share.

The estimated post-acquisition share price of K is 240p. On the assumption that the post-acquisition EPS is 16p, the P/E ratio would be 15.

It would therefore seem that the estimated post-acquisition market price of K shares has been derived by applying the **pre-acquisition P/E ratio** of K to an estimated post-acquisition EPS (assuming no profits growth through synergy).

The estimated post-acquisition equivalent market value of an old H share is 1.5 times 240 pence, because three K shares will be exchanged for two H shares, giving a relative value of 3:2 or 1.5.

These estimates cannot be realistic, because it is incorrect to assume that on a takeover where neither company is minuscule relative to the other, the post-acquisition P/E ratio will be the same as the pre-acquisition P/E ratio of the more highly rated company in the takeover.

K is hoping to take over a public company with a **lower P/E ratio** than its own, and its directors must expect K's post-acquisition P/E ratio to fall accordingly.

A better estimate of the post acquisition P/E ratio would be the *weighted average* of their pre-acquisition P/Es as follows.

	Earnings £'000		*Market value* £'000
K	5,180	(35m × 222p)	77,700
H	2,340	(8m × 322p)	25,760
Combined	7,520		103,460

Weighted average P/E ratio $\frac{103,460}{7,520} = 13.758$

Applying this to a post-acquisition EPS of 16p, an estimated post-acquisition market price of K shares would be (13.758 × 16p) 220p each. This would make the post-acquisition equivalent MV of an old H share (220 × 1.5) = 330p.

There would be a very slight gain for H shareholders at the expense of K shareholders, but not much. This is because the share exchange ratio of three for two reflects almost exactly the pre-acquisition market prices per share of 322:222 = 1.45 or nearly 1.50, which is 3:2.

(b)

	£'000
Value of 35 million K shares:	
Estimated post-acquisition value (× 240p)	84,000
Pre-acquisition value (× 222p)	77,700
Gain to K shareholders from acquisition (× 18p)	6,300

K could raise its offer by £6,300,000 without reducing the wealth of its shareholders, but only assuming that the 240p estimate of the post-acquisition share price is correct. This extra value might be offered in **cash** (£0.7875 per share in H) or in **more shares** in K.

(c) The pre-acquisition market value of K is unchanged at 222p, and so a two-for-one share exchange offer would value each share in H at 444p as well, compared with its current 322p.

	£'000
Offer value for 8,000,000 shares in H (× 444p)	35,520
Current value of 8,000,000 shares in H (× 322p)	25,760
Excess	9,760

The revised offer would only maintain the wealth of current shareholders if the combined share values of the post-acquisition company were to increase by at least £9,760,000.

It is assumed that the value of the post-acquisition company will be increased by the NPV of the asset disposals, savings in running costs and extra redundancy costs, discounted at K's cost of capital of 14% per year.

Year	*Item*	*Amount*	*Discount factor*	*Present value*
		£'000	14%	£'000
0	Redundancy costs	(3,500)	1.000	(3,500.0)
1	Redundancy costs	(8,400)	0.877	(7,366.8)
1	Fixed asset disposals	7,200	0.877	6,314.4
1 – ∞	Savings in running costs	2,750	(1 ÷ 0.14) = 7.14	19,642.9
			Net present value	15,090.5

We might therefore conclude that because of redundancies and rationalisation, the combined value of the post-acquisition companies will increase by about £15,000,000 which is more than the £9,760,000 needed to fund the extra price being offered for their shares to H shareholders. Of the increase in share values, H shareholders would benefit by the first £9,760,000, leaving the remaining £5,240,000 to be shared between all shareholders in the post-acquisition company.

A two for one offer should therefore be made.

(d) Assuming no increase in total post-acquisition earnings, the group will have a fairly low interest cover ratio. The interest cover in the 'old' K is (12,400 ÷ 4,431) 2.8 times and in the 'old' H is (5,800 ÷ 2,200) = 2.6 times. In the combined company it will be (12,400 + 5,800) ÷ (4,431 + 2,200) = 2.75 times.

Although we do not have balance sheet details, this low interest cover indicates **high gearing**, and the cost of the existing debt capital might therefore be high.

The takeover will create an **enlarged company**, and because of this, it is fairly reasonable to assume that the **risk of default** will be less than with either of the 'old' companies taken individually. This **reduction in default risk**, if perceived to be significant, might reduce the return that investors in debt capital seek from the company. A reduction in the required return on marketable fixed interest capital would raise its **market value**. In this respect, the acquisition would have some effect on the **market value** of K's debt.

Of course, K's debt might be **non-marketable bank loans** and **overdrafts**, in which case the acquisition would not have any effect on the market value of the debt, since such debt has no market value.

26 Intergrand

Top tips. This question is slightly tougher than you are likely to see in the exam; it is though a good (though demanding) test of your technique.

In (b) the main calculation is the adjusted present value – debt calculation. Although the free cash flows is the most significant working, in fact these represent only half of the 22 marks available, although the additional tax, which is dependent on the calculations of the free cash flows, is worth a further 3 marks. It is better exam technique to work out the easier figures first before attempting the free cash flow calculations to make sure you get the marks for these.

The publicity costs are discounted at Intergrand's WACC because they are quoted at an equivalent figure for Intergrand.

You have to assume that the exchange rate in 20X6 applies in perpetuity.

The research is a sunk cost and should thus be excluded from the calculation.

There are several possible ways of calculating the tax shield on debt acquired. You can simply calculate the market value x tax relief, and assume that the loans similar to the current bonds will be available to infinity. More prudently, you can take the question at face value and assume that the tax relief on the bonds will be available until 20X9 when the bonds are redeemed, and that further bonds won't be issued. We have discounted the tax relief at the risk-free rate, but it would also be acceptable (though involve more calculations) to discount it at the cost of debt, calculating the cost of debt by an IRR calculation or using the interest yield.

It is definitely easier to round the base case cost of capital to the nearest whole number and thus be able to make use of discount tables.

The sale of assets and the extra investment both relate to Oberberg, so they should be discounted at its cost of capital, but they do not form part of the free cash flows. The interest should also be excluded from the free cash flows but the synergies should be included. The free cash flows and additional tax post 20X6 can be found using the dividend valuation model formula, but don't forget to discount these because they start from 20X7 (year 5).

Easy marks. Despite all the complications in the calculations, you can easily score most of the marks you need on the discussion. (a) is a gentle introduction, and most of the discussion points in (b) will be raised in other investment appraisals.

Examiner's comments. Answers to (a) were generally good. In (b) most candidates were able to identify relevant cash flows, although some undertook a traditional NPV calculation rather than a free cash flow, and few candidates picked up the hints in the requirement that the question required an adjusted present value calculation.

Many candidates wasted time attempting long calculations to ascertain a revised WACC, which was not necessary for this question, or converting euro cash flows into sterling, which was not necessary because the purchase price was in euros.

Some answers only included cash flows for one or two years, rather than the whole (infinite) life of the project.

Other mistakes included omitting factors such as UK tax, investment for expansion, the benefit of the publicity and lost exports. Some did not deduct the loans from the present value. Discussions were generally poor with many answers only discussing one or two points.

(a) (i) **Advantages of organic growth**

(1) The company will be developing a new vehicle that has the group's existing culture rather than acquiring a **subsidiary** with a **different culture**.

(2) Growing organically may be cheaper in the long-run as it is more likely to **be financed** by **retained earnings** rather than new sources with issue costs, and it will not involve paying a premium for a desirable subsidiary.

(3) Planned development of a subsidiary should mean that there is **no duplication of resources** with existing operations.

(4) Organic growth offers **more opportunities** for **current employees**.

(5) Organic growth is more likely to be in areas where a company **currently has expertise**, limiting the risk of failure.

(ii) **Advantages of acquisition**

(1) Acquisition can offer **speedier entry** into an overseas market than organic growth.

(2) Merging with **established firms abroad** can be a means of **purchasing market information**, **market share**, **distribution channels** and **reputation**.

(3) **Other synergies** include **acquisition of management skills** and **knowledge**, **intangibles** such as brands and trademarks, or **additional cash** and **debt capacity**.

(4) Acquiring a subsidiary may be a means of **removing trade barriers**.

(5) Acquisition can be a means of **removing a competitor**.

(6) **Start-up costs** will not be incurred.

Ultimately the risk of acquiring an established operation may well be less than starting up a subsidiary in an area where the company has **not previously operated**.

(b) **Adjusted present value of investment**

	Working	*Euro m*
Redundancy		(5.0)
Publicity	1	7.0
Lost exports	2	(4.3)
Tax shield	3	9.7
Sale of assets	5	7.3
Investment for expansion	6	(6.9)
Free cash flows	7	171.2
Additional tax	8	(10.5)
Adjusted present value		168.5
Value of outstanding loans (30 + ((1230/1000) × 18)		(52.1)
Value of Oberberg		116.4

Using free cash flows and adjusted present value, the value of Oberberg is €116.3 million which suggests an offer of €115 million is reasonable, although the estimate is subject to a large margin of approximation.

Workings

1 **Publicity**

$$\text{Benefit} = \frac{\text{Annual cash flows (1 - t)}}{\text{Intergrand's WACC}}$$

$$= \frac{1(1-0.3)}{0.1}$$

$$= €7\text{million}$$

2 **Lost exports**

Cost of lost exports = £800,000 × 0.5 × (1 – 0.3) = £280,000

However the exchange rate is not constant.

Under purchasing power parity, next year's euro/£ exchange rate is $\frac{1+0.02}{1+0.04}$ of this year's exchange rate

	20X3	*20X4*	*20X5*	*20X6*
Exchange rate	1.594	1.563	1.533	1.504
Cost of lost exports €million	0.45	0.44	0.43	0.42
Discount at Intergrand's WACC, 10%	0.909	0.826	0.751	0.683
Present value	0.41	0.36	0.32	0.29

	€ million
Present value 20X3 – 6	1.38
Present value 20X7 – infinity $(\frac{0.42}{0.1}) - (0.42 \times 3.170)$	2.87
	4.25

3 **Tax shield**

	€ million
Bank loans (30 × 0.25)	7.5
Bonds: Annual interest charge × Tax relief × 4% Cumulative discount factor (18 × 0.08 × 0.25 × 6.002)	2.2
	9.7

The tax shield on the bonds has been discounted at the risk-free rate, on the assumption that tax relief is virtually certain to be received.

4 **Discount rate**

Discount at appropriate rate for Oberberg.

Use $\beta_u = \beta_g \left(\frac{V_E}{V_E + V_D(1-t)}\right) + \beta_d \left(\frac{V_D(1-t)}{V_E + V_D(1-t)}\right)$

Assuming debt is risk-free,

$$\beta_u = \beta_g \left(\frac{V_E}{V_E + V_D(1-t)}\right)$$

V_E – 15 × (300/100) = 45

V_D = 30 + (18 × 1.23) = 52.14

$$\beta_u = 1.4 \frac{45}{45 + 52.14(1-0.25)}$$

$$= 0.749$$

Using CAPM

$k_{eu} = R_f + [R_m - R_f]\beta$
$= 4 + (11 - 4)\ 0.749$
$= 9.24\%$, say 9%.

This is used for the base case free cash flow calculation, before calculation of financing side effects.

5 **Sale of assets**

Present value = 8.0 × 9% Discount factor year 1
= 8.0 × 0.917
= €7.3 million

6 **Investment for expansion**

Present value = 9.0 × 9% Discount factor year 3
= 9.0 × 0.772
= €6.9 million

7 **Free cash flows**

	20X3	20X4	20X5	20X6
	€m	€m	€m	€m
Sales	38.2	41.2	44.0	49.0
Synergies	-	2.0	2.0	2.0
Labour	(11.0)	(12.1)	(13.0)	(14.1)
Materials	(8.3)	(8.7)	(9.0)	(9.4)
Overheads	(3.2)	(3.2)	(3.3)	(3.4)
Tax allowable depreciation	(6.3)	(5.8)	(5.6)	(5.2)
Taxable profit	9.4	13.4	15.1	18.9
Taxation	(2.4)	(3.4)	(3.8)	(4.7)
Add back tax allowable depreciation	6.3	5.8	5.6	5.2
Working capital	(0.7)	(0.9)	(1.0)	(2.0)
Replacement investment	(4.2)	(4.2)	(4.2)	(4.2)
Free cash flows	8.4	10.7	11.7	13.2
Discount factors 9%	0.917	0.842	0.772	0.708
Present value	7.7	9.0	9.0	9.3

Free cash flows 20X3 – 20X6 = €35 million

Free cash flows post 20X6 $= 13.2\dfrac{(1+g)}{k_e - g} \times$ 9% Discount factor year 4

$= 13.2\ \dfrac{(1+0.02)}{0.09-0.02} \times 0.708$

= €136.2 million

Free cash flows = 136.2 + 35
= €171.2 million

8 **Additional tax**

Discount at Intergrand's cost of capital as relates to UK liability.

Taxable profit	9.4	13.4	15.1	18.9
Extra tax at 5%	0.47	0.67	0.76	0.95
Discount factors 10%	0.909	0.826	0.751	0.683
Present value	0.43	0.55	0.57	0.65

Additional tax 20X3 – 20X6 = €2.2 million

Additional tax post 20X6 = $0.95 \frac{(1+g)}{K_e - g} \times$ 10% Discount factor year 4

$$= 0.95 \frac{(1+0.02)}{0.1-0.02} \times 0.683$$

= €8.3 million

Extra tax = 2.2 + 8.3 = €10.5 million

Other factors to be considered

(i) **Assumptions**

The **assumptions** used in the forecasts need to be **examined carefully** and alternative forecasts prepared under different assumptions, for example the need for additional investment at a later date, tax changes or assuming that all the exports will be lost.

(ii) **Risk**

Further work needs to be done on **assessing risks**, as the risk assessments upon which the beta factor calculation is **based** may **not be accurate** and risks may change over time, particularly as we are looking at cash flows to infinity. Sensitivity analysis needs to be **undertaken** to see how much key figures may change before the decision is affected.

(iii) **Timescale**

The majority of the benefits from Oberberg will be **obtained after 20X6**, and the directors of Intergrand must **consider** whether this is **too long a timescale** for its investors.

(iv) **Real options**

The existence of real options, the **chance to take decisions** in the future that could **further enhance** the value of Oberberg should be considered.

(v) **Economic exposure**

If inflation rates stay the same, the value of the euros and hence the value of the investment will **continue to appreciate**. However the investment's value will be affected by a UK decision to join the Euro.

(vi) **Implications of acquisition**

The board needs to consider the implications of diversification. Although the acquisition can **reduce risk by diversification**, it can also create **difficulties of integration**, particularly if Oberberg is significant in size relative to Intergrand. Intergrand's board needs to consider carefully any synergies involved and how reliable forecasts of these are, measured against the costs of changing the structure and culture of Oberberg. Intergrand's board should also consider carefully the attitudes of Oberberg's staff in the light of the planned redundancies, and what will be required to retain staff who are important for Oberberg's continued success.

(vii) **Other strategies**

Intergrand's board should try to **ascertain** whether there are other investments in Germany or elsewhere that offer **higher present values** or are **better strategic fits**.

27 Dalewater

Top tips. The first paragraph gives four different reasons why the company has experienced difficulties. These can be used to add depth to your answer to part (a). Part (b) requires you to consider the relevance of 'asset stripping' to what is a potentially profitable business. In part (c) the main reasons for the increase in share price are described in detail in the question, and part (d) is a common examination topic.

(a) **Going concern value**

A company's **going concern value** is the **present value of the cash surpluses** it is expected to generate if it continues its business operations. The break-up (or broken-up) value is the present value of cash flows if the company is wound up and its assets sold and liabilities paid off.

For a healthy company, the going concern value is higher than the break-up value: the shareholders acquire business assets and use them to produce added value. Most of the factors that cause the going concern value to fall below break up value are due to incompetent management, and include the following.

(i) **Underutilisation of assets**. Non-current assets may be held unused (as in the case of Dalewater's land) or inefficiently used (e.g. plant and equipment) or inventory may be unnecessarily high. A low rate of return on assets drags down the company's value.

(ii) **Unprofitable investment decisions**. For example, investing in cheap substandard equipment which breaks down frequently, or in new products which fail to meet sales targets.

(iii) **Lack of quality systems and procedures**. For example, poor maintenance of machinery, leading to production breakdown, poor training of staff, using staff without appropriate skills, lack of market research, ignoring feedback from customers, etc.

(iv) **Confused corporate image**. Dalewater seems to lack a clear corporate vision and to have ignored considerations of its corporate and product image when it embarked on its marketing plans.

(v) **Poor management of human resources**. For example, disputes with employees leading to stoppages and inefficiencies.

(vi) **Poor financial management**. Incurring unnecessary costs because of lack of financial controls and disciplines.

In addition, **problems may arise which are outside management's control, such as the development of substitute products**, or **health scares** concerning the product (eg pollution caused by another party). However, in the case of Dalewater this does not seem to be the case, and the problems must be seen as the result of poor management. This is significant, as it implies that Dalewater is *potentially* profitable as a going concern.

(b) If Dalewater was genuinely worth £0.80 per share if wound up, then at first sight if would be worthwhile Peakspring bidding a lower figure, such as £0.70, and then breaking up the company, making a profit of £0.10 per share. Although such 'asset stripping' may well have been a practical proposition, there are a number of reasons why Peakspring may have rejected this course of action.

(i) The **estimate** of £0.80 per share made by Dalewater's financial advisors may have been **over-optimistic** compared with the advice received by Peakspring. In particular, the management and administration costs of the break-up may have been under-estimated and Dalewater's value may fall significantly if the lawsuits are successful.

(ii) Although Dalewater is a listed company, there may have been a **strong group of shareholders** (eg original family owners) who were **opposed** to a sale to Peakspring. Peakspring may have decided that a contested bid would be too wasteful of company resources.

(iii) Peakspring may have decided that a purchase for break-up would **divert management attention** from its main business and would contribute nothing to its strategic objectives. The two companies are not the only players in the market, and the shutdown of a potentially profitable company because of its incompetent management would simply encourage competitors to expand their activities or even to set up using Dalewater's facilities.

(iv) Peakspring may **face cash flow limitations** that prevent it bidding above 50%.

(c) Dalewater's shares rose by £0.25 during the time of the bid because of increased demand for its shares. This may have happened for a number of reasons, including the following.

(i) **Demand for shares rose generally**. The stock market index increased.

(ii) When Peakspring made its offer, investors perceived that the company's shares might be a **good short term investment**: the initial offer of £0.50 per share might be increased if an alternative bidder entered the market.

(iii) When Dalewater made its share buy-back offer (worth £0.70 per share), investors immediately saw the prospect of **short term gains** and demand increased further.

(iv) The release of **information about improved operating and marketing methods** helped to increase demand further, as did the sale of the under-utilised land.

(v) The **possible cost of the contingent liabilities** may have **decreased**.

(vi) The **proposed changes in gearing** may reduce Dalewater's cost of capital.

(d) If the takeover was made using cash as purchase consideration instead of shares, the advantages to Peakspring would be as follows.

(i) The total **value of the purchase consideration** could be **less**, because cash is a less risky asset than shares (which might fall in value). The shareholders of Dalewater would be prepared to accept a lower reward in return for the lower risk.

(ii) There would be **no dilution of Peakspring's shareholdings**, and probably no consequent changes in the company's management structure.

The disadvantages might be as follows.

(i) Peakspring is left with **insufficient cash and working capital** to fund its daily operations, or is unable to fund necessary investment in improving Dalewater's facilities.

(ii) Peakspring is forced to **increase borrowings** to raise the cash, which might increase the company's gearing and financial risk.

28 Financial and non-financial appraisal

Top tips. Questions dealing with wider investment issues may well link in with objectives of organisations. Remember this exam is not just about limited companies! Schools can use NPV, but may use different benchmarks, and must always consider the three Es.

Importance of present value

Capital projects of the nature being considered by the two organisations involve long-term **commitment of funds**, in anticipation of a potential **future inflow of cash**. Capital expenditure decisions should be based on an evaluation of future cash flows, **discounted** at an appropriate cost of capital, to arrive at a net present value of the investment. A positive **net present value** indicates a financially viable project.

When looking at the differing objectives of private and public sector organisations, the financial viability (or otherwise) of a project will be more readily associated with private sector preoccupations with **profitability** and **return to shareholders**. A public sector organisation such as a school does however need to ensure that it makes proper use of the **resources** made available to it, so an assessment of the cost of an investment project is going to be important if it is going to be able to measure whether or not it is making the best use of these resources within its necessarily **limited budget**.

That said, **social provision** of school services will be required **regardless of financial viability**, for example in deprived areas, or areas of the community which need special facilities. The return made by the school in such circumstances is more difficult to quantify and therefore measure.

Private sector company

The private sector company is seeking to increase its production capacity with an enlarged factory. This is likely to have been stimulated by **increased demand**, or at least an expectation of **increased future sales** and **market share**. The company may even be finding that it is having to turn customers away because of a lack of capacity. It is driven by clearly **commercial considerations.**

The **incremental** discounted cash flows (both in and out) associated with the factory extension need to be positive if the project is going to add to **shareholder value** and be viable in the financial sense. If the cost of building the extension exceeds the possible future cash flows (taking all expected revenues and tax breaks into account) then the project is simply not worth doing.

The company may expect **economies of scale** to result from the new premises, which will improve profitability via **lower unit costs**. If the industry has high **fixed costs**, significant reductions in unit costs can be achieved by producing on a larger scale.

Non financial considerations for the private sector company may include **quality concerns**. Quality is a key performance measure for manufacturing companies. Without the new premises, future improvements in quality may be compromised. The ability to stay ahead of the competition via **innovation** and **new product development** may also be seen as an important role for the planned new capacity. These factors will not be easily assessed by standard capital appraisal methods, although the company is likely to have some idea of what will be happening to the market in the future, and the likely impact on market share if the company does not keep up on quality, innovation and satisfying customer demand.

In other words, the longer term implications of the project need to be considered.

Publicly funded school

The school will not be charging for its services, so there is no revenue stream by which profitability or financial viability of the project can be measured. However, some kind of **return to the stakeholders** in the school (the local community, the government, the taxpayers) needs to be assessed. A starting point will be an assessment of the costs of the project in **net present value** terms, using an appropriate cost of capital.

This can then be assessed against the perceived **benefit** of the school service, or maybe even the cost of putting the services out to **tender** to a private organisation.

Because public sector funds are limited, the expenditure on school buildings is likely to be diverting funds away from other local projects. The providers of the funds must decide whether the school services are an **appropriate use of money**. Could it be better spent elsewhere, such as on a new wing for the local library? How would the community benefit from the new services (or suffer if they are not provided)? As can be seen, non-financial criteria are very much to the fore.

The new school building may be assessed using a **value for money** audit. Such an audit focuses on **economy, efficiency** and **effectiveness**. Economy and efficiency refer to the way in which the school services will be provided, and effectiveness measures the school's performance in achieving its objectives of bringing educational services to the community. This latter measure is likely to be the most visible and important one in the public sector, where the effectiveness of service provision of all kinds is always under public scrutiny and expectations get higher and higher with each new service provided.

29 Shegdor

Top tips. In (a) the most significant uses that your answer needs to bring out are avoidance of tax and import duties, ensuring proper performance measurement and establishing goal congruent behaviour. Note that whilst all of the objectives are valid in certain contexts, some of them may conflict, for example charging a low transfer price to avoid import duty may conflict with the aim of charging a large enough price to give the transferring division a sufficient return for its efforts. A proforma similar to the one we've used in (b) can help you ensure that you cover all relevant elements of transfer pricing calculations.

(a) **Objectives of transfer pricing strategies**

(i) The transfer price should provide a **selling price** that enables the transferring division to earn a return for its efforts, and the receiving division to incur a cost for benefits received.

(ii) The transfer price should be set at a level that enables **profit centre performance** to be **measured commercially**; thus the transfer price should be a **fair commercial price**.

(iii) The transfer price should encourage profit centre managers to **agree** on the **amounts of goods and services to be transferred**.

(iv) The transfer price should lead to a level **of goods and services being transferred** which is **congruent** with the **objectives** of the organisation, for example **generating retained earnings** in the most advantageous locations or **limiting remittances** of foreign currency between group members.

(v) **Transfer prices** can be used to **minimise the effect of import duties**; the lower the transfer price, the lower the level of import duty.

(vi) Transfer prices can also be used to **minimise tax levels** by ensuring that taxable income is earned in low tax economies.

(vii) **Transfer prices** can be used as a means of **remitting income** if restrictions on dividend remittances are in place.

(b) **Fixed plus variable cost**

	Umbaga	Mazila	Bettuna
	$000	$000	$000
Sales	8,200	16,000	14,800.0
Costs			
Variable costs	6,400	3,600	3,000.0
Fixed costs	1,800	700	900.0
Transfer price	–	8,200	8,200.0
Import duty	–	820	–
	8,200	13,320	12,100.0
Taxable profit	–	2,680	2,700.0
Tax	–	670	864.0
Profit after tax	–	2,010	1,836.0
Withholding tax	–	–	–
Remittance	–	1,206	1,101.6
UK tax on remittance (W)	–	(134)	–
	–	1,072	1,101.6
Retained (40% after tax profit)	–	804	734.4
Total profit		1,876	1,836.0

Total profit

Umbaga + Mazila 0+ 1,876 = $1,876,000

Umbaga + Bettuna 0 + 1,836 = $1,836,000

Working

UK tax = (2,680,000 × 0.3) – 670,000 = 134,000

Fixed plus variable cost plus 30%

	Umbaga	Mazila	Bettuna
	$000	$000	$000
Sales	10,660.00	16,000	14,80.00
Costs			
Variable costs	6,400.00	3,600	3,000.00
Fixed costs	1,800.00	700	900.00
Transfer price	–	10,660	10,660.00
Import duty		1,066	–
	8,200.00	16,026	14,560.00
Taxable profit	2,460.00	(26)	240.00
Tax	984.00	–	76.80
Profit/(Loss) after tax	1,476.00	(26)	163.20
Withholding tax			
(Umbaga 1,476 × 0.6 × 0.15)	132.84	–	–
Remittance			
(Umbaga 1,476 × 0.6 × 0.85)	752.76		97.92
UK tax on remittance	–	–	–
	752.76	–	97.92
Retained (40% after tax profit)	590.40	(26)	65.28
Total profit	1,343.16	(26)	163.20

Total profit

Umbaga + Mazila 1,343.16 – 26 = $1,317,160

Umbaga + Bettuna 1,343.16 + 163.2 = $1,506,360

Conclusion

The best plan is to charge sales at fixed plus variable costs, and manufacture in Mazila. This avoids tax in the country of highest tax, Umbaga.

(c) **Likely government attitudes**

Umbaga

The government may query whether the **transfer price** is at a **commercial rate** and, depending on the tax laws, may be able to impart an artificial profit to the transaction and hence charge tax.

Mazila

The government's attitude is likely to be **favourable** as manufacturing is taking place in the country, and hence boosting its economy. Although the import duty is lower than under the markup scenario, this is more than outweighed by the company tax that the government will be able to collect.

Bettuna

The government can take **no action** against the company as the company is not doing anything. It can try to attract the company by offering a subsidy, which would only need to be greater than $40,000 (1,876,000 – 1,836,000) for the decision to be changed.

UK

The UK government would be happy with this arrangement, since it is the only arrangement of those considered that will mean that the company pays tax.

30 Mezen

Top tips. In (a), if you failed to identify which costs were relevant correctly, make sure you understand why. (c) makes the important point about sensitivity of cash flows. Even if a project has a positive NPV, or an acceptable IRR, a company may not go ahead if the profits are felt to be too marginal, and the risk of loss too great. Although you will have encountered questions on the weaknesses of IRR in lower level papers, they still might sneak into *Financial Strategy*.

(a) **Incremental cash flows**

The survey has been undertaken already, even though it has not yet been paid for, and therefore the £30,000 is a sunk cost.

The depreciation charge of £15,000 is not a cash-flow. The re-allocated fixed overheads will be incurred whether or Mezen goes ahead with the product. Both of these amounts may be subtracted from the £25,000 of fixed overheads in the original calculations.

The company forgoes £70,000 of immediate income from the sale of the machine.

	Time 0 £'000	*Time 1* £'000	*Time 2* £'000	*Time 3* £'000	*Time 4* £'000	*NPV* £'000
Sales		180	200	160	120	
Cost of sales		(115)	(140)	(110)	(85)	
Variable overheads		(27)	(30)	(24)	(18)	
Fixed overheads		(5)	(5)	(5)	(5)	
Machine	(70)				10	
Working capital	(20)				20	
Incremental cash flows	(90)	33	25	21	42	
× 10% discount factor	1.00	0.91	0.83	0.75	0.68	
Present value	(90.00)	30.03	20.75	15.75	28.56	5.09

(b) **Approximate internal rate of return**

	Time 0 £'000	*Time 1* £'000	*Time 2* £'000	*Time 3* £'000	*Time 4* £'000	*NPV* £'000
Incremental cash flows	(90)	33	25	21	42	
× 14% discount factor	1.00	0.88	0.77	0.68	0.59	
Present value	(90.00)	29.04	19.25	14.28	24.78	(2.65)

$$\text{IRR} = A + \left[\frac{N_A}{N_A - N_B} \times (B - A)\right]\%$$

where A is the lower rate of return, B is the higher rate of return, N_A is the NPV discounted at A, and N_B is the NPV discounted at B.

$$\text{IRR} = 10 + \left[\frac{5.09}{5.09 - (-2.65)} \times (14 - 10)\right]\% = 12.63\%$$

(c) The product has a positive net present value and an IRR that exceeds the company's cost of capital, and this suggests that it should be launched.

The decision is very marginal, however. It would certainly not be worthwhile if the market survey had not yet been commissioned, in which case the cost of £30,000 would need to be included. A relatively small drop in sales or a small increase in costs would result in a negative NPV. The company may well be able to find better uses for the £20,000 that will be spent now, and for the immediate income of £70,000 on the sale of the machine.

(d) The **internal rate of return (IRR)** is the rate of return that results in a NPV of zero. The rule with the **internal rate of return (IRR)** method of project evaluation is that a project should be undertaken if it is expected to achieve a return in excess of the company's cost of capital. A project that has an IRR in excess of the cost of capital must have a positive NPV.

Strengths

The main **advantage** of the IRR method is that the information it provides may be more easily understood by managers, especially non-financial managers.

It is sometimes said that IRR is difficult to calculate, but **both** NPV and IRR are actually **very easy to calculate** with a **spreadsheet**.

Weaknesses

However, it might be tempting for some managers to **confuse IRR** and **accounting return** on capital employed (ROCE). The accounting ROCE and the IRR are two completely different measures. If managers were given information about both ROCE (or ROI) and IRR, it might be easy to get their relative meaning and significance mixed up.

The IRR method also ignores the **relative size of investments**: for example a project with an annual return of £50 on an initial investment of £100 would have the same IRR as a project with an annual return of £5,000 on an initial investment of £10,000, although the latter is clearly preferable.

IRR **favours projects that are less sensitive to increases in the discount rate** and therefore the IRR method may sometimes indicate that a project that yields a smaller increase in shareholder wealth should be preferred to one that yields a larger increase, whereas the opposite is the case. NPV should therefore be used to **decide** between **mutually exclusive projects**.

31 DIN

Top tips. In (a) you have to explain why the real rate of return is a significant figure and state the clues that questions will give you about whether cash flows are real or nominal.

In (b) if you are working out the cost element of unit price, a table is always helpful. Brief narrative can also be helpful to show the examiner what you've done and highlight the points for which you will gain marks, such as excluding sunk costs.

(a) The **real rate of return** is the rate of return which an investment would show in the absence of inflation. For example, if a company invests £100, inflation is 0%, and the investment at the end of the year is worth £110, then the real rate of return is 10%.

In reality however, there is likely to be an element of inflation in the returns due to the change in the purchasing power of money over the period. In the example above, if inflation was running at 5%, then to show a real rate of return of 10%, the investment would need to be worth £115.50 at the end of the year. In this case the money rate of return is 15.5% which is made up of the real return of 10% and inflation at 5%.

The relationship between the nominal ('money') rate of return and the real rate of return can be expressed as follows.

$$(1 + \text{nominal rate}) = (1 + \text{real rate}) \times (1 + \text{inflation rate})$$

The rate to be used in discounting cash flows for capital project appraisal will depend on the way in which the **expected cash flows** are **calculated**. If the cash flows are expressed in terms of the actual number of pounds that will be received or paid on the various future dates, then the nominal rate must be used. If however they are expressed in terms of the value of the pound at year 0, then the real rate must be used.

(b) *Workings*

	Year 1	*Year 2*	*Year 3*	*Year 4*
Sales volume	25,000	25,000	25,000	25,000
Unit price (£)	80	84	88	93
Variable material cost (£)	8.00	8.32	8.65	9.00
Variable labour cost (£)	12.00	13.20	14.52	15.97
Variable overhead (£)	12.00	12.48	12.98	13.50

Notes

(i) Development costs of £480,000 are sunk costs and will be excluded from the calculations.

(ii) Depreciation does not involve any movement of cash and will be excluded from the fixed overheads (£600,000 in year 1).

(iii) All figures have been adjusted for the appropriate rate of inflation. The investment will therefore be evaluated using the WACC expressed as a nominal rate of 15%.

Evaluation of investment

(All figures £'000)

	Year 0	*Year 1*	*Year 2*	*Year 3*	*Year 4*
Capital outlay	(2,400)				
Sales		2,000	2,100	2,205	2,315
Direct costs					
Materials		(200)	(208)	(216)	(225)
Labour		(300)	(330)	(363)	(399)
Overhead		(300)	(312)	(324)	(337)
Fixed overheads		(200)	(210)	(221)	(232)
Gross cash flow	(2,400)	1,000	1,040	1,081	1,122
Discount at 15%	1.000	0.870	0.756	0.658	0.572
Present value	(2,400)	870	786	711	642
Cumulative PV	(2,400)	(1,530)	(744)	(33)	609

The investment yields a net present value at the end of four years of £609,000. In the absence of other factors such as capital rationing, production of the Rance should be undertaken.

32 Auriga

Top tips. (a) is another question that requires careful identification of relevant costs. Work carefully through (b) if you didn't get it right as sensitivity analysis is very likely to come up.

Examiner's comments. Part (a) of the question was generally well answered with some candidates scoring very high marks. The main problem however was that some candidates did not select the correct cost of capital as an appropriate discount rate. As the question stated that the project had the same level of risk as the other projects undertaken by the company then the weighted average cost of capital was the appropriate rate to use.

The sensitivity analysis in part (b) of the question, however, was less well answered as a significant number of candidates clearly did not really know how to approach the problem. This was particularly disappointing as similar problems had been included in previous examinations.

The final part of the question, which required comments on the calculations, was generally well answered with candidates managing to make comments that were consistent with their earlier calculations.

(a) **Net present value**

	Time				
	0	*1*	*2*	*3*	*4*
	£000	£000	£000	£000	£000
Machinery	(300.00)				
Advertising		(50.00)	(50.00)	(50.00)	(50.00)
Sales (£22 × 15,000)		330.00	330.00	330.00	330.00
Materials (W1)		(112.50)	(112.50)	(112.50)	(112.50)
Labour (£5.50 × 15,000)		(82.50)	(82.50)	(82.50)	(82.50)
Redundancy cost saving	230.00				
Overheads (W2)		(52.50)	(52.50)	(52.50)	(52.50)
Net cash flow	(70.00)	32.50	32.50	32.50	32.50
Discount factor @ 10% (W3)	1.00	0.91	0.83	0.75	0.68
Present value	(70.00)	29.60	27.00	24.40	22.10
Net present value	33.10				

Workings

1 *Materials*

	£
Cost per unit	
Without polymer (6.50 – 2.0)	4.50
Replacement cost (2 × £1.50)	3.00
	7.50

Total material cost 15,000 × £7.50 £112,500

2 *Overheads*

	£
Total overheads (£8.50 × 15,000)	127,500
Depreciation (300,000/4)	(75,000)
Cash flow	(52,500)

3 *Discount factor*

WACC (12% × 50%) + (8% × 50%) = 10%

(b) X = annual net cash flow from operations

Project becomes unprofitable when NPV is zero ie where net present value of annual cash flows is equal to the initial cash outflow of £70,000.

(X × 4 year annuity factor)	= £70,000
X × (0.91 + 0.83 + 0.75 + 0.68)	= £70,000
3.17X	= £70,000
X	= £22,082

Therefore if the net cash flows reduce from £32,500 per annum to 22,082 per annum the net present value will be zero. This is a reduction of £10,418.

(c) The initial net present value calculation shows that the project is worthwhile: when all of the relevant cash flows are taken into consideration the project has a positive net present value of just over £33,000. Therefore this project will increase shareholder wealth by this amount.

The figures are highly **sensitive to change**, however. Even assuming costs can be fixed at the predicted levels by means of contractual agreements a fall of less than 4% in annual demand (about 600 units) would result in a negative NPV. If extra advertising or a price reduction is required to achieve the maximum sales level this will further impair the viability of the project.

If the appraisal had been conducted **before development and market research costs** had been incurred it would have been **rejected from the outset**, and this would have been more beneficial for shareholders.

33 Fund restrictions

Top tips. In part (a) you should state any further assumptions that you make about the constraints on investment. The Profitability Index approach should be used. In part (c) it is helpful to consider the reasons why cash shortages may arise and to relate these to the capital budget constraints.

(a) It is assumed that the **restriction on investment** applies to the total period under consideration, and that this **amount cannot be incremented** after period 0 by using funds generated from the projects selected earlier. The projects will be ranked using the Profitability Index (PI), which is calculated as the NPV per £1 invested.

Project	*NPV*	*Investment*	*PI*	*Ranking*
	£'000	£'000	£'000	
A	14.22	150	0.0948	4
B	28.27	200	0.1414	1
C	21.74	175	0.1242	2
D	35.01	300	0.1167	3

On this basis, the company should invest £200,000 in project B, £175,000 in project C, and the remaining £75,000 in project D. This will generate an expected NPV of £67,515.

(b) If there are no fund restrictions and the projects are mutually exclusive, the company should select the project that has the **highest NPV** since this will make the greatest contribution to increasing the net worth of the business, and on this basis project D would be chosen.

(c) A period of capital rationing is often associated with more general problems of cash shortage. Possible reasons for this include the following.

(i) The business has become **loss making** and is unable to cover the depreciation charge. Since one purpose of the depreciation charge is to allow for the cost of the assets used in the profit and loss account, the implication is that there will be insufficient cash with which to replace these assets when necessary.

(ii) High inflation may mean that even though the business is profitable in historical cost terms, it is still **failing to generate sufficient funds** to replace assets.

(iii) If the business is growing it may face a **shortage of working capital** with which to finance expansion, and this may result in a period of capital rationing.

(iv) If the business is seasonal or cyclical it may face **times of cash shortage** despite being fundamentally sound. In this situation, there may be a periodic need for capital rationing.

(v) A large one-off item of expenditure such as a property purchase may mean that the company faces a **temporary shortage of cash** for further investment.

A further reason for capital rationing arises in the situation where the company has more investment opportunities available than the funds allocated to the capital budget permit. This means that projects must be ranked for investment, taking into account both financial and strategic factors.

34 ANT

Top tips. A table setting out each element of unit cost is helpful. When doing the NPV calculations it is important to show them, but show them in a way that minimises the writing you have to do. If you were not able to fit your answer to (a) across the page, you could have stated the discount factors at the start of the answer and then done the calculations. Note also that we have taken the short cut of using annuity factors. Don't forget the 'reclaiming of working capital' in year 5.

In (b) you are using **total inflows** to calculate the profitability index, not net present value. When setting out your workings a column on cumulative outlay should help you ensure you take the correct proportion of the partial project.

(c) starts off by stating the **assumptions**, and then goes on to discuss **complications** in which the NPV approach could not be used.

(a) The first step is to calculate the **annual contribution** from each project, together with the working capital cash flows. These cash flows, together with the initial outlay, can then be **discounted** at the **cost of capital** to arrive at the NPV of each project. Development costs already incurred are irrelevant. There are no additional administration costs associated with the projects, and depreciation is also irrelevant since it has no cash effect.

First, calculate annual contribution.

	A	*B*	*C*	*D*
Unit sales	150,000	75,000	80,000	120,000
	£	£	£	£
Selling price per unit	30.00	40.00	25.00	50.00
Material cost per unit	7.60	12.00	4.50	25.00
Labour cost per unit	9.80	12.00	5.00	10.00
Variable overheads per unit	6.00	7.00	2.50	10.50
	£'000	£'000	£'000	£'000
Sales per annum	4,500	3,000	2,000	6,000
Materials	1,140	900	360	3,000
Labour	1,470	900	400	1,200
Variable overheads	900	525	200	1,260
Annual contribution	990	675	1,040	540

	A	B	C	D
	£'000	£'000	£'000	£'000
Working capital requirement (20% annual sales value)	900	600	400	1,200

It is assumed that working capital will be recovered at the end of year 5. The initial outlay will be made in year 0.

The NPV of each project can now be calculated.

Cash flows

Year	*A*		*B*		*C*		*D*		*Discount*
	Gross pa	*Net*	*Gross pa*	*Net*	*Gross pa*	*Net*	*Gross pa*	*Net*	*factor*
	£'000	£'000	£'000	£'000	£'000	£'000	£'000	£'000	18%
0	(3,000)	(3,000)	(2,000)	(2,000)	(2,800)	(2,800)	(1,800)	(1,800)	1
1-4	990	2,663	675	1,816	1,040	2,798	540	1,453	2.690
5	1,890	826	1,275	557	1,440	629	1,740	760	0.437
		489		373		627		413	

(b) The **profitability** index provides a **means** of **optimising the NPV** when there are more projects available which yield a positive NPV than funds to invest in them. The profitability index measures the ratio of the present value of **cash inflows** to the **initial outlay** and represents the net present value per £1 invested.

Project	*PV of inflows*	*Initial outlay*	*Ratio*	*Ranking*
	£'000	£'000		
A	3,489	3,000	1.163	4
B	2,373	2,000	1.187	3
C	3,427	2,800	1.224	2
D	2,213	1,800	1.229	1

Project D has the highest PI ranking and is therefore the first choice for investment. On this basis the funds available should be invested as follows.

Project	*Initial outlay*	*Total NPV*	*% taken*	*Cumulative outlay*	*Actual NPV*
	£'000	£'000		£'000	£'000
D	1,800	413	100	1,800	413
C	2,800	627	100	4,600	627
B	2,000	373	30	5,200	112
A	3,000	491	0	5,200	0
Total NPV generated					1,152

(c) The profitability index (PI) approach can be applied only if the projects under consideration fulfil certain criteria, as follows.

(i) There is **only one constraint on investment**, in this case capital. The PI ensures that maximum return per unit of scarce resource (capital) is obtained.

(ii) **Each investment** can be **accepted** or **rejected** in its entirety or alternatively accepted on a partial basis.

(iii) The NPV generated by a given project is **directly proportional** to the percentage of the investment undertaken.

(iv) Each investment can only be **made once** and not repeated.

(v) The company's aim is to **maximise overall NPV**.

If **additional funds** are **available** but at a higher cost, then the simple PI approach cannot be used since it is not possible to calculate unambiguous individual NPVs.

If certain of the projects that may be undertaken are **mutually exclusive** then **sub-problems** must be **defined** and **calculations made** for different combinations of projects. This can become a very lengthy process. These assumptions place limitations on the use of the ratio approach. It is not appropriate to multi-constraint situations when linear programming techniques must be used. Each project must be infinitely divisible and the company must accept that it may need to undertake a small proportion of a given project. This is frequently not possible in practice. It is also very unlikely that there is a simple linear relationship between the NPV and the proportion of the project undertaken; it is much more likely that there will be discontinuities in returns.

Possibly a more serious constraint is the assumption that the company's only concern is to **maximise NPV**. It is possible that there may be long-term strategic reasons which mean that an investment with a lower NPV should be undertaken instead of one with a higher NPV, and the ratio approach takes no account of the relative degrees of risk associated with making the different investments.

35 Feasibility study

Top tips. This question may seem rather peripheral to the financial strategy syllabus but feasibility studies are a key stage in project implementation and control that you do need to consider. Feasibility studies should identify the wider relevant costs and benefits which you may also have to discuss. (e) is a good example of the sort of question part that you could find in the compulsory question.

(a) A computer feasibility study is intended to evaluate the appropriateness of computerising an application which had been accomplished manually or by using another system. It is intended to accomplish three things.

(i) **Assess the information processing requirements** found in an application.

(ii) **Identify and investigate various alternatives** which could satisfy the requirements identified.

(iii) **Inform management** about the options and the costs, benefits, technology, risks, labour implications etc of each.

(b) **The assessment of needs provides the foundation for all other analysis**. Here one identifies what tasks are to be computerised and quantifies the requirements in terms of volume, speed, accuracy, security etc. Without this understanding of what the system will need to do it is most unlikely that an effective or economical system will be obtained. This phase looks primarily at the **functions to be performed** and the required performance standards.

Given the required tasks and performance standards a **variety of alternatives** may be reviewed and compared. The objective here is to keep an open mind and consider a full range of options. Several options might satisfy all performance criteria and then be referred to management for a final decision, perhaps with a recommendation for one.

The information provided to management on costs, benefits, etc allows them to consider any systems acquisition, development or upgrade. This information allows systems to be **compared more effectively**.

(c) The study would normally be carried out by a **feasibility study team**. This team would include:

(i) Someone from the **software house** having a detailed knowledge of computers and systems design

(ii) One or two **senior managers** having a detailed knowledge of the workings and staff of the departments affected

(iii) An **accountant** to carry out cost-benefit analyses of the proposed system, and prepare a detailed budget for installing it

(d) The best solution for the organisation is best identified through a thorough **investigation**, as would be provided by the feasibility study. The understanding gained by studying an existing system and formalising its operation **will aid in designing** a new system, or in **developing a specification** for one. Any purchase of a package without first developing **a sound specification** is likely to leave the company with a system unsuited to their needs.

(e) Four factors which would justify **introducing a new computer system** for production planning and scheduling would be these.

(i) **Better control over the handling of customer orders** so that these are dealt with more expeditiously.

(ii) **Improved production planning** to allow the company to fill orders more effectively and deliver production in a more timely fashion.

(iii) **Inventories will be more closely monitored** and improved production planning will reduce the amount of work in progress. These reductions will reduce the company's need for working capital to yield a direct improvement in cash flow.

(iv) By improving its production scheduling it will find that **better use of both equipment and labour will result**. This will improve profits, perhaps significantly.

List of key terms and index

Note: Key Terms and their references are given in **bold**

Review Form & Free Prize Draw – Paper P9 Management Accounting Financial Strategy (5/07)

All original review forms from the entire BPP range, completed with genuine comments, will be entered into one of two draws on 31 January 2008 and 31 July 2008. The names on the first four forms picked out on each occasion will be sent a cheque for £50.

Name: ______________________ **Address:** ______________________

How have you used this Interactive Text?
(Tick one box only)

- ☐ Home study (book only)
- ☐ On a course: college ____________
- ☐ With 'correspondence' package
- ☐ Other ____________

Why did you decide to purchase this Interactive Text? *(Tick one box only)*

- ☐ Have used BPP Texts in the past
- ☐ Recommendation by friend/colleague
- ☐ Recommendation by a lecturer at college
- ☐ Saw information on BPP website
- ☐ Saw advertising
- ☐ Other ____________

During the past six months do you recall seeing/receiving any of the following?
(Tick as many boxes as are relevant)

- ☐ Our advertisement in *Financial Management*
- ☐ Our advertisement in *Pass*
- ☐ Our advertisement in *PQ*
- ☐ Our brochure with a letter through the post
- ☐ Our website www.bpp.com

Which (if any) aspects of our advertising do you find useful?
(Tick as many boxes as are relevant)

- ☐ Prices and publication dates of new editions
- ☐ Information on Text content
- ☐ Facility to order books off-the-page
- ☐ None of the above

Which BPP products have you used?

Text	☑	*Success CD*	☐	*Learn Online*	☐
Kit	☐	*i-Learn*	☐	*Home Study Package*	☐
Passcard	☐	*i-Pass*	☐	*Home Study PLUS*	☐

Your ratings, comments and suggestions would be appreciated on the following areas.

	Very useful	*Useful*	*Not useful*
Introductory section (Key study steps, personal study)	☐	☐	☐
Chapter introductions	☐	☐	☐
Key terms	☐	☐	☐
Quality of explanations	☐	☐	☐
Case studies and other examples	☐	☐	☐
Exam focus points	☐	☐	☐
Questions and answers in each chapter	☐	☐	☐
Fast forwards and chapter roundups	☐	☐	☐
Quick quizzes	☐	☐	☐
Question Bank	☐	☐	☐
Answer Bank	☐	☐	☐
OT Bank	☐	☐	☐
Index	☐	☐	☐

Overall opinion of this Study Text *Excellent* ☐ *Good* ☐ *Adeqate* ☐ *Poor* ☐

Do you intend to continue using BPP products? *Yes* ☐ *No* ☐

On the reverse of this page are noted particular areas of the text about which we would welcome your feedback.
The BPP Learning Media author of this edition can be e-mailed at: julietgood@bpp.com

Please return this form to: Nick Weller, CIMA Publishing Manager, BPP Learning Media, FREEPOST, London, W12 8BR

Review Form & Free Prize Draw (continued)

TELL US WHAT YOU THINK

Please note any further comments and suggestions/errors below

Free Prize Draw Rules

1 Closing date for 31 January 2008 draw is 31 December 2007. Closing date for 31 July 2008 draw is 30 June 2008.

2 Restricted to entries with UK and Eire addresses only. BPP Learning Media Ltd employees, their families and business associates are excluded.

3 No purchase necessary. Entry forms are available upon request from BPP Learning Media Ltd. No more than one entry per title, per person. Draw restricted to persons aged 16 and over.

4 Winners will be notified by post and receive their cheques not later than 6 weeks after the relevant draw date.

5 The decision of the promoter in all matters is final and binding. No correspondence will be entered into.